DICTIONARY
FRENCH • ENGLISH
ENGLISH • FRENCH

TIGER BOOKS INTERNATIONAL
LONDON

© Geddes & Grosset Ltd 1994

This edition published in 1994 by
Tiger Books International PLC, London

ISBN 1-85501-372-X

Printed and bound in Slovenia

	Abbreviations	**Abréviations**
abrev	abbreviation	abréviation
adj	adjective	adjectif
adv	adverb	adverbe
art	article	articule
auto	automobile	automobile
aux	auxiliary	auxiliaire
bot	botany	botanique
chem, chim	chemistry	chimie
col	colloquial term	expression familière
com	commerce	commerce
compd	compound	mot composé
comput	computers	informatique
conj	conjunction	conjonction
excl	exclamation	exclamation
f	feminine noun	substantif fémenin
fam	colloquial term	expression familière
fig	figurative	figuré
geol	geology	géologie
gr	grammar	grammaire
imp	impersonal	impersonnel
inform	computers	informatique
interj	interjection	interjection
invar	invariable	invariable
irr	irregular	irrégulier
jur	law term	jurisprudence
law	law term	jurisprudence
ling	linguistics	linguistique
m	masculine noun	substantif masculin
mar	marine term	vocabulaire marin
mat, math	mathematics	matémathiques
med	medicine	médicine
mil	military term	vocabulaire militaire
mus	music	musique
n	noun	substantif

orn	ornithology	ornithologie
pej	pejorative	péjoratif
pl	plural	pluriel
pn	pronoun	pronom
poet	poetical term	vocabulaire poétique
prep	preposition	préposition
rad	radio	radio
rail	railway	chemin de fer
sl	slang	argot
teat	theatre	théâtre
tec	technology	technologie
TV	television	télévision
vi	intransitive verb	verbe intransitif
vr	reflexive verb	verbo réfléchi
vt	transitive verb	verbo transitif
zool	zoology	zoologie

A

à *prép* (in)to; at; on; by, per; **aller ~ l'école** to go to school; **~ neuf heures** at nine o'clock; **c'est ~ toi** it's yours; it's your turn.

abaissement *m* fall, drop.

abaisser *vt* to lower; **s'~ à faire** to stoop to doing.

abandon *m* abandonment, desertion.

abandonné *adj* relaxed.

abandonner *vt to* abandon, leave.

abasourdi *adj* stunned.

abasourdir *vt* to stun.

abats *m pl* giblets.

abat-jour *m* lampshade.

abattement *m* despondency; exhaustion.

abattoir *m* abattoir, slaughterhouse.

abattre *vt* to shoot; to slaughter.

abattu *adj* despondent; exhausted.

abbaye *f* abbey.

abbé *m* abbot.

abbesse *f* abbess.

abcès *m* abscess.

abdiquer *vt, vi* to abdicate.

abdomen *m* abdomen.

abdominal *adj* abdominal.

abeille *f* bee.

aberrant *adj* aberrant; absurd

aberration *f* aberration.

abêtissant *adj* mindless.

abêtissement *m* mindlessness.

abîme *m* chasm.

abîmer *vt* spoil, damage; *** s'~** *vr* to get spoiled *ou* damaged.

abject *adj* abject.

abjection *f* abjectness.

abjurer *vt* to abjure.

ablatif *m* ablative.

ablation *f (med)* removal.

abnégation *f* abnegation.

aboiement *m* bark.

abolir *vt* to abolish.

abolition *f* abolition.

abominable *adj* abominable;

~ment *adv* abominably.

abondamment *adv* abundantly.

abondance *f* abundance.

abondant *adj* abundant, plentiful.

abonder *vi* to be abundant *ou* plentiful.

abonné *m*, **-ée** *f*; * *adj* subscriber.

abonnement *m* subscription.

abonner *vt* **~ à qn** to subscribe, take out a subscription (*à* to); * **s'~** *vr* to subscribe, take out a subscription (*à* to).

abord *m*: **d'~** first (of all).

abordable *adj* affordable.

aborder *vt* to approach.

aborigène *m* aborigine; * *adj* aboriginal.

aboutir *vi* to succeed.

aboutissement *m* outcome; success.

abrasif *adj* abrasive.

abrégé *m* summary; **en ~** briefly

abréger *vt* to shorten; to abridge.

abreuver *vt* to water.

abreuvoir *m* drinking trough.

abréviation *f* abbreviation.

abri *m* shelter.

abricot *m* apricot.

abriter *vt* to shelter; * **s'~** *vr* to shelter

abroger *vt* to repeal.

abrupt *adj* abrupt; **~ement** *adv* abruptly.

abruti *m*, **-ie** *f*; * *adj* idiotic.

abrutir *vt* to make stupid.

abrutissant *adj* stunning; mindnumbing.

abscisse *f (med)* abscissa.

absence *f* absence.

absent *adj* absent.

absenter(s') *vr* to leave, go out.

abside *f* apse.

absolu *adj* absolute; **~ment** *adv* absolutely; * *m* absolute.

absolution *f* absolution.

absolutisme *m* absolutism.

absorbant *adj* absorbent.

absorber *vt to* absorb.

absorption *f* absorption.

absoudre *vt* to absolve.

abstenir(s') *vr* to abstain.

abstention *f* abstention.

abstentionniste *mf* abstainer.

abstinence *f* abstinence.

abstraction *f* abstraction.

abstrait *adj* abstract; **~ement** *adv* in the abstract; * *m* abstract; abstract art.

absurde *adj* absurd; **~ment** *adv* absurdly.

absurdité *f* absurdity.

abus *m* abuse.

abuser *vt* ~ **de** to exploit; to abuse.

abusif *adj* improper.

académicien *m*, **-ienne** *f* academician.

académie *f* academy; learned society.

académique *adj* academic.

acajou *m* mahogany.

acariâtre *adj* quarrelsome.

accablant *adj* overwhelming.

accabler *vt* to overwhelm.

accalmie *f* lull, calm.

accéder *vi*: ~ **à** to reach.

accélérateur *m* accelerator.

accélération *f* acceleration.

accélérer *vi* to speed up, accelerate.

accent *m* accent.

accentuation *f* accentuation.

accentué *adj* pronounced.

accentuer *vt* to accentuate.

acceptable *adj* acceptable.

accepter *vt* to accept.

accès *m* access.

accessible *adj* accessible.

accessoire *adj* secondary; **~ment** *adv* secondarily; if need be; * *m* accessory.

accident *m* accident.

accidentel *adj* accidental; **~lement** *adv* accidentally.

acclamations *fpl* cheers; acclamation.

acclamer *vt* to acclaim, cheer.

acclimater *vt* to acclimatize; **s'~** *vr* to become acclimatized.

accolade *f* embrace.

accommodant *adj* accommodating.

accommoder *vt* to prepare; to adapt.

accompagnateur *m*, **-trice** *f* (*mus*) accompanist; guide.

accompagnement *m* accompaniment.

accompagner *vt* to accompany.

accomplir *vt* to do, accomplish.

accomplissement *m* accomplishment.

accord *m* agreement; **d'~!** okay!, all right!; **être d'~** to agree.

accordéon *m* accordion.

accorder *vt* to give; **s'~** *vr* to agree.

accoster *vt* to accost.

accouchement *m* (*med*) delivery.

accoucher *vi* to give birth.

accoudoir *m* armrest.

accouplement *m* coupling; joining.

accourir *vi* to run up (*à*, *vers* to).

accoutrement *m* outfit, dress.

accréditer *vt* to substantiate.

accroc *m* tear; to breach.

accrocher *vt* to hang up (*à* on).

accroissement *m* increase.

accroître *vt* to increase.

accroupir(s') *vr* to crouch.

accueil *m* welcome, reception.

accueillant *adj* welcoming.

accueillir *vt* to welcome.

accumulateur *m* battery.

accumulation *f* accumulation.

accumuler *vt* to accumulate.

accusateur *adj*, *f* **-trice** accusing.

accusatif *m* accusative (case).

accusation *f* accusation.

accusé *m*, **-ée** *f* accused, defendant.

accuser *vt* to accuse.

acerbe *adj* acerbic, acid.

acétate *m* acetate.

acétone *f* acetone.

acharné *adj* bitter, fierce; unrelenting.

acharnement *m* fierceness; determination.

acharner(s') *vr* ~ **a faire qch** to try desperately to do something; ~ **contre qn** to hound somebody.

achat *m* purchase.

acheminer *vt* to send, forward.

acheter *vt* to buy.

acheteur *m*, **-euse** *f* buyer.

achèvement *m* completion.

achever *vt* to finish; to complete.

acide *adj* acidic; * *m* acid.

acidité *f* acidity.

acidulé *adj* rather acid.

acier *m* steel.

aciérie *f* steelworks.

acné *f* acne.

acompte *m* deposit, down payment.

à-côté *m* side issue.

à-coup *m* jolt.

acoustique *adj* acoustic; * *f* acoustics.

acquéreur *m* buyer.

acquérir *vt* to buy, purchase.

acquiescer *vi* to agree; to acquiesce.

acquis *adj* acquired; * *m* experience.

acquisition *f* acquisition; purchase.

acquittement *m* acquittal; payment.

acquitter *vt* to acquit; to pay.

acre *f* acre.

âcre *adj* acrid.

acrobate *mf* acrobat.

acrobatie *f* acrobatics.

acrobatique *adj* acrobatic.

acrylique *m*, *adj* acrylic.

acte *m* act; deed.

acteur *m*, **actrice** *f* actor.

actif *adj* active; * *m* (*ling*) active (voice).

action *f* act, action; share.

actionnaire *mf* shareholder.

actionner *vt* to activate; to drive.

activement *adv* actively.

activer *vt* to speed up; **s'~** *vr* to bustle about.

activité *f* activity; hustle and bustle.

actualité *f* * l' **actualité** current events.

actuel *adj* current, present; ~**lement** *adv* currently, at present.

acuité *f* acuteness; shrillness.

acuponcture *f* acupuncture.

adaptable *adj* adaptable.

adaptateur *m* adaptor.

adaptation *f* adaptation.

adapter *vt* to adapt (*à* to); **s'~** *vr* to adapt (*à* to).

additif *m* additive.

addition *f* addition; bill.

additionnel *adj* additional.

additionner *vt* to add up.

adepte *mf* follower; enthusiast.

adéquat *adj* suitable, appropriate.

adhérence *f* adhesion.

adhérent *m*, **-e** *f* member, adherent; * *adj* : ~ **à** which adheres *ou* sticks to.

adhérer *vi* to adhere, stick.

adhésif *adj* adhesive.

adhésion *f* adherence; membership.

adjacent *adj* adjacent (*à* to).

adjectif *m* adjective.

adjoint *m* **-e** *f* assistant.

adjudant *m* warrant officer.

adjudication *f* sale by auction.

adjuger *vt* to auction.

admettre *vt* to admit; to accept; to assume.

administrateur *m*, **-trice** *f* administrator.

administratif *adj* administrative.

administration *f* management; administration.

administrer *vt* to run; to administer.

admirable *adj* admirable; **-ment** *adv* admirably, brilliantly.

admiratif *adj* admiring.

admiration *f* admiration.

admirativement *adv* admiringly.

admirer *vt* to admire.

admissible *adj* acceptable.

admission *f* admission.

adolescence *f* adolescence.

adolescent *m*, **-e** *f* adolescent.

adopter *vt* to adopt; to pass.

adoption *f* adoption; passing.

adorable *adj* adorable; **~ment** *adv* delightfully.

adorer *vt* to adore, worship.

adoucir *vt* to soften.

adrénaline *f* adrenalin.

adresse *f* address; skill.

adresser *vt* to address; to send; **s'~** *vr* **s'~ à** to address; to go and see.

adroit *adj* deft, skilful; **~ement** *adv* deftly, skilfully.

aduler *vt* to flatter.

adulte *mf* adult, grown-up; *adj* adult, full-grown.

adultère *m* adultery.

adverbe *m* adverb.

adverbial *adj* adverbial; **~ement** *adv* adverbially.

adversaire *mf* adversary, opponent.

adversité *f* adversity.

aération *f* ventilation.

aérer *vt* to air.

aérien *adj* air; aerial.

aérodrome *m* aerodrome, airfield.

aérodynamique *adj* aerodynamic; * *f* aerodynamics.

aérogare *f* airport; (air) terminal.

aéroglisseur *m* hovercraft.

aéronautique *adj* aeronautic; * *f* aeronautics.

aéronaval *adj*, *pl* **aéronavals** air and sea.

aéroport *m* airport.

aérospatial adj aerospace.

affable *adj* affable.

affaiblir *vt* to weaken; **s'~** *vr* to weaken, grow weaker.

affaiblissement *m* weakening.

affaire *f* matter.

affaissement *m* subsidence.

affaisser *vt* subside; to cave in; **s'~** *vr* to cause to subside *ou* cave in.

affamé *adj* starving.

affamer *vt* to starve.

affectation *f* allocation (*à* to); affectation.

affecté *adj* affected.

affecter *vt* to affect.

affectif *adj* emotional.

affection *f* affection.

affectueux *adj* affectionate.

affectueusement *adv* affectionately.

affermir *vt* to strengthen; firm.

affermissement *m* strengthening.

affichage *m* posting (up).

affiche *f* poster.

afficher *vt* to post *ou* put up.

affiner *vt* to refine.

affinité *f* affinity.

affirmatif *adj* affirmative.

affirmation *f* assertion.

affirmativement *adv* in the affirmative.

affirmer *vt* to assert.

affluent *m* tributary.

affluer *vi* to rush (*à* to).

afflux *m* influx.

affolant *adj* alarming.

affolement *m* panic.

affoler *vt* to throw into a panic; **s'~** *vr* to get into a panic.

affranchir *vt* to frank, stamp; to free.

affranchissement *m* stamping, franking; freeing.

affréter *vt* to charter.

affreux *adj* horrible; awful.

affreusement *adv* horribly, dreadfully.

affrontement *m* confrontation.

affronter *vt* to confront; **s'~** *vr* to confront one another.

afin *prép*: **~ de** (in order) to; **~ qu'il le sache** in order that, so that.

africain *adj*, *mf* African.

Afrique f Africa.
agaçant adj annoying.
agacer vt to annoy, irritate.
âge m age; **quel ~ as-tu?** how old are you?
âgé adj old; **~ de 10 ans** 10 years old.
agence f agency; branch; offices.
agencement m organization, arrangement; equipment.
agencer vt to arrange; to equip.
agenda m diary.
agenouiller(s') vr to kneel (down).
agent m agent; policeman.
agglomération f town, urban area.
aggravant adj aggravating.
aggravation f worsening, aggravation; increase.
aggraver vt to make worse; to increase; **s'~** vr to get worse, worsen; to increase.
agile adj agile, nimble; **~ment** adv nimbly.
agilité f agility.
agir vi to act.
agitateur m, **-trice** f agitator.
agitation f agitation.
agiter vt to shake; to wave; **s'~** vr to move about; to fidget.
agneau m lamb.
agonie f death throes.
agrafe f staple; hook.
agrafer vt to staple (together); to fasten up.
agrafeuse f stapler.
agraire adj agrarian; land.
agrandir vt to make bigger; to widen; to expand; **s'~** vr to get bigger; to widen; to expand.
agrandissement m enlargement.
agréable adj agreeable, pleasant; **~ment** adv agreeably, pleasantly.
agresser vt to attack.
agresseur m attacker.
agressif adj aggressive.
agression f attack.
agressivement adv aggressively.

agressivité f aggressiveness.
agricole adj agricultural.
agriculteur m farmer.
agriculture f agriculture, farming.
agripper vt to grab (hold of); **s'~ à** vr to grab on to.
agronome m agronomist.
agronomie f agronomy.
agrumes m pl citrus fruits.
ahuri adj stunned; stupefied.
ahurissant adj staggering.
aide f help; aid;
aider vt to help.
aigle m eagle.
aigre adj sour, bitter; **~ment** adv sourly.
aigreur f sourness; sharpness.
aigri adj bitter, embittered.
aigu adj, f **aiguë** shrill; acute.
aiguillage m shunting.
aiguille f needle.
aiguiller vt to direct; to shunt.
aiguiser vt to sharpen.
ail m garlic.
ailé adj winged.
aileron m fin; aileron.
ailleurs adv elsewhere; **partout ~** everywhere else; **nulle part ~** nowhere else; **d'~** moreover; by the way.
aimable adj kind; **~ment** adv kindly
aimant m magnet.
aimanter vt to magnetize.
aimer vt to love.
aîné m, **aînée** f eldest ou oldest child; * adj elder, older; eldest, oldest
ainsi adv so, thus; **puisque c'est ~** since this is the way it is ou things are.
air m air; **avoir l'~ content** to look happy; **d'un ~ moqueur** in a mocking fashion.
aire f area.
aise f pleasure.
aisé adj easy; well-off; **~ment** adv easily.
aisselle f armpit.

11

ajournement *m* adjournment; postponment.

ajourner *vt* to adjourn; to defer, postpone.

ajout *m* addition.

ajouter *vt* to add.

ajuster *vt* to adjust.

alarmant *adj* alarming.

alarme *f* alarm.

alarmer *vt* to alarm; **s'~** *vr* to get alarmed (*de* at, about).

albâtre *m* alabaster.

album *m* album.

albumine *f* albumin.

alcalin *adj* alkaline.

alcaloïde *m* alkaloid.

alchimie *f* alchemy.

alchimiste *m* alchemist.

alcool *m* alcohol.

alcoolique *adj* alcoholic; * *mf* alcoholic.

alcoolisme *m* alcoholism.

aléatoire *adj* uncertain; risky.

alentours *mpl* surroundings, neighbourhood.

alerte *adj* alert; agile; * *f* alarm, alert.

alerter *vt* to alert; to notify; to warn.

algèbre *f* algebra.

algébrique *adj* algebraic; **~ment** *adv* algebraically.

algorithme *m* algorithm.

algue *f* seaweed.

alibi *m* alibi.

aliénation *f* alienation.

aliéner *vt* to alienate.

alignement *m* alignment; aligning.

aligner *vt* to align, line up.

aliment *m* food.

alimentaire *adj* alimentary, food.

alimentation *f* feeding; diet; food industry.

alimenter *vt* to feed; **s'~** *vr* to eat.

alinéa *m* paragraph.

allée *f* avenue; path.

alléger *vt* to make lighter; to alleviate.

allégorie *f* allegory.

allégresse *f* exhilaration.

alléguer *vt* to give, put forward.

aller *vi* to go; **comment allez-vous?** how are you?; **allons-y** let's go; **s'en aller** to go away, leave; * *m* outward journey; single ticket.

allergie *f* allergy.

allergique *adj* allergic (*à* to).

alliage *m* alloy.

alliance *f* alliance; marriage; wedding ring.

allié *m*, **-ée** *f* ally; * *adj* allied.

allier *vt* to combine.

allô *excl* hello!

allocation *f* allocation; allowance.

allongé *adj* **être allongé** to be lying (down).

allonger *vt* to lengthen; **s'~** *vr* to lengthen; to lie down.

allouer *vt* to allocate.

allumage *m* ignition.

allumer *vt* to light; to turn *ou* switch on.

allumette *f* match.

allure *f* speed; look.

allusion *f* allusion (*à* to).

alluvions *fpl* alluvium, alluvial deposits.

alors *adv* then; **~ que** while; whereas.

alouette *f* lark.

alourdir *vt* to make heavy; to increase.

alphabet *m* alphabet.

alphabétique *adj* alphabetical; **~ment** *adv* alphabetically.

alpinisme *m* mountaineering.

alpiniste *mf* mountaineer.

altération *f* alteration, change.

altercation *f* altercation.

altérer *vt* to change, alter.

alternance *f* alternation.

alternatif *adj* alternate.

alternative *f* alternative.

alternativement *adv* in turn, alternately.

alterner *vt*, *vi* to alternate.(*avec* with).

altitude *f* altitude, height.

altruisme *m* altruism.

aluminium *m* aluminium.

alvéole *f* cell.

amabilité *f* kindness.

amaigrir *vt* to make thin(ner).

amaigrissant *adj* slimming.

amalgame *m* combination, amalgam.

amalgamer *vt* to combine.

amande *f* almond.

amant *m* lover.

amarrer *vt* to moor.

amas *m* pile, heap.

amasser *vt* to amass, pile up.

amateur *m* amateur; connaisseur.

ambassade *f* embassy.

ambassadeur *m*, **-drice** *f* ambassador.

ambiance *f* atmosphere.

ambigu *adj*, *f* **ambiguë** ambiguous.

ambiguïté *f* ambiguity.

ambitieux *adj* ambitious.

ambition *f* ambition.

ambivalence *f* ambivalence.

ambre *m* amber.

ambulance *f* ambulance.

ambulant *adj* travelling.

âme *f* soul.

amélioration *f* improvement.

améliorer *vt* to improve; **s'~** *vr* to improve.

aménagement *m* fitting out; adjustment; development.

aménager *vt* to fit out; to adjust; to develop.

amende *f* fine.

amendement *m* amendment.

amener *vt* to bring.

amer *adj* bitter.

amèrement *adv* bitterly.

Américain *m*, **-e** *f* American.

américain *adj* American.

Amérique *f* America.

amertume *f* bitterness.

ameublement *m* furniture.

ami *m*, **-ie** *f* friend.

amiante *m* asbestos.

amibe *f* amoeba.

amical *adj* friendly; **~ement** *adv* in a friendly manner.

amincir *vt* to thin (down).

amiral *m* admiral.

amitié *f* friendship.

ammoniac *m* ammonia.

amnésie *f* amnesia.

amnistie *f* amnesty.

amnistier *vt* to grant an amnesty to.

amoindrir *vt* to weaken; to reduce.

amoindrissement *m* weakening; reduction.

amoncellement *m* pile; accumulation.

amorcer *vt* to bait; to begin.

amorphe *adj* passive.

amortir *vt* to soften; to deaden.

amortissement *m* paying off.

amour *m* love.

amoureux *adj* in love (*de* with).

amovible *adj* detachable.

ampère *m* ampere, amp.

amphibie *adj* amphibious.

amphithéâtre *m* amphitheatre.

ample *adj* roomy; wide; **~ment** *adv* amply, fully.

ampleur *f* fullness; range.

amplifier *vt* to increase; to amplify.

amplitude *f* amplitude; magnitude.

ampoule *f* bulb; phial; blister.

amputation *f* amputation.

amputer *vt* to amputate.

amusant *adj* amusing.

amuser *vt* to amuse.

an *m* year; **avoir vingt ~s** to be 20 (years old).

anabolisant *m* anabolic steroid.

anachronisme *m* anachronism.

anagramme *m* anagram.

analgésique *adj* analgesic.

analogie *f* analogy.

analogique *adj* analogical.

analogue *adj* analogous (*à* to).

analphabète *adj* illiterate.

analyse *f* analysis; test.

analyser *vt* to analyse.

analyste *mf* analyst; psychoanalyst.

analytique *adj* analytical; ~**ment** *adv* analytically.

ananas *m* pineapple.

anarchie *f* anarchy.

anarchiste *mf* anarchist.

anathème *m* anathema.

anatomie *f* anatomy.

anatomique *adj* anatomical; ~**ment** *adv* anatomically.

ancestral *adj* ancestral.

ancêtre *m* ancestor.

anchois *m* anchovy.

ancien *adj* old; former; ~**nement** *adv* formerly.

ancienneté *f* (years of) service; seniority; age.

ancrage *m* anchorage.

ancre *f* anchor.

ancrer *vt* to anchor.

âne *m* ass, donkey.

anéantir *vt* to destroy.

anéantissement *m* destruction.

anecdote *f* anecdote.

anémie *f* anemia.

anémone *f* anemone.

anesthésie *f* anaesthetic; anaesthesia.

anesthésique *m* anaesthetic.

ange *m* angel.

angélique *adj* angelic; * *f* angelica.

angine *f* tonsillitis.

Anglais *m*, -e *f* Englishman; Englishwoman.

anglais *adj* English; * *m* (*ling*) English.

angle *m* angle; corner.

Angleterre *f* England.

anglophone *adj* English-speaking; *mf* English speaker.

angoissant *adj* agonizing.

angoisse *f* anguish.

angoisser *vt* to make anxious.

animal *m* animal.

animateur *m*, -**trice** *f* host, compère; leader.

animation *f* animation; hustle and bustle.

animé *adj* busy; lively.

animer *vt* to lead; to host; to liven up; **s'~** *vr* to liven up.

animisme *m* animism.

animosité *f* animosity.

annales *fpl* annals.

anneau *m* ring.

année *f* year; **les ~s soixante** the Sixties

annexe *f* annexe; * *adj* subsidiary.

annexer *vt* to annex; to append.

annihiler *vt* to annihilate.

anniversaire *m* birthday; **joyeux ~!** happy birthday!

annonce *f* advertisement; announcement.

annoncer *vt* to announce (*à* to).

annoter *vt* to annotate.

annuaire *m* telephone directory, phone book.

annuel *adj* annual; ~**lement** *adv* annually.

annulation *f* cancellation; nullification.

annuler *vt* to cancel; to nullify.

anode *f* anode.

anodin *adj* insignificant.

anomalie *f* anomaly.

anonyme *adj* anonymous; impersonal; ~**ment** *adv* anonymously.

anorexie *f* anorexia.

anorexique *adj, mf* anorexic.

anormal *adj* abnormal; ~**ement** *adv* abnormally.

anse *f* handle.

antagonisme *m* antagonism.

antagoniste *adj* antagonistic.

antécédent *m* antecedent.

antenne *f* (*rad, tv*) aerial; (*zool*) feeler.

antérieur *adj* earlier, previous; ~**ement** *adv* earlier, previously.

anthologie *f* anthology.

anthracite *m* anthracite.

anthropologie *f* anthropology.

anthropologue *m* anthropologist.

antiaérien *adj* anti-aircraft; air-raid.

anticancéreux *adj* cancer.

antichambre *f* antechamber.

anticipation *f* anticipation.

anticonceptionnel *adj* contraceptive.

anticonformiste *adj, mf* nonconformist.

anticorps *m* antibody.

anticyclone *m* anticyclone.

antidater *vt* to backdate.

antidépresseur *adj, m* antidepressant.

antidote *m* antidote.

antigel *m* antifreeze.

antimilitariste *adj, mf* antimilitarist.

antinucléaire *adj, mf* antinuclear.

antipathie *f* antipathy.

antipathique *adj* unpleasant.

antipode *m* antipodes; **aux ~s de** the polar opposite of.

antiquaire *mf* antique dealer.

antique *adj* ancient.

antiquité *f* antiquity; antique.

antirouille *adj invar* rustproof.

antisémite *mf* anti-semite; *adj* anti-semitic.

antisepsie *f* antisepsis.

antiseptique *adj* antiseptic.

antisocial *adj* antisocial.

antitétanique *adj* (anti-)tetanus.

antithèse *f* antithesis.

antitoxine *f* antitoxin.

antivol *m invar* anti-theft *ou* security device; lock; * *adj invar* anti-theft.

antonyme *m* antonym.

antre *m* den.

anus *m* anus.

anxiété *f* anxiety.

anxieux *adj* anxious.

aorte *f* aorta.

août *m* August.

apaisant *adj* soothing.

apaisement *m* calm(ing down); relief.

apaiser *vt* to calm (down); to relieve.

apathie *f* apathy.

apathique *adj* apathetic.

apercevoir *vt* to see; to catch a glimpse of.

aperçu *m* (overall *ou* general) idea.

apéritif *m* aperitif.

apesanteur *f* weightlessness.

apeuré *adj* frightened.

aphone *adj* voiceless, hoarse.

aphrodisiaque *adj, m* aphrodisiac.

apiculteur *m* beekeeper.

apitoyer *vt* to rouse one's pity; **s'~** *vr* to feel pity (*sur* for).

aplanir *vt* to level (out); to smooth away.

aplati *adj* flat.

aplatir *vt* to flatten (out).

apocalypse *f* apocalypse.

apocalyptique *adj* apocalyptic.

apogée *m* apogee, peak.

apolitique *adj* apolitical; nonpolitical.

apologie *f* apology.

apoplexie *f* apoplexy.

apostrophe *f* apostrophe.

apothéose *f* apotheosis.

apôtre *m* apostle.

apparaître *vi* to appear.

appareil *m* device; appliance; (tele-)phone; **~-photo** camera.

appareillage *m* casting off; equipment.

appareiller *vi* to cast off.

apparemment *adv* apparently.

apparence *f* appearance.

apparent *adj* apparent.

apparition *f* appearance; apparition.

appartement *m* flat, apartment.

appartenance *f* membership.

appartenir *vi*: **~ à** to belong to.

appât *m* bait.

appâter *vt* to lure; to bait.

appauvrir *vt* to impoverish; **s'~** *vr* to grow poorer.

appauvrissement *m* impoverishment.

appel *m* call; appeal.

appeler *vt* to call; to call out; **s'~**

vr **je m'appelle Léon** my name is Leon.

appellation *f* appellation; name.

appendicite *f* appendicitis.

appesantir *vt* to weigh down; to strengthen; **s'~** *vr* to grow heavier; to grow stronger.

appétissant *adj* appetizing.

appétit *m* appetite (*de* for).

applaudir *vt, vi* to applaude.

applaudissements *mpl* applause.

applicable *adj* applicable (*à* to).

application *f* application; use.

appliqué *adj* thorough, industrious.

appliquer *vt* to apply (*à* to); **s'~** *vr* to apply oneself.

apport *m* supply.

apporter *vt* to bring.

apposer *vt* to append; to affix.

appréciable *adj* appreciable.

appréciatif *adj* evaluative; appreciative.

appréciation *f* estimation, assessment

apprécier *vt* to assess; to appreciate.

appréhender *vt* to apprehend; to dread.

appréhension *f* apprehension.

apprendre *vt* to learn; **~ à lire** to learn to read; **~ à lire à un enfant** to teach a child to read.

apprenti *m*, **-ie** *f* apprentice.

apprentissage *m* apprenticeship.

apprêter *vt* to get ready; **s'~** *vr* to get ready.

apprivoiser *vt* to tame.

approbateur *adj*, *f* **-trice** approving.

approbation *f* approval.

approche *f* approach.

approcher *vt* to move near; to approach; **s'~** *vr* to approach.

approfondir *vt* to deepen.

approfondissement *m* deepening.

approprier(s') *vr* to appropriate.

approuver *vt* to approve of.

approvisionnement *m* supplying.

approvisionner *vt* to supply; **s'~** *vr* to stock up (*de, en* with).

approximatif *adj* approximate.

approximation *f* approximation.

approximativement *adv* approximately.

appui *m* support.

appuie-tête *m invar* headrest.

appuyer *vt* to press; to lean; to support *vi* to press; **s'~** to put up with; to take on; *vr* **s'~ sur** to lean on; to rely on.

âpre *adj* bitter; **~ment** *adv* bitterly.

après *prép* after; **après tout** after all; **d'~ elle** according to her; **collé ~ la vitre** stuck on the window; * *adv* after(wards). **tout de suite ~** immediately after *ou* afterwards.

après-demain *adv* the day after tomorrow.

après-midi *m / f invar* afternoon.

âpreté *f* bitterness.

a priori *m* apriorism; * *adv* a priori.

apte *adj* capable (*à* of).

aptitude *f* aptitude; ability.

aquarium *m* aquarium.

aquatique *adj* aquatic.

aqueduc *m* aqueduct.

aqueux *adj* aqueous.

arabesque *f* arabesque.

arable *adj* arable.

arachide *f* peanut, groundnut.

araignée *f* spider.

arbalète *f* crossbow.

arbitrage *m* arbitration.

arbitraire *adj* arbitrary; **~ment** *adv* arbitrarily.

arbitre *m* arbiter; referee.

arbitrer *vt* to arbitrate; to referee.

arborer *vt* to wear; to bear.

arborescence *f* arborescence.

arboriculture *f* arboriculture, tree cultivation.

arbre *m* tree.

arbrisseau *m* shrub.

arbuste *m* bush.

arc *m* bow; arc; arch.

arcade *f* arch.

arc-bouter(s') *vr* to lean.

arc-en-ciel *m*, *pl* **arcs-en-ciel** rainbow.

archaïque *adj* archaic.

archange *m* archangel.

arche *f* arche.

archéologie *f* archaeology.

archéologue *mf* archaeologist.

archétype *m* archetype.

archevêque *m* archbishop.

archipel *m* archipelago.

architecte *mf* architect.

architectonique *adj* architectonic.

architectural *adj* architectural.

architecture *f* architecture.

archiver *vt* to file, archive.

archives *fpl* archives, records.

archiviste *mf* archiviste.

ardemment *adv* ardently.

ardent *adj* ardent, burning.

ardeur *f* ardour.

ardoise *f* slate.

ardu *adj* difficult.

are *f* are (= a hundred square metres).

arène *f* arena.

arête *f* (fish)bone.

argent *m* silver; money.

argenté *adj* silver; silver-plated.

argenterie *f* silverware.

argile *f* clay.

argot *m* slang.

argument *m* argument.

argumentation *f* argumentation.

argumenter *vi* to argue (*sur* about).

aride *adj* arid.

aridité *f* aridity.

aristocrate *mf* aristocrat.

aristocratie *f* aristocracy.

aristocratique *adj* aristocratic.

arithmétique *f* arithmetic; * *adj* arithmetical; **~ment** *adv* arithmetically.

armature *f* (frame)work.

arme *f* arm, weapon.

armée *f* army.

armement *m* arms, weapons; armaments.

armer *vt* to arm; **s'~** *vr* to arm oneself.

armistice *m* armistice.

armoire *f* cupboard; wardrobe.

armure *f* armour.

aromate *m* herb; spice.

aromatique *adj* aromatic.

aromatiser *vt* to flavour.

arôme *m* aroma; flavour.

arpenteur *m* (land) surveyor.

arqué *adj* curved, arced.

arquebuse *f* arquebus.

arrachement *m* wrench; pulling *ou* tearing off.

arracher *vt* to pull (out); to tear off.

arrangeant *adj* obliging.

arrangement *m* arrangement.

arranger *vt* to arrange; to fix; **cela m'arrangerait** that would suit me; **s'~** *vr* to come to an arrangement; to manage; to get better.

arrestation *f* arrest.

arrêt *m* stopping; stop (button).

arrêté *m* order.

arrêter *vt* to stop; **s'~** *vr* to stop.

arrhes *fpl* deposit.

arrière *m invar* back; **en ~** back-(wards); **à l'~** at the back; * *adj invar* back, rear.

arriéré *adj* backward.

arrière-goût *m* aftertaste.

arrière-grand-mère *f* great-grandmother.

arrière-grand-père *m* great-grandfather.

arrière-pays *m* hinterland.

arrière-pensée *f* ulterior motive; mental reservation.

arrière-petits-enfants *m pl* great-grandchildren.

arrière-plan *m* background.

arrimer *vt* to stow.

arrivage *m* delivery.

arrivant *m*, **-e** *f* newcomer.

arrivée *f* arrival, coming.

arriver *vi* to arrive, come.

arriviste *mf* careerist; social climber.

arrogance *f* arrogance.

arrogant *adj* arrogant.

arroger(s') *vr* to assume (without rights to).

arrondi *adj* round(ed).

arrondir *vt* to make round; to round off.

arrondissement *m* district.

arrosage *m* watering.

arroser *vt* to water.

arsenal *m* arsenal.

arsenic *m* arsenic.

art *m* art.

artère *f* artery; road.

artériel *adj* arterial.

arthrite *f* arthritis.

artichaut *m* artichoke.

article *m* article.

articulation *f* joint; knuckle.

articuler *vt* to articulate.

artifice *m* trick.

artificiel *adj* artificial; **~lement** *adv* artificially.

artillerie *f* artillery.

artisan *m* artisan, craftsman.

artisanal *adj* craft.

artisanat *m* craft industry.

artiste *mf* artist.

artistique *adj* artistic; **~ment** *adv* artistically.

as *m* ace.

ascendance *f* ancestry.

ascendant *adj* upward, rising; * *m* (strong) influence, ascendancy (*sur* over).

ascenseur *m* lift, elevator.

ascension *f* ascent.

ascète *mf* ascetic.

ascétique *adj* ascetic.

aseptiser *vt* to sterilize; to disinfect.

asexué *adj* asexual.

asiatique *adj* Asian.

asile *m* refuge; asylum.

aspect *m* appearance, look.

asperge *f* asparagus.

asperger *vt* to splash (*de* with).

aspérité *f* bump.

asphalte *m* asphalt.

asphyxie *f* asphyxiation, suffocation.

asphyxier *vt* to asphyxiate, suffocate.

aspirateur *m* vacuum cleaner.

aspiration *f* inhalation.

aspirer *vt* to inhale.

aspirine *f* aspirin.

assagir *vt* to quieten (down); **s'~** *vr* to quieten (down).

assaillant *m* assailant.

assaillir *vt* to assail.

assainir *vt* to clean up; to purify.

assainissement *m* cleaning up.

assaisonnement *m* seasoning.

assaisonner *vt* to season.

assassin *m* murderer; assassin.

assassinat *m* murder; assassination.

assassiner *vt* to assassinate.

assaut *m* assault, attack (*de* on).

assécher *vt* to drain; **s'~** *vr* to dry (up *ou* out).

assemblage *m* assembly; assembling.

assemblée *f* meeting.

assembler *vt* to assemble; **s'~** *vr* to assemble.

assentiment *m* assent.

asseoir(s') *vr* to sit down.

assermenté *adj* on oath.

assertion *f* assertion.

asservissement *m* enslavement; slavery.

assez *adv* enough; quite, rather; **avoir ~ d'argent** to have enough money; **~ bien** quite well; **j'en ai assez!** I've had enough!; I'm fed up.

assidu *adj* assiduous; regular.

assiduité *f* assiduity; regularity.

assiéger *vt* to besiege.

assiette *f* plate.

assigner *vt* to assign.

assimilation *f* assimilation; comparison; classification.

assimiler *vt* to assimilate.

assis *adj* seated, sitting (down).

assistance f audience; assistance.

assistant m, **-e** f assistant.

assister vt to attend; to assist.

association f association.

associé m, **-ée** f associate, partner.

associer vt to associate (à with); **s'~** vr to join together.

assombrir vt to darken; **s'~** to darken.

assommer vt to stun.

Assomption f: **l'~** the Assumption.

assortiment m assortment.

assortir vt to match; **s'~** vr to go well together.

assoupir(s') vr to doze off.

assoupissement m doze.

assouplir vt to make supple; to relax.

assouplissement m softening; relaxing.

assourdir vt to deafen; to muffle.

assourdissant adj deafening.

assouvir vt to satisfy.

assouvissement m satisfying, satisfaction.

assujettir vt to subjugate.

assumer vt to assume.

assurance f (self-)assurance; assurance; insurance (policy).

assuré m, **-e** f assured; * adj assured.

assurer vt to assure; **s'~** vr to insure oneself.

assureur m (insurance) agent; insurer(s), insurance company.

astérisque m asterisk.

asthmatique adj, mf asthmatic.

asthme m asthma.

asticot m maggot.

astigmate adj astigmatic.

astiquer vt to polish.

astre m star.

astreignant adj demanding.

astreindre vt to force, compel; **s'~** vr **s'~ à faire** to force ou compel to do.

astrologie f astrology.

astrologique adj astrological.

astrologue m astrologer.

astronaute m astronaut.

astronome m astronomer.

astronomie f astronomy.

astronomique adj astronomical.

astuce f shrewdness; (clever) trick; pun.

astucieux adj astute.

asymétrique adj asymmetric(al).

atelier m workshop; studio.

atermoyer vi to procrastinate.

athée mf atheist; adj atheistic.

athéisme m atheism.

athlète mf athlete.

athlétique adj athletic.

athlétisme m athletics.

atlas m atlas.

atmosphère f atmosphere.

atmosphérique adj atmospheric.

atome m atom.

atomique adj atomic.

atomiseur m spray; atomizer.

atout m trump; advantage, asset.

âtre m hearth.

atroce adj atrocious; dreadful; **~ment** adv atrociously; dreadfully.

atrocité f atrocity.

atrophié adj atrophied.

attachant adj endearing.

attache f fastener.

attaché m, **-e** f attaché; assistant.

attachement m attachment (à to).

attacher vt to tie together; to tie up; to fasten; to attach (à to).

attaque f attack.

attaquer vt to attack; to tackle.

attarder(s') vr to linger.

atteindre vt to reach; to affect; to contact.

atteinte f attack (à on); **hors d'~** beyond ou out of reach.

attenant adj adjoining.

attendre vt to wait; **en attendant** meanwhile, in the meantime; **s'~** vr : **s'~ à qch** to expect something.

attendrir vt to fill with pity; to move; to tenderize; **s'~** vr to be moved (sur by).

attendrissant *adj* touching, moving.

attendrissement *m* emotion.

attendu *adj* expected; long-awaited.

attentat *m* attack (*contre* on); murder attempt.

attente *f* wait; expectation.

attentif *adj* attentive; careful.

attention *f* attention; care.

attentionné *adj* considerate, thoughtful (*pour* towards).

attentivement *adv* attentively; carefully.

atténuation *f* alleviation; easing.

atténuer *vt* to alleviate; to ease.

atterrir *vi* to land, touch down.

atterrissage *m* landing, touchdown.

attester *vt* to testify to.

attirail *m* gear.

attirant *adj* attractive.

attirer *vt* to attract; **s'~ des ennuis à qn** to cause somebody trouble.

attiser *vt* to stir up.

attitude *f* attitude; bearing.

attraction *f* attraction.

attrait *m* attraction, appeal.

attraper *vt* to catch.

attrayant *adj* attractive.

attribuer *vt* to attribute; to award.

attribut *m* attribute.

attribution *f* attribution.

attrister *vt* to sadden.

attroupement *m* crowd.

au = à le.

aube *f* dawn, daybreak.

auberge *f* inn; **~ de jeunesse** youth hostel.

aubergine *f* aubergine.

aucun *adj* no; not any; any; **sans ~ doute** without (any) doubt; **~ement** *adv* in no way; not in the least; * *pron* none; not any; any (one); **~ d'entre eux** none of them.

audace *f* audacity; daring.

audacieux *adj* audacious, bold; daring.

audience *f* audience; hearing.

audiovisuel *adj* audio-visual.

auditeur *m*, **-trice** *f* listener; auditor.

auditoire *m* audience.

augmentation *f* increase, rise (*de* in); increasing, raising (*de* of).

augmenter *vt* to increase, raise.

augure *f* omen; oracle.

aujourd'hui *adv* today.

aumône *f* alms; **demander/faire l'~** to beg for/give alms.

auparavant *adv* before, previously; before, first.

auprès *prép* :**~ de** next to; (compared) with.

auquel = à lequel.

auréole *f* halo, aureole; ring (mark).

auriculaire *adj* auricular; * *m* little finger.

aurore *f* dawn, first light.

ausculter *vt* to auscultate.

aussi *adv* too, also; so; **nous ~** us too; **une ~ belle journée** such a beautiful day; **il est ~ petit qu'elle** he is as small as she is.

aussitôt *adv* immediately; **~ dit, ~ fait** no sooner said than done; **~ que** as soon as.

austère *adj* austere; **~ment** *adv* austerely.

austérité *f* austerity.

autant *adv* as much; as many; so much; such; so many; such a lot of; the same; **~ que je sache** as far as I know; **~ que possible** as much as possible; **elle n'est pas plus heureuse pour ~** she's not any happier for it *ou* for all that.

autel *m* altar.

auteur *m* author.

authenticité *f* authenticity.

authentifier *vt* to authenticate.

authentique *adj* authentic; **~ment** *adv* authentically.

autobiographie *f* autobiography.

autobiographique *adj* autobiographical.

autocar *m* coach.

autocollant *adj* self-adhesive.

autocuiseur *m* pressure cooker.

autodéfense *f* self-defence.

autodestruction *f* self-destruction.

autodidacte *mf* self-taught.

auto-école *f* driving school.

automate *m* automaton.

automatique *adj* automatic; **~ment** *adv* automatically.

automatiser *vt* to automate.

automatisme *m* automatism.

automne *m* autumn.

automobile *f* (motor) car.

automobiliste *mf* motorist.

autonome *adj* autonomous; self-governing.

autonomie *f* autonomy; self-government.

autoportrait *m* self-portrait.

autopsie *f* autopsy, post-mortem (examination).

autoradio *m* car radio.

autorisation *f* authorization, permission; permit.

autoriser *vt* to authorize, give permission for; to allow.

autoritaire *adj* authoritarian.

autorité *f* authority.

autoroute *f* motorway.

autosatisfaction *f* self-satisfaction.

auto-stop *m* hitch-hiking; **faire de l'~** to hitch-hike.

auto-stoppeur *m*, **-euse** *f* hitch-hiker.

autour *prép* **~ de** (a)round; * *adv* (a)round; **il y en a tout ~** there is/are some all around.

autre *adj* other; **~ chose** something else *ou* different; **~ part** somewhere else; **d'~ part** on the other hand; moreover; * *pron* another (one); **j'en veux un ~** I'd like another (one); **encore deux ~s** another two; **les cinq ~s** the five others; the other five.

autrefois *adv* in the past, in days gone by.

autrement *adv* differently; otherwise; **je n'ai pas pu faire ~** I couldn't do differently *ou* otherwise.

autruche *f* ostrich.

autrui *pron* others.

aux = à les.

auxiliaire *adj* auxiliary; * *m* auxiliary; * *mf* assistant.

avachir(s') *vr* to become *ou* grow limp.

avalanche *f* avalanche.

avaler *vt* to swallow.

avance *f* advance; lead; **arriver en ~** to arrive early; **payer d'~** to pay in advance; **réserver à l'~** to book in advance; **avoir de l'~ sur** to have the lead over.

avancement *m* promotion; progress; forward movement.

avancer *vt* to move forward; to bring forward; to put forward; **s'~** *vr* to advance, move forward; * *vi* to make forward, advance; to make progress; to project, stick out.

avant *prép* before; **~ peu** shortly; **~ tout** above all; * *adv* before; **en ~** in front, ahead; * *m* front; bow; forward.

avantage *m* advantage.

avantager *vt* to favour; to flatter.

avantageux *adj* profitable, worthwhile; attractive; flattering.

avant-bras *m invar* forearm.

avant-coureur *adj* precursory.

avant-dernier *m*, **-ière** *f*, *adj* next to last, second last, last but one.

avant-garde *f* avant-garde; vanguard.

avant-goût *m* foretaste.

avant-hier *adv* the day before yesterday.

avant-première *f* preview.

avare *mf* miser; *adj* miserly.

avarice *f* avarice, miserliness.

avarie *f* damage.

avarié *adj* rotting; damaged.

avec *prép* with; to.
avènement *m* accession (*à* to); advent.
avenir *m* future.
aventure *f* adventure; venture; experience; affair.
aventurer(s') *vr* to venture.
aventurier *m*, **-ière** *f* adventurer.
avenue *f* avenue.
avérer(s') *vr* to turn out, prove to be.
averse *f* shower (of rain).
aversion *f* aversion (*pour* to); loathing (*pour* for).
avertir *vt* to warn; to inform (*de* of).
avertissement *m* warning.
aveu *m* admission, confession.
aveuglant *adj* blinding.
aveugle *adj* blind; *mf* blind person (*ou* man *ou* woman).
aveuglement *m* blindness.
aveugler *vt* to blind.
aviateur *m*, **-trice** *f* pilot, aviator.
aviation *f* flying; aviation.
avide *adj* greedy; eager; **~ment** *adv* greedily; eagerly.
avidité *f* greed; eagerness.

avilir *vt* to degrade.
avilissant *adj* degrading.
avion *m* (air)plane, aircraft.
aviron *m* oar; rowing.
avis *m* opinion.
avisé *adj* wise, sensible.
aviser *vt* to advise, inform; to notice; **s'~** *vr* **s'aviser de** to realize suddenly.
aviver *vt* to sharpen; to deepen; to arouse.
avocat *m*, **-e** *f* barrister; * *m* avocado (pear).
avoine *f* oats.
avoir *vt* to have; **il y a** there is/are; **il y a deux mois** two months ago; **qu'as-tu?** what's wrong (with you)?; **il n'avait qu'à le dire** he only had to say (the word); * *m* resources; credit.
avortement *m* abortion.
avorter *vi* to abort; to fail.
avoué *m* solicitor.
avouer *vt* to admit (to); to confess (to).
avril *m* April.
axe *m* axis; axle; main road.
axial *adj* axial.
azote *m* nitrogen.

B

babines *fpl* chops.
babiole *f* trinket, trifle.
bâbord *m* (*naut*) port.
babouin *m* baboon.
bac *m* ferry.
bâche *f* tarpaulin, cover.
bâcler *vt* to botch; to obstruct.
bactérie *f* bacterium.
badaud *m* (*pej*) idle onlooker.
badge *m* badge.
bafouer *vt* to scorn.
bafouiller *vi* to stammer; to babble.
bagage *m* luggage; stock of knowledge.

bagarre *f* fight, brawl.
bagarrer (se) *vr* to fight; to riot.
bagatelle *f* trinket; trifling sum.
bagne *m* penal servitude; (*fig*) grind.
bague *f* ring.
baguette *f* stick; loaf of French bread.
baie *f* (*geog*) bay.
baigner *vt vi* to bathe; * **se ~** *vr* to have a bathe, swim.
baignoire *f* bathtub.
bâiller *vi* to yawn.
bâillon *m* gag.
bâillonner *vt* to gag.

bain *m* bath; bathe, swim.

baiser *m* kiss; * *vt* to kiss.

baisse *f* fall, drop.

baisser *vi* to fall, drop vt to lower.

bal *m* dance.

balade *f (fam)* walk; drive.

balader(se) *vr (fam)* to go for a walk; to go for a drive.

balai *m* broom, brush.

balance *f* balance; scales.

balancement *m* sway; rocking.

balancer *vt* to balance; to swing.

balançoire *f* swing; seesaw.

balayer *vt* to sweep, brush.

balbutiement *m* stammering, mumbling.

balbutier *vt* to stammer, mumble.

balbuzard *m* osprey.

balcon *m* balcony.

baleine *f* whale.

balistique *f* ballistics.

ballast *m* ballast.

balle *f* bullet; ball.

ballet *m* ballet.

ballon *m* ball; balloon.

ballotter *vt* jolt, shake about.

balourd *adj* stupid; clumsy.

balustrade *f* balustrade; handrail.

bambou *m* bamboo.

banal *adj* banal, trite; **~ement** *adv* tritely.

banalisation *f* vulgarizing; standardization.

banalité *f* banality, triteness.

banane *f* banana.

bancaire *adj* banking, bank.

bancal, *pl* **bancals** *adj* lame; rickety.

bandage *m* bandage.

bande *f* band; tape; **~ dessinée** strip cartoon.

bandeau *m* headband; blindfold.

bander *vt* to bandage; to stretch.

banderole *f* banderole, streamer.

bandit *m* bandit.

banlieue *f* suburbs.

bannière *f* banner.

bannir *vt* to banish; to prohibit.

bannissement *m* banishment.

banque *f* bank; banking.

banqueroute *f* bankruptcy.

banquet *m* banquet.

banquette *f* seat, stool.

banquier *m* banker.

banquise *f* ice field.

baptême *m* baptism.

baptiser *vt* to baptise.

bar *m* bar.

barbare *adj* barbarian; barbaric.

barbarie *f* barbarism; barbarity.

barbarisme *.m (Gram)* barbarism.

barbe *f* beard.

barbelé *adj* barbed.

barbiturique *adj* barbituric; * *m* barbiturate.

barboter *vi* to bubble; to splash.

barbouillage *m* scribble; daub.

barbouiller *vt* to smear; to scrawl.

barbu *adj* bearded; * *m* bearded man.

barème *m* list, schedule.

baril *m* barrel, cask.

bariolé *adj* multicoloured, motley.

baromètre *m* barometer.

baron *m*, **-ne** *f* baron.

baroque *adj* baroque; * *m* baroque.

barque *f* small boat.

barrage *m* barrage, barrier.

barre *f* bar, rod.

barré *adj* barred, blocked.

barreau *m* rung; bar (cage).

barrer *vt* to bar, block.

barrette *f* brooch.

barricader *vt* to barricade; **se ~** *vr* to barricade oneself.

barrière *f* barrier; fence.

baryton *m* baritone.

bas *adj* low, base; **~sement** *adv* basely, meanly; * *n* stocking; sock.

basalte *m* basalt.

bas-côté *m* verge; aisle.

bascule *f* weighing machine, scales.

basculer *vi* to overbalance.

base f base; basis.

baser vt to base; **se baser sur** vr to depend on, rely on.

bas-fond m (naut) shallow, shoal.

basilic m (bot) basil.

basilique f basilica.

basket m basketball.

basketteur m, **-euse** f basketball player.

bas-relief m bas relief.

basse f (mus) bass; shoal, reef.

basse-cour f poultry-yard.

bassesse f meanness; vulgarity.

bassin m pond, pool; dock.

bassine f bowl.

basson m bassoon.

bastion m bastion.

bas-ventre m belly, guts.

bataille f battle.

batailler vi to battle.

batailleur adj combative, aggressive.

bataillon m (mil) battalion.

bâtard adj bastard, illegitimate.

bateau m boat, ship.

batelier m boatman.

bâtiment m building.

bâtir vt to build.

bâtisse f building; masonry.

bâton m stick, staff.

batracien m batrachian.

battant m clapper (bell); shutter.

batte f bat; beating.

battement m banging; beating.

batterie f battery.

batteur m drummer; batsman.

battre vt to beat, defeat.

battu adj beaten; frequented.

baudet m donkey.

baume m balm, balsam.

bauxite f bauxite.

bavard m, **-e** f chatterbox; * adj talkative, loquacious.

bavardage m chatting; chattering; gossiping.

bavarder vi to chat, gossip.

bave f dribble, slobber.

baver vi to dribble, drool.

bavure f smudge, flaw.

bazar m bazaar; general store.

B.D. f (**bande dessinée**) strip cartoon.

béant adj gaping, wide open.

béat adj blessed; complacent; **~ement** adv complacently; blissfully.

béatitude f beatitude; bliss.

beau, f **belle** adj beautiful, lovely.

beaucoup adv a lot, a great deal; **~ de monde** a lot of people; **~ de temps** a great deal of time.

beau-fils m son-in-law.

beau-frère m brother-in-law.

beau-père m father-in-law.

beauté f beauty, loveliness.

beaux-arts m pl fine art.

beaux-parents m pl spouse's parents, in-laws.

bébé m baby.

bec m beak, bill.

béchamel f béchamel (sauce).

bée adj open-mouthed, flabbergasted.

bégaiement m stammering, faltering.

bégayer vi to stammer, stutter.

bégonia m begonia.

beige adj beige; * m beige.

beignet m fritter; doughnut.

bêlement m bleating.

bêler vi to bleat.

Belge mf Belgian.

belge adj Belgian.

Belgique f Belgium.

belle-fille f daughter-in-law.

belle-mère f mother-in-law.

belle-sœur f sister-in-law.

belligérant m, **-ante** f belligerent; * adj belligerent.

belliqueux adj aggressive; warlike.

bémol m (mus) flat.

bénédictin m, **-ine** f Benedictine.

bénédiction f benediction, blessing.

bénéfice m profit; benefit.

bénéficiaire mf beneficiary.

bénéficier vi to benefit; to enjoy.

bénévole adj voluntary; unpaid; **~ment** adv voluntarily.

bénin, f bénigne adj benign; minor; harmless.

bénir vt to bless.

bénit adj consecrated, holy.

benne f skip; tipper.

benzène m benzene.

béquille f crutch; prop.

berceau m cradle.

bercement m rocking.

bercer vt to rock, cradle.

berceuse f lullaby; rocking chair.

béret m beret.

berge f riverbank; barge.

berger m shepherd, **-ère** f shepherdess.

bergerie f sheepfold.

berner vt to fool, hoax.

besogne f work; job.

besoin m need; want; **avoir ~ de** to need.

bestial adj bestial; **~ement** adv bestially.

bestialité f bestiality; brutishness.

bétail m livestock; cattle.

bête adj stupid, silly; **~ment** adv stupidly, foolishly; * f animal.

bêtifier vt to play the fool; to prattle stupidly.

bêtise f stupidity, foolishness.

béton m concrete.

betterave f beetroot, beet.

beurre m butter.

beurrer vt to butter.

bévue f blunder.

biais m slant, angle; expedient.

biathlon m biathlon.

bibelot m bibelot, curio.

biberon m baby's bottle.

bible f bible.

bibliographie f bibliography.

bibliothécaire mf librarian.

bibliothèque f library; bookcase.

bicarbonate m bicarbonate.

bicentenaire m bicentenary.

biceps m biceps.

biche f doe; darling, pet.

bicolore adj bi-coloured, two-tone.

bicyclette f bicycle.

bidon m tin, can; flask.

bidonville m shanty town.

bien adv well; properly; very; **c'est ~ cela** that's right; * n property, estate.

bien-être m well-being.

bienfaisant adj beneficial, kind.

bienfaiteur m benefactor, **-trice** f benefactress.

bienheureux adj blessed; lucky; happy.

bientôt adv soon.

bienveillant adj benevolent, kindly.

bienvenu adj welcome.

bienvenue f welcome.

bière f beer; coffin.

bifteck m steak.

bifurcation f bifurcation, fork.

bifurquer vi to fork, branch off.

bigot adj bigoted.

bihebdomadaire adj twice-weekly.

bijou m jewel.

bijouterie f jewellery.

bijoutier m, **-ière** f jeweller.

bilan m balance sheet; assessment.

bilatéral adj bilateral.

bile f bile.

bilingue adj bilingual.

billard m billiards.

bille f marble; billiard ball.

billet m ticket; note.

billetterie f cash dispenser.

billion m billion.

bimensuel adj twice monthly.

bimestriel adj every two months.

binaire adj binary.

biochimie f biochemistry.

biochimiste mf biochemist.

biodégradable adj biodegradable.

bioéthique f bioethics.

biographie f biography.

biologie f biology.

biologique adj biological.

biologiste mf biologist.

biopsie f biopsy.

biosphère f biosphere.

bioxyde *m* dioxide.

bipède *m* biped.

bipolaire *adj* bipolar.

bisannuel *adj* biennial.

biscornu *adj* crooked, misshapen; odd, outlandish.

biscuit *m* cake; biscuit.

bisexuel *adj* bisexual.

bissextile *adj* bissextile, leap (year).

bistouri *m* bistoury.

bitume *m* bitumen.

bitumer *vt* to asphalt, tarmac.

bizarre *adj* bizarre, strange; ~ment *adv* strangely, oddly.

bizarrerie *f* strangeness, singularity.

blafard *adj* pale, pallid.

blague *f* joke, trick.

blaguer *vi* to joke.

blagueur *m*, **-euse** *f* joker, wag; * *adj* jokey, teasing.

blaireau *m* badger.

blâme *m* blame, rebuke.

blâmer *vt* to blame, rebuke.

blanc *adj*, *f* **blanche** white; * *m* white; blank; *mf* white person; * *f* minim.

blancheur *f* whiteness.

blanchir *vi* to turn white; to become lighter; * *vt* to whiten; to lighten.

blanchissage *m* laundering; refining.

blanchisserie *f* laundry.

blasé *adj* blasé.

blason *m* blazon, coat of arms.

blasphème *m* blasphemy.

blasphémer *vi* to blaspheme.

blé *m* wheat.

blême *adj* pale, wan.

blêmir *vi* to turn pale.

blessant *adj* cutting, hurtful.

blessé *adj* injured, wounded.

blesser *vt* to injure, wound.

blessure *f* injury, wound.

bleu *adj* blue; * *n* blue; bruise.

bleuet *m* cornflower.

bleuir *vi* to turn blue; * *vt* to make blue.

bleuté *adj* bluish.

blindage *m* armour plating.

blindé *adj* armoured, reinforced.

bloc *m* block, group, unit.

blocage *m* blocking, freezing.

blocus *m* blockade.

blond *adj* blond, fair.

blondir *vi* to turn blond, turn golden; * *vt* to bleach.

bloquer *vt* to block, blockade.

blottir (se) *vr* to curl up, snuggle up.

blouse *f* blouse; overall.

blouson *m* windcheater, bomber jacket.

bobine *f* reel, bobbin.

bocal *m* jar; bowl.

bœuf *m* ox, bullock.

bohémien *m*, **-ienne** *f* Bohemian; nonconformist.

boire *vt* to drink; * *vi* to drink, tipple.

bois *m* wood.

boisé *adj* wooded.

boisson *f* drink.

boîte *f* box.

boiter *vi* to limp.

boiteux *adj* lame.

boîtier *m* case, body.

boitillant *adj* somewhat lame.

boitiller *vi* to hobble slightly.

bol *m* bowl.

bolet *m* wild mushroom.

bombardement *m* bombardment, bombing.

bombarder *vt* to bombard, bomb.

bombe *f* bomb.

bombé *adj* rounded, domed.

bon *adj*, *f* **bonne** good; * *m* slip, coupon, bond.

bonbon *m* sweet, candy.

bond *m* leap; bounce.

bonde *f* stopper, plug.

bondé *adj* packed.

bondir *vi* to jump, leap; to bounce.

bonheur *m* happiness; luck.

bonhomme *m*, *pl* **bonshommes** chap, fellow.

bonification *f* improvement; bonus.

bonifier *vt* to improve; * **se ~** *vr* to improve.

bonjour *m* hello, good morning.

bonnet *m* bonnet, hat.

bonneterie *f* hosiery.

bonsoir *m* good evening.

bonté *f* goodness, kindness.

bon vivant *m* bon vivant.

bord *m* side, edge.

bordé *adj* edged, bordered.

bordée *f* broadside, volley.

border *vt* to edge, border.

bordereau *m* note; invoice.

bordure *f* frame, border.

borgne *adj* one-eyed.

borne *f* boundary; milestone.

borné *adj* narrow-minded.

borner *vt* to restrict, limit.

bosse *f* hump, knob.

bosseler *vt* to dent, emboss.

bossu *m*, **-ue** *f* hunchback; * *adj* hunchbacked.

botanique *f* botany; * *adj* botanical.

botaniste *f* botanist.

botte *f* boot.

bottine *f* ankle boot, bootee.

bouche *f* mouth.

bouché *adj* cloudy, overcast.

bouchée *f* mouthful.

bouche-à-bouche *m* kiss of life.

boucher *vt* to butcher; * **se ~** *vr* to become cloudy; *m*, **-ère** *f* butcher.

boucherie *f* butcher's (shop); butchery.

bouchon *m* cork.

boucle *f* curl; buckle.

boucler *vt* to buckle; to surround.

bouclier *m* shield.

bouddhisme *m* Buddhism.

boudeur *adj* sullen, sulky.

boudin *m* pudding.

boue *f* mud.

bouée *f* buoy.

boueur *m* dustman.

bouffée *f* whiff, puff.

bouffi *adj* swollen, puffed up.

bouffon *m* buffoon, clown.

bougeoir *m* candlestick.

bouger *vi* to move; * *vt* to move, shift.

bougie *f* candle.

bouillant *adj* boiling.

bouillir *vi* to boil.

bouilloire *f* kettle.

bouillon *m* broth, soup.

bouillonner *vi* to bubble; foam.

bouillotte *f* hot-water bottle.

boulanger *m*, **-ère** *f* baker.

boulangerie *f* bakery.

boule *f* ball, bowl.

boulet *m* cannonball; millstone.

boulevard *m* boulevard.

bouleversant *adj* upsetting, confusing.

bouleversement *m* confusion, disruption.

bouleverser *vt* to confuse, disrupt.

boulimie *f* bulimia.

boulimique *adj* bulimic.

boulon *m* bolt.

bouquet *m* bouquet, posy.

bouquin *m fam* book.

bouquiniste *mf* second-hand bookseller.

bourbeux *adj* muddy.

bourbier *m* quagmire.

bourdon *m* bumblebee.

bourdonnement *m* buzz, buzzing.

bourdonner *vi* to buzz, hum.

bourg *m* market-town.

bourgeois *m*, **-e** *f* bourgeois, middle-class person; * *adj* bourgeois, middle-class.

bourgeoisie *f* bourgeoisie, middle classes.

bourgeon *m* bud.

bourgeonner *vi* to bud.

bourrasque *f* squall, gust.

bourreau *m* torturer, executioner.

bourrelet *m* pad, cushion.

bourrer *vt* to stuff, cram.

bourse *f* purse; stock exchange.

boursier *m*, **-ière** *f* broker; speculator.

boursouflé *adj* bloated, swollen.

bousculade *f* hustle, scramble.

bousculer *vt* to jostle, hustle.
boussole *f* compass.
bout *m* end; piece, scrap.
boutade *f* whim, caprice; jest.
bouteille *f* bottle.
boutique *f* shop, store.
bouton *m* button.
boutonner *vt* to button.
boutonnière *f* buttonhole.
bouture *f* cutting.
bovin *m* bovine.
boxe *f* boxing.
boxer *vi* to box.
boxeur *m* boxer.
boyau *m* guts, insides.
boycottage *m* boycotting.
boycotter *vt* to boycott.
bracelet *m* bracelet.
braconnier *m* poacher.
brader *vt* to sell at a discount.
braderie *f* discount sale.
braguette *f* fly (trousers).
braise *f* embers.
brancard *m* shaft, pole.
branche *f* branch.
branchement *m* branching; connection.
brancher *vt* to connect, link.
branchies *fpl* gills.
brandir *vt* to flourish, brandish.
branlant *adj* loose; shaky.
bras *m* arm.
brasier *m* brazier, furnace.
brasse *f* breaststroke.
brassée *f* armful.
brasser *vt* to brew; to mix.
brasserie *f* bar; brewery.
bravade *f* bravado.
brave *adj* brave, courageous;
~**ment** *adv* bravely, courageously.
braver *vt* to brave, defy.
bravoure *f* bravery, courage.
brebis *f* ewe.
brèche *f* breach, gap.
bredouillant *adj* stammering, mumbling.
bredouille *adj* empty-handed.
bredouiller *vi* to stammer, mumble.

bref *adj*, *f* **brève** brief, concise; **en ~** *adv* in short.
bretelle *f* strap, sling.
brevet *m* licence, patent.
breveté *adj* patented.
bribe *f* bit, scrap.
bric-à-brac *m* bric-a-brac.
bricolage *m* DIY, odd jobs.
bricole *f* small job.
bricoler *vi* to do odd jobs.
bricoleur *m* handyman, **-euse** *f* handywoman.
bride *f* bridle.
bridé *adj* restrained, restricted.
brider *vt* to restrain, restrict.
brièvement *adv* briefly, concisely.
brièveté *f* brevity.
brigade *f* brigade.
brigadier *m* corporal, sergeant.
brillamment *adv* brilliantly.
brillant *adj* brilliant, shining.
briller *vi* to shine.
brin *m* stalk, strand.
brindille *f* twig.
brique *f* brick, slab.
briquet *m* lighter.
brise *f* breeze.
briser *vt* to smash, shatter.
brocante *f* second-hand dealing.
brocanteur *m*, **-euse** *f* second-hand dealer.
broche *f* brooch.
brochure *f* brochure, pamphlet.
broder *vt* to embroider, *vi* to embellish, elaborate.
broderie *f* embroidery.
bronche *f* bronchus.
bronchite *f* bronchitis.
bronzage *m* tan.
bronze *m* bronze.
bronzer *vi* to get a tan.
brosse *f* brush.
brosser *vt* to brush.
brouette *f* wheelbarrow.
brouillard *m* fog, mist.
brouiller *vt* to embroil, confuse.
brouillon *m* rough copy, draft;
* *adj* untidy.
broussaille *f* brushwood, undergrowth.

broussailleux *adj* bushy, overgrown.

brousse *f* undergrowth, bush.

brouter *vt, vi* to graze.

broyer *vt* to grind, pulverize.

broyeur *adj* crushing, grinding.

bruine *f* drizzle.

bruissement *m* rustle.

bruit *m* noise, sound.

bruitage *m* sound-effects.

brûlant *adj* burning, scorching.

brûler *vt, vi* to burn.

brûlure *f* burn.

brume *f* haze, mist.

brumeux *adj* hazy, misty.

brun *m* dark-haired man, **brune** *f* brunette; * *adj* brown.

brusque *adj* brusque, abrupt; **~ment** *adv* brusquely, abruptly.

brusquer *vt* to offend; to hasten.

brut *adj* crude, raw.

brutal *adj* brutal, rough; **~ement** *adv* brutally, roughly.

brutaliser *vt* to brutalize; to bully.

brutalité *f* brutality.

brute *f* brute; animal.

bruyamment *adv* noisily.

bruyant *adj* noisy.

bruyère *f* heather.

bûche *f* log.

bûcheron *m*, **-onne** *f* woodcutter, lumberjack.

budget *m* budget.

budgétaire *adj* budgetary.

buée *f* condensation; steam.

buffet *m* sideboard, buffet.

buisson *m* bush.

bulbe *m* bulb.

bulle *f* bubble; blister.

bulletin *m* bulletin.

buraliste *mf* tobacconist.

bureau *m* office; desk.

bureaucrate *mf* bureaucrat.

bureaucratie *f* bureaucracy.

bureaucratique *adj* bureaucratic.

burin *m* graver, chisel.

bus *m* bus.

buste *m* bust, chest.

but *m* objective, goal.

butane *m* butane.

buté *adj* stubborn.

butin *m* booty, loot.

butte *f* knoll, mound.

buvable *adj* drinkable.

buvard *m* blotting paper.

buvette *f* refreshment-room.

buveur *m*, **-euse** *f* drinker.

C

ça *pron* that; it; **~ va?** How goes it?; **~ y est** that's it; **qui ~** who? (do you mean?); **comment ~** how? (do you mean?); **~ alors!** you don't say!.

cabale *f* cabal, intrigue.

cabane *f* cabin, shed.

cabanon *m* cottage; chalet.

cabaret *m* cabaret; tavern.

cabine *f* cabin, cab; cockpit.

cabinet *m* surgery; office, study.

câble *m* cable.

câbler *vt* to cable.

cabosser *vt* to dent.

cabotage *m* coastal navigation.

cabriolet *m* convertible.

cacahouète *f* peanut.

cacao *m* cocoa.

cache *m* cache; mask; hiding place.

caché *adj* hidden, secluded.

cache-col *m invar* scarf.

cache-nez *m invar* scarf.

cacher *vt* to hide, conceal; **se ~** *vr* to hide oneself.

cacheter *vt* to seal.

cachette *f* hideout, hiding place.

cachot *m* dungeon.

cachottier, -ière *adj* mysterious, secretive.
cactus *m* cactus.
cadavre *m* corpse.
cadeau *m* present.
cadenas *m* padlock.
cadenasser *vt* to padlock.
cadence *f* rhythm, time, cadence.
cadet *m*, **-ette** *f* youngest child.
cadrage *m* centring.
cadran *m* dial, face.
cadre *m* frame; context; scope.
cadrer *vt* to centre; to set the parameters of.
caduc *adj*, *f* **caduque** null and void; obsolete.
cafard *m* hypocrite; cockroach.
café *m* coffee.
cafétéria *f* cafeteria.
cafetière *f* coffeepot.
cage *f* cage.
cageot *m* crate.
cagoule *f* cowl; balaclava.
cahier *m* notebook.
cahot *m* jerk, jolt.
caillot *m* clot.
caillou *m* stone; pebble.
caisse *f* box; till; fund.
caissier *m*, **-ière** *f* cashier.
cajoler *vt* to cajole, coax; to pet.
cajou *m* cashew.
calamité *f* calamity.
calcaire *m* calcareous, chalky.
calcination *f* calcination.
calciner *vt* to calcine; to scorch.
calcium *m* calcium.
calcul *m* sum, calculation.
calculateur *adj*, *f* **-trice** calculating.
calculatrice, calculette *f* calculator.
calculer *vt* to calculate, reckon; *vi* to budget carefully.
cale *f* hold; dock.
caleçon *m* shorts, pants.
calembour *m* pun.
calendrier *m* calendar.
calepin *m* notebook.
caler *vi* to stall; to give up.
calfeutrer *vt* to make airtight,

draughtproof.
calibre *m* calibre, bore.
calibrer *vt* to calibrate.
calice *m* chalice.
câlin *m* cuddle; * *adj* cuddly.
câliner *vt* to cuddle.
calligraphie *f* calligraphy.
callosité *f* callosity.
calmant *m* tranquillizer, sedative; * *adj* tranquillizing.
calmar *m* squid.
calme *m* calm, stillness; * *adj* calm, still; **~ment** *adv* calmly, quietly.
calmer *vt* to calm, soothe, pacify.
calomnie *f* calumny, slander.
calomnier *vt* to slander; to libel.
calomnieux *adj* calumnious, slanderous.
calorie *f* calorie.
calorifique *adj* calorific.
calque *m* tracing; copy.
calquer *vt* to trace; to copy.
calvaire *m* calvary, crucifix.
calvitie *f* baldness.
camarade *mf* companion, friend.
camaraderie *f* camaraderie, friendship.
cambouis *m* grease.
cambré *adj* arched.
cambriolage *m* burglary.
cambrioler *vt* to burgle.
cambrioleur *m*, **-euse** *f* burglar.
caméléon *m* chameleon.
camélia *m* camelia.
caméra *f* camera.
camion *m* lorry.
camionneur *m* lorry driver, trucker.
camomille *f* camomile.
camouflage *m* camouflage.
camoufler *vt* to camouflage.
camp *m* camp.
campagnard *m* countryman, **-e** *f* countrywoman; * *adj* country, rustic.
campagne *f* country, countryside.
campement *m* camp, encampment.
camper *vi* to camp.

campeur *m*, **-euse** *f* camper.

canal *m* canal, channel.

canalisation *f* canalization; mains.

canaliser *vt* to channel; to funnel.

canapé *m* sofa, settee.

canard *m* duck.

cancer *m* cancer.

cancéreux *adj* cancerous.

candeur *f* candour; naïvety.

candidat *m*, **-e** *f* candidate.

candidature *f* candidature, candidacy.

candide *adj* frank, ingenuous; **~ment** *adv* openly, ingenuously.

canevas *m* canvas; framework.

canicule *m* heatwave.

canif *m* penknife.

canine *f* eye tooth.

caniveau *m* gutter.

canne *f* cane, rod.

cannelle *f* cinnamon.

canoë *m* canoe.

canon *m* cannon, gun.

canot *m* boat, dinghy.

cantate *f* cantata.

cantatrice *f* singer.

cantine *f* canteen.

cantique *m* canticle, hymn.

canton *m* canton.

cantonner(se) *vr* to take up position in.

caoutchouc *m* rubber.

cap *f* cape; course.

capable *adj* capable, competent.

capacité *f* capacity.

cape *f* cloak.

capillaire *adj* capillary.

capitaine *m* captain.

capital *adj* capital, cardinal, major; * *m* capital, stock.

capitale *f* capital (letter, city).

capitalisme *m* capitalism.

capitaliste *mf* capitalist.

capiteux *adj* heady, strong.

capitonner *vt* to pad.

capitulation *f* capitulation.

capituler *vt* to capitulate.

caporal *m* corporal.

capot *m* bonnet, hood.

capote *f* greatcoat, hood.

capoter *vt* to capsize, overturn.

câpre *m* cape.

caprice *m* caprice, whim.

capricieusement *adv* capriciously.

capricieux *adj* capricious.

capricorne *m* capricorn.

capsule *f* capsule.

capter *vt* to win; to pick up; to tap.

capteur *m* captor; pick-up.

captif *m*, **-ive** *f* captive; * *adj* captive.

captivant *adj* enthralling, captivating.

captiver *vt* to captivate, enthrall.

captivité *f* captivity.

capture *f* capture.

capturer *vt* to capture.

capuche *f* hood.

car *conj* for; because; * *m* bus; van.

carabine *f* carbine, rifle.

caractère *m* character, disposition.

caractérisé *adj* marked, blatant.

caractériser *vt* to characterize.

caractérisque *f* characteristic, feature; * *adj* characteristic.

carafe *f* carafe.

carambolage *m* affray; pile-up (car).

caramel *m* caramel.

caraméliser *vt* to caramelize.

carapace *f* carapace, shell.

carat *m* carat.

caravane *f* caravan.

caravelle *f* caravel.

carbonate *m* carbonate.

carbone *m* carbon.

carbonique *adj* carbonic.

carboniser *vt* to carbonize.

carburant *m* motor fuel.

carburateur *m* carburettor.

carburation *f* carburation.

carbure *m* carbide.

carcasse *f* carcass.

carcéral *adj* prison.

cardiaque *adj* cardiac.

cardigan *m* cardigan.

cardinal *m* cardinal; * *adj* cardinal.

cardiologie *f* cardiology.

cardiologue *m* cardiologist.

cardio-vasculaire *adj* cardiovascular.

carême *m* fast, fasting.

carence *f* deficiency; insolvency.

caressant *adj* affectionate.

caresse *f* caress.

caresser *vt* to caress, fondle.

cargaison *f* cargo, freight.

cargo *m* cargo boat.

caricatural *adj* caricatural; grotesque.

caricature *f* caricature.

caricaturer *vt* to caricature.

caricaturiste *m* caricaturist.

carie *f* caries.

carié *adj* decayed.

carillon *m* carillon, chime, peal.

caritatif *adj* charitable.

carnage *m* carnage.

carnassier *m* carnivore, **-ière** *f* gamebag; *adj* carnivorous.

carnaval *m* carnival.

carnet *m* notebook; logbook.

carnivore *mf* carnivore; *adj* carnivorous.

carotide *f* carotid.

carotte *f* carrot.

carpe *f* carp.

carpette *f* rug, doormat.

carré *m* square; * *adj* square; straightforward.

carreau *m* tile; pane.

carrefour *m* crossroads.

carrelage *m* tiling.

carrément *adv* bluntly, directly.

carrière *f* career.

carrosse *m* coach.

carrosserie *f* bodywork, coachwork.

carrossier *m* coachbuilder.

carrure *f* build, stature.

cartable *m* satchel.

carte *f* card; map.

cartel *m* cartel.

cartésien *adj* Cartesian.

cartilage *m* cartilage.

cartilagineux *adj* cartilaginous.

cartomancien *m*, **-ienne** *f* fortune-teller.

carton *m* cardboard.

cartonner *vt* to bind (book).

cartouche *f* cartridge.

cas *m* case; circumstance.

casanier *m*, **-ière** *f* homebody.

cascade *f* waterfall.

cascadeur *m*, **-euse** *f* acrobat, stuntman.

case *f* square; box.

caser *vt* (*Fam*) to set up (job, marriage).

caserne *f* barracks.

casier *m* compartment; filing cabinet.

casino *m* casino.

casque *m* helmet.

casquette *f* peaked cap.

cassant *adj* brittle.

casse-croûte *m invar* snack.

casser *vt* to break; **se ~** *vr* to break.

casserole *f* saucepan.

casse-tête *m invar* puzzle, conundrum.

cassette *f* cassette; cash-box.

cassis *m* blackcurrant.

cassure *f* break, crack.

caste *f* caste.

castor *m* beaver.

castration *f* castration.

castrer *vt* to castrate.

cataclysme *m* cataclysm.

catacombe *f* catacomb.

catalogue *m* catalogue.

cataloguer *vt* to catalogue.

catalyseur *m* catalyst.

catalytique *adj* catalytic.

cataplasme *m* cataplasm.

catapulte *f* catapult.

cataracte *f* cataract.

catastrophe *f* catastrophe.

catastrophique *adj* catastrophic.

catéchisme *m* catechism.

catégorie *f* category.

catégorique *adj* categorical; **~ment** *adv* categorically.

cathédrale *f* cathedral.

cathode f cathode.

cathodique adj cathodic.

catholicisme m Catholicism.

catholique adj Catholic.

cauchemar m nightmare.

cause f cause, reason.

causer vt to cause; to chat; * vi to talk, chat.

caustique adj caustic.

caution f security, guarantee.

cautionner vt to guarantee.

cavalerie f cavalry.

cavalier m, **-ière** f rider.

cave f cellar.

caveau m tomb; small cellar.

caverne f cave, cavern.

caverneux adj cavernous.

caviar m caviar.

cavité f cavity.

ce adj **cet** (*before vowel and mute h*), f **cette**, pl **ces** this; these; that; those; **cet homme-là** that man; * pron; **c'est le facteur** it's the postman; ~ **sont mes lunettes** these are my glasses; ~ **que tu veux** what you want; **c'est ~ dont je vous parle** that's what I am speaking to you about.

ceci pron this.

cécité f blindness.

céder vi to give in; * vt to give up; to transfer.

ceindre vt to put round; to encircle.

ceinture f belt, girdle.

ceinturer vt to surround.

ceinturon m belt.

cela pron that; *emphasis* **qui ~?** who? (do you mean)?; **comment ~?** how? (do you mean?).

célébration f celebration.

célèbre adj famous.

célébrer vt to celebrate.

célébrité f fame, celebrity.

célérité f celerity, speed.

céleste adj celestial.

célibat m celibacy.

célibataire mf single person; * adj single, unmarried.

cellulaire adj cellular.

cellule f cell, unit.

cellulite f cellulite.

celluloïde m celluloid.

cellulose f cellulose.

celui pron, f **celle** this one, pl **ceux** these ones.

cendre f ash.

cendrier m ashtray.

censé adj supposed; deemed.

censure f censorship.

censurer vt to censor.

cent adj a hundred; **tu as ~ fois raison** you are absolutely right; **faire les ~ pas** to walk up and down; * m a hundred; ~ **pour ~** per cent.

centaine f around a hundred, a hundred or so.

centenaire m centenarian; * adj a hundred years old.

centésimal adj centesimal.

centième mf hundredth; * adj hundredth.

centigrade m centigrade.

centigramme m centigramme.

centime m centime.

centimètre m centimetre.

central adj central.

centraliser vt to centralize.

centre m centre.

centrer vt to centre; to focus.

centrifuge adj centrifugal.

centuple adj centuple, hundred-fold; * mf centuple.

cependant conj however.

céramique f ceramic.

cerceau m hoop.

cercle m circle, ring.

cercueil m coffin.

céréale f cereal.

cérébral adj cerebral.

cérémonial adj ceremonial.

cérémonie f ceremony.

cérémonieux adj ceremonious.

cerf-volant m kite.

cerise f cherry.

cerisier m cherry tree.

cerne f ring.

cerner vt to circle, encompass.

certain *adj* certain, sure; **~ment**
  adv certainly, most probably; **~s**
  pron some, certain.
certificat *m* certificate.
certifier *vt* to certify; to guarantee.
certitude *f* certainty, certitude.
cerveau *m* brain.
cervelle *f* brain.
cervical *adj* cervical.
césarienne *f* Caesarean.
cesser *f* to cease, stop.
cessez-le-feu *m* cease-fire.
cet *adj*, *f* **cette** *see* **ce**.
cétacé *m* cetacean.
ceux *see* **ce**.
chacun *pron* each one; **~e**
  d'entre elles each of them; **~**
  son tour each in turn.
chagrin *m* sorrow, chagrin.
chahut *m* row, uproar.
chahuter *vi* to make a row.
chaîne *f* chain.
chaînon *m* link.
chair *f* flesh.
chaise *f* chair.
châle *m* shawl.
châlet *m* chalet.
chaleur *f* heat.
chaleureusement *adv* warmly.
chaleureux *adj* warm, cordial.
chalumeau *m* blowlamp.
chalutier *m* trawler.
chambre *f* room.
chameau *m* camel.
champ *m* field.
champêtre *adj* rural, country.
champignon *m* mushroom.
champion *m*, **-onne** *f* champion.
championnat *m* championship.
chance *f* luck.
chancelant *adj* staggering, tot-
  tering.
chanceler *vi* to stagger; to totter.
chancelier *m* chancellor.
chanceux *adj* lucky, fortunate.
chandail *m* sweater.
chandeleur *f* Candlemas.
chandelier *m* candlestick.
chandelle *f* candle.

changeant *adj* changeable, variable.
changement *m* change, changing.
changer *vi* to change; * *vt* to
  change.
chanson *f* song.
chant *m* song; singing.
chantage *m* blackmail.
chanter *vi*, *vt* to sing.
chanteur *m*, **-euse** *f* singer.
chantier *m* building site.
chantonner *vi*, *vt* to hum.
chanvre *m* hemp.
chaos *m* chaos.
chaotique *adj* chaotic.
chapeau *m* hat.
chapelet *m* rosary; string.
chapelle *f* chapel.
chapiteau *m* capital (column).
chapitre *m* chapter.
chaque *adj* each.
char *m* (*mil*) tank; chariot.
charabia *m* gibberish.
charbon *m* coal.
charcuterie *f* pork-meat trade.
charcutier *m*, **-ière** *f* pork
  butcher.
chardon *m* thistle.
charge *f* load; responsibility.
chargé *adj* loaded.
chargement *m* loading; freight.
charger *vt* to load; **se ~ de** to take
  responsibility for; to attend to.
chariot *m* waggon; freight car.
charisme *m* charisma.
charitable *adj* charitable, kind;
  ~ment *adv* charitably.
charité *f* charity.
charlatan *m* charlatan.
charmant *adj* charming, delightful.
charme *m* charm.
charmer *vt* to charm, beguile.
charmeur *m*, **-euse** *f* charmer;
  * *adj* winning, enchanting.
charnel *adj* carnal.
charnière *f* hinge, pivot.
charnu *adj* fleshy.
charogne *f* carrion.

charpente *f* structure, framework.

charpentier *m* carpenter.

charrette *f* cart.

charrier *vt* to cart; to carry.

charrue *f* plough.

chartre *f* prison.

chasse *f* hunting; chase.

chasse-neige *m invar* snowplough.

chasser *vt* to hunt; to chase.

chasseur *m*, **-euse** *f* hunter.

châssis *m* chassis.

chaste *adj* chaste; **~ment** *adv* chastely.

chasteté *f* chastity.

chat *m*, **chatte** *f* cat.

châtaigne *f* chestnut.

châtain *adj* chestnut brown.

château *m* castle, château.

châtiment *m* chastisement, punishment.

chaton *m* kitten.

chatouiller *vt* to tickle.

chatoyant *adj* glistening.

châtrer *vt* to castrate.

chaud *adj* warm, hot; **~ement** *adv* warmly, hotly.

chaudière *f* boiler.

chaudron *m* cauldron.

chauffage *m* heating.

chauffard *m* road-hog.

chauffe-eau *m invar* water-heater.

chauffer *vi* to heat; * *vt* to heat up.

chauffeur *m* driver.

chaumière *f* cottage.

chaussée *f* road, street.

chausse-pied *m* shoehorn.

chaussette *f* sock.

chausson *m* slipper.

chaussure *f* shoe.

chauve *adj* bald.

chauve-souris *f* bat.

chauvin *adj*, *f* **chauvine** chauvinistic.

chauvinisme *m* chauvinism.

chaux *f* lime.

chavirer *vi* to capsize, overturn.

chef *m* head, boss; chef.

chef-d'oeuvre *m* masterpiece.

chemin *m* way, road; **~ de fer** railway.

cheminée *f* chimney.

cheminement *m* progress; course.

chemise *f* shirt.

chemisier *m* shirtmaker.

chêne *m* oak.

chenil *m* kennel.

chenille *f* caterpillar.

chèque *m* cheque.

chéquier *m* chequebook.

cher *adj*, *f* **chère** dear, expensive.

chercher *vt* to look for.

chercheur *m*, **-euse** *f* researcher; seeker.

chéri *m*, **-ie** *f* darling, dearest; * *adj* beloved, cherished.

chétif *adj* puny, paltry.

cheval *m* horse.

chevalet *m* easel.

chevalier *m* knight.

chevelu *adj* long-haired.

chevelure *f* hair, head of hair.

chevet *m* chevet; pillow.

cheveu *m* hair.

cheville *f* ankle.

chèvre *f* goat.

chèvrefeuille *m* honeysuckle.

chevreuil *m* roe deer.

chez *prép* at home: **je rentre ~ moi** I'm going home; **~ ta tante** at my aunt's.

chic *m* style, stylishness; **avoir le ~ pour** to have the knack for.

chicorée *f* chicory.

chien *m*, **chienne** *f* dog.

chiffon *m* rag, cloth.

chiffonné *adj* crumpled, rumpled.

chiffre *m* figure.

chignon *m* chignon, bun.

chimère *f* chimera.

chimérique *adj* chimerical, fanciful.

chimie *f* chemistry.

chimique *adj* chemical; **~ment** *adv* chemically.

chimiste *mf* chemist.
chimpanzé *m* chimpanzee.
chiot *m* puppy.
chipoteur *m*, **-euse** *f* haggler.
chirurgical *adj* surgical.
chirurgie *f* surgery.
chirurgien *m* surgeon.
chlore *m* chlorine.
chloroforme *m* chloroform.
chlorophyle *f* chlorophyll.
chlorure *m* chloride.
choc *m* shock, crash.
chocolat *m* chocolate.
choeur *m* choir, chorus.
choir *vi* to fall.
choisir *vt* to choose.
choix *m* choice.
choléra *m* cholera.
chômage *m* unemployment.
chômeur *m*, **-euse** *f* unemployed person.
choquant *adj* shocking, appalling.
choquer *vt* to shock.
chorale *f* choral.
chorégraphe *mf* choreographer.
choréraphie *f* choreography.
choriste *mf* chorister.
chose *f* thing, matter, object.
chou *m* cabbage.
chouette *f* owl.
chou-fleur *m* cauliflower.
choyer *vt* to cherish.
chrétien *m*, **-ienne** *f* Christian, *adj* christian.
christianisme *m* Christianity.
chrome *m* chromium.
chromosome *m* chromosome.
chronique *adj* chronic; * *f* chronicle, column, page.
chroniqueur *m* chronicler; columnist
chronologie *f* chronology.
chronologique *adj* chronological; **~ment** *adv* chronologically.
chronomètre *m* chronometer.
chronométrer *vt* to time.
chrysanthème *m* chrysanthemum.
chuchotement *m* whisper, rustling.

chuchoter *vi* to whisper.
chuintement *m* hissing.
chuinter *vi* to hiss.
chute *f* fall, drop.
chuter *vi* to fall.
ci *adv*: **ces fleurs-ci** these flowers; **ci-joint** enclosed; **ci-dessous** below; **ci-contre** opposite; in the margin; annexed.
cible *f* target.
cibler *vt* to target.
cicatrice *f* scar.
cicatrisation *f* cicatrization, healing.
cicatriser *vt* to heal; **se ~** *vr* to heal; to form a scar.
cidre *m* cider.
ciel *m*, *pl* **cieux, ciels** sky.
cierge *m* candle.
cigale *f* cicada.
cigare *m* cigar.
cigarette *f* cigarette.
cil *m* eyelash.
ciller *vi* to blink.
cime *f* summit.
ciment *m* cement.
cimenter *vt* to cement.
cimetière *m* cemetery.
cinéaste *mf* film-maker.
cinéma *m* cinema.
cinémathèque *f* film library.
cinématographique *adj* film, cinema.
cinéphile *mf* film enthusiast.
cinétique *adj* kinetic.
cinglant *adj* bitter, lashing, cutting.
cingler *vt* to lash; to sting.
cinq *m* five.
cinquantaine *f* about fifty.
cinquante *m* fifty.
cinquantenaire *m* fiftieth anniversary.
cinquantième *mf* fiftieth, *adj* fiftieth.
cinquième *mf* fifth, *adj* fifth; * **~ment** *adv* in fifth place.
cintre *m* arch.
cirage *m* polish.
circonférence *f* circumference.

circonscription *f* division, constituency.
circonspect *adj* circumspect.
circonstance *f* circumstance.
circuit *m* circuit, tour.
circulaire *adj* circular; **~ment** *adv* circularly.
circulation *f* circulation; traffic.
circuler *vi* to circulate; to move.
cire *f* wax.
cirer *vt* to polish.
cirque *m* circus.
ciseau *m* chisel; scissor(s).
citadelle *f* citadel.
citadin *m*, **-e** *f* city dweller; * *adj* town, urban.
citation *f* citation, summons.
cité *f* city.
citer *vt* to quote, cite.
citerne *f* water tank.
citoyen *m*, **-enne** *f* citizen.
citron *m* lemon.
citrouille *f* pumpkin.
civière *f* stretcher.
civil *adj* civil; **~ement** *adv* civilly.
civilisation *f* civilization.
civilisé *adj* civilized.
civiliser *vt* to civilize.
civique *adj* civic.
clair *adj* clear, bright; **~ement** *adv* clearly.
clairière *f* clearing, glade.
claisemé *adj* scattered.
clairvoyance *f* perspicacity; clairvoyance.
clairvoyant *adj* perceptive; clairvoyant.
clameur *f* clamour.
clan *m* clan.
clandestin *adj* clandestine; **~ement** clandestinely.
clandestinité *f* secrecy.
clapoter *vi* to lap (water).
clapotis *m* lapping.
claque *f* slap, smack.
claquement *m* clapping, slamming.
claquer *vi* to bang; to slam.
clarifier *vt* to clarify; **se ~** *vr* to become clear.

clarinette *f* clarinet.
clarté *f* light, brightness.
classe *f* class, standing.
classement *m* filing; grading.
classer *vt* to file; to classify.
classeur *m* filing cabinet.
classification *f* classification.
classique *adj* classical, standard; **~ment** *adv* classically.
clause *f* clause.
claustrer *vt* to confine.
claustrophobie *f* claustrophobia.
clavecin *m* harpsichord.
clavicule *f* collarbone.
clavier *m* keyboard.
clé, clef *f* key.
clémence *f* clemency, mildness.
clergé *m* clergy.
cliché *m* cliché; negative.
client *m*, **-e** *f* client.
clientèle *f* clientèle.
cligner *vi* to blink.
clignotant *adj* blinking, flickering; * *m* indicator.
clignotement *m* blinking, flickering.
clignoter *vi* to blink; to flicker.
climat *m* climate.
climatique *adj* climatic.
climatisation *f* air conditioning.
climatiser *vt* to air-condition.
clin d'oeil *m* wink.
clinique *f* clinic.
cliqueter *vi* to jingle; to clink.
clitoris *m* clitoris.
clochard *m*, **-e** *f* down-and-out.
cloche *f* bell.
clocher *m* steeple.
clochette *f* hand-bell.
cloison *f* partition.
cloîtrer(se) *vr* to enter the monastic life.
clore *vt* to close, conclude.
clos *adj* closed, enclosed.
clôture *f* fence, hedge.
clou *m* nail.
clouer *vt* to nail.
club *m* club.
coagulation *f* coagulation.
coaguler *vi* to coagulate.

coaliser *vt*, *vi* to form a coalition.
coalition *f* coalition.
cobalt *m* cobalt.
cobaye *m* guinea-pig.
cobra *m* cobra.
cocaïne *f* cocaine.
coccinelle *f* ladybird.
coccyx *m* coccyx.
cocher *vt* to notch; to tick off.
cochon *m*, **-onne** *f* pig.
code *m* code.
coder *vt* to code.
codifier *vt* to codify.
coefficient *m* coefficient.
coéquipier *m*, **-ière** *f* team mate.
coeur *m* heart.
coexister *vi* to coexist.
coffre *m* chest; **~-fort** safe.
coffret *m* casket.
cogner *vi* to hammer; to bang.
cohabitation *f* cohabitation.
cohabiter *vi* to cohabit.
cohérence *f* coherence.
cohérent *adj* coherent.
cohésion *f* cohesion.
cohue *f* crowd.
coiffer *vt* to arrange s.o.'s hair; **se ~** *vr* to do one's hair.
coiffeur *m*, **-euse** *f* hairdresser.
coiffure *f* hairstyle.
coin *m* corner.
coincer *vt* to wedge; to jam.
coïncidence *f* coincidence.
coït *m* coitus.
col *m* neck.
colère *f* anger.
colérique *adj* quick-tempered, irascible.
colibri *m* hummingbird.
colique *f* diarrhoea.
colis *m* parcel.
collaborateur *m*, **-trice** *f* collaborator, colleague.
collaboration *f* collaboration.
collaborer *vi* to collaborate.
collant *adj* clinging, sticky; * *m* leotard.
collecte *f* collection.
collectif *adj* collective.
collection *f* collection.

collectionner *vt* to collect.
collectionneur *m*, **-euse** *f* collector.
collectivement *adv* collectively.
collectivité *f* community; collective ownership.
collège *m* college, school.
collègue *mf* colleague.
coller *vt* to stick; to glue; * *vi* to stick, be sticky.
collier *m* necklace.
colline *f* hill.
collision *f* collision.
colloque *m* colloquium.
collocataire *mf* co-tenant.
colombe *f* dove.
colon *m* colonist.
colonel *m* colonel.
colonie *f* colony.
colonisation *f* colonization.
coloniser *vt* to colonize.
colonne *f* column.
colorant *m* colouring.
coloration *f* colouring, staining.
coloré *adj* coloured.
colorier *vt* to colour in.
coloris *m* colouring, shade.
colossal *adj* colossal.
colporter *vt* to peddle.
colza *m* rape seed.
coma *m* coma.
comateux *adj* comatose.
combat *m* combat, fight.
combatif *adj* combative.
combativité *f* combativeness.
combattant *adj* fighting, combatant.
combattre *vt* to fight; to combat; * *vi* to fight.
combien *adv* how much, how many; **~ de temps** how much time; **~ sont-ils?** how many are they.
combinaison *f* combination.
combiner *vt* to combine.
comble *m* height, peak.
combler *vt* to fill; to fulfil.
combustible *m* fuel.
combustion *f* combustion.
comédie *f* comedy.

comédien m; **-ienne** f actor.
comestible adj edible.
comète f comet.
comique adj comic; **~ment** adv comically.
comité m committee.
commandant m commander.
commande f command, order.
commandement m command, commandment.
commander vt, vi to order, command.
commanditer vt to finance, sponsor.
commando m commando.
comme conj as, like; **~ ci ~ ça** so-so; **~ il faut** properly; adv how.
commémoration f commemoration.
commémorer vt to commemorate.
commencement m beginning, start.
commencer vt to begin; *vi to begin; to start.
comment adv how; **~ dire?** how shall we say?; **~ cela?** what do you mean?.
commentaire m comment; commentary.
commentateur m, **-trice** f commentator.
commenter vt to comment.
commérage m piece of gossip.
commerçant m, **-e** f merchant, trader.
commerce m business, commerce.
commercial adj commercial; **~ement** adv commercially.
commercialiser vt to market.
commère f gossip.
commettre vt to commit.
commissaire m representative; commissioner.
commissariat m commissionership; commissariat.
commission f commission, committee.

commissionnaire m messenger; agent.
commode adj convenient, comfortable.
commodité f convenience.
commun adj common, joint; **~ément** adv commonly.
communal adj council; common, communal.
communautaire adj community.
communauté f community; joint estate.
commune f town, district.
communication f communication.
communier vi to receive communion.
communion f communion.
communiqué m communiqué.
communiquer vt to communicate; to transmit; * vi to communicate.
communisme m communism.
communiste mf communist.
compact adj compact, dense.
compagne f companion.
compagnie f company.
compagnon m companion.
comparable adj comparable.
comparaison f comparison.
comparaître vi to appear.
comparativement adv comparatively.
comparer vt to compare.
compartiment m compartment.
compartimenter vt to compart, partition.
compas m compass.
compassion f compassion.
compatibilité f compatibility.
compatible adj compatible.
compatir vi to sympathize.
compatissant adj compassionate.
compatriote mf compatriot.
compensation f compensation.
compenser vt to compensate; to offset; **se ~** vr to balance each other, to make up for.
compétence f competence.

compétent *adj* competent, capable.

compétitif *adj* competitive.

compétition *f* competition.

compétitivité *f* competitiveness.

complaisance *f* kindness; complacency.

complaisant *adj* kind; complacent.

complément *m* complement; extension.

complémentaire *adj* complementary, supplementary.

complet *adj* complete, full.

complètement *adv* completely, fully.

compléter *vt* to complete; **se ~** *vr* to complement one another.

complexe *adj* complex, complicated.

complexé *adj* mixed-up.

complication *f* complication.

complice *mf* accomplice.

complicité *f* complicity, collusion.

compliment *m* compliment.

complimenter *vt* to compliment; to congratulate.

compliqué *adj* complicated, intricate.

compliquer *vt* to complicate.

complot *m* plot.

comportement *m* behaviour; performance.

comporter *vt* to consist of, comprise; **se ~** *vr* to behave.

composant *m* component, constituent.

composante *f* component.

composer *vt* to compose, make up; **se ~** *vr*: **se ~ de** to be made up of.

compositeur *m*, **-trice** *f* composer; typesetter.

composition *f* composition, formation.

compréhensible *adj* comprehensible.

compréhensif *adj* comprehensive, understanding.

compréhension *f* comprehension, understanding.

comprendre *vt* to understand; to consist of.

compresse *f* compress.

compresseur *m* compressor.

compression *f* compression; reduction.

comprimé *adj* compressed; restrained; * *m* tablet.

comprimer *vt* to compress; to restrain.

compromettant *adj* compromising.

compromettre *vt* to compromise.

compromis *m* compromise.

comptabilité *f* accountancy.

comptable *adj* accounting; * *mf* accountant.

compte *m* account.

compter *vt, vi* to count.

compteur *m* meter.

comptoir *m* counter, bar.

comte *m* count, **comtesse** *f* countess.

concave *adj* concave.

concéder *vt* to grant, concede.

concentration *f* concentration.

concentré *adj* concentrated; reserved.

concentrer *vt* to concentrate; **se ~** *vr* to concentrate.

concept *m* concept.

conception *f* conception, design.

concerner *vt* to concern, regard.

concert *m* concert.

concertation *f* dialogue, consultation.

concession *f* concession; privilege.

concessionnaire *mf* concessionaire, grantee.

concevoir *vt* to imagine; to conceive.

concierge *mf* caretaker, concierge.

conciliant *adj* conciliatory.

conciliation *f* conciliation; reconciliation.

concilier *vt* to reconcile; to attract.

concis *adj* concise.

concision *f* conciseness, brevity.

concluant *adj* conclusive, decisive.

conclure *vt* to conclude; to decide; **se ~** *vr* to conclude, come to an end.

conclusion *f* conclusion.

concombre *m* cucumber.

concordance *f* agreement, accord.

concorder *vi* to agree; to coincide.

concours *m* competition; conjuncture.

concret *adj* concrete, solid.

concrètement *adv* concretely.

concrétiser *vt* to put in concrete form.

concubin *m*, **-e** *f* concubine; cohabitant.

concubinage *m* concubinage; cohabitation.

concurrence *f* competition.

concurrent *m*, **-e** *f* concurrent; competing.

condamnation *f* condemnation; sentencing.

condamné *m*, **-e** *f* convict; sentenced person; * *adj* sentenced.

condamner *vt* to condemn; to sentence.

condensation *f* condensation.

condensé *adj* condensed, evaporated.

condenser *vt* to condense, compress.

condescendant *adj* condescending.

condiment *m* condiment.

condition *f* condition, term.

conditionné *adj* conditioned; packaged.

conditionnement *m* conditioning; packaging.

conditionner *vt* to condition; to package.

condoléances *fpl* condolences.

conducteur *m*, **-trice** *f* driver; operator.

conduire *vt, vi* to lead; to drive.

conduit *m* conduit, pipe.

conduite *f* conduct; driving; running.

cône *m* cone.

confédération *f* confederation.

conférence *f* conference.

conférencier *m*, **-ière** *f* speaker; lecturer.

confesser *vt* to confess; **se ~** *vr* to go to confession.

confession *f* confession.

confiance *f* confidence, trust.

confiant *adj* confident; confiding.

confidence *f* confidence; disclosure.

confident *m*, **-e** *f* confidant.

confidentiel *adj* confidential; **~lement** *adv* confidentially.

confier *vt* to confide; to entrust; **se ~** *vr* to confide in.

confiner *vt* to confine; **se ~** to be confined; *vr:* **se ~ à** to confine oneself to.

confirmation *f* confirmation.

confirmer *vt* to confirm; **se ~** *vr* to be confirmed.

confiserie *f* confectionery.

confisquer *vt* to confiscate, impound.

confiture *f* jam.

conflictuel *adj* conflicting.

conflit *m* conflict, contention.

confondre *vt* to confuse, mingle.

conforme *adj* consistent; true.

conformément *adv* in accordance with.

conformer *vt* to model; **se ~** *vr* to conform.

conformiste *mf* conformist.

conformité *f* conformity; likeness.

confort *m* comfort.

confortable *adj* comfortable, cosy; **~ment** *adv* comfortably.

confrère *m* colleague.

confrontation *f* confrontation; comparison.

confronter *vt* to confront.

confus *adj* confused, indistinct; **~ément** *adv* confusedly, vaguely.

confusion f confusion, disorder.

congé m leave; holiday.

congédier vt to dismiss.

congélateur m freezer.

congeler vt to freeze.

congestion f congestion; stroke.

congratulation f congratulation.

congratuler vt to congratulate.

congrégation f congregation.

congrès m congress, conference.

conifère m conifer.

conjoint m, **-e** f spouse; * adj joint; linked; **~ement** adv jointly.

conjonctivite f conjunctivitis.

conjoncture f conjuncture; situation.

conjugaison f conjugation.

conjugal adj conjugal.

conjuguer vt to conjugate; to combine.

conjuration f conspiracy, plot.

conjurer vt to conspire; to implore.

connaissance f knowledge; consciousness.

connaisseur m, **-euse** f connoisseur; expert.

connaître vt to know, be acquainted with.

connecter vt to connect.

connecteur m connective.

connexion f connection, link.

connivence f connivance.

connotation f connotation.

connu adj known; famous.

conquérant m, **-e** f conqueror; * adj conquering.

conquérir vt to conquer.

conquête f conquest.

conquis adj conquered, vanquished.

consacrer vt to devote, dedicate; **se ~** vr to dedicate oneself to.

consciemment adv consciously, knowingly.

conscience f consciousness; conscience.

consciencieusement adv consciencieously.

consciencieux adv conscientious.

conscient adj conscious, aware.

consécration f consecration.

consécutif adj consecutive.

consécutivement adv consecutively.

conseil m advice, counsel.

conseiller m, **-ère** f counsellor, adviser; * vt to advise, counsel.

consentant adj consenting, willing.

consentement m consent.

consentir vi to consent; to acquiesce.

conséquence f consequence, result.

conséquent adj consequent, logical.

conservateur m, **-trice** f conservative; curator.

conservation f conservation.

conservatoire m conservatory; school.

conserve f canned food.

conserver vt to keep, preserve; **se ~** vr to keep.

considérable adj considerable; notable; **~ment** adv considerably.

considération f consideration, respect.

considérer vt to consider, regard.

consigne f orders, instructions.

consistance f consistency; strength.

consister vi: **~ en** to consist of; **cela consiste à** that consists in doing.

consolation f consolation, solace.

console f console.

consoler vt to console, comfort.

consolidation f consolidation, reinforcement.

consolider vt to consolidate, reinforce.

consommateur m, **-trice** f consumer.

consommation f consumption; accomplishment.

consommé *adj* consummate, accomplished; * *m* consommé.

consommer *vt* to consume; to use.

consonne *f* consonant.

conspirateur *m*, **-trice** *f* conspirator.

conspiration *f* conspiracy, plot.

conspirer *vi* to conspire, plot.

constamment *adv* constantly, continually.

constant *adj* constant, continuous.

constante *f* constant.

constat *m* report; acknowledgement.

constatation *f* authentication, verification.

constater *vt* to record; to verify.

constellation *f* constellation, galaxy.

consternation *f* consternation, dismay.

consterner *vt* to dismay.

constipation *f* constipation.

constituer *vt* to constitute, form.

constitution *f* constitution, formation.

constitutionnel *adj* constitutional; **-lement** *adv* constitutionally.

constructeur *m*, **-trice** *f* builder, maker.

constructif *adj* constructive.

construction *f* building, construction.

construire *vt* to construct, build.

consul *m* consul.

consulaire *adj* consular.

consulat *m* consulate.

consultant *m*, **-e** *f* consultant; * *adj* consulting.

consultation *f* consultation, advice.

consulter *vt* to consult, take advice from.

consumer *vt* to consume; to spend; **se ~** *vr* to decay, waste away.

contact *m* contact, touch.

contacter *vt* to contact, approach.

contagieux *adj* contagious, infectious.

contamination *f* contamination, pollution.

contaminer *vt* to contaminate, pollute.

conte *m* story, tale.

contemplation *f* contemplation, meditation.

contempler *vt* to contemplate, meditate.

contemporain *adj* contemporary.

contenance *f* capacity, volume.

contenir *vt* to contain.

contentement *m* contentment, satisfaction.

contenter *vt* to please; to satisfy; **se ~** *vr*: **se ~ de** to content oneself with.

contenu *m* contents, enclosure.

contestation *f* dispute, controversy.

contester *vt* to contest, dispute.

contexte *m* context.

contigu *adj*, *f* **contiguë** contiguous, adjacent.

continent *m* continent.

continental *adj* continental.

contingent *m* quota; draft (*mil*).

continu *adj* continuous, incessant.

continuation *f* continuation.

continuel *adj* continual, continuous; **-lement** *adv* continuously, continually.

continuer *vt* to continue, proceed with; * *vi* to continue, go on.

contour *m* contour, outline.

contourner *vt* to bypass, skirt.

contraceptif *adj* contraceptive.

contraception *f* contraception.

contracter *vt* to contract; to acquire; **se ~** *vr* to contract, to shrink.

contraction *f* contraction.

contradiction *f* contradiction, discrepancy.

contradictoire *adj* contradictory, conflicting.

contraindre *vt* to constrain, compel.

contrainte *f* constraint, compulsion.

contraire *m* opposite, contrary; * *adj* opposite, contrary; **~ment** *adv* contrarily.

contrariant *adj* contrary; perverse.

contrarier *vt* to annoy; to oppose.

contrariété *f* annoyance, disappointment.

contraste *m* contrast.

contrat *m* contract, agreement.

contre *prép* against; **parier à 10 ~ 1** to bet at 10 to 1; **~ toute attente** contrary to all expectations; **par ~** on the other hand.

contre-attaque *f* counter-attack.

contre-attaquer *vi* to counter-attack.

contrebalancer *vt* to counterbalance.

contrebande *f* contraband, smuggling.

contrebandier *m*, **-ière** *f* smuggler.

contrebasse *f* double bass.

contrecarrer *vt* to thwart, oppose.

contrecoeur: à ~ reluctantly.

contrecoup *m* rebound, repercussion.

contredire *vt* to contradict, refute.

contrefaçon *f* counterfeit, forgery.

contrefaire *vt* to counterfeit, forge.

contre-indication *f* contraindication.

contremaître *m* foreman.

contre-offensive *f* counter-offensive.

contrepartie *f* compensation; consideration.

contre-plaqué *m* plywood.

contrepoison *m* antidote, counter-poison.

contresens *m* nonsense; misunderstanding; mistranslation.

contretemps *m* mishap; contretemps; syncopation.

contribuable *mf* taxpayer.

contribuer *vt*, *vi* to contribute.

contribution *f* contribution; tax.

contrôle *m* control, check.

contrôler *vt* to control, check.

contrôleur *m*, **-euse** *f* inspector; auditor.

controverse *f* controversy.

controversé *adj* disputed.

contusion *f* bruise, contusion.

convaincant *adj* convincing.

convaincre *vt* to convince, persuade.

convaincu *adj* convinced, persuaded.

convalescence *f* convalescence.

convenable *adj* fitting, suitable; **~ment** *adv* suitably, fitly.

convenir *vi* to agree, accord.

convention *f* convention, agreement.

conventionnel *adj* conventional; contractual; **~lement** *adv* conventionally.

convenu *adj* agreed; stipulated.

convergent *adj* convergent.

converger *vi* to converge.

conversation *f* conversation, talk.

conversion *f* conversion.

convertir *vt* to convert; **se ~** *vr* to be converted.

convexe *adj* convex.

conviction *f* conviction.

convier *vt* to invite; to urge.

convivial *adj* convivial; user-friendly.

convocation *f* convoking, summoning.

convoi *m* convoy; train.

convoiter *vt* to covet.

convoquer *vt* to convoke, convene.

convulsion *f* convulsion.

coopératif *adj* cooperative.

coopération *f* cooperation.

coopérative *f* cooperative.

coopérer *vi* to cooperate, collaborate.

coordinateur *m*, **-trice** *f* coordinator.

coordination *f* coordination; committee.

coordonnées *fpl* coordinates.

coordonner *vt* to coordinate.

copain *m* friend, pal.

copeau *m* shaving, chip.

copie *f* copy, reproduction.

copier *vt* to copy, reproduce.

copieusement *adv* copiously, abundantly.

copieux *adj* copious, abundant.

copilote *m* co-pilot.

copine *f* friend, mate.

coproduction *f* coproduction.

copropriété *f* co-ownership, joint ownership.

coq *m* cock, rooster.

coque *f* hull; shell.

coquelicot *m* poppy.

coquet *adj* stylish, smart; **~tement** *adv* stylishly, smartly.

coquetterie *f* smartness, stylishness.

coquillage *m* shellfish.

coquille *f* shell, scallop.

coquin *m*, **-e** *f* naughty, mischievous.

cor *m* horn.

corail *m* coral.

coran *m* Koran.

corbeau *m* crow.

corbeille *f* basket.

corbillard *m* hearse.

cordage *m* rope; rigging.

corde *f* rope; string.

cordée *f* roped mountaineering party.

cordial *adj* cordial, warm; **~ement** *adv* cordially, warmly.

cordialité *f* cordiality, warmth.

cordon *m* cord, string; cordon.

cordonnerie *f* shoemending.

cordonnier *m*, **-ière** *f* shoemender, cobbler.

coriace *adj* tough; tight.

coriandre *m* coriander.

corne *f* horn, antler.

cornée *f* cornea.

corneille *f* crow.

cornemuse *f* bagpipes.

cornet *m* cornet, cone.

corniche *f* cornice; ledge.

cornichon *m* gherkin; greenhorn.

corporatif *adj* corporative, corporate.

corporation *f* corporation, guild.

corporatisme *m* corporatism.

corporel *adj* corporal, bodily.

corps *m* body, corpse.

corpulence *f* corpulence.

corpulent *adj* corpulent.

corpus *m* corpus.

correct *adj* correct, accurate; **~ement** *adv* correctly, accurately.

correcteur *m*, **-trice** *f* examiner; proofreader.

correction *f* correction; proofreading.

corrélation *f* correlation.

correspondance *f* correspondence, communication.

correspondant *m*, **-e** *f* correspondent; * *adj* corresponding.

correspondre *vi* to correspond, communicate.

corridor *m* corridor, passage.

corrigé *m* corrected version, fair copy.

corriger *vt* to correct.

corroborer *vt* to corroborate.

corroder *vt* to corrode.

corrompre *vt* to corrupt, debase.

corrompu *adj* corrupt.

corrosif *adj* corrosive.

corrosion *f* corrosion.

corruption *f* corruption, debasement.

corsage *m* blouse, bodice.

corsaire *m* corsair, pirate.

corsé *adj* rich, full-bodied.

corset *m* corset.

cortège *m* cortège, procession.

cortex *m* cortex.

cortical *adj* cortical.

cortisone *f* cortisone.

corvée *f* fatigue duty; forced labour.

cosmétique *m* cosmetic.

cosmique *adj* cosmic.

cosmonaute *mf* cosmonaut.

cosmopolite *adj* cosmopolitan.

cosmos *m* cosmos.

costume *m* costume, dress.

cotation *f* quotation, valuation.

côte *f* coast; rib; slope.

côté *m* side; point.

coteau *m* hill.

côtelé *adj* ribbed.

côtelette *f* cutlet.

coter *vt* to quote;to classify.

côtier *adj* coastal, inshore.

coton *m* cotton.

cotonneux *adj* fleecy, downy.

côtoyer *vt* to mix with, skirt.

cou *m* neck.

couchant *adj* setting.

couche *f* layer, coat.

coucher *vt* to put to bed; **se ~** *vr* to go to bed.

coucou *m* cuckoo.

coude *m* elbow.

coudé *adj* angled, bent.

coudoyer *vt* mix with, rub shoulders with.

coudre *vt, vi* to sew.

couette *f* bearing; duvet.

coulant *adj* flowing; smooth.

couler *vi* to flow, run.

couleur *f* colour, shade.

couleuvre *f* grass snake.

coulis *m* sauce, purée.

coulissant *adj* sliding.

coulisse *f* groove; wings(*theat*)..

coulisser *vi* to slide, run.

couloir *m* corridor, passage.

coup *m* blow; shot; **~ sur ~** one after another, incessantly; **tout à ~** suddenly; **après ~** afterwards, after the event; **~ de feu** shot; **jeter un ~ d'oeil** to glance; **~ de coude** nudge; **~ de téléphone** phone call; **~ de soleil** sunstroke.

coupable *mf* culprit; * *adj* guilty.

coupant *adj* cutting, sharp.

coupe *f* cut; cutting.

coupe-papier *m invar* paper knife.

couper *vt* to cut, slice.

couple *m* couple, pair.

couplet *m* couplet, verse.

coupole *f* dome.

coupon *m* coupon, voucher, ticket.

coupure *f* cut; break.

cour *f* court, yard, courtyard.

courage *m* courage, daring.

courageusement *adv* courageously.

courageux *adj* courageous.

couramment *adv* fluently; commonly.

courant *adj* current; present; * *m* stream, current.

courbature *f* stiffness; ache.

courbaturé *adj* aching.

courbe *f* curve; contour.

courbé *adj* curved, stooped.

courber *vt* to curve, bend.

coureur *m*, **-euse** *f* runner.

courgette *f* courgette.

courir *vi* to run, race.

couronne *f* crown, wreath.

couronnement *m* coronation.

couronner *vt* to crown.

courrier *m* mail, post.

courroie *f* strap, belt.

cours *m* course; flow; path.

course *f* running; race; flight; journey.

coursier *m*, **-ière** *f* courier, messenger.

court *adj* short, brief.

court-bouillon *m* court-bouillon, wine sauce.

court-circuit *m* short-circuit.

court-circuiter *vt* to short-circuit.

courtier *m*, **-ière** *f* broker, agent.

courtiser *vt* to court.

courtois *adj* courteous; **~ement** *adv* courteously.

courtoisie *f* courtesy, courteousness.

cousin *m*, **-e** *f* cousin.

coussin *m* cushion, pillow.
coussinet *m* pad; bearing.
coût *m* cost, charge.
couteau *m* knife.
coûter *vi, vt* to cost.
coûteusement *adv* expensively.
coûteux *adj* costly, expensive.
coutume *f* custom, habit.
coutumier *adj* customary, usual.
couture *f* sewing, needlework.
couturier *m* couturier, fashion designer.
couturière *f* dressmaker.
couvent *m* convent.
couver *vt* to hatch, incubate; * *vi* to smoulder, lurk.
couvercle *m* lid, cap.
couvert *m* shelter; cover; pretext; * *adj* covered; secret; obscure.
couverture *f* blanket; cover; roofing.
couvre-feu *m* curfew.
couvreur *m* roofer.
couvrir *vt* to cover; **se ~** *vr* to cover up; to become overcast.
crabe *m* crab.
crachement *m* spitting.
cracher *vt* to spit.
crachin *m* drizzle.
craie *f* chalk.
craindre *vt* to fear.
crainte *f* fear, dread.
craintif *adj* timid, cowardly.
crampe *f* cramp.
crampon *m* stud, spike, crampon.
cramponner *vt* to cramp, clamp; **se ~** *vr* to cling, hang on.
cran *m* notch, cog.
crâne *m* cranium, skull.
crânien *adj* cranial.
crapaud *m* toad.
crapule *f* villain.
crapuleux *adj* villainous, vicious.
craquellement *m* cracking.
craquement *m* crack, creaking, snap.
craquer *vi* to creak, squeak, crack.
crasseux *adj* grimy, filthy.
cratère *m* crater.

cravate *f* tie.
créancier *m*, **-ière** *f* creditor.
créateur *m*, **-trice** *f* creator, author.
créatif *adj* creative.
création *f* creation.
créativité *f* creativity.
créature *f* creature.
crèche *f* creche; crib.
crédibilité *f* credibility.
crédible *adj* credible.
crédit *m* credit, trust.
crédit-bail *m* lease; leasing.
crédule *adj* credulous, gullible.
crédulité *f* credulity, gullibility.
créer *vt* to create, produce.
crémaillère *f* rack.
crème *f* cream.
crémerie *f* dairy.
crémeux *adj* creamy.
crémier *m* dairyman, **-ière** *f* dairywoman.
créneau *m* battlement.
crêpe *f* pancake; * *m* crepe, crape.
crêperie *f* pancake restaurant.
crépitement *m* crackling; rattling.
crépiter *vi* to crackle; to rattle.
crépu *adj* frizzy, woolly.
crépuscule *m* twilight, dusk.
cresson *m* watercress.
crête *f* crest, comb.
crétin *m*, **-e** *f* cretin, idiot.
creuser *vi* to dig, burrow; * *vt* to dig, hollow.
creuset *m* crucible.
creux *adj* hollow, empty.
crevaison *f* puncture, flat.
crevé *adj* burst, punctured.
crever *vt* to burst; to gouge; *vi* to burst; to split.
crevette *f* prawn.
cri *m* cry, howl, yell.
criant *adj* crying; striking, glaring.
criard *adj* yelling; scolding.
crible *m* riddle, sieve; **passer au ~** to riddle; to examine closely.
cribler *vt* to sift, riddle.
cric *m* jack (car).

crier *vi* to cry, shout.
crime *m* crime, offence.
criminel *m*, **elle** *f* criminal; * *adj* criminal.
crin *m* horsehair.
crinière *f* mane.
crique *f* creek.
criquet *m* locust.
crise *f* crisis, attack.
crisper *vt* to shrivel; to clench.
cristal *m* crystal, glassware.
cristallin *adj* crystalline.
cristallisation *f* crystallization.
cristalliser *vt* to crystallize.
critère *m* criterion, standard.
critiquable *adj* censurable, open to criticism.
critique *adj* critical, censorious; * *f* criticism; critique.
critiquer *vt* to criticize, censure.
croc *m* fang; hook.
croche *f* quaver.
crochet *m* hook, clip.
crochu *adj* hooked, claw-like.
crocodile *m* crocodile.
croire *vt* to believe; to think.
croisade *f* crusade.
croisement *m* crossing, junction.
croiser *vt* to cross; to fold; **se ~** *vr* to cross, intersect.
croisière *f* cruise.
croissance *f* growth, increase.
croissant *adj* growing, increasing; * *m* croissant; crescent.
croître *vi* to grow, rise.
croix *f* cross.
croque-monsieur *m* toasted cheese and ham sandwich.
croquer *vt* to crunch, munch.
croquette *f* croquette.
croquis *m* sketch, outline.
crosse *f* crozier; butt, grip.
crotte *f* manure, dung.
croupir *vi* to stagnate, wallow.
croustillant *adj* crusty, crisp.
croustiller *vi* to be crusty, crispy.
croûte *f* crust.
croûton *m* crust, crouton.
croyance *f* belief.
croyant *adj* believing.

cru *adj* raw, uncooked; * *m* vineyard; wine.
cruauté *f* cruelty, inhumanity.
cruche *f* pitcher.
crucial *adj* crucial, decisive.
crucifix *m* crucifix.
crucifixion *f* crucifixion.
crudité *f* crudity, coarseness.
crue *f* flood.
cruel *adj* cruel; **~lement** *adv* cruelly.
crustacé *m* crustacean, shellfish.
crypte *m* crypt.
crypter *vt* to encode, scramble.
cube *m* cube, block.
cubique *adj* cubic.
cubisme *m* cubism.
cueillette *f* picking, gathering.
cueillir *vt* to pick, gather.
cuiller, cuillère *f* spoon, spoonful.
cuir *m* leather, hide.
cuirasse *f* cuirass, breastplate.
cuirassé *adj* armoured; * *m* battleship.
cuire *vi* to cook.
cuisine *f* kitchen; cookery.
cuisiner *vt, vi* to cook.
cuisinier *m*, **-ière** *f* cook.
cuisinière *f* cooker, stove.
cuisse *f* thigh.
cuisson *f* cooking, baking.
cuit *adj* cooked.
cuivre *m* copper.
cul *m* bottom, ass.
culasse *f* cylinder-head; breech.
cul-de-jatte *mf* legless cripple.
cul-de-sac *m* blind alley, cul-de-sac.
culinaire *adj* culinary.
culminer *vi* to culminate, tower.
culot *m* cheek, nerve.
culotte *f* knickers; underpants; shorts.
culpabiliser *vt* to make someone feel guilty; **se ~** *vr* to feel guilty.
culpabilité *f* guilt, culpability.
culte *m* cult, veneration.
cultivable *adj* cultivable.
cultivateur *m*, **-trice** *f* farmer.

cultivé *adj* cultured.
cultiver *vt* to cultivate; **se ~** *vr* to improve oneself.
culture *f* culture; cultivation.
culturel *adj* cultural.
culturisme *m* body-building.
cumin *m* cumin.
cumul *m* pluralism; accumulation.
cumuler *vt* to accumulate; to hold concurrently.
cupide *adj* greedy; **~ment** *adv* greedily.
cupidité *f* greed, cupidity.
cure *f* cure; treatment.
curé *m* parish priest, parson.
cure-dents *m* toothpick.
curieusement *adv* curiously.
curieux *m*, **-euse** *f* inquisitive person; onlooker; * *adj* curious, inquisitive.
curiosité *f* curiosity, inquisitiveness.
cursus *m* degree course.

cutané *adj* skin, cutaneous.
cuve *f* vat, tank.
cuvette *f* basin, bowl.
cyanure *m* cyanide.
cybernétique *f* cybernetics.
cyclable *adj* cycle, for cycling.
cyclamen *m* cyclamen.
cycle *m* cycle; stage.
cyclique *adj* cyclical.
cyclisme *m* cycling.
cycliste *mf* cyclist; * *adj* cycle.
cyclomoteur *m* moped.
cyclone *m* cyclone.
cyclope *m* Cyclops.
cygne *m* swan.
cylindre *m* cylinder.
cylindrée *f* capacity (engine).
cylindrique *adj* cylindrical.
cymbale *f* cymbal.
cynique *adj* cynical; **~ment** *adv* cynically.
cynisme *m* cynicism.
cytologie *f* cytology.
cytoplasme *m* cytoplasm.

D

dactylographe *mf* typist.
dactylographie *f* typing, typewriting.
dactylographier *vt* to type.
dada *m* (*fam*) hobby-horse; geegee.
dahlia *m* dahlia.
daigner *vt* to deign, condescend.
daim *m* deer.
dalle *f* flagstone, slab.
dalmatien *m* Dalmatian.
daltonien *adj* colour-blind.
dame *f* lady; dame.
damier *m* draughtboard.
damnation *f* damnation.
damné *adj* damned.
damner *vt* to damn.
danger *m* danger, risk.
dangereusement *adv* dangerously.

dangereux *adj* dangerous, risky.
dans *prép* in; into; **il a ~ les trente ans** he's thirty or so.
dansant *adj* dancing.
danse *f* dance; dancing.
danser *vi* to dance.
danseur *m*, **-euse** *f* dancer.
dard *m* dart; sting.
datation *f* dating.
date *f* date.
dater *vt* to date.
datif *m* dative.
datte *f* (*bot*) date.
dattier *m* date palm.
dauphin *m* dolphin.
daurade *f* sea bream.
davantage *adv* more.
de *prép* of; from; **une femme ~ quarante ans** a forty-year-old woman; **~ bonne heure** early;

deux ~ plus two more; * *art* some, any.

dé *m* die; thimble.

déambuler *vi* to stroll.

débâcle *f* disaster; collapse.

déballage *m* unpacking; display.

déballer *vt* to unpack; to display.

débandade *f* rout, stampede.

débarbouiller *vt* to wash quickly; **se ~** *vr* to wash oneself; to extricate oneself.

débarcadère *m* landing; wharf.

débardeur *m* docker, stevedore.

débarquement *m* landing, disembarkment.

débarquer *vt* to land, unship; * *vi* to disembark, land.

débarrasser *vt* to clear, rid; **se ~** *vr*: **se ~ de** to rid oneself of.

débat *m* debate; dispute, contest.

débattre *vi* to debate, discuss.

débauche *f* debauchery, dissoluteness.

débaucher *vt* to debauch, corrupt.

débile *adj* weak, feeble.

débilitant *adj* debilitating, weakening.

débit *m* debit; turnover; flow.

débiter *vt* to debit; to produce.

débiteur *m*, **-trice** *f* debtor.

déblayer *vt* to clear away, remove.

déblocage *m* unblocking; freeing, releasing.

débloquer *vt* to release, unlock.

déboisement *m* deforestation.

déboiser *vt* to deforest.

déboîtement *m* dislocation.

débordant *adj* exuberant, overflowing.

débordé *adj* overwhelmed.

débordement *m* overflowing; outflanking.

déborder *vi* to overflow; to outflank.

débouché *m* outlet; issue.

déboucher *vt* to open, uncork; * *vi* to pass out, emerge.

debout *adv* upright, standing; être ~ to stand.

déboutonner *vt* to unbutton.

débraillé *adj* untidy, disordered.

débrancher *vt* to disconnect.

débrayer *vi* to declutch; to stop work.

débris *m* debris, waste.

débrouiller *vt* to disentangle, unravel; **se ~** *vr* to cope, manage.

début *m* beginning, outset.

débutant *adj* novice.

débuter *vi* to start, begin; * *vt* to lead, start.

décadence *f* decadence, decline.

décadent *adj* decadent.

décaféiné *adj* decaffeinated.

décagone *m* decagon.

décalage *m* gap, interval; discrepancy.

décalcifier *vt* to decalcify.

décaler *vt* to stagger; to shift.

décalitre *m* decalitre.

décamètre *m* decametre.

décaper *vt* to clean, scour.

décapotable *adj* convertible; * *f* convertible.

décapsuler *vt* to take the lid off.

décapsuleur *m* bottle-opener.

décathlon *m* decathlon.

décéder *vi* to die.

décelable *adj* detectable.

déceler *vt* to detect; to disclose.

décembre *m* December.

décemment *adv* decently.

décence *f* decency.

décennal *adj* decennial.

décennie *f* decade.

décent *adj* decent, proper.

décentralisation *f* decentralization.

décentraliser *vt* to decentralize.

déception *f* disappointment; deceit.

décerner *vt* to award, confer.

décès *m* death, decease.

décevant *adj* disappointing; deceptive.

décevoir *vt* to disappoint; to deceive.

déchaîné *adj* wild, unbridled.

déchaîner *vt* to unleash; **se ~** *vr* to break loose, run wild.

décharge *f* discharge; receipt.

déchargement *m* unloading.

décharger *vt* to unload, discharge.

décharné *adj* lean, emaciated.

déchausser *vt* to take off footwear; **se ~** *vr* to take one's shoes off.

déchéance *f* decay, decline.

déchet *m* loss, waste.

déchiffrer *vt* to decipher, decode.

déchiqueter *vt* to tear; to slash; to shred.

déchirant *adj* harrowing, excruciating.

déchirement *m* tearing, ripping.

déchirer *vt* to tear, rip.

déchirure *f* tear, rip.

déchoir *vi* to decline; to sink.

déchu *adj* fallen; declined; deposed.

décibel *m* decibel.

décidé *adj* decided; determined; **~ment** *adv* positively; resolutely; certainly.

décigramme *m* decigram.

décilitre *m* decilitre.

décimal *adj* decimal.

décimètre *m* decimetre.

décisif *adj* decisive, conclusive.

décision *f* decision.

déclamer *vt* to declaim.

déclamation *f* declamation.

déclaré *adj* professed, avowed.

déclarer *vt* to declare, announce; **se ~** *vr* to speak one's mind.

déclenchement *m* release, setting off.

déclencher *vt* to release, set off; **se ~** *vr* to release itself, go off.

déclic *m* click; trigger.

déclin *m* decline, deterioration.

déclinaison *f* declension; declination.

déclinant *adj* declining.

décliner *vi* to decline, refuse.

déclivité *f* declivity, slope.

décloisonner *vt* to decompartmentalize.

décoder *vt* to decode, decipher.

décodeur *m* decoder, decipherer.

décoiffer *vt* to disarrange so's hair.

décoincer *vt* to loose, release.

décollage *m* take-off, lift-off.

décoller *vi* to unpaste, steam off; to take off; * *vt*; **se ~** *vr* to come unstuck, become detached.

décolleté *adj* low-necked, low-cut; *m* decolletage, low neckline.

décolorant *adj* bleaching, decolorizing; * *m* bleaching substance.

décolorer *vt* to decolour, bleach.

décombres *mpl* rubble, debris.

décomposer *vt* to decompose; to break up; to dissect; **se ~** *vr* to decompose, decay.

décomposition *f* decomposition, breaking up.

décompression *f* decompression.

décomprimer *vt* to decompress.

décompte *m* discount; deduction.

déconcentrer *vt* to devolve; to disperse; **se ~** *vr* to lose concentration.

déconcertant *adj* disconcerting.

déconcerter *vt* to disconcert.

décongeler *vt* to thaw, defrost.

déconnecter *vt* to disconnect.

déconnexion *f* disconnection.

décontenancé *adj* embarrassed; disconcerted.

décontracté *adj* relaxed.

décontracter *vt* to relax; **se ~** *vr* to relax.

décontraction *f* relaxation.

décor *m* scenery; setting.

décorateur *m*, **-trice** *f* decorator; set designer.

décoratif *adj* decorative, ornamental.

décoration *f* decoration, embellishment.

décorer *vt* to decorate, adorn.

décortiquer *vt* to husk, shell.

découler *vi* to flow; to ensue.

découpage *m* cutting up, carving.

découper *vt* to carve, cut up.

décourageant *adj* discouraging, disheartening.

découragement *m* discouragement.

décourager *vt* discourage, dishearten; **se ~** *vr* to become discouraged.

décousu *adj* unsewn; loose; disconnected.

découvert *adj* uncovered; open; * *m* overdraft.

découverte *f* discovery.

découvrir *vt* to discover.

décret *m* decree, enactment.

décréter *vt* to decree, enact.

décrire *vt* to describe.

décrocher *vt* to take down; to unhook.

décroissant *adj* decreasing, lessening.

décroître *vi* to decrease, diminish.

déçu *adj* disappointed.

décupler *vi* to increase tenfold.

dédaigner *vt to* disdain, scorn.

dédaigneusement *adv* disdainfully.

dédaigneux *adj* disdainful, scornful.

dédain *m* disdain, scorn.

dedans *adv* inside, indoors; * *m* inside; **au ~ inside**.

dédicace *f* dedication.

dédier *vt* to consecrate, dedicate to.

dédommagement *m* compensation, damages.

dédommager *vt* to compensate, indemnify.

dédouanement *m* customs clearance.

dédoubler *vt* to divide in two; to remove lining.

déduction *f* deduction.

déduire *vt* to deduct; to deduce.

déesse *f* goddess.

défaillance *f* faintness; exhaustion; blackout.

défaillant *adj* faint; weakening.

défaillir *vi* to faint; to weaken.

défaire *vt* to undo, dismantle.

défaite *m* defeat, overthrow.

défaitiste *adj, mf* defeatist.

défaut *m* defect, fault.

défavorable *adj* unfavourable; **~ment** *adv* unfavourably.

défavoriser *vt* to penalize, treat unfairly.

défection *f* defection.

défectueux *adj* defective, faulty.

défendeur *m*, **-deresse** *f* defendant.

défendre *vt* to defend, protect; to prohibit; **se ~** *vr* to defend oneself.

défense *f* defence; prohibition.

défenseur *m* defender.

défensif *adj* defensive.

défi *m* defiance; challenge.

défiant *adj* mistrustful, distrustful.

déficience *f* deficiency.

déficient *adj* deficient; weak.

déficit *m* deficit, shortfall.

déficitaire *adj* deficient, in deficit.

défier *vt* to challenge, defy.

défilé *m* procession, parade.

défiler *vi* to parade, march.

défini *adj* definite, precise.

définir *vt* to define, specify.

définitif *adj* definitive, final.

définition *f* definition.

définitivement *adv* definitively, finally.

déflagration *f* deflagration, explosion.

déflation *f* deflation.

défoncer *vt* to smash in; to dig deeply.

déformation *f* deformation, distortion.

déformer *vt* to deform, distort; **se ~** *vr* to bend; to lose its shape.

défoulement *m* outlet; release.

défouler *vt* to unwind, relax; **se ~** *vr* to get rid of one's inhibitions.

défricher *vt* to clear; to reclaim.

défunt *m*, **-e** *f* deceased; * *adj* late, deceased.

dégagé *adj* clear; open.

dégagement *m* freeing, clearance.

dégager *vt* to free, clear; **se ~** *vr* to free oneself, extricate oneself.

dégarnir *vt* to empty; to clear.

dégât *m* havoc, damage.

dégel *m* thaw.

dégeler *vt vi* to thaw, melt.

dégénérer *vi* to degenerate, decline.

dégivrer *vt* to de-ice, defrost.

dégonfler *vt* to deflate, empty.

dégourdir *vt* to warm up, revive.

dégourdissement *m* reviving, return of circulation.

dégoût *m* disgust, distaste.

dégouter *vt* to disgust.

dégradant *adj* degrading.

dégradation *f* degradation, debasement.

dégradé *m* shading off; gradation.

dégrader *vt* to degrade, debase; **se ~** *vr* to become degraded, debased.

dégrafer *vt* to unfasten, unhook.

dégraisser *vt* to remove grease.

degré *m* degree; grade.

dégrèvement *m* reduction; redemption.

dégripper *vt* to unblock; to unchoke.

déguisement *m* disguise.

déguiser *vt* to disguise; **se ~** *vr* to disguise oneself.

dégustation *f* tasting, sampling.

dehors *adv* outside, outdoors; **au ~** outwardly; **en ~ de** outside; apart from; * *m* outside, exterior.

déjà *adv* already.

déjeuner *vi* to lunch; * *m* lunch.

déjouer *vt* to elude; to thwart.

delà *adv*: **au ~ de** beyond; **par ~** beyond.

délabré *adj* dilapidated, ramshackle.

délacer *vt* to unlace, undo.

délai *m* delay; respite; time limit.

délaisser *vt* to abandon, quit.

délassant *adj* relaxing, refreshing.

délasser *vt* to refresh, relax; **se ~** *vr* to rest, relax.

délateur *m*, **-trice** *f* informer.

délation *f* denouncement; informing.

délavé *adj* diluted; faded.

délayage *m* dragging-out, spinning-out.

délayer *vt* to thin; to drag out.

délectation *f* delectation, delight.

délecter(se) *vr* to delight, revel.

délégation *f* delegation.

délégué *m*, **-e** *f* delegate, representative; * *adj* delegate, delegated.

déléguer *vt* to delegate.

délibération *f* deliberation; resolution.

délibéré *adj* deliberate; resolute; **~ment** *adv* deliberately.

délicat *adj* delicate, dainty; **~ement** *adv* delicately.

délicatesse *f* delicacy, daintiness.

délice *m* delight, pleasure.

délicieux *adj* delicious, delightful.

délier *vt* to unbind, untie.

délimitation *f* delimitation.

délimiter *vt* to delimit, demarcate.

délinquance *f* delinquency.

délinquant *m*, **-e** *f* delinquent, offender; * *adj* delinquent.

délirant *adj* delirious, frenzied.

délire *m* delirium, frenzy.

délirer *vi* to be delirious.

délit *m* offence, misdemeanour.

délivrance *f* deliverance; release; delivery.

délivrer *vt* to deliver; to release; **se ~** *vr* to free oneself.

déloger *vt* to evict, dislodge.

déloyal *adj* disloyal, unfaithful; **~ement** *adv* disloyally.

déloyauté *f* disloyalty, treachery.

delta *m* delta.

deltaplane *m* hang-glider.

démagogie *f* demagogy.

démagogique *adj* demagogic.

démagogue *m* demagogue.

demain *adv* tomorrow.

demande *f* request, petition; question.

demander *vt* to ask, request; **se ~** *vr* to wonder.

démangeaison *f* itch; longing.

démaquillant *m* make-up remover; * *adj* make-up removing.

démaquiller *vt* to remove make-up; **se ~** *vr* to take one's make-up off.

démarche *f* bearing; gait, walk.

démarrage *m* moving off, casting off.

démarrer *vi* to start up, move off; * *vt* to start, get started.

démarreur *m* starter.

démasquer *vt* to unmask, uncover.

démêlage *m* disentangling; combing.

démêler *vt* to disentangle, unravel; comb.

déménagement *m* removal; moving (house).

déménager *vi* to move house.

déménageur *m* removal man.

démener(se) *vr* to struggle, strive.

dément *adj* mad, insane, crazy.

démenti *m* denial, refutation.

démentir *vt* to deny, refute.

démesuré *adj* excessive, inordinate; **~ment** *adv* excessively, inordinately.

démettre *vt* to dislocate; to dismiss.

demeure *f* residence, dwelling place.

demeurer *vi* to live at, reside, stay.

demi *adj* half; **à ~** halfway; * *m* half.

demi-cercle *m* semicircle.

demi-douzaine *f* half-dozen.

demi-droite *f* half-line.

demi-finale *f* semi-final.

demi-frère *m* half-brother.

demi-heure *f* half hour.

demi-jour *m* half-light, twilight.

démilitariser *vt* to demilitarize.

demi-litre *m* half-litre.

demi-lune *f* half-moon.

demi-mesure *f* half-measure.

demi-mot *m*: **à ~** without spelling out.

demi-pension *f* half-board.

demi-soeur *f* half-sister.

démission *f* resignation.

démissionner *vi* to resign.

demi-tarif *m* half-fare.

demi-tour *m* half-turn.

démocrate *mf* democrat.

démocratie *f* democracy.

démocratique *adj* democratic; **~ment** *adv* democratically.

démocratiser *vt* to democratize.

démodé *adj* old-fashioned, out-of-date.

démographie *f* demography.

démographique *adj* demographic.

demoiselle *f* young lady; spinster; damsel.

démolir *vt* to demolish, knock down.

démolition *f* demolition.

démon *m* demon, fiend.

démoniaque *adj* demoniac, fiendish.

démonstrateur *m*, **-trice** *f* demonstrator.

démonstratif *adj* demonstrative.

démonstration *f* demonstration; proof.

démontable *adj* collapsible, that can be dismantled.

démonte-pneu *m* tyre lever.

démonter *vt* to dismantle, take down, dismount; **se ~** *vr* to come apart, be nonplussed.

démontrer *vt* demonstrate; to prove.

démoralisant *adj* demoralizing.

démoraliser *vt* to demoralize; **se**

~ *vr* to become demoralized.

démouler *vt* to take out of a mould.

démunir *vt* to deprive; to divest.

démystifier *vt* to demystify, disabuse.

dénaturé *adj* denatured, disfigured.

dénégation *f* denial.

déneiger *vt* to clear snow from.

déni *m* denial, refusal.

dénicher *vt* to dislodge; to unearth.

dénier *vt* to deny, disclaim.

dénigrer *vt* to denigrate, disparage.

dénivellation *f* difference in level, unevenness.

dénombrer *vt* to number, enumerate.

dénomination *f* denomination, designation.

dénoncer *vt* to denounce; to inform against.

dénonciation *f* denunciation.

dénouement *m* dénouement; unravelling; outcome.

dénouer *vt* to unravel, untie, undo.

dénoyauter *vt* to stone (fruit).

denrée *f* commodity, provisions, foodstuff.

dense *adj* dense, thick.

densité *f* density, denseness.

dent *f* tooth.

dentaire *adj* dental.

dentelé *adj* jagged, perforated.

dentelle *f* lace.

dentier *m* denture, dental plate.

dentifrice *m* toothpaste.

dentiste *mf* dentist.

dentition *f* dentition, teething.

dénuder *vt* to bare, denude; **se ~** *vr* to strip off.

dénué *adj* devoid, bereft.

dénuement *m* destitution; deprivation.

déodorant *m* deodorant.

déontologie *f* deontology.

dépannage *m* repairing, fixing.

dépanner *vt* to repair, fix.

dépanneur *m*, **-euse** *f* breakdown mechanic.

dépanneuse *f* breakdown lorry.

dépareillé *adj* unmatched; odd.

déparer *vt* to spoil; to disfigure.

départ *m* departure; start.

département *m* department.

dépasser *vt* to exceed; to go past.

dépaysé *adj* disoriented, out of one's element.

dépaysement *m* disorientation.

dépêcher *vt* to dispatch, send; **se ~** *vr* to hurry, rush.

dépendance *f* dependence; dependency.

dépendant *adj* dependent.

dépendre *vi* to depend on, be dependent on.

dépens *mpl*: **aux ~ de** at the expense of.

dépense *f* expenditure, outlay.

dépenser *vt* to expend, spend; **se ~** *vr* to exert oneself.

dépérir *vi* to decline, waste away.

dépeupler *vt* to depopulate; to clear.

dépistage *m* tracking; detection.

dépister *vt* to track.

dépit *m* spite; grudge; **en ~ de** in spite of.

dépité *adj* vexed; frustrated.

déplacé *adj* misplaced; ill-timed.

déplacement *m* displacement; removal.

déplacer *vt* to displace; to move; **se ~** *vr* to change residence.

déplaire *vi* to displease; to offend.

déplaisant *adj* disagreeable, unpleasant.

dépliant *m* prospectus, leaflet; * *adj* extendible; folding.

déplier *vt* to unfold; to open out.

déploiement *m* deployment; display.

déplorable *adj* deplorable, disgraceful.

déplorer *vt* to deplore, bewail.

déployer *vt* to deploy; to display.

dépopulation *f* depopulation.

déportation *f* deportation, transportation.

déporté *m*, **-e** *f* deportee.

déporter *vt* to deport, transport.

déposer *vt* to lodge, deposit.

dépositaire *mf* depository; trustee.

déposition *f* deposition; evidence.

dépôt *m* deposit; warehouse.

dépouillement *m* scrutiny, perusal; despoiling.

dépouiller *vt* to strip; to despoil; to peruse.

dépourvu *adj* lacking, wanting; **au ~** off guard.

dépoussiérer *vt* to dust.

dépravation *f* depravity, corruption.

dépravé *adj* depraved, corrupt.

dépréciation *f* depreciation.

déprécier *vt* to depreciate; to disparage; **se ~** *vr* to depreciate, fall in value.

dépressif *adj* depressive.

dépression *f* depression, slump; dejection.

déprimant *adj* depressing.

déprimer *vt* to depress; to discourage.

depuis *prép* since, from; after.

député *m* deputy, delegate.

déracinement *m* uprooting, eradication.

déraciner *vt* to uproot, eradicate.

déraillement *m* derailment.

dérailler *vi* to be derailed, run off the rails.

dérailleur *m* derailleur, derailer (*rail*).

déraisonner *vi* to talk irrationally, rave.

dérangement *m* derangement; inconvenience.

déranger *vt* to upset, unsettle; **se ~** *vr* to move; to put oneself out.

dérapage *m* skid.

déraper *vi* to skid, slip.

déréglé *adj* out order; irregular; unruly.

dérèglement *m* disturbance; irregularity; dissoluteness.

dérégler *vt* to disturb; to put out of order; to upset.

dérision *f* derision, mockery.

dérisoire *adj* derisory; pathetic.

dérivation *f* derivation; diversion.

dérive *f* drift; **aller à la ~** to go downhill.

dériver *vi* to drift.

dermatologie *f* dermatology.

dermatologue *mf* dermatologist.

derme *m* dermis.

dernier *adj* last; latest; back; * *m*, **-ière** *f* last one; latter.

dernièrement *adv* recently; lately.

dérobade *f* sidestepping; evasion.

dérober *vt* to steal; to hide; **se ~** *vr* to steal away, escape.

dérogation *f* derogation; dispensation.

déroger *vi* to derogate; to detract.

déroulement *m* unfolding; progress, development.

dérouler *vt* to unwind, uncoil; **se ~** *vr* to develop; to unfold.

déroutant *adj* disconcerting.

déroute *f* rout, overthrow.

dérouter *vt* to rout, overthrow.

derrière *prép* behind; * *adv*; **par ~** by the back; * *m* bottom; back; **de ~** back, rear.

des *art* = de les; *see* **un, une**.

dès *prép* from, since; **~ que** when; as soon as.

désabusé *adj* disenchanted; disabused.

désaccord *m* disagreement, discord.

désaffecté *adj* disused.

désagréable *adj* disagreeable, unpleasant; **~ment** *adv* disagreeably, unpleasantly.

désagréger *vt* to break up, separate; **se ~** *vr* to break up, become separated.

désagrément *m* displeasure, annoyance.

désaltérant *adj* thirst-quenching.

désaltérer *vt* to refresh; **se ~** *vi* to quench one's thirst.

désamorcer *vt* to unprime, defuse.

désapprobateur *adj* disapproving.

désapprobation *f* disapproval.

désapprouver *vt* to disapprove, object.

désarçonner *vt* to unsaddle; to nonplus, baffle.

désarmant *adj* disarming.

désarmement *m* disarmament.

désarmer *vt* to disarm; to unload.

désarroi *m* disarray, confusion.

désarticuler *vt* to dislocate; to upset.

désastre *m* disaster.

désastreux *adj* disastrous, unfortunate.

désavantage *m* disadvantage; prejudice.

désavantager *vt* to disadvantage, handicap.

désaveu *m* disavowal, retraction.

désavouer *vt* to disavow, retract.

descendance *f* descent, lineage.

descendant *m*, **-e** *f* descendant; * *adj* falling, descending.

descendre *vi* to descend, go down; * *vt* to take down, bring down.

descente *f* descent, way down.

descriptif *adj* descriptive, explanatory.

description *f* description.

désemparé *adj* helpless; distraught.

désenchantement *m* disenchantment; disillusion.

désenfler *vi* to become less swollen.

désensibiliser *vt* to desensitize.

déséquilibre *m* imbalance, unbalance.

déséquilibré *adj* unbalanced, unhinged.

déséquilibrer *vt* to unbalance, throw off balance.

désert *m* desert, wilderness; * *adj* deserted.

déserter *vt* to desert.

déserteur *m* deserter.

désertification *f* desertification.

désertion *f* desertion.

désertique *adj* desert; barren.

désespérant *adj* desperate, hopeless; discouraging.

désespéré *adj* desperate, hopeless; **~ment** *adv* desperately.

désespérer *vi* to despair, give up hope.

désespoir *m* despair, despondency.

déshabiller *vt* to undress; **se ~** *vr* to undress.

désherbage *m* weeding.

désherbant *m* weed killer.

désherber *vt* to weed.

déshériter *vt* to disinherit.

déshonorant *adj* dishonourable, disgraceful.

déshonorer *vt* to dishonour, disgrace.

déshydraté *adj* dehydrated.

déshydrater *vt* to dehydrate; **se ~** *vr* to become dehydrated.

désignation *f* designation, nomination; name.

désigner *vt* to designate, indicate.

désillusion *f* disillusion; disappointment.

désillusionner *vt* to disillusion; to disappoint.

désincarné *adj* disincarnate, disembodied.

désinfectant *m* disinfectant; * *adj* disinfectant.

désinfecter *vt* to disinfect.

désinfection *f* disinfection.

désinformation *f* disinformation.

désintégration *f* disintegration.

désintégrer *vt* to split, break up; **se ~** *vr* to disintegrate.

désintéressé *adj* disinterested, unselfish.

désintéressement *m* disinterestedness, unselfishness.

désintéresser(se) *vr* to lose interest in.

désintoxiquer *vt* to detoxify; to dry out; **se ~** *vr* to dry out.

désinvolte *adj* easy, offhand, casual.

désinvolture *f* casualness, offhandedness.

désir *m* desire, wish, longing.

désirable *adj* desirable.

désirer *vt* to desire, wish, long.

désobéir *vi* to disobey.

désobéissance *f* disobedience.

désobéissant *adj* disobedient.

désobligeant *adj* disobliging; uncivil.

désodorisant *m* deodorant; * *adj* deodorizing, deodorant.

désodoriser *vt* to deodorize.

désoeuvré *adj* unoccupied, idle.

désoeuvrement *m* idleness.

désolation *f* desolation; ruin; grief.

désolé *adj* desolate; disconsolate, grieved.

désordonné *adj* untidy; inordinate; reckless.

désordre *m* disorder, confusion, disturbance.

désorganisation *f* disorganization.

désorienté *adj* disorientated.

désormais *adv* from now on, henceforth.

désossé *adj* boned.

despote *m* despot.

despotique *adj* despotic; **~ment** *adv* despotically.

dessèchement *m* dryness, drying up, withering.

dessécher *vt* to dry, parch, wither; **se ~** *vr* to dry out, become parched.

dessein *m* design, plan, scheme; **à ~** intentionally.

desserrer *vt* to loosen; to unscrew; to slacken; **se ~** *vr* to work loose, come undone.

dessert *m* dessert, sweet.

desservir *vt* to clear (table); to do a disservice to.

dessin *m* drawing, sketch; draft.

dessinateur *m*, **-trice** *f* drawer, draughtsman.

dessiner *vt* to draw, sketch; to design.

dessous *adv* under, beneath; * *m* underside, bottom.

dessus *adv* over, above; * *m*; **prendre le ~** to gain the upper hand; **le ~ du panier** the upper crust, the pick of the bunch.

destabiliser *vt* to destabilize.

destin *m* destiny, fate, doom.

destinataire *mf* addressee, consignee.

destination *f* destination; purpose.

destinée *f* destiny, fate.

destiner *vt* to determine; to intend, destine, aim.

destituer *vt* to dismiss, depose.

destructeur *adj* destructive, ruinous.

destruction *f* destruction.

désuétude *f* disuse **tomber en ~** to fall into disuse.

détachable *adj* detachable.

détachant *m* cleaner, stain remover.

détaché *m* staccato.

détachement *m* detachment, indifference.

détacher *vt* to detach, unfasten; **se ~** *vr* to become detached.

détail *m* detail, particular.

détaillant *m*, **-e** *f* retailer.

détailler *vt* to detail; to sell retail.

détartrage *m* descaling.

détartrant *m* descaling substance; * *adj* descaling.

détartrer *vt* to descale.

détaxe *f* reduction in tax.

détecter *vt* to detect.

détecteur *m* detector.

détection *f* detection.

détective *m* detective.

déteindre *vi* to lose colour, fade.

détendre *vt* to release, loosen; **se ~** to relax, calm down.

détendu *adj* slack; relaxed.

détenir *vt* to detain; to hold.

détente *f* relaxation, easing.

détenteur *m*, **-trice** *f* holder, possessor.

détergent *m* detergent.

détérioration *f* deterioration.

détériorer *vt* to damage; to impair; **se ~** *vr* to deteriorate; to worsen.

déterminant *adj* determining, deciding.

détermination *f* determination; resolution.

déterminé *adj* determined, resolute.

déterminer *vt* to determine, decide.

déterrer *vt* to dig up, disinter.

détestable *adj* detestable, odious; **~ment** *adv* detestably.

détester *vt* to detest, hate.

détonateur *m* detonator.

détonation *f* detonation, explosion.

détonner *vi* to clash (colour); to go out of tune.

détour *m* detour; curve; evasion.

détourné *adj* indirect, oblique.

détournement *m* diversion, rerouting.

détourner *vt* to divert, reroute.

détracteur *m*, **-trice** *f* detractor, disparager.

détraquer *vt* to upset; to disorder; **se ~** *vr* to become upset; to go wrong.

détresse *f* distress, trouble.

détriment *m*: **au ~ de** to the detriment of.

détritus *m* refuse, rubbish.

détroit *m* strait.

détrôner *vt* to dethrone, depose.

detruire *vt* to destroy, demolish.

dette *f* debt.

deuil *m* mourning, bereavement, grief.

deux *adj* two; * *m* two; **entre les ~** so-so, fair to middling; **en moins de ~** in a jiffy.

deuxième *adj* second; **~ment** *adv* secondly; * *mf* second.

deux-points *m* colon.

deux-roues *m* two-wheeled vehicle.

dévaler *vt vi* to hurry down, tear down.

dévaliser *vt* to burgle; to rifle.

dévalorisation *f* depreciation.

dévaloriser *vt* to depreciate, reduce the value of.

dévaluation *f* devaluation.

devancer *vt* to outstrip, outrun; to precede.

devant *prép* in front of, before; * *adv* in front; * *m* front; **prendre les ~s** to make the first move, pre-empt; **aller au-~ de** to anticipate.

devanture *f* display; shop-front.

dévaster *vt* to devastate, lay waste.

développement *m* development; growth; progress.

développer *vt* to develop, expand; **se ~** *vr* to develop, grow.

devenir *vi* to become, grow.

déverrouiller *vt* to unbolt, unlock.

déverser *vt* to pour; to dump.

dévêtir *vt* to undress; **se ~** *vr* to get undressed.

déviation *f* deviation; diversion.

dévier *vi* to deviate; to turn aside; to swerve.

devin *m*, **-eresse** *f* seer, soothsayer.

deviner *vt* to guess; to solve; to foretell.

devinette *f* riddle, poser.

devis *m* estimate, quotation.

dévisager *vt* to stare at.

devise *f* currency.

dévisser *vt* to unscrew, undo.

dévoiler *vt* to unveil, disclose.

devoir *m* duty; homework; *vt* to owe; to have to.

dévorer *vt* to devour, consume.

dévot *adj* devout, pious.

dévotion *f* devotion, piety.

dévoué *adj* devoted, dedicated.

dévouement *m* devotion, dedication.

dévouer(se) *vr* to devote oneself, sacrifice oneself.

dextérité *f* dexterity, adroitness.

diabète *m* diabetes.

diabétique *adj* diabetic.

diable *m* devil.

diablotin *m* imp; cracker (Christmas).

diabolique *adj* diabolical, devilish; ~**ment** *adv* diabolically.

diagnostic *m* diagnosis.

diagnostiquer *vt* to diagnose.

diagonale *f* diagonal.

diagramme *m* diagram; graph.

dialecte *m* dialect.

dialectique *f* dialectic; * *adj* dialectic.

dialogue *m* dialogue, conversation.

dialoguer *vt* to write in dialogue form.

dialyse *f* dialysis.

diamant *m* diamond.

diamètre *m* diameter.

diaphragme *m* diaphragm.

diarrhée *f* diarrhoea.

dictaphone *m* dictaphone.

dictateur *m*, -**trice** *f* dictator.

dictatorial *adj* dictatorial.

dictature *f* dictatorship.

dictée *f* dictating; dictation.

dicter *vt* to dictate, impose.

dictionnaire *m* dictionary.

dicton *m* saying, dictum.

didactique *adj* didactic.

dièse *f* sharp (*mus*).

diesel *m* diesel.

diète *f* diet.

diététicien *m*, -**ienne** *f* dietician.

diététique *adj* dietary.

dieu *m* god.

diffamation *f* defamation, slandering.

diffamer *vt* to defame, slander.

différé *adj* pre-recorded.

différemment *adv* differently.

différence *f* difference.

différenciation *f* differentiation.

différencier *vt* to differentiate.

différend *m* disagreement, difference of opinion.

différent *adj* different; various.

différer *vt* to differ; to vary.

difficile *adj* difficult; awkward, tricky; ~**ment** *adv* with difficulty.

difficulté *f* difficulty; problem.

difforme *adj* deformed, misshapen.

difformité *f* deformity.

diffuser *vt* to diffuse, circulate, broadcast.

diffusion *f* diffusion, circulation, broadcasting.

digérer *vt* to digest.

digeste *adj* easily digestible.

digestif *adj* digestive.

digestion *f* digestion.

digital *adj* digital.

digne *adj* worthy; dignified; ~**ment** *adv* worthily, deservedly.

dignité *f* dignity.

digression *f* digression.

digue *f* dyke; sea wall.

dilapider *vt* to squander; to embezzle.

dilatation *f* dilation, distension.

dilater *vt* to dilate, distend; **se ~** *vr* to dilate, distend.

dilemme *m* dilemma.

dilettante *mf* dilettante.

diluer *vt* to dilute.

dilution *f* dilution.

dimanche *m* Sunday.

dimension *f* dimension, size.

diminuer *vt* to diminish, reduce; * *vi* to diminish, lessen.

diminutif *m* diminutive.

diminution *f* reduction, lessening.

dinde *f* turkey hen.

dindon *m* turkey cock.

dindonneau *m* young turkey.

dîner *vi* to dine; * *m* dinner.

dinosaure *m* dinosaur.

diocèse *m* diocese.

diode *f* diode.

dioxyde *m* dioxide.

diphtérie *f* diphtheria.

diphtongue *f* diphthong.

diplomate *m* diplomat.

diplomatie *f* diplomacy.

diplomatique *adj* diplomatic;
~**ment** *adv* diplomatically.

diplôme *m* diploma, certificate.

diplômé *m*, -**e** *f* holder of a diploma, *adj* qualified.

dire *vt* to say; to tell; **se ~** to say
to oneself; to call oneself. *vr:* **se
~ que** to be said that.

direct *adj* direct; ~**ement** *adv*
directly; * *m* express.

directeur *m*, -**trice** *f* director.

direction *f* direction, management.

directive *f* directive, order.

dirigeant *m*, -**e** *f* leader, ruler;
* *adj* ruling, executive.

diriger *vt* to run, direct; **se ~** *vr:*
se ~ vers to head for, make for.

discernement *m* discernment,
judgment.

discerner *vt* to discern, distinguish.

disciple *m* disciple.

disciplinaire *adj* disciplinary.

discipline *f* discipline.

discipliné *adj* disciplined.

discontinu *adj* discontinuous.

discordant *adj* discordant, conflicting.

discorde *f* discord, dissension.

discothèque *f* discotheque.

discours *m* speech, talking.

discourtois *adj* discourteous.

discréditer *vt* to discredit.

discret *adj* discreet.

discrétion *f* discretion, prudence.

discrétionnaire *adj* discretionary.

discrimination *f* discrimination.

discriminer *vt* to distinguish; to
discriminate.

disculper *vt* to excuse, exonerate;
se ~ *vr* to justify oneself, excuse
oneself.

discussion *f* discussion, debate.

discutable *adj* debatable, questionable.

discuter *vi, vt* to discuss, debate.

disgrâce *f* disgrace.

disgracieux *adj* awkward,
ungraceful.

disjoncter *vi* to cut off, disconnect.

disjoncteur *m* cutout, circuit
breaker.

disparaître *vi* to disappear, vanish.

disparate *adj* disparate, incongruous.

disparité *f* disparity, incongruity.

disparition *f* disappearance;
death; extinction.

disparu *adj* vanished; bygone;
missing.

dispensaire *m* dispensary.

dispense *f* dispensation, exemption.

dispenser *vt* to dispense, exempt;
se ~ *vr:* **se ~ de** to dispense with;
to avoid.

disperser *vt* to spread, scatter; **se
~** *vr* to disperse, scatter.

dispersion *f* dispersal, scattering.

disponibilité *f* availability.

disponible *adj* available; transferable.

dispos *adj* refreshed; alert; in
form.

disposer *vt* to arrange, dispose;
se ~ *vr:* **se ~ à** to prepare to do;
* *vi* to leave.

dispositif *m* device, mechanism.

disposition *f* arrangement, layout.

disproportionné *adj* disproportionate.

dispute *f* dispute, argument.

disputer *vt* to dispute, rival; **se ~**
vr to quarrel, argue.

disquaire *mf* record-dealer.

disqualifier *vt* to disqualify.

disque *m* disk; record.

disquette *f* diskette.

dissection *f* dissection.

dissemblable *adj* dissimilar; different.

disséminer *vt* to disseminate, scatter.

dissentiment *m* disagreement, dissent.

disséquer *vt* to dissect.

dissertation *f* dissertation.

dissidence *f* dissidence, dissent.

dissident *adj* dissident.

dissimulation *f* dissimulation, double-dealing.

dissimulé *adj* double-faced, dissembling.

dissimuler *vt* to dissemble, conceal; **se ~** *vr* to conceal oneself.

dissipation *f* dissipation, waste.

dissipé *adj* dissipated, undisciplined.

dissiper *vt* to dispel; to dissipate; **se ~** *vr* to disperse, become undisciplined.

dissociation *f* dissociation.

dissocier *vt* to dissociate.

dissolution *f* dissolution.

dissolvant *m* solvent, dissolvent.

dissonant *adj* dissonant; discordant.

dissoudre *vt* to dissolve.

dissuader *vt* to dissuade.

dissuasif *adj* dissuasive, deterrent.

dissuasion *f* dissuasion.

distance *f* distance, interval.

distancier(se) *vr* to distance oneself from.

distant *adj* distant.

distendre *vt* to distend, strain; **se ~** *vr* to become distended.

distillation *f* distillation.

distiller *vt* to distil.

distillerie *f* distillery.

distinct *adj* distinct, different; **~ement** *adv* distinctly.

distinctif *adj* distinctive.

distinction *f* distinction.

distingué *adj* distinguished.

distinguer *vt* to distinguish; to discern; **se ~** *vr* to distinguish oneself.

distorsion *f* distortion.

distraction *f* inattention; absent-mindedness; abstraction.

distraire *vt* to distract; to amuse; **se ~** *vr* to enjoy oneself.

distrait *adj* inattentive, absentminded; **~ement** *adv* absent–mindedly.

distrayant *adj* entertaining, diverting.

distribuer *vt* to distribute.

distributeur *m* distributor.

distribution *f* distribution.

district *m* district.

diurétique *adj* diuretic; * *m* diuretic.

divagation *f* wandering, rambling.

divaguer *vi* to ramble, rave.

divan *m* divan.

divergence *f* divergence.

divergent *adj* divergent.

diverger *vi* to diverge, differ.

divers *adj* diverse, varied; **~ement** *adv* diversely.

diversification *f* diversification.

diversifier *vt* to vary, diversify; **se ~** *vr* to diversify.

diversion *f* diversion.

diversité *f* diversity, variety.

divertir *vt* to amuse, entertain; **se ~** *vr* to amuse oneself.

divertissant *adj* amusing, entertaining.

divertissement *m* diversion, recreation.

dividende *m* dividend.

divin *adj* divine, exquisite; **~ement** *adv* divinely.

divination *f* divination.

divinité *f* divinity.

diviser *vt* to divide, split; **se ~** *vr* to split up, divide into.

division *f* division.

divorce *m* divorce.

divorcé *m*, **-e** *f* divorcee; * *adj* divorced.

divorcer *vi* to get divorced.

divulgation *f* disclosure, divulgence.

divulguer *vt* to divulge, disclose.

dix *adj*, *m* ten.

dix-huit *adj, m* eighteen.
dix-huitième *adj, mf* eighteenth.
dixième *adj* tenth; **~ment** *adv* tenthly; * *mf* tenth.
dix-neuf *adj, m* nineteen.
dix-neuvième *adj, mf* nineteenth.
dix-sept *adj, m* seventeen.
dix-septième *adj, mf* seventeenth.
dizaine *f* ten, ten or so.
docile *adj* docile, submissive; **~ment** *adv* docilely.
docilité *f* docility, submissiveness.
dock *m* dock, dockyard.
docteur *m* doctor.
doctorat *m* doctorate.
doctrine *f* doctrine.
document *m* document.
documentaire *adj* documentary.
documentaliste *mf* researcher.
documentation *f* documentation; information.
documenter *vt* to document; **se ~** *vr* to gather information on.
dogmatique *adj* dogmatic.
dogme *m* dogma.
doigt *m* finger; **être à deux ~s de** to come very close to doing; **obéir au ~ et à l'oeil** to toe the line.
doigté *m* touch; fingering technique.
domaine *m* domain, estate; sphere.
domanial *adj* domainal, belonging to an estate.
dôme *m* dome, vault.
domestique *adj* domestic, household.
domestiquer *vt* to domesticate, tame.
domicile *m* domicile, address.
domicilié *adj* domiciled.
dominant *adj* dominant, prevailing.
dominante *f* dominant characteristic.
dominateur *adj* governing; domineering.

domination *f* domination; to dominion.
dominer *vt* to dominate; to prevail; **se ~** to control oneself.
dominical *adj* Sunday.
dommage *m* damage; harm; **c'est ~** it's a pity.
dompter *vt* to tame, train.
dompteur *m*, **-euse** *f* trainer, tamer.
don *m* gift; talent.
donateur *m*, **-trice** *f* donor.
donation *f* donation.
donc *conj* so, therefore, thus; **pourquoi ~?** why was that?.
donné *adj* given; fixed; **étant ~** seeing that, in view of.
donnée *f* datum.
donner *vt* to give; * *vi* to knock, beat.
donneur *m*, **-euse** *f* giver, donor; dealer.
dont *pron* whose, of which.
dopage *m* doping.
doper *vt* to dope; **se ~** *vr* to take drugs, dope oneself.
doré *adj* gilded; tanned.
dorénavant *adv* from now on, henceforth.
dorer *vt* to gild; to tan.
dorloter *vt* to pamper, pet.
dormir *vi* to sleep, be asleep; to be still.
dortoir *m* dormitory.
dos *m* back; top; ridge.
dosage *m* mixture; balance; proportioning.
dose *f* dose; amount; quantity.
doser *vt* to measure out, proportion; to strike a balance.
dossier *m* dossier, file; case.
dot *f* dowry.
doter *vt* to provide with a dowry; to endow.
douane *f* customs.
douanier *m* custom (s).
double *adj* double, duplicate, dual; **~ment** *adv* doubly; * *m* copy, double, replica; twice as much.

doubler *vt vi* to double, duplicate.

doublure *f* lining; understudy.

doucement *adv* softly, gently.

doucereux *adj* sugary; mawkish; suave.

douceur *f* softness, gentleness.

douche *f* shower.

doucher *vt* to give a shower to; **se ~** *vr* to take a shower.

doué *adj* gifted, endowed with.

douille *f* case; cartridge.

douillet *adj* delicate, tender; soft.

douleur *f* pain, ache; anguish.

douloureusement *adv* painfully, grievously.

douloureux *adj* painful, grievous.

doute *m* doubt, misgiving; **sans ~** without doubt.

douter *vi* to doubt, question; **se ~** *vr* **se ~ de** to suspect someone; **se ~ que** to suspect that, expect that.

douteux *adj* doubtful, dubious.

doux *adj*, *f* **douce** soft; sweet; mild.

douzaine *f* dozen.

douze *adj*, *m* twelve.

douzième *adj* twelfth; **~ment** twelfthly adv; * *mf* twelfth.

doyen *m*, **-enne** *f* dean; doyen.

draconien *adj* draconian, drastic.

dragée *f* bonbon, sugar-almond.

dragon *m* dragon.

dramatique *adj* dramatic, tragic; **~ment** *adv* dramatically.

dramatiser *vt* to dramatize.

dramaturge *mf* playwright.

drame *m* drama.

drap *m* sheet; **~-housse** fitted sheet; **être dans de beaux ~s** to be in a fine mess.

drapeau *m* flag.

draper *vt* to drape.

dressage *m* taming; pitching.

dresser *vt* to draw up; to put up; **se ~** *vr* to stand up; to rear up.

dresseur *m*, **-euse** *f* trainer, tamer.

dribbler *vi* to dribble.

drogue *f* drug.

drogué *m*, **-e** *f* drug addict; * *adj* drugged.

droguer *vt* to drug, administer drugs; **se ~** *vr* to dose up; to take drugs.

droguerie *f* hardware trade.

droguiste *mf* hardware storekeeper.

droit *adj* right; straight; sound; honest; **~ement** *adv* uprightly, honestly; * *adv* straight, straight ahead; * *m* right; law; tax.

droite *f* right side; right (wing); straight line.

droitier *adj* right-handed.

droiture *f* uprightness, honesty.

drôle *adj* funny, amusing; peculiar; **~ment** *adv* funnily, peculiarly.

dromadaire *m* dromedary.

dru *adj* thick, dense; sturdy.

du *art* of the.

dû *adj* owed; due; **~ment** *adv* duly.

dualité *f* duality.

dubitatif *adj* doubtful, dubious.

dubitativement *adv* doubtfully, dubiously.

duc *m* duke, **duchesse** *f* duchess.

duché *m* duchy.

duel *m* duel; dual.

duettiste *mf* duettist.

dune *f* dune.

duo *m* duo; duet.

duodénum *m* duodenum.

dupe *adj* easily duped; * *f* dupe.

duper *vt* to dupe, take in.

duplex *m* duplex, two-way.

dupliquer *vt* to duplicate.

dur *adj* hard, tough; difficult. **~ement** *adv* harshly, severely.

durable *adj* durable, lasting; **~ment** *adv* durably.

duralumin *m* duralumin.

durant *prép* during, for.

durcir *vt vi* to harden; **se ~** *vr* to become hardened.

durcissement *m* hardening.

durée *f* duration, length.

durer *vi* to last.

dureté *f* hardness; austerity, harshness.

durillon *m* callus, corn.

duvet *m* down.

duveté *adj* downy.

dynamique *f* dynamic; dynamics; * *adj* dynamic; **~ment** *adv* dynamically.

dynamiser *vt* to energize; to potentiate.

dynamisme *m* dynamism.

dynamitage *m* dynamiting.

dynamite *f* dynamite.

dynamiter *vt* to dynamite.

dynamo *f* dynamo.

dynastie *f* dynasty.

dynastique *adj* dynastic.

dysenterie *f* dysentery.

dyslexie *f* dyslexia.

dyslexique *adj* dyslexic.

E

eau *f* water; rain.

eau-de-vie *f* brandy.

ébahir *vt* to astonish, stupefy, dumbfound.

ébahissement *m* astonishment, amazement.

ébauche *f* rough draft, rough outline.

ébaucher *vt* to sketch; to roughcast.

ébène *f* ebony.

ébéniste *m* cabinetmaker.

éblouir *vt* to dazzle; to fascinate.

éblouissant *adj* dazzling; amazing.

éblouissement *m* dazzle; bedazzlement.

ébouillanter *vt* to scald; to blanch; **s'~** *vr* to scald oneself.

éboulement *m* collapse, caving in; fall.

ébouriffé *adj* tousled, ruffled.

ébranler *vt* to shake; to unsettle, disturb.

ébrécher *vt* to chip, indent; to break into (fortune).

ébriété *f* intoxication.

ébrouer(s') *vr* to shake oneself.

ébruiter *vt* to disclose, divulge; **s'~** *vr* to spread, be noised abroad.

ébullition *f* boiling; effervescence; turmoil.

écaille *f* scale; shell.

écailler *vt* to scale; to chip; **s'~** *vr* to flake off, peel off.

écarlate *adj* scarlet.

écart *m* distance; interval; discrepancy; **rester à l'~** to steer clear of.

écarteler *vt* to tear apart; to quarter.

écarter *vt* to separate; to avert; to dismiss; **s'~** *vr* to make way; to swerve.

ecchymose *f* bruise, ecchymosis.

ecclésiastique *adj* ecclesiastical; * *m* ecclesiastic, clergyman.

échafaud *m* scaffold.

échafaudage *m* scaffolding.

échange *m* exchange, barter, trade.

échanger *vt* to exchange.

échantillon *m* sample.

échapée *f* breakaway; glimpse.

échappement *m* exhaust; release.

échapper *vi* to escape, avoid, elude; **s'~** *vr* to escape from; to leak.

écharde *f* splinter, sliver.

écharpe *f* scarf; arm-sling.

échassier *m* wader.

échauffement *m* heating; warm-up; constipation.

échauffer *vt* to heat, overheat; to

excite; **s'~** *vr* to warm up; to get worked up.

échéance *f* expiry; maturity date.

échec *m* failure, defeat; chess.

échelle *f* ladder; scale.

échelon *m* rung; grade.

échelonner *vt* to grade; to stagger, set at intervals; **s'~** *vr* to be graduated, staggered.

échine *f* backbone, spine; **courber l'~** to submit.

échiquier *m* chessboard.

écho *m* echo; rumour.

échographie *f* ultrasound.

échoir *vi* to fall due; to befall, fall to someone's lot.

échouer *vi* to fail; to end up; to run aground.

éclabousser *vt* to splash, spatter.

éclair *m* flash; lightning flash; spark.

éclairage *m* lighting, light.

éclairagiste *m* electrician; lighting engineer.

éclaicie *f* clear interval, bright spot; glade.

éclaircir *vt* to lighten; to down; to brighten up; **s'~** *vr* to clear; to clear up.

éclaircissement *m* clearing up, explanation, elucidation.

éclairer *vt* to light, illuminate; clarify, explain.

éclat *m* brightness, glare; splinter; splendour.

éclatant *adj* bright, blazing; resounding; blatant.

éclatement *m* explosion, bursting, rupture.

éclater *vi* to explode; to break out; to exclaim.

éclectique *adj* eclectic.

éclipse *f* eclipse.

éclipser *vt* to eclipse, overshadow; **s'~** *vr* to disappear, vanish.

éclore *vi* to hatch out; to blossom.

éclosion *f* hatching; blooming; birth.

écluse *f* lock.

écoeurant *adj* disgusting, nauseating.

écoeurement *m* nausea, disgust; discouragement.

écoeurer *vt* to nauseate, disgust.

école *f* school, schooling; sect, doctrine.

écolier *m* schoolboy, **-ière** *f* schoolgirl.

écologie *f* ecology.

écologique *adj* ecological.

écologiste *mf* ecologist.

économe *adj* thrifty; * *mf* steward, treasurer.

économie *f* economy, thrift; economics.

économique *adj* economic; **~ment** *adv* economically.

économiser *vt* to economize; to save.

écorce *f* bark, peel, skin.

écorchure *f* scratch; graze.

Ecossais *m* Scotsman, **-e** *f* Scotswoman.

écossais *adj* Scottish.

Ecosse *f* Scotland.

écoulement *m* flow, discharge, outlet; disposal, selling.

écouler *vt* to flow, discharge; to sell; **s'~** *vr* to leak, flow out; to pass by; to sell.

écoute *f* listening, audience.

écouter *vt* to listen to, hear.

écran *m* screen.

écrasant *adj* crushing; overwhelming.

écraser *vt* to crush; to overwhelm; to run over; **s'~** *vr* to crash; to get crushed.

écrémer *vt* to skim, cream.

écrevisse *f* crayfish.

écrin *m* box, casket.

écrire *vt* to write; to spell.

écrit *adj* written; * *m* document; piece of writing.

écriteau *m* notice, sign.

écriture *f* writing; handwriting; script.

écrivain *m* writer.

écrou *m* nut.

écroulement *m* collapse, caving in.

écrouler(s') *vr* to collapse; to crumble.

écru *adj* raw; unbleached; untreated.

ectoplasme *m* ectoplasm.

écueil *m* reef, shelf; peril.

écume *f* foam, froth; scum.

écureuil *m* squirrel.

écurie *f* stable.

écusson *m* badge, shield.

eczéma *m* eczema.

édification *f* erection, construction.

édifice *m* edifice, building.

édifier *vt* to build, construct; to edify.

éditer *vt* to publish, produce; to edit.

éditeur *m*, **-trice** *f* publisher; editor.

édition *f* publishing; edition; editing.

éditorial *m* leading article, editorial.

éducatif *adj* educational.

éducation *f* education; upbringing.

édulcorant *m* sweetener; * *adj* sweetening.

éduquer *vt* to educate; to bring up, raise.

effacer *vt* to efface, erase, wipe off; **s'~** *vr* to wear away, become obliterated.

effaré *adj* alarmed, bewildered.

effaroucher *vt* to frighten; to shock.

effectif *m* staff; size, complement; * *adj* effective, positive.

effectivement *adv* effectively, positively.

effectuer *vt* to effect, execute, carry out.

effervescence *f* effervescence; excitement, ferment.

effervescent *adj* effervescent; excited.

effet *m* effect, impression; spin; bill, note.

efficace *adj* effective; efficient; **~ment** *adv* effectively, efficiently.

efficacité *f* effectiveness, efficiency.

effleurer *vt* to touch lightly, skim across.

effondrement *m* collapse, caving in.

effondrer(s') *vr* to collapse, cave in.

efforcer(s') *vr* to endeavour, do one's best.

effort *m* effort, exertion; stress, strain.

effraction *f* breaking and entering.

effrayant *adj* frightening, fearsome.

effrayer *vt* to frighten, scare.

effriter *vt* to crumble; to exhaust (land); **s'~** *vr* to crumble away, disintegrate.

effroi *m* terror, dismay.

effronté *adj* shameless, impudent, cheeky; **~ment** *adv* shamelessly, impudently.

effroyable *adj* horrifying, appalling; **~ment** *adv* horrifyingly, appallingly.

égal *adj* equal; even, level; equable; **~ement** *adv* evenly; equally; also, as well.

égaler *vt* to equal, match.

égalisation *f* equalization; levelling.

égaliser *vt* to equalize; to level out.

égalitaire *adj* egalitarian.

égalité *f* equality; equableness; evenness.

égard *m* consideration, respect; **à l'~ de** concerning, regarding; **à tous ~s** in all respects.

égarer *vt* to mislead, lead astray; **s'~** *vr* to get lost; to wander from the point.

égayer *vt* to enliven, cheer up.

églantine *f* eglantine, wild rose.

église *f* church.

égocentrique *adj* egocentric, self-centred.

égoïsme *m* selfishness, egoism.

égoïste *mf* egotist; * *adj* egotistic; **~ment** *adv* egotistically.

égout *m* sewer.

égoutter *vt* to strain; to wring out.

égratignure *f* scratch, scrape.

éjecter *vt* to eject, throw out.

élaboration *f* elaboration, development.

élaborer *vt* to elaborate, develop.

élan *m* surge, momentum, speed; spirit, elan.

élancer(s') *vr* to rush, spring, hurl oneself.

élargir *vt* to widen, stretch; **s'~** *vr* to get wider.

élargissement *m* widening, stretching, enlarging.

élastique *adj* elastic; flexible; * *m* elastic, elastic band.

électeur *m*, **-trice** *f* voter, elector.

élection *f* election; choice.

électoral *adj* electoral.

électorat *m* electorate; constituency; franchise.

électricien *m* electrician.

électricité *f* electricity.

électrique *adj* electric.

électrocardiogramme *m* electrocardiogram.

électrode *f* electrode.

électrolyse *f* electrolysis.

électroménager *m* household appliance; * *adj* electrical (household).

électron *m* electron.

électronicien *m* electronics engineer.

électronique *f* electronics; * *adj* electronic.

élégance *f* elegance, stylishness.

élégant *adj* elegant, stylish.

élément *m* element, component; cell; fact.

élémentaire *adj* elementary; basic.

éléphant *m* elephant.

élevage *m* rearing, breeding.

élève *mf* pupil, student.

élevé *adj* high; heavy; lofty, exalted.

élever *vt* to bring up, raise; to put up, lift up.; **s'~** *vr* to rise, go up.

éleveur *m*, **-euse** *f* stockbreeder.

éligible *adj* eligible.

élimination *f* elimination.

éliminatoire *adj* eliminatory; * *f* preliminary heat.

éliminer *vt* to eliminate, discard.

élire *vt* to elect.

élite *f* elite.

élitisme *m* elitism.

elle *pron* she; it; her; **c'est à ~** it's up to her; it's her's; **~-même** herself.

elliptique *adj* elliptic; **~ment** *adv* elliptically.

élocution *f* elocution, diction.

éloge *m* praise; eulogy.

élogieux *adj* laudatory, eulogistic.

éloigné *adj* distant, remote.

éloigner *vt* to move away, take away; **s'~** *vr* to go away; to grow distant.

éloquence *f* eloquence.

éloquent *adj* eloquent.

élu *adj* chosen, elected.

élucider *vt* to elucidate, clear up.

émacié *adj* emaciated, wasted.

émail *m* enamel.

émailler *vt* to enamel.

émancipation *f* emancipation, liberation.

émanciper *vt* to emancipate, liberate; **s'~** *vr* to become emancipated, liberated.

émaner *vi* to emanate, issue.

emballage *m* packing paper, wrapping paper.

emballer *vt* to pack up, wrap up.

embarcadère *m* landing stage, pier.

embarcation *f* boat, craft.

embargo *m* embargo.

embarquement *m* loading; embarkation.

embarquer *vt* to embark; to load; * *vi* to embark, go aboard.

embarras *m* embarrassment, confusion; trouble.

embarrassant *adj* embarrassing, uncomfortable.

embarrassé *adj* embarrassed, self-conscious.

embarrasser *vt* to embarrass; to hinder, hamper; **s'~** *vr* to burden oneself with; to be troubled by.

embaucher *vt* to take on, hire.

embellir *vt* to beautify, make more attractive.

embellissement *m* embellishment, improvement.

embêter *vt* (*fam*) to bore; to get on one's nerves; **s'~** *vr* to be bored, fed up.

emblème *m* symbol, emblem.

emboîter *vt* to fit together; to follow closely; **s'~** *vr* to fit together; to fit into each other.

embonpoint *m* stoutness, plumpness.

embouchure *f* mouth (river); mouthpiece.

embouteillage *m* traffic jam; bottling.

embranchement *m* junction; side road.

embrasser *vt* to kiss, embrace.

embrayage *m* clutch.

embrayer *vi* to engage the clutch.

embrouiller *vt* to tangle up, mix up; **s'~** *vr* to become muddled, confused.

embryon *m* embryo.

embryonnaire *adj* embryonic.

embuscade *f* ambush.

émeraude *f* emerald.

émerger *vi* to emerge; to stand out.

émeri *m* emery.

émerveiller *vt* to astonish, amaze; **s'~** *vr* to marvel at.

émetteur *adj* transmitting.

émettre *vt* to send out, emit, transmit.

émeute *f* riot.

émietter *vt* to crumble; to disperse, break up; **s'~** *vr* to crumble; to disperse, break up.

émigration *f* emigration.

émigré *m*, **-e** *f* émigré, expatriate.

émigrer *vi* to emigrate.

éminence *f* hill, elevation; eminence, distinction.

éminent *adj* eminent, distinguished.

émir *m* emir.

émission *f* sending out; transmission; broadcast; emission.

emmêler *vt* to entangle; confuse; **s'~** *vr* to tangle.

emménager *vi* to move in.

emmener *vt* to take away; to lead.

émoi *m* agitation, emotion.

émotif *adj* emotional; emotive.

émotion *f* emotion; commotion.

émotivité *f* emotionalism.

émouvant *adj* moving, touching.

émouvoir *vt* to move, disturb, upset; **s'~** *vr* to be moved; to get worried, upset.

empailler *vt* to stuff.

empaqueter *vt* to parcel up, pack.

emparer(s') *vr* to seize, grab; to take possession of.

empêchement *m* obstacle, hitch; impediment.

empêcher *vt* to prevent, stop; **s'~** *vr*: **s'~ de** to refrain from doing something.

empereur *m* emperor.

empester *vt* to stink of; to poison, infect.

empêtrer *vt* to entangle,; **s'~** *vr* to get involved in, get mixed up in.

emphase *f* pomposity; emphasis, stress.

empiéter *vi* to encroach, overlap.

empiler *vt* to pile up, stack.

empire *m* empire; influence, ascendancy.

empirer *vi* to get worse, deteriorate.

empirique *adj* empirical; **~ment** *adv* empirically.

emplacement *m* site, location.

emploi *m* use; job, employment.

employé *m*, **-e** *f* employee.

employer *vt* to use; to spend; to employ.

employeur *m*, **euse** *f* employer.

empoisonner *vt* to poison; to annoy.

emporter *vt* to take; to carry off; to involve; **s'~** *vr* to lose one's temper.

empreinte *f* imprint, impression, stamp.

empresser(s') *vi* to rush to; to press around, fuss around.

emprise *f* hold, ascendancy.

emprisonner *vt* to imprison; to trap.

emprunt *m* borrowing, loan.

emprunter *vt* to borrow; to assume; to derive.

ému *adj* moved; filled with emotion; touched; excited.

émulsion *f* emulsion.

en *prép* in; to; by; on; **~ tant que** as; *pron* from there; of it, of them; **je n'~ veux plus** I don't want any more of them; **s'~ faire** to worry; **il ~ va de même pour** the same goes for.

encadré *m* box; framed text.

encadrement *m* framing; training; managerial staff.

encadrer *vt* to frame; to train; to surround.

encaissement *m* collection; receipt; cashing.

encaisser *vt* to collect, receive; to cash.

encastrer *vt* to embed, fit in, encase.

enceinte *f* pregnant.

encens *m* incense.

encenser *vt* to cense; to shower praise on.

encercler *vt* to encircle, surround.

enchaînement *m* linking; link; sequence.

enchaîner *vt* to chain.

enchanté *adj* enchanted, delighted.

enchantement *m* enchantment, delight.

enchanter *vt* to enchant, delight.

enchâsser *vt* to set, imbed.

enchère *f* bid, offer.

enchevêtrement *m* entanglement, confusion.

enclave *f* enclave.

enclencher *vt* to engage; to set in motion.

enclin *adj* inclined, prone.

enclore *vt* to enclose, shut in.

enclume *f* anvil; engine block.

encoder *vt* to encode.

encolure *f* neck; collar size.

encombrant *adj* unwieldy, cumbersome.

encombrement *m* congestion; jumble; obstruction.

encombrer *vt* to clutter, obstruct; **s'~** *vr* to burden oneself.

encore *adv* still; only; again; more; **~ que** even though.

encourageant *adj* encouraging, heartening.

encouragement *m* encouragement.

encourager *vt* to encourage; to incite.

encre *f* ink.

encyclopédie *f* encyclop(a)edia.

endettement *m* indebtedness; debt.

endetter *vt* to get so into debt; **s'~** *vr* to get into debt.

endive *f* chicory.

endoctrinement *m* indoctrination.

endoctriner *vt* to indoctrinate.

endommager *vt* to damage.

endormir *vt* to put to sleep; **s'~** *vr* to fall asleep.

endossement *m* endorsement.

endosser *vt* to put on; to shoulder; to endorse.

endroit *m* place; side part; **à l'~** regarding.

enduire *vt* to coat, smear.

enduit *m* coating.

endurance *f* endurance, stamina.

endurci *adj* hardened; hard-hearted.

endurcir *vt* to harden; **s'~** *vr* to become hardened.

endurer *vt* to endure, bear.

énergétique *adj* energy; energizing.

énergie *f* energy; spirit, vigour.

énergique *adj* energetic, vigorous; **~ment** *adv* energetically.

énervant *adj* enervating; irritating.

énervement *m* irritation; nervousness.

énerver *vt* to irritate, annoy; to get on one's nerves; **s'~** *vr* to get excited, worked up.

enfance *f* childhood; infancy.

enfant *mf* child; native.

enfanter *vt* to give birth to.

enfantillage *m* childishness.

enfantin *adj* childish, infantile.

enfer *m* hell.

enfermer *vt* to lock up; to confine; to box in.

enfiévrer *vt* to stir up, inflame.

enfiler *vt* to string, thread; to put on.

enfin *adv* at last; in short; after all.

enflammer *vt* to set on fire; to inflame, kindle; **s'~** *vr* to catch fire, ignite.

enflé *adj* swollen; bombastic, turgid.

enfler *vi* to swell up, inflate.

enfoncer *vt* to stick in, thrust; to break open; **s'~** *vr* to sink into, disappear into.

enfouir *vt* to bury.

enfuir(s') *vr* to run away, flee.

engagement *m* agreement, commitment, undertaking; engaging; opening.

engager *vt* to bind; to involve; to insert; to open; **s'~** *vr* to undertake to; to take a job.

engelure *f* chilblain.

engendrer *vt* to create, engender; to father.

engin *m* machine; instrument; contraption.

englober *vt* to include, encompass.

engloutir *vt* to wolf down; to engulf.

engorgement *m* obstruction, clogging; glut.

engouement *m* infatuation; fad, craze.

engouffrer *vt* to devour, swallow up, engulf; **s'~** *vr* to sweep, surge.

engourdi *adj* numb; dull.

engourdir *vt* to numb; to dull, blunt; **s'~** *vr* to become numb, to grow sluggish.

engourdissement *m* numbness; sleepiness.

engrais *m* fertilizer; manure.

engraisser *vi* to get fatter; * *vt* to fatten; to fertilize.

engrenage *m* gears, gearing.

énigmatique *adj* enigmatic; **~ment** *adv* enigmatically.

énigme *f* enigma, riddle.

enivrer *vt* to intoxicate, make drunk; **s'~** *vr* to get drunk.

enjeu *m* stake.

enjoliver *vt* to ornament; to embroider (truth).

enlacer *vt* to embrace, intertwine.

enlaidir *vt* to make ugly; **s'~** *vr* to become ugly.

enlèvement *m* abduction, kidnapping; removal.

enlever *vt* to remove; to take off; to deprive; to abduct.

enliser *vt* to get stuck (car); **s'~** *vr* to get bogged down, get sucked into.

enneigé *adj* snowy, snowbound.

enneigement *m* snow coverage.

ennemi *m*, **-e** *f* enemy.

ennui *m* boredom, tedium, weariness.

ennuyer *vt* to bore, bother; **s'~** *vr* to get bored.

71

ennuyeux *adj* boring, tedious.

énorme *adj* enormous, huge.

énormément *adv* enormously.

énormité *f* enormity, hugeness; howler.

enquête *f* inquiry, investigation; survey.

enquêter *vi* to hold an inquiry; to investigate.

enraciner *vt* to implant, root; **s'~** *vr* to take root; to settle down somewhere.

enragé *adj* furious; keen.

enregistrement *m* recording; registration.

enregistrer *vt* to record; to register.

enrichi *adj* improved, enriched; nouveau riche.

enrichir *vt* to enrich, expand; **s'~** *vr* to get rich.

enrichissant *adj* enriching.

enrichissement *m* enrichment.

enrober *vt* to wrap, cover, coat.

enrôler *vt* to enlist, enrol.

enrouement *m* hoarseness.

enrouer *vt* to make hoarse.

enrouler *vt* to roll up, wind up.

enseignant *m*, **-e** *f* teacher.

enseigne *f* sign; ensign.

enseignement *m* education, training, instruction.

enseigner *vt* to teach.

ensemble *adv* together, at the same time; * *m* unity; whole.

ensoleillé *adj* sunny.

ensorceler *vt* to bewitch, enchant.

ensuite *adv* then, next, afterwards.

entaille *f* cut, gash.

entamer *vt* to start, open, make a hole in.

entassement *m* piling up, heaping up.

entasser *vt* to pile up, heap up.

entendement *m* understanding, comprehension.

entendre *vt* to hear; to intend, mean; to understand; **s'~** *vr* to

agree; to know how to.

entendu *adj* agreed; **bien ~** of course.

entente *f* harmony, understanding; accord.

enterrement *m* burial; funeral.

enterrer *vt* to bury, inter.

en-tête *m* heading, header.

entêté *adj* stubborn, obstinate.

entêtement *m* stubbornness, obstinacy.

entêter *vt* to go to the head of; **s'~** *vr* to persist in.

enthousiasme *m* enthusiasm.

enthousiasmer *vt* to fill with enthusiasm; **s'~** *vr* to be enthusiastic about.

enthousiaste *adj* enthusiastic; * *mf* enthusiast.

entier *adj* entire, whole; intact.

entièrement *adv* entirely, wholly, completely.

entité *f* entity.

entonnoir *m* funnel; swallow hole; shell-hole.

entorse *f* sprain.

entortiller *vt* to twist, twine; to hoodwink, wheedle.

entourage *m* set, circle; entourage.

entourer *vt* to surround, frame, encircle; **s'~** *vr*: **s'~ de** to surround oneself with.

entracte *m* interval, intermission.

entraide *f* mutual aid.

entraider(s') *vr* to help one another.

entrailles *fpl* entrails, guts; womb.

entrain *m* spirit, liveliness.

entraînement *m* training, coaching; force, impetus.

entraîner *vt* to drag; to lead; to train; **s'~** *vr* to train oneself.

entraîneur *m* trainer, coach.

entrave *f* hindrance, obstacle; shackle.

entraver *vt* to hold up; to shackle.

entre *prép* between, among, into.

entrebâiller *vt* to half-open; **s'~** *vr* to be half-open.

entrecôte *f* rib steak.

entrecouper *vt* to intersperse, interrupt with.

entrée *f* entry, entrance; admission; insertion; **~ en matière** introduction; **d'~ de jeu** from the outset.

entrejambes *m* crotch.

entrelacer *vt* to intertwine, interlace.

entremêler *vt* to intermingle, intermix.

entremets *m* sweet, dessert.

entreposer *vt* to store, put into storage.

entrepôt *m* warehouse, bonded warehouse.

entreprenant *adj* enterprising.

entreprendre *vt* to embark upon, undertake.

entrepreneur *m*, **-euse** *f* contractor; entrepreneur.

entreprise *f* company; venture, business.

entrer *vi* to enter, go in.

entresol *m* entresol, mezzanine.

entretemps *adv* meanwhile.

entretenir *vt* to maintain, look after; to speak with.

entretien *m* upkeep, maintenance; conversation.

entrevoir *vt* to make out; to glimpse; to anticipate.

entrevue *f* meeting, interview.

entrouvert *adj* half-open.

entrouvrir *vt* to half-open; **s'~** *vr* to half-open; to gape.

énumération *f* enumeration, listing.

énumérer *vt* to enumerate, list.

envahir *vt* to invade, overrun.

envahissant *adj* invasive; intrusive; pervasive.

enveloppe *f* envelope; covering; exterior.

envelopper *vt* to envelop; to wrap up; to veil.

envergure *f* breadth, scope, scale.

envers *prép* towards, to; * *m*; **à l'~** inside out, upside down.

envie *f* desire, longing, inclination; envy.

envier *vt* to envy.

envieux *adj* envious.

environ *adv* about, around; **~s** *mpl* vicinity, neighbourhood.

environnant *adj* surrounding.

environnement *m* environment.

environnemental *adj* environmental.

environner *vt* to surround, encircle.

envisager *vt* to view, envisage.

envoi *m* dispatch, remittance; kick-off.

envol *m* takeoff, flight.

envoler(s') *vr* to fly away; to disappear.

envoûtant *adj* bewitching, entrancing.

envoûter *vt* to bewitch.

envoyé *m*, **-e** *f* messenger, envoy.

envoyer *vt* to send, dispatch; hurl, fire.

enzyme *m* enzyme.

épais *adj* thick; deep.

épaisseur *f* thickness; depth.

épaissir *vi* to thicken; to deepen; * *vt*; **s'~** *vr* to thicken, get thicker.

épanoui *adj* radiant, beaming.

épanouir *vt* to brighten, light up; open out; **s'~** *vr* to bloom.

épanouissement *m* blooming; lighting up; opening out.

épargne *f* saving, savings.

épargner *vt* to save; to spare.

éparpiller *vt* to scatter, distribute; **s'** *vr* to scatter.

épaule *f* shoulder.

épauler *vt* to support, back up.

épave *f* wreck; derelict; ruin.

épée *f* sword.

épeler *vt* to spell.

éperdu *adj* distraught, overcome; **~ment** *adv* frantically, desperately.

éperon *m* spur; cutwater.

épervier *m* sparrowhawk.

éphémère *adj* ephemeral, fleeting.

épi *m* ear; tuft.

épice *m* spice.

épicé *adj* spicy; juicy.

épicerie *f* grocery trade; grocer's shop.

épicier *m*, **-ière** *f* grocer; greengrocer.

épidémie *f* epidemic.

épidémique *adj* epidemic; contagious.

épiderme *m* epidermis; skin.

épier *vt* to spy on.

épiglotte *f* epiglottis.

épilation *f* removal of hair.

épilepsie *f* epilepsy.

épileptique *adj* epileptic.

épiler *vt* to remove hair, pluck.

épilogue *m* epilogue; conclusion.

épinard *m* spinach.

épine *f* spine; thorn; quill.

épineux *adj* thorny, prickly; tricky.

épingle *f* pin.

épiphanie *f* Epiphany.

épique *adj* epic.

épiscopal *adj* episcopal.

épiscopat *m* episcopate.

épisode *m* episode.

épisodique *adj* occasional; transitory; **~ment** *adv* occasionally.

épitaphe *f* epitaph.

épithète *f* epithet.

éplucher *vt* to clean; to peel; to sift.

épluchure *f* peeling, paring.

éponge *f* sponge.

éponger *vt* to sponge, mop.

épopée *f* epic.

époque *f* time, epoch, age, period.

épouser *vt* to marry, wed; espouse.

épousseter *vt* to dust.

épouvantable *adj* terrible, appalling; **~ment** *adv* terribly, appallingly.

épouvantail *m* scarecrow.

épouvante *f* terror, dread.

épouvanter *vt* to terrify, appall.

époux *m*, **épouse** *f* spouse.

éprendre(s') *vr* to fall in love with.

épreuve *f* test; ordeal, trial; proof.

éprouvant *adj* trying, testing.

éprouver *vt* to feel, experience.

éprouvette *f* test tube.

épuisé *adj* exhausted; sold out.

épuisement *m* exhaustion.

épuiser *vt* to exhaust, wear out; **s'~** *vr* to run out; to exhaust oneself.

épuisette *f* landing net.

épurer *vt* to purify, refine.

équateur *m* equator.

équation *f* equation.

équatorial *adj* equatorial.

équerre *f* square; brace.

équestre *adj* equestrian.

équilibre *m* balance, equilibrium; harmony.

équilibrer *vt* to balance; **s'~** *vr* to balance each other.

équipage *m* crew; gear, equipment.

équipe *f* team, crew, gang, staff.

équipement *m* equipment; fitting out, fittings.

équiper *vt* to equip, fit out.

équipier *m*, **-ière** *f* team member.

équitable *adj* equitable, fair; **~ment** *adv* equitably, fairly.

équitation *f* equitation, riding.

équivalence *f* equivalence.

équivalent *adj* equivalent, same; * *m* equivalent.

équivoque *adj* equivocal, questionable.

érable *m* maple.

érafler *vt* to scratch, scrape.

ère *f* era.

érection *f* erection; establishment.

éreintant *adj* exhausting, backbreaking.

ergot *m* spur; lug.

ériger *vt* to erect; to establish.

ermite *m* hermit.

éroder *vt* to erode.

érosion f erosion.

érotique adj erotic.

érotisme m eroticism.

errant adj wandering, stray.

errer vi to wander, roam.

erreur f error, mistake, fault.

erroné adj erroneous.

éructation f eructation.

érudit adj erudite, learned.

érudition f erudition, learning.

éruptif adj eruptive.

éruption f eruption.

escabeau m stool; stepladder.

escadron m squadron, platoon.

escalade f climbing; escalation.

escalader vt to climb, scale.

escale f port of call, touchdown.

escalier m stairs, steps.

escalope f escalope.

escamoter vt to dodge, evade; to pilfer.

escapade f escapade; prank, jaunt.

escargot m snail.

escarpement m escarpment; steepness.

esclavage m slavery, bondage.

esclavagisme m proslavery.

esclave mf slave.

escompte m discount.

escompter vt to discount.

escorte f escort; retinue.

escorter vt to escort.

escrime f fencing.

escrimeur m, **-euse** f fencer.

escroc m crook, con man.

escroquer vt to swindle, con.

ésotérique adj esoteric.

espace m space, interval.

espacement m spacing, interval.

espacer vt to space out.

espadon m swordfish.

espadrille f espadrille, rope-soled sandal.

espèce f sort, kind; species.

espérance f hope, expectation.

espérer vt to hope.

espion m, **-onne** f spy.

espionnage m espionage, spying.

espionner vt to spy.

esplanade f esplanade.

espoir m hope.

esprit m mind, intellect; spirit; wit.

esquimau m, **-aude** f Eskimo.

esquisse f sketch, outline.

esquisser vt to sketch, outline. .

esquiver vt to dodge; to shirk.

essai m test, trial; attempt; essay.

essaim m swarm.

essayage m fitting, trying on.

essayer vt to test, try, try on.

essence f petrol; essential oil.

essentiel adj essential, basic; -**lement** adv essentially, basically.

essieu m axle.

essorage m wringing, mangling.

essorer vt to wring, mangle.

essouffler vt to wind; **s'~** vr to get out of breath.

essuyer vt to wipe, mop; **s'~** vr to wipe oneself.

est m east.

esthète mf aesthete.

esthéticien m, **-ienne** f beautician.

esthétique adj aesthetic; attractive; **~ment** adv aesthetically; * f aesthetics.

estimation f valuation; estimation, reckoning.

estime f esteem, respect, regard.

estimer vt to value, assess, estimate.

estival adj summer.

estivant m, **-e** f holidaymaker, summer visitor.

estomac m stomach.

estomper vt to blur, dim **s'~** vr to become blurred.

estrade f platform, rostrum.

estragon m tarragon.

et conj and.

étable f cowshed.

établi adj established; * m workbench.

établir vt to establish, set up; **s'~** vr to settle; to set oneself up as; to become established.

établissement *m* establishing, building; establishment.

étage *m* floor, storey; stage, level.

étagère *f* shelf.

étalage *m* display, display window; stall.

étalagiste *mf* window dresser; stallholder.

étaler *vt* to spread, strew; to stagger; to display.

étalon *m* stallion.

étanche *adj* waterproof.

étanchéité *f* waterproofness.

étang *m* pond.

étape *f* stage, leg; staging point.

état *m* state, condition; statement.

étatique *adj* under state control.

étatiser *vt* to bring under state control, nationalize.

état-major *m* (*mil*) staff; staff headquarters.

étau *m* vice.

étayer *vt* to prop up, support.

été *m* summer.

éteindre *vt* to put out, extinguish; **s'~** *vr* to go out; to die; to evaporate.

éteint *adj* faded; extinct.

étendard *m* standard.

étendre *vt* to spread, extend; to floor; **s'~** *vr* to spread; to stretch out; to increase.

étendu *adj* extensive, sprawling, wide.

étendue *f* expanse, area; duration.

éternel *adj* eternal, everlasting; **~lement** *adv* eternally.

éterniser *vt* to draw out; to immortalize; **s'~** *vr* to drag on, linger on.

éternité *f* eternity; ages.

éternuer *vi* to sneeze.

éthane *m* ethane.

éther *m* ether.

ethnie *f* ethnic unit.

ethnique *adj* ethnic.

ethnologie *f* ethnology.

ethnologue *mf* ethnologist.

étincelant *adj* sparkling; gleaming.

étinceler *vi* to sparkle, gleam.

étincelle *f* spark; gleam, glimmer.

étiqueter *vt* to label, mark.

étiquette *f* label, ticket; etiquette.

étirement *m* stretching.

étirer *vt* to stretch, draw out; **s'~** *vr* to stretch out.

étoffe *f* material, fabric; stuff.

étoile *f* star.

étoilé *adj* starry.

étonnant *adj* astonishing, surprising.

étonné *adj* astonished, surprised.

étonnement *m* surprise, astonishment.

étonner *vt* to astonish, surprise; **s'~** *vr* to be astonished.

étouffant *adj* stifling.

étouffer *vt* to suffocate; to muffle; **s'~** *vr* to be suffocated, to swelter.

étourderie *f* absentmindedness.

étourdi *adj* absentminded; **~ment** *adv* absentmindedly.

étourdir *vt* to stun, daze; to deafen.

étourdissant *adj* deafening; stunning.

étourdissement *m* blackout, dizzy spell; surprise.

étourneau *m* starling.

étrange *adj* strange, funny; **~ment** *adv* strangely, oddly.

étranger *m*, **-ère** *f* foreigner, stranger, alien; * *adj* foreign, strange, unknown.

étrangeté *f* strangeness, oddness.

étranglement *m* strangulation; bottleneck.

étrangler *vt* to strangle, stifle; **s'~** *vr* to strangle oneself, choke.

être *vi* to be; **c'est-à-dire** namely, that is to say; * *m* being, person, soul.

étreindre *vt* to embrace, hug; to seize.

étreinte *f* embrace; stranglehold.

étrier *m* stirrup.

étroit *adj* narrow; strict; **~ement** *adv* closely; strictly.

étude *f* study; survey; office.

étudier *vt* to study, examine.

étui *m* case; holster.

étymologie *f* etymology.

étymologique *adj* etymological.

eu = *p.p.* avoir had.

eucalyptus *m* eucalyptus.

eucharistie *f* eucharist.

euphémisme *m* euphemism.

euphorie *f* euphoria.

euphorique *adj* euphoric.

européen *m*, **-enne** *f* European; * *adj* European.

euthanasie *f* euthanasia.

eux *pron* they, them; **c'est à ~** it's up to them; it's theirs; **~-mêmes** themselves.

évacuation *f* evacuation; emptying.

évacuer *vt* to evacuate, clear.

évader(s') *vr* to escape.

évaluation *f* evaluation, appraisal.

évaluer *vt* to evaluate, appraise.

évangélique *adj* evangelical.

évangéliser *vt* to evangelize.

évangile *m* gospel.

évanouir(s') *vr* to faint, pass out.

évanouissement *m* faint, blackout.

évaporation *f* evaporation.

évaporer(s') *vr* to evaporate.

évasif *adj* evasive.

évasion *f* escape; escapism.

évasivement *adv* evasively.

évêché *m* bishopric.

éveil *m* awakening; dawning.

éveiller *vt* to waken, arouse; **s'~** *vr* to wake up.

événement *m* event, incident.

éventail *m* fan; range.

éventaire *m* tray; stall.

éventualité *f* eventuality, possibility.

éventuel *adj* possible; **~lement** *adv* possibly.

évêque *m* bishop.

évertuer(s') *vr* to strive to.

évidemment *adv* obviously, evidently.

évidence *f* evidence, proof.

évident *adj* obvious, evident.

évier *m* sink.

évincer *vt* to oust; to evict.

éviter *vt* to avoid; to spare.

évocation *f* evocation, recall.

évolué *adj* developed, advanced; enlightened.

évoluer *vi* to evolve, develop.

évolution *f* evolution, development.

évoquer *vt* to evoke, recall.

exacerber *vt* to exacerbate, aggravate.

exact *adj* exact, accurate; **~ement** *adv* exactly.

exactitude *f* exactness, accuracy.

exagération *f* exaggeration.

exagéré *adj* exaggerated, excessive; **~ment** *adv* exaggeratedly.

exagérer *vt* to exaggerate.

exaltation *f* elation; extolling, praising.

exalter *vt* to exalt, glorify; to elate.

examen *m* examination, survey, investigation.

examinateur *m*, **-trice** *f* examiner.

examiner *vt* to examine, survey.

exaspération *f* exasperation.

exaspérer *vt* to exasperate.

exaucer *vt* to fulfil, grant.

excédent *m* surplus, excess.

excédentaire *adj* surplus, excess.

excellent *adj* excellent.

exceller *vi* to excel.

excentricité *f* eccentricity.

excentrique *adj* eccentric; **~ment** *adv* eccentrically.

excepté *adj* apart, aside; * *prép* except, but for.

exception *f* exception, derogation.

exceptionnel *adj* exceptional; **~lement** *adv* exceptionally.

excès *m* excess, surplus.

excessivement *adv* excessively.
excitant *m* stimulant; * *adj* exciting, stimulating.
excitation *f* excitation, stimulation; incitement.
exciter *vt* to excite, stimulate; **s'~** *vr* to get excited.
exclamation *f* exclamation.
exclamer(s') *vr* to exclaim.
exclu *adj* excluded, outcast.
exclure *vt* to exclude, oust, expel.
exclusif *adj* exclusive.
exclusion *f* exclusion, suspension.
exclusivement *adv* exclusively.
exclusivité *f* exclusive rights.
excrément *m* excrement.
excroissance *f* excrescence, outgrowth.
excursion *f* excursion, trip.
excursionniste *mf* tripper; walker.
excuse *f* excuse, pretext.
excuser *vt* to excuse, forgive; **s'~** *vr* to apologize for.
exécrable *adj* execrable, atrocious; **~ment** *adv* atrociously, execrably.
exécration *f* execration, loathing.
exécrer *vt* to execrate, loathe.
exécuter *vt* to execute, carry out, perform; to produce.
exécution *f* execution, carrying out, performance.
exemplaire *m* copy, archetype; * *adj* model, exemplary; **~ment** *adv* exemplarily.
exemple *m* example, model, instance.
exempt *adj* exempt, free from.
exercer *vt* to exercise, perform, fulfil; **s'~** *vr* to practise.
exercice *m* exercise, practice, use; financial year.
exhaustif *adj* exhaustive.
exhaustivement *adv* exhaustively.
exhiber *vt* to exhibit, show; to produce; **s'~** *vr* to show off; to expose oneself.

exhibition *f* exhibition, show; display.
exhibitionniste *mf* exhibitionist.
exhortation *f* exhortation.
exhorter *vt* to exhort, urge.
exigeant *adj* demanding, exacting.
exigence *f* demand, requirement; exigency.
exiger *vt* to demand, require.
exigu *adj*, *f* **exiguë** scanty, exiguous.
exiguïté *f* exiguity, scantiness.
exil *m* exile.
exilé *m*, **-e** *f* exile;* *adj* exiled.
exiler *vt* to exile, banish; **s'~** *vr* to go into exile.
existant *adj* existing.
existence *f* existence, life.
exister *vi* to exist; to be.
exode *m* exodus; drift, loss.
exonération *f* exemption.
exonérer *vt* to exempt.
exorbitant *adj* exorbitant, outrageous.
exorciser *vt* to exorcise.
exotique *adj* exotic.
exotisme *m* exoticism.
expansif *adj* expansive; outgoing, forthcoming.
expansion *f* expansion, development.
expatrié *m*, **-e** *f* expatriate; * *adj* expatriate.
expatrier *vt* to expatriate; **s'~** *vr* to expatriate oneself.
expectative *f* expectation, hope; **être dans l'~** to be still waiting (to see, to hear).
expédier *vt* to send, dispatch; to dispose of.
expéditeur *m*, **-trice** *f* sender; shipper, consignor.
expéditif *adj* quick, expeditious.
expédition *f* dispatch; consignment.
expérience *f* experience; experiment.
expérimental *adj* experimental; **~ement** *adv* experimentally.

expérimentateur m, **-trice** f experimenter.

expérimentation f experimentation.

expérimenté adj experienced.

expérimenter vt to test; to experiment with.

expert adj expert, skilled in; * m expert; connoisseur; assessor.

expertise f expertise; expert appraisal.

expiation f expiation, atonement.

expier vi to expiate, atone for.

expiration f expiry; expiration, exhalation.

expirer vi to breathe out, expire.

explicatif adj explanatory.

explication f explanation, analysis.

explicite adj explicit ~**ment** adv explicitly.

expliquer vt to explain, account for; to analyse.

exploitant m, **-e** f farmer, smallholder.

exploitation f working; exploitation; operating; concern; smallholding.

exploiter vt to work, exploit; run, operate.

explorateur m, **-trice** f explorer.

exploration f exploration.

explorer vt to explore.

exploser vi to explode.

explosif adj explosive; * m explosive.

explosion f explosion.

exportateur m, **-trice** f exporter.

exportation f export, exportation.

exporter vt to export.

exposé m exposition, overview, statement.

exposer vt to display; to explain, state; to expose; **s'~** vr to expose oneself to, run the risk of.

exposition f display; exposition; exposure.

exprès adj formal, express.

express adj fast; * m fast train.

expressif adj expressive.

expression f expression.

expressionnisme m expressionism.

expressionniste mf expressionist; * adj expressionist, expressionistic.

exprimer vt to express, voice; **s'~** vr to express oneself.

expropriation f expropriation.

expulser vt to expel; to evict.

expulsion f expulsion; éviction.

exquis adj exquisite; ~**ément** adv exquisitely.

extase f ecstasy; rapture.

extasier(s') vr to go into ecstasies.

extensible adj extensible, extendable.

extension f extension; stretching; expansion.

exténuant adj exhausting.

exténuer vt to exhaust; **s'~** vr to exhaust oneself.

extérieur m exterior, outside; * adj outer, external, exterior; ~**ement** adv externally, outwardly.

extérioriser vt to show, express; to exteriorize.

extermination f extermination.

exterminer vt exterminate.

externe adj external, outer.

extincteur m extinguisher.

extinction f extinction, extinguishing.

extraction f extraction; mining.

extradition f extradition.

extraire vt to extract; to mine.

extrait m extract; abstract.

extraordinaire adj extraordinary; ~**ment** adv extraordinarily.

extraterrestre mf extraterrestrial; * adj extraterrestrial.

extravagant adj extravagant, wild.

extraverti m, **-e** f extrovert; * adj extrovert.

extrême adj extreme; ~**ment** adv extremely.

extrémiste *mf, adj* extremist.
extrémité *f* extremity, limit; straits.

exubérance *f* exuberance.
exubérant *adj* exuberant.
exulter *vi* to exult.

F

fable *f* fable, story, tale.
fabricant *m*, **-ante** *f* manufacturer, maker.
fabrication *f* manufacture, production; counterfeiting.
fabrique *f* factory.
fabriquer *vt* to manufacture; to forge; to fabricate.
fabuleux *adj* fabulous, mythical, legendary.
façade *f* façade, front.
face *f* face, side, surface, aspect; **en ~** opposite, over the road; **~ à** facing; **faire ~ à** to confront, face up to; **de ~** fullface, frontal; **~ à ~** face to face.
face à face *m* encounter, interview.
facette *f* facet.
fâché *adj* angry; sorry.
fâcher *vt* to anger, make angry; to grieve; **se ~** *vr* to get angry.
fâcheux *adj* deplorable, regrettable.
facile *adj* easy; facile; **~ment** *adv* easily.
facilité *f* easiness, ease; ability; facility.
faciliter *vt* to make easier, facilitate.
façon *f* way, fashion; make; imitation; **de toute ~** at any rate; **non merci, sans ~** no thanks, honestly; **de ~ à** so that, so as to.
façonner *vt* to shape, fashion, model; to till.
fac-similé *m* facsimile.
facteur *m* postman.
factice *adj* artificial, imitation.
faction *f* faction; sentry-duty.

facturation *f* invoicing.
facture *f* bill, invoice; construction, technique.
facturer *vt* to invoice, charge for.
facultatif *adj* optional.
faculté *f* faculty; power, ability; right.
fade *adj* insipid, bland, dull.
fagot *m* faggot, bundle of firewood.
faible *adj* weak, feeble; slight, poor; **~ment** *adv* weakly, faintly, feebly.
faiblesse *f* weakness, feebleness, faintness.
faiblir *vi* to fail, flag, weaken; to wane.
faïence *f* earthenware, crockery.
faille *f* fault; flaw; weakness.
faillir *vi*: to come close to; to fail **j'ai failli tomber** I almost fell.
faillite *f* bankruptcy; collapse.
faim *f* hunger; appetite; famine.
fainéant *m*, **-ante** *f* idler, loafer.
faire *vt* to do; to make; **rien à ~!** nothing doing!; **se ~ à** to get used to; **s'en ~ à** to worry.
faire-part *m* announcement (birth, marriage, death).
faisable *adj* feasible.
faisan *m* pheasant.
faisceau *m* bundle, stack; beam.
fait *m* event; fact; act.
faîte *m* summit; rooftop.
falaise *f* cliff.
falloir *vi*: to be necessary **il faut que tu partes** you must leave.
falsifier *vt* to falsify, alter.
famélique *adj* starving, scrawny.
fameux *adj* first-rate; downright, out-and-out.

familial *adj* family, domestic.
familiariser *vt* to familiarize; **se ~** *vr* to familiarize oneself.
familiarité *f* familiarity.
familier *adj* familiar; colloquial; informal.
familièrement *adv* familiarly, informally.
famille *f* family.
famine *f* famine.
fanatique *adj* fanatic; **~ment** *adv* fanatically; * *mf* fanatic; zealot.
fanatisme *m* fanaticism.
fané *adj* faded, withered.
faner *vt* to turn (hay); to fade; **se ~** *vr* to wither, fade.
fanfare *f* fanfare, flourish; brass band.
fantaisie *f* whim, extravagance; imagination.
fantasme *m* fantasy.
fantasmer *vi* to fantasize.
fantastique *adj* fantastic; **~ment** *adv* fantastically; eerily.
fantôme *m* ghost, phantom.
faon *m* fawn.
farce *f* joke, prank; farce.
farceur *m*, **-euse** *f* joker; clown.
farci *adj* crammed, packed.
farcir *vt* to stuff, cram.
fard *m* make-up.
fardeau *m* load, burden.
farder *vt* to make up; to disguise; **se ~** *vr* to make oneself up.
farine *f* flour.
farineux *adj* floury, powdery; * *m* starchy food.
farouche *adj* shy, timid; unsociable; fierce; **~ment** *adv* fiercely.
fascicule *m* fascicle, part, instalment.
fascinant *adj* fascinating.
fascination *f* fascination.
fasciner *vt* to fascinate, bewitch.
fascisme *m* fascism.
fasciste *mf*, *adj* fascist.
faste *m* pomp, ostentation.
fastidieux *adj* tedious, boring.
fastueux *adj* sumptuous, luxurious.

fatal *adj* fatal, deadly; fateful; **~ement** *adv* inevitably, unavoidably.
fataliste *mf* fatalist; * *adj* fatalistic.
fatalité *f* fatality; inevitability.
fatidique *adj* fateful; fatal.
fatigant *adj* tiring, fatiguing.
fatigue *f* fatigue, tiredness.
fatigué *adj* tired, weary; overworked, strained.
fatiguer *vt* to tire; to overwork, strain; **se ~** *vr* to get tired.
faubourg *m* suburb.
faucher *vt* to reap; to flatten, knock down.
faucille *f* sickle.
faucon *m* falcon, hawk.
faufiler *vt* to tack; to insinuate, introduce; **se ~** *vr* to worm one's way in.
faune *f* wildlife, fauna.
faussaire *mf* forger.
faussement *adv* wrongly; falsely.
fausser *vt* to distort, alter; to warp.
fausseté *f* falseness; deceitfulness.
faute *f* mistake, foul, fault; **~ de mieux** for lack of anything better.
fauteuil *m* armchair.
fautif *m*, **-ive** *f* culprit, guilty party; * *adj* at fault, guilty; faulty, incorrect.
fauve *m* wildcat; fawn.
faux *adj* false, forged, fake; wrong; bogus.
faux-filet *m* sirloin.
faux-fuyant *m* evasion, equivocation.
faux-semblant *m* sham, pretence.
faveur *f* favour.
favorable *adj* favourable, sympathetic; **~ment** *adv* favourably.
favori *m*, **-ite** *f* favourite; * *adj* favourite.
favoriser *vt* to favour, further.
fébrile *adj* feverish, febrile; **~ment** *adv* feverishly.

fébrilité f feverishness.

fécond adj fertile; prolific, fruitful; creative.

fécondation f impregnation, fertilization.

féconder vt to impregnate; to fertilize, pollinate.

fécondité f fertility, fecundity.

fécule f starch.

féculent adj starchy; * m starchy food.

fédéral adj federal.

fédération f federation.

fée f fairy.

féerique adj magical, fairy.

feindre vt to feign, pretend.

feinte f dummy, feint.

fêlé adj cracked, hare-brained.

félicitation f congratulation.

féliciter vt to congratulate.

félin adj feline; * m feline.

femelle f female.

féminin adj feminine, female.

féminisme m feminism.

féministe mf; * adj feminist.

féminité f femininity.

femme f woman; wife; **~ de ménage** housewife; **~ de chambre** chambermaid.

fémur m femur.

fendiller vt to chink; to crack, craze; **se ~** vr to be covered in small cracks.

fendre vt to split, cleave; to crack; **se ~** vr to crack.

fenêtre f window.

fenouil m fennel.

fente f crack, fissure; slot.

féodal adj feudal.

fer m iron, point, blade; **~ à cheval** horseshoe.

férié adj holiday.

ferme adj firm, steady; definite; **~ment** adv firmly; * f farm.

fermé adj closed; exclusive; inscrutable.

ferment m ferment, leaven.

fermentation f fermentation, fermenting.

fermenter vi to ferment, work.

fermer vt to close; block; turn off; **se ~** vr to close, shut up; to close one's mind to.

fermeté f firmness, steadiness.

fermeture f closing, shutting; latch; fastener.

fermier m, **-ière** f farmer.

féroce adj ferocious, savage; **~ment** adv ferociously, savagely.

férocité f ferocity, fierceness.

ferraille f scrap iron.

ferronnerie f ironworks; ironwork.

ferroviaire adj railway.

fertile adj fertile, productive.

fertilisation f fertilization.

fertiliser vt to fertilize.

fertilité f fertility.

fervent adj fervent, ardent.

ferveur f fervour, ardour.

fesse f buttock.

festin m feast.

festival m festival.

fête f feast, holiday.

fêter vt to celebrate, fête.

fétichisme m fetishism.

fétichiste mf; * adj fetishist.

fétide adj fetid.

feu m fire; light; hearth; **en ~** on fire.

feuillage m foliage, greenery.

feuille f leaf.

feuillet m leaf, page, layer.

feuilleté adj foliated; laminated.

feuilleter vt to leaf through; to glance at.

feuilleton m serial, series.

feutre m felt; felt hat.

fève f broad bean.

fiabilité f accuracy; dependability.

fiable adj reliable; dependable.

fiançailles fpl engagement, betrothal.

fiancer(se) vr to become engaged.

fiasco m fiasco.

fibre f fibre.

fibreux adj fibrous, stringy.

fibrome m fibroid, fibroma.

ficeler *vt* to tie up.

ficelle *f* string; stick (bread).

fiche *f* card; sheet; certificate.

ficher *vt* to file, put on file.

fichier *m* catalogue;file.

fictif *adj* fictitious; imaginary.

fiction *f* imagination, fiction.

fidèle *adj* faithful, loyal; **~ment** *adv* faithfully; * *mf* believer.

fidélité *f* fidelity, loyalty.

fief *m* fief; stronghold, preserve.

fier(se) *vr* to trust, rely on.

fier *adj* proud, haughty; noble.

fièrement *adv* proudly.

fierté *f* pride; arrogance.

fièvre *f* fever, temperature; excitement.

fiévreux *adj* feverish.

figer *vt* to congeal, freeze; clot; **se ~** *vr* to congeal, freeze; clot.

figue *f* fig.

figuier *m* fig tree.

figurant *m*, **-e** *f* extra, walk-on; stooge.

figuratif *adj* figurative, representational.

figure *f* face; figure; illustration, diagram.

figuré *adj* figurative, metaphorical, diagrammatic; * *m*: **au ~** in the figurative sense.

figurer *vt* to represent; * *vi* to appear, feature; **se ~** *vr* to imagine.

figurine *f* figurine.

fil *m* thread; wire; cord; **~ de fer** wire; **~ à plomb** plumb line; **au ~ des jours** with the passing days.

filament *m* filament, strand, thread.

filature *f* spinning; mill; tailing.

file *f* line, queue; **à la ~** in line, in succession; **stationner en double ~** to double-park.

filer *vt* to spin; to tail; to draw out; * *vi* to run, trickle; to fly by; to make off.

filet *m* dribble, trickle; fillet; net.

filiation *f* filiation; relation.

filière *f* path; procedures; network.

fille *f* daughter, girl.

fillette *f* (small) girl.

filleul *m*, **-eule** *f* godson, godchild.

film *m* film, picture.

filmer *vt* to film.

filon *m* vein, seam.

fils *m* son.

filtre *m* filter.

filtrer *vt* to filter; to screen.

fin *f* end, finish; **prendre ~** to terminate, come to an end; * *adj* thin, fine; delicate; **~ement** *adv* finely, delicately.

final *adj* final; **~ement** *adv* finally.

finale *f* finale.

finance *f* finance.

financement *m* financing.

financer *vt* to finance.

financier *m*, **-ière** *f* financier.

financièrement *adv* financially.

finesse *f* fineness; sharpness; neatness; delicacy.

fini *adj* finished, over, complete.

finir *vt* to finish, complete; * *vi* to finish, end; to die.

finition *f* finish, finishing.

fisc *m* tax department.

fiscal *adj* fiscal, tax.

fissure *f* crack, fissure.

fixation *f* fixation; fixing, fastening.

fixe *adj* fixed, permanent, set; **~ment** *adv* fixedly, steadily.

fixer *vt* to fix, fasten; to arrange; **se ~** *vr* to settle.

flacon *m* bottle, flask.

flageolant *adj* shaky.

flageolet *m* flageolet.

flagrant *adj* flagrant, blatant.

flair *m* sense of smell, nose; intuition.

flairer *vt* to smell, sniff; to scent.

flambeau *m* torch; candlestick.

flamboyant *adj* blazing; flamboyant.

flamboyer *vi* to blaze, flash, gleam.

flamme f flame; fervour; ardour.
flan m custard tart; mould.
flanc m flank, side.
flanelle f flannel.
flâner vi to stroll; to lounge about.
flasque adj flaccid; spineless.
flatter vt t flatter, gratify; to pander; to delight.
flatterie f flattery.
flatteur m, **-euse** f flatterer.
fléau m scourge; plague.
flèche f arrow.
fléchir vi to bend, yield, weaken; * vt to bend, sway.
fléchissement m bending; flexing; bowing.
flegmatique adj phlegmatic.
flegme m composure, phlegm.
flétrir vt to wither, fade; to stigmatize; **se ~** vr to wither, wilt.
fleur f flower.
fleuri adj in bloom; flowery.
fleurir vi to blossom, flower; * vt to decorate with flowers.
fleuriste mf florist.
fleuve m river. .
flexibilité f flexibility.
flexible adj flexible, pliant.
flic m (fam) cop, policeman.
flocon m fleck, flake.
floraison f flowering, blossoming.
floral adj floral, flower.
flore f flora.
florissant adj flourishing, blooming.
flot m stream, flood; floodtide; wave.
flotte f fleet; rain.
flottement m wavering; vagueness, imprecision.
flotter vi to float; to drift; to wander; to waver.
flotteur m float.
flou adj blurred, hazy.
fluctuant adj fluctuating.
fluctuation f fluctuation.
fluide adj fluid, flowing.
fluidité f fluidity.
fluor m fluorine.
fluorescent adj fluorescent.

fluorure m fluoride.
flûte f flute; French stick.
flûtiste mf flautist.
flux m flood; flow; flux.
focaliser vt to focus; **se ~** vr to be focused on.
foetus m foetus.
foi f faith, trust.
foie m liver.
foin m hay.
foire f fair, trade fair.
fois f time, occasion.
folie f madness, insanity; extravagance.
folklore m folklore.
folklorique adj outlandish.
follement adv madly, wildly.
foncé adj dark, deep (colours).
foncer vi to hammer along, rush at; * vt to make darker; to sink, bore.
foncier adj land, landed, property.
foncièrement adv fundamentally, basically.
fonction f post, duty; function.
fonctionnaire mf civil servant.
fonctionnement m working, functioning, operation.
fonctionner vi to work, function, operate.
fond m bottom, back; **au ~** basically, in fact; **à ~** thoroughly, in depth; **dans le ~** in reality, basically; **~ de teint** foundation cream.
fondamental adj fundamental, basic; **~ement** adv fundamentally.
fondamentalisme m fundamentalism.
fondamentaliste mf; * adj fundamentalist.
fondant adj thawing, melting.
fondateur m, **-trice** f founder.
fondation f foundation.
fondement m foundation; ground.
fonder vt to found; to base.
fondre vi to melt; to vanish; to

slim; * *vt* to melt; to cast; to merge.

fonds *m* business; fund; money; stock.

fondu *adj* melted; molten; cast.

fontaine *f* fountain, spring.

fonte *f* melting; casting; smelting.

football *m* football, soccer.

forage *m* drilling, boring.

forain *m*, **-e** *f* stallholder; fairground entertainer; * *adj* fairground.

force *f* strength, force, violence, energy; **à ~ de** by dint of.

forcé *adj* forced; emergency; **~ment** *adv* inevitably.

forcené *adj* deranged, frenzied.

forcer *vt* to force, compel; track down; *vi* to overdo, strain; **se ~ vr** to force oneself to.

forestier *adj* forest; forestry.

forêt *f* forest.

forfait *m* set price, package; withdrawal.

forfaitaire *adj* fixed, set, inclusive.

forge *f* forge, smithy.

forger *vt* to forge, form, mould.

forgeron *m* blacksmith, smith.

formaliser(se) *vr* to take offence at.

formalité *f* formality.

format *m* format, size.

formation *f* formation; training.

forme *f* form, shape; mould, fitness; **être en ~** to be on form; **en ~ de** forming.

formel *adj* definite, positive; formal; **~lement** *adv* positively, definitely; formally.

former *vt* to form, make up; to train; **se ~ vr** to form, gather; to train oneself.

formidable *adj* tremendous; fantastic; **~ment** *adv* tremendously, fantastically.

formulaire *m* form.

formule *f* formula; phrase; system.

formuler *vt* to formulate; express.

fort *adj* strong; high; loud; pronounced; **~ement** *adv* strongly; highly; very much; * *adv* loudly; greatly; most; * *m* fort; strong point, forte.

forteresse *f* fortress.

fortifiant *m* tonic; * *adj* fortifying; invigorating.

fortification *f* fortification.

fortifier *vt* to fortify, strengthen; **se ~ vr** to grow stronger.

fortuit *adj* fortuitous, chance; **~ement** *adv* fortuitously.

fortune *f* fortune, luck.

fortuné *adj* wealthy; fortunate.

fosse *f* pit; grave.

fossé *m* ditch; gulf.

fossette *f* dimple.

fossile *m* fossil.

fou *adj*, *f* **folle** mad, wild; tremendous; erratic.

foudre *f* lightning, thunderbolt.

foudroyant *adj* lightning; thundering; violent.

foudroyer *vt* to strike (lightning).

fouet *m* whip; whisk.

fouetter *vt* to whip, flog.

fougère *f* fern.

fougue *f* ardour, spirit.

fougueux *adj* fiery, ardent.

fouille *f* frisking; excavations.

fouiller *vt* to search, scour.

foulard *m* scarf.

foule *f* crowd; masses, heaps.

four *m* oven; furnace; fiasco.

fourbe *adj* deceitful, two-faced.

fourbu *adj* exhausted.

fourche *f* pitchfork; crotch.

fourchette *f* fork .

fourchu *adj* forked; cloven.

fourgon *m* coach, wagon, van.

fourmi *f* ant.

fourmilière *f* anthill.

fourmillement *m* swarming, milling.

fourmiller *vi* to swarm, teem.

fourneau *m* stove.

fournir *vt* to supply, provide.

fournisseur *m*, **-euse** *f* purveyor, supplier.

fourniture *f* supplying, provision.
fourrage *m* fodder, forage.
fourré *adj* filled; fur-lined; * *m* thicket.
fourrer *vt* to stuff; to line.
fourrière *f* pound (car).
fourrure *f* coat, fur.
foutu *adj* bloody, damned; lousy.
foyer *m* home; fireplace; club; focus.
fracas *m* crash; roar, din.
fraction *f* fraction, part.
fractionnement *m* splitting up, division.
fracture *f* fracture.
fracturer *vt* to fracture, break open.
fragile *adj* fragile, delicate.
fragilité *f* fragility, flimsiness.
fragment *m* fragment.
fragmentation *f* fragmentation; splitting up.
fragmenter *vt* to break up, fragment; **se ~** *vr* to fragment, break up.
fraîcheur *f* freshness, coolness.
frais *mpl* expenses; * *adj*, *f* **fraîche** fresh, cool.
fraise *f* strawberry.
framboise *f* raspberry.
franc *adj*, *f* **franche** frank, open; clear; absolute.
Français *m* Frenchman, **-e** *f* Frenchwoman.
français *adj* French; * *m* French.
France *f* France.
franchement *adv* frankly, openly; boldly; clearly.
franchir *vt* to clear, get over, cross.
franchise *f* frankness, openness; exemption; franchise.
francophone *mf* French-speaker, *adj* French-speaking.
francophonie *f* French-speaking communities.
frange *f* fringe; threshold.
frappant *adj* striking.
frapper *vt* to hit; to strike down; to infringe; * *vi* to strike, knock.

fraternel *adj* fraternal; **~lement** *adv* fraternally.
fraterniser *vi* to fraternize.
fraternité *f* fraternity.
fraude *f* fraud, cheating.
frauduleux *adj* fraudulent.
frayeur *f* fright.
frein *m* brake; check.
freinage *m* braking; slowing down.
freiner *vi* (*auto*) to brake; to slow down; * *vt* (*auto*) to slow down; to curb, check.
frêle *adj* flimsy, fragile.
frémir *vi* to quiver, tremble.
frémissant *adj* quivering, trembling.
frémissement *m* shudder, quiver.
frénétique *adj* frenetic; **~ment** *adv* frenetically.
fréquemment *adv* frequently.
fréquence *f* frequency.
fréquent *adj* frequent.
frère *m* brother.
fresque *f* fresco.
friand *adj* partial to, fond of.
friandise *f* delicacy, sweetmeat.
fric *m* (*fam*) cash, lolly.
friction *f* friction.
frigidaire *m* refrigerator.
frigide *adj* frigid.
frileux *adj* susceptible to cold; chilly.
frire *vt* to fry.
frisé *adj* curly, curly-haired.
friser *vi* to curl, be curly; * *vt* to curl; to graze, skim.
frisson *m* shiver, shudder.
frissonnant *adj* shivering, shuddering.
frissonnement *m* shuddering, shivering.
frissonner *vi* to shudder, tremble, shiver.
frite *f* chip.
friteuse *f* chip pan.
friture *f* frying; frying fat.
frivole *adj* frivolous, shallow.
frivolité *f* frivolity.
froid *adj* cold, cool; **~ement** *adv*

coldly, coolly; * *m* cold; coolness; refrigeration.

froideur *f* coldness, chilliness.

froissement *m* creasing; rustling, rustle.

froisser *vt* to crease; to offend; **se ~** *vr* to crease; to take offence.

frôler *vt* to brush against; to verge on.

fromage *m* cheese.

front *m* forehead; face; front.

frontal *adj* frontal.

frontalier *adj* border, frontier.

frontière *f* border, frontier.

frottement *m* rubbing, scraping.

frotter *vt* to rub, scrape.

fructifier *vi* to bear fruit.

fructueux *adj* fruitful, profitable.

frugal *adj* frugal; **~ement** *adv* frugally.

frugalité *f* frugality.

fruit *m* fruit, result.

fruité *adj* fruity.

frustration *f* frustration.

frustrer *vt* to frustrate, deprive.

fugace *adj* fleeting, transient.

fugitif *m*, **-ive** *f* fugitive; * *adj* fugitive, runaway.

fugue *f* running away.

fuir *vi* to avoid; to flee; to leak.

fuite *f* flight, escape; leak.

fulgurant *adj* lightning; dazzling.

fumant *adj* smoking, fuming.

fumé *adj* smoked.

fumée *f* smoke; vapour.

fumer *vi* to smoke, steam, give off smoke; * *vt* to smoke.

fumet *m* aroma.

fumeur *m*, **-euse** *f* smoker.

fumier *m* dung, manure.

funèbre *adj* funeral; funerary.

funérailles *fpl* funeral.

funéraire *adj* funeral, funerary.

funeste *adj* disastrous; harmful.

fureur *f* fury; violence.

furie *f* shrew; fury, rage.

furieusement *adv* furiously.

furieux *adj* furious, violent.

furtif *adj* furtive; stealthy.

furtivement *adj* furtively.

fusée *f* rocket, missile.

fusible *m* fuse.

fusil *m* rifle, gun.

fusillade *f* fusillade; gunfire; shoot-out.

fusiller *vt* to shoot.

fusion *f* fusion; melting; merger; blending.

fusionner *vt* to merge, combine.

fût *m* trunk; shaft; barrel.

futé *adj* crafty, cunning.

futile *adj* futile; **~ment** *adv* futilely.

futilité *f* futility.

futur *adj* future; * *m* intended, fiancé; future.

fuyant *adj* fleeting; evasive.

fuyard *m*, **-e** *f*; * *adj* runaway.

G

gabarit *m* size, build; calibre.

gâcher *vt* to mix; to waste.

gachette *f* trigger.

gâchis *m* mess.

gadget *m* gadget; gimmick.

gaffe *f* blunder; boat hook.

gage *m* security; pledge; proof.

gagnant *m*, **-e** *f* winner; * *adj* winning.

gagner *vt* to earn, to win, beat; to gain; * *vi* to win; to spread.

gai *adj* cheerful, happy, gay; **~ement** *adv* cheerfully, happily.

gaieté *f* cheerfulness, gaiety.

gain *m* earnings; gain, profit, benefit; saving.

gaine *f* girdle; sheath.

gala *m* official reception; gala.

galamment *adv* courteously, gallantly.

galant *adj* gallant, courteous.

galanterie *f* gallantry.

galaxie *f* galaxy.
galère *f* galley.
galerie *f* gallery; tunnel.
galet *m* pebble.
galette *f* pancake.
Gallois *m* Welshman, **-e** *f* Welshwoman.
gallois *adj* Welsh; * *m* Welsh (language).
galon *m* braid; stripe.
galop *m* gallop; canter.
galoper *vi* to gallop; to run wild.
galvaniser *vt* to galvanize.
gambas *fpl* prawns.
gamin *m*, **-e** *f* kid, street urchin.
gaminerie *f* playfulness; childishness.
gamme *f* range; scale.
ganglion *m* ganglion.
gangrène *f* gangrene.
gant *m* glove.
gap *m* gap; difference, discrepancy.
garage *m* garage.
garagiste *mf* garage owner.
garant *m*, **-e** *f* guarantor.
garantie *f* guarantee, surety.
garantir *vt* to guarantee, secure.
garçon *m* boy; assistant; waiter.
garde *f* custody; guard; surveillance; * *m* guard, warder.
garde-à-vous *m* standing to attention.
garde-boue *m* mudguard.
garde-chasse *m* gamekeeper.
garde-fou *m* railing; parapet; safeguard.
garder *vt* t look after; to stay in; to keep on.
garderie *f* day nursery.
garde-robe *f* wardrobe.
gardien *m*, **-ienne** *f* guard, guardian, warden; protector; **~ de but** *m* goalkeeper.
gare *f* rail station; basin; depot.
garer *vt* to park; to dock; **se ~** *vr* to avoid, steer clear of.
gargariser(se) *vr* to gargle; to crow about.
gargarisme *m* gargle.

gargouillement *m* gurgling; rumbling.
gargouiller *vi* to gurgle; to rumble.
garnir *vt* to fit with; to trim, decorate.
garnison *f* (*mil*) garrison.
garniture *f* trimming, lining; garnish.
garrot *m* garrotte; tourniquet.
gars *m* (*fam*) lad; bloke.
gaspillage *m* waste; squandering.
gaspiller *vt* to waste, squander.
gastrique *adj* gastric.
gastronome *m* gourmet, gastronome.
gastronomie *f* gastronomy.
gâté *adj* ruined; spoiled.
gâteau *m* cake.
gâter *vt* to ruin; to spoil; **se ~** *vr* to go bad, go off.
gâteux *adj* senile; doddering.
gauche *adj* left; awkward, clumsy; **~ment** *adv* awkwardly; * *f* left; left wing.
gaucher *adj* left-handed.
gauchisant *m*, **-e** *f* leftist; * *adj* of leftist tendencies.
gauchiste *mf*; * *adj* leftist.
gaufre *f* waffle.
gaver *vt* to force-feed; to fill up; **se ~** *vr* to stuff oneself; to devour.
gaz *m invar* gas; fizz; wind.
gaze *f* gauze.
gazelle *f* gazelle.
gazeux *adj* gaseous; fizzy.
gazon *m* lawn; turf.
gazouiller *vi* to chirp, warble.
géant *m* giant, **-e** *f* giantess.
geindre *vi* to groan; to whine.
gel *m* frost; gel.
gélatine *f* gelatine.
gelé *adj* cold, unresponsive.
gelée *f* frost; jelly.
geler *vi* to freeze, be frozen; * *vt* to freeze, turn to ice; to suspend.
gélule *f* capsule.
gémeaux *mpl* Gemini.
gémir *vi* to groan, moan.

gémissement *m* groan, moan; groaning.

gênant *adj* annoying; awkward.

gencive *f* gum.

gendarme *m* policeman; gendarme.

gendarmerie *f* police force, constabulary.

gendre *m* son-in-law.

gêne *f* discomfort; trouble; embarrassment; **être sans ~** to be inconsiderate.

généalogie *f* genealogy.

généalogique *adj* genealogist.

gêner *vt* to bother; to hinder; to make uneasy; **se ~** *vr* to put oneself out.

général *adj* general, broad; common; **~ement** *adv* generally; * *m* general, **-e** *f* general's wife; call to arms.

généralisation *f* generalization.

généraliser *vt* to generalize; **se ~** *vr* to become widespread.

généraliste *m* general practitioner; * *adj* general-interest; non-specialized.

généralité *f* majority; general points.

générateur *m* generator.

génération *f* generation.

générer *vt* to generate

généreusement *adv* generously; nobly.

généreux *adj* generous; noble; magnanimous.

générosité *f* generosity; nobility; magnanimity.

génétique *adj* genetic; **~ment** *adv* genetically.

génial *adj* inspired, of genius.

génie *m* genius; spirit; genie.

génital *adj* genital.

génocide *m* genocide.

genou *m* knee.

genre *m* kind, type; gender; genre.

gens *mpl* people, folk.

gentil *adj*, *f* **gentille** kind; good; pleasant.

gentillesse *f* kindness; favour.

gentiment *adv* kindly; nicely.

géographe *mf* geographer.

géographie *f* geography.

géographique *adj* geographic.

géologie *f* geology.

géologue *mf* geologist.

géomètre *m* surveyor.

géométrie *f* geometry.

géométrique *adj* geometric; **~ment** *adv* geometrically.

géranium *m* geranium.

gérant *m*, **-e** *f* manager.

gerbe *f* sheaf, bundle; collection.

gercer *vt* to chap, crack; **se ~** *vr* to chap, crack.

gerçure *f* (small) crack.

gérer *vt* to manage, administer.

germe *m* germ; seed.

germer *vi* to sprout, germinate.

gérondif *m* gerundive; gerund.

gésier *m* gizzard.

gestation *f* gestation.

geste *m* gesture; act, deed.

gesticuler *vi* to gesticulate.

gestion *f* management, administration.

gestionnaire *adj* administrative, management.

ghetto *m* ghetto.

gibier *m* game; prey.

gicler *vi* to spurt, squirt.

gicleur *m* jet.

gifle *f* slap, smack.

gifler *vt* to slap, smack.

gigantesque *adj* gigantic, immense.

gigot *m* leg (mutton/lamb), haunch.

gilet *m* waistcoat.

gingembre *m* ginger.

girafe *f* giraffe.

giratoire *adj* gyrating, gyratory.

girouette *f* weather vane.

gisement *m* deposit; mine; pool.

gitan *m*, **-e** *f* gipsy.

gîte *m* shelter; home; gîte.

givre *m* frost, rime.

givré *adj* covered in frost.

glace *f* ice; ice cream; mirror.

glacé *adj* icy; frozen; glazed; chilly.

glacer *vt* to freeze; to chill; to glaze.

glacial *adj* icy; freezing.

glacier *m* glacier; ice cream maker.

glacière *f* icebox.

glaçon *m* icicle; ice cube.

glaïeul *m* gladiola.

glaise *f* clay.

gland *m* acorn.

glande *f* gland.

glaner *vt* to glean.

glauque *adj* blue-green; shabby, run-down.

glissade *f* slide, skid.

glissant *adj* slippery.

glissement *m* sliding; gliding; downturn, downswing.

glisser *vi* to slide, slip, skid.

glissière *f* slide; runner.

global *adj* global, overall; **~ement** *adv* globally.

globe *m* globe, sphere; earth.

globulaire *adj* global; corpuscular.

globule *m* globule; corpuscle.

globuleux *adj* globular; protruding.

gloire *f* glory; distinction; celebrity.

glorieux *adj* glorious.

glorifier *vt* to glory, honour; **se ~** *vr* to glory in; to boast.

glossaire *m* glossary.

glouton *m*, **-onne** *f* glutton; * *adj* gluttonous, ravenous; **~nement** *adv* gluttonously.

gluant *adj* sticky, gummy.

glucide *m* glucide.

glucose *m* glucose.

glycérine *f* glycerine.

gobelet *m* beaker, tumbler.

gober *vt* to swallow.

goéland *m* seagull, gull.

goinfre *m* pig, *adj* piggish.

golf *m* golf.

golfeur *m*, **-euse** *f* golfer.

gomme *f* gum; rubber, eraser.

gommer *vt* to rub out; to gum.

gond *m* hinge.

gondole *f* gondola.

gondoler *vi* to crinkle, warp, buckle; **se ~** *vr* to crinkle; to split one's sides laughing.

gonflable *adj* inflatable.

gonflement *m* inflation, swelling.

gonfler *vt* to pump up, inflate; **se ~** *vr* to swell; to be puffed up.

gong *m* gong; bell.

gorge *f* throat.

gorgée *f* mouthful.

gorille *m* gorilla.

gosier *m* throat, gullet.

gosse *mf* (*fam*) kid.

gothique *m*, *adj* Gothic.

goudron *m* tar.

goudronner *vt* to tar.

gouffre *m* gulf, chasm, abyss.

goulu *adj* greedy, gluttonous.

goulûment *adv* greedily, gluttonously.

goupille *f* pin.

gourd *adj* numb (with cold).

gourde *f* gourd; flask.

gourdin *m* club, cudgel.

gourmand *adj* greedy.

gourmandise *f* greed, greediness.

gourmet *m* gourmet.

gourmette *f* chain bracelet.

gousse *f* pod.

goût *m* taste; liking; style.

goûter *vt* to taste; to appreciate; * *vi* to have a snack; to taste good; * *m* snack.

goutte *f* drop; dram; gout.

gouttière *f* gutter; drainpipe.

gouvernail *m* rudder; helm.

gouvernement *m* government.

gouvernemental *adj* government, governmental.

gouverner *vt* to govern, rule; to control; to steer.

gouverneur *m* governor.

goyave *f* guava.

grâce *f* grace; favour; mercy; pardon; **~ à** thanks to.

gracier *vt* to pardon.

gracieusement *adv* gracefully; kindly.

gracieux *adj* gracious.

grade *m* rank; grade; degree.

gradé *m* officer; * *adj* promoted.

gradin *m* tier; step; terrace.

graduel *adj* gradual; progressive; ~**lement** *adv* gradually.

graduer *vt* to step up; to graduate.

graffiti *mpl* graffiti.

grain *m* grain, seed; bead.

graine *f* seed.

graissage *m* greasing, lubricating.

graisse *f* grease, fat.

graisser *vt* to grease, lubricate.

grammaire *f* grammar.

grammairien *m*, **-ienne** *f* grammarian.

grammatical *adj* grammatical; ~**ement** *adv* grammatically.

gramme *m* gramme.

grand *adj* big; tall; great; leading; **pas ~-chose** not a lot, not up to much; ~**ement** *adv* greatly; a great deal; nobly.

grandeur *f* size; greatness; magnitude.

grandiose *adj* imposing, grandiose.

grandir *vi* to grow bigger, increase; * *vt* to magnify; exaggerate.

grand-mère *f* grandmother.

grand-père *m* grandfather.

grand-parents *mpl* grandparents

granit(e) *m* granite.

granulé *m* granule; * *adj* granular.

granuleux *adj* granular; grainy.

graphique *m* graph; * *adj* graphic; ~**ment** *adv* graphically.

graphite *m* graphite.

grappe *f* cluster, bunch.

gras *adj*, *f* **grasse** fatty; fat; greasy; crude.

gratification *f* gratuity; bonus.

gratin *m* cheese dish, gratin.

gratis *adv* free, gratis.

gratitude *f* gratitude, gratefulness.

gratter *vt* to scratch, scrape.

gratuit *adj* free, gratuitous; disinterested; ~**ement** *adv* free; gratuitously.

grave *adj* grave, solemn; ~**ment** *adv* gravely, solemnly.

graver *vt* to engrave, imprint.

graveur *m* engraver, woodcutter.

gravier *m* stone, gravel.

gravir *vt* to climb.

gravitation *f* gravitation.

gravité *f* gravity.

gravure *f* engraving, carving.

gré *m*: liking, taste; **au ~ de** depending on, at the mercy of; **bon ~ mal ~** like it or not, willy-nilly; **savoir ~** to be grateful.

greffe *f* transplant, graft.

greffer *vt* to transplant, graft.

grégaire *adj* gregarious.

grêle *f* hail.

grêlon *m* hailstone.

grelotter *vi* to shiver.

grenade *f* pomegranate; grenade.

grenat *m* garnet.

grenier *m* attic, garret.

grenouille *f* frog.

grès *m* sandstone; stoneware.

grésiller *vi* to sizzle; splutter.

grève *f* strike; shore.

gribouillage *m* scrawl, scribble.

gribouiller *vi* to doodle; * *vt* to scribble, scrawl.

grièvement *adv* seriously.

griffe *f* claw.

griffer *vt* to scratch.

griffonner *vt* to scribble, jot down.

grignoter *vi* to nibble at, pick at; * *vt* to nibble at; to eat away.

gril *m* grill pan; rack.

grillade *f* grill.

grillage *m* toasting; grilling.

grille *f* railings; gate; grill.

grille-pain *m invar* toaster.

griller *vt* to toast, scorch; to put bars on; * *vi* to toast, grill.

grillon *m* cricket.

grimace *f* grimace

grimper *vi* to climb up.

grincement *m* grating, creaking.

grincer *vi* to grate, creak.

grincheux *adj* grumpy.

griotte *f* Morello cherry; marble.

grippe *f* flu, influenza.

grippé *adj* suffering from flu.

gris *adj* grey.

grisant *adj* exhilarating; intoxicating.

griser *vt* to intoxicate; **se ~** *vr* to get drunk.

grisonnant *adj* greying.

grive *f* thrush.

grog *m* grog.

grognement *m* grunt, grunting.

grogner *vi* to grumble, moan.

grognon *m* grumbler, moaner, *adj* grumpy, surly.

grommeler *vi* to mutter; to grumble; * *vt* to mutter.

grondement *m* rumbling, growling.

gronder *vt* to scold; * *vi* to rumble, growl.

gros *adj*, *f* **grosse** big; fat; thick; serious; heavy; coarse; **en ~** in bulk; * *m* bulk; wholesale; fat man.

groseille *f* currant.

grossesse *f* pregnancy.

grosseur *f* thickness; weight; fatness.

grossier *adj* coarse; unrefined; base.

grossièrement *adv* roughly; coarsely.

grossièreté *f* rudeness; coarseness.

grossir *vi* to get fatter; to swell, grow; * *vt* to magnify; to exaggerate.

grossiste *mf* wholesaler.

grotesque *adj* grotesque, ludicrous; **~ment** *adv* grotesquely.

grotte *f* cave; grotto.

grouiller *vi* to mill about; to swarm; **se ~** *vr* (*fam*) to get a move on.

groupe *m* group; party; cluster.

groupement *m* grouping; group.

grouper *vt* to group together; to bulk; **se ~** *vr* to gather.

grue *f* crane.

grumeau *m* lump.

gruyère *m* gruyère (cheese).

guenon *f* female monkey; hag.

guépard *m* cheetah.

guêpe *f* wasp.

guêpier *m* trap; wasp's nest.

guère *adv* hardly, scarcely.

guéri *adj* cured.

guéridon *m* pedestal table.

guérir *vi* to get better; to heal; * *vt* to cure, heal; **se ~** *vr* to get better; to recover from.

guérison *f* recovery; curing.

guérisseur *m*, **-euse** *f* healer.

guerre *f* war; warfare.

guerrier *m*, **-ière** *f* warrior.

guet *m* watch; **faire le ~** to be on the watch.

guetter *vt* to watch; to lie in wait for.

gueule *f* mouth; face; muzzle.

gueuler *vi* (*fam*) to bawl; bellow.

guichet *m* counter; ticket office, booking office.

guichetier *m*, **-ière** *f* counter clerk.

guidage *m* guides; guidance.

guide *m* guide.

guider *vt* to guide; **se ~** *vr* to be guided by.

guidon *m* handlebars.

guignol *m* puppet; puppet show.

guillemet *m* inverted comma; quotation mark.

guillotine *f* guillotine.

guimauve *f* marshmallow.

guindé *adj* stiff, uptight.

guirlande *f* garland.

guise *f* manner, way. **en ~ de** by way of; **à ta ~** as you please.

guitare *f* guitar.

guitariste *mf* guitarist.

guttural *adj* guttural

gymnase *m* gymnasium; secondary school.

gymnastique *f* gymnastic.

gynécologie *f* gynaecology.

gynécologue, gynécologiste *mf* gynaecologist.

gyrophare *m* revolving light.

H

habile *adj* skilful, skilled; clever;
~**ment** *adv* skilfully.
habileté *f* skill, skilfulness; clever
move.
habiliter *vt* to qualify; to authorize.
habillement *m* clothing, dress,
outfit.
habiller *vt* to dress, clothe; **s'~** *vr*
to get dressed.
habit *m* clothes; apparel; dress–
coat; outfit.
habitable *adj* inhabitable.
habitant *m*, **-e** *f* inhabitant; occupant; dweller.
habitat *m* habitat; housing con-
ditions.
habitation *f* dwelling; residence;
house.
habité *adj* manned.
habiter *vi* to live; * *vt* to live in;
occupy.
habitude *f* habit, custom, routine.
habituel *adj* usual, customary;
~**lement** *adv* usually, generally.
habituer *vt* to accustom; to teach;
s'~ *vr* to get used to.
hache *f* axe, hatchet.
hacher *vt* to chop, mince.
hachoir *m* chopper, cleaver.
hachure *f* hatching, hachure.
hagard *adj* wild; haggard; distraught.
haie *f* hedge.
haine *f* hatred.
haineux *adj* full of hatred; malevolent.
haïr *vt* to hate, detest.
hâle *m* tan, sunburn.
hâlé *adj* tanned, sunburnt.
haleine *f* breath, breathing.
haletant *adj* panting, gasping.
haleter *vi* to pant, gasp for
breath.
hall *m* hall, foyer.
halle *f* covered market; hall.
hallucination *f* hallucination.

halo *m* halo.
halte *f* stop, break; stopping place.
haltère *f* dumbbell.
hamac *m* hammock.
hameçon *m* fish-hook.
hamster *m* hamster.
hanche *f* hip; haunch.
hand-ball *m* handball.
handballeur *m*, **-euse** *f* handball
player.
handicap *m* handicap.
handicaper *vt* to handicap
hangar *m* shed, barn; hangar.
hanneton *m* maybug.
hanter *vt* to haunt.
happer *vt* to snap up, snatch.
harassant *adj* exhausting, wearing.
harcèlement *m* harassing; pes-
tering.
harceler *vt* to harass; to pester;
to plague.
hardi *adj* bold, daring; brazen;
~**ment** *adv* boldly, daringly; bra-
zenly.
hareng *m* herring.
hargne *f* spite.
hargneux *adj* aggressive, belligerent.
haricot *m* bean.
harmonica *m* harmonica.
harmonie *f* harmony; wind section.
harmonieusement *adv* harmo-
niously.
harmonieux *adj* harmonious;
well-matched.
harmoniser *vt* to harmonize; **s'~**
vr to be in harmony.
harnacher *m* to harness.
harnais *m* harness; equipment.
harpe *f* harp.
harpiste *mf* harpist.
harpon *m* harpoon.
hasard *m* chance; accident; hazard; risk.
hasardeux *adj* hazardous, risky.

hâte *f* haste; impatience.

hâter *vt* to hasten; to quicken; **se ~** *vr* to hurry.

hâtif *adj* precocious; early; hasty.

hâtivement *adv* hastily.

hausse *f* rise, increase.

hausser *vt* to raise; to heighten.

haut *adj* high, tall; upper; superior; **~ement** *adv* highly.

hautain *adj* haughty, lofty.

hautbois *m* oboe.

hauteur *f* height; elevation; haughtiness; bearing.

haut-parleur *m* loudspeaker.

hebdomadaire *adj*; * *m* weekly.

hébergement *m* accommodation; lodging.

héberger *vt* to accommodate, lodge.

hectare *m* hectare.

hectogramme *m* hectogram.

hectolitre *m* hectolitre.

hectomètre *m* hectometre.

hélice *f* propeller; helix.

hélicoptère *m* helicopter.

hélium *m* helium.

hématome *m* severe bruise, haematoma.

hémicycle *m* semicircle, hemicycle; amphitheatre.

hémiplégique *mf* person paralysed on one side, hemiplegic; * *adj* hemiplegic.

hémisphère *m* hemisphere.

hémoglobine *f* haemoglobin.

hémophile *adj* haemophiliac.

hémophilie *f* haemophilia.

hémorragie *f* bleeding, haemorrhage.

hémorroïde *f* haemorrhoid, pile.

henné *m* henna.

hépatique *adj* hepatic.

hépatite *f* hepatitis.

herbe *f* grass; **en ~** under grass.

herbivore *m* herbivore; *adj* herbivorous.

herboriste *mf* herbalist.

héréditaire *adj* hereditary.

hérédité *f* heredity; heritage; right of inheritance.

hérésie *f* heresy.

hérétique *adj* heretical.

hérissé *adj* bristling; spiked.

hérisser *vt* to bristle; to spike; * **se ~** *vr* to stand on end; to bristle.

hérisson *m* hedgehog.

héritage *m* inheritance; heritage, legacy.

hériter *vi* to inherit.

héritier *m* heir, **-ière** *f* heiress.

hermaphrodite *m* hermaphrodite; * *adj* hermaphrodite.

hermétique *adj* airtight, watertight, hermetic; **~ment** *adv* hermetically.

hermine *f* ermine.

hernie *f* hernia, rupture.

héroïne *f* heroine; heroin.

héroïque *adj* heroic; **~ment** *adv* heroically.

héroïsme *m* heroism.

héron *m* heron.

héros *m* hero.

herpès *m* herpes; cold sore.

hésitant *adj* hesitant.

hésitation *f* hesitation.

hésiter *vi* to hesitate.

hétéroclite *adj* heterogeneous; sundry; eccentric.

hétérogène *adj* heterogeneous.

hétérosexuel *adj* heterosexual.

hêtre *m* beech.

heure *f* hour; time of day; **de bonne ~** early; **tout à l'~** a short time ago, just now.

heureusement *adv* luckily; happily.

heureux *adv* lucky; happy.

heurter *vt* to strike, hit; to jostle.

hexagone *m* hexagon.

hibernation *f* hibernation.

hibou *m* owl.

hideux *adj* hideous.

hier *adv* yesterday.

hiérarchie *f* hierarchy.

hiérarchique *adj* hierarchical; **~ment** *adv* hierarchically

hilarant *adj* hilarious, side-splitting.

hilarité *f* hilarity, laughter.

hindouisme *m* Hinduism.

hippisme *m* riding, equestrianism.

hippocampe *m* sea horse.

hippodrome *m* racecourse.

hippopotame *m* hippopotamus.

hirondelle *f* swallow.

hirsute *adj* hirsute, hairy.

hisser *vt* to hoist, haul up.

histoire *f* history; story; business; **~ de dire** just to say.

historien *m*, **-ienne** *f* historian.

historique *adj* historic; historical; **~ment** *adv* historically.

hiver *m* winter.

hivernal *adj* winter; wintry.

H.L.M. (habitation à loyer modéré) *f/m* public sector housing.

hocher *vt* to nod; to shake one's head.

hochet *m* rattle; toy.

holocauste *m* holocaust.

homard *m* lobster.

homéopathe *mf* homeopath.

homéopathie *f* homeopathy.

homicide *m* homicide

hommage *m* homage, tribute; **rendre ~ à** to pay homage to.

homme *m* man.

homme-grenouille *m* frogman.

homogène *adj* homogeneous.

homogénéiser *vt* to homogenize.

homogénéité *f* homogeneity.

homologue *adj* homologous; equivalent.

homologuer *vt* to ratify; to approve.

homonyme *m* homonym; * *adj* homonymous.

homosexualité *f* homosexuality.

homosexuel *m*, **-elle** *f* homosexual.

honnête *adj* honest; decent; honourable; **~ment** *adv* honestly, decently.

honnêteté *f* honesty, decency.

honneur *m* honour; integrity; credit; **en l'~ de** in honour of.

honorable *adj* honourable; reputable; **~ment** *adv* honourably.

honoraire *adj* honorary.

honoraires *mpl* fees.

honorer *vt* to honour; to esteem; to do credit to; **s'~** *vr*: **s'~ de** to pride oneself on.

honte *f* shame, disgrace.

honteusement *adv* shamefully; disgracefully.

honteux *adj* shameful; disgraceful.

hôpital *m* hospital.

hoquet *m* hiccough.

horaire *m* timetable; * *adj* hourly.

horizon *m* horizon.

horizontal *adj* horizontal; **~ement** *adv* horizontally.

horloge *f* clock.

horloger *m*, **-ère** *f* watchmaker, clockmaker.

hormone *f* hormone.

horoscope *m* horoscope.

horreur *f* horror.

horrible *adj* horrible; dreadful; **~ment** *adv* horribly

horrifier *vt* to horrify.

hors *prép* outside; beyond; save; except; **~ série** incomparable, outstanding.

hors-bord *m invar* speedboat.

hors-d'oeuvre *m invar* hors' oeuvre, starter.

hors-jeu *m invar* offside.

hors-piste *m invar* off-piste.

hortensia *m* hydrangea.

horticulteur *m* horticulturist.

horticulture *f* horticulture.

hospice *m* home, asylum; hospice.

hospitalier *adj* hospital; hospitable.

hospitalisation *f* hospitalization.

hospitaliser *vt* to hospitalize.

hospitalité *f* hospitality.

hostie *f* host.

hostile *adj* hostile; **~ment** *adv* hostilely.

hostilité *f* hostility.

hôte *m*, **hôtesse** *f* host; landlord.

hôtel *m* hotel.

hôtelier *m*, **-ière** *f* hotelier; * *adj* hotel.

hôtellerie *f* inn; hotel business.

hotte *f* basket.

houblon *m* hop.

houille *f* coal.

houle *f* swell.

houleux *adj* stormy; turbulent.

houppe *f* tuft; tassel.

housse *f* cover, dust-sheet.

houx *m* holly.

hublot *m* porthole.

huer *vt* to boo.

huile *f* oil; petroleum.

huissier *m* bailiff; usher.

huit *adj*, *m* eight.

huitaine *f* eight or so.

huitième *adj* eighth; **-ment** *adv* eighthly; * *mf* eighth.

huître *f* oyster.

humain *adj* human; humane; **-ement** *adv* humanly; humanely; * *m* human.

humanisme *m* humanism.

humaniste *m* humanist; * *adj* humanist.

humanitaire *adj* humanitarian.

humanité *f* humanity.

humble *adj* humble; modest; **-ment** *adv* humbly.

humecter *vt* to dampen, moisten.

humeur *f* mood, humour; temper.

humide *adj* humid.

humidité *f* humidity.

humiliant *adj* humiliating.

humiliation *f* humiliation.

humilier *vt* to humiliate.

humilité *f* humility.

humoristique *adj* humorous.

humour *m* humour.

hurlement *m* roar, yell; howl.

hurler *vi*; * *vt* to roar, yell.

hutte *f* hut.

hybride *adj* ; * *m* hybrid.

hydratant *adj* moisturizing.

hydratation *f* hydration; moisturizing.

hydrater *vt* to hydrate; to moisturize.

hydraulique *adj* hydraulic.

hydravion *m* seaplane.

hydrocarbure *m* hydrocarbon.

hydrogène *m* hydrogen.

hydrolyse *f* hydrolysis.

hydrophile *adj* hydrophilic.

hydroxyde *m* hydroxide.

hyène *f* hyena.

hygiène *f* hygienics; hygiene.

hygiénique *adj* hygienic; **-ment** *adv* hygienically.

hymne *m* hymn.

hyperbole *f* hyperbole; hyperbola.

hypermarché *m* hypermarket.

hypermétrope *adj* long-sighted; * *mf* long-sighted person.

hypertension *f* hypertension.

hypertrophié *adj* hypertrophied.

hypnose *f* hypnosis.

hypnotique *adj* hypnotic.

hypnotiser *vt* to hypnotize.

hypocondriaque *mf* ; * *adj* hypochondriac.

hypocrisie *f* hypocrisy.

hypocrite *mf* hypocritical; * *adj* hypocrite; **-ment** *adv* hypocritically.

hypophyse *f* pituitary gland, hypophysis.

hypothalamus *m* hypothalamus.

hypothèque *f* mortgage.

hypothéquer *vt* to mortgage.

hypothèse *f* hypothesis; assumption.

hypothétique *adj* hypothetical; **-ment** *adv* hypothetically.

hystérie *f* hysteria.

hystérique *mf* hysterical; * *adj* hysteric.

I

ibis *m* ibis.
iceberg *m* iceberg.
idéal *adj;* * *m* ideal.
idéaliser *vt* to idealize.
idéaliste *mf* idealistic; * *adj* idealist.
idée *f* idea.
identifier *vt* to identify; **s'~** *vr* to identify with.
identique *adj* identical; **~ment** *adv* identically.
identité *f* identity; similarity.
idéologie *f* ideology.
idiot *m,* **-e** *f* idiot, fool; * *adj* idiotic, stupid; **~ement** *adv* idiotically.
idole *f* idol.
igloo, iglou *m* igloo.
ignoble *adj* ignoble, mean, base.
ignorance *f* ignorance.
ignorant *adj* ignorant; unacquainted; uninformed.
ignorer *vt* to be ignorant of; to be unaware of; to ignore.
iguane *m* iguana.
il *pron* he, it.
île *f* island, isle.
illégal *adj* illegal; unlawful; **~ement** *adv* illegally.
illégalité *f* illegality.
illégitime *adj* illegitimate; unwarranted.
illettré *adj* illiterate.
illicite *adj* illicit; **~ment** *adv* illicitly.
illimité *adj* unlimited; limitless.
illisible *adj* illegible, unreadable.
illogique *adj* illogical.
illumination *f* illumination, lighting.
illuminer *vt* to light up, illuminate; to enlighten.
illusion *f* illusion
illusoire *adj* illusory; illusive; **~ment** *adv* illusorily.
illustration *f* illustration.
illustre *adj* illustrious, renowned.

illustrer *vt* to illustrate.
îlot *m* islet; block (flats).
image *f* image, picture; reflection.
imagé *adj* colourful; full of imagery.
imaginaire *adj* imaginary.
imagination *f* imaginative.
imaginer *vt* to imagine; to suppose; to devise; **s'~** *vr* to imagine oneself; to think.
imbattable *adj* unbeatable.
imbécile *mf* idiot, imbecile; * *adj* stupid, idiotic.
imbiber *vt* to soak, moisten.
imbriquer *vt* to fit into; to overlap; **s'~** *vr* to be linked.
imbuvable *adj* undrinkable; unbearable.
imitation *f* imitation; mimicry; forgery.
imiter *vt* to imitate.
immaculé *adj* spotless, immaculate.
immangeable *adj* inedible.
immatriculation *f* registration.
immatriculer *vt* to register.
immédiat *adj* immediate; instant; **~ement** *adv* immediately, instantly.
immense *adj* immense, boundless.
immensément *adv* immensely; hugely.
immensité *f* immensity; immenseness.
immergé *adj* submerged.
immersion *f* immersion; submersion.
immeuble *m* building; block of flats; real estate.
immigrant *m,* **-e** *f* immigrant.
immigration *f* immigration.
immigré *m,* **-e** *f* immigrant.
imminent *adj* imminent, impending.
immobile *adj* motionless, still.
immobilier *adj* property; * *m* property business.

immobiliser *vt* to immobilize; to bring to a standstill; **s'~** *vr* to stop, stand still.

immobilité *f* stillness; immobility; permanence.

immonde *adj* squalid; base, vile.

immoral *adj* immoral.

immoralité *f* immorality.

immortaliser *vt* to immortalize.

immortel *adj* immortal.

immuable *adj* unchanging, immutable; **~ment** *adv* immutably.

immuniser *vt* to immunize.

immunité *f* immunity.

impact *m* impact.

impair *adj* odd, uneven.

impalpable *adj* impalpable.

impardonnable *adj* unforgivable, unpardonable.

imparfait *adj* imperfect; **~ement** *adv* imperfectly.

impartial *adj* impartial; **~ement** *adv* impartially.

impartialité *f* impartiality.

impasse *f* dead end, cul-de-sac; impasse.

impassible *adj* impassive.

impatiemment *adv* impatiently.

impatience *f* impatience.

impatient *adj* impatient.

impatienter *vt* to irritate, annoy; **s'~** *vr* to grow, get impatient.

impeccable *adj* perfect; faultless, impeccable; **~ment** *adv* perfectly, impeccably.

impénétrable *adj* impenetrable; inscrutable.

impensable *adj* unthinkable.

impératif *adj* imperative; mandatory; * *m* requirement; demand; constraint.

impératrice *f* empress.

imperceptible *adj* imperceptible; **~ment** *adv* imperceptibly.

imperfection *f* imperfection.

impérial *adj* imperial.

impérialisme *m* imperialism.

imperméable *adj* impermeable, waterproof; impervious to.

impersonnel *adj* impersonal.

impertinence *f* impertinence.

impertinent *adj* impertinent.

imperturbable *adj* unshakeable; imperturbable; **~ment** *adv* imperturbably.

impétueux *adj* impetuous.

impitoyable *adj* merciless, pitiless; **~ment** *adv* mercilessly, pitilessly.

implacable *adj* implacable; **~ment** *adv* implacably.

implantation *f* implantation; establishment; introduction.

implanter *vt* to introduce; to establish; to implant; **s'~** *vr* to be established; to become implanted.

implication *f* implication; involvement.

implicite *adj* implicit; **~ment** *adv* implicitly.

impliquer *vt* to imply; to necessitate; to implicate; **s'~** *vr* to get involved in one's work.

impoli *adj* impolite, rude.

impolitesse *f* impoliteness, rudeness.

impopulaire *adj* unpopular.

importance *f* importance, significance; size.

important *adj* important, significant; sizeable.

importateur *m*, **-trice** *f* importer; * *adj* importing.

importation *f* import, importation.

importer *vt* to import; * *vi* to matter; **que m'importe que** what does it matter to me that; **peu importe** whatever; **n'importe qui** anybody; **n'importe quoi** anything; **n'importe comment** anyhow; **n'importe quel** any.

importuner *vt* to importune, bother.

imposant *adj* imposing; stately.

imposer *vt* to impose, lay down; to fix (prices); **s'~** *vr* to be essential; to assert oneself.

impossibilité f impossibility.

impossible adj impossible.

imposteur m impostor.

impôt m tax, duty.

impotent adj disabled, crippled.

imprégner vt impregnate; to permeate; to imbue; **s'~** vr to become impregnated with; to become imbued with.

impresario m manager, impresario.

impression f feeling, impression.

impressionnant adj impressive; upsetting.

impressionner vt to impress; to upset.

impressionisme m impressionism.

impressioniste mf; * adj impressionist.

imprévisible adj unforeseeable; unpredictable.

imprévoyant adj improvident.

imprévu adj unforeseen, unexpected.

imprimante f printer.

imprimé adj printed; * m printed form; printed material.

imprimer vt to print.

imprimerie f printing works; printing house.

imprimeur m printer.

improbable adj improbable, unlikely.

improductif adj unproductive.

improvisation f improvisation.

improviser vt to improvise.

improviste(à l') adv unexpectedly.

imprudence f carelessness, imprudence.

imprudent adj careless, imprudent.

impudence f impudence; shamelessness.

impudique adj immodest, shameless.

impuissance f powerlessness, helplessness.

impuissant adj powerless, helpless.

impulsif adj impulsive.

impulsion f impulse; impetus.

impulsivement adv impulsively.

impunément adv with impunity.

impur adj impure; mixed.

impureté f impurity.

inacceptable adj unacceptable.

inaccessible adj inaccessible; obscure; incomprehensible.

inaccoutumé adj unusual.

inachevé adj unfinished, uncompleted.

inactif adj inactive, idle.

inaction f inactivity, idleness.

inactivité f inactivity.

inadapté adj unsuitable; maladjusted.

inadéquat adj inadequate.

inadmissible adj inadmissible.

inaltérable adj stable; unchanging, permanent.

inamovible adj irremovable; fixed.

inanimé adj inanimate; unconscious.

inaperçu adj: unnoticed **passer ~** to go unnoticed.

inappréciable adj invaluable, inestimable.

inapte adj incapable.

inattaquable adj unassailable; irrefutable.

inattendu adj unexpected, unforeseen.

inattention f inattention, lack of attention.

inauguration f inauguration, opening.

inaugurer vt to inaugurate, open.

inavouable adj shameful; undisclosable.

incapable adj incapable; incompetent.

incapacité f incompetence; disability; **être dans l'~ de** to be unable to do.

incarcérer vt to incarcerate.

incarnation f incarnation.

incarner *vt* to incarnate, embody.

incendiaire *adj* incendiary; inflammatory; * *mf* arsonist.

incendie *m* fire, blaze.

incendier *vt* to set alight; to kindle.

incertain *adj* uncertain, unsure.

incertitude *f* uncertainty; **être dans l'~** to feel uncertain.

incessant *adj* incessant, ceaseless.

inceste *m* incest.

incident *m* incident, point of law.

incinération *f* incineration; cremation.

inciser *vt* to incise; to lance.

incisive *f* incisive; piercing.

incitation *f* incitement; incentive.

inciter *vt* to incite, urge.

inclinaison *f* incline; gradient.

incliner *vt* to bend; to slope; to bow.

inclure *vt* to include; to insert.

inclus *adj* enclosed; included; **ci-~** herein enclosed.

incohérence *f* incoherence; inconsistency.

incohérent *adj* incoherent; inconsistent.

incolore *adj* colourless; clear.

incommode *adj* inconvenient; awkward.

incommoder *vt* to disturb, bother.

incomparable *adj* incomparable; **~ment** *adv* incomparably.

incompatibilité *f* incompatibility.

incompatible *adj* incompatible.

incompétence *f* incompetence.

incompétent *adj* incompetent; inexpert.

incomplet *adj* incomplete.

incompréhensible *adj* incomprehensible.

incompréhension *f* lack of understanding.

inconcevable *adj* inconceivable.

inconciliable *adj* irreconcilable.

inconditionnel *adj* unconditional; unreserved; unquestioning.

inconfortable *adj* uncomfortable; awkward; **~ment** *adv* uncomfortably.

incongru *adj* unseemly; incongruous.

inconnu *m*, **-e** *f* stranger, unknown person; * *m* unknown?; * *adj* unknown.

inconsciemment *adv* unconsciously; thoughtlessly.

inconscience *f* unconsciousness; thoughtlessness.

inconscient *adj* unconscious; thoughtless, reckless; * *m* subconscious, unconscious.

inconsidéré *adj* inconsiderate; thoughtless; **~ment** *adv* inconsiderately.

inconsistant *adj* flimsy; colourless; watery.

inconsolable *adj* disconsolate; inconsolable.

inconstant *adj* fickle; variable, inconstant.

incontestable *adj* incontestable, unquestionable; **~ment** *adv* incontestably, unquestionably.

inconvénient *m* drawback, inconvenience.

incorporation *f* incorporation; integration; blending.

incorporer *vt* to incorporate, integrate.

incorrect *adj* faulty, incorrect; **~ement** *adv* incorrectly.

incorrigible *adj* incorrigible.

incorruptible *adj* incorruptible.

incrédule *adj* incredulous; * *mf* unbeliever, non-believer.

incrédulité *f* incredulity, lack of belief.

incroyable *adj* incredible; unbelievable; **~ment** *adv* incredibly, unbelievably.

incruster *vt* to inlay; to superimpose; **s'~** *vr* to become imbedded in; to become rooted in.

inculpation *f* inculcation, instilling.

inculpé *m*, **-e** *f* accused; * *adj* accused.

incurable *adj* incurable.

indécent *adj* incurably, hopelessly.

indéchiffrable *adj* indecipherable; incomprehensible.

indécis *adj* indecisive; unsettled; undefined.

indéfini *adj* undefined; indefinite; **~ment** *adv* indefinitely.

indéfinissable *adj* indefinable.

indemne *adj* unharmed, unhurt.

indemniser *vt* to indemnify; to compensate.

indemnité *f* compensation; indemnity.

indéniable *adj* undeniable, indisputable; **~ment** *adv* undeniably.

indépendance *f* independence.

indépendant *adj* independent.

indestructible *adj* indestructible.

indéterminé *adj* undetermined; unspecified; undecided.

index *m* index; index finger.

indexer *vt* to index.

indicatif *m* signature tune; dialling code; * *adj* indicative.

indication *f* indication; piece of information; instruction.

indice *m* indication; clue; sign.

indifféremment *adv* indiscriminately, equally.

indifférence *f* indifference.

indifférent *adj* indifferent; immaterial.

indigène *mf* native; local; * *adj* indigenous, native.

indigeste *adj* indigestible.

indigestion *f* indigestion.

indigne *adj* unworthy; undeserving.

indigner *vt* to annoy, make indignant; **s'~** *vr* to be indignant.

indiquer *vt* to indicate, point out; to tell.

indirect *adj* indirect; circumstantial; collateral; **~ement** *adv* indirectly.

indiscipliné *adj* undisciplined.

indiscret *adj* indiscreet; inquisitive.

indiscrétion *f* indiscretion; inquisitiveness.

indiscutable *adj* indisputable; unquestionable; **~ment** *adv* indisputably.

indispensable *adj* indispensable; essential.

indisponible *adj* unavailable.

indistinct *adj* indistinct, vague; **~ement** *adv* indistinctly.

individu *m* individual.

individuel *adj* individual; **~lement** *adv* individually.

indolore *adj* painless.

indubitable *adj* indubitable; certain; **~ment** *adv* indubitably.

indulgence *f* indulgence; leniency.

indulgent *adj* indulgent; lenient.

industrialisation *f* industrialization.

industrie *f* industry; dexterity, ingenuity.

industriel *m*, **-elle** *f* industrialist, manufacturer; * *adj* industrial.

inébranlable *adj* steadfast, unwavering.

inédit *adj* unpublished; original.

inefficace *adj* ineffective; inefficient.

inefficacité *f* ineffectiveness; inefficiency.

inégal *adj* unequal; uneven; irregular; **~ement** *adv* unequally; unevenly.

inégalité *f* inequality; difference, disparity.

inéluctable *adj* ineluctable, unavoidable; **~ment** *adv* ineluctably.

inépuisable *adj* inexhaustible.

inerte *adj* inert; lifeless.

inertie *f* inertia, apathy.

inespéré *adj* unexpected.

inestimable *adj* inestimable, invaluable.

inévitable *adj* inevitable, unavoidable.

inexact *adj* inexact, inaccurate.

inexactitude *f* inaccuracy.

inexistant *adj* nonexistent.

inexorable *adj* inexorable; ~**ment** *adv* inexorably.

inexpérimenté *adj* inexperienced; inexpert.

inexplicable *adj* inexplicable; ~**ment** *adv* inexplicably.

inexprimable *adj* inexpressible.

infaillible *adj* infallible.

infâme *adj* infamous; base, vile.

infantile *adj* infantile, childish.

infatigable *adj* indefatigable, tireless; ~**ment** *adv* indefatigably.

infect *adj* vile; revolting; filthy.

infecter *vt* to infect; to contaminate; **s'~** *vr* to become infected.

infection *f* infection.

inférieur *adj* inferior; lower.

infériorité *f* inferiority.

infernal *adj* infernal, diabolical.

infester *vt* to infest;overrun.

infidèle *adj* unfaithful, disloyal.

infidélité *f* infidelity.

infiltration *f* infiltration.

infini *adj* infinite; interminable; ~**ment** *adv* infinitely.

infinitif *m* infinitive.

infirme *adj* feeble; crippled, disabled.

infirmerie *f* infirmary; sick bay.

infirmier *m*, **-ière** *f* nurse.

infirmité *f* disability; infirmity.

inflammation *f* inflammation.

inflation *f* inflation.

inflexible *adj* inflexible, rigid.

infliger *vt* to inflict; to impose.

influence *f* influence.

influencer *vt* to influence, sway.

informaticien *m*, **-ienne** *f* computer scientist.

information *f* piece of information; information; inquiry.

informatique *f* computing; data processing; * *adj* computer.

informer *vt* to inform, tell; **s'~** *vr* to find out, inquire.

infraction *f* infraction, infringement; offence.

infranchissable *adj* impassable; insuperable.

infrarouge *adj* infrared.

infrastructure *f* infrastructure; substructure.

infructueux *adj* fruitless, unsuccessful.

infusion *f* infusion, herb tea.

ingénieur *m* engineer.

ingénieux *adj* ingenious, clever.

ingénu *adj* ingenuous, naive.

ingrat *adj* ungrateful; unprofitable.

ingratitude *f* ingratitude.

ingrédient *m* ingredient; component.

inhabité *adj* uninhabited, unoccupied.

inhabituel *adj* unusual, unaccustomed.

inhumain *adj* inhuman.

inimaginable *adj* unimaginable.

inimitable *adj* inimitable.

ininterrompu *adj* uninterrupted; unbroken.

initial *adj* initial; ~**ement** *adv* initially.

initiation *f* initiation.

initiative *f* initiative; enterprise.

initier *vt* to initiate.

injecter *vt* to inject.

injection *f* injection.

injure *f* injury; insult.

injurier *vt* to abuse; insult.

injuste *adj* unjust, unfair; ~**ment** *adv* unjustly.

injustice *f* injustice.

injustifié *adj* unjustified.

inné *adj* innate, inborn.

innocence *f* innocence.

innocent *m*, **-e** *f* innocent person; simpleton; * *adj* innocent.

innocenter *vt* to clear, prove innocent.

innovation *f* innovation.

innover *vi* to innovate, make innovations.

inodore *adj* odourless, scentless.

inoffensif *adj* inoffensive, harmless.

inondation *f* inundation.

inonder *vt* to flood, inundate.

inopportun *adj* ill-timed, inopportune.

inoubliable *adj* unforgettable.

inouï *adj* unprecedented, unheard of.

inox *m* stainless steel.

inqualifiable *adj* unspeakable.

inquiet *adj* worried, anxious, uneasy.

inquiéter *vt* to worry, disturb **s'~** *vr* to get worried.

inquiétude *f* restlessness, uneasiness.

insaisissable *adj* elusive; imperceptible.

insalubre *adj* insalubrious; unhealthy.

insatiable *adj* insatiable; **~ment** *adv* insatiably.

insatisfaction *f* dissatisfaction.

inscription *f* inscription; registration; matriculation.

inscrire *vt* to inscribe; to enter; to set down; to register; **s'~** *vr* to join; to register, enrol.

insecte *m* insect.

insecticide *m* insecticide.

insémination *f* insemination.

insensé *adj* insane, demented.

insensible *adj* insensible, unfeeling, insensitive; imperceptible; **~ment** *adv* imperceptibly; insensibly.

inséparable *adj* inseparable.

insérer *vt* to insert.

insertion *f* insertion, inserting.

insidieux *adj* insidious

insignifiant *adj* insignificant, trifling.

insinuation *f* insinuation.

insinuer *vt* to insinuate, imply; **s'~** *vr* to insinuate oneself into; to creep into.

insipide *adj* insipid, tasteless.

insister *vi* to insist, be insistent; to stress.

insolence *f* insolence.

insolent *adj* insolent; brazen.

insolite *adj* unusual; strange.

insomnie *f* insomnia.

insouciance *f* unconcern; carelessness.

insouciant *adj* carefree; careless.

insoutenable *adj* unbearable; untenable.

inspecter *vt* to inspect, examine.

inspecteur *m*, **-trice** *f* inspector

inspection *f* inspection.

inspiration *f* inspiration; suggestion.

inspirer *vt* to inspire; to breathe in; **s'~** *vr*: **s'~ de** to be inspired by.

instable *adj* unstable; unsettled.

installation *f* installation; installing.

installer *vt* to install; to fit out; **s'~** *vr* to set oneself up as; to settle down.

instant *m* moment, instant.

instantané *adj* instant, instantaneous; **~ment** *adv* instantly.

instaurer *vt* to institute; to impose.

instinct *m* instinct.

instinctif *adj* instinctive.

instinctivement *adv* instinctively.

institut *m* institute; school.

instituteur *m*, **-trice** *f* teacher.

institution *f* institution; establishment.

instructif *adj* instructive.

instruction *f* instruction; education; inquiry.

instruire *vt* to instruct; to teach; to conduct an inquiry; **s'~** *vr* to educate oneself; to obtain information about.

instrument *m* instrument, implement.

insuffisance *f* insufficiency, inadequacy.

insuffisant *adj* insufficient, inadequate.

insuline *f* insulin.

insulte *f* insult.

insulter *vt* to insult, affront.

insupportable *adj* unbearable, intolerable; **~ment** *adv* unbearably, intolerably.

insurrection *f* insurrection, revolt.

intact *adj* intact.

intégral *adj* integral; uncut; complete; **~ement** *adv* integrally; in full.

intégralité *f* whole; entirety.

intégrer *vt* to integrate; **s'~** *vr* to become integrated; to fit in.

intégrité *f* integrity.

intellectuel *m*, **-uelle** *f* intellectual; * *adj* intellectual, mental.

intelligence *f* intelligence; understanding.

intelligent *adj* intelligent, shrewd, bright.

intelligible *adj* intelligible.

intempéries *fpl* bad weather.

intendant *m*, **-e** *f* bursar; steward, stewardess.

intense *adj* intense; severe.

intensément *adv* intensely.

intensif *adj* intensive.

intensifier *vt* to intensify; **s'~** *vr* to intensify.

intensité *f* intensity; severity.

intention *f* intention; purpose, intent.

interaction *f* interaction.

intercaler *vt* to intercalate; to interpolate.

intercepter *vt* to intercept.

interchangeable *adj* interchangeable.

interdiction *f* interdiction, prohibition, ban.

interdire *vt* to forbid, ban, prohibit.

interdit *adj* forbidden, prohibited; dumbfounded.

intéressant *adj* interesting; attractive, worthwhile.

intéresser *vt* to interest; to affect; **s'~** *vr*: **s'~ à** to be interested in, take an interest in.

intérêt *m* interest; significance, importance.

interférence *f* interference; conjunction.

intérieur *adj* interior, internal; inland; **à l'~** inside; within; **~ement** *adv* inwardly.

intérimaire *adj* acting; interim; temporary.

interligne *m* line space; interlining; lead.

interlocuteur *m*, **-trice** *f* interlocutor, speaker.

intermède *m* interlude.

intermédiaire *adj* intermediate; intermediary.

interminable *adj* interminable; endless; **~ment** *adv* interminably, endlessly.

intermittent *adj* intermittent, sporadic.

international *adj* international.

interne *adj* internal; * *mf* boarder; house doctor.

interpeller *vt* to call out to; to interpellate.

interphone *m* intercom, interphone.

interposer *vt* to interpose; **s'~** *vr* to intervene.

interprétation *f* interpretation, rendering.

interprète *mf* interpreter.

interpréter *vt* to interpret; to perform.

interrogation *f* interrogation, questioning; question.

interrogatoire *m* questioning; cross-examination.

interroger *vt* to question; to interrogate; **s'~** *vr* to wonder.

interrompre *vt* to interrupt, break; **s'~** *vr* to break off, interrupt oneself.

interrupteur *m* switch.

interruption *f* interruption, break.

intervalle *m* interval; space, distance.

intervenir *vi* to intervene; to take part in.

intervention *f* intervention; operation.

intestinal *adj* intestinal

intestin *m* intestine.

intime *adj* intimate; private; **~ment** *adv* intimately; * *mf* close friend.

intimider *vt* to intimidate.

intimité *f* intimacy; privacy.

intituler *vt* to call, entitle; **s'~** *vr* to be called; to call oneself.

intolérable *adj* intolerable.

intolérance *f* intolerance.

intolérant *adj* intolerant.

intonation *f* intonation.

intoxication *f* poisoning; indoctrination.

intransigeant *adj* intransigent, uncompromising.

intransitif *adj* intransitive.

intrépide *adj* intrepid, fearless; **~ment** *adv* intrepidly.

intrigant *adj* scheming.

introduction *f* introduction; launching; institution.

introduire *vt* to introduce, insert; to present; **s'~** *vr* to find one's way in; to be introduced.

introuvable *adj* undiscoverable; not to be found.

introverti *m*, **-e** *f* introvert; * *adj* introverted.

intrus *m*, **-e** *f* intruder; * *adj* intruding, intrusive.

intuitif *adj* intuitive.

intuition *f* intuition.

inutile *adj* useless; unavailing; pointless; **~ment** *adv* uselessly, needlessly.

inutilisable *adj* unusable.

invalide *adj* disabled; invalid.

invariable *adj* invariable; unvarying; **~ment** *adv* invariably.

invasion *f* invasion.

inventaire *m* inventory; stock list.

inventer *vt* to invent; to devise; to make up.

inventeur *m*, **-trice** *f* inventor.

invention *f* invention; inventiveness.

inverse *adj* opposite; * *m* opposite, reverse.

inverser *vt* to reverse, invert.

inversion *f* inversion; reversal.

investir *vt* to invest; to surround.

investissement *m* investment; investing.

invincible *adj* invincible, indomitable.

invisible *adj* invisible; unseen.

invitation *f* invitation.

invité *m*, **-e** *f* guest.

inviter *vt* to invite, ask.

involontaire *adj* involuntary; unintentional; **~ment** *adv* involuntarily.

invoquer *vt* to invoke; to call up; to plead.

invraisemblable *adj* unlikely, improbable; **~ment** *adv* improbably.

invulnérable *adj* invulnerable.

iode *m* iodine.

ion *m* ion.

iris *m* iris.

Irlandais *m* Irishman, **-e** *f* Irishwoman

irlandais *adj* Irish.

Irlande *f* Ireland.

ironie *f* irony.

ironique *adj* ironic; **~ment** *adv* ironically.

irradiation *f* irradiation; radiation.

irrationnel *adj* irrational.

irrécupérable *adj* irretrievable.

irréel *adj* unreal.

irréfléchi *adj* unconsidered; hasty.

irrégularité *f* irregularity; variation; unevenness.

irrégulier *adj* irregular; varying; uneven.

irrégulièrement *adv* irregularly; unevenly.

irrémédiable *adj* irreparable; incurable; **~ment** *adv* irreparably.

irremplaçable *adj* irreplaceable.

irréparable *adj* irreparable; irretrievable; **~ment** *adv* irreparably.

irrésistible *adj* irresistible; **~ment** *adv* irresistibly.

irresponsable *adj* irresponsible

irréversible *adj* irreversible; **~ment** *adv* irreversibly.

irrigation *f* irrigation.

irriguer *vt* to irrigate.

irriter *vt* to irritate; to provoke.

irruption *f* irruption.

Islam *m* Islam

isolement *m* loneliness; isolation; insulation.

isoler *vt* to isolate; to insulate; **s'~** *vr* to cut oneself off.

issu *adj* descended from; stemming from.

issue *f* outlet; solution; outcome.

ivoire *m* ivory.

ivre *adj* drunk, inebriated.

ivresse *f* drunkenness.

ivrogne *mf* drunkard.

J

jachère *f* fallow; leaving land fallow.

jade *m* jade.

jadis *adv* formerly, long ago.

jaguar *m* jaguar.

jaillir *vi* to spout, gush; to spring.

jalon *m* staff; landmark, milestone.

jalonner *vt* to mark out.

jalousie *f* jealousy, envy.

jaloux *m*, **-ouse** *f* jealous person; * *adj* jealous, envious.

jamais *adv* never, not ever; **à ~** for ever.

jambe *f* leg.

jambon *m* ham.

janvier *m* January.

jardin *m* garden.

jardinage *m* gardening.

jardiner *vi* to garden.

jardinier *m*, **-ière** *f* gardener.

jargon *m* jargon, slang; gibberish.

jarret *m* hock; shin.

jaser *vi* to chatter; to twitter; to babble.

jasmin *m* jasmine.

jauge *f* gauge; capacity; tonnage.

jauger *vt* to gauge the capacity of; to size up.

jaunâtre *adj* yellowish.

jaune *adj* yellow; * *m* yellow.

jaunir *vi* to yellow, turn yellow; * *vt* to make yellow.

jaunisse *f* jaundice.

jazz *m* jazz.

je, j' *pron* I.

jésuite *m* Jesuit.

jet *m* jet, spurt; throwing.

jetable *adj* disposable.

jetée *f* pier.

jeter *vt* to throw; to discard; to give out; **se ~** *vr* to throw oneself; to rush at.

jeton *m* token; counter.

jeu *m* play; game; gambling; **~ de jambes** footwork; **~ de mots** pun, play on words; **cacher son ~** to conceal one's intentions.

jeudi *m* Thursday.

jeun(à) *adv* on an empty stomach.

jeune *adj* young; junior; new; youthful; * *m* youth, young man; *f* young girl.

jeûne *m* fast.

jeûner *vi* to fast.

jeunesse *f* youth, youthfulness.

joaillerie *f* jewelling; jewellery.

joaillier *m*, **-ière** *f* jeweller.

joie *f* joy, happiness; pleasure.

joindre *vt* to join, link; to attach;

se ~ *vr* to join, join in.
joint *m* joint; join.
jointure *f* joint *(anat)*.
joli *adj* pretty; good, handsome;
~ment *adv* nicely, attractively.
jonc *m* rush; cane.
joncher *vt* to strew with.
jonction *f* junction.
jongler *vi* to juggle.
jongleur *m*, **-euse** *f* juggler.
jonquille *f* daffodil, jonquil.
joue *f* cheek
jouer *vi* to play; to gamble; to act.
jouet *m* toy.
joueur *m*, **-euse** *f* player; gambler.
jouffflu *adj* chubby; round-faced.
joug *m* yoke.
jouir *vi* to enjoy; to delight in.
jouissance *f* enjoyment; use.
jour *m* day; daylight; **tous les
~s** every day; **à ~** up to date;
vivre au ~ le ~ to live from day
to day; **~ férié** public holiday;
mise à ~ updating; update; **du
~ au lendemain** overnight.
journal *m* newspaper; bulletin,
journal; **~ de bord** logbook; **~
télévisé** television news.
journalisme *m* journalism.
journaliste *mf* journalist.
journée *f* day; day's work.
jovial *adj* jovial, jolly.
jovialité *f* joviality.
joyau *m* jewel, gem.
joyeusement *adv* joyfully, cheerfully.
joyeux *adj* joyful, cheerful.
jubiler *vi* to be jubilant, exult.
judaïsme *m* Judaism.
judiciaire *adj* judicial, legal.
judicieusement *adv* judicious-
ly.
judicieux *adj* judicious.
judo *m* judo
judoka *mf* judoka.
juge *m* judge.

jugement *m* judgment; sentence;
opinion.
juger *vt* to judge; to decide; to consider.
juif *m* Jew; Jewish; **juive** *f* Jewess; Jewish.
juillet *m* July.
juin *m* June.
jumeau *m*, **-elle** *f* twin; * *adj*
twin; double.
jumelage *m* twinning.
jumelé *adj* twinned, twin.
jumelle(s) *f(pl)* binoculars.
jument *f* mare.
jungle *f* jungle.
jupe *f* skirt.
jurer *vt* to swear, pledge.
juridiction *f* jurisdiction; court of
law.
juridique *adj* legal, juridical;
~ment *adv* juridically, legally.
jurisprudence *f* case law, jurisprudence.
juriste *m* lawyer; jurist.
juron *m* oath, curse.
jury *m* jury; board of examiners.
jus *m* juice.
jusque, jusqu' *prép* to, as far as;
until.
justaucorps *m* jerkin; leotard.
juste *adj* just, fair; exact; sound;
~ment *adv* exactly, precisely
justesse *f* accuracy; aptness;
soundness.
justice *f* justice, fairness.
justicier *m*, **-ière** *f* justiciary; dispenser of justice.
justificatif *adj* supporting, justi-
ficatory.
justification *f* justification; proof.
justifier *vt* to justify, prove; **se ~**
vr to justify oneself.
jute *m* jute.
juteux *adj* juicy; lucrative.
juvénile *adj* young, youthful.
juxtaposer *vt* to juxtapose.
juxtaposition *f* juxtaposition.

K

kaki *adj* khaki.
kaléidoscope *m* kaleidoscope.
kangourou *m* kangaroo.
karaté *m* karate.
kayac, kayak *m* kayak.
képi *m* kepi.
kermesse *f* fair; bazaar.
kérosène *m* kerosene, aviation fuel.
kidnapper *vt* to kidnap, abduct.
kidnappeur *m*, **-euse** *f* kidnapper.
kilogramme *m* kilogramme.
kilohertz *m* kilohertz.

kilométrage *m* total kilometres travelled (mileage).
kilomètre *m* kilometre.
kimono *m* kimono.
kinésithérapeute *mf* physiotherapist.
kiosque *m* kiosk, stall.
kiwi *m* kiwi, Chinese gooseberry.
klaxon *m* horn.
klaxonner *vi* to sound one's horn.
kleptomane *mf* kleptomaniac.
kleptomanie *f* kleptomania.
koala *m* koala.
kyste *m* cyst.

L

la *art, pron: see* **le**.
là *adv* there; over there; then; **par ~** that way; **~-dedans** inside, in there; **~-dessous** underneath, under there; **~-dessus** on that; thereupon; **~-haut** up there, up on top; **celui-~** that one.
label *m* label; seal.
labeur *m* labour, toil.
laboratoire *m* laboratory.
laborieux *adj* laborious, toilsome.
labourer *vt* to plough; to dig over; to rip open.
labyrinthe *m* labyrinth.
lac *m* lake.
lacer *vt* to lace up; to tie up.
lacérer *vt* to lacerate; to tear.
lacet *m* lace.
lâche *adj* slack; loose; lax; cowardly; **~ment** *adv* loosely; in a cowardly manner.
lâcher *vt* to loosen; to release.
lâcheté *f* cowardice; meanness.
laconique *adj* laconic; **~ment** *adv* laconically.
lacté *adj* milky, lacteal.

lactique *adj* lactic.
lacune *f* lacuna; gap.
lagon *m* lagoon.
lagune *f* lagoon.
laïc *m* layman, **laïque** *f* laywoman; * **laïque** *adj* lay, civil.
laid *adj* ugly, unsightly.
laideur *f* ugliness, unsightliness.
lainage *m* woollen article.
laine *f* wool.
laisse *f* leash, string, lead.
laisser *vt* to leave; to let; **~ tomber** to drop; **se ~ aller** to let oneself go.
laisser-passer *m invar* pass, permit.
lait *m* milk.
laitage *m* milk; milk products.
laiton *m* brass.
laitue *f* lettuce.
lama *m* llama; lama.
lambeau *m* shred; tatter.
lambris *m* plastering; panelling.
lame *f* blade; strip; metal plate.
lamelle *f* slide, lamella.
lamentable *adj* lamentable, dis-

tressing; **~ment** *adv* lamentably.

lamentation *f* lamentation; wailing.

lamenter(se) *vr* to lament, bewail.

laminer *vt* to laminate.

lampadaire *m* standard-lamp; street lamp.

lampe *f* lamp, light; bulb.

lance *f* lance, spear.

lance-flammes *m* *invar* flamethrower.

lancement *m* launching; starting up; throwing.

lance-pierres *m* *invar* catapult.

lancer *vt* to throw; to launch; **se ~** *vr* to leap, jump; to embark on.

lancinant *adj* piercing; haunting.

lande *f* moor.

langage *m* language, speech.

langoureux *adj* languid, languorous.

langouste *f* spiny lobster.

langoustine *f* Dublin bay prawn.

langue *f* tongue; language.

languette *f* tongue; tongue-like strip.

langueur *f* languor.

languir *vi* to languish; to linger.

lanière *f* thong; lash.

lanoline *f* lanolin.

lanterne *f* lantern; lamp.

lapin *m*, **-e** *f* rabbit.

lapsus *m* slip, mistake.

laque *f* shellac, lacquer; * *m* lacquer article.

lard *m* fat; bacon.

lardon *m* lardon.

large *adj* wide; generous; lax; great; **~ment** *adv* widely; greatly.

largeur *f* width, breadth.

larguer *vt* to loose, release; cast off.

larme *f* tear.

larmoyant *adj* tearful, weeping.

larve *f* larva, grub.

laryngite *f* laryngitis.

larynx *m* larynx.

las *adj*, *f* **lasse** weary, tired.

lasagne *f* lasagne.

laser *m* laser.

lasser *vt* to tire; **se ~** *vr* to grow tired of.

lassitude *f* tiredness, weariness.

latent *adj* latent.

latéral *adj* lateral, side; **~ement** *adv* laterally.

latex *m* latex.

latin *adj* Latin; * *m* Latin.

latitude *f* latitude; margin.

latte *f* lath.

lauréat *m*, **-e** *f* prize winner.

laurier *m* bay-tree, laurel.

lavabo *m* washbasin.

lavage *m* washing; bathing.

lavande *f* lavender.

lave *f* lava.

lavement *m* enema.

laver *vt* to wash; to cleanse; **se ~** *vr* to wash oneself.

laverie *f* laundry.

lave-vaisselle *m* *invar* dishwasher.

laxatif *adj* laxative; * *m* laxative.

laxisme *m* laxness.

layette *f* baby clothes.

le *art*, *f* **la**, *devant voyelle* **l'**, *pl* **les** the; * *pron* him, her, them.

lécher *vt* to lick.

leçon *f* lesson; reading; class.

lecteur *m*, **-trice** *f* reader.

lecture *f* reading; perusal.

légal *adj* legal, lawful; **~ement** *adv* legally.

légaliser *vt* to legalize.

légalité *f* legality, lawfulness.

légendaire *adj* legendary.

légende *f* legend; inscription.

léger *adj* light; slight; faint; inconsiderate.

légèrement *adv* lightly; thoughtlessly

légèreté *f* lightness; nimbleness; thoughtlessness.

légion *f* legion

législatif *adj* legislative; * *m* legislature.

législation *f* legislation, laws.

légitime *adj* legitimate, lawful; **~ment** *adv* legitimately.

légitimité *f* legitimacy.

legs *m* legacy, bequest.

léguer *vt* to bequeath; to devise.

légume *m* vegetable.

lendemain *m* next day, day after.

lent *adj* slow; tardy; sluggish; **~ement** *adv* slowly.

lente *f* nit.

lenteur *f* slowness.

lentille *f* lentil; lens.

léopard *m* leopard.

lèpre *f* leprosy.

lépreux *m*, **-euse** *f* leper; * *adj* leprous.

lequel *pron*, *f* **laquelle**, *pl* **lesquels, lesquelles** who, whom, which.

lesbienne *f* lesbian.

léser *vt* to wrong; to damage.

lésion *f* wrong; lesion, wound.

lessive *f* washing powder.

leste *adj* nimble, agile; **~ment** *adv* nimbly.

lester *vt* to fill; to ballast.

léthargie *f* lethargy.

léthargique *adj* lethargic.

lettre *f* letter, note; literature; **en toutes ~s** in black and white; **suivre à la ~** to carry out to the letter; **avant la ~** in advance, premature.

leucémie *f* leukaemia.

leucocyte *m* leucocyte.

leur *pron* them; **le ~, la ~, les ~s** theirs.

leurrer *vt* to deceive; to lure; **se ~** *vr* to delude oneself.

levain *m* leaven.

lever *vt* to lift, raise; to levy; **se ~** *vr* to get up; * *m* rising; getting up.

levier *m* lever.

lèvre *f* lip.

lévrier *m* greyhound.

levure *f* yeast.

lexique *m* vocabulary, lexis.

lézard *m* lizard.

lézarde *f* crack.

liaison *f* affair; connection; liaison, link.

liasse *f* bundle.

libellule *f* dragonfly.

libéral *adj* liberal; **~ement** *adv* liberally; * *m* liberal.

libéraliser *vt* to liberalize.

libéralisme *m* liberalism.

libéralité *f* liberality, generosity.

libération *f* release, liberation.

libérer *vt* to release; to liberate; **se ~** *vr* to free oneself.

liberté *f* liberty, freedom.

libido *f* libido.

libraire *mf* bookseller.

librairie *f* bookshop; bookselling.

libre *adj* free; independent; **~ment** *adv* freely.

licence *f* degree; permit; licentiousness.

licenciement *m* redundancy; dismissal.

licencier *vt* to make redundant; to dismiss.

lichen *m* lichen.

licorne *f* unicorn.

lie *f* dregs, sediment.

liège *m* cork.

lien *m* bond; link, connection; tie.

lier *vt* to bind; to link; **se ~** *vr*: **se ~ avec** to make friends.

lierre *m* ivy.

lieu *m* place, position; cause; occasion; **avoir ~** to take place; **en premier ~** in the first place; **au ~ de** instead of.

lieutenant *m* (*mil*) lieutenant.

lièvre *m* hare.

ligament *m* ligament

ligature *f* ligature; tying up.

ligne *f* line; row; range.

lignée *f* lineage; offspring.

lignite *m* lignite.

ligoter *vt* to bind hand and foot.

ligue *f* league.

lilas *m* lilac; * *adj* lilac.

limace *f* slug.

limande *f* sole.

lime *f* file.

limer *vt* to file down.

limitation *f* limitation, restriction.

limite *f* boundary, limit; **à la ~** ultimately.

limiter *vt* to limit, restrict; **se ~** *vr* to limit oneself to.

limitrophe *adj* border.

limon *m* silt, mud.

limonade *f* lemonade.

limpide *adj* limpid, clear.

limpidité *f* limpidity, clearness.

lin *m* flax; linen.

linceul *m* shroud.

linéaire *adj* linear.

linge *m* linen; washing.

lingerie *f* linen room; underwear, lingerie.

lingot *m* ingot.

linguiste *mf* linguist.

linguistique *f* linguistics; * *adj* linguistic.

lion *m* lion, **lionne** *f* lioness

lionceau *m* lion cub.

lipide *m* lipid.

liquéfier *vt* to liquefy; **se ~** *vr* to liquefy.

liqueur *f* liqueur; liquid.

liquidation *f* liquidation; winding up; elimination.

liquide *m* liquid.

liquider *vt* to settle; to wind up; to eliminate

lire *vt* to read.

lis *m* lily.

lisible *adj* legible; readable; **~ment** *adv* legibly.

lisière *f* edge; border; selvage; outskirts.

lisse *adj* smooth, glossy.

lisser *vt* to smooth, gloss.

liste *f* list; schedule.

lit *m* bed; layer.

litanie *f* litany.

literie *f* bedding.

lithographie *f* lithography.

litière *f* litter.

litige *m* lawsuit; dispute.

litigieux *adj* litigious.

litre *m* litre.

littéraire *adj* literary.

littéral *adj* literal; **~ement** *adv* literally.

littérature *f* literature; writing.

littoral *m* coast; * *adj* coastal, littoral.

liturgie *f* liturgy.

livide *adj* livid, pale.

livraison *f* delivery; number, issue.

livre *m* book; * *f* pound (weight, currency).

livrer *vt* to deliver, hand over; to give away; **se ~** *vr* to abandon oneself; to practise.

livret *m* libretto; booklet.

livreur *m* delivery man, **-euse** *f* delivery woman.

lobe *m* lobe.

lobotomie *f* lobotomy.

local *adj* local; **~ement** *adv* locally.

localisation *f* localization.

localiser *vt* to localize.

localité *f* locality; town.

locataire *mf* tenant; lodger.

location *f* renting; lease, leasing.

locomotion *f* locomotion.

locomotive *f* locomotive, engine; dynamo.

locution *f* locution, idiom.

logarithme *m* logarithm.

loge *f* lodge; dressing room; box.

logement *m* housing; accommodation.

loger *vt* to accommodate; to billet; * *vi* to live in.

logiciel *m* software.

logique *f* logic; * *adj* logical; **~ment** *adv* logically.

logistique *f* logistics.

logo *m* logo.

loi *f* law; act, statute; rule.

loin *adv* far, a long way; * *m* distance; background; **au ~** in the distance; **de ~** from a distance; **moins ~** not so far; **plus ~** further, farther.

lointain *adj* distant, remote; * *m* distance; background

loir *m* dormouse.

loisir *m* leisure, spare time.

lombaire *adj* lumbar; * *f* lumbar vertebra.

lombric *m* earthworm.

long *adj*, *f* **longue** long, lengthy; **~uement** *adv* at length.

longer *vt* to border; to walk along.

longévité *f* longevity.

longitude *f* longitude.

longtemps *adv* for a long time.

longueur *f* length.

longue-vue *f* telescope.

loquace *adj* loquacious, talkative.

loque *f* rag.

loquet *m* latch; clasp.

lorgner *vt* to leer, ogle.

lors *adv*: then **~ de** at the time of; **dès ~** from that time.

lorsque *conj* when.

losange *m* lozenge, diamond.

lot *m* prize; lot; portion.

loterie *f* lottery; raffle.

lotion *f* lotion.

lotissement *m* allotment; site, housing development.

lotus *m* lotus.

louange *f* praise, commendation.

louche *adj* dubious; suspicious, shady.

loucher *vi* to squint; to ogle.

louer *vt* to rent, lease; to book.

loup *m* wolf.

loupe *f* magnifying glass.

louper *vt* (*fam*) to botch, bungle; to flunk.

lourd *adj* heavy; sultry; unwieldy; **~ement** *adv* heavily.

lourdeur *f* heaviness.

loutre *f* otter.

louve *f* she-wolf; sling.

louveteau *m* wolf-cub.

loyal *adj* loyal, faithful; **~ement** *adv* loyally.

loyauté *f* loyalty

loyer *m* rent.

lubrifiant *m* lubricant; * *adj* lubricating.

lubrifier *vt* to lubricate.

lubrique *adj* lustful, lecherous; **~ment** *adv* lustfully.

lucarne *f* skylight

lucide *adj* lucid, clear; **~ment** *adv* lucidly.

lucidité *f* lucidity, clearness.

lucratif *adj* lucrative.

ludique *adj* play.

lueur *f* glimmer, gleam; glimpse.

luge *f* sledge, toboggan.

lugubre *adj* lugubrious, gloomy; **~ment** *adv* lugubriously.

lui *pron* him, her, it; **c'est à ~** it is his; **~-même** himself, herself, itself.

luire *vt* to shine, gleam.

luisant *adj* gleaming, shining.

lumbago *m* lumbago.

lumière *f* light; daylight; lamp; insight.

lumineux *adj* luminous; illuminated.

lunaire *adj* lunar, moon.

lunatique *adj* fantastical, whimsical, quirky.

lundi *m* Monday.

lune *f* moon.

lunette *f* telescope; sight; **~s** glasses.

lustré *adj* glossy; shiny.

luth *m* lute.

luthérien *adj* Lutheran.

luthiste *mf* lutanist.

lutin *m* mischievous, impish.

lutte *f* struggle; contest; strife.

lutter *vi* to struggle, fight.

lutteur *m*, **-euse** *f* wrestler, fighter.

luxation *f* dislocation, luxation.

luxe *m* luxury, excess.

luxueusement *adv* luxuriously.

luxueux *adj* luxurious.

luxure *f* lust.

luxuriance *f* luxuriance.

luxuriant *adj* luxuriant.

luzerne *f* lucerne.

lycée *m* secondary school.

lycéen *m* secondary schoolboy, **-éenne** *f* secondary schoolgirl

lymphatique *adj* lymphatic.

lymphe *f* lymph.

lymphocyte *m* lymphocyte.

lyncher *vt* to lynch.
lynx *m* lynx.
lyre *f* lyre.

lyrique *adj* lyric; **~ment** *adv* lyrically.
lyrisme *m* lyricism.

M

---

macabre *adj* macabre, deathly.
macadam *m* tarmac.
macaque *m* macaque.
macédoine *f* medley, hotchpotch; macedoine.
macérer *vt* to macerate; to mortify oneself; * *vi* to macerate, steep.
mâche *f* corn-salad.
mâcher *vt* to chew.
machiavélique *adj* Machiavellian.
machin *m* (*fam*) gadget; thingamajig.
machinal *adj* mechanical, automatic; **~ement** *adv* mechanically.
machination *f* machination, plot.
machine *f* machine; engine; apparatus.
machinerie *f* machinery, plant.
machiniste *m* machinist; driver; stagehand.
mâchoire *f* jaw.
maçon *m* builder, mason.
maçonnerie *f* masonry; building.
macrobiotique *adj* macrobiotic; * *f* macrobiotics
madame *f* Madam; Mrs; lady.
madeleine *f* madeleine.
mademoiselle *f* Miss; young lady.
magasin *m* shop, store; warehouse.
magazine *m* magazine.
mage *m* magus; seer.
magicien *m*, **-ienne** *f* magician.
magie *f* magic
magique *adj* magic; magical; **~ment** *adv* magically.
magistral *adj* masterly; authoritativ•; **~ement** *adv* in a masterly fashion.

magistrat *m* magistrate.
magistrature *f* magistracy; magistrature.
magnanime *adj* magnanimous; **~ment** *adv* magnanimously.
magnanimité *f* magnanimity.
magnat *m* magnate.
magnésium *m* magnesium.
magnétique *adj* magnetic.
magnétiser *vt* to magnetize; to hypnotize.
magnétisme *m* magnetism; hypnotism.
magnétophone *m* tape recorder.
magnétoscope *m* video recorder; videotape.
magnifique *adj* magnificent; sumptuous; **~ment** *adv* magnificently.
magnolia *m* magnolia.
magot *m* (*fam*) savings, hoard, nest egg.
magouille *f* (*fam*) fiddle, scam; scheming.
mai *m* May.
maigre *adj* thin; meagre, scarce; **~ment** *adv* meagrely.
maigreur *f* thinness; meagreness; sparseness.
maigrir *vi* to get thinner; to waste away.
maille *f* stitch; mesh; link.
maillet *m* mallet.
maillon *m* link; shackle.
maillot *m* jersey; leotard.
main *f* hand; **avoir la ~** to have the lead; **passer la ~** to make way for so.
main-d'œuvre *f* workforce.
maintenance *f* maintenance, servicing.
maintenant *adv* now; **à partir**

de ~ from now on.

maintenir *vt* to keep, maintain; preserve; **se ~** *vr* to persist; to hold one's own.

maintien *m* maintenance; preservation; keeping up.

maire *m* mayor, **-esse** *f* mayoress.

mairie *f* mayoralty; town hall.

mais *conj* but.

maïs *m* maize.

maison *f* house; home; building; premises.

maître *m* **-esse** *f* master; ruler; lord; proprietor.

maîtresse *f* mistress; teacher

maîtrise *f* mastery; control; expertise.

maîtriser *vt* to control; to master; **se ~** *vr* to control oneself.

majesté *f* majesty, grandeur.

majestueusement *adv* majestically.

majestueux *adj* majestic.

majeur *adj* major; main; chief; superior; * *m* major *mf* adult.

majoration *f* increased charge; overestimation.

majordome *m* major-domo.

majorer *vt* to increase, raise.

majorette *f* majorette.

majoritaire *adj* majority.

majorité *f* majority.

majuscule *f* capital letter.

mal *adv* wrong, badly; * *m* evil, wrong; harm; pain.

malachite *f* malachite.

malade *adj* sick, ill; diseased; * *mf* invalid, sick person.

maladie *f* illness; malady, complaint; disorder.

maladresse *f* clumsiness; awkwardness.

maladroit *adj* clumsy, awkward; **~ement** *adv* clumsily.

malaise *m* uneasiness, discomfort; indisposition.

malchance *f* ill luck; misfortune; mishap.

malchanceux *adj* unlucky, unfortunate.

mâle *m* male; * *adj* male; manly, virile.

malédiction *f* malediction, curse.

maléfique *adj* hurtful; malignant; baleful.

malencontreux *adj* unfortunate, untoward.

malentendu *m* misunderstanding.

malfaisant *adj* malevolent; harmful; wicked.

malfaiteur *m* criminal; malefactor.

malgré *prép* in spite of; despite.

malheur *m* misfortune; calamity.

malheureusement *adv* unfortunately.

malheureux *adj* unfortunate; unlucky; unhappy.

malhonnête *adj* dishonest, crooked; uncivil; **~ment** *adv* dishonestly.

malhonnêteté *f* dishonesty; incivility.

malice *f* malice, spite; mischievousness.

malicieux *adj* malicious, spiteful; mischievous.

malin *adj* shrewd, cunning, crafty; malignant.

malintentionné *adj* ill-disposed, spiteful.

malle *f* trunk.

malléable *adj* malleable.

malmener *vt* to ill-treat, maltreat.

malnutrition *f* malnutrition.

malsain *adj* unhealthy, unwholesome; immoral.

malt *m* malt.

maltraiter *vt* to abuse; to handle roughly.

malveillance *f* malevolence, spite.

malveillant *adj* malevolent, spiteful.

maman *f* mother, mummy, mum.

mamelle *f* breast; udder.

mamelon *m* nipple, teat.

mammifère *m* mammal.

manche *f* sleeve; game, round; * *m* handle, shaft.

manchot *m*, **-e** *f* one-armed person; * *adj* one-armed; * *m* penguin.

mandarin *m* mandarin, Mandarin.

mandarine *f* tangerine.

mandat *m* mandate; money order; proxy.

mandataire *mf* proxy; representative.

mandibule *f* mandible, jaw.

mandoline *f* mandolin.

manège *m* roundabout, merry-go-round.

manette *f* lever, tap.

manganèse *m* manganese.

mangeable *adj* edible.

manger *vt* to eat; to consume, squander

mangeur *m*, **-euse** *f* eater.

mangouste *f* mongoose.

mangue *f* mango.

maniable *adj* handy, workable, tractable; amenable.

maniaque *adj* eccentric; fussy.; * *mf* maniac;fusspot; fanatic.

manie *f* mania

maniement *m* handling; management, use.

manier *vt* to handle; to manipulate.

manière *f* manner, way, style.

maniéré *adj* affected.

manifestation *f* demonstration; expression, manifestation.

manifeste *adj* manifest, evident, obvious; **~ment** *adv* manifestly, obviously; * *m* manifesto.

manifester *vt* to display, make known; to demonstrate; **se ~** *vr* to make oneself known; to appear; to express itself.

manigancer *vt* to contrive; to scheme.

manipulation *f* handling; manipulation.

manipuler *vt* to handle; to manipulate

manivelle *f* crank.

mannequin *m* model; dummy.

manoeuvre *f* manoeuvre, operation; scheme; * *m* labourer.

manoeuvrer *vt* to manoeuvre; to operate; * *vi* to manoeuvre, move.

manoir *m* manor.

manomètre *m* manometer.

manquant *adj* missing.

manque *m* lack, shortage; shortcoming, deficiency.

manquer *vt* to miss; to fail; to be absent.

mansarde *f* attic, garret.

manteau *m* coat; mantle, blanket; cloak.

manuel *m* manual, handbook; * *adj* manual; **~lement** *adv* manually.

manufacture *f* factory; manufacture.

manufacturier *m*, **-ière** *f* factory owner; manufacturer; * *adj* manufacturing.

manuscrit *m* manuscript; typescript; * *adj* handwritten.

manutention *f* handling.

mappemonde *f* map of the world.

maquereau *m* mackerel.

maquette *f* model; mock-up; dummy; sketch.

maquillage *m* make-up.

maquiller *vt* to make up;to fake; to fiddle; **se ~** *vr* to put on one's make-up.

marais *m* marsh, swamp.

marasme *m* stagnation; depression, slump.

marathon *m* marathon.

marbre *m* marble; marble statue.

marbré *adj* marbled; mottled, blotchy.

marbrier *m* marble-cutter; monumental mason.

marchand *m*, **-e** *f* shopkeeper; dealer; merchant; * *adj* market, trade.

marchandage *m* bargaining, haggling.

marchander *vi* to bargain over, haggle.

marchandise *f* merchandise, commodity; goods.

marche *f* walk; journey; progress; movement; **mettre en ~** to start up; to turn on.

marché *m* market; transaction, contract.

marcher *vi* to walk, march; to progress; to work.

marcheur *m*, **-euse** *f* walker, pedestrian.

mardi *m* Tuesday.

mare *f* pool, pond.

marécage *m* marsh, swamp.

maréchal *m* marshal.

marée *f* tide/

margarine *f* margarine.

marge *f* margin; latitude, freedom; mark-up.

marginal *adj* marginal.

marginaliser *vt* to marginalize.

marguerite *f* daisy.

mari *m* husband.

mariage *m* marriage.

marié *m* bridegroom; * *adj* married.

marier *vt* to marry; blend, harmonize; **se ~** *vr* to get married.

marin *m* sailor.

marine *f* navy; seascape; marine.

mariner *vi* to marinate; to hang about; * *vt* to marinate.

marionnette *f* puppet; puppet show.

maritime *adj* maritime; seaboard.

marjolaine *f* marjoram.

marmelade *f* compote; marmalade.

marmite *f* pot.

marmonner *vt* to mumble, mutter.

marmotte *f* marmot.

maroquinerie *f* tannery; fine leather craft.

maroquinier *m* leather craftsman; dealer in fine leather.

marquant *adj* outstanding, vivid.

marque *f* mark, sign; brand; make.

marquer *vt* to mark; to note down; to score.

marquis *m* marquis, **-e** *f* marchioness.

marraine *f* godmother; sponsor.

marron *m* chestnut; brown; * *adj* brown.

marronnier *m* chestnut tree.

mars *m* March.

marsouin *m* porpoise.

marteau *m* hammer; knocker.

marteler *vt* to hammer; to beat.

martial *adj* martial, warlike.

martin-pêcheur *m* kingfisher.

martyr *m*, **-e** *f* martyr; * *adj* martyred.

martyre *m* martyrdom.

martyriser *vt* to torture, martyr..

mascarade *f* farce, mascarade.

masculin *adj* masculine.

masochisme *m* masochism.

masochiste *mf* masochist; * *adj* masochistic.

masque *m* mask; facade, front.

masquer *vt* to mask, conceal; to disguise.

massacre *m* massacre; slaughter.

massacrer *vt* to massacre, slaughter.

massage *m* massage.

masse *f* mass, heap; bulk; mob.

masser *vt* to mass, assemble; to massage.

masseur *m* masseur, **euse** *f* masseuse.

massif *adj* massive, solid, heavy; * *m* massif; clump.

massivement *adv* en masse, massively, heavily.

massue *f* club.

mastic *m* mastic; cement; putty.

mastiquer *vt* to chew, masticate.

masturbation *f* masturbation.

masturber *vt*; **se ~** *vr* to masturbate.

mat *adj* matt, dull; dead, dull-sounding.

mât *m* mast; pole.

match *m* match; game.

matelas *m* mattress.

matelassé *adj* stuffed; padded, cushioned.

matelot *m* sailor; seaman.

mater *vt* to subdue; to control, curb; to spy on; to ogle.

matérialiser *vt* to make materialize, embody; **se ~** *vr* to materialize.

matériaux *mpl* material, materials.

matériel *adj* material, physical; practical; **~lement** *adv* materially, practically.

maternel *adj* maternal, motherly; **~lement** *adv* maternally.

maternité *f* motherhood; pregnancy; maternity hospital.

mathématicien *m*, **-ienne** *f* mathematician.

mathématique *adj* mathematical; **~ment** *adv* mathematically; * *f* mathematics.

matière *f* material, matter; subject; **~ première** raw material.

matin *m* morning; dawn.

matinal *adj* morning.

matinée *f* morning; matinée.

matraque *f* truncheon; cosh.

matrice *f* womb; mould; matrix.

matricule *m* reference number; * *f* roll, register.

matrimonial *adj* matrimonial, marriage.

maturation *f* maturing; maturation.

maturité *f* maturity; prime.

maudire *vt* to curse.

maudit *adj* cursed; blasted; damned.

maussade *adj* sulky, sullen; **~ment** *adv* sulkily, sullenly.

mauvais *adj* bad; wicked; faulty; hurtful; poor.

mauve *adj* mauve; * *f* mallow.

maximal *adj* maximal.

maxime *f* maxim.

maximum *m* maximum.

mayonnaise *f* mayonnaise.

me, m' *pron* me; myself.

mécanicien *m*, **-ienne** *f* mechanic; engineer.

mécanique *f* mechanics; mechanical engineering; * *adj* mechanical; **~ment** *adv* mechanically.

mécanisme *m* mechanism, working.

mécène *m* patron.

méchamment *adv* spitefully; wickedly.

méchanceté *f* spitefulness; wickedness; mischievousness.

méchant *adj* spiteful; wicked; mischievous.

mèche *f* wick, fuse; tuft.

méconnaissable *adj* unrecognizable.

méconnu *adj* unrecognized; misunderstood.

mécontent *adj* discontent, displeased.

mécontentement *m* discontent; displeasure.

médaille *f* medal; stain, mark.

médaillon *m* medallion; locket.

médecin *m* doctor, physician.

médecine *f* medicine

médiateur *m*, **-trice** *f* mediator; arbitrator.

médiatique *adj* media.

médical *adj* medical; **~ement** *adv* medically.

médicament *m* medicine, drug.

médicinal *adj* medicinal.

médiéval *adj* medieval.

médiocre *adj* mediocre; passable; indifferent; **~ment** *adv* indifferently; poorly.

médisant *adj* slanderous.

méditation *f* meditation.

méditer *vi* to meditate; * *vt* to contemplate, have in mind.

médium *m* medium.

méduse *f* jellyfish.

méfiance *f* distrust, mistrust.

méfiant *adj* distrustful, mistrustful.

méfier(se) *vr* to mistrust, distrust; to be suspicious.

mégalomane *adj* megalomaniac; * *mf* megalomaniac.

mégaphone *m* megaphone.

mégot *m* cigarette-end, stub.

meilleur *adj* better, preferable; **le ~, la ~e** the best.

mélancolie *f* melancholy, gloom.

mélancolique *adj* melancholy; melancholic; **~ment** *adv* melancholically.

mélange *m* mixing, blending; mixture.

mélanger *vt* to mix, blend; to muddle.

mêlée *f* melée, fray; scrum.

mêler *vt* to mix; to combine; **se ~** *vr* to mix, mingle; **se ~ à** to join; **se ~ de** to get mixed up in.

mélisse *f* balm.

mélodie *f* melody, tune.

mélodieusement *adv* melodiously, tunefully.

mélodieux *adj* melodious, tuneful.

mélomane *mf* music lover.

melon *m* melon.

membrane *f* membrane.

membre *m* member; limb.

même *adv* even; **tout de ~** nevertheless, all the same; * *adj* same, identical; * *pron*: **le ~, la ~, les ~s** the same, the same one.

mémoire *f* memory; * *m* memorandum, report.

mémorable *adj* memorable.

mémoriser *vt* to memorize.

menaçant *adj* menacing, threatening.

menace *f* threat; intimidation; danger.

menacer *vt* to threaten, menace; to impend.

ménage *m* housework, housekeeping; household.

ménager *vt* to treat with caution; to manage; to arrange.; **se ~** *vr* to take care of oneself; * *adj* household, domestic.

ménagère *f* housewife.

ménagerie *f* menagerie.

mendiant *m*, **-e** *f* beggar, mendicant.

mendier *vt* to beg; to implore.

mener *vt* to lead, guide; to steer; to manage.

meneur *m*, **-euse** *f* leader; agitator.

menhir *m* menhir, standing stone.

méningite *f* meningitis.

ménopause *f* menopause.

menottes *fpl* handcuffs.

mensonge *m* lie, falsehood; error, illusion.

menstruation *f* menstruation.

mensuel *adj* monthly.

mental *adj* mental; **~ement** *adv* mentally.

mentalité *f* mentality.

menteur *m*, **-euse** *f* liar; * *adj* lying, deceitful.

menthe *f* mint.

menthol *m* menthol.

mention *f* mention; comment; grade.

mentionner *vt* to mention.

mentir *vi* to lie; to be deceptive.

menton *m* chin.

menu *m* menu; meal; * *adj* slender, thin; petty, minor.

menuiserie *f* joinery, carpentry.

menuisier *m* joiner, carpenter.

mépris *m* contempt, scorn.

méprisant *adj* contemptuous, scornful.

mépriser *vt* to scorn, despise.

mer *f* sea; tide.

mercenaire *m* mercenary.

mercerie *f* haberdashery.

merci *m* thank you; * *f* mercy; **sans ~** merciless; **être à la ~ de** to be at the mercy of.

mercredi *m* Wednesday.

mercure *m* mercury.

mère *f* mother.

méridien *m* meridian; midday.

méridional *adj* southern.

meringue *f* meringue.

merisier *m* wild cherry.

mérite *m* merit, worth; quality.

mériter *vt* to deserve, merit.

merlan *m* whiting.

merle *m* blackbird

merveille *f* marvel, wonder.

merveilleusement *adv* marvellously, wonderfully.

merveilleux *adj* marvellous, wonderful.

mésange *f* tit (*orn*).

mésentente *f* misunderstanding.

mesquin *adj* mean, niggardly; petty; **~ement** *adv* meanly, pettily.

message *m* message.

messager *m*, **-ère** *f* messenger.

messagerie *f* parcels office, parcels service.

messe *f* mass

messie *m* messiah.

mesure *f* measure; gauge; measurement; moderation; step; **au fur et à ~** as; one by one; **sans commune ~ avec** there is no possible comparison with; **dans la mesure où** insofar as; **en ~** in time.

mesurer *vt* to measure; to assess; to limit; **se ~** *vr* to try one's strength; **se ~ à** to pit oneself against, measure one's strength against.

métabolisme *m* metabolism.

métal *m* metal.

métallique *adj* metallic.

métallisé *adj* metallic, metallized.

métallurgie *f* metallurgy.

métallurgiste *m* steelworker, metalworker.

métamorphose *f* metamorphosis.

métamorphoser *vt* to transform, metamorphose; **se ~** *vr* to be metamorphosed.

métaphore *f* metaphor.

métaphorique *adj* metaphorical; **~ment** *adv* metaphorically.

métaphysique *adj* metaphysical; * *f* metaphysics.

météore *m* meteor.

météorite *m / f* meteorite.

météoroloque, météorologiste *mf* meteorologist.

méthane *m* methane.

méthode *f* method, way.

méthodique *adj* methodical; **~ment** *adv* methodically.

méthylène *m* methyl alcohol; methylene.

méticuleusement *adv* meticulously.

méticuleux *adj* meticulous

métier *m* job; occupation; **~ à tricoter** knitting machine; **~ à tisser** weaving loom.

métis *m*, **-isse** *f* half-caste; hybrid; mongrel; * *adj* half-caste; hybrid, mongrel.

mètre *m* metre.

métro *m* underground, metro.

métronome *m* metronome.

métropole *f* metropolis.

métropolitain *adj* metropolitan; underground.

mets *m* dish.

metteur en scène *m* director (*cin*)

mettre *vt* to put, place; to put on; **~ en marche** to start up; **se ~** *vr* to place oneself; to sit down; **se ~ à** to begin to; **se ~ en route** to start off.

meuble *m* piece of furniture.

meubler *vt* to furnish.

meule *f* millstone; grindstone.

meurtrier *m* murderer, **-ière** *f* murderess.

meurtrir *vt* to bruise.

meute *f* pack.

mezzanine *f* mezzanine.

mi- *adj* half; **à ~chemin** halfway; **~clos** half-closed; **à ~jambe** up to the knees; **à ~voix** in a low voice.

miauler *vi* to mew.

miche *f* round loaf.

microbe *m* germ, microbe.

microbien *adj* microbial, microbic.

microclimat *m* microclimate.

microfilm *m* microfilm.

micro-informatique *f* microcomputing.

micro-onde *f* microwave; * *m* **micro-ondes** microwave oven.

micro-ordinateur *m* microcomputer.

microphone *m* microphone.

microprocesseur *m* microprocessor.

microscope *m* microscope.

microscopique *adj* microscopic.

midi *m* midday, noon.

mie *f* crumb, soft part of a loaf.

miel *m* honey.

mien *pron*, *f* **mienne**: le ~, la mienne, les ~s, les miennes mine, my own.

miette *f* crumb; remnant; morsel.

mieux *m* improvement; **le** ~ the best; **de** ~ **en** ~ better and better.

mignon *adj* sweet, pretty.

migraine *f* headache; migraine.

migrateur *m* migrant.

migration *f* migration.

mijoter *vi* to simmer, be brewing; * *vt* to simmer; to scheme, plot.

milice *f* militia.

milieu *m* middle, centre; medium; environment.

militaire *m* serviceman; * *adj* military, army.

militant *m*, **-e** *f* militant; * *adj* militant.

militer *vi* to militate; to be a militant.

mille *m* one thousand; * *adj* one thousand.

millénaire *m* millennium, a thousand years; thousandth anniversary * *adj* thousand-year-old; millennial.

mille-pattes *m* millipede.

millésime *m* year, date; vintage.

millet *m* millet.

milliard *m* thousand million; milliard.

milliardaire *adj* worth (many)

millions; * *mf* multimillionaire.

milliardième *adj* thousand millionth; * *m* thousand millionth.

millième *adj* thousandth; * *m* thousandth.

millier *m* thousand.

milligramme *m* milligramme.

millilitre *m* millilitre.

millimètre *m* millimetre.

million *m* million.

millionième *adj* millionth; * *m* millionth.

millionnaire *adj* millionaire; worth millions; * *mf* millionaire.

mime *m* mime ; * *mf* mimic.

mimer *vt* to mime; to mimic, imitate.

mimétisme *m* mimicry; mimetism.

mimosa *m* mimosa.

minable *adj* seedy, shabby; **~ment** *adv* shabbily.

mince *adj* thin, slender; meagre, trivial.

mincir *vi* to get slimmer, get thinner.

mine *f* expression; appearance; mine; **avoir bonne** ~ to look good.

mineral *m* ore.

minéral *adj* mineral; inorganic; * *m* mineral.

minéralogique *adj* mineralogical.

mineur *m*, **-e** *f* minor; * *adj* minor; * *m* miner.

miniature *f* miniature.

mini-jupe *f* miniskirt.

minimal *adj* minimal, minimum.

minime *adj* minor, minimal.

minimum *m* minimum.

ministère *m* ministry; agency.

ministériel *adj* ministerial.

ministre *m* minister; clergyman.

minoritaire *adj* minority.

minorité *f* minority.

minuit *m* midnight.

minuscule *adj* minuscule, tiny, minute.

minute *f* minute, moment.

minuterie *f* time switch; regulator.

minutieux *adj* meticulous; minute.

mirabelle *f* plum.

miracle *m* miracle, wonder.

miraculeux *adj* miraculous.

mirage *m* mirage.

miroir *m* mirror, reflection.

misanthrope *mf* misanthrope; misanthropist; * *adj* misanthropic.

mise *f* putting, placing; stake; deposit; investment; **~ en scène** production, staging; **~ en liberté** release; **~ en ordre** ordering, arrangement; **~ en oeuvre** implementation.

miser *vt* to stake, to bet.

misérable *adj* miserable; destitute; pitiable; **~ment** *adv* miserably.

misère *f* misery; poverty; destitution.

miséricorde *f* mercy, forgiveness.

misogyne *mf* misogynist; * *adj* misogynous.

missile *m* missile.

mission *f* mission, assignment.

missionnaire *m* missionary.

mi-temps *f* half-time; half.

miteux *adj* dingy, shabby, poverty-stricken.

mitigé *adj* mitigated; lukewarm.

mitoyen *adj* common; semi-detached.

mitrailler *vt* to machine-gun.

mitraillette *f* submachine gun.

mitrailleuse *f* machine gun.

mixer *vt* to mix; to blend.

mixte *adj* mixed; joint; combined.

mixture *f* mixture, concoction.

mobile *adj* moving; movable; mobile; nimble; * *m* motive; moving body.

mobilier *m* furniture; * *adj* movable; personal; transferable.

mobilisation *f* mobilization, calling up.

mobilité *f* mobility.

mobylette *f* moped.

moche *adj* (*fam*) ugly, lousy.

mode *f* fashion; custom; * *m* form, mode; way.

modèle *m* model; pattern; design; example.

modeler *vt* to model; to shape; **se ~** *vr*: **se ~ sur** to model oneself on.

modem *m* modem.

modération *f* moderation; diminution.

modéré *adj* ; **~ment** *adv*

modérer *vt* to moderate, restrained; **se ~** *vr* to control oneself, keep one's temper.

moderne *adj* modern, up-to-date.

moderniser *vt* to modernize.

modeste *adj* modest, simple; unassuming; **~ment** *adv* modestly.

modestie *f* modesty.

modification *f* modification, alteration.

modifier *vt* to modify, alter; **se ~** *vr* to be modified.

modulation *f* modulation; adjustment.

moelle *f* marrow; core.

moelleux *adj* mellow; soft; smooth.

moeurs *fpl* morals; customs.

moi *pron* me, I; **c'est à ~** it is mine, it is my turn; **~-même** myself.

mois *m* month.

moisi *adj* mouldy, mildewed; * *m* mould.

moisir *vi* to go mouldy.

moisissure *f* mould, mildew.

moisson *f* harvest.

moissonner *vt* to reap, mow.

moite *adj* moist, damp.

moitié *f* half.

molaire *f* molar.

molécule *f* molecule.

mollement *adv* softly; gently.

mollusque *m* mollusc.

moment *m* moment, instant, while; time; opportunity.

momentané *adj* momentary;

brief; **~ment** *adv* momentarily.
momie *f* mummy.
mon *pron*, *f* **ma**, *pl* **mes** my, my own.
monarchie *f* monarchy.
monastère *m* monastery.
mondain *adj* worldly, mundane; society, fashionable.
monde *m* world, earth; society, company; **il y a du ~** there are some people there.
mondial *adj* world, world-wide; **~ement** *adv* the world over.
monétaire *adj* monetary.
moniteur *m*, **-trice** *f* instructor, coach; supervisor.
monnaie *f* currency; coin; change.
monoculture *f* single-crop farming, monoculture.
monologue *m* monologue.
monopole *m* monopoly.
monopoliser *vt* to monopolize.
monotone *adj* monotonous
monotonie *f* monotony, sameness.
monseigneur *m* my lord, your grace.
monsieur *m* sir, gentleman, Mr, *pl* **messieurs** gentlemen, Messrs.
monstre *m* monster.
monstrueux *adj* monstrous.
mont *m* mountain; mount.
montage *m* assembly; setting up; editing.
montagnard *m*, **-e** *f* mountain dweller.
montagne *f* mountain.
montagneux *adj* mountainous.
montant *m* upright; total, total sum; * *adj* upward, rising; upstream.
montée *f* climb, climbing; ascent; rise.
monter *vi* to go up, ascend; get into (vehicle); * *vt* to go up; to carry/bring up.
monteur *m*, **-euse** *f* fitter; editor.
montre *f* watch.
montrer *vt* to show, point to; to

prove; **se ~** *vr* to appear; to prove oneself.
monture *f* mount; setting; frame.
monument *m* monument, memorial.
monumental *adj* monumental, colossal.
moquer(se) *vr* to make fun, jeer, laugh at.
moqueur *m*, **-euse** *f* mocker, scoffer; * *adj* mocking.
moral *adj* moral, ethical; intellectual; **~ement** *adv* morally.
moralité *f* morals, morality.
morbide *adj* morbid, unhealthy.
morceau *m* piece, morsel, fragment; extract.
mordant *adj* cutting, mordant; * *m* mordant.
mordre *vt* to bite, gnaw; to grip.
morgue *f* morgue; mortuary.
morille *f* morel.
morne *adj* gloomy, dismal.
morose *adj* sullen, morose.
morphine *f* morphine.
morphologie *f* morphology.
morse *m* Morse (code); (*zool*) walrus.
morsure *f* bite.
mort *m* dead man, **-e** *f* dead woman; * *adj* dead; * *f* death.
mortalité *f* mortality; death rate.
mortel *adj* mortal; fatal; **~lement** *adv* mortally.
mortier *m* mortar.
mortuaire *adj* mortuary; funeral.
morue *f* cod.
mosaïque *f* mosaic.
mosquée *f* mosque
mot *m* word; saying; **~s croisés** crossword.
moteur *m* engine, motor; * *adj* motor, driving.
motif *m* motive, grounds; motif, design.
motion *f* motion; **~ de censure** censure motion.
motivation *f* motivation.
motiver *vt* to justify; to motivate.
moto *f* motorbike.

moto-cross *m* motocross, scrambling.

motte *f* clod, lump; slab.

mou *adj*, *f* **molle** soft; gentle; muffled.

mouche *f* fly.

moucher *vt* to wipe so's nose; **se ~** *vr* to blow one's nose.

moucheron *m* midge, gnat.

moucheté *adj* speckled; flecked.

mouchoir *m* handkerchief.

moudre *vt* to mill, grind.

moue *f* pout; **faire la ~** to pout.

mouette *f* gull.

moufle *f* mitten.

mouillé *adj* wet, soaked.

mouiller *vt* to wet; to water down; **se ~** *vr* to get wet.

moulage *m* moulding, casting.

moule *m* mould; * *f* mussel.

mouler *vt* to mould; to model.

moulin *m* mill.

moulu *adj* ground; bruised

mourant *m* dying man, **-e** *f* dying woman; * *adj* dying.

mourir *vi* to die.

mousse *f* moss; foam, froth.

mousser *vi* to froth, foam

mousseux *adj* sparkling; frothy; * *m* sparkling wine.

moustache *f* moustache; whiskers.

moustachu *adj* moustached; * *m* moustached man.

moustiquaire *f* mosquito net.

moustique *m* mosquito.

moutarde *f* mustard.

mouton *m* sheep; mutton.

mouvement *m* movement, motion; animation.

mouvementé *adj* eventful; turbulent.

mouvoir *vt* to drive, power; **se ~** *vr* to move.

moyen *m* means; way; * *adj* average, medium, moderate; **~nement** *adv* fairly, moderately; **~ âge** Middle Ages.

moyenne *f* average.

moyeu *m* hub; boss.

mue *f* moulting; shedding.

muer *vi* to moult; to slough.

muet *m* mute (man), **muette** *f* mute (woman); * *adj* dumb; silent, mute.

mufle *m* muffle; muzzle.

muguet *m* thrush.

mule *f* she-mule.

mulet *m* mule.

multicolore *adj* multicoloured.

multinationale *f* multinational.

multiple *adj* numerous, multiple; * *m* multiple.

multiplication *f* multiplication.

multiplier *vt* ; **se ~** *vr* to multiply, increase.

multitude *f* multitude, crowd.

municipal *adj* municipal; local.

municipalité *f* town, municipality.

munir *vt* to provide, equip with; **se ~** *vr* to equip oneself.

munition *f* munition, ammunition.

mur *m* wall.

mûr *adj* ripe, mature; worn out.

muraille *f* city wall, rampart.

mûre *f* blackberry.

mûrir *vi* to ripen, mature.

murmure *m* murmur; muttering; grumbling.

murmurer *vi* to murmur; to whisper; grumble; to babble * *vt* to murmur.

muscle *m* muscle.

musclé *adj* muscular, brawny.

musculaire *adj* muscular.

muse *f* muse.

museau *m* muzzle, snout.

musée *m* art gallery, museum.

musicien *m*, **-ienne** *f* musician; * *adj* musical.

musique *f* music.

musulman *m*, **-e** *f* Moslem; * *adj* Moslem.

mutant *m*, **-e** *f* mutant; * *adj* mutant.

mutation *f* transfer; transformation; mutation.

muter *vt* to transfer, move.

mutilation *f* mutilation, maiming.

mutiler *vt* to mutilate; **se ~** *vr* to injure oneself.

mutisme *m*

mutuel *adj* ; **~lement** *adv*

mutuelle *f* mutual insurance company

mycose *f* mycosis.

mygale *f* mygale, trap-door spider.

myope *mf* short-sighted person; * *adj* short-sighted.

myopie *f* short-sightedness.

myosotis *m* forget-me-not.

myrtille *f* bilberry.

mystère *m* mystery.

mystérieusement *adv* mysteriously.

mystérieux *adj* mysterious.

mystifier *vt* to mystify; to hoax.

mystique *adj* mystical; * *mf* mystic.

mythe *m* myth.

mythique *adj* mythical.

mythologie *f* mythology.

N

nacre *f* mother-of-pearl.

nacré *adj* nacreous, pearly, iridescent.

nageoire *f* fin, flipper.

nager *vi* to swim.

nageur *m*, **-euse** *f* swimmer; rower.

naïf *adj* naïve, artless, ingenuous.

nain *m*, **-e** *f* dwarf; * *adj* dwarfish, dwarf.

naissance *f* birth, extraction; dawn, beginning.

naître *vi* to be born; to arise, spring up.

naïvement *adj* naïvely.

naïveté *f* naïvety, artlessness, gullibility.

nanti *m* rich man, *adj* rich, well-to-do.

nappe *f* tablecloth; layer; sheet, expanse.

napper *vt* to top with.

napperon *m* tablemat.

narcisse *m* narcissus.

narcotique *m* drug, narcotic; * *adj* narcotic.

narguer *vt* to flout, defy; to cheek.

narine *f* nostril.

narrateur *m*, **-trice** *f* narrator.

narration *f* narration, narrative.

nasal *adj* nasal.

naseau *m* nostril.

natalité *f* birth rate.

natation *f* swimming.

nation *f* nation.

national *adj* national; domestic.

nationaliser *vt* to nationalize.

nationaliste *mf* nationalist; * *adj* nationalist.

nationalité *f* nationality.

natte *f* plait, braid.

naturalisation *f* naturalization.

naturaliser *vt* to naturalize; to stuff.

naturaliste *mf* naturalist; taxidermist; * *adj* naturalistic.

nature *f* nature; kind, sort; temperament.

naturel *adj* natural; bodily; native; unsophisticated; **~lement** *adv* naturally; of course.

naufrage *m* shipwreck; ruin, foundering.

nausée *f* nausea.

nautique *adj* nautical, water.

naval *adj* naval, shipbuilding.

navet *m* turnip.

navette *f* shuttle; **faire la ~** to shuttle between.

navigateur *m* navigator, sailor.

navigation *f* sailing, navigation.

navire *m* ship, vessel.

navrant *adj* distressing, upsetting.

ne *adv* no, not.

né *adj* born

néanmoins *adv* nevertheless.

néant *m* nothing, nothingness, emptiness.

nécessaire *adj* necessary; requisite; indispensable; **~ment** *adv* necessarily.

nécessité *f* necessity; need; inevitability.

nécessiter *vt* to require, necessitate.

nécropole *f* necropolis.

nectar *m* nectar.

nectarine *f* nectarine.

néfaste *adj* harmful; unlucky; ill-fated.

négatif *adj* negative.

négation *f* negation; negative.

négativement *adv* negatively.

négligemment *adv* negligently; carelessly; nonchalantly.

négligence *f* negligence, carelessness.

négligent *adj* negligent, careless; nonchalant.

négliger *vt* to neglect; to be negligent about.

négociant *m*, **-e** *f* merchant.

négociation *f* negotiation.

négocier *vi* to negotiate; to trade; * *vt* to negotiate.

neige *f* snow.

neiger *vi* to snow, be snowing.

nénuphar *m* water lily.

néophyte *mf* neophyte; novice * *adj* newly converted.

nerf *m* nerve.

nerveusement *adv* nervously; irritably.

nerveux *adj* nervous; vigorous; excitable.

nervosité *f* nervousness; excitability.

nervure *f* nervure, vein; rib.

net *adj*, *f* **nette** clean; clear; plain; sharp; net; **~tement** *adv* cleanly; clearly; plainly.

netteté *f* neatness; clearness; sharpness.

nettoyage *m* cleaning; clearing up.

nettoyer *vt* to clean; to ruin, clean out.

neuf *adj* nine; * *m* nine.

neurologie *f* neurology.

neurone *m* neuron.

neutraliser *vt* to neutralize.

neutralité *f* neutrality.

neutre *adj* neutral; neuter.

neutron *m* neutron.

neuvième *adj* ninth; **~ment** *adv* ninthly; * *mf* ninth.

neveu *m* nephew.

névralgie *f* neuralgia.

névrose *f* neurotic

nez *m* nose; flair; **avoir du ~** to have flair.

niais *adj* silly, simple, inane; **~ement** *adv* inanely.

niche *f* niche, nook; kennel; trick.

nickel *m* nickel.

nicotine *f* nicotine.

nid *m* nest; den; berth.

nièce *f* niece.

nier *vt* to deny; to repudiate.

nigaud *m*, **-e** *f* simpleton.

nitrate *m* nitrate.

nitroglycérine *f* nitroglycerine.

niveau *m* level; standard; par; gauge.

niveler *vt* to level; to even out, equalize.

noble *adj* noble, dignified; **~ment** *adv* nobly.

noblesse *f* nobleness, nobility.

noce *f* wedding, wedding feast; marriage ceremony.

nocif *adj* noxious, harmful.

noctambule *mf* night reveller, night owl; sleepwalker; * *adj* enjoying night life; noctambulant.

nocturne *adj* nocturnal, night; * *f* evening fixture; late night opening.

nodule *m* nodule.

Noël *m* Christmas.

noeud *m* knot, bow; crux.

noir *adj* black; dark; * *m* black; darkness; black man

noircir *vt* to blacken; to dirty; *vi* to tan; to ripen; **se ~** *vr* to darken, grow black.

noire *f* black woman.

noisetier *m* hazel tree.

noisette *f* hazel.

noix *f* walnut

nom *m* name; fame; noun

nomade *mf* nomad.

nombre *m* number, quantity.

nombreux *adj* numerous, frequent.

nombril *m* navel.

nomenclature *f* list, catalogue; nomenclature.

nominal *adj* nominal; noun; **~ement** *adv* nominally.

nominatif *m* nominative.

nomination *f* appointment; nomination.

nommer *vt* to appoint; nominate.

non *adv* no; not.

nonchalance *f* nonchalance.

nonchalant *adj* nonchalant.

non-conformiste *mf* nonconformist; * *adj* nonconformist.

non-lieu *m* insufficient ground to prosecute.

non-sens *m* nonsense.

non-violence *f* non-violence.

nord *m* north, northerly (wind)

nordique *adj* Nordic; Scandinavian.

normal *adj* normal, usual; standard-sized; **~ement** *adv* normally, usually.

norme *f* norm; standard.

nostalgie *f* nostalgia.

nostalgique *adj* nostalgic.

notable *adj* notable; noteworthy; **~ment** *adv* notably.

notaire *m* notary; solicitor.

notamment *adv* notably; in particular.

note *f* note; minute; mark; bill.

noter *vt* to note down; to notice; to mark.

notice *f* note; directions; instructions.

notion *f* notion, idea.

notoire *adj* notorious; well-known, acknowledged; **~ment** *adv* notoriously.

notoriété *f* notoriety; fame.

notre *adj*, *pl* **nos** ours, our own.

nôtre *pron*: **le ~, la ~, les ~s** ours, our own.

nouer *vt* to tie, knot; **se ~** *vr* to join together.

nouille *f* piece of pasta.

nourrice *f* child-minder, nanny.

nourrir *vt* to feed, provide for; to stoke; **se ~** *vr* to feed oneself.

nourrissant *adj* nourishing, nutritious.

nourrisson *m* infant, nursling.

nourriture *f* food; sustenance.

nous *pron* we; us; **c'est à ~** it's ours; it's our turn; **~-mêmes** ourselves.

nouveau *adj* new; recent; additional.

nouveau-né *m*, **-e** *f* new-born child.

nouveauté *f* novelty; newness.

nouvelle *f* piece of news; short story.

novembre *m* November.

novice *mf* novice, beginner; * *adj* novice, unpractised, inexperienced.

noyade *f* drowning, drowning incident.

noyau *m* stone, pit; core; nucleus

noyer *vt* to drown; to flood; **se ~** *vr* to drown, drown oneself; * *m* walnut (tree).

nu *adj* naked, nude; plain, unadorned.

nuage *m* cloud.

nuageux *adj* cloudy, overcast.

nuance *f* shade, hue; faint difference, nuance.

nucléaire *adj* nuclear; * *m* nuclear energy.

nudiste *mf* nudist; * *adj* nudist.

nudité *f* nakedness, nudity.

nuée *f* thick cloud; horde, swarm.
nuire *vi* to harm, injure; to prejudice.
nuisible *adj* harmful; noxious;
~**ment** *adv* harmfully.
nuit *f* night, darkness.
nul *adj* no; nil; null and void; non-existent; ~**lement** *adv* not at all, not in the least.
nullité *f* nullity; uselessness.
numéral *adj* numeral; * *m* numeral.

numérique *adj* numerical; digital.
numéro *m* number; issue.
numérotation *f* numbering, numeration.
numéroter *vt* to number.
nuptial *adj* nuptial, wedding.
nuque *f* nape (of the neck).
nutritif *adj* nutritious, nourishing.
nutrition *f* nutrition.
nylon *m* nylon.
nymphe *f* nymph.

O

oasis *m* oasis.
obéir *vt* to obey, be obedient; to comply.
obéissance *f* obedience; compliance.
obéissant *adj* obedient.
obèse *adj* obese.
obésité *f* obesity.
objecter *vt* to object.
objectif *adj* objective, unbiased;
* *m* objective, target.
objection *f* objection.
objectivement *adv* objectively.
objet *m* object, thing; purpose; matter.
obligation *f* obligation, duty; bond.
obligatoire *adj* obligatory, compulsory; ~**ment** *adv* obligatorily.
obligé *adj* obliged, compelled; inevitable; necessary.
obliger *vt* to oblige, require; to bind.
oblique *adj* oblique, sidelong.
oblitérer *vt* to obliterate; to cancel (stamp)
obscène *adj* obscene.
obscénité *f* obscenity.
obscur *adj* obscure, dark, gloomy;
~**ément** *adv* obscurely.
obscurcir *vt* to darken; to obscure; **s'~** *vr* to get dark.

obscurité *f* obscurity; darkness.
obséder *vt* to obsess, haunt
obsèques *fpl* funeral.
observateur *m*, **-trice** *f* observer;
* *adj* observant.
observation *f* observation; remark.
observatoire *m* observatory.
observer *vt* to observe, watch; to notice; to comply with.
obsession *f* obsession.
obstacle *m* obstacle, hindrance.
obstétrique *f* obstetrics.
obstination *f* obstinacy, stubbornness.
obstiné *adj* obstinate, stubborn;
~**ment** *adv* obstinately.
obstiner(s') *vr* to insist, persist.
obtenir *vt* to obtain, procure, get; to achieve.
obturation *f* stopping, closing up, obturation.
obus *m* shell.
occasion *f* occasion, opportunity; cause; bargain.; **d'~** casual.
occident *m* west.
occidental *adj* western; Occidental.
occulte *adj* occult.
occupant *m*, **-e** *f* occupant, occupier.
occupation *f* occupation, pursuit;

127

work, job; occupancy.

occuper *vt* to occupy; to employ; to inhabit; **s'~** *vr* to keep busy.

océan *m* ocean.

ocre *m* ochre; * *adj* ochre.

octane *m* octane.

octave *f* octave.

octet *m* byte.

octobre *m* October.

octroyer *vt* to grant, bestow; **s'~** *vr* to allow oneself.

oculaire *adj* ocular.

odeur *f* smell, odour.

odieux *adj* hateful, obnoxious.

odorat *m* smell (sense).

oedème *m* oedema.

œil *m*, *pl* **yeux** eye; look; bud.

œillet *m* carnation.

oesophage *m* oesophagus.

œuf *m* egg.

œuvre *f* work; action, deed; production.

offense *f* offence; injury, wrong.

offenser *vt* to offend; to injure, shock; **s'~** *vr* to take offence.

offensif *adj* offensive; forceful, aggressive.

offensive *f* offensive, attack.

office *m* office, bureau; duty; function.

officiel *adj* official; **~lement** *adv* officially.

officier *m* officer.

officieusement *adv* officiously; unofficially.

officieux *adj* officious, over-obliging; unofficial.

offrande *f* offering.

offre *f* offer, tender, bid.

offrir *vt* to offer.

offusquer *vt* to offend; **s'~** *vr* to take offence.

ogive *f* ogive, pointed arch.

ogre *m* ogre, **-esse** *f* ogress.

ohm *m* ohm.

oie *f* goose.

oignon *m* onion; bulb.

oiseau *m* bird.

oisif *adj* idle.

oisiveté *f* idleness.

oléagineux *adj* oleaginous, oily.

oléoduc *m* oil pipeline.

olfactif *adj* olfactory.

oligarchie *f* oligarchy.

oligo-élément *m* trace element.

olive *f* olive.

olivier *m* olive tree.

olympique *adj* Olympic.

ombilical *adj* umbilical.

ombragé *adj* shaded, shady.

ombre *f* shade, shadow.

omelette *f* omelette.

omettre *vt* to leave out, miss out.

omission *f* omission.

omnibus *m* local train; omnibus.

omnipotent *adj* omnipotent.

omniprésent *adj* omnipresent.

omoplate *f* shoulder blade.

on *pron* one; someone, anyone.

once *f* ounce.

oncle *m* uncle.

onctueux *adj* smooth, creamy.

onde *f* wave.

ondoyant *adj* undulating, flowing; changeable.

ondulation *f* undulation; wave.

onduler *vi* to undulate; to ripple.

onéreux *adj* onerous; expensive, costly.

ongle *m* nail; claw, talon; hoof.

onomatopée *f* onomatopoeia.

onyx *m* onyx.

onze *adj* eleven; * *m* eleven.

onzième *adj* eleventh; **~ment** *adv* in eleventh place; * *mf* eleventh.

opale *f* opal.

opaque *adj* opaque; impenetrable.

opéra *m* opera.

opération *f* operation, performance; transaction, deal.

opérationnel *adj* operational.

opératoire *adj* operating; operative, surgical.

opérer *vt* to operate; to carry out, implement.

opérette *f* operetta, light opera.

ophtalmie *f* ophthalmia.

opiniâtre *adj* stubborn; persistent; **~ment** *adv* stubbornly; persistently.

opinion *f* opinion, view.

opium *m* opium.

opportun *adj* timely, opportune; **~ément** *adv* opportunely.

opportuniste *mf* opportunist; * *adj* opportunist.

opportunité *f* opportuneness, expediency, timeliness.

opposant *m*, **-e** *f* opponent; * *adj* opposing.

opposé *adj* opposite, contrary; facing; * *m*; **à l'~** contrary to; conversely.

opposer *vt* to oppose; to contrast; to object; **s'~** *vr* to be opposed to; to clash, conflict.

opposition *f* opposition; conflict.

oppresser *vt* to oppress, weigh down.

oppressif *adj* oppressive.

oppression *f* oppression.

opprimer *vt* to oppress, crush.

opticien *m*, **-ienne** *f* optician.

optimisme *m* optimism.

optimiste *mf* optimist; * *adj* optimistic.

option *f* option, choice.

optionnel *adj* optional.

optique *adj* optical; * *f* optics.

opulence *f* opulence, wealth.

opulent *adj* opulent, wealthy.

or *m* gold; * *conj* now.

oracle *m* oracle.

orage *m* storm, tempest, thunderstorm.

orageux *adj* stormy.

oral *adj* oral, verbal; **~ement** *adv* orally.

orange *f* orange; * *adj invar* orange.

oranger *m* orange tree.

orang-outan(g) *m* orang-utan.

orateur *m*, **-trice** *f* orator.

orbite *f* orbit; socket; sphere.

orchestral *adj* orchestral.

orchestre *m* orchestra.

orchestrer *vt* to orchestrate, score.

orchidée *f* orchid.

ordinaire *adj* ordinary, common, usual; **~ment** *adv* ordinarily, usually; * *m* custom, usual routine; **d'~, à l'~** ordinarily, usually.

ordinateur *m* computer.

ordonnance *f* prescription, order, edict.

ordonner *vt* to arrange; to order; to prescribe

ordre *m* order, command; class.

ordure *f* filth, dirt; excrement; rubbish.

oreille *f* ear; hearing; wing; handle.

oreiller *m* pillow.

oreillons *mpl* mumps.

orfèvre *m* silversmith, goldsmith

orfèvrerie *f* silversmith's (goldsmith's) craft.

organe *m* organ; instrument; medium.

organigramme *m* organizational chart.

organique *adj* organic.

organisateur *m*, **-trice** *f* organizer.

organisation *f* organization.

organiser *vt* to organize, arrange; **s'~** *vr* to organize o.s.

organisme *m* organism.

organiste *mf* organist.

orgasme *m* orgasm.

orge *f* barley.

orgie *f* orgy.

orgue *m* (*mus*) organ

orgueil *m* pride, arrogance.

orgueilleux *adj* proud, arrogant.

orient *m* orient, east.

oriental *adj* eastern, oriental.

orientation *f* orientation; positioning; directing; trend.

orienter *vt* to orientate; to position; to direct; **s'~** *vr* to ascertain one's position; to turn towards.

orifice *m* orifice; aperture, opening.

originaire *adj* originally from,

native to; ~ment adv originally, primitively.

original adj original, novel; peculiar, bizarre; * m original; top copy.

originalité f originality; oddness.

origine f origin, source, derivation; **à l'~** originally.

originel adj original, primitive.

orme m elm.

ornement m ornament, embellishment.

ornemental adj ornamental.

orner vt to adorn, decorate.

ornière f rut.

ornithologie f ornithology.

ornithologiste, ornithologue mf ornithologist.

orphelin m, -e f orphan.

orphelinat m orphanage.

orteil m toe.

orthodoxe adj orthodox; * mf orthodox.

orthogonal adj orthogonal.

orthographe f orthography.

orthopédie f orthopaedics.

orthopédique adj orthopaedic.

ortie f nettle.

orvet m slow worm.

os m bone.

oscillation f oscillation, swinging.

osciller vi to oscillate, swing.

oseille f sorrel.

oser vt to dare.

osier m osier, willow.

osmose f osmosis.

ossature f skeleton; framework.

ossements mpl bones.

ostensible adj open, conspicuous; ~ment adv openly; conspicuously.

ostentation f ostentation.

ostéopathe mf osteopath.

ostracisme m ostracism.

otage m hostage.

otarie f sea-lion.

ôter vt to take away, remove; to deprive, deduct.

otite f ear infection.

oto-rhino-laryngologie f otorhinolaryngology.

oto-rhino(-laryngologiste) mf ear, nose and throat specialist.

ou conj or.

où adv where, in which; pron where.

ouate f cotton wool.

oubli m forgetfulness; oblivion; oversight, omission.

oublier vt to forget;to omit, neglect.

oubliette f oubliette.

ouest m west; adj west.

oui adv yes.

ouïe f hearing.

ouragan m hurricane, whirlwind.

ourlet m hem.

ours m, -e f bear.

oursin m sea urchin.

ourson m bear cub.

outil m tool, implement.

outillage m (set of) tools; equipment.

outiller vt to equip; to provide with tools.

outrage m outrage, insult, wrong.

outrageant adj outrageous, insulting.

outre prép as well as, besides; **en ~** moreover; **~ mesure** to excess, inordinately; **passer ~** to go on, to take no notice; * f goatskin, leather bottle.

outré adj excessive, exaggerated.

outremer m lapis lazuli; ultramarine.

outrepasser vt to exceed; to transgress.

ouvert adj open; exposed; frank; ~ement adv openly, overtly.

ouverture f opening; mouth; overture; means, way.

ouvrable adj working, business.

ouvrage m work; piece of work.

ouvre-boîte m tin-opener.

ouvre-bouteille m bottle-opener.

ouvrier m, -ière f worker; * adj working-class; industrial; labour.

ouvrir *vt* to open; to unlock; to broach; **s'~** *vr* to open; to open one's mind; to cut o.s.
ovaire *m* ovary.
ovale *adj* oval; * *m* oval.
ovation *f* ovation.
ovni *m* UFO.
ovulation *f* ovulation.

ovule *m* ovum; ovule.
oxydation *f* oxidization, oxidation.
oxyde *m* oxide.
oxyder *vt* to oxidize; **s'~** *vr* to become oxidized.
oxygène *m* oxygen.
ozone *f* ozone.

P

pacifier *vt* to pacify.
pacifique *adj* peaceful, pacific; **~ment** *adv* peacefully, pacifically.
pacifiste *mf* pacifist; * *adj* pacifist.
pacte *m* pact, treaty.
pactiser *vi* to covenant; to come to terms with.
pagaie *f* paddle.
pagayer *vi* to paddle.
page *f* page; passage.
pagne *m* loincloth.
paiement *m* payment
païen *m*, **-ïenne** *f* pagan; * *adj* pagan.
paillasse *f* straw mattress.
paillasson *m* doormat.
paille *f* straw.
paillette *f* sequin; spangle.
pain *m* bread; loaf; bar
pair *adj* even; * *m* peer; par; **hors ~** outstanding, matchless.
paire *f* pair; yoke; brace.
paisible *adj* peaceful; calm; **~ment** *adv* peacefully; calmly.
paître *vi* to graze.
paix *f* peace; quiet; stillness; tranquillity.
palais *m* palace; law courts; palate
palan *m* hoist.
pâle *adj* pale, pallid.
palette *f* palette; pallet; paddle.
pâleur *f* paleness, pallor.
palier *m* landing; level; degree.

pâlir *vi* to turn pale; to dim; to fade.
palissade *f* fence; boarding; stockade.
palliatif *m* palliative; * *adj* palliative.
pallier *vt* to palliate; to offset.
palmarès *m* prize list; medal record.
palme *f* palm leaf; palm.
palmé *adj* palmate; webbed.
palmeraie *f* palm grove.
palmier *m* palm tree.
palmipède *m* palmiped.
palpable *adj* palpable.
palper *vt* to feel, touch; to palpate.
palpitation *f* palpitation; throbbing; quivering.
palpiter *vi* to palpitate; to beat; to race.
paludisme *m* malaria.
pamplemousse *m* grapefruit.
panache *m* panache; gallantry
panaché *adj* variegated; motley.
pancarte *f* sign, notice; placard.
pancréas *m* pancreas.
panda *m* panda.
pané *adj* covered in breadcrumbs.
panier *m* basket; pannier.
panique *f* panic.
paniquer *vi* to panic, get panicky.
panne *f* breakdown; fault, problem.
panneau *m* panel; sign, notice.
panoplie *f* outfit; display.
panorama *m* panorama.

panoramique *adj* panoramic.
pansement *m* dressing, bandage.
panser *vt* to dress, bandage.
pantalon *m* trousers; pants; knickers.
panthéon *m* pantheon.
panthère *f* panther.
pantin *m* jumping-jack; puppet.
pantomime *f* pantomime; mime.
pantoufle *f* slipper.
paon *m* peacock.
papa *m* dad; daddy.
papauté *f* papacy.
papaye *f* papaya.
pape *m* pope.
papeterie *f* stationery; stationer's shop; paper mill.
papetier *m*, **-ière** *f* stationer; paper-maker.
papier *m* paper; article; wrapper.
papillon *m* butterfly.
papillote *f* sweet wrapper
papoter *vi* to chatter.
Pâques *fpl* Easter.
paquebot *m* liner, steamer.
pâquerette *f* daisy.
paquet *m* packet, pack; bag; parcel.
par *prép* by, with, through; from; along; **~-ci**, **~-là** here and there, now and then; **~-derrière** the back; **~-dessous** underneath; **~-dessus** over, above.
parabole *f* parabola; parable.
parachever *vt* to perfect; to complete.
parachute *m* parachute.
parachuter *vt* to parachute.
parachutiste *mf* parachutist.
parade *f* parade, show; parry.
paradis *m* paradise; gallery.
paradoxal *adj* paradoxical; **~ement** *adv* paradoxically.
paradoxe *m* paradox.
paraffine *f* paraffin.
parages *mpl*: vicinity; waters. **dans les ~** in the area.
paragraphe *m* paragraph; section.
paraître *vi* to appear; to be pub-

lished; to look, seem; **il paraît que** apparently.
parallèle *adj* parallel; **~ment** *adv* parallel; at the same time.
paralyser *vt* to paralyse.
paralysie *f* paralysis.
paralytique *mf* paralytic; * *adj* paralytic.
paramètre *m* parameter.
paranoïa *f* paranoia.
paranoïaque *adj* paranoiac, paranoid; * *mf* paranoiac, paranoid.
paraphraser *vt* to paraphrase.
parapluie *m* umbrella.
parasite *m* parasite, sponger.
parasol *m* parasol; sunshade.
paratonnerre *m* lightning conductor.
paravent *m* folding screen, partition.
parc *m* park; grounds; depot.
parcelle *f* fragment, particle; parcel.
parce que *conj* because
parchemin *m* parchment.
parcimonie *f* parsimony.
parcmètre *m* meter (parking).
parcourir *vt* to travel through; to scour; to traverse.
pardon *m* pardon, forgiveness.
pardonner *vt* to pardon; to excuse, overlook.
pare-brise *m invar* windscreen.
pare-chocs *m invar* bumper.
pareil *m*, **-eille** *f* equal; match **sans ~** unparalleled, unequalled; * *adj* like, equal, similar; identical; **~lement** *adv* likewise, equally.
parent *m*, **-e** *f* relative, relation; (*pl*) parents.
parental *adj* parental.
parenté *f* relationship, kinship.
parenthèse *f* parenthesis, digression.
parer *vt* to adorn, deck out; to ward off; to parry; **~ à** to deal with, overcome.
paresse *f* laziness; sluggishness.

paresseux *m*, **-euse** *f* lazy person, loafer; * *adj* lazy.

parfaire *vt* to perfect, bring to perfection.

parfait *adj* perfect, flawless; **~ement** *adv* perfectly; completely, absolutely.

parfois *adv* sometimes, occasionally.

parfumer *vt* to perfume, scent; **se ~** *vr* to use perfume.

parfumerie *f* perfumery.

parfumeur *m*, **-euse** *f* perfumer.

pari *m* bet, wager.

parier *vt* to bet, wager.

parking *m* car park; parking.

parlement *m* Parliament.

parlementaire *adj* parliamentary; * *mf* member of parliament.

parler *vi* to talk, speak; * *vt* to speak.

parmesan *m* parmesan (cheese).

parmi *prép* among.

parodie *f* parody.

paroi *f* wall; surface.

paroisse *f* parish.

parole *f* word; speech; voice; lyrics.

paroxysme *m* paroxysm; crisis.

parquer *vt* to park; to enclose, pen.

parquet *m* floor, floorboards.

parrain *m* godfather; patron; promoter.

parrainage *m* sponsorship; promoting; sponsorship.

parrainer *vt* to sponsor, propose.

parsemer *vt* to sprinkle, strew.

part *f* part; share; portion; **prendre ~ à** to participate in; **faire ~ de** to announce; **de sa part** for his part; **autre ~** elsewhere; **nulle ~** nowhere; **d'autre ~** moreover.

partage *m* sharing, distribution; portion.

partager *vt* to divide up, share out.

partenaire *mf* partner.

parti *m* party; option; match.

partial *adj* partial, biased; **~ement** *adv* in a biased way.

participant *m*, **-e** *f* participant, member; * *adj* participant, participating.

participation *f* participation; involvement.

participe *m* participle.

participer *vi* to take part in, participate.

particularité *f* particularity, characteristic.

particule *f* particle.

particulier *adj* particular, specific; peculiar, characteristic; * *m* person, private individual; character.

particulièrement *adv* particularly, especially.

partie *f* part; subject; game; party; **faire ~ de** to be a part of.

partiel *adj* part, partial; **~lement** *adv* partially, in part.

partir *vi* to leave, set off; to start up; **à ~ de** from.

partisan *m*, **-e** *f* partisan, supporter, proponent.

partition *f* partition; score.

partout *adv* everywhere.

parvenir *vi*: **~ à** to reach; to achieve.

pas *m* step; pace; footprint; gait; * *adv* no, not.

passable *adj* passable, tolerable; **~ment** *adv* tolerably; reasonably.

passage *m* passage, passing by; transit.

passager *m*, **-ère** *f* passenger; * *adj* passing, transitory.

passant *m*, **-e** *f* passer-by, wayfarer; * *adj* much frequented, busy.

passe *f* pass; permit; channel.

passé *m* past.

passeport *m* passport.

passer *vi* to pass; to elapse; to disappear, fade; **se ~** *vr* to pass; to take place; **se ~ de** to do without.

passerelle f footbridge; bridge; gangway.

passe-temps m *invar* pastime

passif *adj* passive; * m passive.

passion f passion; suffering; fondness.

passionnant *adj* fascinating; exciting.

passionné *adj* passionate, impassioned; **~ment** *adv* passionately.

passionner *vt* to fascinate; to interest deeply, impassion; **se ~** *vr* to be fascinated by, have a passion for.

passivement *adv* passively.

passivité f passivity, passiveness.

pastel m pastel.

pastèque f watermelon.

pasteur m minister, pastor.

pasteuriser *vt* to pasteurize.

pastiche m pastiche.

pastille f pastille, lozenge.

patate f (*fam*) spud; sweet potato.

patauger *vi* to wade about, splash about.

pâte f pastry, pasta, dough, batter.

pâté m pâté.

paternel *adj* paternal, fatherly; **~lement** *adv* paternally.

paternité f paternity; fatherhood.

pathétique *adj* pathetic.

patiemment *adv* patiently.

patience f patience, endurance.

patient *adj* patient, enduring.

patienter *vi* to wait.

patin m skate; **~ à glace** iceskate; **~ à roulettes** roller skate.

patinage m skating; slipping; spinning.

patiner *vi* to skate; to slip; to spin.

patineur m, **-euse** f skater.

patinoire f ice rink.

pâtisserie f cake shop, confectioner's.

pâtissier m, **-ière** f pastry cook, confectioner.

patois m patois, provincial dialect.

patrie f homeland, country.

patrimoine m inheritance, patrimony.

patriote mf patriot; * *adj* patriotic.

patriotisme m patriotism.

patron m owner, boss, proprietor. **-onne** f owner, boss, proprietress.

patronat m employers.

patronner *vt* to patronize, sponsor.

patrouille f patrol.

patte f leg, paw, foot.

pâturage m pasture, pasturage, grazing.

pâture f pasture; food.

paume f palm.

paumer *vt* (*fam*) to lose; **se ~** *vr* to get lost.

paupière f eyelid.

paupiette f stuffed slice of meat.

pause f pause; half-time.

pauvre *adj* poor; indigent; scanty; weak; **~ment** *adv* poorly; * mf poor person, pauper.

pavé m cobblestone, paving stone.

pavillon m house; pavilion; flag.

pavot m poppy.

paye f pay, wages.

payer *vt* to pay, settle; to reward.

pays m country; region; village; land.

paysage m landscape; scenery.

paysan m countryman, farmer, **-anne** f countrywoman.

P.D.G. (président-directeur général) m chairman and managing director.

péage m toll; tollgate.

peau f skin; hide, pelt.

pêche f peach; fishing.

pécher *vi* to sin.

pêcher *vt* to fish; to catch; * m peach tree.

pécheur m, **-eresse** f sinner

pêcheur m fisherman, **-euse** f fisherwoman.

pectoral *adj* pectoral; throat, cough.

pectoraux *mpl* pectorals.

pédagogie *f* education; educational methods.

pédagogue *mf* teacher; educationalist; * *adj* pedagogic.

pédale *f* pedal; treadle.

pédaler *vi* to pedal.

pédalier *m* pedal-board, crank-gear.

pédestre *adj* pedestrian.

pédiatre *mf* paediatrician.

pédicure *mf* chiropodist.

peigne *m* comb.

peigner *vt* to comb; to card; **se ~** *vr* to comb one's hair.

peignoir *m* dressing gown.

peindre *vt* to paint; to depict, portray.

peine *f* effort; sadness; pain; punishment; difficulty.

peiner *vi* to toil; to struggle.

peintre *m* painter; portrayer.

peinture *f* painting, picture; paintwork.

péjoratif *adj* pejorative.

pelage *m* coat, fur.

peler *vi* to peel.

pèlerin *m* pilgrim; peregrine falcon.

pèlerinage *m* pilgrimage.

pélican *m* pelican.

pelle *f* shovel; spade.

pellicule *f* film; thin layer.

pelote *f* ball; pelota.

peloton *m* pack; squad; platoon.

pelouse *f* lawn, field; ground.

pelure *f* peeling, piece of peel.

pénal *adj* penal; criminal.

pénaliser *vt* to penalize.

pénalité *f* penalty.

penalty *m* penalty (kick).

pencher *vi* to lean; to tilt; to list; * *vt* to tip up; tilt; **se ~** *vr* to bend down; to study, look at.

pendant *prép* during; for; **~ que** while, whilst; * *adj* hanging, drooping; pending.

pendentif *m* pendant; *(archit)* pendentive.

pendre *vi* to hang, dangle; * *vt* to hang; **se ~** *vr* to hang oneself.

pendule *f* clock; * *m* pendulum.

pénétrant *adj* penetrating, piercing; searching; acute.

pénétration *f* penetration; perception.

pénétrer *vi* to enter, penetrate; * *vt* to penetrate, pierce; to pervade.

pénible *adj* hard, tiresome; difficult; laborious; **~ment** *adv* painfully; with difficult

péniche *f* barge.

péniciline *f* penicillin.

péninsule *f* peninsula.

pénis *m* penis.

pénitence *f* penitence, penance; punishment.

pénitent *m*, **-e** *f* penitent; * *adj* penitent.

pénitencier *m* prison, penitentiary.

pénombre *f* half-light; penumbra.

pensée *f* thought; thinking; mind.

penser *vt* to think, suppose, believe; * *vi* to think.

pensif *adj* pensive, thoughtful.

pension *f* pension; boarding house.

pensionnaire *mf* boarder; lodger.

pensionnat *m* boarding school.

pensivement *adv* pensively, thoughtfully.

pentagone *m* pentagon.

pentathlon *m* pentathlon.

pente *f* slope; gradient.

Pentecôte *f* Pentecost.

pénurie *f* shortage, scarcity; penury.

pépère *m* granddad, grandpa.

pépin *m* pip; snag, hitch.

pépinière *f* tree nursery; breeding-ground.

pépite *f* nugget.

perçant *adj* piercing, shrill.

percée *f* opening, clearing; breach; breakthrough.

perce-oreille *m* earwig.

perception *f* perception; collection.

percer *vt* to pierce; to drill; to see through.

percevoir *vt* to perceive, detect; to collect.

percher *vt* to stick; to place on; **se ~** *vr* to perch.

percussion *f* percussion.

percussionniste *mf* percussionist.

percuter *vt* to strike; to crash into.

perdant *m*, **-e** *f* loser; * *adj* losing.

perdre *vt* to lose; to waste; to miss; * *vi* to lose; **se ~** *vr* to lose one's way.

perdrix *f* partridge.

perdu *adj* lost; wasted; missed.

père *m* father; sire.

péremptoire *adj* peremptory.

perfection *f* perfection.

perfectionnement *m* perfection, perfecting; improvement.

perfectionner *vt* to improve, perfect; **se ~** *vr* to improve, improve oneself.

perfectionniste *mf* perfectionist; * *adj* perfectionist.

perfide *adj* perfidious, treacherous; **~ment** *adv* perfidiously.

perforation *f* perforation.

perforer *vt* to perforate; to pierce.

performance *f* result, performance.

performant *adj* outstanding; high-performance, high-return.

péricliter *vi* to collapse; to be in jeopardy.

péril *m* peril, danger.

périlleux *adj* perilous.

périmé *adj* out-of-date; expired.

périmètre *m* perimeter.

période *f* period; epoch, era; wave, spell.

périodique *adj* periodic; **~ment** *adv* periodically.

péripétie *f* event, episode.

périphérie *f* periphery.

périphérique *adj* peripheral, outlying; * *m* ring road; peripheral.

périple *m* voyage; journey.

périr *vi* to perish, die.

périscope *m* periscope.

périssable *adj* perishable.

perle *f* pearl; bead; gem.

permanence *f* permanence; permanency.

permanent *adj* permanent, continuous.

permanente *f* perm.

permanenter *vt* to perm.

perméable *adj* permeable; pervious.

permettre *vt* to allow, permit; **se ~** *vr* to allow oneself.

permis *adj* permitted; * *m* permit, licence.

permission *f* permission; leave.

permutation *f* permutation.

permuter *vt* to change, switch round; to permutate.

pernicieux *adj* pernicious.

perpendiculaire *adj* perpendicular; **~ment** *adv* perpendicularly.

perpétuel *adj* perpetual; permanent; **~lement** *adv* perpetually.

perpétuer *vt* to perpetuate, carry on; **se ~** *vr* to be perpetuated; to survive.

perpétuité *f* perpetuity.

perplexe *adj* perplexed, confused.

perplexité *f* perplexity, confusion.

perquisition *f* search.

perquisitionner *vt* to make a search.

perron *m* steps, perron.

perroquet *m* parrot.

perruche *f* budgerigar; chatterbox.

perruque *f* wig.

persécuter *vt* to persecute; to harass.

persécution *f* persecution.

persévérance *f* perseverance.

persévérant *adj* persevering.

persévérer *vi* to persevere; to persist in.

persil *m* parsley.

persistance *f* persistence.

persistant *adj* persistent; evergreen.

persister *vi* to persist, keep up.

personnage *m* character, individual.

personnaliser *vt* to personalize.

personnalité *f* personality.

personne *f* person; self; appearance; **en ~** in person; * *pron* anyone, anybody; nobody.

personnel *adj* personal; selfish; **~lement** *adv* personally.

personnifier *vt* to personify.

perspective *f* perspective; view; angle.

perspicace *adj* shrewd, perspicacious.

perspicacité *f* insight, perspicacity.

persuader *vt* to persuade; to convince.

persuasif *adj* persuasive; convincing.

persuasion *f* persuasion; conviction.

perte *f* loss, losing; ruin.

pertinent *adj* pertinent.

perturbation *f* disruption; perturbation.

perturber *vt* to disrupt, disturb.

pervenche *f* periwinkle.

pervers *adj* perverse; perverted.

perversité *f* perversity.

pesant *adj* heavy, weighty; deep.

pesanteur *f* gravity; heaviness.

pèse-personne *m* scales.

peser *vt* to weigh; to press; to evaluate; * *vi* to weigh, weigh down; to hang over; **se ~** to weigh in.

pessimisme *m* pessimism.

pessismiste *mf* pessimist; * *adj* pessimistic.

peste *f* pest, nuisance; plague.

pesticide *m* pesticide.

pétale *f* petal.

pétanque *f* petanque.

pétard *m* firecracker; detonator; charge; racket, row.

pétillant *adj* bubbly, fizzy.

pétiller *vi* to crackle; to bubble; to sparkle.

petit *adj* small, tiny; slim; young.

petitesse *f* smallness, modesty; meanness.

petit-fils *m* grandson.

petite-fille *f* granddaughter.

pétition *f* petition.

petits-enfants *mpl* grandchildren.

pétrifié *adj* petrified; transfixed; fossilized.

pétrin *m* kneading trough; scrape, mess, tight spot.

pétrir *vt* to knead; to mould, shape.

pétrole *m* oil, petroleum.

pétrolier *m* oil tanker; * *adj* petroleum, oil, oil-producing.

pétrolifère *adj* oil-bearing.

pétunia *m* petunia.

peu *adv* little, not much, few; **un petit ~** a little bit; **quelque ~** a little; **pour ~ que** however little; **~ de** little, few.

peuplade *f* tribe, people.

peuple *m* people, nation; crowd.

peuplement *m* populating; stocking.

peupler *vt* to populate, stock; to plant.

peuplier *m* poplar.

peur *f* fear, terror, apprehension; **avoir ~** to be afraid.

peureux *adj* fearful, timorous.

peut-être *adv* perhaps.

phalange *f* phalanx.

phallocrate *m* male chauvinist.

pharaon *m* pharaoh.

phare *m* lighthouse; headlight.

pharmaceutique *adj* pharmaceutical.

pharmacie *f* pharmacy; pharmacology.

pharmacien *m*, **-ienne** *f* pharmacist; chemist.

pharynx *m* pharynx.

phase *f* phase, stage.

phénoménal *adj* phenomenal.

phénomène *m* phenomenon;

freak; character.

philanthrope *mf* philanthropist.

philatélie *f* philately, stamp collecting.

philologie *f* philology.

philosophe *mf* philosopher; * *adj* philosophical.

philosopher *vi* to philosophize.

philosophie *f* philosophy.

philosophique *adj* philosophical; **~ment** *adv* philosophically.

phobie *f* phobia.

phonétique *f* phonetics; * *adj* phonetic; **~ment** *adv* phonetically.

phoque *m* seal; sealskin.

phosphate *m* phosphate.

phosphore *m* phosphorus.

phosphorescent *adj* luminous, phosphorescent.

photo *f* photo.

photocopie *f* photocopy.

photocopier *vt* to photocopy.

photocopieur *m*, **photocopieuse** *f* photocopier.

photogénique *adj* photogenic.

photographe *mf* photograph.

photographie *f* photography.

photographier *vt* to photograph.

photographique *adj* photographic

phrase *f* sentence; phrase.

physicien *m*, **-ienne** *f* physicist.

physiologie *f* physiology.

physiologique *adj* physiological.

physionomie *f* countenance, physiognomy.

physionomiste *adj* good at remembering faces.

physiothérapie *f* physiotherapy.

physique *f* physics; * *adj* physical; **~ment** *adv* physically.

pianiste *mf* pianist.

piano *m* piano.

pic *m* peak; **à ~** vertically, sheer.

pichet *m* pitcher, jug.

picorer *vt* to peck; to nibble.

picot *m* picot, burr.

picotement *m* tickle; prickling.

picoter *vt* to tickle; to prickle; to

smart, sting.

pictural *adj* pictorial.

pie *f* magpie; chatterbox.

pièce *f* piece; object; component; room; paper, document.

pied *m* foot; track; hoof; bottom; **à ~** on foot; **être sur ~** to be underway.

pied-à-terre *m invar* pied-à-terre.

piédestal *m* pedestal.

piège *m* trap; pit; snare.

piéger *vt* to trap, set a trap.

pierre *f* stone.

piété *f* piety.

piétiner *vi* to stamp (one's foot); * *vt* to trample on.

piéton *m* pedestrian; * *adj* pedestrian.

pieu *m* post, stake, pile.

pieusement *adv* piously, devoutly.

pieux *adj* pious, devout.

pigeon *m* pigeon; dupe, mug.

pigment *m* pigment.

pigmentation *f* pigmentation.

pignon *m* gable; cogwheel.

pile *f* pile; pier; battery; * *adv* dead; just, right, exactly.

piler *vt* to crush, pound.

pilier *m* pillar.

pillage *m* pillaging, looting.

piller *vt* to pillage, loot.

pilon *m* pestle; wooden leg.

pilote *m* pilot; driver.

piloter *vt* to pilot, fly; to drive.

pilotis *m* pile, pilotis.

pilule *f* pill.

piment *m* pepper, capsicum.

pimenter *vt* to add spice.

pin *m* pine.

pince *f* crowbar; pincer; dart.

pinceau *m* brush, paintbrush.

pincée *f* pinch.

pincer *vt* to pinch, nip; to grip.

pinède *f* pine forest.

pingouin *m* penguin.

ping-pong *m* table tennis.

pintade *f* guinea-fowl.

pinte *f* pint.

pioche *f* pick, pickaxe.

piocher *vt* to use a pick; to swot.

piolet *m* ice axe.

pion *m* pawn; draught.

pionnier *m* pioneer.

pipe *f* pipe.

pipette *f* pipette.

piquant *adj* prickly; pungent; piquant; * *m* quill, spine; prickle.

pique *f* pike, lance.

pique-nique *m* picnic.

pique-niquer *vi* to picnic.

piquer *vt* to sting, bite; to goad; to puncture.

piquet *m* post, picket.

piqûre *f* prick; sting; bite.

pirate *m* pirate.

pire *adj* worse; **le ~, la ~, les ~s** the worst.

pirogue *f* pirogue, dugout canoe.

pirouette *f* pirouette; about-turn.

pis *m* udder.

pis-aller *m invar* last resort, stopgap.

piscine *f* swimming pool.

pissenlit *m* dandelion.

pistache *f* pistachio.

piste *f* track, trail; course; runway; lead, clue.

pistolet *m* pistol, gun.

piston *m* piston.

pistonner *vt* to pull strings for, recommend.

piteux *adj* pitiful, pathetic.

pitié *f* pity, mercy.

pitoyable *adj* pitiful, pitiable.

pittoresque *adj* picturesque.

pivoine *f* peony.

pivot *m* pivot; mainspring.

pivoter *vi* to revolve, pivot.

placard *m* cupboard; poster, notice.

place *f* place; square; seat; space; position; **à la ~ de** instead of.

placebo *m* placebo.

placement *m* placing; investment.

placenta *m* placenta; afterbirth.

placer *vt* to place, put; to fit; to seat; to sell; to invest; **se ~** *vr* to take up position; to stand; to find a job.

placide *adj* placid, calm.

placidité *f* placidity, calmness.

plafond *m* ceiling; roof.

plafonner *vi* to reach a ceiling/maximum.

plage *f* beach.

plagiat *m* plagiarism, plagiary.

plagier *vt* to plagiarize.

plaider *vt* to plead; to defend; * *vi* to plead for, go to court.

plaidoirie *f* defence speech; plea.

plaidoyer *m* defence speech; plea.

plaie *f* wound, cut; scourge.

plaignant *m*, **-e** *f* plaintiff.

plaindre *vt* to pity; to begrudge; **se ~** *vr* to complain.

plaine *f* plain.

plainte *f* complaint; moan, groan.

plaintif *adj* plaintive, complaining.

plaire *vi* to please, be pleasant; **se ~** *vr* to enjoy, take pleasure in.

plaisant *adj* pleasant, agreeable.

plaisanter *vi* to joke, jest.

plaisanterie *f* joking; pleasantry; humour.

plaisir *m* pleasure; delight; entertainment; **faire ~** to please.

plan *m* plan, scheme, project; plane, level.

planche *f* plank, board; plate; shelf.

plancher *m* floor.

planchette *f* small board, small shelf.

plancton *m* plankton.

planer *vi* to glide, soar; to hover over.

planétaire *adj* planetary.

planète *f* planet.

planeur *m* glider.

planifier *vt* to plan.

planisphère *m* planisphere.

planning *m* programme, schedule.

plantation *f* plantation; planting.

plante *f* plant.

planter *vt* to plant; to hammer in; to stick, dump.

plantureux *adj* copious, ample.

plaque *f* sheet, plate; plaque; slab.

plaqué *m* plated.

plaquer *vt* to plate, veneer; to jilt; to tackle.

plaquette *f* plaque; tablet; slab.

plasma *m* plasma.

plastifier *vt* to coat with plastic.

plastique *m* plastic; * *adj* plastic.

plat *adj* flat; straight; dull, insipid; **~ement** *adv* dully, insipidly; * *m* plate, dish; course.

platane *m* plane tree.

plateau *m* tray; turntable; plateau; stage.

plate-bande *f* border, flower-bed.

plate-forme *f* platform.

platine *m* platinum; * *f* deck; turntable; stage.

platitude *f* platitude; flatness, dullness.

platonique *adj* platonic.

plâtre *m* plaster.

plâtrer *vt* to plaster; to set in plaster.

plâtrier *m* plasterer.

plausible *adj* plausible.

plébiscite *m* plebiscite.

plébisciter *vt* to elect by plebiscite.

plein *adj* full; entire, whole; busy; **~ement** *adv* fully, in full; wholly; * *m* filling up; full house; height, middle.

plénitude *f* plenitude, fullness.

pléonasme *m* pleonasm.

pleur *m* tear, sob; **en ~s** in tears.

pleurer *vi* to cry, weep; * *vt* to mourn for, lament.

pleurésie *f* pleurisy.

pleuvoir *vi* to rain; to shower down, rain down.

plexus *m* plexus.

pli *m* fold; crease; wrinkle; envelope.

pliant *adj* collapsible, folding.

plier *vt* to fold; to bend; * *vi* to bend; to yield; **se ~** *vr* to fold up; to submit.

plinthe *f* plinth; skirting board.

plissement *m* creasing, folding; puckering.

plisser *vt* to pleat, fold; to pucker; * *vi* to become creased.

pliure *f* fold; bend.

plomb *m* lead; sinker; fuse.

plombage *m* weighting; leading; filling.

plomber *vt* to weight; to fill.

plomberie *f* plumbing.

plombier *m* plumber.

plongée *f* diving, dive.

plongeoir *m* diving board.

plongeon *m* dive.

plonger *vi* to dive; to plunge, dip sharply.

plongeur *m*, **-euse** *f* diver; washer-up.

ployer *vi* to bend, to sag.

pluie *f* rain; shower.

plumage *m* plumage, feathers.

plume *f* feather.

plumeau *m* feather duster.

plumer *vt* to pluck.

plupart *f* most, most part, majority **la ~ de** most of.

pluriel *m* plural; * *adj* plural.

plus *adv* more, most; **~ grand que** bigger than; **de ~ en ~** more and more; **de ~** besides, moreover; **non ~** neither, not either.

plusieurs *adj* several.

plus-que-parfait *m* pluperfect.

plus-value *f* appreciation; increase in value.

plutonium *m* plutonium.

plutôt *adv* rather, quite, fairly; sooner.

pluvieux *adj* rainy, wet.

pneu *m* tyre.

pneumatique *adj* pneumatic; * *m* tyre.

pneumonie *f* pneumonia.

poche *f* pocket; pouch; bag.

pocher *vt* to poach.

pochette *f* pocket handkerchief; wallet; envelope.

pochoir *m* stencil.
podium *m* podium.
poêle *m* stove; * *f* frying pan.
poème *m* poem.
poésie *f* poetry.
poète *m* poet.
poétique *adj* poetic; **~ment** *adv* poetically.
poids *m* weight, influence; **~ lourd** heavyweight; **~ plume** feather weight.
poignant *adj* poignant.
poignard *m* dagger.
poignarder *vt* to stab.
poigne *f* grip; hand.
poignée *f* handful; **~ de mains** handshake.
poignet *m* wrist; cuff.
poil *m* hair;coat; bristle.
poilu *adj* hairy.
poinçon *m* hallmark, style; awl.
poinçonner *vt* to stamp;to hallmark.
poindre *vi* to break, dawn; to afflict.
poing *m* fist; **coup de ~** punch.
point *m* point, spot; stage; full stop; **mettre au ~** to finalize; to perfect; **faire le ~** to take a bearing; **être sur le ~ de** to be about to; **à~** medium, just right, when due; **~~virgule** semicolon; **~ de vue** point of view.
pointage *m* checking off; sighting; scrutiny.
pointe *f* point, head; spike, tack; **tailler en ~** to cut to a point; **sur la ~ des pieds** on tiptoe.
pointer *vi* to clock in; to soar up; to peep out; * *vt* to check off; to clock in; to stick into.
pointillé *m* stipple engraving; dotted line.
pointilleux *adj* particular, fastidious.
pointu *adj* pointed, sharp; subtle.
pointure *f* size, number.
poire *f* pear.
poireau *m* leek.
poirier *m* pear tree.

pois *m* pea; **~ chiche** chickpea; **petits ~** garden peas.
poison *m* poison.
poisseux *adj* sticky.
poisson *m* fish.
poissonnerie *f* fishmonger's, fish shop.
poissonnier *m*, **-ière** *f* fishmonger.
poitrail *m* breast, chest.
poitrine *f* chest, breast; bosom.
poivre *m* pepper.
poivrer *vt* to pepper, put pepper in.
poivrière *f* pepperpot.
poivron *m* green pepper, capsicum.
polaire *adj* polar.
polariser *vt* to polarize; to attract.
polarité *f* polarity.
polaroïd *m* polaroid; * *adj* polaroid.
pôle *m* pole; centre.
polémique *f* controversy, polemic; * *adj* controversial, polemic.
poli *adj* polite; polished, smooth; **~ment** *adv* politely.
police *f* police; policing; regulations.
polichinelle *m* buffoon.
policier *m* policeman, **-ière** *f* policewoman.
poliomyélite *f* poliomyelitis.
polir *vt* to polish; to refine.
politesse *f* politeness, courtesy.
politicien *m*, **-ienne** *f* politician; * *adj* politicking.
politique *f* politics; policy; * *adj* political; **~ment** *adv* politically.
politiser *vt* to politicize; to make a political issue of.
pollen *m* pollen.
polluant *adj* polluting; * *m* pollutant.
polluer *vt* to pollute.
pollution *f* pollution.
polo *m* polo.
poltron *m*, **-onne** *f* coward; * *adj* cowardly, craven.

polyamide *m* polyamide.
polycopier *vt* to duplicate, stencil.
polyester *m* polyester.
polygame *m* polygamist.
polygamie *f* polygamy.
polyglotte *adj* polyglot; * *mf* polyglot.
polygone *m* polygon.
polymère *m* polymer; * *adj* polymeric.
polyvalent *adj* polyvalent; varied; versatile.
pommade *f* pomade; ointment.
pomme *f* apple.
pomme de terre *f* potato.
pommette *f* cheekbone.
pommier *m* apple tree.
pompe *f* pump.
pomper *vt* to pump.
pompeux *adj* pompous; pretentious.
pompier *m* fireman.
pompiste *mf* pump attendant.
poncer *vt* to sand down, rub down.
ponction *f* puncture.
ponctualité *f* punctuality.
ponctuation *f* punctuation.
ponctuel *adj* punctual; **~lement** *adv* punctually.
ponctuer *vt* to punctuate; to phrase.
pondéré *adj* weighted.
pondre *vt* to lay; to produce.
poney *m* pony.
pont *m* bridge; deck; axle.
ponte *f* laying; clutch.
pontifical *adj* pontifical.
ponton *m* pontoon; landing stage.
populaire *adj* popular; working-class; vernacular.
populariser *vt* to popularize.
popularité *f* popularity.
population *f* population.
porc *m* pig; pork.
porcelaine *f* porcelain.
porc-épic *m* porcupine.
porche *m* porch.
porcherie *f* pigsty.
pore *m* pore.

poreux *adj* porous.
pornographique *adj* pornographic.
port *m* port, harbour; pass; carrying, wearing.
portail *m* portal.
portatif *adj* portable.
porte *f* door; gate; threshold.
porte-avions *m invar* aircraft carrier.
porte-bagages *m invar* luggage rack.
porte-bonheur *m invar* lucky charm.
porte-clefs, porte-clés *m invar* key ring.
porte-documents *m invar* briefcase.
portée *f* reach, range; capacity; impact, significance; **à la ~ de** within reach; **hors de ~** out of reach.
portefeuille *m* wallet; portfolio.
porte-jarretelles *m invar* suspender belt.
portemanteau *m* coat hanger; hat stand.
porte-parole *m invar* spokesperson.
porte-plume *m invar* penholder.
porter *vt* to carry; to take; to wear; to hold, keep; **se ~** *vr* to put oneself forward; to go
porteur *m*, **-euse** *f* porter; carrier; * *adj* booster; strong, buoyant
portier *m* commissionaire.
portière *f* door.
portillon *m* gate, barrier.
portion *f* portion, share.
portique *m* portico.
portrait *m* portrait.
portraitiste *mf* portraitist.
pose *f* pose, posture; laying, fitting, setting.
poser *vt* to put; to install; to set out; to ask; **se ~** *vr* to land, settle; to come up, arise.
positif *adj* positive, definite.
position *f* position; situation; state; stance.

positionner *vt* to position, locate.

positivement *adv* positively.

posologie *f* posology.

posséder *vt* to possess, have; to know inside out.

possesseur *m* possessor, owner.

possessif *adj* possessive.

possession *f* possession, ownership.

possibilité *f* possibility; potential.

possible *adj* possible, feasible; potential; * *m*; **faire son ~** to do one's best.

postal *adj* postal, mail.

poste *f* post office, post; * *m* post, position; station; job.

poster *vt* to post, mail; to station; **se ~** *vr* to take up a position.

postérieur *adj* later, subsequent; back, posterior.

postérité *f* posterity; descendants.

posthume *adj* posthumous.

postiche *adj* false; postiche; pretended; * *m* hairpiece; toupee.

postier *m*, **-ière** *f* post office worker.

postillon *m* postilion.

postulant *m*, **-e** *f* applicant.

postuler *vt* to apply for; to postulate.

posture *f* posture, position.

pot *m* jar; pot; can.

potable *adj* drinkable; passable.

potage *m* soup.

potager *m* kitchen garden; * *adj* vegetable, edible.

potassium *m* potassium.

pot-au-feu *m invar* stew.

pot-de-vin *m* bribe.

poteau *m* post, stake.

potée *f* hotpot.

potelé *adj* plump, chubby.

potence *f* gallows; bracket.

potentiel *adj* potential; * *m* potential.

poterie *f* pottery, piece of pottery.

potiche *f* figurehead.

potier *m* potter.

potion *f* potion.

potiron *m* pumpkin.

pou *m* louse.

poubelle *f* dustbin.

pouce *m* thumb; big toe; inch.

poudre *f* powder, dust.

poudrer *vt* to powder.

poudrière *f* powder magazine.

poulailler *m* henhouse.

poulain *m* foal; protegé.

poule *f* hen, fowl.

poulet *m* chicken.

poulie *f* pulley.

poulpe *m* octopus.

pouls *m* pulse.

poumon *m* lung.

poupe *f* stern.

poupée *f* doll.

poupon *m* baby.

pouponnière *f* day nursery, creche

pour *prép* for; to; in favour of; on account of; in order; **~ que** so that, in order that; **être ~** to be in favour of.

pourboire *m* tip.

pourceau *m* pig, swine.

pourcentage *m* percentage.

pourchasser *vt* to pursue; to harry.

pourparlers *mpl* talks, negotiations.

pourpre *adj* crimson; * *m* crimson

pourquoi *adv* why; **~ pas?** why not?; * *m* reason, question.

pourri *adj* rotten, decayed; corrupt; * *m* rotten part, rottenness.

pourrir *vi* to rot, go rotten; to deteriorate.

pourriture *f* rot, rottenness

poursuite *f* pursuit; prosecution.

poursuivant *m*, **-e** *f* pursuer; plaintiff.

poursuivre *vt* to pursue; to seek; to prosecute.

pourtant *adv* however, yet, nevertheless.

pourtour *m* circumference, perimeter.

pourvoir *vt* to provide, equip.

pourvu *conj*: ~ **que** provided that.

pousse *f* shoot; sprouting.

poussée *f* pressure, pushing; thrust; upsurge.

pousser *vt* to push; to drive; to incite; * *vi* to push; to grow, expand; **se ~ vr** to move, shift.

poussette *f* push chair.

poussière *f* dust.

poussiéreux *adj* dusty.

poussin *m* chick; junior.

poutre *f* beam.

pouvoir *vi* can, be able; may, be allowed; * *m* power, ability; authority; proxy.

pragmatique *adj* pragmatic.

prairie *f* meadow, prairie.

pralin *m* praline.

praline *f* praline, sugared almond.

praticable *adj* practicable; passable.

pratiquant *m*, **-e** *f* churchgoer; * *adj* practising.

pratique *f* practice; exercise; observance; * *adj* practical; **~ment** *adv* practically.

pratiquer *vt* to practise, exercise; to carry out.

pré *m* meadow.

préalable *adj* preliminary; previous; **~ment** *adv* previously, first.

préambule *m* preamble, prelude.

préau *m* covered playground; inner yard.

préavis *m* notice, advance warning.

précaire *adj* precarious.

précarité *f* precariousness.

précaution *f* precaution; care.

précautionneux *adj* cautious, careful.

précédent *adj* previous, preceding; * *m* precedent.

précéder *vt* to precede, go before.

précepte *m* precept.

prêcher *vt* to preach; * *vi* to preach, sermonize.

prêcheur *m*, **-euse** *f* preacher.

précieux *adj* precious; invaluable.

précipice *m* precipice; abyss.

précipitamment *adv* hurriedly, hastily.

précipitation *f* haste, violent hurry.

précipiter *vt* to throw, push down; to hasten, precipitate; **se ~ vr** to rush forward; to speed up.

précis *adj* precise, exact; **~ément** *adv* precisely.

préciser *vt* to specify; to clarify; **se ~ vr** to become clear.

précision *f* precision, preciseness.

précoce *adj* precocious, premature.

préconçu *adj* preconceived.

préconiser *vt* to recommend; to advocate.

précurseur *m* forerunner, precursor; * *adj* precursory, preceding.

prédateur *m* predator.

prédécesseur *m* predecessor.

prédestiné *adj* predestined, fated.

prédiction *f* prediction.

prédire *vt* to predict, foretell.

prédisposition *f* predisposition.

prédominance *f* predominance.

prédominant *adj* predominant.

prédominer *vi* to predominate.

préfabriqué *adj* prefabricated.

préface *f* preface, prelude.

préfecture *f* prefecture.

préférable *adj* preferable; better; **~ment** *adv* preferably.

préféré *m*, **-e** *f* favourite; *adj* favourite, preferred.

préférence *f* preference.

préférer *vt* to prefer.

préfet *m* prefect.

préfigurer *vt* to prefigure.

préhistoire *f* prehistory.

préhistorique *adj* prehistoric.

préjudice *m* loss; harm; wrong; damage.

préjudiciable *adj* prejudicial, detrimental.

préjudicier *vt* to be prejudicial.

préjugé *m* prejudice.

prélasser(se) *vr* to sprawl, lounge.

prélèvement *m* taking; levying; imposition.

prélever *vt* to take; to levy; to deduct.

préliminaire *m* preliminary; * *adj* preliminary.

prélude *m* prelude; warm-up.

prématuré *adj* premature; untimely; **~ment** *adv* prematurely.

préméditation *f* premeditation.

prémédité *adj* premeditated.

premier *m* first, first floor, **-ière** *f* first, first gear; * *adj* first; former; chief; early; primary

première *f* première.

premièrement *adv* firstly, in first place.

prémonition *f* premonition.

prémonitoire *adj* premonitory.

prénatal *adj* prenatal.

prendre *vt* to take; to pick up; to catch; * *vi* to take root; to harden; to start; **se ~** *vr* to consider oneself; **s'y ~ mal** to set about the wrong way; **s'en ~ à** to set upon, take it out on.

prénom *m* first name, forename.

préoccuper *vt* to worry; to preoccupy; **se ~** *vr* to concern oneself.

préparatif *m* preparation.

préparation *f* preparation; making up; training.

préparatoire *adj* preparatory.

préparer *vt* to prepare, get ready; to train **se ~** *vr* to prepare oneself.

prépondérant *adj* preponderant, dominating.

préposition *f* preposition.

prérogative *f* prerogative.

près *adv* near, close; nearly, almost; **de ~** closely; **à peu ~** just about, near enough; **à peu de**

choses ~ more or less.

présage *m* omen, sign, presage.

presbytère *m* presbytery.

presbytie *f* long-sightedness, presbyopia.

prescrire *vt* to prescribe; to stipulate.

présélection *f* preselection.

présence *f* presence.

présent *m* present, gift **-e** *f* this letter, the present letter; * *adj* present; * *m* present; **à ~** just now.

présentable *adj* presentable.

présentateur *m*, **-trice** *f* host, compere; presenter.

présentation *f* presentation; introduction; **faire les ~s** to make the introductions.

présenter *vt* to introduce; to present; to explain; **se ~** *vr* to appear; to come forward; to introduce oneself.

présentoir *m* display shelf.

préservatif *m* condom.

préserver *vt* to preserve; to protect; **se ~** *vr* to protect oneself.

présidence *f* presidency; chairmanship.

président *m*, **-e** *f* president.

présidentiel *adj* presidential.

présider *vt* to preside, chair; to direct.

présomption *f* presumption, assumption.

présomptueux *adj* presumptuous.

presque *adv* almost, nearly; hardly, scarcely.

presqu'île *f* peninsula.

pressant *adj* urgent, pressing.

presse *f* press, newspapers; throng.

pressé *adj* hurried, urgent.

presse-citron *m invar* lemon squeezer.

pressentiment *m* presentiment, foreboding.

pressentir *vt* to have a presentiment of.

presse-papiers *m invar* paperweight.

presser *vt* to press; to squeeze; to hurry up; **se ~** *vr* to hurry; to crowd around.

pression *f* pressure.

pressoir *m* press (wine, cider)

prestation *f* benefit; service; payment; allowance.

prestidigitateur *m*, **-trice** *f* conjurer; magician.

prestige *m* prestige.

prestigieux *adj* prestigious.

présumer *vt* to presume; to assume.

prêt *adj* ready; prepared, willing; * *m* loan, lending.

prêt-à-porter *m* ready-to-wear.

prétendant *m*, **-e** *f* candidate.

prétendre *vt* to claim, maintain; to want; to intend, mean.

prétendu *adj* so-called, supposed; **~ment** supposedly, allegedly.

prétentieux *adj* pretentious.

prétention *f* pretension, claim; pretentiousness.

prêter *vt* to lend; to attribute; to give.

prétérit *m* preterite tense.

prétexte *m* pretext, excuse.

prêtre *m* priest.

preuve *f* proof, evidence.

prévaloir *vi* to prevail.

prévenant *adj* considerate, thoughtful.

prévenir *vt* to prevent; to warn, inform; to anticipate.

préventif *adj* preventive.

prévention *f* prevention.

prévisible *adj* foreseeable.

prévision *f* prediction; forecast.

prévoir *vt* to anticipate; to plan; to provide for.

prévoyance *f* foresight, forethought.

prévoyant *adj* provident.

prévu *adj* provided for.

prier *vi* to pray; * *vt* to pray to; to beg; to invite.

prière *f* prayer; entreaty.

primaire *adj* primary; elementary.

primate *m* primate.

primauté *f* primacy.

prime *f* premium, subsidy; free gift.

primer *vi* to dominate; to take first place; * *vt* to outdo; to prevail.

primeurs *fpl* early fruit and vegetable.

primevère *f* primrose.

primitif *adj* primitive.

primordial *adj* primordial, essential.

prince *m* prince.

princesse *f* princess.

principal *m* principal; headmaster; * *adj* main, principal; **~ement** *adv* principally.

principe *m* principle; origin; element; **en ~** in principle.

printanier *adj* spring.

printemps *m* spring.

prioritaire *adj* having priority, priority.

priorité *f* priority.

pris *adj* taken; busy, engaged.

prise *f* hold, grip; catch; plug; dose; **lâcher ~** to let go one's hold; **~ de sang** blood sample; **~ de courant** plug, power point; **~ de conscience** awareness, realization.

prisme *m* prism.

prison *f* prison; jail.

prisonnier *m*, **-ière** *f* prisoner; * *adj* captive.

privation *f* deprivation; forfeiture.

privatiser *vt* to privatize.

privé *adj* private; unofficial; independent.

priver *vt* to deprive; **se ~** *vr* to go without.

privilège *m* privilege.

privilégié *m*, **-e** *f* privileged person; * *adj* privileged, favoured.

privilégier *vt* to favour.

prix *m* price, cost; prize.

probabilité *f* probability, likelihood.

probable *adj* probable, likely; **~ment** *adv* probably.

problématique *adj* problematical; * *f* problem; problematics.

problème *m* problem, issue.

procédé *m* process; behaviour.

procéder *vi* to proceed.

procédure *f* procedure; proceedings.

procès *m* proceedings; lawsuit, trial.

procession *f* procession.

processus *m* process; progress.

procès-verbal *m* minutes; report.

prochain *adj* next; imminent; **~ement** *adv* soon, shortly; * *m* neighbour.

proche *adj* nearby; close, imminent.

proclamation *f* proclamation.

proclamer *vt* to proclaim, declare.

procuration *f* proxy, power of attorney.

procurer *vt* to procure, provide; **se ~** *vr* to procure, obtain for oneself.

procureur *m* prosecutor.

prodige *m* marvel, wonder.

prodigieusement *adv* prodigiously, incredibly.

prodigieux *adj* prodigious.

prodiguer *vt* to be lavish, be unsparing; to squander

producteur *m*, **-trice** *f* producer; * *adj* producing, growing.

productif *adj* productive.

production *f* production; generation; output.

productivité *f* productivity.

produire *vt* to produce; to grow;to generate; **se ~** *vr* to happen, take place.

produit *m* product; goods; yield, profit.

proéminent *adj* prominent.

profane *adj* secular, profane; * *mf* layman, lay person.

profaner *vt* to profane; to defile.

proférer *vt* to utter, pronounce.

professeur *m* teacher, professor.

profession *f* profession; occupation, trade.

professionnel *m*, **-elle** *f* professional; skilled worker; * *adj* professional; occupational; technical; **~lement** *adv* professionally.

profil *m* profile, outline.

profiler *vt* to profile; to streamline; **se ~** *vr* to stand out, be profiled.

profit *m* profit; advantage, benefit.

profitable *adj* profitable; **~ment** *adv* profitably.

profiter *vi* to profit; to thrive.

profiteur *m*, **-euse** *f* profiteer.

profond *adj* deep, profound; heavy; **~ément** *adv* deeply, profoundly.

profondeur *f* depth; profundity.

profusion *f* profusion, wealth; **à ~** plenty, in profusion.

programme *m* programme; syllabus; schedule.

programmer *vt* to programme; to schedule.

progrès *m* progress; improvement; advance.

progresser *vi* to progress; to advance.

progression *f* progress; progression, spread.

progressivement *adv* progressively.

prohiber *vt* to prohibit, ban.

proie *f* prey, victim.

projecteur *m* projector; spotlight, floodlight.

projectile *m* projectile; missile.

projection *f* projection, casting; showing.

projet *m* plan; draft.

projeter *vt* to plan; to throw out; to cast, project.

prolétaire *mf* proletarian.

prolétariat *m* proletariat.

prolifération *f* proliferation.

proliférer *vi* to proliferate.

prologue *m* prologue.

prolongation *f* prolongation, extension.

prolongement *m* continuation, extension.

prolonger *vt* to prolong, extend; **se ~** *vr* to go on, persist.

promenade *f* walk, stroll; drive, spin.

promener *vt* to take out for a walk; **se ~** *vr* to go for a walk.

promeneur *m*, **-euse** *f* walker.

promesse *f* promise.

prometteur *adj* promising.

promettre *vt* to promise.

promontoire *m* promontory, headland.

promoteur *m*, **-trice** *f* promoter, instigator.

promotion *f* promotion; advancement.

promouvoir *vt* to promote, upgrade.

prompt *adj* prompt; swift; ready; **~ement** *adv* promptly; swiftly.

promptitude *f* promptness; swiftness.

promulgation *f* promulgation.

promulguer *vt* to promulgate.

prôner *vt* to laud; to advocate.

pronom *m* pronoun.

prononcer *vt* to pronounce, utter; **se ~** *vr* to reach a verdict.

prononciation *f* pronunciation.

pronostic *m* forecast; prognosis; tip.

pronostiquer *vt* to forecast, prognosticate.

propagande *f* propaganda.

propagation *f* propagation; spreading.

propager *vt* to propagate, spread; **se ~** *vr* to spread, be propagated.

propane *m* propane.

prophète *m* prophet.

prophétie *f* prophecy.

prophétique *adj* prophetic.

prophétiser *vt* to prophesy.

propice *adj* propitious, favourable.

proportion *f* proportion, ratio.

proportionné *adj* proportional; proportionate.

proportionnel *adj* proportional; **~lement** *adv* proportionally.

propos *m* talk, remarks; intention; **à ~ de** about, on the subject of; **hors de ~** irrelevant.

proposer *vt* to propose, suggest; **se ~** *vr* to offer one's services; to intend to.

proposition *f* proposition, suggestion

propre *adj* clean, neat; honest; own; peculiar; suitable; **~ment** *adv* cleanly; exactly; specifically.

propreté *f* cleanliness; tidiness.

propriétaire *mf* owner; landlord.

propriété *f* ownership, property; appropriateness, suitability.

propulser *vt* to propel, power.

propulsion *f* propulsion.

prorogation *f* prorogation; deferment; extension.

proroger *vt* to prorogue; to defer; to extend.

prosaïque *adj* mundane, prosaic.

proscrire *vt* to proscribe; to prohibit.

prose *f* prose.

prospecter *vt* to prospect; to canvass.

prospecteur *m*, **-trice** *f* prospector.

prospection *f* prospecting; canvassing.

prospectus *m* leaflet; prospectus.

prospère *adj* prosperous, flourishing.

prospérer *vi* to prosper, flourish.

prospérité *f* prosperity.

prostate *f* prostate.

prosterner(se) *vr* to prostrate oneself.

prostituée *f* prostitute.

prostitution *f* prostitution.

prostré *adj* prostrate, prostrated.

protagoniste m protagonist

protecteur m, **-trice** f protector; patron; * adj protective; patronizing.

protection f protection; patronage.

protectionnisme m protectionism.

protégé m, **-e** f favourite, protegé; * adj protected, sheltered.

protéger vt to protect; to patronize; **se ~** vr to protect oneself.

protéine f protein.

protestant m, **-e** f Protestant; * adj Protestant.

protestantisme m Protestantism.

protestation f protest, protestation.

protester vi to protest; to affirm.

prothèse f prosthesis; prosthetics.

protocole m protocol; etiquette.

prototype m prototype.

protubérance f protuberance, bulge.

proue f prow; bows.

prouesse f prowess.

prouver vt to prove; to demonstrate.

provenir vi to come from; to be due to.

proverbe m proverb.

proverbial adj proverbial.

providence f providence.

providentiel adj providential.

province f province.

provincial m, **-e** f provincial; * adj provincial

provision f provision; supply, stock.

provisoire adj provisional, temporary; **~ment** adv provisionally.

provocant adj provocative.

provocation f provocation.

provoquer vt to provoke; to cause.

proximité f proximity, closeness; imminence.

prudemment adv prudently, carefully.

prudence f prudence, care.

prudent adj prudent, careful.

prune f plum.

pruneau m prune.

prunelle f sloe; pupil, eye.

prunier m plum tree.

psaume m psalm.

pseudonyme m pseudonym; pen name; alias.

psoriasis m psoriasis.

psychanalyse f psychoanalysis.

psychanalyser vt to psychoanalyse

psychanalyste mf psychoanalyst.

psychédélique adj psychedelic.

psychiatre mf psychiatrist

psychiatrie f psychiatry.

psychiatrique adj psychiatric.

psychique adj psychic, psychological.

psychisme m psyche, mind.

psychologie f psychology.

psychologique adj psychological; **~ment** adv psychologically.

psychologue mf psychologist; * adj psychological.

psychopathe mf psychopath; mentally ill person.

psychose f psychosis; obsessive fear.

psychosomatique adj psychosomatic.

psychothérapie f psychotherapy.

puberté f puberty.

pubis m pubis.

public adj, f **publique** public, state; * m public, audience; public sector.

publication f publication, publishing.

publicité f publicity.

publier vt to publish; to make public.

publiquement adv publicly.

puce f flea.

puceron m aphid, greenfly.

pudeur f modesty, decency.

pudique *adj* modest; chaste;
~**ment** *adv* modestly.
puer *vi* to stink; * *vt* to stink.
puéricultrice *f* paediatric nursing.
puéril *adj* puerile, childish;
~**ement** *adv* puerilely, child-
ishly.
puérilité *f* puerility, childishness.
puis *adv* then, next.
puiser *vt* to draw from, extract.
puisque *conj* since; as; seeing
that.
puissance *f* power, strength; output; force.
puissant *adj* powerful; potent.
puits *m* well; shaft.
pull-over *m* pullover, sweater.
pulluler *vi* to swarm, pullulate.
pulmonaire *adj* pulmonary, lung.
pulpe *f* pulp.
pulsation *f* beat; beating; pulsation.
pulsion *f* drive, urge.
pulvériser *vt* to pulverize; to
powder.
puma *m* puma.
punaise *f* bug.
punir *vt* to punish.

punition *f* punishment.
pupille *f* pupil; ward.
pupitre *m* desk; console; lectern.
pur *adj* pure; neat; clear; ~**ement**
adv purely.
purée *f* mashed potatoes; purée.
pureté *f* purity, pureness.
purge *f* purge; purgative; drain-
ing.
purger *vt* to purge; to drain.
purifier *vt* to purify, cleanse.
purin *m* liquid manure.
puritain *m*, -**e** *f* puritan; * *adj*
puritan.
puritanisme *m* puritanism.
pur-sang *m invar* thoroughbred.
purulent *adj* purulent.
pus *m* pus.
putois *m* polecat.
putréfaction *f* putrefaction.
putréfier *vt* to putrefy, rot.
pyjama *m* pyjamas.
pylône *m* pylon.
pyramide *f* pyramid.
pyrex *m* Pyrex.
pyromane *mf* pyromaniac; arsonist.
python *m* python.

Q

quadragénaire *adj mf* forty-
year-old.
quadrangle *m* quadrangle.
quadrature *f* quadrature.
quadriceps *m* quadriceps.
quadrilatère *m* quadrilateral.
quadrillage *m* covering, control;
check pattern.
quadriller *vt* to mark out in
squares; to cover, control.
quadrupède *adj m* quadruped.
quadruple *adj m* quadruple.
quai *m* quay, wharf; platform.
qualificatif *adj* qualifying.
qualification *f* qualification.

qualifier *vt* to describe; to qualify;
se ~ *vr* to qualify for; to call oneself.
qualitatif *adj* qualitative.
qualitativement *adv* qualita-
tively.
qualité *f* quality; skill; position.
quand *conj* when, whenever,
while.
quant *prep*: ~ **à lui** as for him, it.
quantifier *vt* to quantify.
quantitatif *adj* quantitative.
quantitativement *adv* quantita-
tively.
quantité *f* quantity, amount.

quarantaine *f* about forty; **avoir la ~** to be in one's forties.

quarante *adj, m inv* forty.

quarantième *adj, mf* fortieth.

quart *m* quarter; beaker; watch.

quartette *m* quartet.

quartier *m* district, neighbourhood; quarters; quarter.

quartz *m* quartz.

quasi *adv* almost, nearly.

quasiment *adv* almost, nearly.

quaternaire *adj* quaternary, *m* Quaternary.

quatorze *adj, m* fourteen.

quatorzième *adj, mf* fourteenth; **~ment** *adv* in fourteenth place.

quatre *adj, m* four.

quatre-vingt(s) *adj, m* eighty.

quatre-vingt-dix *adj, m* ninety.

quatre-vingtième *adj, mf* eightieth.

quatrième *adj, mf* fourth; **~ment** *adv* in fourth place.

quatuor *m* quartet.

que *conj* that; than; * *pron* that; whom; what; which.

quel, *f* **quelle** *adj* who, what, which.

quelconque *adj* some, any; least, slight; poor, indifferent.

quelque *adj* some; **~ part** somewhere.

quelque chose *pron* something.

quelquefois *adv* sometimes

quelqu'un, *f* **-une** someone, somebody, *pl* **quelques-uns, -unes** *pron* some, a few; il y a ~? is there someone there?

quémander *vt* to beg for.

querelle *f* quarrel; row; debate.

quereller (se) *vp* to quarrel, squabble.

question *f* question; matter, issue.

questionnaire *m* questionnaire.

questionner *vt* to question.

quête *m* quest, search; collection; **en ~ de** in search of.

quêter *vi* to seek; to collect money.

queue *f* tail; stalk; queue; **faire la ~** to queue.

qui *pron* who, whom; which.

quiche *f* quiche.

quiconque *pron* whoever, whosoever.

quiétude *f* quiet; peace; tranquillity.

quille *f* skittle; keel.

quincaillerie *f* hardware, ironmongery.

quinine *f* quinine.

quinquagénaire *adj mf* fifty-year-old.

quinquennal *adj* five-year, quinquennial.

quinquina *m* cinchona.

quinte *f* fifth (*mus*); coughing fit.

quintette *m* quintet.

quintuple *adj* quintuple; * *m* quintuple.

quintupler *vt* to multiply by five; * *vi* to quintuple, increase fivefold.

quintuplés *m pl*, **-ées** *f pl* quintuplets.

quinzaine *f* about fifteen; fortnight.

quinze *adj, m* fifteen.

quinzième *adj, mf* fifteenth; **~ment** *adv* in fifteenth place.

quiproquo *m* mistake; misunderstanding.

quittance *f* receipt; bill.

quitte *adj* even, quits; **être ~ envers** to be quits, all square with; **~ à** even if it means, although it may mean; **~ ou double** double or quits.

quitter *vt* to leave; to give up; **se ~** *vr* to part company, separate.

quoi *pron* what; **~ que** whatever.

quoique *conj* although, though.

quolibet *m* gibe, jeer.

quote-part *f* share.

quotidien *adj* daily, everyday; **~nement** *adv* daily, every day; * *m* everyday life.

quotient *m* quotient.

R

rabâcher *vi* to harp on, keep on;
  * *vt* to rehearse, harp on.
rabais *m* reduction, discount; **au
  ~** at a reduced price.
rabaisser *vt* to humble, disparage; to reduce; **se ~** *vr* to belittle oneself.
rabattre *vt* to close;to pull down;
  to reduce; **se ~** *vr* to cut across,
  pull in front of; **se ~ sur** to fall
  back on.
rabbin *m* rabbi.
rabot *m* plane.
raboter *vt* to plane; to scrape.
rabougri *adj* stunted, puny.
racaille *f* rabble, scum.
raccommodage *m* mending, repairing.
raccommoder *vt* to mend, repair.
raccompagner *vt* to see back to;
  to accompany home.
raccord *m* join; link; pointing.
raccordement *m* linking; joining; connecting.
raccorder *vt* to link up, join up;
  se ~ *vr* to link, join up.
raccourci *m* shortcut; **en ~** in
  miniature.
raccourcir *vt* to shorten, curtail;
  * *vi* to shrink; to grow shorter.
raccrocher *vt* to ring off; to hang
  up;to grab; **se ~** *vr* to catch; to
  cling to.
race *f* race; stock; breed.
rachat *m* repurchase, purchase.
racheter *vt* to repurchase; to redeem; to ransom.
rachitique *adj* rachitic; scrawny.
racial *adj* racial.
racine *f* root; **~ carrée** square
  root.
racisme *m* racism.
raciste *mf* racist; * *adj* racist.
racler *vt* to scrape; to rake.
racoler *vt* to accost; to solicit.
raconter *vt* to tell, recount.
radar *m* radar.

rade *f* harbour, roads.
radeau *m* raft.
radiateur *m* radiator; heater.
radiation *f* radiation.
radical *adj* radical; **~ement** *adv*
  radically.
radieux *adj* radiant, dazzling.
radin *m*, **-e** *f* skinflint; * *adj*
  mean, stingy.
radio *f* radio; X-ray.
radioactif *adj* radioactive.
radioactivité *f* radioactivity.
radiodiffuser *vt* to broadcast (radio).
radiodiffusion *f* broadcasting
  (radio).
radiographie *f* radiography; X-
  ray photography.
radiologie *f* radiology.
radiologue *mf* radiologist.
radiophonique *adj* radiote-
  lephony.
radioscopie *f* radioscopy.
radio-taxi *m* radio taxi.
radis *m* radish.
radium *m* radium.
radoter *vi* to ramble; to dote.
radoucir *vt* to soften; **se ~** *vr* to
  calm down; to mellow.
rafale *f* gust, blast; flurry.
raffermir *vt* to harden; to
  strengthen; **se ~** *vr* to become
  strengthened.
raffinage *m* refining.
raffiné *adj* refined, sophisticated.
raffinement *m* refinement, so-
  phistication.
raffiner *vt* to refine.
raffoler *vi*: **~ de** to be crazy about.
rafle *f* raid, round-up.
rafraîchir *vt* to cool, freshen,
  chill; **se ~** *vr* to freshen up; to
  get colder.
rafraîchissant *adj* refreshing,
  cooling.
rafraîchissement *m* cooling; cold
  drink.

rage f rage, fury; mania; rabies.

rageur adj quick-tempered; bad-tempered.

ragot m (fam) malicious gossip.

ragoût m ragout; stew.

raid m raid; trek.

raide adj stiff; steep; rough; broke.

raideur f stiffness; steepness; roughness.

raidir vt to stiffen; to tighten; to harden.

raie f line; furrow; scratch.

raifort m horseradish.

rail m rail; railway.

railler vt to scoff at, mock.

raillerie f mockery, scoffing.

railleur adj mocking, scoffing.

rainette f tree frog.

raisin m grape.

raison f reason; motive; sense; ground; ratio; **avoir ~** to be right; **en ~ de** because of.

raisonnable adj reasonable, sensible; **~ment** adv reasonably.

raisonnement m reasoning; argument.

raisonner vi to reason; to argue.

rajeunir vi to feel younger; to be modernized; * vt to rejuvenate.

rajouter vt to put in; to add; **en ~** to exaggerate.

rajuster vt to readjust, rearrange; to tidy up.

râle m groan; death rattle.

ralenti adj slow; slackened; * m slow motion; **au ~** ticking over, idling.

ralentir vi to slow down, let up; * vt to slow down, check.

ralentissement m slowing down; slowing up.

râler vi to groan, moan.

ralliement m rallying, winning over; uniting.

rallier vt to rally; to win over; **se ~** vr to join; to side with.

rallonge f extension, lengthening; extension lead.

rallumer vt to relight; to switch on again; to revive.

ramadan m Ramadan.

ramage m song; foliage.

ramassage m collection; gathering.

ramasser vt to pick up; to collect, gather.

rambarde f guardrail.

rame f oar; underground train; stake.

rameau m branch; ramification.

ramener vt to bring back, restore.

ramer vi to row.

rameur m, **euse** f rower.

ramification f ramification.

ramifier(se) vr to ramify; to branch out.

ramollir vt to soften; to weaken; **se ~** vr to go soft.

ramoner vt to sweep.

ramoneur m chimney sweep.

rampant adj crawling, creeping.

rampe f ramp, slope; gradient.

ramper vi to crawl, slither.

rance adj rancid, rank.

rancoeur f rancour, resentment.

rançon f ransom.

rancune f grudge, rancour.

rancunier adj rancorous, spiteful.

randonnée f drive; ride; ramble.

randonneur m, **-euse** f hiker, rambler.

rang m row, line; rank; class.

rangée f row, range, tier.

rangement m arranging, putting in order.

ranger vt to arrange, array; to put in order; **se ~** vr to line up; to make room; to park.

ranimer vt to reanimate, revive; to rekindle.

rapace m bird of prey.

rapatrié m, **-e** f repatriate; * adj repatriated.

rapatriement m repatriation.

rapatrier vt to repatriate.

râpe f rasp, rough file.

râper vt to grate; to rasp.

râpeux adj rough.

rapide *adj* rapid, quick; steep; **~ment** *adv* rapidly, quickly.

rapidité *f* rapidity, quickness.

rapiécer *vt* to patch up.

rappel *m* recall; reminder

rappeler *vt* to recall; to remind; **se ~** *vr* to remember.

rapport *m* report; relation; reference; profit; **en ~ avec** in touch with.

rapporter *vt* to report; to bring back; to yield; **se ~** *vr*: **se ~ à** to relate to.

rapporteur *m*, **-euse** *f* reporter; tell-tale; * *adj* tell-tale; * *m* protractor.

rapprochement *m* drawing closer; reconciliation.

rapprocher *vt* to bring nearer; to reconcile; **se ~** *vr* to approach; to come together, to be reconciled.

rapt *m* abduction.

raquette *f* racket.

rare *adj* rare; few, odd; exceptional; **~ment** *adv* rarely, seldom.

raréfier(se) *vr* to rarefy; become scarce.

rareté *f* rarity; scarcity; infrequency.

rarissime *adj* extremely rare.

ras *adj* close-shaven, shorn; **à ~** short; level with; **à ~ bords** to the brim; **en avoir ~ le bol** (*fam*) to be fed up.

rasage *m* shaving; shearing.

raser *vt* to shave off; to scrape; to raze; **se ~** *vr* to have a shave.

rasoir *m* razor.

rassasier *vt* to satisfy.

rassemblement *m* assembling, mustering; crowd; political group.

rassembler *vt* to rally, gather together; **se ~** *vr* to gather, assemble.

rasseoir(se) *vr* to sit down again.

rasséréner *vt* to clear up, restore serenity to.

rassis *adj* settled; calm; stale.

rassurant *adj* reassuring, comforting.

rassurer *vt* to reassure; to comfort; **se ~** *vr* to be reassured.

rat *m* rat.

ratatiner *vt* to shrivel; to wrinkle; **se ~** *vr* to become wrinkled.

ratatouille *f* ratatouille.

rate *f* spleen.

raté *m*, **-e** *f* failure; * *m* misfire.

râteau *m* rake.

râtelier *m* rack; denture.

rater *vt* to miss; to spoil; to fail; * *vi* to misfire; to miss.

ratification *f* ratification.

ratifier *vt* to ratify, confirm.

ration *f* ration, allowance.

rationnel *adj* rational.

rationnement *m* rationing.

rationner *vt* to ration, put on rations; **se ~** *vr* to ration oneself.

ratisser *vt* to rake; to comb.

rattacher *vt* to refasten; to attach; to link.

rattraper *vt* to catch again, retake; to recover; **se ~** *vr* to catch hold of; to make up for.

rature *f* deletion, erasure.

raturer *vt* to delete, erase.

rauque *adj* hoarse, raucous.

ravage *m* havoc; ravaging, laying waste.

ravager *vt* to ravage; devastate.

ravaler *vt* to swallow again; to restore.

ravi *adj* delighted.

ravin *m* ravine, gully.

ravir *vt* to delight.

raviser (se) *vr* to think better of it, change one s mind.

ravissant *adj* ravishing, delightful; ravenous.

ravitaillement *m* revictualling; refuelling.

ravitailler *vt* to revictual; to resupply; **se ~** *vr* to be resupplied; to refuel.

raviver *vt* to revive, reanimate; **se ~** *vr* to be revived.

rayer *vt* to scratch; to rule; to cross out.

rayon *m* ray, beam; spoke; shelf.

rayonnant *adj* radiant, beaming.

rayonnement *m* radiance, effulgence; influence.

rayonner *vi* to radiate, shine; to be influential.

rayure *f* stripe; streak; groove.

réaccoutumer *vt* to reaccustom; **se ~** *vr* to become reaccustomed.

réacteur *m* reactor; jet-engine.

réaction *f* reaction.

réactionnaire *adj* reactionary; * *mf* reactionary.

réactiver *vt* reactivate.

réadaptation *f* rehabilitation; readjustment.

réadapter *vt* to readjust; to rehabilitate.

réagir *vi* to react.

réalisateur *m*, **-trice** *f* director, film-maker.

réalisation *f* realization; carrying out; achievement.

réaliser *vt* to realize; to carry out; to achieve; **se ~** *vr* to be realized, come true.

réalisme *m* realism.

réaliste *adj* realistic; * *mf* realist.

réalité *f* reality; **en ~** in fact, in reality.

réanimation *f* resuscitation.

réanimer *vt* to reanimate; to resuscitate.

réapparaître *vi* to reappear.

rébarbatif *adj* stern, grim, forbidding.

rebattu *adj* hackneyed.

rebelle *mf* rebel; * *adj* rebel, rebellious.

rebeller(se) *vr* to rebel.

rébellion *f* rebellion.

reboisement *m* reafforestation.

reboiser *vt* to reafforest.

rebondir *vi* to bounce; to rebound.

rebondissement *m* rebound; bouncing.

rebord *m* rim, edge; hem.

rebrousser *vt* to brush back; **~ chemin** to turn back.

rébus *m* rebus, puzzle.

rebut *m* scrap; repulse, rebuff.

récalcitrant *adj* recalcitrant, stubborn.

récapituler *vt* to recapitulate, sum up.

receler *vt* to receive; to harbour.

récemment *adv* recently.

recensement *m* census, inventory.

recenser *vt* to make a census of; to record.

récent *adj* recent; new.

récépissé *m* receipt.

récepteur *m* receiver.

réceptif *adj* receptive.

réception *f* reception, welcome; receipt.

réceptionniste *mf* receptionist.

récession *f* recession.

recette *f* recipe; formula; receipt.

receveur *m*, **-euse** *f* recipient; collector.

recevoir *vt* to receive, welcome; to take, collect.

rechange *m*: change; spare **de ~** spare.

recharge *f* recharging; reloading.

rechargeable *adj* rechargeable; reloadable.

recharger *vt* to recharge; to reload.

réchaud *m* stove; dish-warmer.

réchauffer *vt* to reheat; to warm up; **se ~** *vr* to get warmer.

rêche *adj* rough, harsh.

recherche *f* search; inquiry; investigation; research; **être à la ~ de** to be in search of.

recherché *adj* sought after, in demand; choice, exquisite.

rechercher *vt* to seek; to investigate.

rechigner *vi* to look sulky; to balk.

rechute *f* relapse; lapse.

récidive *f* second offence, relapse into crime; recidivism.

récidiver *vi* to offend again; (*med*) to recur.

récidiviste *mf* recidivist, habitual criminal.

récif *m* reef.

récipient *m* container, receptacle.

réciproque *adj* reciprocal, mutual; **~ment** *adv* reciprocally.

récit *m* account, story.

récital *m*, *pl* **-als** recital.

récitation *f* recitation; recital.

réciter *vt* to recite.

réclamation *f* complaint; demand; claim.

réclame *f* advertisement; publicity; **en ~** on offer.

réclamer *vt* to claim, demand, ask for; * *vi* to complain.

reclus *adj* shut up, secluded.

réclusion *f* reclusion; confinement.

recoiffer *vt* to do somebody's s hair; **se ~** *vr* to do one s hair.

recoin *m* corner, nook.

recoller *vt* to restick.

récolte *f* harvest; collection; result.

récolter *vt* to harvest; to collect.

recommandation *f* recommendation, reference.

recommander *vt* to recommend; to commend; to register (letter).

recommencement *m* renewal; fresh beginning.

recommencer *vi* to begin again; * *vt* to begin again, resume.

récompense *f* reward; award.

réconciliation *f* reconciliation.

réconcilier *vt* to reconcile; **se ~** *vr* to become reconciled.

reconduire *vt* to bring back; to see home, escort.

réconfort *m* comfort.

réconfortant *adj* comforting; tonic.

réconforter *vt* to comfort; to fortify; **se ~** *vr* to take some refreshment.

reconnaissance *f* recognition; acknowledgement; gratitude.

reconnaissant *adj* grateful.

reconnaître *vt* to recognize; to acknowledge; to be grateful.

reconnu *adj* recognized, accepted.

reconquérir *vt* to reconquer; to recover.

reconsidérer *vt* to reconsider.

reconstituer *vt* to reconstitute; rebuild, restore.

reconstitution *f* reconstitution; rebuilding, restoration.

reconstruire *vt* to reconstruct, rebuild.

reconversion *f* reconversion, redeployment.

recopier *vt* to copy again.

record *m* record.

recoudre *vt* to sew up again.

recoupement *m* crosscheck.

recourbé *adj* curved, hooked.

recourir *vi* to run again ~ **à** to appeal.

recours *m* recourse; redress; appeal.

recouvrir *vt* to cover again; to cover up.

récréatif *adj* recreative; entertaining.

récréation *f* recreation; break.

récrimination *f* recrimination, remonstration.

récriminer *vi* to recriminate, remonstrate.

recroqueviller(se) *vr* to shrivel up.

recrudescence *f* recrudescence; upsurge; further outbreak.

recrue *f* recruit.

recrutement *m* recruiting, recruitment.

recruter *vt* to recruit.

rectal *adj* rectal.

rectangle *m* rectangle.

rectangulaire *adj* rectangular.

recteur *m* priest, rector.

rectificatif *m* correction; * *adj* corrected, rectified.

rectification *f* rectification; correction.

rectifier *vt* to rectify, correct; to adjust.

rectiligne *adj* straight; rectilinear.

recto *m* recto, first side; front .

rectum *m* rectum.

reçu *p.p.* **recevoir** accepted, successful; * *m* receipt.

recueil *m* collection, miscellany.

recueillement *m* meditation.

recueillir *vt* to gather, collect; to record; **se ~** *vr* to collect one s thoughts.

recul *m* retreat; recession; decline.

reculer *vi* to fall back, retreat; * *vt* to move back; to defer.

récupération *f* recovery; retrieval.

récupérer *vt* to recover, retrieve; to recuperate; * *vi* to recover.

récurer *vt* to scour.

recycler *vt* to recycle.

rédacteur *m*, **-trice** *f* editor, compiler; drafter; writer; sub-editor.

rédaction *f* drafting, drawing up.

rédemption *f* redemption.

redescendre *vi* to go down again; * *vt* to bring down again, go down again.

redevable *adj* indebted, owing; liable.

redevance *f* rent; tax; fees.

rediffusion *f* repeat, reshowing.

rédiger *vt* to write; to compile; to draft.

redire *vt* to repeat, say again; **trouver à ~ à** to find fault with.

redoubler *vt* to increase, intensify; * *vi* to increase, intensify; **~ de** to redouble.

redoutable *adj* redoubtable, formidable.

redouter *vt* to dread, fear.

redresser *vt* to rectify; to true; to set up again; **se ~** *vr* to stand up; to right itself.

réduction *f* reduction; discount; mitigation.

réduire *vt* to reduce, diminish; **se ~** *vr*: **se ~ à** to boil down to.

réduit *adj* reduced, limited; miniature; * *m* retreat; recess; small room.

rééducation *f* re-education; rehabilitation.

rééduquer *vt* to re-educate; to rehabilitate.

réel *adj* real, genuine; **~lement** *adv* really.

réélire *vt* to re-elect.

rééquilibrer *vt* to restabilize.

réévaluer *vt* to revalue.

refaire *vt* to redo; to remake; to renew.

réfectoire *m* canteen, refectory.

référence *f* reference.

référendum *m* referendum.

refermer *vt* to close again.

réfléchi *adj* well-considered; reflective, thoughtful.

réfléchir *vi* to think, reflect; * *vt* to realize; to mirror.

reflet *m* reflection; reflex.

refléter *vt* to reflect, mirror.

réflexe *m* reflex.

réflexion *f* thought, reflection; remark; **à la ~** on reflection; **~ faite** all things considered.

reflux *m* reflux, ebb.

réforme *f* reform, amendment; discharge.

réformer *vt* to reform, correct; to invalid out; to scrap.

refouler *vt* to drive back, repel.

réfraction *f* refraction.

refrain *m* refrain, chorus.

réfréner *vt* to curb, hold in check.

réfrigérateur *m* refrigerator.

réfrigérer *vt* to refrigerate.

refroidir *vt* to cool; * *vi* to cool down, get cold.

refroidissement *m* cooling; chill.

refuge *m* refuge, shelter; lay-by.

réfugié *m*, **-e** *f* refugee; * *adj* refugee.

réfugier(se) *vr* to take refuge.

refus *m* refusal.

refuser *vt* to refuse; to reject; to deny; **se ~** *vr* to deny oneself; **se ~ à** to reject.

réfuter *vt* to refute.

regagner *vt* to regain, win back.

regain *m* renewal; revival.

régal *m* delight, treat.

régaler *vt* to regale; to treat; **se ~ vr** to treat oneself.

regard *m* look; glance; expression; peephole.

regardant *adj* particular, meticulous; stingy.

regarder *vt* to look at; to glance; to be opposite; to concern; **~ à to** think about.

régates *fpl* regattas.

régénération *f* regeneration.

régénérer *vt* to regenerate, revive.

régent *m*, **-e** *f* regent.

régenter *vt* to rule over, domineer.

régie *f* administration; state control.

régime *m* system, régime; scheme; diet; rate, speed.

régiment *m* regiment.

région *f* region, area.

régional *adj* regional.

régir *vt* to govern, rule.

régisseur *m* manager; steward; bailiff.

registre *m* register, record; style; compass.

réglable *adj* adjustable.

réglage *m* regulation, adjustment; tuning.

règle *f* rule; order; regularity; period.

règlement *m* regulation, rules; settlement.

réglementaire *adj* regulation; statutory.

réglementation *f* regulations; control.

réglementer *vt* to regulate, control.

régler *vt* to settle, pay; to regulate.

réglisse *f* liquorice.

règne *m* reign.

régner *vi* to reign; to prevail.

regorger *vi*: **~ de** to overflow with, abound in.

régresser *vi* to regress; to recede.

régression *f* regression.

regret *m* regret, yearning; **à ~** regretfully.

regrettable *adj* regrettable.

regretter *vt* to regret, be sorry; to miss.

regroupement *m* gathering together; reassembly

regrouper *vt* to group together; to reassemble; **se ~ vr** to assemble.

régulariser *vt* to regularize; straighten out.

régularité *f* regularity; consistency.

régulier *adj* regular; consistent; steady; even; legitimate.

régulièrement *adv* regularly; consistently; lawfully.

réhabilitation *f* rehabilitation; discharge; reinstatement.

réhabiliter *vt* to rehabilitate; to discharge; to reinstate.

réhabituer *vt* to reaccustom somebody to; **se ~ vr** to reaccustom oneself to.

rehausser *vt* to heighten, raise.

rein *m* kidney.

réincarnation *f* reincarnation.

reine *f* queen.

reine-claude *f* greengage.

réinsertion *f* reinsertion, reintegration.

réintégrer *vt* to reinstate; to return to.

réitérer *vt* to reiterate, repeat.

rejaillir *vi* to gush out; to rebound on.

rejet *m* rejection, dismissal; throwing up.

rejeter *vt* to reject, dismiss; throw up.

rejoindre *vt* to rejoin; to catch up with.

rejouer *vt* to replay; to perform again; * *vi* to play again.

réjouir *vt* to delight; to entertain;

se ~ *vr* to rejoice, be delighted.

réjouissance *f* rejoicing, merry-making.

relâche *f* intermission, respite; **faire ~** to be closed; **sans ~** without intermission.

relâchement *m* relaxation, loosening; laxity.

relâcher *vt* to relax, slacken; **se ~ vi** to relax; to become lax.

relais *m* relay; shift; staging post.

relatif *adj* relative; relating to.

relation *f* relation, relationship; reference; acquaintance; account; **être en ~ avec** to be in contact with.

relativement *adv* relatively.

relativisme *m* relativism.

relativité *f* relativity.

relaxant *adj* relaxing.

relaxation *f* relaxation.

relaxer *vt* to relax; to acquit; to release; **se ~** *vr* to relax.

relayer *vt* to relieve, take the place of; to relay; **se ~** *vr* to take turns.

relecture *f* rereading.

reléguer *vt* to relegate; to banish.

relève *f* relief; relief party.

relevé *m* statement; list; bill; * *adj* turned up, rolled up; elevated.

relever *vt* to set up again, raise again, right; to rebuild; to relieve; **se ~** *vr* to stand up again; to get up.

relief *m* relief; contours; depth.

relier *vt* to link up, connect; to bind.

religieux *m* monk, **-euse** *f* nun; * *adj* religious.

religion *f* religion.

relique *f* relic.

relire *vt* to reread.

reliure *f* binding; bookbinding.

reluire *vi* to gleam, shine.

remaniement *m* recasting; altering; revision; amendment.

remanier *vt* to recast, revise; to amend.

remarquable *adj* remarkable, notable; **~ment** *adv* remarkably.

remarque *f* remark, comment.

remarquer *vt* to remark; to notice.

rembourrer *vt* to stuff; to pad.

remboursement *m* reimbursement, repayment.

rembourser *vt* to reimburse, pay back.

remède *m* remedy, cure.

remédier *vi*: **~ à** to remedy, cure.

remerciement *m* thanks; thanking.

remercier *vt* to thank.

remettre *vt* to put back; to replace; to restart; to revive; **se ~ vr** to recover, get better; **se ~ à** to start doing something again; **se ~ de** to get over something.

réminiscence *f* reminiscence.

remise *f* delivery; remittance; discount; deferment; **~ en état** repairing; **~ à neuf** restoration; **~ en jeu** throw-in; **~ en question** calling into question; **~ en cause** calling into question; **~ de peine** reduction in sentence.

remmener *vt* to take back.

remontant *m* tonic; * *adj* invigorating, fortifying.

remonte-pente *m* ski tow.

remonter *vi* to go up again; to rise, increase; to return; * *vt* to go up; to take up.

remontrance *f* remonstrance.

remords *m* remorse.

remorque *f* trailer; towrope.

remorquer *vt* to tow.

remorqueur *m* tug.

rémouleur *m* knife-grinder.

remous *m* back-wash; eddy, swirl.

rempailler *vt* to reseat (chair).

rempart *m* rampart; defence.

remplaçant *m*, **-e** *f* replacement.

remplacement *m* replacing; substitution.

remplacer *vt* to replace; stand in for.

remplir *vt* to fill; to fill in; to fulfil; **se ~** *vr* to fill up.

remplissage *m* filling up; padding.

remporter *vt* to take away.

remuant *adj* restless, fidgety.

remue-ménage *m invar* commotion; hullabaloo.

remuer *vi* to move; to fidget; * *vt* to move, shift; to stir; **se ~** *vr* to move; to shift oneself.

rémunération *f* remuneration, payment.

rémunérer *vt* to remunerate, pay.

renaissance *f* rebirth, Renaissance.

renaître *vi* to be reborn; to be revived; to reappear.

renard *m* fox.

renchérir *vi* to go further, go one better; to bid higher.

renchérissement *m* increase in price.

rencontre *f* meeting, encounter; conjuncture; collision.

rencontrer *vt* to meet; to find; to strike; **se ~** *vr* to meet each other.

rendement *m* yield; output.

rendez-vous *m* appointment; date; meeting place.

rendormir *vt* to put to sleep again; **se ~** *vr* to go back to sleep.

rendre *vt* to render; to give back, return; to yield; **se ~** *vr* to surrender; to give way.

rêne *f* rein.

renfermé *adj* withdrawn, close; * *m* fusty/close smell.

renfermer *vt* to contain, hold.

renflement *m* bulge.

renflouer *vt* to refloat; to bail out.

renfoncement *m* recess.

renfoncer *vt* to drive further in; to recess.

renforcer *vt* to strengthen, reinforce.

renfort *m* reinforcement; help.

renfrogné *adj* frowning, glum.

renier *vt* to repudiate, disown.

renifler *vt* to sniff, snuffle.

renne *m* reindeer.

renom *m* renown, fame.

renommée *f* renowned, famed.

renoncement *m* renouncement; renunciation.

renoncer *vi* to renounce, give up.

renonciation *f* renunciation; waiver.

renouer *vt* to tie again; to renew.

renouveau *m* spring; renewal.

renouveler *vt* to renew; to revive; **se ~** *vr* to be renewed.

renouvellement *m* renewal; revival.

rénovation *f* renovation; renewal.

rénover *vt* to renovate.

renseignement *m* information; intelligence.

renseigner *vt* to inform, give information to; **se ~** *vr* to ask for information.

rentabiliser *vt* to make profitable.

rentable *adj* profitable.

rente *f* rent; profit; annuity.

rentier *m*, **-ière** *f* stockholder, fundholder; rentier.

rentrée *f* reopening; reassembly; reappearance.

rentrer *vi* to re-enter; to return home; to begin again; * *vt* to bring in.

renversement *m* inversion; reversal; overturning.

renverser *vt* to turn upside down; to reverse; to overturn.

renvoi *m* sending back; returning; dismissal.

renvoyer *vt* to send back; to return;to dismiss.

réorganisation *f* reorganization.

réorganiser *vt* to reorganize.

réouverture *f* reopening.

repaire *m* den, lair.

répandre *vt* to pour out; to scatter, spread; **se ~** *vr* to spread; to be spilled.

répandu *adj* widespread.

réparateur *m*, **-trice** *f* repairer.

réparation *f* repairing; restoration.

réparer *vt* to repair; to restore; to make up for.

repartie *f* retort **avoir de la ~ to** be quick at repartee.

repartir *vi* to set off again; to start up again.

répartir *vt* to share out; to distribute; **se ~** *vr* to be divided.

répartition *f* sharing out; allocation.

repas *m* meal.

repassage *m* ironing; grinding, sharpening.

repasser *vt* to cross again; to resit; * *vi* to go past again.

repêcher *vt* to fish out, retrieve.

repeindre *vt* to repaint.

repenti *adj* repentant.

repentir *m* repentance, contrition.

repentir(se) *vr* to repent, rue.

répercussion *f* repercussion.

répercuter *vt* to reverberate; to echo; **se ~** *vr* to reverberate; to echo.

repère *m* line, mark; **point de ~** indication, reference mark.

repérer *vt* to spot, pick out; to mark out.

répertoire *m* index, catalogue; repertory.

répertorier *vt* to itemize; to index.

répéter *vt* to repeat; to rehearse; **se ~** *vr* to repeat oneself; to reoccur.

répétitif *adj* repetitive.

répétition *f* repetition; rehearsal.

repiquer *vt* to plant out, transplant.

répit *m* respite, rest.

repli *m* fold, coil, meander; withdrawal; downturn.

replier *vt* to fold up; to withdraw; **se ~** *vr* to coil up, curl up.

réplique *f* reply, retort; counterattack.

répliquer *vt* to reply; to retaliate.

répondant *m*, **-e** *f* guarantor; bail, surety.

répondeur *m* answering machine.

répondre *vt* to answer, reply.

réponse *f* response, reply.

report *m* postponement, deferment; carrying forward.

reportage *m* report; commentary; reporting.

reporter *vt* to take back; to carry forward; to transfer; * *m* reporter.

repos *m* rest; tranquillity; landing.

reposant *adj* restful, refreshing.

reposer *vt* to put back; to rest; to ask again; **se ~** *vr* to rest oneself.

repoussant *adj* repulsive; repellent.

repousser *vt* to push again; to repel.

reprendre *vt* to retake, recapture; to resume; **se ~** *vr* to correct oneself; to pull oneself together.

représailles *fpl* reprisals; retaliation.

représentant *m* representative.

représentatif *adj* representative.

représentation *f* representation; performance.

représenter *vt* to represent, depict; to perform; to symbolize.

répressif *adj* repressive.

répression *f* repression.

réprimande *f* reprimand, rebuke.

réprimander *vt* to reprimand, rebuke.

réprimer *vt* to repress; to quell.

reprise *f* resumption; recapture, taking back; **à plusieurs ~s** several times.

repriser *vt* to darn.

réprobation *f* reprobation.

reproche *m* reproach; objection.

reprocher *vt* to reproach, blame.

reproduction *f* reproduction; copy; duplicate.

reproduire *vt* to reproduce, copy; to repeat; **se ~** *vr* to reproduce, breed.

reptile *m* reptile.

repu *adj* full, satiated.

républicain *m*, **-e** *f* republican; * *adj* republican.

république *f* republic.

répudier *vt* to repudiate; to renounce.

répugnance *f* repugnance, disgust.

répugnant *adj* repugnant, disgusting.

répulsion *f* repulsion, repugnance.

réputation *f* reputation; character; fame.

réputé *adj* reputable, renowned; supposed, reputed.

requérir *vt* to call for, request.

requête *f* petition, request.

requin *m* shark.

requis *adj* required, requisite.

réquisition *f* requisition; conscription.

réquisitionner *vt* to requisition; to conscript.

rescapé *m*, **-e** *f* survivor.

réseau *m* network, net.

réservation *f* reservation, booking.

réserve *f* reserve; reservation, caution.

réservé *f* reserved.

réserver *vt* to reserve, save; to book; to lay by.

réservoir *m* tank; reservoir.

résidence *f* residence; apartment block.

résidentiel *adj* residential

résider *vi* to reside, dwell.

résidu *m* residue.

résignation *f* resignation.

résigner(se) *vr* to resign oneself.

résilier *vt* to terminate; to annul.

résine *f* resin.

résistance *f* resistance.

résistant *adj* resistant; tough, unyielding.

résister *vi* to resist, withstand.

résolu *adj* resolved, determined; **~ment** *adv* resolutely.

résolution *f* resolution, determination; solution.

résonner *vi* to resound, resonate.

résorber *vt* to reduce; to absorb; **se ~** *vr* to be reduced.

résoudre *vt* to solve; to resolve; to annul; **se ~** *vr*: **se ~ à** to decide to do.

respect *m* respect, regard, deference.

respectable *adj* respectable; sizeable.

respecter *vt* to respect; to comply with.

respectif *adj* respective.

respectivement *adv* respectively.

respectueusement *adv* respectfully.

respectueux *adj* respectful.

respirable *adj* breathable.

respiration *f* breathing, respiration.

respiratoire *adj* respiratory.

respirer *vi* to breathe, respire; to rest; * *vt* to breathe in.

resplendissant *adj* shining, radiant.

responsabilité *f* responsibility; liability.

responsable *adj* responsible; liable; * *mf* official, manager.

resquiller *vi* to sneak in; to take a free ride.

ressaisir(se) *vr* to regain one s self-control.

ressemblance *f* resemblance, likeness; similarity.

ressemblant *adj* lifelike.

ressembler *vi* to resemble, be like; **se ~** *vr* to be alike.

ressemelage *m* soling, resoling.

ressentiment *m* resentment.

ressentir *vt* to feel, experience; **se ~** *vr*: **se ~ de** to feel the effects of.

resserrement *m* contraction, tightening; narrowing.

resserrer *vt* to tighten; to strengthen; **se ~** *vr* to grow tighter.

ressort *m* spring; motivation.

ressortir *vi* to go out again; to stand out.

ressortissant *m*, **-e** *f* national.

ressource *f* resource, resort, expedient.

ressusciter *vi* to revive, reawaken; to come back to life; * *vt* to resuscitate; to revive.

restant *adj* remaining; * *m* rest, remainder.

restaurant *m* restaurant.

restaurateur *m*, **-trice** *f* restaurateur; restorer

restauration *f* restoration, rehabilitation; catering.

restaurer *vt* to restore; to feed; **se ~** *vr* to take refreshment.

reste *m* rest, left-over, remainder; **du ~** besides; **être en ~** to be outdone.

rester *vi* to remain, stay; to be left; to continue; to pause.

restituer *vt* to return, restore; to refund.

restitution *f* restoration; restitution.

restreindre *vt* to restrict, curtail; **se ~** *vr* to restrain oneself.

restreint *adj* restricted, limited.

restrictif *adj* restrictive.

restriction *f* restriction, limitation; reserve.

restructurer *vt* to restructure.

résultat *m* result, outcome; profit.

résulter *vi*: **~ de** to result, follow from, ensue.

résumé *m* summary, recapitulation; **en ~** in brief.

résumer *vt* to sum up; **se ~** *vr*: **se ~ à** to amount to.

résurrection *f* resurrection.

rétablir *vt* to re-establish, restore; **se ~** *vr* to recover, get well again.

rétablissement *m* re-establishment, restoring.

retard *m* lateness; delay; **être en ~** to be behind; to be backward.

retardataire *mf* latecomer; * *adj* obsolete.

retardé *adj* backward, slow.

retarder *vt* to delay; to hinder; to put back; * *vi* to be out of touch.

retenir *vt* to hold back, retain; to remember; **se ~** *vr* to control oneself.

rétention *f* retention; withholding.

retentir *vi* to resound; to ring.

retentissant *adj* resounding; ringing.

retenue *f* discretion; deduction, stoppage; reservoir.

réticence *f* reticence.

réticent *adj* reticent.

rétine *f* retina.

retiré *adj* remote, isolated.

retirer *vt* to take off; to take out, withdraw; to redeem; **se ~** *vr* to retire, withdraw; to stand down.

retombée *f* fallout; repercussions.

retomber *vi* to fall again; to have a relapse; **~ sur** to come across.

rétorquer *vt* to retort.

retouche *f* touching up; alteration.

retoucher *vt* to touch up; to alter.

retour *m* return; recurrence; vicissitude, reversal; **être de ~** to be back.

retournement *m* reversal; turnaround.

retourner *vt* to reverse, turn over; to return; * *vi* to return, go back; **se ~** *vr* to turn over; to overturn.

rétracter *vt* to retract, take back; **se ~** *vr* to retract, withdraw one s evidence.

retrait *m* ebb; retreat; withdrawal; **être en ~** to be set back.

retraite *f* retreat; retirement; refuge; **à la ~** retired.

retraité *m*, **-e** *f* pensioner; * *adj* retired.

retranchement *m* curtailment; entrenchment.

retrancher *vt* to curtail; to entrench.

retransmettre *vt* to retransmit.

retransmission *f* retransmission.

rétrécir *vi* to narrow; to shrink; * *vt* to take in, make narrower; **se ~** *vr* to narrow; to shrink.

rétrécissement *m* narrowing; shrinking.

rétribuer *vt* to remunerate.

rétribution *f* retribution.

rétroactif *adj* retrospective; retroactive.

rétroaction *f* retroaction; retrospective action.

rétrograde *adj* reactionary, backward.

rétrograder *vi* to go backward, regress.

rétroprojecteur *m* overhead projector.

rétrospectif *adj* retrospective.

rétrospective *f* retrospective.

rétrospectivement *adv* retrospectively.

retrousser *vt* to roll up, hitch up.

retrouvailles *fpl* reunion.

retrouver *vt* to find again, to regain; to recover; to recognize; **se ~** *vr* to meet up; to end up in.

rétroviseur *m* rear-view mirror.

réunifier *vt* to reunify.

réunion *f* collection, gathering.

réunir *vt* to unite; to collect, gather; to combine; **se ~** *vr* to meet; to assemble.

réussir *vi* to succeed, be a success; * *vt* to make a success of.

réussite *f* success, successful outcome.

revanche *f* revenge; **en ~** on the other hand.

rêvasser *vi* to daydream.

rêve *m* dream, dreaming; illusion.

réveil *m* waking, awaking; alarm clock.

réveiller *vt* to wake; **se ~** *vr* to awaken.

réveillon *m* midnight feast.

révélation *f* revelation, disclosure; developing.

révéler *vt* to reveal, disclose; **se ~** *vr* to be revealed; to prove to be

revenant *m*, **-e** *f* ghost.

revendeur *m*, **-euse** *f* retailer; dealer.

revendication *f* claiming; claim; demand.

revendiquer *vt* to claim; to demand.

revendre *vt* to resell

revenir *vi* to come back, reappear; to happen again; **ne pas en ~** to not recover from, not pull through; **~ à soi** to come round.

revenu *m* income, revenue.

rêver *vi* to dream; to muse; * *vt* to dream of.

réverbération *f* reverberation.

réverbère *m* street lamp.

révérence *f* bow, curtsey.

révérend *adj* reverend.

révérer *vt* to revere.

rêverie *f* reverie, musing.

revers *m* back, reverse; counterpart.

réversible *adj* reversible.

revêtement *m* coating, surface.

revêtir *vt* to don; to assume.

rêveur *m*, **-euse** *f* dreamer; * *adj* dreamy

revigorer *vt* to invigorate; to revive.

revirement *m* change of mind; reversal; turnaround.

réviser *vt* to review; to revise.

révision *f* review; auditing; revision.

revivre *vt* to relive; * *vi* to live again, come alive again.

révocation *f* removal; dismissal; revocation.

revoir *vt* to see again; **se ~** *vr* to meet each other again.

révoltant *adj* revolting, appalling.

révolte *f* revolt, rebellion.

révolter *vt* to revolt, outrage; **se ~** *vr* to rebel, revolt.

révolu *adj* past, bygone.

révolution *f* revolution.

révolutionnaire *mf* revolutionary; * *adj* revolutionary.

révolutionner *vt* to revolutionize; to upset.

revolver *m* revolver.

révoquer *vt* to revoke; to dismiss.

revue *f* review; inspection.

rez-de-chaussée *m invar* ground floor.

rhabiller *vt* to dress somebody again; to fit somebody out again; **se ~** *vr* to dress oneself again.

rhésus *m* rhesus.

rhétorique *f* rhetoric; * *adj* rhetorical.

rhinocéros *m* rhinoceros.

rhododendron *m* rhododendron.

rhubarbe *f* rhubarb.

rhum *m* rum.

rhumatisme *m* rheumatism.

rhume *m* cold.

riant *adj* smiling; cheerful.

ribambelle *f* swarm, herd.

ricanement *m* snigger, sniggering.

ricaner *vi* to snigger, giggle

riche *adj* rich, wealthy; abundant; **~ment**; * *mf* rich person.

richesse *f* richness; wealth; abundance.

ricochet *m* ricochet; rebound.

rictus *m* grin; grimace.

ride *f* wrinkle; ripple; ridge.

ridé *adj* wrinkled

rideau *m* curtain.

ridicule *adj* ridiculous; * *m* ridiculousness; absurdity; ridicule.

ridiculiser *vt* to ridicule.

rien *pron* nothing; **de ~** don t mention it; **il n en est ~** he s nothing of the sort; * *m* nothingness; mere nothing; pinch, shade; **en un ~ de temps** in no time **pour un ~** at the slightest little thing.

rieur *adj* cheerful; laughing.

rigide *adj* rigid; **~ment** *adv* rigidly.

rigidité *f* rigidity, stiffness.

rigole *f* channel; rivulet.

rigoler *vi* (*fam*) to have a good laugh.

rigoureusement *adv* harshly, rigorously.

rigoureux *adj* rigorous, harsh.

rigueur *f* rigour; harshness, severity.

rime *f* rhyme.

rimer *vi* to rhyme (with)

rince-doigts *m invar* finger-bowl.

rincer *vt* to rinse out; to rinse.

ring *m* boxing ring.

riposte *f* riposte, retort.

riposter *vi* to answer back, retaliate.

rire *vi* to laugh; to smile; to joke; * *m* laughter, laugh.

risée *f* laugh; ridicule; mockery, derision.

risible *adj* laughable, ridiculous.

risque *m* risk, hazard.

risqué *adj* risky, hazardous; risqué.

risquer *vt* to risk; to venture; **se ~** *vr* to venture; dare.

ristourne *f* discount, rebate.

rite *m* rite.

rituel *adj* ritual.

rivage *m* shore

rival *m*, **-e** *f* rival; **sans ~** unrivalled; * *adj* rival.

rivaliser *vi* to rival, compete with; **~ de** to vie with.

rivalité *f* rivalry.

rive *f* shore, bank.

river *vt* to clinch; to rivet.

riverain *m*, **-e** *f* lakeside resident; riverside resident; * *adj* lakeside, riverside.

rivière *f* river.

riz *m* rice.

robe *f* dress; gown; **~ de chambre** dressing gown.

robinet *m* tap.

robot *m* robot.

robotique *f* robotics.
robuste *adj* robust.
robustesse *f* robustness.
roc *m* rock.
rocaille *f* loose stones; rocky ground.
rocailleux *adj* rocky.
roche *f* rock.
rocher *m* rock, boulder.
rodage *m* grinding, polishing; running in, breaking in.
roder *vt* to grind, polish; to run in
rôder *vi* to roam; to prowl about.
rôdeur *m*, **-euse** *f* prowler.
rogner *vt* to pare, prune, clip.
rognon *m* kidney.
roi *m* king
rôle *m* role, character; roll, catalogue.
roman *m* novel; romance.
romancier *m*, **-ière** *f* novelist.
romanesque *adj* fabulous; storybook; novelistic.
romantique *adj* romantic.
romantisme *m* romanticism.
rompre *vt* to break; to snap; to dissolve; * *vi* to break; to burst.
ronce *f* bramble.
rond *m* circle, ring; slice, round; * *adj* round; chubby, plump; frank; **~ement** *adv* briskly, frankly.
ronde *f* patrol; round; beat.
rondelle *f* slice, round; disc.
rondeur *f* plumpness; roundness.
rondin *m* log.
rond-point *m* roundabout.
ronflement *m* snore, snoring; humming; roaring.
ronfler *vi* to snore; to hum; to roar.
ronger *vt* to gnaw.
ronronner *vi* to purr; to hum.
rosbif *m* roast beef.
rose *f* rose; * *adj* pink; * *m* pink.
roseau *m* reed.
rosée *f* dew.
rosier *m* rosebush.
rossignol *m* nightingale.

rot *m* belch, burp.
roter *vi* to belch, burp.
rotation *f* rotation; turnover.
rôti *m* joint, roast.
rotin *m* rattan.
rôtir *vt* to roast.
rôtisserie *f* rotisserie, steakhouse.
rotonde *f* rotunda; roundhouse.
rotule *f* kneecap, patella.
rouage *m* cog; gearwheel.
roucouler *vi* to coo; to bill.
roue *f* wheel.
rouge *adj* red; * *m* red; **~ à lèvres** lipstick.
rouge-gorge *m* robin.
rougeole *f* measles.
rougeur *f* redness, blushing.
rougir *vi* to blush, go red; * *vt* to make red, redden.
rouille *f* rust.
rouiller *vi* to rust; * *vt* to make rusty.
roulant *adj* on wheels; moving.
rouleau *m* roll; roller.
roulement *m* rotation; movement; rumble, rumbling.
rouler *vt* to wheel, roll along; * *vi* to go, run (train); to drive.
roulette *f* castor; trundle; roulette.
roulis *m* rolling.
roulotte *f* caravan.
rouquin *m*, **-e** *f* redhead; * *adj* red-haired.
route *f* road; way; course, direction.
routier *adj* road; * *m* lorry driver; transport cafe.
routine *f* routine.
routinier *adj* humdrum, routine.
roux *m*, **rousse** *f* redhead; * *adj* red, auburn.
royal *adj* royal, regal; **~ement** *adv* royally.
royaliste *mf* royalist; * *adj* royalist.
royaume *m* kingdom.
royauté *f* monarchy.
ruade *f* kick (horse).

ruban *m* ribbon;tape, band.
rubéole *f* rubella.
rubis *m* ruby.
rubrique *f* column; heading, rubric.
ruche *f* hive.
rude *adj* rough; hard; unrefined; **~ment** *adv* roughly, harshly.
rudesse *f* roughness; harshness.
rudiment *m* rudiment; principle.
rudimentaire *adj* rudimentary.
rudoyer *vt* to treat harshly.
rue *f* street.
ruée *f* rush, stampede.
ruelle *f* alley.
ruer *vi* to kick (horse); **se ~** *vr* to pounce on.
rugby *m* rugby.
rugbyman *m* rugby player.
rugir *vi* to roar.
rugissement *m* roar, roaring.
rugueux *adj* rough; coarse.

ruine *f* ruin; wreck.
ruiner *vt* to ruin.
ruineux *adj* ruinous; extravagant.
ruisseau *m* stream, brook.
ruisseler *vi* to stream, flow.
ruissellement *m* streaming; cascading.
rumeur *f* rumour; murmur; hum.
ruminer *vt* to ruminate; to brood over.
rupture *f* break, rupture; breach; split.
rural *adj* rural, country.
ruse *f* cunning, slyness.
rusé *adj* cunning, crafty.
rustine ® *f* rubber repair patch.
rustique *adj* rustic.
rutilant *adj* gleaming, rutilant.
rythme *m* rhythm; rate, speed.
rythmique *adj* rhythmic.

S

sabbatique *adj* sabbatical.
sable *m* sand.
sablé *m* shortbread biscuit; * *adj* sandy, sanded.
sablier *m* hourglass, sandglass.
sabot *m* clog; hoof.
sabotage *m* sabotage.
saboter *vt* to sabotage; to mess up.
saboteur *m*, **-euse** *f* saboteur; bungler.
sabre *m* sabre
sac *m* bag, sack; **~ à main** handbag; **~ de voyage** travelling bag.
saccade *f* jerk, jolt.
saccadé *adj* jerky, broken, staccato.
saccager *vt* to sack; to wreck, devastate.
saccharine *f* saccharin.
sacerdoce *m* priesthood.

sacerdotal *adj* priestly, sacerdotal.
sachet *m* bag; sachet; packet.
sacoche *f* saddlebag, satchel.
sacre *m* coronation; consecration.
sacré *adj* sacred, holy; damned, confounded.
sacré-coeur *m* Sacred Heart.
sacrer *vt* to crown; to consecrate.
sacrifice *m* sacrifice.
sacrifier *vt* to sacrifice; to give up; **se ~** *vr* to sacrifice oneself.
sacrilège *m* sacrilege.
sacristie *f* sacristy.
sacrum *m* sacrum.
sadique *adj* sadistic; * *mf* sadist.
sadisme *m* sadism.
sadomasochiste *adj* sadomasochistic; * *mf* sadomasochistic.
safari *m* safari.
safran *m* saffron.
saga *f* saga.

sagace *adj* sagacious, shrewd.

sagacité *f* sagacity, shrewdness.

sage *adj* wise, sensible; well-behaved; **~ment** *adv* wisely, sensibly; * *m* sage, wise man.

sage-femme *f* midwife.

sagesse *f* wisdom, sense; good behaviour.

sagittaire *m* archer; Sagittarius.

saignant *adj* bleeding; underdone.

saignement *m* bleeding.

saigner *vi* to bleed; * *vt* to bleed; to stick.

saillant *adj* prominent, protruding.

saillie *f* projection; sally; flash of wit.

saillir *vi* to gush out; to project, jut.

sain *adj* healthy; sound; sane; **~ement** *adv* healthily; soundly.

saindoux *m* lard.

saint *m*, **-e** *f* saint; * *adj* holy, saintly; **Saint-Sylvestre** New Year's Eve; **Saint-Esprit** Holy Spirit.

saint-bernard *m* St Bernard.

sainteté *f* saintliness; holiness.

saisie *f* seizure, distraint; capture.

saisir *vt* to take hold of; to seize, distrain; to capture.

saisissant *adj* gripping, startling, striking.

saison *f* season.

saisonnier *adj* seasonal.

salade *f* salad; jumble, miscellany.

saladier *m* salad bowl.

salaire *m* salary, pay; reward.

salamandre *f* salamander.

salarié *m*, **-e** *f* salaried employee; * *adj* salaried.

sale *adj* dirty, filthy; obscene; nasty; **~ment** *adv* dirtily.

salé *adj* salty, salted; savoury.

saler *vt* to salt, add salt.

saleté *f* dirtiness, dirt; rubbish; obscenity.

salière *f* saltcellar.

salin *adj* saline.

salir *vt* to make dirty, soil; **se ~** *vr* to get dirty.

salissant *adj* dirty; that gets dirty easily.

salive *f* saliva.

saliver *vi* to salivate; to drool.

salle *f* room; hall; theatre; audience; **~ de séjour** living room; **~ à manger** dining room; **~ de bain** bathroom; **~ de cinéma** cinema.

salon *m* lounge, sitting room; exhibition.

salopette *f* overalls.

salpêtre *m* saltpetre.

salsifis *m* salsify, oyster-plant.

salubre *adj* healthy, salubrious.

saluer *vt* to greet; to salute.

salut *m* safety, salvation; welfare; wave (hand); salute.

salutaire *adj* salutary; profitable; healthy.

salutation *f* salutation, greeting.

samedi *m* Saturday.

sanatorium *m* sanatorium.

sanctifier *vt* to sanctify, bless.

sanction *f* sanction, penalty; approval.

sanctionner *vt* to punish; to sanction, approve.

sanctuaire *m* sanctuary.

sandale *f* sandal.

sandwich *m* sandwich.

sang *m* blood; race; kindred

sang-froid *m* sangfroid, cool, calm.

sanglant *adj* bloody, gory; bloodshot; blood-red.

sangle *f* strap; girth.

sanglier *m* wild boar.

sanglot *m* sob.

sangloter *vi* to sob.

sangsue *f* leech.

sanguinaire *adj* sanguinary, bloodthirsty.

sanitaire *adj* health, sanitary.

sans-abris *mf invar* homeless person.

sans-gêne *adj* inconsiderate; * *m*

invar inconsiderate type.

santal *m* sandalwood.

santé *f* health, healthiness.

saper *vt* to undermine, sap.

sapeur-pompier *m* fireman.

saphir *m* sapphire.

sapin *m* fir tree, fir.

sarcasme *m* sarcasm.

sarcastique *adj* sarcastic.

sarcler *vt* to weed; to hoe.

sarcophage *m* sarcophagus.

sardine *f* sardine.

sardonique *adj* sardonic.

S.A.R.L. (société à responsabilité limitée) *f* limited liability company.

sarrasin *m* buckwheat.

sas *m* airlock; sieve.

satanique *adj* satanic, diabolical.

satellite *m* satellite.

satiété *f* satiety, satiation; **à ~ ad** nauseam.

satin *m* satin.

satiné *adj* satiny, satin-smooth; glazed.

satire *f* satire, lampoon.

satirique *adj* satirical.

satisfaction *f* satisfaction; gratification; appeasement.

satisfaire *vt* to satisfy; to gratify; to appease.

satisfaisant *adj* satisfactory; satisfying.

satisfait *adj* satisfied.

saturation *f* saturation.

saturé *adj* saturated; overloaded, jammed.

saturer *vt* to saturate; to surfeit; to congest.

satyre *m* satyr.

sauce *f* sauce, dressing.

saucière *f* sauceboat.

saucisse *f* sausage.

saucisson *m* large sausage; salami.

sauf *prép* save, except; unless; * *adj* safe, unhurt.

sauge *f* sage.

saugrenu *adj* preposterous, absurd.

saule *m* willow.

saumon *m* salmon.

sauna *m* sauna.

saupoudrer *vt* to sprinkle; to dust.

saut *m* jump, bound; waterfall.

sauté *adj* sauté.

sauter *vi* to jump, leap; to blow up; to get sacked.

sauterelle *f* grasshopper.

sautiller *vi* to hop, skip.

sauvage *adj* savage, wild; unsociable; **~ment** *adv* savagely.

sauvegarde *f* safeguard; backup.

sauvegarder *vt* to safeguard.

sauver *vt* to save, rescue; to preserve; **se ~** *vr* to save oneself; to escape.

sauvetage *m* rescue; salvage.

sauveteur *m* rescuer.

savant *adj* learned; expert; skilled; * *m* scientist, scholar.

savate *f* old shoe.

saveur *f* flavour; savour.

savoir *vt* to know; to be aware; to understand; to be able; * *m* learning, knowledge.

savoir-faire *m* know-how.

savoir-vivre *m* good manners, good breeding.

savon *m* soap.

savonner *vt* to soap, lather.

savonnette *f* bar of soap.

savoureux *adj* tasty, savoury.

saxophone *m* saxophone.

saxophoniste *mf* saxophonist.

scabreux *adj* scabrous; dangerous; improper.

scalpel *m* scalpel.

scandale *m* scandal.

scandaleux *adj* scandalous.

scandaliser *vt* to scandalize, shock deeply; **se ~** *vr* to be scandalized.

scanner *m* scanner; * *vt* to digitize.

scaphandre *m* diving suit.

scarabée *m* beetle, scarab.

scarlatine *f* scarlet fever.

sceau *m* seal.

scélérat *m*, **-e** *f* villain, rascal;
* *adj* villainous, wicked.
sceller *vt* to seal.
scénario *m* scenario; screenplay.
scénariste *mf* scriptwriter.
scène *f* stage; scenery, scene.
scepticisme *m* scepticism.
sceptique *adj* sceptical; * *mf*
sceptic.
sceptre *m* sceptre.
schéma *m* diagram, sketch; outline.
schématique *adj* diagrammatic,
schematic; **~ment** *adv* diagram-
matically.
schématiser *vt* to schematize.
schisme *m* schism; split.
schiste *m* schist, shale.
schizophrène *mf* schizophrenic;
* *adj* schizophrenic.
schizophrénie *f* schizophrenia.
sciatique *f* sciatica.
scie *f* saw; bore.
sciemment *adv* knowingly, on
purpose.
science *f* science; skill; knowledge.
science-fiction *f* science fiction.
scientifique *adj* scientific;
~ment *adv* scientifically.
scierie *f* sawmill.
scinder *vt* to split, divide up.
scintillant *adj* sparkling, glistening.
scintillement *m* sparkling, glistening.
scintiller *vi* to sparkle, glisten.
scission *f* split, scission.
sciure *f* sawdust.
sclérose *f* sclerosis.
scléroser(se) *vr* to become scle-
rotic.
scolaire *adj* school; academic.
scolariser *vt* to send to school; to
provide schools.
scolarité *f* schooling.
scoliose *f* scoliosis, curvature of
the spine.
scooter *m* scooter.
score *m* score.

scorie *f* slag, scoria.
scorpion *m* scorpion.
scout *m* scout, boy scout.
script *m* printing; script.
scrupule *m* scruple, qualm,
doubt.
scrupuleusement *adv* scrupu-
lously.
scrupuleux *adj* scrupulous.
scruter *vt* to scrutinize, scan.
scrutin *m* ballot, poll.
sculpter *vt* to sculpt; to carve.
sculpteur *m* sculptor.
sculpture *f* sculpture.
se *pron* oneself, himself, herself,
itself, themselves.
séance *f* meeting, sitting, session;
seat.
seau *m* bucket, pail.
sec *adj*, *f* **sèche** dry, arid; barren;
unfeeling; curt; neat.
sécateur *m* secateurs.
séchage *m* drying; seasoning.
sèche-cheveux *m invar* hair-
drier
sèchement *adv* dryly; curtly.
sécher *vi* to dry, dry out; * *vt* to
dry, wipe.
sécheresse *f* drought; dryness.
séchoir *m* drying room; **~ à linge**
clothes horse
second *adj* second, in second
place; * *m* second; second floor;
second in command.
secondaire *adj* secondary.
seconde *f* second.
seconder *vt* to assist, help.
secouer *vt* to shake, toss; **se ~** *vr*
to shake oneself.
secourir *vt* to help, assist.
secouriste *mf* first-aid worker.
secours *m* help, assistance; relief;
rescue.
secousse *f* jolt, bump.
secret *m* secret; privacy; mystery;
* *adj* secret; private; discreet.
secrétaire *mf* secretary; * *m* writing desk.
secrétariat *m* office of secretary;
secretariat.

secrètement *adv* secretly.

secréter *vt* to secrete, exude.

sécrétion *f* secretion.

secte *f* sect.

secteur *m* sector, section, district.

section *f* section, division; branch.

sectionner *vt* to sever; to divide into sections.

séculaire *adj* secular, century-old, once a century.

sécurisant *adj* reassuring, lending security.

sécuriser *vt* to make somebody feel secure.

sécuritaire *adj* security.

sécurité *f* security; safety.

sédatif *m* sedative; * *adj* sedative.

sédentaire *adj* sedentary; * *m* sedentary.

sédiment *m* sediment.

sédimentation *f* sedimentation.

séducteur *m* seducer, **-trice** *f* seductress.

séduction *f* seduction; captivation

séduire *vt* to seduce; to charm, captivate.

séduisant *adj* seductive; enticing, attractive.

segment *m* segment.

segmenter *vt* to segment.

ségrégation *f* segregation.

seigle *m* rye.

seigneur *m* lord, nobleman; master.

sein *m* breast, bosom; womb; **au ~ de** within.

séisme *m* earthquake, seism.

seize *adj, m* sixteen.

seizième *adj, mf* sixteenth; **~ment** *adv* in sixteenth place.

séjour *m* stay, sojourn; abode; **salle de ~** living room.

séjourner *vi* to stay, sojourn.

sel *m* salt; wit.

sélecteur *m* selector; gear lever.

sélectif *adj* selective.

sélection *f* choosing, selection.

sélectionner *vt* to select, pick.

sélectivement *adv* selectively.

self-service *m* self-service restaurant.

selle *f* saddle.

selon *prép* according to; pursuant to.

semaine *f* week.

semblable *adj* like, similar, alike; such.

semblant *m* appearance, look; pretence; **faire ~ (de)** to pretend to.

sembler *vi* to seem, appear.

semelle *f* sole.

semence *f* seed; semen.

semer *vt* to sow; to scatter, strew.

semestre *m* half-year; semester.

semestriel *adj* half-yearly; semestral.

semi-conducteur *m* semiconductor.

séminaire *m* seminary; seminar.

semi-remorque *f* trailer, semitrailer.

semis *m* seedling; sowing; seedbed.

semoule *f* semolina.

sénat *m* senate.

sénateur *m* senator.

sénile *adj* senile.

sénilité *f* senility.

sens *m* sense; judgement; consciousness; meaning; direction;; **bon ~** good sense.

sensation *f* sensation, feeling.

sensationnel *adj* fantastic, sensational.

sensé *adj* sensible.

sensibiliser *vt* to make sensitive to, heighten awareness of.

sensibilité *f* sensitivity, sensitiveness.

sensible *adj* sensitive; perceptive; appreciable; **~ment** *adv* approximately; noticeably.

sensoriel *adj* sensory.

sensualité *f* sensuality.

sensuel *adj* sensual.

sentence *f* sentence.

sentencieux *adj* sententious.

sentier *m* path, track.

sentiment *m* feeling, sentiment; emotion.

sentimental *adj* sentimental.

sentimentalisme *m* sentimentalism.

sentinelle *f* sentry, sentinel.

sentir *vt* to feel; to perceive, guess; to smell.

séparation *f* separation; division; pulling apart.

séparatiste *mf* separatist.

séparément *adv* separately.

séparer *vt* to separate, divide; to pull off; to split; **se** ~ *vr* to separate, divide; to part with.

sept *adj*, *m* seven.

septembre *m* September

septième *adj*, *mf* seventh; ~**ment** *adv* in seventh place.

sépulture *f* sepulture, burial.

séquelle *f* gang, crew; after-effects.

séquence *f* sequence.

séquestre *m* sequestration, confiscation.

séquestrer *vt* to sequester, impound.

serein *adj* serene, calm; ~**ement** *adv* serenely.

sérénade *f* serenade.

sérénité *f* serenity, calmness.

sergent *m* sergeant; police constable.

série *f* series, string; class; rank.

sérieusement *adv* seriously, responsibly.

sérieux *adj* serious; responsible; * *m* seriousness, reliability.

seringue *f* syringe.

serment *m* oath; pledge.

sermon *m* sermon.

sermonner *vt* to lecture, reprimand.

séropositif *adj* HIV positive, seropositive.

serpe *f* billhook, bill.

serpent *m* serpent, snake.

serpenter *vi* to meander, wind.

serpentin *m* coil, worm (still).

serre *f* greenhouse; claw.

serré *adj* tight; close, compact.

serrer *vt* to tighten, fasten; to clench; **se** ~ *vr* to crowd, huddle.

serrure *f* lock.

serrurerie *f* locksmithing.

serrurier *m* locksmith.

sérum *m* serum.

servante *f* servant, maidservant.

serveur *m* waiter, -**euse** *f* waitress.

serviable *adj* obliging, helpful.

service *m* service; function; department; operation; **rendre** ~ to do a favour; ~ **militaire** national service.

serviette *f* towel; serviette, napkin.

servile *adj* servile, slavish; ~**ment** *adv* servilely, slavishly.

servilité *f* servility.

servir *vi* to be of use, be useful; * *vt* to serve, attend to; **se** ~ *vr* to help oneself; **se** ~ **de** to use, make use of.

servitude *f* servitude; easement.

sésame *m* sesame.

session *f* session, sitting.

seuil *m* threshold.

seul *adj* alone; single; sole; ~**ement** *adv* only; but; solely.

sève *f* sap; pith, vigour.

sévère *adj* severe, austere; ~**ment** *adv* severely; strictly.

sévérité *f* severity; strictness

sévir *vi* to deal severely; to rage, hold sway.

sevrer *vt* to wean; to deprive.

sexe *m* sex; genitals.

sexiste *mf* sexist; * *adj* sexist.

sexualité *f* sexuality.

sexuel *adj* sexual, sex; ~**lement** *adv* sexually.

sexy *adj* sexy.

seyant *adj* becoming.

shampooing *m* shampoo.

shooter *vt* to shoot, make a shot.

shopping *m* shopping.

short *m* shorts.

si *adv* so, so much, however much; yes; * *conj* if; whether.

siamois *adj* Siamese.

sida *m* Aids.

sidéral *adj* sidereal.

sidérer *vt* to flabbergast, stagger.

sidérurgie *f* steel metallurgy

sidérurgique *adj* steel-making.

sidérurgiste *mf* steel maker.

siècle *m* century; period.

siège *m* seat, bench; head office.

siéger *vi* to sit; to be located.

sien *pron*, *f* **sien**: **le ~ his**, its, his own, its own, **la sienne** her, its, her own, its own, **les ~s**, **les siennes** their, their own.

sieste *f* nap, snooze; siesta.

sifflement *m* whistling; hissing.

siffler *vi* to whistle; to hiss; * *vt* to whistle for; to hiss, boo.

sifflet *m* whistle; catcall.

sigle *m* abbreviation; acronym.

signal *m* signal, sign.

signalement *m* description, particulars.

signaler *vt* to signal, indicate; to point out.

signalisation *f* signalling system; installing signs.

signature *f* signature; signing.

signe *m* sign; mark; indication; symptom.

signer *vt* to sign; to hallmark.

signet *m* bookmark.

significatif *adj* significant, revealing.

signification *f* significance; meaning.

signifier *vt* to mean, signify; to make known; to serve notice.

silence *m* silence; stillness.

silencieusement *adv* silently.

silencieux *adj* silent; still.

silhouette *f* silhouette, outline.

silice *f* silica.

silicone *f* silicone.

sillage *m* wake; slipstream; trail.

sillon *m* furrow; fissure.

sillonner *vt* to plough, furrow; to criss-cross.

silo *m* silo.

similaire *adj* similar.

similarité *f* similarity.

similitude *f* similitude.

simple *adj* simple; mere; single; common; **~ment** *adv* simply, merely.

simplicité *f* simplicity; simpleness.

simplification *f* simplification.

simplifier *vt* to simplify.

simpliste *adj* simplistic.

simulation *f* simulation, simulation.

simuler *vt* to simulate, feign.

simultané *adj* simultaneous; **~ment** *adv* simultaneously.

sincère *adj* sincere, honest; **~ment** *adv* sincerely.

sincérité *f* sincerity, honesty.

singe *m* monkey.

singulariser *vt* to singularize; make conspicuous; **se ~** *vr* to make oneself conspicuous.

singularité *f* singularity; peculiarity.

singulier *adj* singular, peculiar; remarkable.

singulièrement *adv* singularly; remarkably.

sinistre *m* disaster; accident; * *adj* sinister; **~ment** *adv* in a sinister way.

sinistré *m*, **-e** *f* disaster victim; * *adj* disaster-stricken.

sinon *conj* otherwise, if not; except.

sinueux *adj* sinuous, winding.

sinus *m* sinus; sine.

sinusite *f* sinusitis.

siphon *m* siphon.

sirène *f* mermaid; siren, hooter.

sirop *m* syrup.

sirupeux *adj* syrupy.

sismique *adj* seismic.

site *m* setting, beauty spot.

sitôt *adv* so soon, as soon; **pas de ~** not for a while; **~ que** as soon as.

situation *f* situation, position; state of affairs.

situer *vt* to site, situate; **se ~** *vr*

to place oneself; to be situated.
six *adj, m* six.
sixième *adj, mf* sixth; **~ment** *adv* in sixth place.
sketch *m* sketch.
ski *m* ski, skiing.
skier *vi* to ski.
skieur *m*, **-euse** *f* skier.
slalom *m* slalom.
slip *m* briefs, panties, swimming trunks.
slogan *m* slogan.
snack(-bar) *m* snack bar.
snob *adj* snobbish.
snobisme *m* snobbery, snobbishness.
sobre *adj* sober, temperate; **~ment** *adv* soberly, temperately.
sobriété *f* sobriety, temperance.
sobriquet *m* nickname.
sociable *adj* sociable; social.
social *adj* social; **~ement** *adv* socially.
social-démocrate *mf* social democrat; * *adj* social democrat.
socialisme *m* socialism.
socialiste *mf* socialist; * *adj* socialist.
sociétaire *mf* associate; member.
société *f* society; company; partnership.
socio-économique *adj* socio-economic.
sociologie *f* sociology.
sociologique *adj* sociological; **~ment** *adv* sociologically.
sociologue *mf* sociologist.
socle *m* socle, plinth; base.
socquette *f* ankle sock.
sodium *m* sodium.
sodomie *f* sodomy.
soeur *f* sister; nun.
sofa *m* sofa.
soi *pron* one(self); self; **~-même** oneself, himself, herself, itself; **~-disant** so called.
soie *f* silk.
soif *f* thirst
soigné *adj* neat, well-kept.
soigner *vt* to look after, care for;

se ~ *vr* to take care of oneself.
soigneusement *adv* neatly; carefully.
soigneux *adj* neat; careful.
soin *m* care; attention; trouble.
soir *m* evening; night; afternoon.
soirée *f* evening; evening party.
soit *conj* either; or; whether; * *adv* granted; that is to say.
soixantaine *f* about sixty.
soixante *adj, m* sixty.
soixantième *adj, mf* sixtieth.
soja *m* soya.
sol *m* ground; floor; soil.
solaire *adj* solar.
soldat *m* soldier
solde *f* pay; * *m* balance; clearance sale.
solder *vt* to pay; to settle, discharge; **se ~** *vr*: **se ~ par** to show (profit, loss).
sole *f* sole; hearth.
soleil *m* sun, sunshine; sunflower.
solennel *adj* solemn; **~lement** *adv* solemnly.
solfège *m* musical theory; sol-fa.
solidaire *adj* jointly and separately liable; interdependent; **~ment** *adv* jointly and severally.
solidarité *f* solidarity.
solide *adj* solid; stable; sound; **~ment** *adv* solidly; soundly.
solidifier *vt* to solidify; **se ~** *vr* to solidify.
solidité *f* solidity; soundness.
soliste *mf* soloist.
solitaire *mf* recluse, hermit; * *adj* solitary, lone; **~ment** *adv* alone.
solitude *f* solitude; loneliness.
sollicitation *f* entreaty, appeal.
solliciter *vt* to seek, solicit; to appeal to.
sollicitude *f* solicitude, concern.
solo *m* solo.
solstice *m* solstice.
soluble *adj* soluble, solvable.
solution *f* solution; solving; answer.
solvable *adj* solvent; creditworthy.

solvant *m* solvent.

somatique *adj* somatic.

sombre *f* dark; gloomy, dismal.

sombrer *vi* to sink, founder.

sommaire *m* summary, argument; * *adj* basic, brief, summary; **~ment** *adv* basically, summarily.

sommation *f* summons; demand.

somme *m* nap, snooze.

sommeil *m* sleep; sleepiness, drowsiness.

sommeiller *vi* to slumber, doze.

sommelier *m* wine waiter.

sommet *m* summit; top; crest; apex.

sommier *m* springs, divan base; ledger.

sommité *f* leading light, eminent person.

somnambule *mf* sleepwalker; * *adj* sleepwalking.

somnifère *m* sleeping pill, soporific.

somnolent *adj* sleepy, drowsy.

somnoler *vi* to doze, drowse.

somptueux *adj* sumptuous, lavish.

son *m* sound; * *adj*, *f* **sa**; *pl* **ses** his, her, its.

sonate *f* sonata.

sondage *m* drilling; probing; sounding.

sonde *f* sounding line; probe; drill.

sonder *vt* to sound; to probe; to drill.

songe *m* dream.

songer *vt* to dream; to imagine; to consider.

songeur *adj* pensive.

sonner *vi* to ring; to go off; * *vt* to ring, sound.

sonnerie *f* ringing, bells; chimes.

sonnette *f* small bell; house-bell.

sonore *adj* resonant, deep-toned.

sonorisation *f* sound recording; sound system.

sonorité *f* sonority, tone; resonance.

sophistiqué *adj* sophisticated.

soporiphique *m* sleeping drug; soporific; * *adj* soporific.

soprano *mf* soprano.

sorbet *m* sorbet, water ice.

sorcellerie *f* witchcraft, sorcery.

sorcier *m* sorcerer.

sorcière *f* witch, sorceress.

sordide *adj* sordid, squalid; **~ment** *adv* sordidly, squalidly.

sort *m* fate, destiny, lot.

sortant *adj* outgoing, retiring.

sorte *f* sort, kind, manner.

sortie *f* exit, way out; trip; sortie; outburst; export.

sortilège *m* spell (magical).

sortir *vi* to go out, emerge; to result; to escape; **se ~ *vr*** to get out of; to extricate oneself; **s'en ~** to get over, pull through.

sosie *m* double, second self.

sot *adj*, *f* **sotte** silly, foolish; **~tement** *adv* foolishly, stupidly.

sottise *f* stupidity; stupid remark, action.

sou *m* five centimes; cent.

soubresaut *m* jolt; start.

souche *f* stump; stock.

souci *m* worry; concern.

soucier(se) *vr*: **se ~ de** to care about.

soucieux *adj* concerned, worried.

soucoupe *f* saucer.

soudain *adj* sudden, unexpected; **~ement** *adv* suddenly.

soude *f* soda.

souder *vt* to solder; to weld.

soudeur *m*, **-euse** *f* solderer; welder.

soudoyer *vt* to bribe, buy over.

soudure *f* soldering, welding.

souffle *m* blow, puff; breath.

soufflé *m* soufflé; flabbergasted.

souffler *vi* to blow; to breathe; to puff.

soufflerie *f* bellows.

soufflet *m* slap in the face; affront.

souffrance *f* suffering; pain; suspense.

souffrant *adj* suffering; in pain.

souffrir *vi* to suffer, be in pain.

souhait *m* wish.

souhaitable *adj* desirable.

souhaiter *vt* to wish for, desire.

souiller *vt* to soil, dirty; to tarnish.

soulagement *m* relief.

soulager *vt* to relieve, soothe.

soulèvement *m* relief.

soulever *vt* to lift, raise; to excite, stir up; **se ~** *vr* to rise; to revolt.

soulier *m* shoe.

souligner *vt* to underline.

soumettre *vt* to subdue, subjugate; to submit, deliver; **se ~** *vr* to subject oneself to.

soumis *adj* submissive.

soumission *f* submission.

soupape *f* valve; safety valve.

soupçon *m* suspicion, conjecture; hint.

soupçonner *vt* to suspect, surmise.

soupçonneux *adj* suspicious.

soupe *f* soup.

soupeser *vt* to feel the weight of; to weigh up.

soupière *f* soup tureen.

soupir *m* sigh; gasp.

soupirail *m* ventilator; basement window.

soupirer *vi* to sigh; to gasp.

souple *adj* supple; pliable; **~ment** *adv* supply, flexibly.

souplesse *f* suppleness; flexibility.

source *f* source; origin; spring.

sourcil *m* eyebrow.

sourd *m*, **-e** *f* deaf person; * *adj* deaf; muted; veiled; **~ement** *adv* dully; silently.

sourdine *f* mute.

sourd(e)-muet(te) *m(f)* deafmute; * *adj* deaf and dumb.

souriant *adj* smiling, cheerful.

sourire *m* smile, grin.

souris *f* mouse.

sournois *adj* deceitful; sly; **~ement** *adv* deceitfully.

sous *prép* under, beneath, below.

sous-alimenté *adj* undernourished.

sous-bois *m* undergrowth.

sous-chef *m* second-in-command.

souscrire *vi* to subscribe.

sous-développé *adj* underdeveloped.

sous-directeur *m*, **-trice** *f* submanager.

sous-entendre *vt* to imply, infer.

sous-entendu *m* implied, understood.

sous-estimer *vt* to underestimate.

sous-jacent *adj* subjacent, underlying.

sous-louer *vt* to sublet.

sous-marin *m* submarine; * *adj* underwater.

sous-multiple *m* submultiple.

sous-officier *m* non-commissioned officer.

sous-préfecture *f* sub-prefecture.

sous-préfet *m* sub-prefect.

soussigné *adj* undersigned.

sous-sol *m* subsoil; basement.

sous-titre *m* subtitle.

sous-titrer *vt* to subtitle.

soustraction *f* subtraction.

soustraire *vt* to subtract; to remove; **se ~** *vr*: **se ~ à** to escape, elude.

sous-traitance *f* subcontracting.

sous-traitant *m* subcontractor.

sous-traiter *vi* to be subcontracted.

sous-vêtement *m* undergarment.

soutane *f* cassock, soutane.

soute *f* hold; baggage hold.

soutenir *vt* to hold up; to sustain; to endure.

souterrain *m* underground passage; * *adj* underground.

soutien *m* support.

soutien-gorge *m* bra.

soutirer *vt* to extract from.

souvenir *m* memory; recollection; reminder.

souvenir(se) *vr* to remember, recollect.

souvent *adv* often, frequently.

souverain *m*, **-e** *f* sovereign; * *adj* sovereign; supreme;; **~ement** *adv* supremely.

soyeux *adj* silky.

spacieux *adj* spacious, roomy.

spaghettis *mpl* spaghetti.

sparadrap *m* sticking plaster.

spasme *m* spasm.

spasmophilie *f* spasmophilia.

spatial *adj* spatial; space.

spatule *f* spatula.

spécial *adj* special, particular; **~ement** *adv* specially.

spécialisation *f* specialization.

spécialiser *vt* to specialize; **se ~** *vr* to be a specialist.

spécialiste *mf* specialist.

spécialité *f* speciality; specialism.

spécieux *adj* specious.

spécification *f* specification.

spécifier *vt* to specify, determine.

spécifique *adj* specific; **~ment** *adv* specifically.

spécimen *m* specimen; sample.

spectacle *m* spectacle, scene.

spectaculaire *adj* spectacular.

spectateur *m*, **-trice** *f* spectator.

spectre *m* ghost.

spéculateur *m*, **-trice** *f* speculator.

spéculation *f* speculation.

spéculer *vi* to speculate.

spéléologie *f* speleology; caving.

spermatozoïde *m* sperm; spermatozoon.

sperme *m* sperm, semen.

sphère *f* sphere.

sphérique *adj* spherical.

sphinx *m* sphinx.

spirale *f* spiral.

spiritisme *m* spiritualism.

spiritualité *f* spirituality.

spirituel *adj* witty; spiritual; **~lement** *adv* wittily; spiritually.

splendeur *f* splendour, brilliance.

splendide *adj* splendid, magnificent **~ment** *adv* splendidly.

spongieux *adj* spongy.

sponsor *m* sponsor.

sponsoriser *vt* to sponsor.

spontané *adj* spontaneous; **~ment** *adv* spontaneously.

sporadique *adj* sporadic.

sport *m* sport.

sportif *m* sportsman, **-ive** *f* sportswoman; * *adj* sports *compd*; competitive; athletic.

square *m* square.

squatter *vi* to squat in.

squelette *m* skeleton.

squelettique *adj* skeleton-like, scrawny.

stabiliser *vt* to stabilize, consolidate; **se ~** *vr* to stabilize, become stabilized.

stabilité *f* stability.

stable *adj* stable, steady.

stade *m* stadium; stage.

stage *m* training course; articles; probation.

stagiaire *mf* trainee.

stagnation *f* stagnation.

stagner *vi* to stagnate.

standard *m* standard; switchboard; * *adj* standard.

standardiser *vt* to standardize.

standardiste *mf* switchboard operator.

star *f* star.

starter *m* choke.

station *f* station; stage, stop; resort; posture.

stationnaire *adj* stationary.

stationnement *m* parking.

stationner *vi* to park.

station-service *f* service station.

statique *adj* static.

statistique *f* statistics; * *adj* statistical.

statue *f* statue.

statuer *vt* to rule, give a verdict.

statu quo *m* status quo.

statut *m* statute, ordinance; status.

statutaire *adj* statutory; **~ment** *adv* statutorally.

stencil *m* stencil.

sténodactylo *mf* shorthand typist.

sténographie f shorthand.
stentor m **une voix de** stentorian voice.
steppe f steppe.
stère m stere.
stéréo(phonique) adj stereophonic.
stéréotype m stereotype.
stérile adj sterile, infertile.
stérilet m coil, I.U.D.
stériliser vt to sterilize.
stérilité f sterility.
sternum m breastbone, sternum.
stéroïde adj steroidal; * m steroid.
stigmate m mark, scar; stigmata.
stimulant adj stimulating; * m stimulant, stimulus.
stimulation f stimulation.
stimuler vt to stimulate, spur on.
stipuler vt to stipulate, specify.
stock m stock, supply.
stockage m stocking; stockpiling.
stocker vt to stock, stockpile.
stoïcisme m stoicism.
stoïque adj stoical; **~ment** adv stoically; * mf stoic.
stop m stop; stop sign; brakelight.
stopper vt to stop, halt; * vi to stop, halt.
store m blind, shade.
strabisme m squinting; strabismus.
strapontin m foldaway seat; minor role.
stratégie f strategy.
stratégique adj strategic; **~ment** adv strategically.
stratifié adj strategy.
stress m stress.
stressant adj stessful.
stresser vt to cause stress to.
strict adj strict, severe; **~ement** adv strictly.
strident adj strident, shrill.
strié adj streaked, striped, ridged.
stroboscope m stroboscope.
strophe f verse, stanza.
structural adj structural.

structure f structure.
structurel adj structural.
structurer vt to structure; se ~ vr to develop a structure.
stuc m stucco.
studieux adj studious.
studio m studio; film theatre.
stupéfaction f stupefaction, amazement.
stupéfait adj astounded, dumbfounded.
stupéfiant adj astounding, amazing; drug, stupefacient.
stupéfier vt to stupefy; to astound.
stupeur f amazement; stupor.
stupide adj stupid, foolish; **~ment** adv stupidly.
stupidité f stupidity.
style m style; stylus.
stylet m stiletto.
styliste mf designer; stylist.
stylo m pen.
su m knowledge.
suave adj suave, smooth.
subalterne mf subordinate; * adj subordinate.
subconscient m subconscious; * adj subconscious.
subdiviser vt to subdivide.
subdivision f subdivision.
subir vt to sustain, support; to undergo, suffer.
subit adj sudden; **~ement** adv suddenly.
subjectif adj subjective.
subjectivement adv subjectively.
subjectivité f subjectivity.
subjonctif m subjunctive; * adj subjunctive.
subjuguer vt to subjugate; to captivate.
sublime adj sublime; * m sublime.
sublimer vt to sublimate.
subliminal adj subliminal.
submerger vt to submerge, flood; to engulf.
submersible m submarine; * adj submarine.

subordination f subordination.

subordonné m, **-e** f subordinate; * adj subordinate.

subordonner vt to subordinate.

subreptice adj surreptitious; **~ment** adv surreptitiously.

subséquent adj subsequent.

subside m grant.

subsidiaire adj subsidiary.

subsistance f subsistence, maintenance, sustenance.

subsister vi to subsist; to live on.

substance f substance.

substantiel adj substantial; **~lement** adv substantially.

substantif m noun, substantive; * adj substantival, nominal.

substituer vt to substitute, replace.

substitut m substitute.

substitution f substitution.

subterfuge m subterfuge.

subtil adj subtle; **~ement** adv subtly.

subtiliser vt to steal, spirit away.

subtilité f subtlety.

subvenir vi: **~ à** to provide for.

subvention f grant, subsidy.

subventionner vt to subsidize.

subversif adj subversive.

suc m sap; juice.

succéder vi: **~ à** to succeed, follow; * **se ~** vr to succeed one another.

succès m success; hit.

successeur m successor.

successif adj successive.

succession f succession; inheritance, estate.

successivement adv successively.

succinct adj succinct; **~ement** adv succinctly.

succomber vi to succumb, give way.

succulent adj succulent, delicious.

sucursale f branch.

sucer vt to suck.

sucette f lollipop; dummy.

suçon m love bite.

sucre m sugar.

sucrer vt to sugar, sweeten.

sucrerie f sugar refinery.

sucrier m sugar bowl; * adj sugar; sugar-producing.

sud m south.

suer vi to sweat, perspire.

sueur f sweat.

suffire vi to suffice, be sufficient; **il suffit de** it is enough to, it only takes.

suffisamment adv sufficiently, enough.

suffisant adj sufficient, adequate.

suffoquer vi to choke, suffocate; * vt to choke, stifle.

suffrage m suffrage; vote; commendation, approval.

suggérer vt to suggest, put forward.

suggestion f suggestion.

suicidaire adj suicidal; * mf person with suicidal tendencies.

suicide m suicide.

suicider(se) vr to commit suicide.

suie f soot.

suif m tallow.

suintement m oozing; sweating.

suinter vi to ooze; to sweat.

suite f rest; sequel; continuation; series; connection; progress; **tout de ~** at once; **deux fois de ~** two times in a row; **et ainsi de ~** and so on; **à la suite de ~** after, behind; **par la ~** afterwards; **donner ~ à** to follow up.

suivant m, **-e** f next one; attendant; * adj following, next; * prép according to; **~ que** according to whether.

suivi adj steady, regular; widely adopted; * m follow-up.

suivre vt to follow; to attend, accompany; to exercise; **~ son cours** to take its course; **à suivre** to be continued; **se ~** vr to follow each other; to be continuous.

sujet m subject, topic; ground;

reason; * *adj:* **être ~ à** to be subject to, liable to.

sujétion *f* subjection; constraint.

sulfate *m* sulphate.

sulfater *vt* to apply copper sulphate.

sulfure *m* sulphur.

sulfureux *adj* sulphurous.

sulfurique *adj* sulphuric.

sultan *m* sultan, **-e** *f* sultana.

summum *m* climax, height.

super *m* super, four-star petrol; * *adj (fam)* ultra, super.

superbe *adj* superb, splendid; **~ment** *adv* superbly.

supercarburant *m* high-octane petrol.

supercherie *f* trick, trickery.

superficie *f* area, surface.

superficiel *adj* superficial; **~lement** *adv* superficially.

superflu *adj* superfluous.

supérieur *adj* upper; superior; higher, greater; **~ement** *adv* exceptionally well.

supériorité *f* superiority.

superlatif *m* superlative; * *adj* superlative.

superposer *vt* to superpose, stack; to superimpose; **se ~** *vr* to be superimposed.

superposition *f* superposing; superimposition.

supersonique *adj* supersonic.

superstitieux *adj* superstitious.

superstition *f* superstition.

superviser *vt* to supervise.

supplanter *vt* to supplant, oust.

suppléant *m*, **-e** *f* substitute, understudy; * *adj* substitute.

supplément *m* supplement; extra charge.

supplémentaire *adj* supplementary, additional.

suppliant *adj* beseeching, entreating.

supplication *f* supplication; entreaty.

supplice *m* corporal punishment; torture.

supplier *vt* to beseech, entreat.

support *m* support, prop; stand.

supporter *vt* to support; to endure, bear.

supporter *m* supporter.

supposer *vt* to suppose; to assume; to imply.

supposition *f* supposition, surmise.

suppositoire *m* suppository.

suppression *f* suppression; deletion; cancellation.

supprimer *vt* to suppress; to cancel.

suppurer *vi* to suppurate.

suprématie *f* supremacy.

suprême *adj* supreme.

sur *prép* on;over, above; into; out of, from.

sûr *adj* sure, certain; secure; **~ de soi** self-assured; **bien ~** of course; **à coup ~** for sure; **~ement** *adv* surely, certainly.

surabondance *f* overabundance.

suranné *adj* outmoded, outdated.

surcharge *f* overloading; excess; surcharge.

surcharger *vt* to overload.

surchauffe *f* overheating.

surcroît *m*: surplus, excess **de ~** in addition.

surdité *f* deafness.

sureau *m* elder tree.

surélever *vt* to raise, heighten.

surenchérir *vi* to outbid.

surestimer *vt* to overestimate; to overvalue.

sûreté *f* safety; guarantee, surety; **être en ~** to be safe.

surexcité *adj* overexcited.

surface *f* surface.

surgeler *vt* to deep-freeze.

surgir *vi* to rise, appear; to arise, crop up.

surhomme *m* superman.

surintendant *m* superintendent

surlendemain *m* day after tomorrow.

surmenage *m* overwork; overtaxing.

surmener *vt* to overwork; **se ~** *vr* to overwork.

surmonter *vt* to surmount, overcome.

surnager *vi* to float.

surnaturel *adj* supernatural.

surnom *m* nickname.

surnommer *vt* to nickname.

surpasser *vt* to surpass, outdo.

surplomb overhang m: **en ~ overhanging**.

surplomber *vt* to overhang.

surplus *m* surplus, remainder, excess.

surpopulation *f* overpopulation.

surprenant *adj* surprising, amazing.

surprendre *vt* to surprise, amaze.

surprise *f* surprise.

surproduction *f* overproduction.

surréalisme *m* surrealism.

surréaliste *mf* surrealist; * *adj* surrealistic.

sursaut *m* start, jump.

sursauter *vi* to start, jump.

sursis *m* reprieve; deferment.

sursitaire *adj* deferred; suspended.

surtaxe *f* surcharge.

surtout *adv* especially; above all.

surveillance *f* surveillance; supervision; inspection.

surveillant *m*, **-e** *f* warder, guard.

surveiller *vt* to watch; to supervise; to inspect.

survenir *vi* to take place, occur.

survêtement *m* tracksuit.

survie *f* survival.

survivant *m*, **-e** *f* survivor; * *adj* surviving.

survivre *vi* to survive.

survoler *vt* to fly over.

susceptible *adj* sensitive; susceptible; capable; likely; **être ~ de** to be liable to.

susciter *vt* to arouse, incite.

suspect *m*, **-e** *f* suspect; * *adj* suspicious, suspect.

suspecter *vt* to suspect.

suspendre *vt* to hang up; to suspend, defer.

suspendu *adj* hanging; suspended.

suspens *m*: **en ~** in abeyance; shelved.

suspense *m* suspense.

suspension *f* suspension; deferment; adjournment.

suspicieux *adj* suspicious.

suspicion *f* suspicion.

susurrer *vt* to whisper.

suture *f* suture; **points de ~** stitches.

svelte *adj* svelte, slim.

S.V.P. *abrév de* s'il vous plaît. please.

syllabe *f* syllable.

sylvestre *adj* forest.

symbole *m* symbol

symbolique *adj* symbolic; token; nominal; **~ment** *adv* symbolically.

symboliser *vt* to symbolize.

symbolisme *m* symbolism.

symétrie *f* symmetry.

symétrique *adj* symmetrical; **~ment** *adv* symmetrically.

sympa *adj invar* (*fam*) nice, friendly.

sympathie *f* liking; fellow feeling; sympathy.

sympathique *adj* likeable, nice; friendly.

sympathisant *m*, **-e** *f* sympathizer; * *adj* sympathizing.

sympathiser *vi* to get on well with.

symphonie *f* symphony.

symphonique *adj* symphonic.

symptomatique *adj* symptomatic.

symptôme *m* symptom.

synagogue *f* synagogue.

synchronisation *f* synchronization.

synchroniser *vt* to synchronize.

syncope *f* blackout, syncope.

syncopé *adj* syncopated.

syndical *adj* trade-union.

syndicalisme *m* trade unionism.
syndicaliste *mf* trade unionist;
  * *adj* trade union.
syndicat *m* trade union; association.
syndiquer *vt* to unionize; **se ~** *vr*
  to form a trade union.
syndrome *m* syndrome.
synonyme *m* synonym; * *adj* synonymous.

syntaxe *f* syntax.
synthèse *f* synthesis.
synthétique *adj* synthetic.
synthétiser *vt* to synthesize.
synthétiseur *m* synthesizer.
syphilis *f* syphilis.
systématique *adj* systematic;
  ~ment *adv* systematically.
système *m* system.

T

tabac *m* tobacco.
tabagisme *m* nicotine addiction.
tabatière *f* snuffbox; skylight.
table *f* table; **~ de nuit** bedside
  table; **~ ronde** round-table conference.
tableau *m* table; chart; timetable;
  scene; **~ de bord** dashboard.
tablette *f* bar; tablet; block.
tablier *m* apron; pinafore; overall.
tabou *m* taboo.
tabouret *m* stool.
tache *f* mark; stain; spot.
tâche *f* task, assignment; work.
taché *adj* stained, blemished.
tâcher *vi* to endeavour.
tacheté *adj* spotted; freckled.
tachycardie *f* tachycardia.
tacite *adj* tacit; **~ment** *adv* tac-
  itly.
taciturne *adj* taciturn, silent.
tact *m* tact; **avoir du ~** to have
  tact, be tactful.
tactile *adj* tactile.
tactique *f* tactics; * *adj* tactical.
taffetas *m* taffeta.
tagliatelles *fpl* tagliatelli.
taillader *vt* to slash, gash.
taille *f* height, stature, seize; **de
  ~** considerable, sizeable; **être de
  ~ à** to be up to it.
taille-crayons *m* pencil sharp-
  ener.
tailler *vt* to cut; to carve; to

sharpen; **se ~** *vr* (*fam*) to clear
  off, split.
tailleur *m* tailor; cutter, hewer.
taillis *m* copse, coppice.
taire *vt* to hush up; to conceal; **se
  ~** *vr* to be quiet; to fall silent.
talc *m* talc, talcum powder.
talent *m* talent, ability.
talentueux *adj* talented.
talisman *m* talisman.
talon *m* heel; crust; spur.
talonner *vt* to follow closely; to
  hound.
talquer *vt* to put talcum powder
  on.
talus *m* embankment.
tambour *m* drum; barrel.
tambourin *m* tambourine.
tambouriner *vi* to drum; to beat,
  hammer.
tamis *m* sieve; riddle.
tamiser *vt* to sieve; to sift.
tampon *m* stopper, plug; tampon;
  buffer.
tamponner *vt* to mop up; to
  stamp.
tam-tam *m* tom-tom; row.
tandem *m* tandem; duo.
tandis *conj*: **~ que** while;
  whereas.
tangent *adj* tangent, tangential.
tangible *adj* tangible.
tango *m* tango.
tanguer *vi* to pitch (ship).
tanière *f* den, lair.

tank *m* tank.

tanné *adj* tanned; weathered.

tanner *vt* to tan, weather.

tanneur *m* tanner.

tant *adv* so much; ~ **que** as long as; ~ **soit peu** ever so slightly; ~ **mieux** so much the better; that's a good job; ~ **pis** too bad; ~ **bien que mal** as well as can be expected.

tante *f* aunt.

tantôt *adv* sometimes; this afternoon; shortly.

taon *m* horsefly, gadfly.

tapage *m* din, uproar, racket.

tapageur *adj* noisy, rowdy; showy.

tape *f* slap.

taper *vi* to hit, tap, stamp; to beat down; * *vt* to beat; to slap; to type.

tapioca *m* tapioca.

tapir(se) *vr* to crouch; to hide away.

tapir *m* tapir.

tapis *m* carpet; rug; cloth.

tapisser *vt* to wallpaper; to cover; to carpet.

tapisserie *f* tapestry; tapestry-making; **faire ~** to stand on the sidelines.

tapoter *vt* to pat; to tap; to strum.

taquin *adj* teasing.

taquiner *vt* to tease; to plague.

tarauder *vt* to tap; to thread.

tard *adv* late.

tarder *vi* to delay, put off; to dally.

tardif *adj* late; tardy; slow; backward.

tardivement *adv* late; tardily.

tare *f* tare; defect, flaw.

taré *adj* tainted, corrupt; sickly.

tari *adj* dried up.

tarif *m* tariff; price-list.

tarir *vt* to dry up; to exhaust; **se ~** *vr* to dry up.

tarot *m* tarot.

tartare *adj* Tartar.

tarte *f* tart, flan.

tartelette *f* tartlet, tart.

tartine *f* slice of buttered bread.

tartiner *vt* to spread with butter, jam, etc.

tartre *m* tartar; fur, scale.

tas *m* heap, pile; lot, set.

tasse *f* cup; coffee cup.

tassement *m* settling, sinking.

tasser *vt* to heap up; **se ~** *vr* to sink; subside.

tata *f* auntie.

tâter *vt* to feel, try; **se ~** *vr* to feel oneself.

tatonnement *m* trial and error; experimentation.

tatonner *vi* to feel one's way, grope along.

tatouage *m* tattooing; tattoo.

tatouer *vt* to tattoo.

taudis *m* hovel, slum.

taupe *f* mole.

taureau *m* bull.

tauromachie *f* bullfighting.

taux *m* rate; ratio; ~ **de change** exchange rate.

taverne *f* tavern.

taxation *f* taxation, taxing.

taxe *f* tax; duty; rate.

taxer *vt* to tax; to fix the price of.

taxi *m* taxi.

tchin-tchin! *interj* cheers!

te *pron* you, yourself.

technicien *m*, **-ienne** *f* technician.

technique *f* technique; * *adj* technical; **~ment** *adv* technically.

technocrate *m* technocrat.

technocratie *f* technocracy.

technologie *f* technology.

technologique *adj* technological.

téflon *m* teflon.

teigne *f* moth.

teindre *vt* to dye.

teint *m* complexion, colouring.

teinte *f* tint, colour, shade.

teinter *vt* to tint; to stain.

teinture *f* dye; dyeing.

teinturerie *f* dyeing; dye-works; dry cleaner's.

teinturier *m*, **-ère** *f* dyer; dry cleaner.

tel *adj* such; like, similar; **~ quel** such as it is; **en tant que ~** as such, in such a capacity; **il n'y a rien de ~** there's nothing like....

télé *f* TV, telly.

télécarte *f* phonecard.

télécommande *f* remote control.

télécommunication *f* telecommunication.

télécopie *f* facsimile transmission; fax.

télécopieur *m* fax machine.

télédiffusion *f* television broadcasting.

téléphérique *m* cableway; cablecar.

télégramme *m* telegram; cable.

télégraphier *vt* to telegraph, cable.

téléguider *vt* to radio-control.

télématique *f* telematics.

téléobjectif *m* telephoto lens.

télépathie *f* telepathy.

téléphone *m* telephone.

téléphoner *vi* to telephone.

téléphonique *adj* telephone; telephonic.

télescope *m* telescope.

télescopique *adj* telescopic.

télésiège *m* chairlift.

téléski *m* lift, tow.

téléspectateur *m*, **-trice** *f* television viewer.

téléviseur *m* television set.

télévision *f* television.

télex *m* telex.

tellement *adj* so, so much; **~ de** so many, so much.

téméraire *adj* rash, reckless; **~ment** *adv* rashly; recklessly.

témérité *f* rashness; recklessness.

témoignage *m* testimony; evidence; certificate.

témoigner *vi* to testify.

témoin *m* witness; evidence; proof.

témpérament *m* constitution; temperament; character.

tempérance *f* temperance.

température *f* temperature

tempéré *adj* temperate; tempered.

tempérer *vt* to temper; to assuage, soothe.

tempête *f* tempest.

temple *m* temple.

tempo *m* tempo, pace.

temporaire *adj* temporary; **~ment** *adv* temporarily.

temporel *adj* worldly, temporal.

temporiser *vi* to temporize, delay.

temps *m* time; while; tense; beat; weather; **de ~ en ~** from time to time; **entre ~** meanwhile.

tenace *adj* tenacious, stubborn, persistent; **~ment** *adv* tenaciously.

ténacité *f* tenacity; stubbornness.

tenaille *f* pincers; tongs.

tenailler *vt* to torture; to rack.

tendance *f* tendency; leaning; trend.

tendancieux *adj* tendentious.

tendinite *f* tendinitis.

tendon *m* tendon, sinew.

tendre *adj* tender, soft; delicate; **~ment** *adv* tenderly, affectionately.

tendresse *f* tenderness; fondness.

tendu *adj* tight; stretched; concentrated; delicate, fraught.

ténèbres *fpl* darkness, gloom.

ténébreux *adj* dark, gloomy.

teneur *f* terms; content; grade.

tenir *vt* to hold, keep; to stock; to run; * *vi* to hold, stay in place; **à** to value, care about; **~ de** to take after; **se ~** *vr* to hold on to; to behave; **s'en ~ à** to limit oneself to, stick to.

tennis *m* tennis; **~ de table** table tennis.

ténor *m* tenor; leading light.

tentacule *m* tentacle.

tentant *adj* tempting, inviting.

tentation *f* temptation.

tentative *f* attempt, bid.

tente *f* tent.

tenter *vt* to tempt.

tenture *f* hanging; curtain.

tenue *f* holding; session; deportment, good behaviour; dress, appearance.

tergal *m* terylene.

tergiverser *vi* to procrastinate, beat about the bush.

terme *m* term; termination, end; word, expression; **au ~ de** the end of.

terminaison *f* ending.

terminal *adj* terminal; * *m* terminal.

terminer *vt* to terminate; to finish off; **se ~** *vr* to terminate; to come to an end.

terminologie *f* terminology.

termite *m* termite.

terne *adj* colourless; lustreless, drab; spiritless.

ternir *vt* to tarnish, dull.

terrain *m* ground, soil, earth; plot; position; site; field.

terrasse *f* terrace.

terrasser *vt* to floor, knock down; to strike down, overcome.

terre *f* earth; world; ground, land; **mettre pied à ~** to land, alight.

terre à terre *adj* down to earth, commonplace.

terreau *m* compost.

terre-plein *m* terreplein; platform; central reservation.

terrer(se) *vr* to crouch down; to lie low, go to ground.

terrestre *adj* land; terrestrial.

terreur *f* terror, dread.

terreux *adj* earthy; dirty; ashen.

terrible *adj* terrible, dreadful; terrific, great; **~ment** *adv* terribly.

terrien *m* countryman; earthling. **-ienne** *f* countrywoman; earthling.

terrier *m* burrow; earth; terrier.

terrifiant *adj* terrifying, fearsome.

terrifier *vt* to terrify.

terrine *f* earthenware dish, terrine.

territoire *m* territory, area.

territorial *adj* land, territorial.

terroir *m* soil.

terroriser *vt* to terrorize.

terrorisme *m* terrorism.

terroriste *mf* terrorist; * *adj* terrorist.

tertiaire *adj* tertiary.

test *m* test.

testament *m* will, testament.

tester *vt* to test; to make out one's will.

testicule *m* testicle, testis.

tétanos *m* tetanus; lockjaw.

tétard *m* tadpole.

tête *f* head; face; front; top; sense, judgment; **tenir ~** to cope; **faire la ~** to pout, sulk; **~ de turc** whipping boy; **~ de mort** skull and crossbones; **être en ~** to head.

tête à tête *m* private conversation; **en ~** in the lead.

tétée *f* sucking; nursing.

téter *vt* to suck.

tétine *f* teat; udder; dummy.

téton *m* breast.

têtu *adj* headstrong, stubborn.

texte *m* text; theme; passage.

textile *adj* textile.

textuel *adj* textual, literal, exact; **~lement** *adv* literally; word for word.

texture *f* texture.

thé *m* tea.

théâtral *adj* theatrical, dramatic.

théâtre *m* theatre; drama.

théière *f* teapot.

thématique *adj* thematic.

thème *m* theme.

théologie *f* theology.

théorème *m* theorem.

théoricien *m*, **-ienne** *f* theoretician, theorist.

théorie *f* theory.

théorique *adj* theoretical; **~ment** *adv* theoretically.

thérapeute *mf* therapist.

thérapie *f* therapy.

thermal *adj* thermal; hydropathic.

thermique *adj* thermal; thermic.

thermomètre *m* thermometer.

thermos *f/m* thermos.

thermostat *m* thermostat.

thésaurus *m* thesaurus.

thèse *f* thesis.

thon *m* tuna.

thoracique *adj* thoracic; **cage ~** ribcage.

thorax *m* thorax.

thrombose *f* thrombosis.

thym *m* thyme.

thyroïde *f* thyroid.

tibia *m* tibia.

tic *m* twitch, tic; mannerism.

ticket *m* ticket.

tiède *adj* lukewarm, tepid.

tien *pron*, *f* **tienne**: **le ~, la tienne, les ~s, les tiennes** yours, your own.

tiercé *m* tierce.

tiers *adj* third; **~-monde** Third World; * *m* third; third party.

tige *f* stem, stalk.

tigre *m* tiger.

tigresse *f* tigress.

tilleul *m* lime, linden.

timbale *f* kettledrum.

timbre *m* stamp; postmark; bell; tone, timbre.

timbré *adj* stamped; resonant.

timbrer *vt* to stamp; to postmark.

timide *adj* timid, shy; **~ment** *adv* timidly.

timidité *f* timidity, shyness.

timonier *m* (*mar*) helmsman.

tintamarre *m* hubbub, uproar.

tintement *m* ringing; chiming; toll.

tinter *vi* to ring, toll; to chime.

tique *f* tick.

tiquer *vi* to make a face; to wink.

tir *m* shooting, firing, fire; shot; **~ à l'arc** archery.

tirade *f* tirade; monologue.

tirage *m* drawing, drawing off; printing; circulation; friction.

tiraillement *m* tugging; pulling.

tirailler *vt* to tug; to plague; to pester.

tire-bouchon *m* corkscrew.

tire-fesses *m* ski tow.

tirelire *f* moneybox.

tirer *vt* to pull; to draw; to extract; **se ~** *vr* (*fam*) to clear off; **bien s'en ~** to make a good job of st.

tiret *m* dash; hyphen.

tireur *m*, **-euse** *f* gunner, sharpshooter; printer; drawer (of cheque).

tiroir *m* drawer.

tison *m* brand.

tisonnier *m* poker.

tissage *m* weaving.

tisser *vt* to weave.

tissu *m* texture, fabric; tissue.

titan *m* titan.

titane *m* titanium.

titanesque *adj* titanic.

titre *m* title; heading; denomination; claim, right; deed; **à ~ de** by right of; **à juste ~** deservedly, justly; **en ~** titular, acknowledged.

tituber *vi* to stagger.

titulaire *mf* incumbent, holder; * *adj* titular; entitled.

toast *m* slice of toast; toast; **porter un ~** to drink a toast.

toboggan *m* toboggan.

toc *m* tap, knock; imitation jewellery, etc; **en ~** imitation, fake.

toi *pron* you; **~-même** yourself; **c'est à ~** it's your's; it's your turn.

toile *f* cloth; canvas; sheet

toilette *f* cleaning, grooming; washstand; **faire sa ~** to wash oneself; **cabinet de ~** bathroom.

toiser *vt* to survey; to evaluate.

toison *f* fleece.

toit *m* roof; home.

toiture *f* roof, roofing.

tôle *f* sheet metal.

tolérable *adj* tolerable, bearable.

tolérance *f* tolerance.

tolérant *adj* tolerant.

tolérer *vt* to tolerate; to put up with.

tomate *f* tomato.

tombe *f* tomb; grave.

tombeau *m* tomb.

tomber *vi* to fall; to sink; to decay; **laisser ~** to drop; **~ malade** to fall sick; **~ amoureux** to fall in love; **~ sur** to come across; **bien/mal ~** to be lucky/unlucky.

tombola *f* tombola.

tome *m* book;volume.

ton *adj*, *f* **ta**, *pl* **tes** your; * *m* tone; pitch; shade.

tonalité *f* tonality; key.

tondeuse *f* clippers, shears; mower.

tondre *vt* to shear, clip; mow.

tonifiant *m* tonic; * *adj* bracing; invigorating.

tonifier *vt* to tone up; to invigorate.

tonique *adj* tonic; fortifying; invigorating *m* tonic.

tonitruant *adj* thundering.

tonnage *m* tonnage; displacement.

tonne *f* ton, tonne.

tonneau *m* barrel, cask.

tonnelle *f* bower, arbour.

tonnerre *m* thunder.

tonton *m (fam)* uncle.

tonus *m* tone; energy.

top *m* pip, stroke.

topaze *f* topaz.

topographie *f* topography.

toquade *f* infatuation; fad, craze.

toque *f* fur hat; cap.

toquer *vi* to tap, rap.

torche *f* torch.

torcher *vt* to wipe, mop up; **se ~** *vr* to wipe oneself.

torchon *m* cloth; duster.

tordre *vt* to twist, contort; **se ~** *vr* to bend, twist; to sprain.

tordu *adj* twisted, crooked, bent.

tornade *f* tornado.

torpeur *f* torpor.

torpille *f* torpedo.

torpiller *vt* to torpedo.

torréfaction *f* roasting; toasting.

torrent *m* torrent.

torrentiel *adj* torrential.

torride *adj* torrid; scorching.

torsade *f* twist; cable moulding.

torse *m* chest; torso.

torsion *f* twisting; torsion.

tort *m* fault; wrong; prejudice; **avoir ~** to be wrong; **en ~** in the wrong; **à ~ ou à raison** wrongly or rightly; **faire du ~** to harm; **à ~ et à travers** wildly, here there and everywhere.

torticolis *m* torticollis; stiff neck.

tortiller *vt* to twist; **se ~** *vr* to wriggle; to squirm.

tortionnaire *mf* torturer; * *adj* pertaining to torture.

tortue *f* tortoise.

tortueux *adj* tortuous, winding, meandering.

torture *f* torture.

torturer *vt* to torture.

tôt *adv* early; soon, quickly; **au plus ~** as soon as possible; **plus ~** sooner.

total *adj* total; absolute; **~ement** *adv* totally.

totaliser *vt* to totalize, add up.

totalitaire *adj* totalitarian.

totalitarisme *m* totalitarianism.

totalité *f* totality; whole.

totem *m* totem.

touchant *adj* touching, moving.

touche *f* touch; trial; stroke; key.

toucher *vt* to touch; to feel; * *m* touch, feeling.

touffe *f* tuft, clump.

touffu *adj* bushy, thick.

toujours *adv* always; still; all the same; **pour ~** for ever; **~ est-il que** the fact remains that.

toupet *m* quiff, tuft; cheek.

toupie *f* spinning top.

tour *f*; * *m* turn, round; circuit; tour; trick; **faire un ~** to take a stroll; **faire le tour de** to go around; **fermer à double ~** to double-lock; **jouer un ~** to play a trick; **~ à ~** by turns.

tourbe f peat.

tourbillon m whirlwind, whirl-pool.

tourbillonner vi to whirl, eddy.

tourisme m tourism.

touriste mf tourist.

touristique adj tourist.

tourment m torment, agony.

tourmente f storm, tempest.

tourmenter vt to rack, torment; **se ~** vr to fret; to worry.

tournage m turning; (cin) shooting.

tournant m bend; turning point; * adj revolving, swivel; winding.

tournedos m fillet steak.

tournée f tour; round.

tourner vt to turn; to round; * vi to turn; to work; to change; **se ~** vr to turn round; to change.

tournesol m sunflower.

tourneur m turner.

tournevis m screwdriver.

tourniquet m tourniquet; turnstile.

tournis m: sturdy, staggers **avoir le ~** to feel giddy.

tournoi m tournament.

tournoyer vi to whirl, swirl.

tournure f turn; turn of phrase.

tourte f pie.

tourerelle f turtledove.

tourtière f pie tin.

Toussaint f All Saints' Day.

tousser vi to cough.

tout adj, pl **tous**, **toutes** all; whole; every; **~ le monde** everybody; * pron everything; all; **c'est ~** that is all; * m whole, only thing; **pas du ~** not at all; **du ~ au ~** completely; * adv entirely, quite; **~ droit** straight on; **~ à fait** completely, quite; **~ de suite** immediately.

toutefois adv however.

tout-puissant adj all-powerful.

toux f cough.

toxicomane mf drug addict; * adj drug addicted.

toxicomanie f drug addiction.

toxine f toxin.

toxique adj toxic.

trac m nerves, stage fright.

tracas m bustle, turmoil; worry.

tracasser vt to worry; to harass.

trace f track, impression; outline, sketch; vestige, trace.

tracé m layout, plan.

tracer vt to draw, trace; to open up.

trachée f trachea, windpipe.

tract m leaflet, tract.

tractation f transaction; bargaining.

tracteur m tractor.

traction f traction; pulling.

tradition f tradition.

traditionaliste mf traditionalist; * adj traditionalist.

traditionnel adj traditional; usual; **~lement** adv traditionally.

traducteur m, **-trice** f translator.

traduction f translation.

traduire vt to translate.

trafic m traffic; trading; dealings.

trafiquant m, **-ante** f trafficker.

trafiquer vi to traffic, trade.

tragédie f tragedy.

tragédien m, **-ienne** f tragedian, tragic actor.

tragique adj tragic; **~ment** adv tragically.

trahir vt to betray.

trahison f betrayal, treason.

train m train; pace, rate; **être en ~ de** to be in the act of doing st.

traînasser vi to dawdle; to loiter.

traîne f dragging; train; **être à la ~** to be in tow.

traîneau m sleigh, sledge.

traînée f trail, track; drag.

traîner vi to lag, dawdle; to drag on; * vt to drag, pull; to protract; **se ~** vr to drag oneself; to crawl along.

train-train m humdrum routine.

traire vt to milk.

trait m trait, feature; deed; relation; **avoir ~ à** to have reference; ~ **d'union** hyphen, connecting link.

traite *f* trade; draft, bill; milking.

traité *m* treaty; treatise, tract.

traitement *m* treatment; salary, processing.

traiter *vt* to treat; to process; * *vi* to treat, negotiate.

traiteur *m* caterer; trader.

traître *m* traitor, **-esse** *f* traitress.

traîtrise *f* treachery, treacherousness.

trajectoire *f* trajectory.

trajet *m* distance; journey; course, path.

trame *f* framework; web.

tramer *vt* to plot; to weave.

trampoline *m* trampoline.

tramway *m* tram, tramway.

tranchant *adj* sharp, cutting.

tranche *f* slice; edge; section.

tranchée *f* trench; cutting.

trancher *vt* to cut, sever; to conclude; to settle; * *vi* to cut; to resolve; to stand out.

tranquille *adj* quiet, tranquil; **~ment** *adv* quietly, tranquilly.

tranquillisant *m* tranquillizer; * *adj* soothing, tranquillizing.

tranquilliser *vt* to reassure.

tranquillité *f* tranquillity.

transaction *f* transaction, arrangement.

transatlantique *m* transatlantic liner; * *adj* transatlantic.

transcendant *adj* transcendent; transcendental.

transcender *vt* to transcend.

transcription *f* transcription; copy.

transcrire *vt* to transcribe; copy out.

transe *f* trance.

transept *m* transept.

tranférer *vt* to transfer.

transfert *m* transfer; conveyance.

transfiguration *f* transfiguration.

transfigurer *vt* to transfigure.

transformateur *m* transformer.

transformation *f* transformation.

transformer *vt* to transform, change; **se ~** *vr* to be transformed; to change.

transfuge *mf* renegade.

transfuser *vt* to transfuse.

transfusion *f* transfusion.

transgresser *vt* to transgress, infringe.

transgression *f* transgression, infringement.

transi *adj* numb, paralysed.

transiger *vi* to compromise, come to terms.

transistor *m* transistor.

transit *m* transit.

transiter *vi* to pass in transit.

transitif *adj* transitive.

transition *f* transition.

transitoire *adj* transitory.

translucide *adj* translucent.

transmettre *vt* to transmit; to pass on, hand down.

transmissible *adj* transmissible.

transmission *f* transmission; passing on; handing down.

transmuter *vt* to transmute.

transparaître *vi* to show through.

transparence *f* transparency.

transparent *adj* transparent.

transpercer *vt* to pierce; to penetrate.

transpiration *f* transpiration; perspiration.

transpirer *vi* to perspire; to come to light.

transplanter *vt* to transplant.

transport *m* carrying; transport; conveyance; transfer.

transportable *adj* transportable.

transporter *vt* to carry; to transport

transporteur *m* haulier; carrier.

transposer *vt* to transpose.

transposition *f* transposition.

transsexuel *adj* transsexual.

transvaser *vt* to decant.

transversal *adj* transverse;

~**ement** *adv* crosswise; transversely.

transvider *vt* to pour into another container.

trapèze *m* trapeze.

trapéziste *mf* trapeze artist.

trappe *f* trap door.

trappeur *m* trapper.

trapu *adj* squat; thickset.

traquer *vt* to track; to hunt down.

traumatisant *adj* traumatizing.

traumatiser *vt* to traumatize.

traumatisme *m* traumatism.

travail *m* work; job, occupation; labour pl **travaux** work, labour.

travailler *vi* to work; to endeavour; * *vt* to work, shape; to cultivate; to fatigue

travailleur *m*, **-euse** *f* worker; * *adj* diligent; hard-working.

travers *m* breadth; irregularity; fault; **à ~** through, across; **de ~** obliquely, askew; **en ~** across, crosswise.

traversée *f* crossing, going through; traverse.

traverser *vt* to cross, traverse.

traversin *m* bolster.

travesti *m* drag artist; transvestite; * *adj* disguised.

trébucher *vi* to stumble, trip up.

trèfle *m* clover.

tréfonds *m* subsoil, bottom.

treille *f* climbing vine.

treillis *m* trellis; wire mesh.

treize *adj, m* thirteen.

treizième *adj, mf* thirteenth; ~**ment** *adv* in thirteenth place.

tréma *m* dieresis.

tremblant *adj* trembling, shaking.

tremblement *m* trembling; shiver; vibration; ~ **de terre** earthquake.

trembler *vi* to tremble, shake.

trembloter *vi* to tremble slightly, flicker.

trémousser(se) *vr* to wriggle.

tremper *vt* to soak; to dip; * *vi* to soak; to take part in.

tremplin *m* springboard; skijump.

trentaine *f* about thirty.

trente *adj, m* thirty.

trentième *adj, mf* thirtieth.

trépasser *vi* to pass away.

trépidant *adj* pulsating, quivering.

trépied *m* tripod.

trépigner *vi* to stamp one's feet.

très *adv* very; most; very much.

trésor *m* treasure.

trésorerie *f* treasury.

trésorier *m*, **-ière** *f* treasurer.

tressaillir *vi* to thrill; to shudder; to wince.

tressauter *vi* to start, jump.

tresse *f* plait, braid.

tresser *vt* to plait, braid.

tréteau *m* trestle.

treuil *m* winch.

trêve *f* truce; respite, rest.

tri *m* sorting out; selection; grading.

triage *m* sorting out.

triangle *m* triangle.

triangulaire *adj* triangular.

triathlon *m* triathlon.

tribal *adj* tribal.

tribord *m* starboard.

tribu *f* tribe.

tribunal *m* court, tribunal.

tribune *f* gallery, stand; rostrum.

tribut *m* tribute.

tributaire *adj* dependent, tributary.

tricher *vi* to cheat.

tricheur *m*, **-euse** *f* cheater.

trichloréthylène *m* trichlorethylene.

tricolore *adj* three-coloured, tricolour.

tricot *m* jumper; knitting.

tricoter *vt* to knit.

tridimensionnel *adj* three-dimensional.

triennal *adj* triennial; three-yearly.

trier *vt* to sort out; to pick over.

trifouiller *vi* (*fam*) to rummage

about; * *vt* to rummage about in.

trigonométrie *f* trigonometry.

trilingue *adj* trilingual.

trilogie *f* trilogy.

trimer *vi* to slave away.

trimestre *m* quarter; term.

trimestriel *adj* quarterly; three-monthly.

tringle *f* rod.

trinité *f* trinity.

trinquer *vi* to toast; to booze.

trio *m* trio.

triomphal *adj* triumphal; ~**ement** *adv* triumphantly.

triomphant *adj* triumphant.

triomphe *m* triumph, victory.

triompher *vi* to triumph.

triparti, tripartite *adj* tripartite.

tripe *f* tripe; guts.

triple *adj* triple, treble.

tripler *vi* to triple, increase three-fold; * *vt* to triple, treble.

tripoter *vt* to play with, speculate with.

trique *f* cudgel.

triste *adj* sad, melancholy; ~**ment** *adv* sadly.

tristesse *f* sadness; melancholy.

triton *m* triton; tritone.

triturer *vt* to grind up, triturate.

trivial *adj* mundane, trivial; coarse, crude.

trivialité *f* triviality; crudeness.

troc *m* exchange; barter.

troglodyte *m* cave dweller, troglodyte.

trognon *m* core; stalk.

trois *adj, m* three.

troisième *adj, mf* third; ~**ment** *adv* thirdly.

trombe *f*: ~ **d'eau** cloudburst, downpour; **entrer/sortir en** ~ to dash in/out.

trombone *m* trombone.

trompe *f* trumpet; trunk, snout.

trompe-l'œil *m invar* trompe-l'oeil.

tromper *vt* to deceive, trick; **se** ~ *vr* to be mistaken.

tromperie *f* deception, deceit.

trompette *f* trumpet.

trompettiste *mf* trumpet player.

trompeur *adj* deceitful; deceptive.

tronc *m* trunk, shaft.

tronçon *m* section, part.

tronçonner *vt* to cut up, cut into sections.

tronçonneuse *f* chain saw.

trône *m* throne.

trôner *vi* to sit on the throne.

tronquer *vt* to truncate, curtail.

trop *adv* too; too much, unduly; *m* ~ too much, too many.

trophée *m* trophy.

tropical *adj* tropical.

tropique *m* tropic.

trop-plein *m* overflow; excess.

troquer *vt* to barter, swap.

trot *m* trot.

trotter *vi* to trot; to run about; to toddle.

trottiner *vi* to jog along; to trot along.

trottinette *f* scooter.

trottoir *m* pavement.

trou *m* hole; gap; cavity.

troublant *adj* disturbing, disquieting.

trouble *adj* unclear; murky, suspicious; * *m* disturbance, confusion; disorder.

trouble-fête *mf* spoilsport, killjoy.

troubler *vt* to disturb, disconcert; to cloud, darken; **se** ~ *vr* to become cloudy; to become flustered.

trouer *vt* to make a hole in; to pierce.

trouille *f*: **avoir la** ~ to have the wind up.

troupe *f* troupe; troop, band.

troupeau *m* herd, drove.

trousse *f* case, kit; wallet.

trousseau *m* trousseau; outfit.

trouvaille *f* windfall; inspired idea..

trouver *vt* to find, detect; to think; **se** ~ *vr* to find oneself; to be located; **il se trouve que** it happens that.

truand *m* (*fam*) gangster; tramp.

truc *m* (*fam*) trick; gadget, thingummy.

truculent *adj* truculent; colourful, vivid.

truelle *f* trowel.

truffe *f* truffle.

truie *f* sow.

truite *f* trout.

truquage *m* rigging, fixing; fiddling.

truquer *vt* to rig, fix; to fiddle.

tsar *m* tsar.

tu *pron* you.

tuant *adj* exhausting; exasperating.

tuba *m* tuba, snorkel.

tube *m* tube, pipe; duct.

tuberculose *f* tuberculosis.

tuer *vt* to kill; **se ~** *vr* to be killed; to kill oneself.

tuerie *f* slaughter.

tueur *m*, **-euse** *f* killer.

tuile *f* tile.

tulipe *f* tulip.

tulle *m* tulle.

tuméfié *adj* puffed-up, swollen.

tumeur *f* tumour.

tumulte *m* tumult, commotion.

tumultueux *adj* tumultuous, stormy.

tungstène *m* tungsten.

tunique *f* tunic; smock.

tunnel *m* tunnel.

turban *m* turban.

turbine *f* turbine.

turbo *m* turbo.

turbulence *f* turbulence; excitement.

turbulent *adj* turbulent.

turpitude *f* turpitude, baseness.

tutelle *f* guardianship, supervision.

tuteur *m*, **-trice** *f* guardian; * *m* stake, prop.

tutoyer *vt* to address somebody as '*tu*'.

tuyau *m* pipe.

tuyauterie *f* piping.

T.V.A. (taxe à la valeur ajoutée) *f* VAT.

tympan *m* eardrum, tympanum.

type *m* type; model; sample; bloke, chap.

typé *adj* typical.

typhoïde *f* typhoid; * *adj* typhoid.

typhon *m* typhoon.

typhus *m* typhus.

typique *adj* typical; **~ment** *adv* typically.

tyran *m* tyrant.

tyrannie *f* tyranny.

tyrannique *adj* tyrannical.

tyranniser *vt* to tyrannize.

U

ulcère *m* ulcer.

ulcérer *vt* to sicken; to embitter.

ultérieur *adj* later, subsequent; **~ement** *adv* later, subsequently.

ultimatum *m* ultimatum.

ultime *adj* ultimate, final.

ultra-violet *m* ultraviolet ray; * *adj* ultraviolet.

un, une *art* a, an; (number) one; **les ~** some; **l'~ l'autre, les ~s**

les autres one another.

unanime *adj* unanimous; **~ment** *adj* unanimously.

uni *adj* plain, self-coloured; close; smooth; **~ment** *adv* plainly, smoothly.

unification *f* unification; standardization.

unifier *vt* to unify; to standardize.

uniforme *adj* uniform, regular; * *m* uniform.

uniformément *adv* uniformly, regularly.

uniformité *f* uniformity; regularity.

unilatéral *adj* unilateral.

union *f* union; combination, blending.

unique *adj* only, single; unique; **~ment** *adv* only, solely, exclusively; only, merely.

unir *vt* to unite; to join; to combine; **s'~** *vr* to unite; to be joined in marriage.

unisson *m* unison; **à l'~** in unison.

unitaire *adj* unitary, unit.

unité *f* unity; unit.

univers *m* universe; world.

universalité *f* universality.

universel *adj* universal; all-purpose; **~lement** *adv* universally.

universitaire *adj* university; * *mf* academic.

université *f* university.

uranium *m* uranium.

urbain *adj* urban, city.

urbanisation *f* urbanization.

urbaniser *vt* to urbanize.

urbanisme *m* town planning.

urbaniste *mf* town planner.

urée *f* urea.

urgence *f* urgency; emergency.

urgent *adj* urgent.

urinaire *adj* urinary.

urine *f* urine.

uriner *vi* to urinate.

urne *f* ballot box; urn.

urticaire *f* hives, urticaria.

usage *m* use; custom; usage; practice; wear; **faire ~ de** to exercise; to make use of.

usagé *adj* worn, old; second-hand.

usager *m* **ère** *f* user.

usé *adj* worn; threadbare; banal, trite.

user *vt* to make use of, enjoy; to wear out; **~ de** to exercise; to employ; **s'~** *vr* to wear out.

usine *f* factory.

usiner *vt* to machine; to manufacture.

usité *adj* in common use, common.

ustensile *m* implement; utensil.

usuel *adj* ordinary; everyday; **~lement** *adv* ordinarily.

usufruit *m* usufruct.

usure *f* usury.

usurier *m*, **-ière** *f* usurer.

usurper *vt* to usurp.

utérus *m* womb, uterus.

utile *adj* useful; **~ment** *adv* usefully.

utilisateur *m*, **-trice** *f* user.

utilisation *f* use, utilization.

utiliser *vt* to use, utilize; to make use of.

utilitaire *adj* utilitarian.

utilité *f* usefulness; use; profit.

utopie *f* utopia.

utopique *adj* utopian.

V

vacance *f* vacancy; **~s** holiday, vacation.

vacancier *m*, **-ière** *f* holidaymaker.

vacant *adj* vacant, unoccupied.

vacarme *m* racket, row.

vaccin *m* vaccine.

vaccination *f* vaccination.

vacciner *vt* to vaccinate.

vache *f* cow; cowhide

vachement *adv* (*fam*) damned, bloody.

vacher *m*, **-ère** *f* cowherd.

vacherie *f* (*fam*) rottenness, meanness; nasty remark/trick.

vaciller *vi* to sway, totter; to falter.

va-et-vient *m invar* comings and goings; to and fro.

vagabond *m*, **-e** *f* tramp, vagabond.

vagabondage *m* wandering, roaming; vagrancy.

vagabonder *vi* to wander, roam.

vagin *f* vagina.

vaginal *adj* vaginal.

vague *adj* vague, hazy, indistinct; **~ment** vaguely; * *m* vagueness; * *f* wave.

vaguer *vi* to wander, roam.

vaillamment *adv* bravely, courageously.

vaillant *adj* brave, courageous.

vain *adj* vain; empty, hollow; shallow; **en ~** in vain; **~ement** *adv* vainly.

vaincre *vt* to defeat, overcome.

vaincu *adj* defeated, beaten.

vainqueur *m* conqueror, victor.

vaisseau *m* vessel; ship.

vaisselle *f* crockery; dishes; **faire la ~** to do the washing up.

valable *adj* valid, legitimate; worthwhile.

valet *m* valet; servant.

valeur *f* value, worth; security, share; meaning.

valide *adj* able, able-bodied; **~ment** *adv* validly.

valider *vt* to validate.

validité *f* validity.

valise *f* suitcase.

vallée *f* valley.

vallon *m* vale, dale.

vallonné *adj* undulating.

valoir *vt* to be worth; to be valid; **il vaut mieux** it is better to; **~ la peine** to be worth the trouble.

valoriser *vt* to develop; to enhance; to actualize.

valse *f* waltz.

valser *vi* to waltz.

valve *f* valve.

vampire *m* vampire.

vandale *mf* vandal.

vandalisme *m* vandalism.

vanille *f* vanilla.

vanité *f* vanity, conceit.

vaniteux *adj* vain, conceited.

vanne *f* gate, sluice.

vannerie *f* basketry; wickerwork.

vantard *adj* boastful, bragging.

vantardise *f* boastfulness; boast.

vanter *vt* to praise, vaunt; **se ~** *vr* to boast, brag.

vapeur *f* haze, vapour.

vaporeux *adj* filmy, vaporous.

vaporisateur *m* spray, atomizer.

vaporiser *vt* to spray; to vaporize.

varappe *f* rock-climbing.

variable *adj* variable, changeable.

variante *f* variant; variation.

variation *f* variation, change.

varice *f* varicose vein.

varicelle *f* chickenpox.

varié *adj* varied; variegated; various.

varier *vi* to vary, change; * *vt* to vary.

variété *f* variety, diversity.

variole *f* smallpox.

vasculaire *adj* vascular.

vase *m* vase, bowl; * *f* silt, mud.

vaseline *f* vaseline.

vaseux *adj* woolly, muddled; muddy, silty.

vasistas *m* fanlight.

vaste *adj* vast, huge.

vaudeville *m* vaudeville.

vaudou *m* voodoo.

vaurien *m*, **-ienne** *f* good-for-nothing.

vautour *m* vulture.

vautrer(se) *vr* to wallow in.

veau *m* calf; veal.

vecteur *m* vector.

vécu *adj* real, true-life; lived; * *m* real-life.

vedette *f* star; leading light.

végétal *adj* vegetable.

végétarien *m*, **-ienne** *f* vegetarian; * *adj* vegetarian.

végétatif *adj* vegetative.

végétation *f* vegetation.

végéter *vi* to vegetate; to stagnate.

véhémence *f* vehemence.

véhément *adj* vehement.

véhicule *m* vehicle.

veille *f* wakefulness; watch; eve.

veillée *f* evening; evening meeting.

veiller *vi* to stay up, sit up.

veilleur *m* watchman.

veilleuse *f* night light; sidelight.

veinard *m*, **-e** *f* lucky person; * *adj* lucky, jammy.

veine *f* vein, seam; inspiration; luck.

vêler *vi* to calve.

velléité *f* vague desire, vague impulse.

vélo *m* cycle.

vélodrome *m* velodrome.

vélomoteur *m* motorized bike.

velours *m* velvet.

velouté *adj* velvety, downy.

velu *adj* hairy.

vénal *adj* venal, mercenary.

vendange *f* wine harvest; vintage.

vendanger *vt* to harvest grapes from; * *vi* to harvest the grapes.

vendangeur *m*, **-euse** *f* grapepicker.

vendetta *f* vendetta.

vendeur *m*, **-euse** *f* seller, salesperson.

vendre *vt* to sell.

vendredi *m* Friday.

vénéneux *adj* poisonous.

vénérable *adj* venerable.

vénération *f* veneration.

vénérer *vt* to venerate.

vénérien *adj* venereal.

vengeance *f* vengeance, revenge.

venger *vt* to avenge; **se ~** *vr* to avenge oneself.

venimeux *adj* venomous, poisonous; vicious.

venin *m* venom; poison.

venir *vi* to come; to happen; to grow; **~ de** to come from; to derive from; **~ au monde** to be born.

vent *m* wind; breath; emptiness, vanity.

vente *f* sale; selling; auction; **en ~** for sale.

ventilateur *m* ventilator, fan.

ventiler *vt* to ventilate; to divide up

ventouse *f* sucker; suction disc.

ventre *m* stomach, belly; womb.

ventricule *m* ventricle.

ventriloque *mf* ventriloquist; * *adj* ventriloquous.

venue *f* coming.

ver *m* worm; grub; **~ de terre** earthworm.

véracité *f* veracity; truthfulness.

véranda *f* veranda.

verbal *adj* verbal; **~ement** *adv* verbally.

verbe *m* verb; language, word.

verbiage *m* verbiage.

verdeur *f* vigour, vitality.

verdict *m* verdict.

verdir *vi* to go green; * *vt* to turn green.

verdure *f* greenery, verdure.

verge *f* stick, cane.

verger *m* orchard.

verglas *m* black ice.

véridique *adj* truthful, veracious; **~ment** *adv* truthfully.

vérification *f* check; verification.

vérifier *vt* to verify, check; to audit.

véritable *adj* real, genuine; **~ment** *adv* really, genuinely.

vérité *f* truth; truthfulness, sincerity; **en ~** really, actually.

vermeil *adj* vermilion, ruby, cherry; * *m* vermeil.

vermicelle *m* vermicelli.

vermillon *m* vermilion; scarlet.

vermine *f* vermin.

vermisseau *m* vermicule, small worm.

vermoulu *adj* worm-eaten.

verni *adj* varnished.

vernis *m* varnish; glaze; shine.

vernissage *m* varnishing; glazing.

verre *m* glass; lens; drink.
verrerie *f* glassworks; glass-making.
verrière *f* window; glass roof.
verrou *m* bolt.
verrouillage *m* bolting; locking.
verrouiller *vt* to bolt; to lock.
verrue *f* wart, verruca.
vers *prép* towards; around; about; * *m* line, verse.
versatile *adj* versatile.
verse *f*: **pleuvoir à ~** to pour down.
verseau *m* Aquarius.
verser *vt* to pour, shed; to pay; to assign.
verset *m* verse.
version *f* version.
verso *m* back.
vert *m* green; * *adj* green; **langue ~e** slang; **~ement** *adv* sharply, brusquely.
vertébral *adj* vertebral.
vertèbre *f* vertebra.
vertical *adj* vertical; **~ement** *adv* vertically.
vertige *m* vertigo; dizziness.
vertigineux *adj* vertiginous, breathtaking.
vertu *f* virtue; courage; **en ~ de** in accordance with.
vertueux *adj* virtuous.
verve *f* verve, vigour.
verveine *f* vervain, verbena.
vésicule *f* vesicle.
vessie *f* bladder, vesica.
veste *f* jacket.
vestiaire *m* cloakroom; changing-room.
vestibule *m* hall, vestibule.
vestige *m* relic; trace, vestige.
veston *m* jacket.
vêtement *m* garment.
vétéran *m* veteran.
vétérinaire *mf* veterinary surgeon; * *adj* veterinary.
vêtir *vt* to clothe, dress; **se ~** *vr* to dress oneself.
veto *m* veto.
vêtu *adj* dressed; clad, wearing.

vétuste *adj* dilapidated, ancient.
veuf *m* widower; * *adj* widowed.
veuve *f* widow; * *adj* widowed.
veule *adj* spineless.
vexant *adj* annoying, vexing.
vexer *vt* to annoy; to hurt.
viable *adj* viable.
viaduc *m* viaduct.
viande *f* meat.
vibration *f* vibration.
vibrer *vi* to vibrate; to quiver.
vibromasseur *m* vibrator.
vicaire *m* curate, vicar.
vice *m* vice; fault, defect.
vice-président *m* vice-president; deputy chairman.
vice-versa *adv* vice versa.
vicieux *adj* licentious; dissolute; incorrect.
vicissitude *f* vicissitude, change; trial.
vicomte *m* viscount, **-esse** *f* viscountess.
victime *f* victim, casualty; **être ~ de** to be the victim of.
victoire *f* victory.
victorieusement *adv* victoriously.
victorieux *adj* victorious.
vidange *f* emptying; waste outlet.
vidanger *vt* to empty; to drain off.
vide *adj* empty, vacant, devoid; * *m* vacuum; gap; void.
vidéo *f* video; * *adj invar* video.
vidéocassette *f* videocassette.
vide-ordures *m invar* rubbish chute.
vider *vt* to empty; to drain; to vacate; to gut.
videur *m* bouncer.
vie *f* life; living; **être en ~** to be alive.
vieillard *m* old man.
vieillesse *f* old age; the elderly; oldness.
vieillir *vi* to get old; * *vt* to age; to put years on.
vieillissement *m* ageing; obsolescence.
vierge *f* virgin; * *adj* virgin;

blank; unexposed.

vieux adj, f **vieille** old; ancient; obsolete.

vif adj alive, lively; quick; eager; passionate.

vigilance f vigilance.

vigilant adj vigilant.

vigile m vigil.

vigne f vine; vineyard.

vigneron m, **-onne** f wine grower.

vignette f vignette; illustration; seal.

vignoble m vineyard.

vigoureusement adv vigorously, energetically.

vigoureux adj vigorous.

vigueur f vigour, strength, energy.

vil adj vile; lowly.

vilain m naughty boy, **-e** f naughty girl.

villa f villa, detached house.

village m village.

villageois m, **-e** f village, rustic.

ville f town, city.

villégiature f holiday; vacation.

vin m wine.

vinaigre m vinegar.

vinaigrette f vinaigrette, oil and vinegar dressing.

vindicatif adj vindictive.

vingt adj, m twenty.

vingtaine f about twenty.

vingtième adj, mf twentieth; **-ment** adv in twentieth place.

vinicole adj wine, wine-growing.

vinyl m vinyl.

viol m rape.

violation f violation; transgression.

violemment adv violently.

violence f violence; force, duress.

violent adj violent; considerable, excessive.

violer vt to violate, desecrate; to rape.

violet adj purple, violet; * m purple, violet.

violette f (bot) violet.

violeur m rapist.

violon m violin.

violoncelle m cello, violoncello.

violoncelliste mf cello player.

violoniste mf violinist.

vipère f viper, adder.

virage m turn, bend; tacking.

viral adj viral.

virement m turning, tacking; transfer, clearance.

virer vt to transfer; * vi to turn, tack.

virevolter vi to spin round, pirouette.

virginité f virginity; purity.

virgule f comma; point.

viril adj virile; male, masculine; **-ement** adv in a virile way.

virilité f virility; masculinity.

virtuel adj virtual; potential; **-lement** adv virtually.

virtuose mf virtuoso, master.

virulence f virulence, viciousness.

virulent adj virulent, vicious.

virus m virus.

vis f screw.

visa m stamp, visa.

visage m face; expression.

vis-à-vis prép: opposite; **~ de** towards; as regards; * m encounter; person opposite; **en ~** opposite each other.

viscéral adj visceral; deep-rooted.

viscère f viscera; intestines.

viser vt to aim, target; to visa.

viseur m sights; viewfinder.

visibilité f visibility.

visible adj visible; evident, obvious; **-ment** adv visibly; obviously.

visière f peak; eyeshade; visor.

vision f eyesight; vision.

visionnaire mf visionary; * adj visionary.

visite f visit; visiting, inspection; visitor.

visiter vt to visit; to examine, inspect.

visiteur m, **-euse** f visitor; representative.

vison *m* mink.

visqueux *adj* viscous, thick.

visser *vt* to screw on.

visuel *adj* visual.

vital *adj* vital.

vitalité *f* energy, vitality.

vitamine *f* vitamin.

vite *adv* quickly, fast; soon. *adj* swift; quick.

vitesse *f* speed, swiftness; gear.

viticole *adj* wine, wine-growing.

viticulteur *m* wine grower.

vitrage *m* glazing; windows.

vitrail *m* stained-glass window.

vitre *f* pane, window.

vitreux *adj* glassy, glazed, vitreous.

vitrier *m* glazier.

vitrine *f* shop window; display cabinet.

vitriol *m* vitriol.

vitupérer *vi* to vituperate, reprimand.

vivace *adj* inveterate, steadfast; hardy, perennial.

vivacité *f* vivacity, liveliness; vividness; acuteness.

vivant *adj* alive, living; lively.

vivement *adv* quickly, briskly; keenly, acutely.

vivier *m* fishpond.

vivifiant *adj* refreshing, invigorating.

vivifier *vt* to enliven, invigorate, refresh.

vivre *vi* to live, be alive; to last, endure; **vive la mariée!** three cheers for the bride; * *vt* to live, spend; to live through.

vivres *mpl* victuals, supplies.

V.O. (version originale) *f* original version.

vocabulaire *m* vocabulary.

vocal *adj* vocal; **~ement** *adv* vocally.

vocalise *f* singing exercise.

vocation *f* vocation, calling.

vociférer *vi* to vociferate, bawl.

voeu *m* vow; wish.

vogue *f* fashion, vogue; **en ~** in fashion.

voici *prép* here is, here are; ago; past.

voie *f* way, road; means; process; **~ ferrée** railway; **~ d'eau** leak; **en ~ de** in the process of.

voilà *prép* there is, there are; ago; **et ~!** so there!

voile *f* sail; * *m* veil.

voilé *adj* veiled; hazy, blurred.

voiler *vt* to veil, shroud; **se ~** *vr* to wear a veil; to mist over.

voilier *m* sailing boat, yacht.

voir *vt* to see; to deal with; to understand; **avoir à ~ avec** to have to do with; **se ~** *vr* to find oneself; to show.

voisin *m*, **-e** *f* neighbour; fellow; * *adj* neighbouring, next.

voisinage *m* neighbourhood, vicinity.

voiture *f* car; carriage; cart.

voix *f* voice; vote; **parler à ~ basse/haute** to speak in a low/high voice.

vol *m* flight; flock; **à ~ d'oiseau** as the crow flies.

volaille *f* fowl, poultry.

volant *m* steering wheel; * *adj* flying.

volatile *adj* volatile.

volatiliser *vt* to volatilize; to extinguish; **se ~** *vr* to volatilize; to vanish.

volcan *m* volcano.

volcanique *adj* volcanic.

volée *f* flight; volley; **à la ~** in midair; rashly, at random; **demi-~** half-volley.

voler *vi* to fly; **~ en éclats** to smash into pieces; * *vt* to steal; to rob.

volet *m* shutter; flap, paddle.

voleur *m*, **-euse** *f* thief; * *adj* dishonest, thieving.

volley-ball *m* volleyball.

volleyeur *m*, **-euse** *f* volleyball player.

volontaire *adj* voluntary; intentional; **~ment** *adv* voluntarily; intentionally.

volonté *f* will, wish; willingness; willpower.

volontiers *adv* willingly; gladly.

volt *m* volt.

volte-face *f invar* volte-face, about-turn **faire ~** to turn round.

voltige *f* acrobatics; trick riding.

voltiger *vi* to flutter about.

volubile *adj* voluble.

volume *m* volume.

volumineux *adj* voluminous, bulky.

volupté *f* voluptuousness, sensual pleasure.

voluptueux *adj* voluptuous.

volute *f* volute, scroll; wreath.

vomir *vi* to vomit, be sick; * *vt* to vomit, bring up.

vomissement *m* vomiting.

vorace *adj* voracious; **~ment** *adv* voraciously.

voracité *f* voracity, voraciousness.

vos = *pl* votre.

votant *m*, **-e** *f* voter.

vote *m* vote; voting.

voter *vi* to vote.

votre *adj*, *pl* **vos** your, your own.

vôtre *pron*: **le ~, la ~, les ~s** yours, your own.

vouer *vt* to vow; to devote, dedicate.

vouloir *vt* to want, wish; to require; to try; **~ du mal à** to wish somebody harm; **en ~ à** to have something against somebody; **bien ~** to be happy that.

voulu *adj* required; deliberate.

vous *pron* you, you yourself.

voûte *f* vault.

voûté *adj* vaulted.

vouvoyer *vt* to use the *'vous'* form.

voyage *m* journey, trip; travelling.

voyager *vi* to travel, journey.

voyageur *m*, **-euse** *f* traveller, passenger.

voyant *m*, **-e** *f* visionary, seer; * *m* signal light; * *adj* gaudy, showy.

voyelle *f* vowel.

voyeur *m*, **-euse** *f* voyeur.

voyou *m* lout, loafer, hoodlum.

vrac *adv*: **en ~** in bulk.

vrai *adj* true, genuine; **~ment** *adv* truly, really.

vraisemblable *adj* likely, probable; **~ment** *adv* probably.

vrille *f* tendril; spiral; **descendre en ~** to come down in a spin.

vrombir *vi* to roar, hum.

vu *adj* seen; considered, regarded; **être bien/mal ~** to be well/poorly thought of; **ni ~ ni connu** you won't discover anything; * *prép* in view of.

vue *f* sight, eyesight; **en ~ de** with a view to; **avoir des ~s sur** to have designs on.

vulgaire *adj* vulgar, crude; **~ment** *adv* vulgarly.

vulgariser *vt* to popularize; to coarsen.

vulgarité *f* vulgarity, coarseness.

vulnérable *adj* vulnerable.

vulve *f* vulva.

W

wagon *m* wagon, truck, freight car; wagonload.

wagon-citerne *m* tanker.

wagon-lit *m* sleeper.

wagon-restaurant *m* restaurant car.

water-polo *m* water polo.

watt *m* watt.

W.-C. (water-closet) *mpl* lavatory.

week-end *m* weekend.

western *m* western.

whisky *m* whisky.

X

xénophobe *mf* xenophobe; * *adj* xenophobic.

xénophobie *f* xenophobia.
xylophone *m* xylophone.

Y

yacht *m* yacht.
yang *m* yang.
yaourt *m* yoghurt.
yard *m* yard.
yeux = *pl* oeil
yin *m* yin.

yoga *m* yoga
yoghurt *m* = **yaourt**.
yogi *m* yogi.
yo-yo *m* yo-yo.
yucca *m* yucca.
yuppie *mf* yuppy.

Z

zèbre *m* zebra.
zébu *m* zebu.
zèle *m* zeal.
zélé *adj* zealous.
zen *m* Zen.
zénith *m* zenith.
zéro *m* zero, nought, nothing.
zézayer *vi* to lisp.
zigzag *m* zigzag.
zigzaguer *vi* to zigzag.
zinc *m* zinc.
zizanie *f* ill-feeling.
zizi *m* (*fam*) willy.
zodiaque *m* zodiac.

zona *m* shingles.
zone *f* zone, area.
zoo *m* zoo.
zoologie *f* zoology.
zoologiste *mf* zoologist.
zoom *m* zoom; zoom lens.
zoophile *adj* zoophilic, zoophilous.
zozoter *vi* (*fam*) to lisp.
Z.U.P. (**zone à urbaniser en priorité**) *f* urban development zone.
zut *interj* damn! rubbish! shut up!

English-French
Dictionary

A

a *art* un, une.
aback *adv* to be taken ~ *vi* être décontenancé.
abacus *n* abaque, boulier *m*.
abandon *vt* abandonner, laisser.
abandonment *n* abandon *m*.
abase *vt* avilir; humilier.
abasement *n* avilissement *m*; humiliation *f*.
abash *vt* couvrir de honte.
abate *vt* baisser; * *vi* baisser; se calmer.
abatement *n* baisse, réduction *f*.
abbess *n* abbesse *f*.
abbey *n* abbaye *f*.
abbot *n* abbé *m*.
abbreviate *vt* abréger, raccourcir.
abbreviation *n* abréviation *f*.
abdicate *vt* abdiquer; renoncer à.
abdication *n* abdication *f*; renonciation *f*.
abdomen *n* abdomen *m*.
abdominal *adj* abdominal.
abduct *vt* kidnapper, enlever.
abductor *n* abducteur *m*.
abed *adv* au lit.
aberrant *adj* aberrant.
aberration *n* aberration *f*.
abet *vt*: to aid and ~ être complice de.
abeyance *n* suspension *f*.
abhor *vt* abhorrer, exécrer.
abhorrence *n* exécration, horreur *f*.
abhorrent *adj* exécrable.
abide *vt* supporter, souffrir.
ability *n* capacité, aptitude *f*; abilities *pl* talents *mpl*.
abject *adj* misérable; abject, méprisable; ~ly *adv* misérablement.
abjure *vt* abjurer; renoncer à.
ablative *n* (*gr*) ablatif *m*.
ablaze *adj* enflammé.
able *adj* capable; to be ~ pouvoir.
able-bodied *adj* robuste.

ablution *n* ablution *f*.
ably *adv* habilement.
abnegation *n* renoncement *m*.
abnormal *adj* anormal.
abnormality *n* anomalie *f*.
aboard *adv* à bord.
abode *n* domicile *m*.
abolish *vt* abolir, supprimer.
abolition *n* abolition, suppression *f*.
abominable *adj* abominable; ~bly *adv* abominablement.
abomination *n* abomination *f*.
aboriginal *adj* aborigène.
aborigines *npl* aborigènes *mpl*.
abort *vi* avorter.
abortion *n* avortement *m*.
abortive *adj* raté.
abound *vi* abonder; to ~ with abonder en.
about *prep* au sujet de; vers; I carry no money ~ me je n'ai pas d'argent sur moi; * *adv* çà et là; to be ~ to être sur le point de; to go ~ aller de- ci de- là; to go ~ a thing entreprendre quelque chose; all ~ partout.
above *prep* au-dessus de; * *adv* au-dessus; ~ all surtout, principalement; ~ mentioned mentionné ci-dessus.
aboveboard *adj* légitime.
abrasion *n* écorchure *f*.
abrasive *adj* abrasif.
abreast *adv* de front.
abridge *vt* abréger, raccourcir.
abridgment *n* abrégement *m*; version abrégée *f*.
abroad *adv* à l'étranger; to go ~ se rendre à l'étranger.
abrogate *vt* abroger.
abrogation *n* abrogation *f*.
abrupt *adj* abrupt; brusque; ~ly *adv* brusquement; rudement.
abscess *n* abcès *m*.
abscond *vi* s'enfuir.

absence n absence f.
absent adj absent; * vi s'absenter.
absentee n absent m, -e f.
absenteeism n absentéisme m.
absent-minded adj distrait.
absolute adj absolu; **~ly** adv absolument.
absolution n absolution f.
absolutism n absolutisme m.
absolve vt absoudre.
absorb vt absorber.
absorbent adj absorbant.
absorbent cotton n coton hydrophile m.
absorption n absorption f.
abstain vi s'abstenir.
abstemious adj sobre; **~ly** adv sobrement.
abstemiousness n sobriété f.
abstinence n abstinence f.
abstinent adj abstinent.
abstract adj abstrait; * n abrégé m; **in the ~** dans l'abstrait.
abstraction n abstraction f; extraction f.
abstractly adv abstraitement.
abstruse adj abstrus, obscur; **~ly** adv obscurément.
absurd adj absurde; **~ly** adv absurdement.
absurdity n absurdité f.
abundance n abondance f.
abundant adj abondant; **~ly** adv abondamment.
abuse vt abuser de; insulter; maltraiter; * n abus m; injures fpl; mauvais traitements mpl.
abusive adj injurieux; **~ly** adv injurieusement.
abut vi confiner.
abysmal adj abominable.
abyss n abîme m.
acacia n acacia m.
academic adj universitaire; scolaire; théorique.
academician n universitaire mf.
academy n académie f.
accede vi accéder.
accelerate vt accélérer.
accelerator n accélérateur m.

acceleration n accélération f.
accent n accent m; * vt accentuer.
accentuate vt accentuer.
accentuation n accentuation f.
accept vt accepter.
acceptable adj acceptable.
acceptability n acceptabilité f.
acceptance n acceptation f.
access n accès m.
accessible adj accessible.
accession n augmentation f; accession f.
accessory n accessoire m; (law) complice m.
accident n accident m; hasard m.
accidental adj accidentel; **~ly** adv par hasard.
acclaim vt acclamer.
acclamation n acclamation f.
acclimate vt acclimater.
accommodate vt loger; accommoder.
accommodating adj obligeant.
accommodations npl logement m.
accompaniment n (mus) accompagnement m.
accompanist n (mus) accompagnateur m, -trice f.
accompany vt accompagner.
accomplice n complice mf.
accomplish vt accomplir.
accomplished adj accompli.
accomplishment n accomplissement m; **~s** pl talents mpl.
accord n accord m; **with one ~** d'un commun accord; **of one's own ~** de son propre chef.
accordance n: **in ~ with** conformément à.
according prep selon; **~ as** selon que; **~ly** adv en conséquence.
accordion n (mus) accordéon m.
accost vt accoster.
account n compte m; **on no ~** en aucun cas; **on ~ of** en raison de; **to call to ~** demander des comptes; **to turn to ~** mettre à profit; * vt **to ~ for** expliquer; représenter.

accountability n responsabilité f.

accountable adj responsable.

accountancy n comptabilité f.

accountant n comptable mf.

account book n livre de comptes m.

account number n numéro de compte m.

accrue vi s'accumuler; revenir.

accumulate vt accumuler; * vi s'accumuler.

accumulation n accumulation f.

accuracy n exactitude f.

accurate adj exact; ~ly adv exactement.

accursed adj maudit.

accusation n accusation f.

accusative n (gr) accusatif m.

accusatory adj accusateur.

accuse vt accuser.

accused n accusé m, -e f.

accuser n accusateur m, -trice f.

accustom vt accoutumer.

accustomed adj accoutumé.

ace n as m; **within an ~ of** à deux doigts de.

acerbic adj acerbe.

acetate n (chem) acétate m.

ache n douleur f; * vi faire mal.

achieve vt réaliser; obtenir.

achievement n réalisation f; exploit m.

acid adj acide; aigre; * n acide m.

acidity n acidité f.

acknowledge vt reconnaître, admettre.

acknowledgment n reconnaissance f.

acme n apogée m.

acne n acné f.

acorn n gland m.

acoustics n acoustique f.

acquaint vt informer, aviser.

acquaintance n connaissance f.

acquiesce vi acquiescer, consentir.

acquiescence n consentement m.

acquiescent adj consentant.

acquire vt acquérir.

acquisition n acquisition f.

acquit vt acquitter.

acquittal n acquittement m.

acre n acre f.

acrid adj âcre; acerbe.

acrimonious adj acrimonieux.

acrimony n acrimonie f.

across adv en travers, d'un côté à l'autre; * prep à travers; **to come ~** tomber sur.

act vt jouer; * vi agir; jouer la comédie; * n acte m; **~s of the apostles** Actes des Apôtres mpl.

acting adj provisoire.

action n action f; combat m.

action replay n répétition f.

activate vt activer.

active adj actif; ~ly adv activement.

activity n activité f.

actor n acteur m.

actress n actrice f.

actual adj réel; concret; ~ly adv en fait; réellement.

actuary n actuaire mf.

acumen n perspicacité f.

acute adj aigu; perspicace; **~ accent** n accent aigu m; **~ angle** n angle aigu m; **~ly** adv vivement; avec perspicacité.

acuteness n perspicacité f.

ad n annonce f.

adage n adage m.

adamant adj inflexible.

adapt vt adapter, ajuster.

adaptability n facilité d'adaptation f.

adaptable adj adaptable.

adaptation n adaptation f.

adaptor n adaptateur m.

add vt ajouter; **to ~ up** additionner.

addendum n addendum m.

adder n vipère f.

addict n intoxiqué m, -e f.

addiction n dépendance f.

addictive adj qui crée une dépendance.

addition n addition f.

additional *adj* additionnel; **~ly** *adv* de plus.

additive *n* additif *m*.

address *vt* adresser; s'adresser à; * *n* adresse *f*; discours *m*.

adduce *vt* mentionner, citer.

adenoids *npl* végétations *fpl*.

adept *adj* adroit.

adequacy *n* suffisance *f*; capacité *f*.

adequate *adj* adéquat; suffisant; **~ly** *adv* convenablement; suffisamment.

adhere *vi* adhérer.

adherence *n* adhérence *f*.

adherent *n* adhérent, partisan *m*.

adhesion *n* adhérence *f*; adhésion *f*.

adhesive *adj* adhésif.

adhesive tape *n* (*med*) sparadrap *m*.

adhesiveness *n* adhérence *f*.

adieu *adv* adieu; * *n* adieux *mpl*.

adipose *adj* adipeux.

adjacent *adj* adjacent, contigu.

adjectival *adj* adjectival; **~ly** *adv* adjectivalement.

adjective *n* adjectif *m*.

adjoin *vi* être contigu.

adjoining *adj* contigu.

adjourn *vt* reporter, remettre.

adjournment *n* ajournement *m*.

adjudicate *vt* décider; juger.

adjunct *n* adjoint *m*, -e *f*.

adjust *vt* ajuster, adapter.

adjustable *adj* ajustable, adaptable.

adjustment *n* ajustement *m*; réglage *m*.

adjutant *n* (*mil*) adjudant *m*.

ad lib *vt* improviser.

administer *vt* administrer; distribuer; **to ~ an oath** faire prêter serment.

administration *n* administration *f*; gouvernement *m*.

administrative *adj* administratif.

administrator *n* administrateur *m*, -trice *f*.

admirable *adj* admirable; **~bly** *adv* admirablement.

admiral *n* amiral *m*.

admiralship *n* amirauté *f*.

admiralty *n* ministère de la Marine *m*.

admiration *n* admiration *f*.

admire *vt* admirer.

admirer *n* admirateur *m*, -trice *f*.

admiringly *adv* avec admiration.

admissible *adj* admissible.

admission *n* admission, entrée *f*.

admit *vt* admettre; **to ~ to** reconnaître.

admittance *n* admission *f*.

admittedly *adv* il est vrai (que).

admixture *n* mélange *m*.

admonish *vt* admonester, réprimander.

admonition *n* admonestation *f*; conseil *m*.

admonitory *adj* d'admonestation.

ad nauseam *adv* à saturation.

ado *n* agitation *f*.

adolescence *n* adolescence *f*.

adopt *vt* adopter.

adopted *adj* adoptif.

adoption *n* adoption *f*.

adoptive *adj* adoptif.

adorable *adj* adorable.

adorably *adv* adorablement.

adoration *n* adoration *f*.

adore *vt* adorer.

adorn *vt* orner.

adornment *n* ornement *m*.

adrift *adv* à la dérive.

adroit *adj* adroit, habile.

adroitness *n* adresse *f*.

adulation *n* adulation *f*.

adulatory *adj* adulateur.

adult *adj* adulte; * *n* adulte *mf*.

adulterate *vt* falsifier; * *adj* falsifié.

adulteration *n* falsification *f*.

adulterer *n* adultère *m*.

adulteress *n* adultère *f*.

adulterous *adj* adultère.

adultery *n* adultère *m*.

advance *vt* avancer; * *vi* avancer;

faire des progrès; * n avance f.

advanced adj avancé.

advancement n avancement m.

advantage n avantage m; **to take ~ of** profiter de.

advantageous adj avantageux; **~ly** adv avantageusement.

advantageousness n avantage m.

advent n venue f; **Advent** n Avent m.

adventitious adj accidentel.

adventure n aventure f.

adventurer n aventurier m, -ière f.

adventurous adj aventureux; **~ly** adv aventureusement.

adverb n adverbe m.

adverbial adj adverbial; **~ly** adv adverbialement.

adversary n adversaire mf.

adverse adj défavorable, contraire.

adversity n adversité f; malheur m.

advertise vt faire de la publicité pour; mettre une annonce pour.

advertisement n publicité f; annonce f.

advertising n publicité f.

advice n conseil m; avis m.

advisability n opportunité f.

advisable adj prudent, conseillé.

advise vt conseiller; aviser.

advisedly adv de manière avisée.

advisory adj consultatif.

advocacy n défense f.

advocate n avocat m; * vt plaider pour.

advocateship n barreau m.

aerial n antenne f.

aerobics npl aérobic m.

aerometer n aéromètre m.

aeroplane n avion m.

aerosol n aérosol m.

aerostat n aérostat m.

afar adv au loin; **from ~** de loin.

affability n affabilité f.

affable adj affable; **~bly** adv affablement.

affair n affaire f.

affect vt toucher; affecter.

affectation n affectation f.

affected p adj affecté; **~ly** adv avec affectation.

affectingly adv avec affection.

affection n affection f.

affectionate adj affectueux; **~ly** adv affectueusement.

affidavit n déclaration sous serment f.

affiliate vt affilier.

affiliation n affiliation f.

affinity n affinité f.

affirm vt affirmer, déclarer.

affirmation n affirmation f.

affirmative adj affirmatif; **~ly** adv affirmativement.

affix vt coller; apposer; * n (gr) affixe m.

afflict vt affliger.

affliction n affliction f.

affluence n abondance f.

affluent adj riche; abondant.

afflux n afflux m, affluence f.

afford vt fournir; **to be able to ~** avoir les moyens d'acheter.

affray n bagarre f.

affront n affront m, injure f; * vt affronter; insulter.

aflame adv en flammes.

afloat adv à flot.

afore prep avant; * adv d'abord.

afraid adj apeuré; **I am ~** j'ai peur.

afresh adv à nouveau.

aft adv (mar) en poupe.

after prep après; * adv après; **~ all** après tout.

afterbirth n placenta m.

after-crop n deuxième récolte f.

after-effects npl répercussions fpl.

afterlife n vie après la mort f.

aftermath n conséquences fpl.

afternoon n après-midi mf.

afterpains npl tranchées utérines fpl.

aftershave n après-rasage m.

aftertaste n arrière-goût m.

afterward(s) adv ensuite.

again *adv* à nouveau; ~ **and** ~ de nombreuses fois; **as much** ~ la même chose.

against *prep* contre; ~ **the grain** à contre fil; de mauvaise volonté.

agate *n* agate *f*.

age *n* âge *m*; vieillesse *f*; **under** ~ mineur; * *vt* vieillir.

aged *adj* âgé.

agency *n* agence *f*.

agenda *n* ordre du jour *m*.

agent *n* agent *m*.

agglomerate *vt* agglomérer.

agglomeration *n* agglomération *f*.

aggrandizement *n* agrandissement *m*.

aggravate *vt* aggraver; énerver.

aggravation *n* aggravation *f*; énervement *m*.

aggregate *n* agrégat *m*.

aggregation *n* agrégation *f*.

aggression *n* agression *f*.

aggressive *adj* agressif.

aggressor *n* agresseur *m*.

aggrieved *adj* offensé.

aghast *adj* horrifié.

agile *adj* agile; adroit.

agility *n* agilité *f*; adresse *f*.

agitate *vt* agiter.

agitation *n* agitation *f*.

agitator *n* agitateur *m*, -trice *f*.

ago *adv*: **how long** ~? il y a combien de temps?

agog *adj* ému.

agonizing *adj* atroce.

agony *n* agonie *f*.

agrarian *adj* agraire.

agree *vt* convenir; * *vi* être d'accord.

agreeable *adj* agréable; ~**bly** *adv* agréablement; ~ **with** conforme à.

agreeableness *n* caractère agréable *m*.

agreed *adj* convenu; ~! *adv* d'accord!

agreement *n* accord *m*.

agricultural *adj* agricole.

agriculture *n* agriculture *f*.

agriculturist *n* agriculteur *m*.

aground *adv* (*mar*) échoué.

ah! *excl* ah!

ahead *adv* en avant; à l'avance; (*mar*) sur l'avant.

ahoy! *excl* (*mar*) ohé!

aid *vt* aider, secourir; **to** ~ **and abet** être complice de; * *n* aide *f*, secours *m*; aide *mf*.

aide-de-camp *n* (*mil*) aide de camp *m*.

AIDS *n* SIDA *m*.

ail *vt* affliger.

ailing *adj* souffrant.

ailment *n* maladie *f*.

aim *vt* pointer; viser; aspirer à;* *n* but *m*; cible *f*.

aimless *adj* sans but; ~**ly** à la dérive, sans but.

air *n* air *m*; * *vt* aérer.

air balloon *n* ballon *m*.

airborne *adj* aéroporté.

air-conditioned *adj* climatisé.

air-conditioning *n* climatisation *f*.

aircraft *n* avion *m*.

air cushion *n* coussin d'air *m*.

air force *n* armée de l'air *f*.

air freshener *n* appareil de conditionnement d'air *m*.

air gun *n* carabine à air comprimé *f*.

air hole *n* trou d'aération *m*.

airiness *n* aération, ventilation *f*.

airless *adj* mal aéré, mal ventilé.

airlift *n* pont aérien *m*.

airline *n* ligne aérienne *f*.

airmail *n*: **by** ~ par avion.

aeroplane *n* avion *m*.

airport *n* aéroport *m*.

air pump *n* compresseur *m*.

airsick *adj*: **to be** ~ avoir le mal de l'air.

airstrip *n* piste d'atterrissage *f*.

air terminal *n* aérogare *f*.

airtight *adj* hermétique.

airy *adj* aéré; léger.

aisle *n* nef d'église *f*.

ajar *adj* entrouvert.

akimbo adj les poings sur les hanches.

akin adj ressemblant.

alabaster n albâtre m; * adj d'albâtre.

alacrity n vivacité f.

alarm n alarme f; * vt alarmer; inquiéter.

alarm bell n sonnette d'alarme f.

alarmist n alarmiste mf.

alas adv hélas.

albeit conj bien que.

album n album m.

alchemist n alchimiste m.

alchemy n alchimie f.

alcohol n alcool m.

alcoholic adj alcoolisé; * n alcoolique mf.

alcove n alcôve f.

alder n aulne m.

ale n bière f.

alehouse n taverne, brasserie f.

alert adj vigilant; vif; * n alerte f.

alertness n vigilance f; vivacité f.

algae npl algues fpl.

algebra n algèbre f.

algebraic adj algébrique.

alias adj alias.

alibi n (law) alibi m.

alien adj étranger; * n étranger m, -ère f; extra-terrestre mf.

alienate vt aliéner.

alienation n aliénation f.

alight vi mettre pied à terre; * adj en feu.

align vt aligner.

alike adj semblable, égal; * adv de la même façon.

alimentation n alimentation f.

alimony n aliments mpl.

alive adj en vie, vivant; actif.

alkali n alcali m.

alkaline adj alcalin.

all adj tout; * adv totalement; ~ at once, ~ of a sudden soudain; ~ the same cependant; ~ the better tant mieux; not at ~! pas du tout!; il n'y a pas de quoi!; once for ~ une fois pour toutes; * n tout m.

allay vt apaiser.

all clear n feu vert m.

allegation n allégation f.

allege vt alléguer.

allegiance n loyauté, fidélité f.

allegorical adj allégorique; ~ly adv allégoriquement.

allegory n allégorie f.

allegro n (mus) allegro m.

allergy n allergie f.

alleviate vt alléger.

alleviation n allègement m.

alley n ruelle f.

alliance n alliance f.

allied adj allié.

alligator n alligator m.

alliteration n allitération f.

all-night adj ouvert toute la nuit.

allocate vt allouer.

allocation n allocation f.

allot vt assigner.

allow vt permettre; accorder; to ~ for tenir compte de.

allowable adj admissible, permis.

allowance n allocation f; concession f.

alloy n alliage m.

all-right adv bien.

all-round adj complet.

allspice n poivre de la Jamaïque m.

allude vi faire allusion à.

allure n charme, attrait m.

alluring adj attrayant; ~ly adv avec charme.

allurement n attrait m.

allusion n allusion f.

allusive adj allusif; ~ly adv par allusion.

alluvial adj alluvial.

ally n allié m, -e f; * vt allier.

almanac n almanach m.

almighty adj omnipotent, tout-puissant.

almond n amande f.

almond-milk n lait d'amandes m.

almond tree n amandier m.

almost adv presque.

alms *n* aumône *f*.

aloft *prep* au-dessus.

alone *adj* seul; * *adv* seul; **to leave ~** laisser tranquille.

along *adv* le long (de); **~ side** à côté.

aloof *adv* à l'écart.

aloud *adj* à voix haute.

alphabet *n* alphabet *m*.

alphabetical *adj* alphabétique; **~ly** *adv* par ordre alphabétique, alphabétiquement.

alpine *adj* alpin.

already *adv* déjà.

also *adv* aussi.

altar *n* autel *m*.

altarpiece *n* retable *m*.

alter *vt* modifier.

alteration *n* modification *f*.

altercation *n* altercation *f*.

alternate *adj* alterné; * *vt* alterner; **~ly** *adv* alternativement.

alternating *adj* alterné.

alternation *n* alternance *f*.

alternator *n* alternateur *m*.

alternative *n* alternative *f*; * *adj* alternatif; **~ly** *adv* sinon.

although *conj* bien que, malgré.

altitude *n* altitude *f*.

altogether *adv* complètement.

alum *n* alun *m*.

aluminium *n* aluminium *m*.

aluminous *adj* alumineux.

always *adv* toujours.

a.m. *adv* du matin.

amalgam *n* amalgame *m*.

amalgamate *vt* amalgamer; *vi* s'amalgamer.

amalgamation *n* amalgamation *f*.

amanuensis *n* secrétaire *mf*.

amaryllis *n* (*bot*) amaryllis *f*.

amass *vt* accumuler, amasser.

amateur *n* amateur *m*.

amateurish *adj* d'amateur.

amatory *adj* amoureux; érotique.

amaze *vt* stupéfier.

amazement *n* stupéfaction *f*.

amazing *adj* stupéfiant; **~ly** *adv* incroyablement.

amazon *n* amazone *f*.

ambassador *n* ambassadeur *m*.

ambassadress *n* ambassadrice *f*.

amber *n* ambre *m*; * *adj* ambré.

ambidextrous *adj* ambidextre.

ambient *adj* ambiant.

ambiguity *n* ambiguïté *f*.

ambiguous *adj* ambigu; **~ly** *adv* de manière ambiguë.

ambition *n* ambition *f*.

ambitious *adj* ambitieux; **~ly** *adv* ambitieusement.

amble *vi* marcher tranquillement.

ambulance *n* ambulance *f*.

ambush *n* embuscade *f*; **to lie in ~** être embusqué; * *vt* tendre une embuscade à.

ameliorate *vt* améliorer.

amelioration *n* amélioration *f*.

amenable *adj* responsable.

amend *vt* modifier; amender.

amendable *adj* réparable, corrigible.

amendment *n* modification *f*; amendement *m*.

amends *npl* compensation *f*.

amenities *npl* commodités *fpl*.

America *n* Amérique *f*.

American *adj* américain.

amethyst *n* améthyste *f*.

amiability *n* amabilité *f*.

amiable *adj* aimable.

amiableness *n* amabilité *f*.

amiably *adv* aimablement.

amicable *adj* amical; **~bly** *adv* amicalement.

amid(st) *prep* entre, parmi.

amiss *adv*: **something's ~** il se passe quelque chose.

ammonia *n* ammoniaque *m*.

ammunition *n* munitions *fpl*.

amnesia *n* amnésie *f*.

amnesty *n* amnistie *f*.

among(st) *prep* entre, parmi.

amoral *adj* amoral.

amorous *adj* amoureux; **~ly** *adv* amoureusement.

amorphous *adj* informe.

amount *n* montant *m*; quantité *f*; * *vi* se monter.

amp(ere) *n* ampère *m*.

amphibian *n* amphibie *m*.

amphibious *adj* amphibie.

amphitheatre *n* amphithéâtre *m*.

ample *adj* spacieux; en quantité abondante.

ampleness *n* abondance *f*.

amplification *n* amplification *f*.

amplifier *n* amplificateur *m*.

amplify *vt* amplifier.

amplitude *n* amplitude *f*.

amply *adv* amplement.

amputate *vt* amputer.

amputation *n* amputation *f*.

amulet *n* amulette *f*.

amuse *vt* distraire, divertir.

amusement *n* distraction *f*, divertissement *m*.

amusing *adj* divertissant; **~ly** *adv* de manière divertissante.

an *art* un, une.

anachronism *n* anachronisme *m*.

anaemia *n* anémie *f*.

anaemic *adj* (*med*) anémique.

anaesthetic *n* anesthésique *m*.

analog *adj* (*comput*) analogique.

analogous *adj* analogue.

analogy *n* analogie *f*.

analysis *n* analyse *f*.

analyst *n* analyste *mf*.

analytical *adj* analytique; **~ly** *adv* analytiquement.

analyze *vt* analyser.

anarchic *adj* anarchique.

anarchist *n* anarchiste *mf*.

anarchy *n* anarchie *f*.

anatomical *adj* anatomique; **~ly** *adv* anatomiquement.

anatomize *vt* disséquer.

anatomy *n* anatomie *f*.

ancestor *n* ancêtre *mf*.

ancestral *adj* ancestral.

ancestry *n* ascendance *f*.

anchor *n* ancre *f*; * *vi* jeter l'ancre.

anchorage *n* ancrage *m*.

anchovy *n* anchois *m*.

ancient *adj* ancien, antique; **~ly** *adv* anciennement.

ancientness *n* ancienneté *f*.

ancillary *adj* auxiliaire.

and *conj* et.

anecdotal *adj* anecdotique.

anecdote *n* anecdote *f*.

anemone *n* (*bot*) anémone *f*.

anew *adv* de nouveau.

angel *n* ange *m*.

angelic *adj* angélique.

anger *n* colère *f*; * *vt* mettre en colère, irriter.

angle *n* angle *m*; * *vi* pêcher à la ligne.

angled *adj* anguleux.

angler *n* pêcheur à la ligne *m*.

anglicism *n* anglicisme *m*.

angling *n* pêche à la ligne *f*.

angrily *adv* avec colère.

angry *adj* en colère, irrité.

anguish *n* angoisse *f*.

angular *adj* angulaire.

angularity *n* caractère anguleux *m*.

animal *n adj* animal *m*.

animate *vt* animer; * *adj* vivant.

animated *adj* animé.

animation *n* animation *f*.

animosity *n* animosité *f*.

animus *n* haine *f*.

anise *n* anis *m*.

aniseed *n* graine d'anis *f*.

ankle *n* cheville *f*; **~ bone** astragale *m*.

annals *n* annales *fpl*.

annex *vt* annexer; * *n* annexe *f*.

annexation *n* annexion *f*.

annihilate *vt* annihiler, anéantir.

annihilation *n* anéantissement *m*.

anniversary *n* anniversaire *m*.

annotate *vt* annoter.

annotation *n* annotation *f*.

announce *vt* annoncer.

announcement *n* annonce *f*.

announcer *n* présentateur *m*, -trice *f*.

annoy *vt* ennuyer.

annoyance *n* ennui *m*.

annoying *adj* ennuyeux.

annual *adj* annuel; **~ly** *adv* annuellement.

annuity *n* rente viagère *f.*
annul *vt* annuler.
annulment *n* annulation *f.*
annunciation *n* annonciation *f.*
anodyne *adj* calmant.
anoint *vt* oindre.
anomalous *adj* anormal.
anomaly *n* anomalie, irrégularité *f.*
anon *adv* plus tard.
anonymity *n* anonymat *m.*
anonymous *adj* anonyme; **~ly** *adv* anonymement.
anorexia *n* anorexie *f.*
another *adj* un autre; **one ~** l'un l'autre.
answer *vt* répondre à; **to ~ for** répondre de; **to ~ to** répondre à; * *n* réponse *f.*
answerable *adj* responsable.
answering machine *n* répondeur téléphonique *m.*
ant *n* fourmi *f.*
antagonism *n* antagonisme *m*; rivalité *f.*
antagonist *n* antagoniste *mf.*
antagonize *vt* provoquer.
antarctic *adj* antarctique.
anteater *n* fourmilier *m.*
antecedent *n*: **~s** *pl* antécédents *mpl.*
antechamber *n* antichambre *f.*
antedate *vt* antidater.
antelope *n* antilope *f.*
antenna *n* antenne *f.*
anterior *adj* antérieur, précédent.
anthem *n* hymne *m.*
ant-hill *n* fourmilière *f.*
anthology *n* anthologie *f.*
anthracite *n* anthracite *m.*
anthropology *n* anthropologie *f.*
anti-aircraft *adj* antiaérien.
antibiotic *n* antibiotique *m.*
antibody *n* anticorps *m.*
Antichrist *n* Antéchrist *m.*
anticipate *vt* prévoir.
anticipation *n* attente *f*; prévision *f.*
anticlockwise *adv* dans le sens

contraire des aiguilles d'une montre.
antidote *n* antidote *m.*
antifreeze *n* antigel *m.*
antimony *n* antimoine *m.*
antipathy *n* antipathie *f.*
antipodes *npl* antipodes *fpl*
antiquarian *n* antiquaire *mf.*
antiquated *adj* vieux; suranné.
antique *n* antiquité *f.*
antiquity *n* antiquité *f.*
antiseptic *adj* antiseptique.
antisocial *adj* antisocial.
antithesis *n* antithèse *f.*
antler *n* corne *f.*
anvil *n* enclume *f.*
anxiety *n* anxiété *f*; désir *m.*
anxious *adj* anxieux; **~ly** *adv* anxieusement.
any *adj pn* n'importe quel, n'importe quelle; un, une; tout; **~body** quelqu'un; n'importe qui; personne; **~how** de toute façon; de n'importe quelle manière; **~more** plus; **~place** n'importe où; nulle part; **~thing** quelque chose; n'importe quoi; rien.
apace *adv* rapidement.
apart *adv* séparément.
apartment *n* appartement *m.*
apartment house *n* immeuble *m.*
apathetic *adj* apathique.
apathy *n* apathie *f.*
ape *n* singe *m*; * *vt* singer.
aperture *n* ouverture *f.*
apex *n* sommet *m*; apex *m.*
aphorism *n* aphorisme *m.*
apiary *n* rucher *m.*
apiece *adv* chacun, chacune.
aplomb *n* aplomb *m.*
Apocalypse *n* Apocalypse *f.*
apocrypha *npl* apocryphes *mpl.*
apocryphal *adj* apocryphe.
apologetic *adj* d'excuse.
apologist *n* apologiste *mf.*
apologize *vt* excuser.
apology *n* apologie, défense *f.*
apoplexy *n* apoplexie *f.*
apostle *n* apôtre *m.*
apostolic *adj* apostolique.

apostrophe *n* apostrophe *f*.
apotheosis *n* apothéose *f*.
appall *vt* horrifier, atterrer.
appalling *adj* horrible.
apparatus *n* appareil *m*.
apparel *n* vêtements *mpl*.
apparent *adj* évident, apparent;
 ~ly *adv* apparemment.
apparition *n* apparition, vision *f*.
appeal *vi* faire appel; * *n* (*law*) appel *m*.
appealing *adj* attrayant.
appear *vi* paraître.
appearance *n* apparence *f*.
appease *vt* apaiser.
appellant *n* (*law*) appelant *m*.
append *vt* annexer.
appendage *n* appendice *m*.
appendicitis *n* appendicite *f*.
appendix *n* appendice *m*.
appertain *vi* appartenir (à).
appetite *n* appétit *m*.
appetizing *adj* appétissant.
applaud *vt, vi* applaudir.
applause *n* applaudissements *mpl*.
apple *n* pomme *f*.
apple pie *n* tourte aux pommes *f*;
 in ~ order parfaitement en ordre.
apple tree *n* pommier *m*.
appliance *n* appareil *m*.
applicability *n* applicabilité *f*.
applicable *adj* applicable.
applicant *n* candidat *m*, -e *f*.
application *n* application *f*; candidature *f*.
applied *adj* appliqué.
apply *vt* appliquer; * *vi* s'adresser.
appoint *vt* nommer.
appointee *n* personne nommée *f*.
appointment *n* rendez-vous *m*;
 nomination *f*.
apportion *vt* répartir.
apportionment *n* répartition *f*.
apposite *adj* adapté.
apposition *n* apposition *f*.
appraisal *n* estimation *f*.
appraise *vt* évaluer.
appreciable *adj* appréciable, sensible.

appreciably *adv* sensiblement.
appreciate *vt* apprécier; être conscient de.
appreciation *n* appréciation *f*.
appreciative *adj* reconnaissant.
apprehend *vt* appréhender.
apprehension *n* appréhension *f*;
 arrestation *f*.
apprehensive *adj* appréhensif.
apprentice *n* apprenti *m*; * *vt* mettre en apprentissage.
apprenticeship *n* apprentissage *m*.
apprise, apprize *vt* informer.
approach *vi* approcher(s'); * *vt* (s')approcher de; * *n* approche *f*.
approachable *adj* accessible, approchable.
approbation *n* approbation *f*.
appropriate *vt* s'approprier;
 * *adj* approprié, adéquat.
approval *n* approbation *f*.
approve (of) *vt* approuver.
approximate *vi* s'approcher;
 * *adj* approximatif; **~ly** *adv* approximativement.
approximation *n* approximation *f*.
apricot *n* abricot *m*.
April *n* avril *m*.
apron *n* tablier *m*.
apse *n* abside *f*.
apt *adj* idéal; susceptible; **~ly** *adv* opportunément.
aptitude *n* aptitude *f*.
aqualung *n* scaphandre autonome *m*.
aquarium *n* aquarium *m*.
Aquarius *n* Verseau *m* (signe du zodiaque).
aquatic *adj* aquatique.
aqueduct *n* aqueduc *m*.
aquiline *adj* aquilin.
arabesque *n* arabesque *f*.
arable *adj* arable.
arbiter *n* arbitre *m*.
arbitrariness *n* caractère arbitraire *m*.
arbitrary *adj* arbitraire.
arbitrate *vt* arbitrer.

arbitration *n* arbitrage *m*.
arbitrator *n* arbitre *m*.
arbor *n* tonnelle *f*.
arcade *n* galerie *f*.
arch *n* arc *m*; * *adj* malicieux.
archaic *adj* archaïque.
archangel *n* archange *m*.
archbishop *n* archevêque *m*.
archbishopric *n* archevêché *m*.
archeological *adj* archéologique.
archeology *n* archéologie *f*.
archer *n* archer *m*.
archery *n* tir à l'arc *m*.
architect *n* architecte *mf*.
architectural *adj* architectural.
architecture *n* architecture *f*.
archives *npl* archives *fpl*.
archivist *n* archiviste *mf*.
archly *adv* malicieusement.
archway *n* arcade, voûte *f*.
arctic *adj* arctique.
ardent *adj* ardent; **~ly** *adv* ardemment.
ardor *n* ardeur *f*.
arduous *adj* ardu, difficile.
area *n* région *f*; domaine *m*.
arena *n* arène *f*.
arguably *adv* peut-être.
argue *vi* se disputer; * *vt* soutenir.
argument *n* argument *m*; dispute *f*.
argumentation *n* argumentation *f*.
argumentative *adj* raisonneur.
aria *n* (*mus*) aria *f*.
arid *adj* aride.
aridity *n* aridité *f*.
Aries *n* Bélier *m* (signe du zodiaque).
aright *adv* bien; **to set ~** rectifier.
arise *vi* se lever; survenir.
aristocracy *n* aristocratie *f*.
aristocrat *n* aristocrate *mf*.
aristocratic *adj* aristocratique;
~ally *adv* aristocratiquement.
arithmetic *n* arithmétique *f*.
arithmetical *adj* arithmétique;
~ly *adv* arithmétiquement.

ark *n* arche *f*.
arm *n* bras *m*; arme *f*; * *vt* armer;
* *vi* (s')armer.
armament *n* armement *m*.
armchair *n* fauteuil *m*.
armed *adj* armé.
armful *n* brassée *f*.
armhole *n* emmanchure *f*.
armistice *n* armistice *m*.
armour *n* armure *f*.
armoured car *n* voiture blindée *f*.
armoury *n* arsenal *m*.
armpit *n* aisselle *f*.
armrest *n* accoudoir *m*.
army *n* armée *f*.
aroma *n* arôme *m*.
aromatic *adj* aromatique.
around *prep* autour de; * *adv* autour.
arouse *vt* éveiller; exciter.
arraign *vt* accuser.
arraignment *n* accusation *f*;
procès criminel *m*.
arrange *vt* arranger, organiser.
arrangement *n* arrangement *m*.
arrant *adj* absolu.
array *n* série *f*.
arrears *npl* arriéré *m*; retard *m*.
arrest *n* arrestation *f*; * *vt* arrêter.
arrival *n* arrivée *f*.
arrive *vi* arriver.
arrogance *n* arrogance *f*.
arrogant *adj* arrogant; **~ly** *adv*
avec arrogance.
arrogate *vt* s'arroger.
arrogation *n* usurpation *f*.
arrow *n* flèche *f*.
arsenal *n* (*mil*) arsenal *m*.
arsenic *n* arsenic *m*.
arson *n* incendie criminel *m*.
art *n* art *m*.
arterial *adj* artériel.
artesian well *n* puits artésien *m*.
artery *n* artère *f*.
artful *adj* malin, astucieux.
artfulness *n* astuce *f*; habileté *f*.
art gallery *n* musée d'art *m*.
arthritis *n* arthrite *f*.
artichoke *n* artichaut *m*.
article *n* article *m*.

articulate *vt* articuler.
articulated *adj* articulé.
articulation *n* articulation *f*.
artifice *n* artifice *m*.
artificial *adj* artificiel; **~ly** *adv* artificiellement.
artificiality *n* caractère artificiel *m*.
artillery *n* artillerie *f*.
artisan *n* artisan *m*.
artist *n* artiste *mf*.
artistic *adj* artistique.
artistry *n* habileté *f*.
artless *adj* naturel, simple; **~ly** *adv* naturellement, simplement.
artlessness *n* simplicité *f*, naturel *m*.
art school *n* école des beaux-arts *f*.
as *conj* comme; pendant que; aussi; **~ for, ~ to** quant à.
asbestos *n* asbeste *m*, amiante *f*.
ascend *vi* monter.
ascendancy *n* ascendant *m*.
ascension *n* ascension *f*.
ascent *n* montée *f*.
ascertain *vt* établir.
ascetic *adj* ascétique; * *n* ascète *mf*.
ascribe *vt* attribuer.
ash *n* (*bot*) frêne *m*; cendre *f*.
ashcan *n* poubelle *f*.
ashamed *adj* honteux.
ashore *adv* à terre; **to go ~** débarquer.
ashtray *n* cendrier *m*.
Ash Wednesday *n* mercredi des Cendres *m*.
aside *adv* de côté.
ask *vt* demander; **to ~ after** demander des nouvelles de; **to ~ for** demander; **to ~ out** inviter.
askance *adv* avec méfiance.
askew *adv* de côté.
asleep *adj* endormi; **to fall ~** s'endormir.
asparagus *n* asperge *f*.
aspect *n* aspect *m*.
aspen *n* tremble *m*.
aspersion *n* calomnie *f*.

asphalt *n* asphalte *m*.
asphyxia *n* (*med*) asphyxie *f*.
asphyxiate *vt* asphyxier.
asphyxiation *n* asphyxie *f*.
aspirant *n* aspirant *m*, -e *f*.
aspirate *vt* aspirer; * *n* aspiration *f*.
aspiration *n* aspiration *f*.
aspire *vi* aspirer, désirer.
aspirin *n* aspirine *f*.
ass *n* âne *m*; **she ~** ânesse *f*.
assail *vt* assaillir, attaquer.
assailant *n* assaillant, agresseur *m*.
assassin *n* assassin *m*.
assassinate *vt* assassiner.
assassination *n* assassinat *m*.
assault *n* assaut *m*; agression *f*; * *vt* agresser.
assemblage *n* assemblage *m*.
assemble *vt* assembler; * *vi* s'assembler.
assembly *n* assemblée *f*.
assembly line *n* chaîne de montage *f*.
assent *n* assentiment *m*; * *vi* donner son assentiment.
assert *vt* soutenir; affirmer.
assertion *n* assertion *f*.
assertive *adj* péremptoire.
assess *vt* évaluer.
assessment *n* évaluation *f*.
assessor *n* assesseur *m*.
assets *npl* biens *mpl*.
assiduous *adj* assidu; **~ly** *adv* assidûment.
assign *vt* assigner.
assignation *n* rendez-vous *m*; allocation *f*.
assignment *n* allocation *f*; mission *f*.
assimilate *vt* assimiler.
assimilation *n* assimilation *f*.
assist *vt* assister, aider; secourir.
assistance *n* assistance, aide *f*; secours *m*.
assistant *n* aide *mf*, assistant *m*, -e *f*.
associate *vt* associer; * *adj* associé; * *n* associé *m*, -e *f*.

association n association f.

assonance n assonance f.

assorted adj assorti.

assortment n assortiment m.

assuage vt calmer, adoucir.

assume vt assumer; supposer.

assumption n supposition f; **Assumption** n Assomption f.

assurance n assurance f.

assure vt assurer.

assuredly adv assurément

asterisk n astérisque m.

astern adv (mar) en poupe.

asthma n asthme m.

asthmatic adj asthmatique.

astonish vt surprendre, stupéfier.

astonishing adj stupéfiant; ~ly adv incroyablement.

astonishment n surprise, stupéfaction f.

astound vt ébahir.

astraddle adv à cheval.

astray adv: **to go** ~ s'égarer; **to lead** ~ détourner du droit chemin.

astride adv à cheval.

astringent adj astringent.

astrologer n astrologue mf.

astrological adj astrologique.

astrology n astrologie f.

astronaut n astronaute mf.

astronomer n astronome mf.

astronomical adj astronomique.

astronomy n astronomie f.

astute adj malin.

asylum n asile, refuge m.

at prep à; en; ~ **once** tout de suite; ~ **all** du tout; ~ **all events** en tout cas; ~ **first** au début, d'abord; ~ **last** enfin.

atheism n athéisme m.

atheist n athée mf.

athlete n athlète mf.

athletic adj athlétique.

atlas n atlas m.

atmosphere n atmosphère f.

atmospheric adj atmosphérique.

atom n atome m.

atom bomb n bombe atomique f.

atomic adj atomique.

atone vt expier.

atonement n expiation f.

atop adv en haut.

atrocious adj atroce; ~**ly** adv atrocement.

atrocity n atrocité, énormité f.

atrophy n (med) atrophie f.

attach vt joindre.

attaché n attaché m, -e f.

attachment n attachement m.

attack vt attaquer; * n attaque f.

attacker n attaquant m, -e f.

attain vt atteindre, obtenir.

attainable adj accessible.

attempt vt essayer; * n essai m, tentative f.

attend vt servir; assister à; **to** ~ **to** s'occuper de; * vi faire attention.

attendance n service m; assistance f; présence f.

attendant n serviteur m.

attention n attention f; soin m.

attentive adj attentif; ~**ly** adv attentivement.

attenuate vt atténuer.

attest vt attester.

attic n grenier m.

attire n atours mpl.

attitude n attitude f.

attorney n avocat m.

attract vt attirer.

attraction n attraction f; attrait m.

attractive adj attrayant.

attribute vt attribuer; * n attribut m.

attrition n frottement m; usure f.

auburn adj auburn.

auction n vente aux enchères f.

auctioneer n commissaire-priseur m.

audacious adj audacieux, téméraire; ~**ly** adv audacieusement.

audacity n audace, témérité f.

audible adj audible; ~**ly** adv audiblement.

audience n audience f; auditoire m.

audit n audit m; * vt vérifier.

auditor n vérificateur(-trice) de comptes m(f); auditeur m, -trice f.

auditory adj auditif.

augment vt, vi augmenter.

augmentation n augmentation f.

August n août m.

august adj auguste, majestueux.

aunt n tante f.

au pair n (jeune fille) au pair f.

aura n aura f.

auspices npl auspices mpl.

auspicious adj favorable, propice; ~ly adv favorablement.

austere adj austère, sévère; ~ly adv austèrement.

austerity n austérité f.

authentic adj authentique; ~ly adv authentiquement.

authenticate vt légaliser.

authenticity n authenticité f.

author n auteur m.

authoress n femme auteur f, auteur m.

authoritarian adj autoritaire.

authoritative adj autoritaire; ~ly adv autoritairement.

authority n autorité f.

authorization n autorisation f.

authorize vt autoriser.

authorship n paternité f.

auto n voiture f.

autocrat n autocrate mf.

autocratic adj autocratique.

autograph n autographe m.

automated adj automatisé.

automatic adj automatique.

automaton n automate m.

autonomy n autonomie f.

autopsy n autopsie f.

autumn n automne m.

autumnal adj automnal.

auxiliary adj auxiliaire.

avail vt: **to ~ oneself of** profiter de; * n: **to no ~** en vain.

available adj disponible.

avalanche n avalanche f.

avarice n avarice f.

avaricious adj avare.

avenge vt venger.

avenue n avenue f.

aver vt affirmer, déclarer.

average vt atteindre la moyenne de; * n moyenne f, moyen terme m.

aversion n aversion f, dégoût m.

avert vt détourner, écarter.

aviary n volière f.

avoid vt éviter; échapper à.

avoidable adj évitable.

await vt attendre.

awake vt réveiller; * vi se réveiller; * adj éveillé.

awakening n réveil m.

award vt attribuer; * n prix m; décision f.

aware adj conscient; au courant.

awareness n conscience f.

away adv absent; loin; ~! va-t-en!; allez-vous-en! **far and ~** de loin.

away game n match à l'extérieur m.

awe n peur, crainte f.

awe-inspiring, awesome adj terrifiant; imposant.

awful adj horrible, terrible; ~ly adv horriblement, terriblement.

awhile adv un moment.

awkward adj gauche, maladroit; délicat; ~ly adv maladroitement.

awkwardness n maladroitesse f; difficulté f.

awl n alêne f.

awning n (mar) taude f.

awry adv de travers.

axe n hache f; * vt licencier; supprimer.

axiom n axiome m.

axis n axe m.

axle n axe m.

ay(e) excl oui.

B

baa n bêlement m; * vi bêler.

babble vi bavarder, babiller; ~,
   babbling n bavardage, babil-
   lage m.

babbler n bavard m.

babe, baby n bébé, enfant en bas-
   âge m; nourrisson m.

baboon n babouin m.

babyhood n petite enfance f.

babyish adj enfantin; puéril.

baby carriage n voiture d'enfant
   f.

baby linen n layette f.

bachelor n célibataire m; licencié m, -e f.

bachelorship n célibat m.

back n dos m; * adv en arrière, à
   l'arrière; **a few years** ~ il y a
   quelques années, quelques années en arrière; * vt soutenir,
   appuyer, renforcer.

backbite vt médire de, sur.

backbiter n détracteur m, -trice f.

backbone n colonne vertébrale,
   épine dorsale f.

backdate vt antidater.

backdoor n porte de derrière f.

backer n partisan m, -e f.

backgammon n (jeu de) jacquet
   m.

background n fond m.

backlash n réaction violente f.

backlog n accumulation de travail en retard f.

back number n vieux numéro
   (magazine, journal) m.

backpack n sac à dos m.

back payment n rappel de
   salaire m.

backside n derrière m.

back-up lights npl (auto) feux de
   marche arrière mpl.

backward adj rétrograde; retardé; lent; * adv en arrière.

bacon n lard m.

bad adj mauvais, de mauvaise

qualité; méchant; malade; ~**ly**
   adv mal.

badge n plaque f, insigne m,
   badge m; symbole m; signe m.

badger n blaireau m; * vt harceler; importuner.

badminton n badminton m.

badness n mauvaise qualité f;
   méchanceté f.

baffle vt déconcerter, confondre.

bag n sac m; valise f.

baggage n bagages mpl; équipement m.

bagpipe n cornemuse f.

bail n mise en liberté sous caution, caution f; * vt mettre en liberté sous caution; mettre en
   dépôt.

bailiff n huissier m; régisseur m.

bait vt tourmenter; appâter; * n
   appât m; amorce f.

baize n serge f.

bake vt faire cuire au four.

bakery n boulangerie f.

baker n boulanger m, -ère f; ~'**s**
   dozen treize à la douzaine.

baking n cuisson f; fournée f.

baking powder n levure f.

balance n balance f; équilibre m;
   solde d'un compte m; **to lose**
   one's ~ perdre l'équilibre; * vt
   peser; peser le pour et le contre;
   solder; équilibrer.

balance sheet n bilan m.

balcony n balcon m.

bald adj chauve.

baldness n calvitie f.

bale n balle f; * vt emballer; écoper.

baleful adj sinistre, funeste,
   maléfique; ~**ly** adv sinistre-
   ment; lugubrement.

ball n balle f; boule f; ballon m.

ballad n ballade f.

ballast n lest m; * vt lester.

ballerina n ballerine f.

ballet *n* ballet *m*.

ballistic *adj* balistique.

balloon *n* montgolfière *f*, aérostat *m*.

ballot *n* scrutin *m*; vote *m*; * *vi* voter au scrutin secret.

ballpoint (pen) *n* stylo à bille *m*.

ballroom *n* salle de bal *f*.

balm, balsam *n* baume *m*; * *vt* enduire de baume.

balmy *adj* balsamique, parfumé; doux.

balustrade *n* balustrade *f*.

bamboo *n* bambou *m*.

bamboozle *vt* (*fam*) embobiner.

ban *n* interdiction *f*; * *vt* interdire.

banal *adj* banal.

banana *n* banane *f*.

band *n* bande *f*; reliure *f*; courroie de transmission *f*; orchestre *m*.

bandage *n* bande *f*, bandage *m*; * *vt* bander.

bandaid *n* pansement *m*.

bandit *n* bandit *m*.

bandstand *n* kiosque à musique *m*.

bandy *vt* échanger; discuter.

bandy-legged *adj* aux jambes arquées.

bang *n* coup violent, claquement *m*, détonation *f*; * *vt* frapper violemment; claquer.

bangle *n* bracelet *m*.

bangs *npl* frange (courte et droite) *f*.

banish *vt* bannir, exiler, chasser, expatrier.

banishment *n* exil, bannissement *m*.

banister(s) *n*(*pl*) rampe d'escalier *f*.

banjo *n* banjo *m*.

bank *n* rive *f*; remblai *m*; banque *f*; banc *m*; digue *f*; * *vt* déposer de l'argent à la banque; **to ~ on** compter sur.

bank account *n* compte en banque *m*.

bank card *n* carte bancaire *f*.

banker *n* banquier *m*, -ière *f*.

banking *n* opérations bancaires *f pl*.

banknote *n* billet de banque *m*.

bankrupt *adj* failli; * *n* banqueroute *f*, failli *m*.

bankruptcy *n* banqueroute, faillite *f*.

bank statement *n* relevé de compte *m*.

banner *n* bannière *f*; étendard *m*.

banquet *n* banquet *m*.

baptism *n* baptême *m*.

baptismal *adj* de baptême, baptismal.

baptistery *n* baptistère *m*.

baptize *vt* baptiser.

bar *n* bar *m*; barre *f*; obstacle *m*; (law) barreau *m*; * *vt* empêcher; interdire; exclure.

barbarian *n* barbare *mf*; * *adj* barbare, cruel.

barbaric *adj* barbare.

barbarism *n* (*gr*) barbarisme *m*; barbarie *f*.

barbarity *n* barbarie, atrocité *f*.

barbarous *adj* barbare, cruel.

barbecue *n* barbecue *m*.

barber *n* coiffeur (pour hommes) *m*.

bar code *n* code barres *m*.

bard *n* barde *m*; poète *m*.

bare *adj* nu, dépouillé; simple; pur; * *vt* dénuder, découvrir.

barefaced *adj* éhonté, impudent.

barefoot(ed) *adj* aux pieds nus.

bareheaded *adj* nu-tête.

barelegged *adj* aux jambes nues.

barely *adv* à peine, tout juste.

bareness *n* nudité *f*.

bargain *n* affaire *f*; contrat, marché *m*; occasion *f*; * *vi* conclure un marché; négocier; **to ~ for** s'attendre à.

barge *n* péniche *f*.

baritone *n* (*mus*) baryton *m*.

bark *n* écorce *f*; aboiement *m*; * *vi* aboyer.

barley *n* orge *m*.

barmaid *n* serveuse *f*.

barman *n* barman *m*.

barn n grange f; étable f.

barnacles npl anatife m.

barometer n baromètre m.

baron n baron m.

baroness n baronne f.

baronial adj de baron.

barracks npl caserne f.

barrage n barrage m; (fig) torrent m.

barrel n tonneau, fût m; canon de fusil m.

barrelled adj (firearms) chargé.

barrel organ n orgue de Barbarie m.

barren adj stérile, infertile, improductif.

barricade n barricade f; barrière f; * vt barricader, barrer.

barrier n barrière f; obstacle m.

barring adv excepté, sauf.

barrow n brouette f.

bartender n barman m.

barter vi faire du troc; * vt troquer, échanger.

base n base f; partie inférieure f; pied m; point de départ m; * vt fonder sur; * adj vil, abject.

baseball n baseball m.

baseless adj sans fondement, injustifié.

basement n sous-sol m.

baseness n bassesse, vilenie f.

bash vt frapper.

bashful adj timide, modeste; ~ly adv timidement.

basic adj fondamental, de base; ~ally adv fondamentalement.

basilisk n basilic m.

basin n cuvette f; lavabo m.

basis n base f; fondement m.

bask vi se faire dorer au soleil.

basket n panier m, corbeille f.

basketball n basket-ball m.

bass n (mus) contrebasse f.

bassoon n basson m.

bass viol n viole de gambe f.

bass voice n voix de basse f.

bastard n, adj bâtard m.

bastardy n bâtardise f.

baste vt arroser la viande de son jus; bâtir.

basting n bâti m; jus (de viande) m; rossée f.

bastion n (mil) bastion m.

bat n chauve-souris f.

batch n fournée f.

bath n bain m.

bathe vt (vi) (se) baigner.

bathing suit n maillot de bain m.

bathos n platitudes (dans un texte littéraire) fpl.

bathroom n salle de bain f.

baths npl piscine f.

bathtub n baignoire f.

baton n bâton m.

battalion n (mil) bataillon m.

batter vt battre; frapper, martyriser; * n pâte à frire f.

battering ram n (mil) bélier m.

battery n pile, batterie f.

battle n bataille f; combat m; * vi se battre, combattre.

battle array n ordre de bataille m.

battlefield n champ de bataille m.

battlement n remparts m pl.

battleship n cuirassé m.

bawdy adj paillard.

bawl vi brailler, (fam) gueuler.

bay n baie f; laurier m; * vi aboyer, hurler; * adj bai.

bayonet n baïonnette f.

bay window n fenêtre en saillie f.

bazaar n bazar m.

be vi être.

beach n plage f.

beacon n phare, signal lumineux m.

bead n perle f; ~s npl chapelet m.

beagle n beagle m.

beak n bec m.

beaker n gobelet m.

beam n rayon m; poutre f; * vi rayonner, resplendir.

bean n haricot m; **French ~** haricot vert m.

beansprouts npl germes de soja m pl.

bear vt porter, supporter, produire; * vi se diriger.

bear n ours m; **she ~** ourse f.

bearable *adj* supportable.
beard *n* barbe *f*.
bearded *adj* barbu.
bearer *n* porteur *m*, -euse *f*; arbre fructifère *m*.
bearing *n* relation *f*; maintien, port *m*.
beast *n* bête *f*; brute *f*; ~ **of burden** bête de somme *f*.
beastliness *n* bestialité, brutalité *f*.
beastly *adj* bestial, brutal; abominable; * *adv* terriblement.
beat *vt* battre; * *vi* battre, palpiter; * *n* battement *m*; pulsation *f*.
beatific *adj* béatifique; béat.
beatify *vt* béatifier, sanctifier.
beating *n* correction, raclée *f*; battement *m*.
beatitude *n* béatitude *f*.
beautiful *adj* beau, belle, magnifique; ~**ly** *adv* à la perfection, merveilleusement.
beautify *vt* embellir; décorer.
beauty *n* beauté *f*; ~ **salon** *n* institut de beauté *m*; ~ **spot** *n* site touristique *m*.
beaver *n* castor *m*.
because *conj* parce que; * *prép*: ~ **of** en raison de.
beckon *vi* faire signe.
become *vt* convenir, aller à; * *vi* devenir, se faire.
becoming *adj* convenable, seyant.
bed *n* lit *m*.
bedclothes *npl* couvertures et draps *mpl*.
bedding *n* literie *f*.
bedecked *adj* orné.
bedlam *n* maison de fous *f*.
bed-post *n* colonne de lit *f*.
bedridden *adj* cloué au lit; grabataire.
bedroom *n* chambre *f*.
bedspread *n* dessus-de-lit *m invar*.
bedtime *n* heure d'aller au lit *f*.
bee *n* abeille *f*.

beech *n* hêtre *m*.
beef *n* boeuf (viande) *m*.
beefburger *n* hamburger *m*.
beefsteak *n* bifteck *m*.
beehive *n* ruche *f*.
beeline *n* ligne droite *f*.
beer *n* bière *f*.
beeswax *n* cire *f*.
beet *n* betterave *f*.
beetle *n* scarabée *m*.
befall *vi* arriver, survenir; * *vt* arriver à.
befit *vt* convenir à.
before *adv, prep* avant; devant; * *conj* avant de, avant que.
beforehand *adv* à l'avance, au préalable.
befriend *vt* traiter en ami; aider.
beg *vt* mendier; solliciter; supplier; * *vi* demander la charité.
beget *vt* engendrer.
beggar *n* mendiant *m*, -e *f*.
begin *vt*, *vi* commencer.
beginner *n* débutant *m*, -e *f*; novice *mf*.
beginning *n* commencement, début *m*, origine *f*.
begrudge *vt* donner à contrecoeur; envier.
behalf *n* faveur *f*, intérêt *m*; nom *m*, part *f*.
behave *vi* se comporter, se conduire.
behavior *n* conduite *f*; comportement *m*.
behead *vt* décapiter.
behind *prep* derrière; * *adv* derrière, par-derrière, en arrière.
behold *vt* voir; contempler; observer.
behove *vi* incomber à.
beige *adj* beige.
being *n* existence *f*; être *m*.
belated *adj* tardif.
belch *vi* éructer; * *vt* vomir; * *n* éructation *f*, rot *m*.
belfry *n* beffroi, clocher *m*.
belie *vt* démentir, tromper.
belief *n* foi, croyance *f*; conviction, opinion *f*, credo *m*.

believable adj croyable.

believe vt croire; * vi penser, croire.

believer n croyant m, -e f; adepte mf, partisan m, -e f.

belittle vt rabaisser.

bell n cloche f.

bellicose adj belliqueux.

belligerent adj belligérant.

bellow vi beugler, mugir; hurler; * n beuglement, mugissement m.

bellows npl soufflet m.

belly n ventre m.

bellyful n ventrée f; ras-le-bol m.

belong vi appartenir à.

belongings npl affaires fpl.

beloved adj chéri, bien-aimé.

below adv en dessous, en bas; * prep sous, au-dessous de, en dessous.

belt n ceinture f.

beltway n périphérique m.

bemoan vt déplorer; pleurer.

bemused adj déconcerté.

bench n banc m.

bend vt courber, plier; incliner; * vi se courber, s'incliner; * n courbe f.

beneath adv au-dessous; * prep sous, au-dessous de.

benediction n bénédiction f.

benefactor n bienfaiteur m, -trice f.

benefice n bénéfice m; bénéfice ecclésiastique m.

beneficent adj bienfaisant.

beneficial adj profitable, salutaire, utile.

beneficiary n bénéficiaire mf.

benefit n intérêt, avantage m; profit m; bienfait m; * vt profiter à; * vi bénéficier.

benefit night n soirée de bienfaisance f.

benevolence n bienveillance f; générosité f.

benevolent adj bienveillant; de bienfaisance.

benign adj bienveillant, doux, affable; bénin.

bent n penchant m.

benzine n (chem) benzine f.

bequeath vt léguer à.

bequest n legs m.

bereave vt priver.

bereavement n perte f; deuil m.

beret n béret m.

berm n accotement m.

berry n baie f.

berserk adj fou furieux.

berth n (mar) couchette f.

beseech vt supplier, implorer, conjurer.

beset vt assaillir.

beside(s) prep à côté de; excepté; * adv de plus, en outre.

besiege vt assiéger, assaillir.

best adj le meilleur, la meilleure; * adv le mieux; * n le meilleur, le mieux m.

bestial adj bestial, brutal; ~ly adv bestialement.

bestiality n bestialité, brutalité f.

bestow vt accorder, conférer; consacrer.

bestseller n best-seller m.

bet n pari m; * vt parier.

betray vt trahir.

betrayal n trahison f.

betroth vt promettre en mariage.

betrothal n fiançailles f pl.

better adj, adv meilleur, mieux; **so much the ~** tant mieux; * vt améliorer.

betting n pari m.

between prep entre;* adv au milieu.

bevel n biseau m.

beverage n boisson f.

bevy n bande f.

beware vi prendre garde.

bewilder vt déconcerter , dérouter.

bewilderment n perplexité f.

bewitch vt ensorceler, enchanter.

beyond prep au-delà de; au-dessus de; plus de; sauf; * adv au-delà, plus loin.

bias n préjugé m; tendance, inclination f.

bib *n* bavoir *m*.

Bible *n* Bible *f*.

biblical *adj* biblique.

bibliography *n* bibliographie *f*.

bicarbonate of soda *n* bicarbonate de soude *m*.

bicker *vi* se chamailler.

bicycle *n* bicyclette *f*.

bid *vt* ordonner, commander; offrir; * *n* offre, tentative *f*.

bidding *n* ordre *m*; enchère, offre *f*.

bide *vt* attendre, supporter.

biennial *adj* biennal, bisannuel.

bifocals *npl* verres à double foyer *m pl*.

bifurcated *adj* divisé en deux branches.

big *adj* grand, gros; important.

bigamist *n* bigame *mf*.

bigamy *n* bigamie *f*.

big dipper *n* Grande Ourse *f*.

bigheaded *adj* frimeur.

bigness *n* grandeur, grosseur *f*.

bigot *n* fanatique *mf*.

bigoted *adj* fanatique.

bike *n* vélo *m*.

bikini *n* bikini *m*.

bilberry *n* airelle *f*.

bile *n* bile *f*.

bilingual *adj* bilingue.

bilious *adj* bilieux.

bill *n* bec (d'oiseau) *m*; addition *f*; billet *m*.

billboard *n* panneau d'affichage *m*.

billet *n* logement *m*.

billfold *n* portefeuille *m*.

billiards *npl* billard *m*.

billiard-table *n* table de billard *f*.

billion *n* mil milliard *m*.

billy *n* matraque *f*.

bin *n* coffre *m*.

bind *vt* attacher; lier; entourer; relier.

binder *n* relieur *m*, -euse *f*.

binding *n* reliure *f*, extra-fort *m*.

binge *n* beuverie, bringue *f*.

bingo *n* loto *m*.

biochemistry *n* biochimie *f*.

binoculars *npl* jumelles *f pl*.

biographer *n* biographe *mf*.

biographical *adj* biographique.

biography *n* biographie *f*.

biological *adj* biologique.

biology *n* biologie *f*.

biped *n* bipède *m*.

birch *n* bouleau *m*.

bird *n* oiseau *m*.

bird's-eye view *n* vue d'ensemble *f*.

bird-watcher *n* ornithologue *mf*.

birth *n* naissance *f*.

birth certificate *n* extrait de naissance *m*.

birth control *n* limitation des naissances *f*.

birthday *n* anniversaire *m*.

birthplace *n* lieu de naissance *m*.

birthright *n* droit de naissance *m*.

biscuit *n* biscuit *m*.

bisect *vt* couper en deux.

bishop *n* évêque *m*.

bison *n* bison *m*.

bit *n* morceau *m*; peu *m*.

bitch *n* chienne *f*; (*fig*) plainte *f*.

bite *vt* mordre; ~ **the dust** (*fam*) mordre la poussière; * *n* morsure *f*.

bitter *adj* amer, âpre; cuisant, acerbe; glacial; ~**ly** *adv* amèrement; avec amertume; âprement.

bitterness *n* amertume *f*; rancoeur *f*.

bitumen *n* bitume *m*.

bizarre *adj* étrange, bizarre.

blab *vi* jacasser; lâcher le morceau.

black *adj* noir, obscur; * *n* noir *m*.

blackberry *n* mûre *f*.

blackbird *n* merle *m*.

blackboard *n* tableau (noir) *m*.

blacken *vt* noircir, ternir.

black ice *n* verglas *m*.

blackjack *n* vingt-et-un *m*.

blackleg *n* jaune *m*.

blacklist *n* liste noire *f*.

blackmail *n* chantage *m*; * *vt* faire chanter.

black market *n* marché noir *m*.

blackness n couleur noire f; obscurité f; noirceur f.

black pudding n boudin m.

black sheep n brebis galeuse f.

blacksmith n forgeron m.

blackthorn n épine noire f.

bladder n vessie f.

blade n lame f.

blame vt blâmer; * n faute f.

blameless adj irréprochable; ~ly adv irréprochablement.

blanch vt blanchir.

bland adj affable, suave; doux; apaisant.

blank adj blanc; vide, déconcerté; * n blanc m.

blank check n chèque en blanc m.

blanket n couverture f.

blare vi retentir.

blase adj blasé.

blaspheme vt blasphémer.

blasphemous adj blasphématoire.

blasphemy n blasphème m.

blast n souffle d'air m; explosion f; * vt faire sauter.

blast-off n lancement m, mise à feu f.

blatant adj flagrant.

blaze n flamme f; * vi flamber; resplendir.

bleach vt blanchir; décolorer; * vi blanchir; * n eau de Javel f.

bleached adj blanchi; décoloré.

bleachers npl gradins m pl.

bleak adj morne, lugubre, glacial, désolé.

bleakness n froid m; austérité f.

bleary(-eyed) adj larmoyant.

bleat n bêlement m; * vi bêler.

bleed vi, vt saigner.

bleeding n saignement m.

bleeper n bip m.

blemish vt gâter; ternir; * n tache f; infamie f.

blend vt mélanger.

bless vt bénir.

blessing n bénédiction f; bienfait m.

blight vt détruire.

blind adj aveugle; ~ alley n impasse f; * vt aveugler; éblouir; * n aveugle mf; (Venetian) ~ store vénitien m.

blinders npl oeillères f pl.

blindfold vt bander les yeux de; ~ed adj les yeux bandés.

blindly adv à l'aveuglette, aveuglément.

blindness n cécité f.

blind side n côté faible de quelqu'un m.

blind spot n angle mort m.

blink vi clignoter.

blinkers npl clignotants m pl.

bliss n bonheur extrême m; félicité f.

blissful adj heureux; béat, bienheureux; ~ly adv heureusement.

blissfulness n bonheur extrême m, félicité f.

blister n ampoule f; * vi se couvrir de cloques.

blitz n bombardement aérien m.

blizzard n tempête de neige f.

bloated adj gonflé, boursouflé, bouffi.

blob n goutte, tache f.

bloc n bloc m.

block n bloc m; encombrement, blocage m; pâté de maisons m; ~ (up) vt bloquer.

blockade n blocus m; * vt faire le blocus, bloquer.

blockage n obstruction f.

blockbuster n grand succès m.

blockhead n lourdaud, sot, crétin m.

blond adj blond; * n blond m, -e f.

blood n sang m.

blood donor n donneur(-euse) de sang m(f).

blood group n groupe sanguin m.

bloodhound n limier m.

bloodily adv cruellement.

bloodiness n (fig) cruauté f.

bloodless adj exangue, anémié; sans effusion de sang.

blood poisoning *n* empoisonnement du sang *m*.

blood pressure *n* pression artérielle *f*.

bloodshed *n* effusion de sang *f*; carnage *m*.

bloodshot *adj* injecté de sang.

bloodstream *n* système sanguin *m*.

bloodsucker *n* sangsue *f*; (*fig*) vampire *m*.

blood test *n* analyse de sang *f*.

bloodthirsty *adj* sanguinaire.

blood transfusion *n* transfusion sanguine *f*.

blood vessel *n* veine *f*; vaisseau sanguin *m*.

bloody *adj* sanglant, ensanglanté; cruel; ~ **minded** *adj* sanguinaire; pas commode.

bloom *n* fleur *f*; (also fig); * *vi* éclore, fleurir.

blossom *n* fleur *f*.

blot *vt* tacher; sécher; effacer; * *n* tache *f*.

blotchy *adj* marbré; couvert de taches.

blotting pad *n* buvard *m*.

blotting paper *n* papier buvard *m*.

blouse *n* chemisier *m*.

blow *vi* souffler; sonner; * *vt* souffler; faire voler; jouer de; **to ~ up** exploser; * *n* coup *m*.

blowout *n* éclatement *m*.

blowpipe *n* sarbacane *f*.

blubber *n* blanc de baleine *m*; * *vi* pleurnicher.

bludgeon *n* gourdin *m*; matraque *f*.

blue *adj* bleu.

bluebell *n* campanule *f*.

bluebottle *n* (*bot*) bleuet *m*; mouche bleue *f*.

blueness *n* bleu *m*.

blueprint *n* (*fig*) projet *m*.

bluff *n* esbrouffe *f*; * *vt* faire de l'esbrouffe.

bluish *adj* bleuâtre.

blunder *n* gaffe *f*; * *vi* faire une gaffe.

blunt *adj* émoussé, obtus; direct; * *vt* émousser.

bluntly *adv* carrément; sans ménagements.

bluntness *n* brusquerie, rudesse *f*.

blur *n* tache *f*; * *vt* tacher.

blurt out *vt* laisser échapper.

blush *n* rougeur *f*; fard à joues *m*; * *vi* rougir.

blustery *adj* de tempête, violent.

boa *n* boa *m* (serpent).

boar *n* verrat *m*; **wild ~** sanglier *m*.

board *n* planche *f*; table *f*; conseil *m*; * *vt* monter à bord de.

boarder *n* pensionnaire *mf*.

boarding card *n* carte d'embarquement *f*.

boarding house *n* internat *m*; pension (de famille) *f*.

boarding school *n* pensionnat *m*.

boast *vi* se vanter; * *n* vantardise *f*; rodomontade *f*.

boastful *adj* vantard.

boat *n* bateau *m*; canot *m*; barque *f*.

boating *n* canotage *m*; promenade en bateau *f*.

bobsleigh *n* bobsleigh *m*.

bode *vt* présager, augurer.

bodice *n* corsage *m*.

bodily *adj*, *adv* physique(ment).

body *n* corps *m*; cadavre *m*; **any ~** n'importe qui; **every ~** tout le monde.

body-building *n* culturisme *m*.

bodyguard *n* garde du corps *m*.

bodywork *n* (*auto*) carrosserie *f*.

bog *n* marécage *m*.

boggy *adj* marécageux.

bogus *adj* faux.

boil *vi* bouillir; * *vt* faire bouillir; * *n* furoncle *m*; ébullition *f*.

boiled egg *n* oeuf à la coque *m*.

boiled potatoes *npl* pommes de terre à l'eau *f pl*.

boiler *n* casserole *f*; chaudière *f*.

boiling point *n* point d'ébullition *m*.

boisterous adj bruyant; turbulent; tumultueux; **~ly** adv bruyamment, tumultueusement.

bold adj audacieux, téméraire, osé, hardi; **~ly** adv audacieusement, hardiment.

boldness n intrépidité f; audace f; effronterie f.

bolster n traversin m; * vt soutenir.

bolt n verrou m; * vt verrouiller, fermer au verrou.

bomb n bombe f; **~ disposal** déminage m.

bombard vt bombarder.

bombardier n bombardier m.

bombardment n bombardement m.

bombshell n (fig) bombe f.

bond n lien m; attache f; engagement m; obligation f.

bondage n esclavage, asservissement m.

bond holder n obligataire mf.

bone n os m; * vt désosser.

boneless adj désossé, sans os.

bonfire n feu (de joie) m.

bonnet n bonnet m.

bonny adj joli.

bonus n prime f.

bony adj osseux.

boo vt huer.

booby trap n mine f.

book n livre m; **to bring to ~** vt obliger à rendre des comptes.

bookbinder n relieur(-euse) de livres m(f).

bookcase n bibliothèque f.

bookkeeper n comptable mf.

bookkeeping n comptabilité f.

bookmaking n prise des paris f.

bookmarker n signet m.

bookseller n libraire mf.

bookstore n librairie f.

bookworm n rat de bibliothèque m.

boom n grondement m; essor m; * vi gronder.

boon n bienfait m, aubaine f; faveur f.

boor n rustre m; brute f.

boorish adj rustre, rustique.

boost n stimulation f; * vt stimuler.

booster n propulseur m.

boot n botte f; coffre m; **to ~** adv de plus, de surcroît.

booth n cabine f; baraque f.

booty n butin m.

booze vi se saôuler; * n alcool m.

border n bord m; bordure f; lisière f; frontière f; * vt border, avoisiner.

borderline n limite f.

bore vt forer, percer; ennuyer; * n perceuse f; calibre m; raseur m.

boredom n ennui m.

boring adj ennuyeux.

born adj né; originaire.

borrow vt emprunter.

borrower n emprunteur m, -euse f.

bosom n sein m, poitrine f.

bosom friend n ami(e) intime m(f).

boss n chef m; patron(ne) m(f).

botanic(al) adj botanique.

botanist n botaniste mf.

botany n botanique f.

botch vt cochonner.

both pron tou(te)s les deux, l'un(e) et l'autre; * adj les deux; * conj à la fois; autant que.

bother vt ennuyer, déranger; * n ennui, problème m.

bottle n bouteille f; * vt mettre en bouteille.

bottleneck n embouteillage m; goulot m.

bottle-opener n ouvre-bouteille m invar.

bottom n fond m; fondement m; * adj du bas; dernier.

bottomless adj sans fond, insondable; inépuisable.

bough n branche f; rameau m.

boulder n gros galet m.

bounce vi rebondir; bondir, faire des bonds; * n bond, rebond m.

bound n limite f; saut m; répercussion *f*; * *vi* bondir, sauter; * *adj* à destination de.

boundary *n* limite *f*; frontière *f*.

boundless *adj* illimité, infini.

bounteous, bountiful *adj* abondant; prodigue, généreux; bienfaisant.

bounty *n* libéralité, générosité *f*.

bouquet *n* bouquet *m*.

bourgeois *adj* bourgeois.

bout *n* attaque *f*; accès *m*; combat *m*.

bovine *adj* bovin.

bow *vt* incliner, baisser; * *vi* se courber; faire une révérence; * *n* salut *m*, révérence *f*.

bow *n* arc *m*; archet *m*; nœud *m*.

bowels *npl* intestins *m pl*; entrailles *f pl*.

bowl *n* bol, saladier *m*; boule *f*; * *vi* jouer aux boules.

bowling *n* boules *fpl*.

bowling alley *n* bowling *m*.

bowling green *n* terrain de boules *m*.

bowstring *n* corde (d'arc) *f*.

bow tie *n* nœud papillon *m*.

box *n* boîte, caisse *f*; loge *f*; ~ **on the ear** gifle *f*; * *vt* mettre en boîte; * *vi* boxer.

boxer *n* boxeur *m*.

boxing *n* boxe *f*.

boxing gloves *npl* gants de boxe *m pl*.

boxing ring *n* ring *m*.

box office *n* guichet *m*.

box-seat *n* place à côté du siège du cocher *f*.

boy *n* garçon *m*.

boycott *vt* boycotter; * *n* boycottage *m*.

boyfriend *n* petit ami *m*.

boyish *adj* d'enfant, puéril; de garçon.

bra *n* soutien-gorge *m*.

brace *n* attache *f*; bretelle *f*; appareil dentaire *m*.

bracelet *n* bracelet *m*

bracing *adj* vivifiant, tonifiant.

bracken *n* (*bot*) fougère *f*.

bracket *n* tranche *f*; parenthèse *f*; crochet *m*; * **to ~ with** *vt* réunir par une accolade; mettre ensemble.

bracing *adj* vivifiant, tonifiant.

brag *n* fanfaronnade *f*; * *vi* se vanter, fanfaronner.

braid *n* tresse *f*; * *vt* tresser.

brain *n* cerveau *m*; tête *f*; * *vt* assommer, défoncer le crâne à.

brainchild *n* invention personnelle *f*.

brainwash *vt* faire un lavage de cerveau à.

brainwave *n* idée lumineuse *f*.

brainy *adj* intelligent.

brainless *adj* stupide.

brake *n* frein *m*; * *vi* freiner.

brake fluid *n* liquide de frein *m*.

brake light *n* feu de stop *m*.

bramble *n* ronce *f*.

bran *n* son *m*.

branch *n* branche *f*; ramification *f*; * *vi* se ramifier.

branch line *n* (*rail*) ligne d'embranchement *f*.

brand *n* marque *f*; marque au fer *f*; * *vt* marquer au fer.

brandish *vt* brandir.

brand-new *adj* flambant-neuf.

brandy *n* cognac *m*.

brash *adj* grossier; impertinent.

brass *n* cuivre *m*.

brassiere *n* soutien-gorge *m*.

brat *n* môme, gosse *mf*.

bravado *n* bravade *f*.

brave *adj* courageux, brave, vaillant; * *vt* braver; * *n* brave *m*; ~**ly** *adv* bravement, courageusement.

bravery *n* bravoure *f*; courage *m*; magnificence *f*.

brawl *n* bagarre, rixe *f*; * *vi* se bagarrer.

brawn *n* muscle *m*; fromage de tête *m*.

bray *vi* braire; * *n* braiment *m*.

braze *vt* souder au laiton.

brazen *adj* de cuivre; impudent, effronté; * *vi* crâner.

brazier n brasero m.

breach n rupture f; brèche f; violation f.

bread n pain m; (also fig); **brown ~** pain bis m.

breadbox n panière f.

breadcrumbs npl miettes de pain f pl.

breadth n largeur f.

breadwinner n soutien de famille m.

break vt casser; briser; violer; interrompre; * vi se casser; **to ~ into** entrer par effraction; **to ~ out** s'échapper; * n cassure, rupture f; interruption f; **~ of day** point du jour m, aube f.

breakage n rupture f.

breakdown n panne f; dépression nerveuse f. .

breakfast n petit déjeuner m; * vi déjeuner.

breaking n bris m; violation f; fracture f.

breakthrough n percée, innovation f.

breakwater n digue f.

breast n poitrine f, sein m; coeur m.

breastbone n sternum m.

breastplate n pectoral m; plastron m.

breaststroke n brasse f.

breath n haleine f; respiration f; souffle m.

breathe vt, vi respirer; exhaler.

breathing n respiration f; souffle m.

breathing space n moment de répit m.

breathless adj hors d'haleine.

breathtaking adj stupéfiant.

breed n race, espèce f; * vt élever, engendrer; produire; éduquer; * vi se reproduire.

breeder n éleveur m, -euse f.

breeding n élevage m; éducation f.

breeze n brise f.

breezy adj frais.

brethren npl frères m pl.

breviary n bréviaire m.

brevity n brièveté f; concision f.

brew vt faire infuser; brasser; comploter * vi infuser; se tramer; * n infusion f.

brewer n brasseur m.

brewery n brasserie f.

briar, brier n ronce f.

bribe n pot-de-vin m; * vt acheter, soudoyer.

bribery n corruption f.

bric-a-brac n bric-à-brac m.

brick n brique f; * vt bâtir en briques.

bricklayer n maçon m.

bridal adj de noces, nuptial.

bride n mariée f.

bridegroom n marié m.

bridesmaid n demoiselle d'honneur f.

bridge n pont m; arête du nez f; chevalet m; **to ~ (over)** vt relier par un pont.

bridle n bride f; frein m; * vt brider; réfréner.

brief adj bref, concis, succinct; * n affaire f; résumé m.

briefcase n serviette f.

briefly adv brièvement, en peu de mots.

brier n = briar

brigade n (mil) brigade f.

brigadier n (mil) général de brigade m.

brigand n bandit, brigand m.

bright adj clair, brillant, éclatant; **~ly** adv avec éclat.

brighten vt faire briller; * vi s'éclairer.

brightness n éclat, brillant m.

brilliance n éclat m.

brilliant adj éclatant; génial; **~ly** adv avec éclat.

brim n bord m.

brimful adj plein jusqu'au bord.

bring vt apporter; amener; persuader; **to ~ about** entraîner, provoquer; **to ~ forth** produire; provoquer; **to ~ up** élever.

brink n bord m.

brisk adj vif, rapide, frais.

brisket n poitrine de boeuf f.

briskly adj vivement; rapidement.

bristle n poil m; soie f; * vi se hérisser.

bristly adj hérissé.

brittle adj cassant, fragile.

broach vt aborder.

broad adj large.

broadbeans npl fèves fpl.

broadcast n émission f; * vt, vi diffuser, émettre.

broadcasting n radiodiffusion f; émission de télévision f.

broaden vt élargir; * vi s'élargir.

broadly adv généralement.

broad-minded adj tolérant, aux idées larges.

broadness n largeur f.

broadside n flanc (d'un navire) m; dépliant m.

broadways adv en large, dans le sens de la largeur.

brocade n brocart m.

broccoli n brocoli m.

brochure n brochure f, dépliant m.

brogue n accent m.

broil vt griller.

broken adj cassé; interrompu; ~ **English** mauvais anglais m.

broker n courtier m.

brokerage n courtage m.

bronchial adj des bronches.

bronchitis n bronchite f.

bronze n bronze m; * vt bronzer, brunir.

brooch n broche f.

brood vi couver; ruminer; * n couvée f; nichée f.

brood-hen n couveuse f.

brook n ruisseau m.

broom n genêt m; balai m.

broomstick n manche à balai m.

broth n bouillon de viande et de légumes m.

brothel n bordel m.

brother n frère m.

brotherhood n fraternité f.

brother-in-law n beau-frère m.

brotherly adj fraternel; adv fraternellement.

brow n sourcil m; front m; sommet m.

browbeat vt rudoyer.

brown adj marron; brun; ~ **paper** n papier d'emballage m; ~ **bread** n pain bis m; ~ **sugar** n cassonade f; * n marron m; * vt brunir.

browse vt brouter; * vi paître.

bruise vt faire un bleu à; * n bleu m, ecchymose f.

brunch n brunch m.

brunette n brune f.

brunt n choc m.

brush n brosse f; pinceau m; accrochage m; * vt brosser.

brushwood n broussailles fpl; brindilles fpl.

brusque adj brusque.

Brussels sprout n chou de Bruxelles m.

brutal adj brutal; ~**ly** adv brutalement.

brutality n brutalité f.

brutalize vt brutaliser.

brute n brute f; * adj bestial, féroce.

brutish adj brutal, bestial; féroce; ~**ly** adv brutalement.

bubble n bulle f; * vi faire des bulles, bouillonner; pétiller.

bubblegum n bubble-gum m.

bucket n seau m.

buckle n boucle f; * vt attacher, boucler; * vi se déformer.

bucolic adj bucolique.

bud n bourgeon, bouton m; * vi bourgeonner.

Buddhism n bouddhisme m.

budding adj en bouton.

buddy n copain m.

budge vi bouger, remuer; céder.

budgerigar n perruche f.

budget n budget m.

buff n mordu m.

buffalo n bison m.

buffers *npl* (*rail*) pare-chocs *m invar*.

buffet *n* buffet *m*; * *vt* gifler; frapper.

buffoon *n* bouffon *m*.

bug *n* punaise *f*.

bugbear *n* épouvantail, croquemitaine *m*.

bugle(horn) *n* clairon *m*.

build *vt* construire, bâtir.

builder *n* constructeur *m*; entrepreneur *m*.

building *n* bâtiment *m*; immeuble, édifice *m*.

building society *n* organisme de crédit immobilier *m*.

bulb *n* bulbe *m*; oignon *m*.

bulbous *adj* bulbeux.

bulge *vi* se renfler; * *n* gonflement, renflement *m*.

bulk *n* masse *f*; volume *m*; grosseur *f*; majeure partie *f*; **in ~** en gros.

bulky *adj* volumineux; encombrant.

bull *n* taureau *m*.

bulldog *n* bouledogue *m*.

bulldozer *n* bulldozer *m*.

bullet *n* balle *f*.

bulletin board *n* panneau d'affichage *m*.

bulletproof *adj* pare-balles, blindé.

bullfight *n* corrida *f*.

bullfighter *n* torero *m*.

bullfighting *n* tauromachie *f*.

bullion *n* or en barre *m*.

bullock *n* bouvillon *m*.

bullring *n* arène *f*.

bull's-eye *n* centre de la cible *m*.

bully *n* tyran *m*; * *vt* tyraniser.

bulwark *n* rempart *m*.

bum *n* clochard *m*.

bumblebee *n* bourdon *m*.

bump *n* heurt *m*; secousse *f*; bosse *f*; * *vt* heurter.

bumpkin *n* rustre *m*; plouc *m*.

bumpy *adj* cahoteux, bosselé.

bun *n* petit pain *m*; chignon *m*.

bunch *n* botte *f*; groupe *m*.

bundle *n* paquet *m*, liasse *f*; ballot *m*; fagot *m*; * *vt* empaqueter, mettre en liasse.

bung *n* bonde *f*; * *vt* boucher.

bungalow *n* bungalow *m*.

bungle *vt* bousiller; * *vi* faire mal les choses.

bunion *n* oignon *m*.

bunk *n* couchette *f*.

bunker *n* abri *m*; bunker *m*.

buoy *n* (*mar*) bouée *f*.

buoyancy *n* flottabilité *f*; optimisme *m*.

buoyant *adj* flottable; gai, enjoué.

burden *n* charge *f*; fardeau *m*; * *vt* charger.

bureau *n* commode *f*; bureau *m*.

bureaucracy *n* bureaucratie *f*.

bureaucrat *n* bureaucrate *mf*.

burglar *n* cambrioleur *m*, -euse *f*.

burglar alarm *n* signal d'alarme, signal antivol *m*.

burglary *n* cambriolage *m*.

burial *n* enterrement *m*; obsèques *f pl*.

burial place *n* lieu de sépulture *m*.

burlesque *n* caricature, parodie *f*; * *adj* burlesque, caricatural.

burly *adj* robuste, de forte carrure.

burn *vt* brûler; incendier, mettre le feu à; * *vi* brûler; * *n* brûlure *f*.

burner *n* brûleur *m*.

burning *adj* brûlant.

burrow *n* terrier *m*; * *vi* se terrer.

bursar *n* intendant(e) *m(f)*.

burse *n* bourse *f*.

burst *vi* éclater; **to ~ into tears** éclater en sanglots; **to ~ out laughing** éclater de rire; * *vt* **to ~ into** faire irruption dans; * *n* éclatement *m*; explosion *f*.

bury *vt* enterrer, inhumer.

bus *n* (auto)bus *m*.

bush *n* buisson, taillis *m*.

bushy *adj* touffu, plein de buissons.

busily *adv* activement, avec empressement.

business *n* entreprise *f*; commerce *m*; affaires *f pl*; activité *f*.

businesslike *adj* sérieux.

businessman *n* homme d'affaires *m*.

business trip *n* voyage d'affaires *m*.

businesswoman *n* femme d'affaires *f*.

bust *n* buste *m*.

bus-stop *n* arrêt d'autobus *m*.

bustle *vi* s'affairer; s'activer; * *n* remue-ménage *m*; animation *f*.

bustling *adj* animé.

busy *adj* occupé; actif.

busybody *n* mouche du coche *f*.

but *conj* mais; sauf, excepté, seulement.

butcher *n* boucher *m*, -ère *f*; * *vt* abattre, massacrer.

butcher's (shop) *n* boucherie *f*.

butchery *n* boucherie *f*, carnage *m*.

butler *n* majordome *m*.

butt *n* butte *f*; mégot *m*; * *vt* donner un coup de tête à.

butter *n* beurre *m*; * *vt* beurrer.

buttercup *n* (*bot*) bouton d'or *m*.

butterfly *n* papillon *m*.

buttermilk *n* babeurre *m*.

buttocks *npl* fesses *f pl*.

button *n* bouton *m*; * *vt* boutonner.

buttonhole *n* boutonnière *f*.

buttress *n* contre-fort *m*; soutien *m*; * *vt* soutenir.

buxom *adj* bien en chair.

buy *vt* acheter.

buyer *n* acheteur *m*, -euse *f*.

buzz *n* bourdonnement, murmure *m*; * *vi* bourdonner.

buzzard *n* buse *f*.

buzzer *n* interphone *m*.

by *prep* à côté de, près de; par; de; ~ **and** ~ bientôt; ~ **the** ~ à propos; ~ **much** de loin; ~ **all means** certainement; * *adv* près.

bygone *adj* passé.

by-law *n* arrêté municipal *m*.

bypass *n* route de contournement *f*.

by-product *n* sous-produit *m*.

by-road *n* chemin de traverse *m*.

bystander *n* spectateur *m* -trice *f*.

byte *n* (*comput*) octet *m*.

byword *n* proverbe, dicton *m*.

C

cab *n* taxi *m*.

cabbage *n* chou *m*.

cabin *n* cabine *f*; cabane *f*.

cabinet *n* conseil des ministres *m*; meuble de rangement *m*; console *f*.

cabinet-maker *n* ébéniste *m*.

cable *n* (*mar*) câble *m*.

cable car *n* téléphérique *m*.

cable television *n* télévision par câble *f*.

caboose *n* (*mar*) coquerie *f*.

cabstand *n* station de taxis *f*.

cache *n* cachette *f*.

cackle *vi* caqueter, jacasser; * *n* caquetage *m*; jacasserie *f*.

cactus *n* cactus *m*.

cadence *n* (*mus*) cadence *f*.

cadet *n* cadet *m*.

cadge *vt* taper (*fam*).

cafe *n* café *m*.

cafeteria *n* cafétéria *f*.

caffein(e) *n* caféine *f*.

cage *n* cage *f*; prison *f*; * *vt* mettre en cage; emprisonner.

cagey *adj* circonspect.

cajole *vt* cajoler pour amadouer.

cake *n* gâteau *m*.

calamitous *adj* calamiteux, catastrophique.

calamity *n* calamité *f*, désastre *m*.

calculable *adj* calculable.

calculate *vt* calculer, compter.

calculation *n* calcul *m*.

calculator n calculatrice f.

calculus n calcul m.

calendar n calendrier m.

calf n veau m; vachette f; mollet m.

calibre n calibre m.

calisthenics npl gymnastique rythmique f.

call vt appeler; appeler au téléphone; convoquer; **to ~ for** demander, nécessiter ; aller chercher quelqu'un; **to ~ on** rendre visite à; **to ~ attention** demander l'attention; **to ~ names** insulter; * n appel m; cri m; visite f; nomination f; vocation f; profession f.

caller n visiteur m, -euse f.

calligraphy n calligraphie f.

calling n profession, vocation f.

callous adj dur ; insensible.

calm n calme m, tranquillité f; * adj calme, tranquille; * vt calmer; apaiser ; **~ly** adv calmement.

calmness n calme m, tranquillité f.

calorie n calorie f.

calumny n calomnie f.

Calvary n Calvaire m.

calve vi vêler, mettre bas.

Calvinist n calviniste mf.

camel n chameau m.

cameo n camée m.

camera n appareil photographique m; caméra f.

cameraman n cameraman, cadreur m.

camomile n camomille f.

camouflage n camouflage m.

camp n camp m; * vi camper.

campaign n campagne f; * vi faire campagne.

campaigner n militant, candidat en campagne électorale m.

camper n campeur m, -euse f.

camping n camping m.

camphor n camphre m.

campsite n camping m.

campus n campus m.

can v aux pouvoir; * n boîte de conserve f.

canal n conduit m; canal m.

cancel vt annuler.

cancellation n annulation f.

cancer n cancer m.

Cancer n Cancer m (signe du zodiaque).

cancerous adj cancéreux.

candid adj candide, simple, sincère; **~ly** adv candidement, franchement.

candidate n candidat(e) m(f).

candied adj confit.

candle n bougie f; cierge m.

candlelight n lueur d'une bougie f.

candlestick n bougeoir m.

candor n candeur f; sincérité f.

candy n bonbon m.

cane n canne f; bâton m.

canine adj canin.

canister n boîte f.

cannabis n cannabis m.

cannibal n cannibale mf; anthropophage mf.

cannibalism n cannibalisme m.

cannon n canon m.

cannonball n boulet de canon m.

canny adj rusé; prudent.

canoe n canoë m.

canon n canon m; règle f; **~law** droit canon m.

canonization n canonisation f.

canonize vt canoniser.

can opener n ouvre-boîte m.

canopy n baldaquin m, marquise f.

cantankerous adj acariâtre, atrabilaire.

canteen n cantine f.

canter n petit galop m.

canvas n toile f.

canvass vt sonder, examiner; débattre; * vi solliciter des voix; faire du démarchage.

canvasser n prospecteur m, -trice f, démarcheur m, -euse f.

canyon n canyon m.

cap n casquette f.

capability n capacité, aptitude, faculté f; potentiel m.

capable adj capable.

capacitate vt rendre capable.

capacity n capacité, aptitude f; potentiel m.

cape n cap, promontoire m.

caper n cabriole f; gambade f; * vi cabrioler; gambader.

capillary adj capillaire.

capital adj capital; principal; * n capital m; capitale f; majuscule f.

capitalism n capitalisme m.

capitalist n capitaliste mf.

capitalize vt capitaliser; **to ~ on** profiter de.

capital punishment n peine de mort, peine capitale f.

Capitol n Capitole m.

capitulate vi capituler.

capitulation n capitulation f.

caprice n caprice m.

capricious adj capricieux; **~ly** adv capricieusement.

Capricorn n Capricorne m (signe du zodiaque).

capsize vt (mar) chavirer.

capsule n capsule f.

captain n capitaine m.

captaincy, captainship n grade de capitaine m; statut de capitaine m.

captivate vt captiver.

captivation n fascination f.

captive n captif m, -ive f, prisonnier m, -ière f.

captivity n captivité f.

capture n capture f; * vt prendre, capturer.

car n voiture f, automobile f; wagon m.

carafe n carafe f.

caramel n caramel m.

carat n carat m.

caravan n caravane f.

caraway n (bot) cumin m.

carbohydrates npl hydrates de carbone m pl.

carbon n carbone m.

carbon copy n copie carbone f, double carbone m.

carbonize vt carboniser.

carbon paper n papier carbone m.

carbuncle n escarboucle f; furoncle m, tumeur maligne f.

carburetor n carburateur m.

carcass n cadavre m.

card n carte f.

cardboard n carton m.

card game n jeu de cartes m.

cardiac adj cardiaque.

cardinal adj cardinal, principal; * n cardinal m.

card table n table de jeu f.

care n soin m; souci m; * vi se soucier de, être concerné par; **what do I ~?** qu'est-ce que cela peut me faire ? **to ~ for** vt soigner; aimer.

career n carrière f; cours m; * vi aller à toute vitesse.

carefree n insouciant.

careful adj soigneux, consciencieux , prudent; **~ly** adv soigneusement.

careless adj insouciant, négligent; indolent; **~ly** adv négligemment.

carelessness n négligence, indifférence f.

caress n caresse f; * vt caresser.

caretaker n gardien m, -ienne f, concierge mf.

car-ferry n ferry m.

cargo n cargaison de navire f.

car hire n location de voiture f.

caricature n caricature f; * vt caricaturer.

caries n carie f.

caring adj aimant; humanitaire.

Carmelite n carmélite f.

carnage n carnage m.

carnal adj charnel; sensuel; **~ly** adv charnellement.

carnation n œillet m.

carnival n carnaval m.

carnivorous adj carnivore.

carol n chant m.

carpenter n charpentier m; **~'s**

bench banc de menuisier *m*.
carpentry *n* charpenterie *f*.
carpet *n* tapis *m*; * *vt* recouvrir d'un tapis; moquetter.
carpeting *n* moquette *f*.
carriage *n* port *m*; voiture *f*; wagon *m*.
carriage-free *adj* franco de port.
carrier *n* porteur, transporteur *m*.
carrier pigeon *n* pigeon voyageur *m*.
carrion *n* charogne *f*.
carrot *n* carotte *f*.
carry *vt* porter; transporter; conduire; * *vi* porter; **to ~ the day** être victorieux; **to ~ on** continuer.
cart *n* charrette *f*; chariot *m*; * *vt* charrier.
cartel *n* cartel *m*.
carthorse *n* cheval de trait *m*.
Carthusian *n* chartreux *m*.
cartilage *n* cartilage *m*.
cartload *n* charretée *f*.
carton *n* pot *m*; boîte *f*.
cartoon *n* dessin animé *m*.
cartridge *n* cartouche *f*.
carve *vt* tailler, sculpter, ciseler.
carving *n* sculpture *f*.
carving knife *n* couteau à découper *m*.
car wash *n* station de nettoyage pour voitures *f*.
case *n* boîte *f*; valise *f*; cas *m*; étui *m*; enveloppe *f*; **in ~** au cas où.
cash *n* espèces *fpl*; * *vt* encaisser.
cash card *n* carte bancaire *f*.
cash dispenser *n* distributeur automatique de billets *m*.
cashier *n* caissier *m*, -ière *f*.
cashmere *n* cachemire *m*.
casing *n* chambranle *m*; enveloppe *f*.
casino *n* casino *m*.
cask *n* tonneau, fût *m*.
casket *n* cercueil *m*.
casserole *n* cocotte *f*.
cassette *n* cassette *f*.
cassette player, recorder *n* lecteur de cassettes, magnétophone *m*.
cassock *n* soutane *f*.
cast *vt* jeter, lancer; couler; * *n* coup *m*; moule *m*.
castanets *npl* castagnettes *f pl*.
castaway *n* réprouvé, paria *m*.
caste *n* caste *f*.
castigate *vt* punir sévèrement.
casting vote *n* voix prépondérante *f*.
cast iron *n* fonte *f*.
castle *n* château *m*.
castor oil *n* huile de ricin *f*.
castrate *vt* castrer.
castration *n* castration *f*.
cast steel *n* acier fondu *m*.
casual *adj* accidentel, fortuit; **~ly** *adv* par hasard, fortuitement.
casualty *n* victime *f*, mort *m*, -e *f*.
cat *n* chat *m*, chatte *f*.
catalog *n* catalogue *m*.
catalyst *n* catalyseur *m*.
cataplasm *n* cataplasme *m*.
catapult *n* catapulte *f*.
cataract *n* cascade *f*; déluge *m*.
catarrh *n* rhume *m*; catarrhe *m*.
catastrophe *n* catastrophe *f*.
catcall *n* sifflet *m*.
catch *vt* attraper, saisir; prendre; surprendre; **to ~ cold** attraper froid; **to ~ fire** prendre feu; * *n* prise *f*; capture *f*; (*mus*) canon *m*; attrape *f*.
catching *adj* contagieux, communicatif.
catchphrase *n* rengaine *f*.
catchword *n* slogan *m*.
catchy *adj* qui attire l'attention; accrocheur.
catechism *n* catéchisme *m*.
catechize *vt* cathéchiser; interroger.
categorical *adj* catégorique; **~ly** *adv* catégoriquement.
categorize *vt* classer par catégories.
category *n* catégorie *f*.
cater *vi* approvisionner en nourriture.

caterer n fournisseur, traiteur m.

catering n restauration f.

caterpillar n chenille f.

catgut n boyau de chat m.

cathedral n cathédrale f.

catholic adj, n catholique mf.

Catholicism n catholicisme m.

cattle n bétail m.

cattle show n exposition bovine f.

caucus n réunion d'un comité électoral f.

cauliflower n chou-fleur m.

cause n cause f; raison f; motif m; procès m; * vt causer.

causeway n chaussée f.

caustic adj, n caustique m/f.

cauterize vt cautériser.

caution n prudence, précaution f; avertissement m; * vt avertir.

cautionary adj d'avertissement.

cautious adj prudent, circonspect.

cavalier adj arrogant.

cavalry n cavalerie f.

cave n grotte f; caverne f.

caveat n avertissement m; mise en garde f; (law) notification f.

cavern n caverne f.

cavernous adj caverneux.

caviar n caviar m.

cavity n cavité f.

cease vt cesser, arrêter; * vi cesser.

ceasefire n cessez-le-feu m.

ceaseless adj incessant, continuel; ~ly adv continuellement.

cedar n cèdre m.

cede vt céder.

ceiling n plafond m.

celebrate vt célébrer, fêter.

celebration n fête f.

celebrity n célébrité f.

celery n céleri m.

celestial adj céleste, divin.

celibacy n célibat m.

celibate adj célibataire.

cell n cellule f.

cellar n cave f; cellier m.

cello n violoncelle m.

cellophane n cellophane f.

cellular adj cellulaire.

cellulose n (chem) cellulose f.

cement n ciment m; (also fig); * vt cimenter.

cemetery n cimetière m.

cenotaph n cénotaphe m.

censor n censeur m, critique mf.

censorious adj sévère, critique.

censorship n censure f.

censure n censure, critique f; * vt censurer, condamner; critiquer.

census n recensement m.

cent n centime m.

centenarian n centenaire mf.

centenary n centenaire m; * adj centenaire.

centennial adj centenaire.

centigrade n centigrade m.

centilitre n centilitre m.

centimetre n centimètre m.

centipede n mille-pattes m invar.

central adj central; ~ly adv de façon centralisée; dans le centre.

centralize vt centraliser.

centre n centre m; * vt centrer; concentrer; * vi se concentrer.

centrifugal adj centrifuge.

century n siècle m.

ceramic adj en céramique.

cereals npl céréales f pl.

cerebral adj cérébral.

ceremonial adj, n cérémonial m; rituel m.

ceremonious adj cérémonieux; ~ly adv solennellement.

ceremony n cérémonie f; cérémonies fpl.

certain adj certain, sûr; ~ly adv certainement, sans aucun doute.

certainty, certitude n certitude, conviction f.

certificate n certificat, acte m.

certification n authentification f.

certified mail n envoi avec accusé de réception m.

certify vt certifier, assurer.

cervical adj cervical.

cesarean section, ~ operation n (med) césarienne f.

cessation n cessation f.

cesspool *n* cloaque *m*; fosse d'aisances *f*.

chafe *vt* irriter; frotter.

chaff *n* menue paille *f*.

chaffinch *n* pinson *m*.

chagrin *n* dépit *m*.

chain *n* chaîne *f*; série, suite *f*; * *vt* enchaîner; attacher avec une chaîne.

chain reaction *n* réaction en chaîne *f*.

chainstore *n* grand magasin à succursales *m*.

chair *n* chaise *f*; * *vt* présider.

chairman *n* président *m*.

chalice *n* calice *m*.

chalk *n* craie *f*.

challenge *n* défi *m*; * *vt* défier.

challenger *n* provocateur *m*, -trice *f*.

challenging *adj* provocateur.

chamber *n* pièce *f*; chambre *f*.

chambermaid *n* femme de chambre *f*.

chameleon *n* caméléon *m*.

chamois leather *n* peau de chamois *f*.

champagne *n* champagne *m*.

champion *n* champion *m*, -ionne *f*; * *vt* défendre.

championship *n* championnat *m*.

chance *n* hasard *m*; chance *f*; occasion *f*; **by ~** par hasard; * *vt* faire par hasard.

chancellor *n* chancelier *m*.

chancery *n* chancellerie *f*.

chandelier *n* lustre *m*.

change *vt* changer; * *vi* changer, se transformer; * *n* changement *m*, modification *f*; variété *f*; change *m*.

changeable *adj* changeant, variable; inconstant.

changeless *adj* constant, immuable.

changing *adj* variable, changeant.

channel *n* canal *m*; chaîne *f*; * *vt* canaliser.

chant *n* chant *m*; * *vt* chanter.

chaos *n* chaos *m*.

chaotic *adj* chaotique.

chapel *n* chapelle *f*.

chaplain *n* chapelain *m*.

chapter *n* chapitre *m*.

char *vt* carboniser.

character *n* caractère *m*; personnage *m*.

characteristic *adj* caractéristique; **~ally** *adv* typiquement.

characterize *vt* caractériser.

characterless *adj* sans caractère.

charade *n* charade *f*.

charcoal *n* charbon de bois *m*.

charge *vt* charger; accuser; * *n* fardeau *m*; accusation *f*; (*mil*) attaque *f*; prix *m*.

chargeable *adj* passible.

charge card *n* carte de crédit *f*.

charitable *adj* caritatif; charitable; **~bly** *adv* charitablement.

charity *n* charité, bienfaisance *f*; aumône *f*.

charlatan *n* charlatan *m*.

charm *n* charme *m*; attrait *m*; * *vt* charmer, enchanter.

charming *adj* charmant.

chart *n* carte de navigation *f*; diagramme *m*.

charter *n* charte *f*; privilège *m*; * *vt* affréter.

charter flight *n* vol charter *m*.

chase *vt* donner la chasse à; poursuivre; * *n* chasse *f*.

chasm *n* abîme *m*.

chaste *adj* chaste; pur; sobre.

chasten *vt* châtier, corriger.

chastise *vt* châtier, punir, corriger.

chastisement *n* châtiment *m*.

chastity *n* chasteté, pureté *f*.

chat *vi* causer; * *n* petite conversation *f*, bavardage *m*.

chatter *vi* bavarder; jacasser; * *n* bavardage *m*; jacasserie *f*.

chatterbox *n* moulin à paroles *m*, pipelette *f*.

chatty *adj* bavard.

chauffeur *n* chauffeur *m*.

chauvinist *n* chauvin *m*, -e *f*.

cheap *adj* bon marché, peu cher;
~**ly** *adv* bon marché.

cheapen *vt* baisser le prix de.

cheaper *adj* moins cher.

cheat *vt* tromper, frauder; * *n*
fraude, tricherie *f*; tricheur *m*,
-euse *f*.

check *vt* vérifier; contrôler;
réprimer, enrayer; stopper; enregistrer; * *n* contrôle *m*.

checkmate *n* échec et mat *m*.

checkout *n* caisse *f*.

checkpoint *n* poste de contrôle *m*.

checkroom *n* consigne *f*.

checkup *n* bilan de santé *m*.

cheek *n* joue *f*; culot (*fam*) *m*.

cheekbone *n* pommette *f*.

cheer *n* gaieté *f*; joie *f*; applaudissement *m*; * *vt* réconforter, égayer.

cheerful *adj* gai, enjoué, joyeux;
~**ly** *adv* gaiement.

cheerfulness, cheeriness *n* gaieté *f*; bonne humeur *f*.

cheese *n* fromage *m*.

chef *n* chef (de cuisine) *m*.

chemical *adj* chimique.

chemist *n* chimiste *mf*; pharmacien *m*, -ienne *f*.

chemistry *n* chimie *f*.

cheque *n* chèque *m*.

cheque account *n* compte courant *m*.

chequerboard *n* échiquier *m*.

chequered *adj* à carreaux.

cherish *vt* chérir, aimer.

cheroot *n* petit cigare *m*.

cherry *n* cerise *f*; * *adj* vermeil.

cherrytree *n* cerisier *m*.

cherub *n* chérubin *m*.

chess *n* échecs *mpl*.

chessboard *n* échiquier *m*.

chessman *n* pièce de jeu d'échecs
f.

chest *n* poitrine *f*; cage thoracique
f; ~ **of drawers** commode *f*.

chestnut *n* châtaigne *f*.

chestnut tree *n* châtaigner *m*.

chew *vt* mâcher, mastiquer.

chewing gum *n* chewing-gum *m*.

chic *adj* chic.

chicanery *n* chicane, chicanerie
f.

chick *n* poussin *m*; (*fig*) poulette
fam), nana (*fam*) *f*.

chicken *n* poulet *m*.

chickenpox *n* varicelle *f*.

chickpea *n* pois chiche *m*.

chicory *n* chicorée *f*.

chide *vt* gronder, réprimander.

chief *adj* principal, en chef; ~**ly**
adv principalement; * *n* chef *m*.

chief executive *n* directeur
général *m*.

chieftain *n* chef *m*.

chiffon *n* mousseline de soie *f*.

chilblain *n* engelure *f*.

child *n* enfant *m*; **from a ~** tout
enfant; **with ~** enceinte.

childbirth *n* accouchement *m*.

childhood *n* enfance *f*.

childish *adj* enfantin, puéril; ~**ly**
adv puérilement.

childishness *n* enfantillage *m*,
puérilité *f*.

childless *adj* sans enfants.

childlike *adj* d'enfant.

children *npl* de **child**: enfants
mpl.

chill *adj* froid, frais, *f* fraîche; * *n*
froid *m*; * *vt* refroidir; glacer.

chilly *adj* froid, très frais.

chime *n* carillon *m*; harmonie *f*;
* *vi* sonner; s'accorder.

chimney *n* cheminée *f*.

chimpanzee *n* chimpanzé *m*.

chin *n* menton *m*.

china(ware) *n* porcelaine *f*.

chink *n* fente *f*; tintement *m*; * *vi*
tinter.

chip *vt* ébrécher; * *vi* s'ébrécher;
* *n* fragment, éclat *m*; puce *f*;
frite *f*.

chiropodist *n* pédicure *mf*.

chirp *vi* pépier, gazouiller; * *n*
pépiement, gazouillis *m*.

chirping *n* chant des oiseaux *m*.

chisel *n* ciseau *m*; * *vt* ciseler.

chitchat *n* bavardage, papotage
m.

chivalrous *adj* chevaleresque.
chivalry *n* chevalerie *f*.
chives *npl* ciboulette *f*.
chlorine *n* chlore *m*.
chloroform *n* chloroforme *m*.
chock-full *adj* plein à craquer, comble.
chocolate *n* chocolat *m*.
choice *n* choix *m*, préférence *f*; assortiment *m*; sélection *f*; * *adj* de choix, de qualité.
choir *n* choeur *m*.
choke *vt* étrangler; étouffer.
cholera *n* choléra *m*.
choose *vt* choisir, élire.
chop *vt* trancher, couper, hacher; * *n* côtelette *f*; ~s *pl* (*sl*) babines *f pl*.
chopper *n* hélicoptère *m*.
chopping block *n* billot *m*.
chopsticks *npl* baguettes *f pl*.
chore *n* corvée *f*; travail routinier *m*.
choral *adj* choral.
chord *n* corde *f*.
chorist, chorister *n* choriste *mf*.
chorus *n* choeur *m*.
Christ *n* Jésus-Christ.
christen *vt* baptiser.
Christendom *n* christianisme *m*; chrétienté *f*.
christening *n* baptême *m*.
Christian *adj, n* chrétien *m*, -ne *f*; ~ **name** prénom *m*.
Christianity *n* christianisme *m*; chrétienté *f*.
Christmas *n* Noël *f*.
Christmas card *n* carte de Noël *f*.
Christmas Eve *n* veille de Noël *f*.
chrome *n* chrome *m*.
chronic *adj* chronique.
chronicle *n* chronique *f*.
chronicler *n* chroniqueur *m*.
chronological *adj* chronologique; ~**ly** *adv* chronologiquement.
chronology *n* chronologie *f*.
chronometer *n* chronomètre *m*.
chubby *adj* potelé.
chuck *vt* lancer, jeter.
chuckle *vi* rire, glousser.

chug *vi* souffler, haleter.
chum *n* copain *m*, copine *f*.
chunk *n* gros morceau *m*.
church *n* église *f*.
churchyard *n* cimetière *m*.
churlish *adj* fruste, grossier; hargneux.
churn *n* baratte *f*; * *vt* baratter.
cider *n* cidre *m*.
cigar *n* cigare *m*.
cigarette *n* cigarette *f*.
cigarette case *n* étui à cigarettes *m*.
cigarette end *n* mégot *m*.
cigarette holder *n* fume-cigarette *m invar*.
cinder *n* cendre *f*.
cinema *n* cinéma *m*.
cinnamon *n* cannelle *f*.
cipher *n* chiffre *m*.
circle *n* cercle *m*; groupe *m*; * *vt* encercler; tourner autour de * *vi* décrire des cercles.
circuit *n* circuit *m*; tour *m*; tournée *f*.
circuitous *adj* détourné, indirect.
circular *adj* circulaire; * *n* circulaire *f*.
circulate *vi* circuler.
circulation *n* circulation *f*.
circumcise *vt* circoncire.
circumcision *n* circoncision *f*.
circumference *n* circonférence *f*.
circumflex *n* accent circonflexe *m*.
circumlocution *n* circonlocution *f*.
circumnavigate *vt* contourner.
circumnavigation *n* circumnavigation *f*.
circumscribe *vt* circonscrire.
circumspect *adj* circonspect.
circumspection *n* circonspection *f*.
circumstance *n* circonstance, situation *f*.
circumstantial *adj* circonstancié; accessoire.
circumstantiate *vt* détailler.
circumvent *vt* circonvenir.

circumvention *n* tromperie *f*; tricherie *f*.

circus *n* cirque *m*.

cistern *n* citerne *f*.

citadel *n* citadelle *f*.

citation *n* citation *f*.

cite *vt* citer.

citizen *n* citoyen *m*, -enne *f*.

citizenship *n* citoyenneté *f*.

city *n* ville *f*.

civic *adj* civique.

civil *adj* civil, courtois; **~ly** *adv* poliment.

civil defence *n* défense passive *f*.

civil engineer *n* ingénieur des travaux publics *m*.

civilian *n* civil *m*, -e *f*.

civility *n* civilité, courtoisie *f*.

civilization *n* civilisation *f*.

civilize *vt* civiliser.

civil law *n* droit civil *m*.

civil war *n* guerre civile *f*.

clad *adj* vêtu, habillé.

claim *vt* revendiquer, réclamer; * *n* demande *f*; réclamation *f*.

claimant *n* demandeur *m*.

clairvoyant *n* voyant *m*, -e *f*.

clam *n* palourde *f*.

clamber *vi* grimper (avec difficulté).

clammy *adj* moite.

clamor *n* clameur *f*, cris *m pl*; * *vi* vociférer, crier.

clamp *n* attache *f*; * *vt* serrer; imposer; **to ~ down on** resserrer le contrôle.

clan *n* clan, groupe *m*.

clandestine *adj* clandestin.

clang *n* bruit métallique *m*; * *vi* faire un bruit métallique.

clap *vt, vi* applaudir.

clapping *n* applaudissements *m pl*.

claret *n* vin rouge de Bordeaux *m*.

clarification *n* clarification *f*, éclaircissement *m*.

clarify *vt* clarifier, éclaircir.

clarinet *n* clarinette *f*.

clarity *n* clarté *f*.

clash *vi* se heurter; s'entrechoquer;

* *n* choc *m*; affrontement *m*.

clasp *n* fermoir *m*; boucle *f*; étreinte *f*; * *vt* agrafer; étreindre.

class *n* classe *f*; catégorie *f*; * *vt* classer, classifier.

classic(al) *adj* classique; * *n* auteur classique *m*.

classification *n* classification *f*.

classified advertisement *n* petite annonce *f*.

classify *vt* classifier, classer.

classmate *n* camarade de classe *mf*.

classroom *n* salle de classe *f*.

clatter *vi* résonner; cliqueter; * *n* cliquetis *m*.

clause *n* (*gram*) proposition *f*; clause *f*.

claw *n* griffe *f*; serre *f*; pince *f*; * *vt* griffer; agripper.

clay *n* argile *m*.

clean *adj* propre; net; * *vt* nettoyer.

cleaning *n* nettoyage *m*.

cleanliness *n* propreté, pureté *f*.

cleanly *adj* propre; * *adv* proprement, nettement.

cleanness *n* propreté *f*.

cleanse *vt* nettoyer.

clear *adj* clair; net; transparent; évident; * *adv* distinctement; * *vt* clarifier, éclaircir; dégager; disculper; * *vi* s'éclaircir.

clearance *n* déblaiement *m*; autorisation *f*.

clear-cut *adj* net.

clearly *adv* clairement; manifestement.

cleaver *n* couperet *m*.

clef *n* clé *f*.

cleft *n* fissure, crevasse *f*.

clemency *n* clémence *f*.

clement *adj* clément.

clenched *adj* serré.

clergy *n* clergé *m*.

clergyman *n* ecclésiastique *m*.

clerical *adj* clérical, ecclésiastique.

clerk *n* ecclésiastique *m*; employé *m*.

clever *adj* intelligent; habile; astucieux ; ~**ly** *adv* intelligemment, habilement.

click *vt* claquer; * *vi* faire un bruit sec.

client *n* client *m*, -e *f*.

cliff *n* falaise *f*.

climate *n* climat *m*.

climatic *adj* climatique.

climax *n* point culminant *m*, apogée *m*.

climb *vt* grimper, escalader; * *vi* grimper, escalader.

climber *n* alpiniste *mf*.

climbing *n* alpinisme *m*.

clinch *vt* serrer fort.

cling *vi* s'accrocher (à), se cramponner (à); adhérer, (se) coller.

clinic *n* clinique *f*.

clink *vt* faire tinter; * *vi* tinter, résonner; * *n* tintement *m*.

clip *vt* couper; * *n* clip *m*; pince *f*.

clipping *n* coupure *f*.

clique *n* clique *f*.

cloak *n* cape *f*; prétexte *m*; * *vt* masquer.

cloakroom *n* vestiaire *m*.

clock *n* horloge *f*.

clockwork *n* mécanisme d'horloge *m*; * *adj* précis.

clod *n* motte (de terre) *f*.

clog *n* sabot *m*; * *vi* se boucher.

cloister *n* cloître *m*.

close *vt* fermer; clore, conclure; terminer; * *vi* se fermer; * *n* fin *f*; conclusion *f*; * *adj* proche; étroit; ajusté; dense; réservé; * *adv* de près. ~ **by** tout près.

closed *adj* fermé.

closely *adv* étroitement; de près.

closeness *n* proximité *f*; fidélité, exactitude *f*; intimité *f*; minutie *f*.

closet *n* placard *m*.

close-up *n* gros plan *m*.

closure *n* fermeture *f*; clôture *f*.

clot *n* caillot *m*; grumeau *m*.

cloth *n* tissu *m*; chiffon *m*; toile *f*; clergé *m*.

clothe *vt* habiller, vêtir.

clothes *npl* vêtements *mpl*; linge *m*; **bed ~** draps et couvertures *mpl*.

clothes basket *n* panière à linge *f*.

clotheshorse *n* séchoir à linge *m*.

clothesline *n* corde à linge *f*.

clothespin *n* pince à linge *f*.

clothing *n* vêtements *mpl*.

cloud *n* nuage *m*; nuée *f*; * *vt* rendre trouble; assombrir; * *vi* se couvrir; s'obscurcir.

cloudiness *n* nébulosité *f*; obscurité *f*.

cloudy *adj* nuageux, nébuleux; obscur; sombre, trouble.

clout *n* coup de poing *m*.

clove *n* clou de girofle *m*.

clover *n* trèfle *m*.

clown *n* clown *m*.

club *n* matraque *f*; club *m*.

club car *n* wagon-restaurant *m*.

clue *n* indice *m*, indication *f*; idée *f*.

clump *n* massif *m*.

clumsily *adv* gauchement.

clumsiness *n* gaucherie *f*.

clumsy *adj* gauche, maladroit; lourd.

cluster *n* bouquet *m*; grappe *f*; groupe *m*; * *vt* grouper; * *vi* se rassembler.

clutch *n* prise *f*; embrayage *m*; * *vt* empoigner, agripper.

clutter *vt* encombrer.

coach *n* autocar *m*; wagon *m*; entraîneur *m*; * *vt* entraîner, donner des cours particuliers à.

coach trip *n* excursion en car *f*.

coagulate *vt* coaguler; agglutiner; * *vi* se coaguler; s'agglutiner.

coal *n* charbon *m*.

coalesce *vi* s'unir, se fondre.

coalfield *n* gisement charbonnier *m*.

coalition *n* coalition *f*.

coalman *n* charbonnier *m*.

coalmine *n* mine de charbon, houillère *f*.

coarse *adj* rude; grossier; ~**ly** *adv* grossièrement.

coast *n* côte *f*.
coastal *adj* côtier.
coastguard *n* gendarmerie maritime *f*.
coastline *n* littoral *m*.
coat *n* manteau *m*; pelage *m*; couche *f*; * *vt* enduire, revêtir.
coat hanger *n* cintre *m*.
coating *n* revêtement *m*.
coax *vt* cajôler.
cob *n* épi de maïs *m*.
cobbler *n* cordonnier *m*.
cobbles, cobblestones *npl* pavés ronds *mpl*.
cobweb *n* toile d'araignée *f*.
cocaine *n* cocaïne *f*.
cock *n* coq *m*; macho *m*; * *vt* armer; dresser.
cock-a-doodle-doo *n* cocorico *m*.
cockcrow *n* chant du coq *m*.
cockerel *n* jeune coq *m*.
cockfight(ing) *n* combat de coqs *m*.
cockle *n* (*mar*) coque *f*.
cockpit *n* cabine de pilotage *f*.
cockroach *n* cafard *m*.
cocktail *n* cocktail *m*.
cocoa *n* cacao *m*.
coconut *n* noix de coco *f*.
cocoon *n* cocon *m*.
cod *n* morue *f*.
code *n* code *m*; indicatif *m*.
cod-liver oil *n* huile de foie de morue *f*.
coefficient *n* coefficient *m*.
coercion *n* coercition, contrainte *f*.
coexistence *n* coexistence *f*.
coffee *n* café *m*.
coffee break *n* pause-café *f*.
coffee house *n* café *m*.
coffeepot *n* cafetière *f*.
coffee table *n* table basse *f*.
coffer *n* coffre *m*; caisse *f*.
coffin *n* cercueil *m*.
cog *n* dent d'engrenage *f*.
cogency *n* puissance, force *f*.
cogent *adj* convaincant, puissant; ~ly *adv* d'une manière convaincante.
cognac *n* cognac *m*.

cognate *adj* apparenté.
cognition *n* connaissance *f*; cognition *f*.
cognizance *n* connaissance *f*; compétence *f*.
cognizant *adj* instruit; (*law*) compétent.
cogwheel *n* roue dentée *f*.
cohabit *vi* cohabiter.
cohabitation *n* cohabitation *f*.
cohere *vi* se tenir; être cohérent.
coherence *n* cohérence *f*.
coherent *adj* cohérent; logique.
cohesion *n* cohésion *f*.
cohesive *adj* cohésif.
coil *n* rouleau *m*; bobine *f*; * *vt* enrouler.
coin *n* pièce de monnaie *f*; * *vt* frapper.
coincide *vi* coïncider.
coincidence *n* coïncidence *f*.
coincident *adj* coïncident.
coke *n* coke *m*.
colander *n* passoire *f*.
cold *adj* froid; indifférent; ~ly *adv* froidement; avec froideur; * *n* froid *m*; rhume *m*.
cold-blooded *adj* insensible.
coldness *n* froideur *f*.
cold sore *n* bouton de fièvre *m*.
coleslaw *n* salade de chou cru *f*.
colic *n* coliques *fpl*.
collaborate *vi* collaborer.
collaboration *n* collaboration *f*.
collapse *vi* s'écrouler; * *n* écroulement; (*med*) évanouissement *m*.
collapsible *adj* pliant.
collar *n* col *m*.
collarbone *n* clavicule *f*.
collate *vt* collationner, confronter.
collateral *adj* concomitant; parallèle; * *n* nantissement subsidiaire *m*.
collation *n* collation *f*.
colleague *n* collègue *mf*, confrère *m*, consoeur *f*.
collect *vt* rassembler; collectionner.
collection *n* collection *f*.

collective *adj* collectif; **~ly** collectivement.

collector *n* collectionneur *m*, -euse *f*.

college *n* collège *m*.

collide *vi* entrer en collision, se heurter.

collision *n* collision *f*, heurt *m*.

colloquial *adj* familier; parlé; **~ly** *adv* familièrement.

colloquialism *n* expression familière *f*.

collusion *n* collusion *f*.

colon *n* deux-points *m invar*; (*med*) colon *m*.

colonel *n* (*mil*) colonel *m*.

colonial *adj* colonial.

colonist *n* colon *m*.

colonize *vt* coloniser.

colony *n* colonie *f*.

colossal *adj* colossal.

colossus *n* colosse *m*.

colour *n* couleur *f*; prétexte *m*; **~s** *pl* drapeau *m*; * *vt* colorer; * *vi* se colorer.

colour-blind *adj* daltonien.

colourful *adj* coloré.

colouring *n* teint *m*; coloris *m*.

colourless *adj* sans couleur, incolore.

colour television *n* télévision en couleur *f*.

colt *n* poulain *m*.

column *n* colonne *f*.

columnist *n* chroniqueur *m*.

coma *n* coma *m*.

comatose *adj* comateux.

comb *n* peigne *m*; * *vt* peigner.

combat *n* combat *m*; **single ~** duel *m*; * *vt* combattre.

combatant *n* combattant *m*, -e *f*.

combative *adj* combatif.

combination *n* combinaison, association *f*.

combine *vt* combiner; * *vi* s'unir.

combustion *n* combustion *f*.

come *vi* venir; **to ~ across, ~ upon** *vt* rencontrer par hasard, tomber sur; **to ~ by** *vt* obtenir; **to ~ down** *vi* descendre; se

résumer à; **to ~ from** *vt* provenir de; être originaire de; **to ~ in for** *vt* être l'objet de; **to ~ into** *vt* hériter de; **to ~ round, ~ to** *vi* revenir à soi; **to ~ up with** *vt* suggérer.

comedian *n* comédien *m*; comique *m*.

comedienne *n* comédienne *f*; comique *f*.

comedy *n* comédie *f*.

comet *n* comète *f*.

comfort *n* confort *m*; aises *fpl*; commodités *fpl*; consolation *f*; * *vt* réconforter; soulager; consoler.

comfortable *adj* confortable; réconfortant.

comfortably *adv* confortablement; agréablement.

comforter *n* personne qui réconforte *f*; édredon *m*.

comic(al) *adj* comique; **~ly** *adv* comiquement.

coming *n* venue, arrivée *f*; * *adj* à venir.

comma *n* (*gr*) virgule *f*.

command *vt* ordonner, commander; * *n* ordre *m*.

commander *n* commandant *m*.

commandment *n* commandement *m*.

commando *n* commando *m*.

commemorate *vt* commémorer.

commemoration *n* commémoration *f*.

commence *vt*, *vi* commencer.

commencement *n* commencement *m*.

commend *vt* recommander, confier à; louer.

commendable *adj* louable.

commendably *adv* élogieusement.

commendation *n* louange *f*; recommandation *f*.

commensurate *adj* proportionné.

comment *n* commentaire *m*; * *vt* commenter.

commentary n commentaire m; observation f.
commentator n commentateur m, -trice f.
commerce n commerce m, affaires fpl; relations fpl.
commercial adj commercial.
commiserate vt compatir avec.
commiseration n commisération, pitié f.
commissariat n intendance f, ravitaillement m.
commission n commission f; * vt commissionner; commander.
commissioner n commissionnaire, coursier m.
commit vt commettre; confier à; engager.
commitment n engagement m.
committee n comité m.
commodity n produit m, denrée f.
common adj commun; ordinaire; **in** ~ en commun; * n terrain communal m.
commoner n roturier m, -ière f.
common law n droit coutumier m.
commonly adv communément, généralement.
commonplace n lieux communs mpl; * adj banal.
common sense n bon sens m.
Commonwealth n Commonwealth m.
commotion n vacarme m; perturbation f.
commune vi discuter avec sincérité.
communicable adj communicable, transmissible.
communicate vt communiquer, transmettre; * vi communiquer.
communication n communication f.
communicative adj communicatif.
communion n communion f.
communique n communiqué m.
communism n communisme m.
communist n communiste mf.

community n communauté f.
community center n centre social m.
community chest n fonds commun m.
commutable adj interchangeable, permutable.
commutation ticket n carte d'abonnement f.
commute vt échanger.
compact adj compact, serré, dense; * n accord, contrat m; ~ly adv de façon compacte; en peu de mots.
compact disc n disque compact m.
companion n compagnon m, compagne f.
companionship n camaraderie f; compagnie f.
company n compagnie, fréquentation f; société f.
comparable adj comparable.
comparative adj comparatif; ~ly adv comparativement.
compare vt comparer.
comparison n comparaison f.
compartment n compartiment m.
compass n boussole f.
compassion n compassion f.
compassionate adj compatissant.
compatibility n compatibilité f.
compatible adj compatible.
compatriot n compatriote mf.
compel vt contraindre, obliger, forcer.
compelling adj irrésistible.
compensate vt compenser.
compensation n compensation f; dédommagement m.
compere n animateur m, -trice f.
compete vi rivaliser (avec), faire concurrence (à).
competence n compétence f; aptitude f.
competent adj compétent; suffisant; ~ly adv avec compétence.
competition n compétition f; concurrence f.

competitive *adj* concurrentiel, compétitif.

competitor *n* concurrent *m*, -e *f*.

compilation *n* compilation *f*.

compile *vt* compiler.

complacency *n* suffisance *f*.

complacent *adj* suffisant.

complain *vi* se plaindre; déposer une plainte.

complaint *n* plainte *f*; réclamation *f*.

complement *n* complément *m*.

complementary *adj* complémentaire.

complete *adj* complet; achevé; **~ly** *adv* complètement; * *vt* achever, mener à bien, compléter.

completion *n* achèvement *m*.

complex *adj* complexe.

complexion *n* teint *m*; aspect *m*.

complexity *n* complexité *f*.

compliance *n* conformité *f*; soumission *f*.

compliant *adj* docile, soumis.

complicate *vt* compliquer.

complication *n* complication *f*.

complicity *n* complicité *f*.

compliment *n* compliment *m*; * *vt* complimenter.

complimentary *adj* flatteur; à titre gracieux.

comply *vi* se soumettre, se plier, se conformer.

component *adj* composant.

compose *vt* composer; constituer.

composed *adj* calme, posé.

composer *n* auteur *m*; compositeur *m*, -trice *f*.

composite *adj* composite, composé.

composition *n* composition *f*.

compositor *n* compositeur *m*, -trice *f*.

compost *n* compost *m*.

composure *n* maîtrise de soi *f*, calme *m*, sang-froid *m*.

compound *vt* composer, combiner; * *adj*, *n* composé *m*.

comprehend *vt* comprendre; englober.

comprehensible *adj* compréhensible; **~ly** *adv* intelligiblement.

comprehension *n* compréhension *f*; inclusion *f*.

comprehensive *adj* global; complet; compréhensif; **~ly** *adv* globalement.

compress *vt* comprimer, concentrer; * *n* compresse *f*.

comprise *vt* comprendre, embrasser.

compromise *n* compromis *m*; * *vt* compromettre; * *vi* adopter un compromis.

compulsion *n* contrainte *f*; compulsion *f*.

compulsive *adj* compulsif; **~ly** *adv* compulsivement.

compulsory *adj* obligatoire.

compunction *n* remords, scrupule *m*.

computable *adj* computable, calculable.

computation *n* computation *f*, calcul *m*.

compute *vt* calculer.

computer *n* ordinateur *m*.

computerize *vt* traiter par ordinateur, informatiser.

computer programing *n* programmation *f*.

computer science *n* informatique *f*.

comrade *n* camarade *mf*, compagnon *m*, compagne *f*.

comradeship *n* camaraderie *f*.

con *vt* duper; * *n* duperie *f*.

concave *adj* concave.

concavity *n* concavité *f*.

conceal *vt* cacher, dissimuler.

concealment *n* dissimulation *f*; recel *m*.

concede *vt* concéder, accorder.

conceit *n* vanité *f*; trait d'esprit *m*.

conceited *adj* vaniteux, prétentieux.

conceivable *adj* concevable.

conceive *vt* concevoir; * *vi* concevoir.

concentrate *vt* concentrer.

concentration *n* concentration *f*.

concentration camp *n* camp de concentration *m*.

concentric *adj* concentrique.

concept *n* concept *m*.

conception *n* conception *f*.

concern *vt* concerner, toucher; * *n* affaire *f*; souci *m*.

concerning *prep* en ce qui concerne, concernant.

concert *n* concert *m*.

concerto *n* concerto *m*.

concession *n* concession *f*.

conciliate *vt* concilier.

conciliation *n* conciliation *f*.

conciliatory *adj* conciliateur, conciliant.

concise *adj* concis, succinct; ~**ly** *adv* avec concision.

conclude *vt* conclure; décider; déduire.

conclusion *n* conclusion, déduction *f*; fin *f*.

conclusive *adj* décisif, concluant; ~**ly** *adv* de façon concluante.

concoct *vt* confectionner, fabriquer.

concoction *n* préparation *f*; élaboration *f*.

concomitant *adj* concomitant.

concord *n* entente, harmonie *f*.

concordance *n* accord *m*.

concordant *adj* concordant.

concourse *n* rassemblement *m*; carrefour *m*; foule *f*.

concrete *n* béton *m*; * *vt* bétonner.

concubine *n* concubine *f*.

concur *vi* coïncider; s'entendre.

concurrence *n* consentement *m*, coïncidence *f*; union *f*.

concurrently *adv* simultanément.

concussion *n* commotion *f*.

condemn *vt* condamner; désapprouver.

condemnation *n* condamnation *f*.

condensation *n* condensation *f*.

condense *vt* condenser.

condescend *vi* condescendre; daigner.

condescending *adj* condescendant.

condescension *n* condescendance *f*.

condiment *n* condiment *m*.

condition *vt* conditionner; * *n* condition, situation *f*; état *m*.

conditional *adj* conditionnel, hypothétique; ~**ly** *adv* conditionnellement.

conditioned *adj* conditionné.

conditioner *n* après-shampoing *m*.

condolences *npl* condoléances *fpl*.

condom *n* préservatif *m*.

condominium *n* condominium *m*, copropriété *f*.

condone *vt* pardonner, fermer les yeux sur.

conducive *adj* propice, opportun.

conduct *n* conduite *f*; comportement *m*; * *vt* conduire, mener.

conductor *n* receveur *m*; chef d'orchestre *m*; conducteur *m*.

conduit *n* conduit *m*; tuyau *m*.

cone *n* cône *m*.

confection *n* sucrerie, confiserie *f*; confection *f*.

confectioner *n* confiseur *m*, -euse *f*.

confectioner's (shop) *n* confiserie *f*; pâtisserie *f*.

confederacy *n* confédération *f*.

confederate *vi* se confédérer; * *adj*, *n* confédéré *m*.

confer *vt, vi* conférer.

conference *n* conférence *f*.

confess *vt* confesser; * *vi* se confesser.

confession *n* confession *f*.

confessional *n* confessionnal *m*.

confessor *n* confesseur *m*.

confetti *n* confetti *m*.

confidant *n* confident *m*, -e *f*.

confide *vt* confier; ~ **in** se confier à.

confidence n confiance f; assurance f.

confidence trick n abus de confiance m, escroquerie f.

confident adj confiant, assuré, sûr (de soi).

confidential adj confidentiel.

configuration n configuration f.

confine vt limiter; emprisonner.

confinement n détention f; alitement m.

confirm vt confirmer; ratifier.

confirmation n confirmation f; ratification f; corroboration f.

confirmed adj invétéré, endurci.

confiscate vt confisquer.

confiscation n confiscation f.

conflagration n incendie m; conflagration f.

conflict n conflit m; lutte f; dispute f.

conflicting adj contradictoire.

confluence n confluence f; rencontre f.

conform vt conformer, adapter; * vi se conformer (à), s'adapter (à).

conformity n conformité f, accord m.

confound vt confondre.

confront vt confronter; affronter.

confrontation n affrontement m, confrontation f.

confuse vt confondre; embarrasser; embrouiller.

confusing adj déroutant.

confusion n confusion f; désordre m.

congeal vt solidifier, congeler; * vi se solidifier, se congeler.

congenial adj sympathique; similaire.

congenital adj congénital.

congested adj encombré, congestionné.

congestion n encombrement m, congestion f.

conglomerate vt conglomérer, agglomérer; * adj aggloméré; * n (com) conglomérat m.

conglomeration n agglomération f.

congratulate vt complimenter, féliciter.

congratulations npl félicitations fpl.

congratulatory adj de félicitations.

congregate vt rassembler, réunir.

congregation n assemblée f, rassemblement m.

congress n congrès m; conférence f.

congressman n membre du Congrès m.

congruity n congruence f.

congruous adj congru, approprié.

conic(al) adj conique.

conifer n conifère m.

coniferous adj (bot) conifère.

conjecture n conjecture, supposition f; * vt conjecturer, supposer.

conjugal adj conjugal.

conjugate vt (gr) conjuguer.

conjugation n conjugaison f.

conjunction n conjonction f; union f.

conjuncture n conjoncture f; occasion f.

conjure vt conjurer; exorciser.

conjurer n magicien m, -ienne f, illusionniste mf.

con man n escroc m.

connect vt relier, joindre, rattacher.

connection n liaison, connexion f.

connivance n connivence f.

connive vi fermer les yeux (sur); être de connivence.

connoisseur n connaisseur m, -euse f.

conquer vt conquérir; vaincre.

conqueror n vainqueur m; conquérant m.

conquest n conquête f.

conscience n conscience f.

conscientious adj consciencieux; de conscience; ~ly adv consciencieusement.

conscious adj conscient; intentionnel; ~**ly** *adv* consciemment, sciemment.

consciousness *n* conscience *f*.

conscript *n* conscrit *m*.

conscription *n* conscription *f*.

consecrate *vt* consacrer.

consecration *n* consécration *f*.

consecutive *adj* consécutif; ~**ly** *adv* consécutivement.

consensus *n* consensus *m*.

consent *n* consentement *m*; assentiment *m*; * *vi* consentir.

consequence *n* conséquence *f*; importance *f*.

consequent *adj* consécutif; ~**ly** *adv* par conséquent.

conservation *n* conservation *f*.

conservative *adj* conservateur.

conservatory *n* conservatoire *m*.

conserve *vt* conserver; * *n* conserve *f*.

consider *vt* considérer, examiner; * *vi* penser, délibérer.

considerable *adj* considérable; important; ~**bly** *adv* considérablement.

considerate *adj* prévenant, attentionné; prudent; ~**ly** *adv* avec prévenance; prudemment.

consideration *n* considération *f*; réflexion *f*; estime *f*; rémunération *f*.

considering *conj* étant donné que; ~ **that** vu que; étant donné que.

consign *vt* confier, remettre, expédier.

consignment *n* expédition *f*, envoi *m*.

consist *vi* consister (en).

consistency *n* consistance *f*; cohérence *f*; constance *f*.

consistent *adj* constant; cohérent; compatible; ~**ly** *adv* régulièrement.

consolable *adj* consolable.

consolation *n* consolation *f*; réconfort *m*.

consolatory *adj* consolateur.

console *vt* consoler.

consolidate *vt* consolider, grouper; * *vi* se consolider.

consolidation *n* consolidation *f*.

consonant *adj* en accord; * *n* (*gr*) consonne *f*.

consort *n* consort *m*; associé *m*, -e *f*.

conspicuous *adj* voyant, manifeste; notable; ~**ly** *adv* manifestement .

conspiracy *n* conspiration *f*.

conspirator *n* conspirateur *m*, -trice *f*.

conspire *vi* conspirer.

constancy *n* constance, fermeté d'âme *f*; persévérance *f*.

constant *adj* constant; persévérant; ~**ly** *adv* constamment.

constellation *n* constellation *f*.

consternation *n* consternation *f*.

constipated *adj* constipé.

constituency *n* électorat *m*; circonscription *f*.

constituent *n* composant *m*; * *adj* constituant.

constitute *vt* constituer; établir.

constitution *n* constitution *f*.

constitutional *adj* constitutionnel.

constrain *vt* contraindre, forcer, obliger.

constraint *n* contrainte *f*.

constrict *vt* serrer; gêner.

construct *vt* construire, bâtir.

construction *n* construction *f*.

construe *vt* interpréter, analyser.

consul *n* consul *m*.

consular *adj* consulaire.

consulate, consulship *n* consulat *m*.

consult *vt* consulter; * *vi* (se) consulter.

consultation *n* consultation, délibération *f*.

consume *vt* consommer; dissiper; consumer, brûler; * *vi* se consommer.

consumer *n* consommateur *m*, -trice *f*.

consumer goods *npl* biens de consommation *mpl.*

consumerism *n* consumérisme *m.*

consumer society *n* société de consommation *f.*

consummate *vt* consommer, accomplir; perfectionner; * *adj* accompli, consommé.

consummation *n* consommation *f*; perfection *f.*

consumption *n* consommation *f.*

contact *n* contact *m.*

contact lenses *npl* lentilles de contact *fpl.*

contagious *adj* contagieux.

contain *vt* contenir, renfermer; réfréner.

container *n* récipient *m.*

contaminate *vt* contaminer; **~d** *adj* contaminé.

contamination *n* contamination *f.*

contemplate *vt* contempler.

contemplation *n* contemplation *f.*

contemplative *adj* contemplatif.

contemporaneous, contemporary *adj* contemporain.

contempt *n* mépris, dédain *m.*

contemptible *adj* méprisable, vil; **~bly** *adv* vilement.

contemptuous *adj* méprisant, dédaigneux; **~ly** *adv* dédaigneusement.

contend *vi* combattre, lutter; * *vt* affirmer.

content *adj* content, satisfait; * *vt* contenter, satisfaire; * *n* contentement *m*; **~s** *pl* contenu *m*; table des matières *f.*

contentedly *adv* avec contentement.

contention *n* querelle, altercation *f.*

contentious *adj* litigieux; querelleur; **~ly** *adv* en chicanant.

contentment *n* contentement *m*, satisfaction *f.*

contest *vt* contester, discuter, disputer ; * *n* concours *m*; altercation *f.*

contestant *n* concurrent *m*, -e *f.*

context *n* contexte *m.*

contiguous *adj* contigu, voisin.

continent *adj* continent, chaste; * *n* continent *m.*

continental *adj* continental.

contingency *n* contingence *f*; événement imprévu *m*; éventualité *f.*

contingent *n* contingent *m*; * *adj* contingent, éventuel; **~ly** fortuitement.

continual *adj* continuel; **~ly** *adv* continuellement.

continuation *n* continuation, reprise, suite *f.*

continue *vt, vi* continuer.

continuity *n* continuité *f.*

continuous *adj* continu; **~ly** *adv* sans interruption.

contort *vt* tordre, déformer.

contortion *n* contorsion *f.*

contour *n* contour *m.*

contraband *n* contrebande *f*; * *adj* de contrebande.

contraception *n* contraception *f.*

contraceptive *n* contraceptif *m*; * *adj* contraceptif.

contract *vt* contracter; *vi* se contracter; * *n* contrat *m.*

contraction *n* contraction *f.*

contractor *n* entrepreneur *m.*

contradict *vt* contredire.

contradiction *n* contradiction *f.*

contradictory *adj* contradictoire.

contraption *n* gadget, bidule (*fam*) *m.*

contrariness *n* esprit de contradiction *m.*

contrary *adj* contraire, opposé; * *n* contraire *m*; **on the ~** au contraire.

contrast *n* contraste *m*; * *vt* contraster, mettre en constrasse.

contrasting *adj* contrasté, opposé.

contravention *n* infraction *f.*

contributary *adj* contributif.

contribute *vt* contribuer.

contribution *n* contribution *f*; cotisation *f.*

contributor *n* souscripteur(-trice), collaborateur(-trice) *m(f)*.

contributory *adj* contribuant.

contrite *adj* contrit, repentant.

contrition *n* contrition *f*, repentir *m*.

contrivance *n* dispositif *m*; invention *f*.

contrive *vt* inventer, combiner; trouver le moyen de.

control *n* contrôle *m*; maîtrise *f*; autorité *f*; * *vt* maîtriser; réguler; contrôler; gouverner.

control room *n* salle des commandes *f*.

control tower *n* tour de contrôle *f*.

controversial *adj* polémique.

controversy *n* polémique *f*.

contusion *n* contusion *f*.

conundrum *n* énigme *f*.

conurbation *n* conurbation *f*.

convalesce *vi* être en convalescence.

convalescence *n* convalescence *f*.

convalescent *adj* convalescent.

convene *vt* convoquer; réunir; * *vi* se réunir.

convenience *n* commodité, convenance *f*.

convenient *adj* commode, pratique; qui convient; ~**ly** *adv* commodément.

convent *n* couvent *m*.

convention *n* convention *f*; contrat *m*; assemblée *f*.

conventional *adj* conventionnel.

converge *vi* converger.

convergence *n* convergence *f*.

convergent *adj* convergent.

conversant *adj* au courant; compétent.

conversation *n* conversation *f*.

converse *vi* converser.

conversely *adv* inversement, réciproquement.

conversion *n* conversion; transformation *f*.

convert *vt* convertir; * *n* converti *m*, -e *f*.

convertible *adj* convertible; * *n* décapotable *f*.

convex *adj* convexe.

convexity *n* convexité *f*.

convey *vt* transporter; transmettre, communiquer.

conveyance *n* transport *m*; transfert *m*; cession *f*.

conveyancer *n* notaire *m*.

convict *vt* déclarer coupable; * *n* détenu *m*, -e *f*.

conviction *n* condamnation *f*; conviction *f*.

convince *vt* convaincre, persuader.

convincing *adj* convaincant.

convincingly *adv* de façon convaincante.

convivial *adj* jovial.

conviviality *n* jovialité *f*.

convoke *vt* convoquer.

convoy *n* convoi *m*.

convulse *vt* ébranler.

convulsion *n* convulsion *f*; bouleversement *m*; forte agitation *f*.

convulsive *adj* convulsif; ~**ly** *adv* convulsivement.

coo *vt, vi* roucouler.

cook *n* cuisinier *m*, -ière *f*; * *vt* cuire; falsifier; * *vi* faire la cuisine, cuisiner.

cookbook *n* livre de cuisine *m*.

cooker *n* cuisinière *f*.

cookery *n* cuisine *f*.

cookie *n* petit gâteau *m*.

cool *adj* frais; calme; * *n* fraîcheur *f*; * *vt* rafraîchir, refroidir.

coolly *adv* fraîchement; de sang-froid.

coolness *n* fraîcheur *f*; froideur *f*; sang-froid *m*.

cooperate *vi* coopérer.

cooperation *n* coopération *f*.

cooperative *adj* coopératif.

coordinate *vt* coordonner.

coordination *n* coordination *f*.

cop *n* (*fam*) flic *m*.

copartner *n* coassocié *m*, -e *f*.

cope *vi* se débrouiller.

copier *n* photocopieuse *f*.

copious *adj* copieux, abondant; **~ly** *adv* abondamment.

copper *n* cuivre *m*.

coppice, copse *n* taillis *m*.

copulate *vi* copuler.

copy *n* copie *f*; reproduction *f*; exemplaire *m*; * *vt* copier; imiter.

copybook *n* cahier *m*.

copying machine *n* photocopieuse *f*.

copyist *n* copiste *mf*.

copyright *n* droit d'auteur *m*.

coral *n* corail *m*.

coral reef *n* récif de corail *m*.

cord *n* corde *f*, cordon *m*.

cordial *adj* cordial, chaleureux; **~ly** *adv* cordialement.

corduroy *n* velours côtelé *m*.

core *n* trognon *m*; noyau, centre, coeur, *m*.

cork *n* liège *m*; bouchon *m*; * *vt* boucher.

corkscrew *n* tire-bouchon *m*.

corn *n* maïs *m*; grain *m*; blé *m*.

corncob *n* épi de maïs *m*.

cornea *n* cornée *f*.

corned beef *n* corned-beef *m*.

corner *n* coin *m*; angle *m*.

cornerstone *n* pierre angulaire *f*.

cornet *n* cornet *m*.

cornfield *n* champ de maïs *m*.

cornflakes *npl* flocons de maïs, cornflakes *mpl*.

cornice *n* corniche *f*.

cornstarch *n* farine de maïs *f*.

corollary *n* corollaire *m*.

coronary *n* infarctus *m*.

coronation *n* couronnement *m*.

coroner *n* coroner *m*.

coronet *n* couronne *f*.

corporal *n* caporal *m*.

corporate *adj* en commun; d'entreprise.

corporation *n* corporation *f*; société par actions *f*.

corporeal *adj* corporel.

corps *n* corps *m*.

corpse *n* cadavre *m*.

corpulent *adj* corpulent.

corpuscle *n* corpuscule *m*; électron *m*.

corral *n* corral *m*.

correct *vt* corriger; rectifier; * *adj* correct, juste; **~ly** *adv* correctement.

correction *n* correction *f*; rectification *f*.

corrective *adj* correcteur, correctif; * *n* correcteur *m*.

correctness *n* correction *f*.

correlation *n* corrélation *f*.

correlative *adj* corrélatif.

correspond *vi* correspondre.

correspondence *n* correspondance *f*.

correspondent *adj* correspondant; * *n* correspondant *m*, -e *f*.

corridor *n* couloir, corridor *m*.

corroborate *vt* corroborer.

corroboration *n* corroboration *f*.

corroborative *adj* qui corrobore.

corrode *vt* corroder.

corrosion *n* corrosion *f*.

corrosive *adj*, *n* corrosif *m*.

corrugated iron *n* tôle ondulée *f*.

corrupt *vt* corrompre; * *vi* se corrompre, se pourrir; * *adj* corrompu; dépravé.

corruptible *adj* corruptible.

corruption *n* corruption *f*; dépravation *f*.

corruptive *adj* qui corrompt.

corset *n* corset *m*, gaine *f*.

cortege *n* cortège *m*.

cosily *adv* confortablement, douillettement.

cosmetic *adj*, *n* cosmétique *m*.

cosmic *adj* cosmique.

cosmonaut *n* cosmonaute *mf*.

cosmopolitan *adj* cosmopolite.

cosset *vt* dorloter.

cost *n* prix, coût *m*; * *vi* coûter.

costly *adj* coûteux, cher.

costume *n* costume *m*.

cottage *n* cottage *m*.

cotton *n* coton *m*.

cotton candy *n* barbe à papa *f*.

cotton mill *n* filature de coton *f*.

cotton wool *n* coton hydrophile *m*.

couch *n* canapé, divan *m*.

couchette *n* couchette *f*.

cough *n* toux *f*; * *vi* tousser.

council *n* conseil *m*.

councilor *n* membre du conseil *m*; conseiller *m*, -ère *f*.

counsel *n* conseil *m*; avocat *m*.

counselor *n* conseiller *m*, -ère *f*; avocat *m*.

count *vt* compter, dénombrer; calculer; **to ~ on** compter sur; * *n* compte *m*; calcul *m*; chef d'accusation *m*.

countdown *n* compte à rebours *m*.

countenance *n* visage *m*; aspect *m*; mine *f*.

counter *n* comptoir *m*; jeton *m*.

counteract *vt* contrecarrer; neutraliser; contrebalancer.

counterbalance *vt* contrebalancer; compenser; * *n* contrepoids *m*.

counterfeit *vt* contrefaire; * *adj* faux.

countermand *vt* annuler.

counterpart *n* contrepartie *f*; homologue *mf*.

counterproductive *adj* qui va à l'encontre du but visé.

countersign *vt* contresigner.

countess *n* comtesse *f*.

countless *adj* innombrable.

countrified *adj* rustique; campagnard.

country *n* pays *m*; patrie *f*; campagne *f*; région *f*; * *adj* rustique; campagnard.

country house *n* maison de campagne *f*.

countryman *n* campagnard *m*; compatriote *m*.

county *n* comté *m*.

coup *n* coup *m*.

coupé *n* coupé *m*.

couple *n* couple *m*; **a ~ of** deux; * *vt* unir, associer.

couplet *n* distique *m*; couplet *m*.

coupon *n* coupon *m*.

courage *n* courage *m*.

courageous *adj* courageux; **~ly** *adv* courageusement.

courier *n* messager *m*; guide *m*.

course *n* cours *m*; route *f*; chemin *m*; plat *m*; marche à suivre *f*; **of ~** bien sûr, naturellement.

court *n* cour *f*; tribunal *m*; * *vt* courtiser; solliciter.

courteous *adj* courtois; poli; **~ly** *adv* courtoisement.

courtesan *n* courtisane *f*.

courtesy *n* courtoisie *f*.

courthouse *n* palais de justice *m*.

courtly *adj* élégant, raffiné.

court martial *n* conseil de guerre *m*.

courtroom *n* salle de tribunal *f*.

courtyard *n* cour *f*.

cousin *n* cousin *m*, -e *f*; **first ~** cousin(e) germain(e) *m(f)*.

cove *n* (*mar*) crique, anse *f*.

covenant *n* contrat *m*; convention *f*; * *vi* convenir, stipuler par contrat.

cover *n* couverture *f*; abri *m*; prétexte *m*; * *vt* (re)couvrir; dissimuler; protéger.

coverage *n* reportage *m*, couverture *f*.

coveralls *npl* bleu de travail *m*.

covering *n* couverture *f*; couche *f*.

cover letter *n* lettre explicative *f*.

covert *adj* voilé; caché, secret; **~ly** *adv* secrètement.

cover-up *n* dissimulation *f*.

covet *vt* convoiter.

covetous *adj* avide, cupide.

cow *n* vache *f*.

coward *n* lâche *mf*.

cowardice *n* lâcheté *f*.

cowardly *adj* lâche; *adv* lâchement.

cowboy *n* cowboy *m*.

cower *vi* se tapir.

cowherd *n* vacher *m*.

coy *adj* timide ; coquet; évasif; **~ly** *adv* évasivement.

coyness *n* timidité *f*; modestie *f*.

cozy *adj* douillet.

crab *n* crabe *m*.

crab apple n pomme sauvage f; **crab-apple tree** n pommier sauvage m.

crack n craquement m; fente, fissure f; * vt fêler, craquer; **to ~ down on** réprimer; * vi se fêler; craquer.

cracker n pétard m ; biscuit salé m.

crackle vi crépiter, pétiller.

crackling n crépitement m; friture f.

cradle n berceau m; * vt bercer.

craft n habileté f; métier manuel m; barque f.

craftily adv astucieusement.

craftiness n astuce, ruse f.

craftsman n artisan m.

craftsmanship n artisanat m.

crafty adj astucieux, rusé.

crag n rocher escarpé m.

cram vt bourrer; fourrer; * vi s'entasser.

crammed adj bourré.

cramp n crampe f; * vt entraver.

cramped adj à l'étroit.

crampon n crampon m.

cranberry n canneberge f.

crane n grue f.

crash vi s'écraser; * n fracas m; collision f.

crash helmet n casque m.

crash landing n atterrissage en catastrophe m.

crass adj grossier, crasse.

crate n caisse f; cageot m.

crater n cratère m.

cravat n foulard m, cravate f.

crave vt avoir extrêmement besoin de.

craving adj désespéré; insatiable; * n désir extrême m.

crawfish n écrevisse f.

crawl vi ramper; **to ~ with** grouiller.

crayfish n écrevisse f.

crayon n crayon de couleur m.

craze n manie f, engouement m.

craziness n folie f.

crazy adj fou.

creak vi grincer, craquer.

cream n crème f; * adj crème.

creamy adj crémeux.

crease n pli m; * vt froisser.

create vt créer; causer.

creation n création f.

creative adj créatif.

creator n créateur m, -trice f.

creature n créature f.

credence n croyance, foi f; créance f.

credentials npl lettres de créance fpl; preuves d'identité fpl.

credibility n crédibilité f.

credible adj crédible.

credit n crédit m; honneur m; reconnaissance f; * vt croire, reconnaître; créditer.

creditable adj estimable, honorable; **~bly** adv honorablement.

credit card n carte de crédit f.

creditor n créancier m, -ière f.

credulity n crédulité f.

credulous adj crédule; **~ly** adv avec crédulité.

creed n credo m.

creek n ruisseau m.

creep vi ramper; avancer lentement.

creeper n (bot) plante grimpante f.

creepy adj terrifiant, qui donne la chair de poule.

cremate vt incinérer.

cremation n incinération, crémation f.

crematorium n crématoire m.

crescent adj croissant; * n croissant de lune m.

cress n cresson m.

crest n crête f.

crested adj à crête.

crestfallen adj découragé, abattu.

crevasse n crevasse f.

crevice n fissure, lézarde f.

crew n bande, équipe f; équipage m.

crib n berceau m; mangeoire f.

cricket n grillon m.

crime n crime m; délit m.

criminal *adj* criminel; **~ly** *adv* criminellement; * *n* criminel *m*, -elle *f*.
criminality *n* criminalité *f*.
crimson *adj*, *n* cramoisi *m*.
cripple *n*, *adj* invalide *mf*; * *vt* estropier; (*fig*) paralyser.
crisis *n* crise *f*.
crisp *adj* frais; croquant.
crispness *n* croquant *m*.
criss-cross *adj* entrecroisé.
criterion *n* critère *m*.
critic *n* critique *m*.
critic(al) *adj* critique; exigeant, sévère; **~ally** *adv* d'un oeil critique; sévèrement.
criticism *n* critique *f*.
criticize *vt* critiquer.
croak *vi* coasser, croasser.
crochet *n* crochet *m*; * *vt* faire au crochet; *vi* faire du crochet.
crockery *n* poterie *f*.
crocodile *n* crocodile *m*.
crony *n* copain (copine) de longue date *m(f)*.
crook *n* (*fam*) escroc *m*; filou *m*.
crooked *adj* tordu; malhonnête.
crop *n* culture *f*; récolte *f*; * *vt* récolter.
cross *n* croix *f*; croisement *m*; * *adj* de mauvaise humeur, fâché; * *vt* traverser, croiser; **to ~ over** traverser.
crossbar *n* barre transversale *f*.
crossbreed *n* hybride *m*.
cross-country *n* cross-country *m*.
cross-examine *vt* soumettre à un contre-interrogatoire.
crossfire *n* feux croisés *mpl*.
crossing *n* traversée *f*; passage pour piétons *m*.
cross-purpose *n* malentendu *m*; quiproquo *m*; **to be at ~s** comprendre (quelqu'un) de travers.
cross-reference *n* renvoi *m*, référence *f*.
crossroad *n* carrefour *m*.
crosswalk *n* passage clouté *m*.
crotch *n* entre-jambes *m*.
crouch *vi* s'accroupir, se tapir.

crow *n* corbeau *m*; chant du coq *m*; * *vi* chanter victoire.
crowd *n* foule *f*; monde *m*; * *vt* entasser; * *vi* s'entasser.
crown *n* couronne *f*; sommet *m*; * *vt* couronner.
crown prince *n* prince héritier *m*.
crucial *adj* crucial.
crucible *n* creuset *m*.
crucifix *n* crucifix *m*.
crucifixion *n* crucifixion *f*.
crucify *vt* crucifier.
crude *adj* brut, grossier; **~ly** *adv* crûment.
cruel *adj* cruel; **~ly** *adv* cruellement.
cruelty *n* cruauté *f*.
cruet *n* huilier-vinaigrier *m*.
cruise *n* croisière *f*; * *vi* croiser.
cruiser *n* croiseur *m*.
crumb *n* miette *f*.
crumble *vt* émietter; effriter; * *vi* s'émietter; se désintégrer.
crumple *vt* froisser.
crunch *vt* croquer; * *n* (*fig*) crise *f*.
crunchy *adj* croquant.
crusade *n* croisade *f*.
crush *vt* écraser; opprimer; * *n* cohue *f*.
crust *n* croûte *f*.
crusty *adj* croustillant; hargneux, bourru.
crutch *n* béquille *f*.
crux *n* coeur *m*.
cry *vt*, *vi* crier; pleurer; * *n* cri *m*; sanglot *m*.
crypt *n* crypte *f*.
cryptic *adj* énigmatique.
crystal *n* cristal *m*.
crystal-clear *adj* clair comme de l'eau de roche.
crystalline *adj* cristallin; pur.
crystallize *vi* se cristalliser; * *vt* cristalliser.
cub *n* petit *m*.
cube *n* cube *m*.
cubic *adj* cubique.
cuckoo *n* coucou *m*.
cucumber *n* concombre *m*.

cud *n*: to chew the ~ ruminer; (*also fig*).

cuddle *vt* embrasser; * *vi* s'enlacer; * *n* étreinte *f*.

cudgel *n* gourdin *m*, trique *f*.

cue *n* queue de billard *f*.

cuff *n* manchette *f*; revers de pantalon *m*.

culinary *adj* culinaire.

cull *vt* sélectionner; éliminer.

culminate *vi* culminer.

culmination *n* point culminant *m*.

culpability *n* culpabilité *f*.

culpable *adj* coupable; blâmable; ~bly *adv* coupablement.

culprit *n* coupable *mf*.

cult *n* culte *m*.

cultivate *vt* cultiver; améliorer, perfectionner.

cultivation *n* culture *f*.

cultural *adj* culturel.

culture *n* culture *f*.

cumbersome *adj* encombrant; lourd, pesant.

cumulative *adj* cumulatif.

cunning *adj* astucieux, rusé; ~ly *adv* astucieusement; habilement; * *n* astuce, finesse *f*.

cup *n* tasse, coupe *f*; (*bot*) corolle *f*.

cupboard *n* placard *m*.

curable *adj* guérissable.

curate *n* vicaire *m*.

curator *n* conservateur *m*; curateur *m*.

curb *n* frein *m*; bord du trottoir *m*; * *vt* freiner, juguler, modérer.

curd *n* lait caillé *m*.

curdle *vt* cailler, figer; *vi* se cailler, se figer.

cure *n* remède *m*; cure *f*; * *vt* guérir.

curfew *n* couvre-feu *m*.

curing *n* salaison *f*.

curiosity *n* curiosité *f*.

curious *adj* curieux; ~ly *adv* avec curiosité; curieusement.

curl *n* boucle de cheveux *f*; * *vt* boucler; friser; * *vi* friser.

curling iron *n*, **curling tongs** *npl* fer à friser *m*.

curly *adj* frisé, bouclé.

currant *n* groseille *f*.

currency *n* monnaie *f*; circulation *f*; cours *m*.

current *adj* courant; actuel; * *n* cours *m*; tendance *f*; courant *m*.

current affairs *npl* actualité *f*; problèmes actuels *mpl*.

currently *adv* actuellement.

curriculum vitae *n* curriculum vitae *m*.

curry *n* curry *m*.

curse *vt* maudire; * *vi* jurer; * *n* malédiction *f*.

cursor *n* curseur *m*.

cursory *adj* superficiel; hâtif.

curt *adj* succinct; sec.

curtail *vt* réduire; écourter.

curtain *n* rideau *m*.

curtain rod *n* tringle à rideaux *f*.

curtsy *n* révérence *f*; * *vi* faire une révérence.

curvature *n* courbure *f*.

curve *vt* courber; * *n* courbe *f*.

cushion *n* coussin *m*.

custard *n* crème anglaise *f*.

custodian *n* gardien *m*, -ienne *f*.

custody *n* garde *f*; emprisonnement *m*.

custom *n* coutume *f*, usage *m*.

customary *adj* habituel, coutumier, ordinaire.

customer *n* client *m*, -e *f*.

customs *npl* douane *f*.

customs duty *n* droits de douane *mpl*.

customs officer *n* douanier *m*.

cut *vt* découper ; couper; tailler; réduire; blesser; **to ~ short** écourter; interrompre; **to ~ a tooth** percer une dent; * *vi* couper; se couper; * *n* coup *m*; coupure *f*; réduction *f*; ~ **and dried** *adj* arrangé.

cutback *n* réduction *f*.

cute *adj* mignon.

cutlery *n* couverts *mpl*.

cutlet *n* côtelette *f*.

cut-rate *adj* à prix réduit.

cut-throat *n* assassin *m*; * *adj* acharné.

cutting *n* coupure *f*; * *adj* coupant; tranchant.

cyanide *n* cyanure *m*.

cycle *n* cycle *m*; bicyclette *f*; * *vi* aller à bicyclette.

cycling *n* cyclisme *m*.

cyclist *n* cycliste *mf*.

cyclone *n* cyclone *m*.

cygnet *n* jeune cygne *m*.

cylinder *n* cylindre *m*; rouleau *m*.

cylindric(al) *adj* cylindrique.

cymbals *n* cymbale *f*.

cynic(al) *adj* cynique; sceptique; * *n* cynique *mf*.

cynicism *n* cynisme *m*.

cypress *n* cyprès *m*.

cyst *n* kyste *m*.

czar *n* tsar *m*.

D

dab *n* petit peu *m*; touche *f*.

dabble *vi* barboter.

Dacron *n* térylène *m*.

dad(dy) *n* papa *m*.

daddy-long-legs *n* cousin *m*.

daffodil *n* narcisse *m*, jonquille *f*.

dagger *n* poignard *m*.

daily *adj* quotidien; * *adv* quotidiennement, tous les jours; * *n* quotidien *m*.

daintily *adv* délicatement.

daintiness *n* élégance *f*; délicatesse *f*.

dainty *adj* délicat; élégant.

dairy *n* laiterie *f*.

dairy farm *n* laiterie *f*.

dairy produce *n* produits laitiers *mpl*.

daisy *n* marguerite *f*.

daisy wheel *n* marguerite *f*.

dale *n* vallée *f*.

dally *vi* traîner.

dam *n* barrage *m*; * *vt* endiguer.

damage *n* dommage *m*; tort *m*; * *vt* endommager; faire du tort à.

damask *n* damas *m*; * *adj* damassé.

dame *n* dame *f*; fille *f*.

damn *vt* condamner; * *adj* maudit.

damnable *adj* maudit; **~bly** *adv* terriblement.

damnation *n* damnation *f*.

damning *adj* accablant.

damp *adj* humide; * *n* humidité *f*; * *vt* humidifier.

dampen *vt* humidifier.

dampness *n* humidité *f*.

damson *n* prune de Damas *f*.

dance *n* danse *f*; soirée dansante *f*; * *vi, vt* danser.

dance hall *n* dancing *m*.

dancer *n* danseur *m*, -euse *f*.

dandelion *n* pissenlit *m*.

dandruff *n* pellicules *fpl*.

dandy *adj* génial.

danger *n* danger *m*.

dangerous *adj* dangereux; **~ly** *adv* dangereusement.

dangle *vi* pendre.

dank *adj* humide.

dapper *adj* soigné.

dappled *adj* tacheté.

dare *vi* oser; * *vt* défier.

daredevil *n* casse-cou *m invar*.

daring *n* audace *f*; * *adj* audacieux; **~ly** *adv* audacieusement.

dark *adj* sombre, obscur; * *n* obscurité *f*; ignorance *f*.

darken *vt* assombrir, obscurcir; * *vi* s'assombrir, s'obscurcir.

dark glasses *npl* lunettes de soleil *fpl*.

darkness *n* osbcurité *f*.

darkroom *n* chambre noire *f*.

darling *n, adj* chéri *m*, -e *f*.

darn *vt* repriser.

dart *n* dard *m*.

dartboard n jeu de fléchettes m.

dash vi se dépêcher; * n goutte f;
tiret, trait m; **at one ~** tout d'un
coup.

dashboard n tableau de bord m.

dashing adj impétueux; élégant.

dastardly adj lâche.

data n données fpl.

database n base de données f.

data processing n traitement de
données m.

date n date f; rendez-vous m; (bot)
datte f; * vt dater; sortir avec.

dated adj démodé.

dative n (gr) datif m.

daub vt barbouiller.

daughter n fille f; **~ in-law** belle-
fille f.

daunting adj décourageant.

dawdle vi traîner.

dawn n aube f; * vi se lever.

day n jour m, journée f; **by ~** de
jour; **~ by ~** de jour en jour.

daybreak n aube f.

day laborer n journalier m.

daylight n lumière du jour, lumière naturelle f; **~ saving
time** n heure d'été f.

daytime n journée f, jour m.

daze vt étourdir.

dazed adj étourdi.

dazzle vt éblouir.

dazzling adj éblouissant.

deacon n diacre m.

dead adj mort; **~wood** n bois
mort m; **~ silence** n silence de
mort m; **the ~** npl les morts mpl.

dead-drunk adj ivre-mort.

deaden vt amortir.

dead heat n arrivée ex-aequo f.

deadline n date limite f.

deadlock n impasse f.

deadly adj mortel; * adv terriblement.

dead march n marche funèbre f.

deadness n inertie f.

deaf adj sourd.

deafen vt assourdir.

deaf-mute n sourd(e)-muet(te) mf.

deafness n surdité f.

deal n accord m; marché m; **a
great ~** beaucoup; **a good ~** pas
mal; * vt distribuer, donner; * vi
to ~ in être dans le commerce
de; **to ~ with** avoir affaire à.

dealer n commerçant m; trafiquant m; donneur m.

dealings npl rapports mpl; tran-
sactions fpl.

dean n doyen m.

dear adj, **~ly** adv cher.

dearness n cherté f.

dearth n pénurie f.

death n mort f.

deathbed n lit de mort m.

deathblow n coup mortel m.

death certificate n acte de décès
m.

death penalty n peine de mort f.

death throes npl agonie f.

death warrant n condamnation
à mort f.

debacle n débâcle f.

debar vt exclure.

debase vt dégrader.

debasement n dégradation f.

debatable adj discutable.

debate n débat m; * vt discuter;
examiner.

debauched adj débauché.

debauchery n débauche f.

debilitate vt débiliter.

debit n débit m; * vt (com) débiter.

debt n dette f; **to get into ~**
s'endetter.

debtor n débiteur m, -trice f.

debunk vt démystifier.

decade n décennie f.

decadence n décadence f.

decaffeinated adj décaféiné.

decanter n carafe f.

decapitate vt décapiter.

decapitation n décapitation f.

decay vi décliner; pourrir; * n déclin m; pourrissement m; carie f.

deceased adj décédé.

deceit n tromperie f.

deceitful adj trompeur; **~ly** adv
faussement.

deceive vt tromper.

December n décembre m.
decency n décence f; pudeur f.
decent adj décent; bien, bon; **~ly** adv décemment.
deception n tromperie f.
deceptive adj trompeur.
decibel n décibel m.
decide vt decider; * vi se décider.
decided adj décidé.
decidedly adv décidément.
deciduous adj (bot) à feuilles caduques.
decimal adj décimal.
decimate vt décimer.
decipher vt déchiffrer.
decision n décision, détermination f.
decisive adj décisif; **~ly** adv avec décision.
deck n pont m; * vt orner.
deckchair n chaise longue f.
declaim vt, vi déclamer.
declamation n déclamation f.
declaration n déclaration f.
declare vt déclarer.
declension n déclinaison f.
decline vt (gr) décliner; refuser; * vi décliner; * n déclin m; décadence f.
declutch vi débrayer.
decode vt décoder.
decompose vt décomposer.
decomposition n décomposition f.
decor n décor m; décoration f.
decorate vt décorer, orner.
decoration n décoration f.
decorative adj décoratif.
decorator n décorateur m, -trice f.
decorous adj correct, convenable; **~ly** adv convenablement.
decorum n décorum m.
decoy n leurre m.
decrease vt diminuer; * n diminution f.
decree n décret m; * vt décréter; ordonner.
decrepit adj décrépit.
decry vt décrier.
dedicate vt dédier; consacrer.

dedication n dédicace f; consacration f.
deduce vt déduire, conclure.
deduct vt déduire, soustraire.
deduction n déduction f.
deed n action f; exploit m.
deem vt juger.
deep adj profond.
deepen vt approfondir.
deep-freeze n congélateur m.
deeply adv profondément.
deepness n profondeur f.
deer n cerf m.
deface vt défigurer.
defacement n défiguration f.
defamation n diffamation f.
default n défaut m; manque m; * vi manquer à ses engagements.
defaulter n (law) défaillant m, -e f.
defeat n défaite f; * vt vaincre; frustrer.
defect n défaut m.
defection n désertion f.
defective adj défectueux.
defend vt défendre; protéger.
defendant n accusé m, -e f.
defense n défense f; protection f.
defenseless adj sans défense.
defensive adj défensif; **~ly** adv défensivement.
defer vt déférer.
deference n déférence f.
deferential adj respectueux.
defiance n défi m.
defiant adj provocant.
deficiency n défaut m; manque m.
deficient adj insuffisant.
deficit n déficit m.
defile vt salir.
definable adj définissable.
define vt définir.
definite adj sûr; précis; **~ly** adv sans aucun doute.
definition n définition f.
definitive adj définitif; **~ly** adv définitivement.
deflate vt dégonfler.

deflect vt dévier.

deflower vt déflorer.

deform vt déformer.

deformity n déformité f.

defraud vt frauder.

defray vt payer.

defrost vt dégivrer; décongeler.

defroster n dégivreur m.

deft adj habile; **~ly** adv habilement.

defunct adj défunt.

defuse vt désamorcer.

degenerate vi dégénérer; * adj dégénéré.

degeneration n dégénération f.

degradation n dégradation f.

degrade vt dégrader.

degree n degré m; diplôme m.

dehydrated adj déshydraté.

de-ice vt dégivrer.

deign vi daigner.

deity n divinité f.

dejected adj découragé.

dejection n découragement m.

delay vt retarder; * n retard m.

delectable adj délectable.

delegate vt déléguer; * n délégué m, -e f.

delegation n délégation f.

delete vt effacer.

deliberate vt examiner; * adj délibéré; **~ly** adv délibérément, exprès.

deliberation n délibération f.

deliberative adj délibérant.

delicacy n délicatesse f.

delicate adj délicat; **~ly** adv délicatement.

delicious adj délicieux, exquis; **~ly** adv délicieusement.

delight n délice m; enchantement m; * vt enchanter; * vi adorer.

delighted adj enchanté.

delightful adj charmant; **~ly** adv merveilleusement.

delineate vt tracer; détailler.

delineation n tracé m; détail m.

delinquency n délinquance f.

delinquent n délinquant m, -e f.

delirious adj délirant.

delirium n délire m.

deliver vt livrer; délivrer; prononcer.

deliverance n libération f.

delivery n livraison f; accouchement m.

delude vt tromper.

deluge n déluge m.

delusion n tromperie f; illusion f.

delve vi creuser; chercher.

demagog(ue) n démagogue m.

demand n demande f; * vt exiger; réclamer.

demanding adj exigeant.

demarcation n démarcation f.

demean vi s'abaisser.

demeanor n conduite f, comportement m.

demented adj dément.

demise n disparition f.

democracy n démocratie f.

democrat n démocrate mf.

democratic adj démocratique.

demolish vt démolir.

demolition n démolition f.

demon n démon, diable m.

demonstrable adj démontrable; **~bly** adv manifestement.

demonstrate vt démontrer, prouver; * vi manifester.

demonstration n démonstration f; manifestation f.

demonstrative adj démonstratif.

demonstrator n manifestant m, -e f.

demoralization n démoralisation f.

demoralize vt démoraliser.

demote vt rétrograder.

demur vi émettre une objection; hésiter.

demure adj réservé; **~ly** adv avec réserve.

den n antre m.

denatured alcohol n alcool dénaturé m.

denial n dénégation f.

denims npl jean m.

denomination n valeur f; dénomination f.
denominator n (math) dénomi-
nateur m.
denote vt dénoter, indiquer.
denounce vt dénoncer.
dense adj dense, épais.
density n densité f.
dent n bosse f; * vt cabosser.
dental adj dentaire.
dentifrice n dentifrice m.
dentist n dentiste mf.
dentistry n dentisterie f.
denture n dentier m.
denude vt dénuder, dépouiller.
denunciation n dénonciation f.
deny vt nier.
deodorant n déodorant m.
deodorize vt déodoriser.
depart vi partir.
department n département m;
service m.
department store n grand magasin m.
departure n départ m.
departure lounge n salle
d'embarquement f.
depend vi dépendre; ~ on/upon
compter sur.
dependable adj fiable; sûr.
dependant n personne à charge f.
dependency n dépendance f.
dependent adj dépendant.
depict vt dépeindre, décrire.
depleted adj réduit.
deplorable adj déplorable, lamentable; ~bly adv déplorable-
ment.
deplore vt déplorer, lamenter.
deploy vt (mil) déployer.
depopulated adj dépeuplé.
depopulation n dépopulation f.
deport vt déporter; expulser.
deportation n déportation f; expulsion f.
deportment n comportement m.
deposit vt déposer; * n dépôt m;
caution f.
deposition n déposition f.
depositor n déposant m, -e f.

depot n dépôt m.
deprave vt dépraver, corrompre.
depraved adj dépravé.
depravity n dépravation f.
deprecate vt désapprouver.
depreciate vi se déprécier.
depreciation n dépréciation f.
depredation n pillage m.
depress vt déprimer.
depressed adj déprimé.
depression n dépression f.
deprivation n privation f.
deprive vt priver.
deprived adj défavorisé.
depth n profondeur f.
deputation n députation f.
depute vt députer, déléguer.
deputize vi remplacer.
deputy n remplaçant m, -e f;
député m; délégué m, -e f.
derail vt faire dérailler.
deranged adj dérangé.
derby n chapeau melon m.
derelict adj abandonné.
deride vt se moquer de.
derision n dérision f.
derisive adj ridicule; moqueur.
derivable adj déductible.
derivation n dérivation f.
derivative n dérivé m.
derive vt, vi dériver.
derogatory adj désobligeant.
derrick n derrick m.
descant n (mus) déchant m.
descend vi descendre.
descendant n descendant m, -e f.
descent n descente f.
describe vt décrire.
description n description f.
descriptive adj descriptif.
descry vt distinguer.
desecrate vt profaner.
desecration n profanation f.
desert n désert m; * adj désert.
desert vt abandonner; déserter;
* n mérite m.
deserter n déserteur m.
desertion n désertion f.
deserve vt mériter.
deservedly adv à juste titre.

deserving *adj* méritant.

deshabille *n* déshabillé *m*.

desideratum *n* desideratum *m*.

design *vt* concevoir; dessiner; * *n* dessein *m*; design *m*; dessin *m*.

designate *vt* désigner.

designation *n* désignation *f*.

designedly *adv* exprès, délibérément.

designer *n* créateur *m*, -trice *f*; styliste *mf*.

desirability *n* avantage *m*; attrait *m*.

desirable *adj* désirable.

desire *n* désir *m*; * *vt* désirer.

desirous *adj* désireux.

desist *vi* abandonner.

desk *n* bureau *m*.

desolate *adj* désert, désolé.

desolation *n* désolation *f*.

despair *n* désespoir *m*; * *vi* se désespérer.

despairingly *adj* désespérément.

despatch = dispatch.

desperado *n* bandit *m*.

desperate *adj* désespéré; ~ly *adv* désespérément; extrêmement.

desperation *n* désespoir *m*.

despicable *adj* méprisable.

despise *vt* mépriser.

despite *prep* malgré.

despoil *vt* dépouiller.

despondency *n* abattement *m*.

despondent *adj* abattu.

despot *n* despote *m*.

despotic *adj* despotique; ~ally *adv* despotiquement.

despotism *n* despotisme *m*.

dessert *n* dessert *m*.

destination *n* destination *f*.

destine *vt* destiner.

destiny *n* destin, sort *m*.

destitute *adj* indigent.

destitution *n* indigence *f*.

destroy *vt* détruire.

destruction *n* destruction *f*.

destructive *adj* destructeur.

desultory *adj* irrégulier; sans méthode.

detach *vt* séparer, détacher.

detachable *adj* détachable.

detachment *n* (*mil*) détachement *m*.

detail *n* détail *m*; **in** ~ en détail; * *vt* détailler.

detain *vt* retenir; détenir.

detect *vt* détecter.

detection *n* détection *f*; découverte *f*.

detective *n* détective *m*.

detector *n* détecteur *m*.

detention *n* détention *f*.

deter *vt* dissuader.

detergent *n* détergent *m*.

deteriorate *vt* détériorer.

deterioration *n* détérioration *f*.

determination *n* détermination *f*.

determine *vt* déterminer, décider.

determined *adj* déterminé.

deterrent *n* force de dissuasion *f*.

detest *vt* détester.

detestable *adj* détestable.

dethrone *vt* détrôner.

dethronement *n* détrônement *m*.

detonate *vi* détoner.

detonation *n* détonation *f*.

detour *n* déviation *f*.

detract *vt* détourner.

detriment *n* détriment *m*.

detrimental *adj* préjudiciable.

deuce *n* deux *m*; égalité *f*.

devaluation *n* dévaluation *f*.

devastate *vt* dévaster.

devastating *adj* dévastateur.

devastation *n* dévastation *f*.

develop *vt* développer.

development *n* développement *m*.

deviate *vi* dévier.

deviation *n* déviation *f*.

device *n* mécanisme *m*.

devil *n* diable, démon *m*.

devilish *adj* diabolique; ~ly *adv* diaboliquement.

devious *adj* tortueux.

devise *vt* inventer; concevoir.

devoid *adj* dépourvu.

devolve *vt* déléguer.

devote *vt* consacrer.

devoted *adj* dévoué.

devotee *n* partisan *m*, -e *f*.

devotion n dévotion f.

devotional adj dévot.

devour vt dévorer.

devout adj dévot, pieux; ~**ly** adv pieusement.

dew n rosée f.

dewy adj couvert de rosée; ingénu.

dexterity n dextérité f.

dexterous adj adroit, habile.

diabetes n diabète m.

diabetic n diabétique mf.

diabolic adj diabolique; ~**ally** adv diaboliquement.

diadem n diadème m.

diagnosis n (med) diagnostic m.

diagnostic adj diagnostique; * npl ~**s** diagnostic m.

diagonal adj diagonal; ~**ly** adv diagonalement; * n diagonale f.

diagram n diagramme m.

dial n cadrant m.

dial code n code m.

dialect n dialecte m.

dialog(ue) n dialogue m.

dial tone n tonalité f.

diameter n diamètre m.

diametrical adj diamétral; ~**ly** adv diamétralement.

diamond n diamant m.

diamond-cutter n tailleur de diamant m.

diamonds npl (cards) carreaux mpl.

diaper n couche f.

diaphragm n diaphragme m.

diarrhoea n diarrhée f.

diary n journal m.

dice npl dés mpl.

dictate vt dicter; * n ordre m.

dictation n dictée f.

dictatorial adj dictatorial.

dictatorship n dictature f.

diction n diction f

dictionary n dictionnaire m.

didactic adj didactique.

die vi mourir; **to ~ away** s'affaiblir; **to ~ down** s'éteindre.

die n (sing de **dice**) dé m.

diehard n réactionnaire mf.

diesel n diesel m.

diet n diète f; régime m; * vi être au régime.

dietary adj diététique.

differ vi différer.

difference n différence f.

different adj différent; ~**ly** adv différemment.

differentiate vt différencier.

difficult adj difficile.

difficulty n difficulté f.

diffidence n timidité f; manque d'assurance m.

diffident adj timide; mal assuré; ~**ly** adv avec timidité.

diffraction n diffraction f.

diffuse vt diffuser, répandre; * adj diffus.

diffusion n diffusion f.

dig vt creuser; * n coup m.

digest vt digérer.

digestible adj digestible.

digestion n digestion f.

digestive adj digestif.

digger n excavatrice f.

digit n chiffre m.

digital adj digital.

dignified adj digne.

dignitary n dignitaire m.

dignity n dignité f.

digress vi faire une digression.

digression n digression f.

dike n digue f.

dilapidated adj délabré.

dilapidation n délabrement m.

dilate vt dilater; * vi se dilater.

dilemma n dilemme m.

diligence n assiduité f.

diligent adj assidu; ~**ly** adv avec assiduité.

dilute vt diluer.

dim adj indistinct; faible; sombre; * vt affaiblir; troubler.

dime n pièce de dix cents f.

dimension n dimension f.

diminish vt, vi diminuer.

diminution n diminution f.

diminutive n diminutif m.

dimly adv indistinctement; faiblement.

dimmer *n* interrupteur d'intensité *m*.

dimple *n* fossette *f*.

din *n* vacarme *m*.

dine *vi* dîner.

diner *n* restaurant (économique) *m*.

dinghy *n* canot pneumatique *f*.

dingy *adj* sale; miteux.

dinner *n* dîner *m*.

dinner time *n* heure du dîner *f*.

dinosaur *n* dinosaure *m*.

dint *n*: **by ~ of** à force de.

diocese *n* diocèse *m*.

dip *vt* tremper.

diphtheria *n* diphtérie *f*.

diphthong *n* diphtongue *f*.

diploma *n* diplôme *m*.

diplomacy *n* diplomatie *f*.

diplomat *n* diplomate *m*.

diplomatic *adj* diplomatique.

dipsomania *n* dipsomanie *f*.

dipstick *n* (*auto*) jauge *f*.

dire *adj* atroce, affreux.

direct *adj* direct; * *vt* diriger.

direction *n* direction *f*; instruction *f*.

directly *adj* directement; immédiatement.

director *n* directeur *m*, -trice *f*.

directory *n* annuaire *m*.

dirt *n* saleté *f*.

dirtiness *n* saleté *f*.

dirty *adj* sale.

disability *n* incapacité *f*; infirmité *f*.

disabled *adj* infirme.

disabuse *vt* détromper.

disadvantage *n* désavantage *m*; * *vt* désavantager.

disadvantageous *adj* désavantageux.

disaffected *adj* mécontent.

disagree *vi* ne pas être d'accord.

disagreeable *adj* désagréable; **~bly** *adv* désagréablement.

disagreement *n* désaccord *m*.

disallow *vt* rejeter.

disappear *vi* disparaître.

disappearance *n* disparition *f*.

disappoint *vt* décevoir.

disappointed *adj* déçu.

disappointing *adj* décevant.

disappointment *n* déception *f*.

disapproval *n* désapprobation *f*.

disapprove *vt* désapprouver.

disarm *vt* désarmer.

disarmament *n* désarmement *m*.

disarray *n* désordre *m*.

disaster *n* désastre *m*.

disastrous *adj* désastreux.

disband *vt* disperser.

disbelief *n* incrédulité *f*.

disbelieve *vt* ne pas croire.

disburse *vt* débourser.

discard *vt* jeter.

discern *vt* discerner, percevoir.

discernible *adj* perceptible.

discerning *adj* perspicace.

discernment *n* perspicacité *f*.

discharge *vt* décharger; régler (une dette); remplir; * *n* décharge *f*; règlement *m*.

disciple *n* disciple *m*.

discipline *n* discipline *f*; * *vt* discipliner.

disclaim *vt* nier.

disclaimer *n* dénégation *f*.

disclose *vt* révéler.

disclosure *n* révélation *f*.

disco *n* discothèque *f*.

discoloration *n* décoloration *f*.

discolour *vt* décolorer.

discomfort *n* incommodité *f*.

disconcert *vt* déconcerter.

disconnect *vt* débrancher.

disconsolate *adj* inconsolable; **~ly** *adv* inconsolablement.

discontent *n* mécontentement *m*; * *adj* mécontent.

discontented *adj* mécontent.

discontinue *vt* interrompre.

discord *n* discorde *f*.

discordant *adj* discordant.

discount *n* escompte *m*; remise *f*; * *vt* escompter.

discourage *vt* décourager.

discouraged *adj* découragé.

discouragement *n* découragement *m*.

discouraging *adj* décourageant.
discourse *n* discours *m*.
discourteous *adj* discourtois; ~**ly** *adv* de manière discourtoise.
discourtesy *n* manque de courtoisie *m*.
discover *vt* découvrir.
discovery *n* découverte *f*.
discredit *vt* discréditer.
discreditable *adj* peu honorable.
discreet *adj* discret; ~**ly** *adv* discrètement.
discrepancy *n* contradiction *f*.
discretion *n* discrétion *f*.
discretionary *adj* discrétionnaire.
discriminate *vt* distinguer; discriminer.
discrimination *n* discrimination *f*.
discursive *adj* discursif.
discuss *vt* discuter.
discussion *n* discussion *f*.
disdain *vt* dédaigner; * *n* dédain, mépris *m*.
disdainful *adj* dédaigneux, méprisant; ~**ly** *adv* dédaigneusement, avec mépris.
disease *n* maladie *f*.
diseased *adj* malade.
disembark *vt*, *vi* débarquer.
disembarkation *n* (*mil*) débarquement *m*.
disenchant *vt* désenchanter.
disenchanted *adj* désenchanté.
disenchantment *n* désenchantement *m*.
disengage *vt* dégager.
disentangle *vt* démêler.
disfigure *vt* défigurer.
disgrace *n* honte *f*; scandale *m*; * *vt* déshonorer.
disgraceful *adj* honteux; scandaleux; ~**ly** *adv* honteusement.
disgruntled *adj* mécontent.
disguise *vt* déguiser; * *n* déguisement *m*.
disgust *n* dégoût *m*; * *vt* dégoûter.
disgusting *adj* dégoûtant.
dish *n* plat *m*; assiette *f*; * *vt* servir dans un plat; **to ~ up** servir.

dishcloth *n* torchon à vaisselle *m*.
dishearten *vt* démoraliser.
disheveled *adj* ébouriffé.
dishonest *adj* malhonnête; ~**ly** *adv* malhonnêtement.
dishonesty *n* malhonnêteté *f*.
dishonor *n* déshonneur *m*; * *vt* déshonorer.
dishonorable *adj* déshonorable; ~**bly** *adv* de manière déshonorante.
dishtowel *n* torchon à vaisselle *m*.
dishwarmer *n* chauffe-plats *m*.
dishwasher *n* lave-vaisselle *m*; plongeur *m*, -euse *f*.
disillusion *vt* désillusionner.
disillusioned *adj* désillusionné.
disincentive *n* élément dissuasif *m*.
disinclination *n* aversion *f*.
disinclined *adj* peu enclin.
disinfect *vt* désinfecter.
disinfectant *n* désinfectant *m*.
disinherit *vt* déshériter.
disintegrate *vi* se désintégrer.
disinterested *adj* désintéressé; ~**ly** *adv* de manière désintéressée.
disjointed *adj* déréglé; décousu.
disk *n* disque *m*; disquette *f*.
diskette *n* disque *m*, disquette *f*.
dislike *n* aversion *f*; * *vt* ne pas aimer.
dislocate *vt* disloquer.
dislocation *n* dislocation *f*.
dislodge *vt* déloger.
disloyal *adj* déloyal; ~**ly** *adv* déloyalement.
disloyalty *n* déloyauté *f*.
dismal *adj* triste, lugubre.
dismantle *vt* démonter.
dismay *n* consternation *f*.
dismember *vt* démembrer.
dismiss *vt* renvoyer; écarter.
dismissal *n* renvoi *m*; rejet *m*.
dismount *vt* désarçonner; * *vi* descendre.
disobedience *n* désobéissance *f*.
disobedient *adj* désobéissant.
disobey *vt* désobéir.

disorder n désordre m.
disorderly adj en désordre, confus.
disorganization n désorganisation f.
disorganized adj désorganisé.
disorientated adj désorienté.
disown vt renier.
disparage vt dénigrer.
disparaging adj désobligeant.
disparity n disparité f.
dispassionate adj impartial; calme.
dispatch vt envoyer; * n envoi m; dépêche f.
dispel vt dissiper.
dispensary n dispensaire m.
dispense vt dispenser; distribuer.
disperse vt disperser.
dispirited adj démoralisé.
displace vt déplacer.
display vt exposer; faire preuve de; * n exposition f; déploiement m.
displeased adj mécontent.
displeasure n mécontentement m.
disposable adj à jeter.
disposal n disposition f.
dispose vt disposer.
disposed adj disposé.
disposition n disposition f.
dispossess vt déposséder.
disproportionate adj disproportionné.
disprove vt réfuter.
dispute n dispute f; controverse f; * vt mettre en cause.
disqualify vt rendre incapable; disqualifier.
disquiet n inquiétude f.
disquieting adj inquiétant.
disquisition n étude f.
disregard vt ne pas tenir compte de; mépriser; * n dédain m.
disreputable adj de mauvaise réputation.
disrespect n irrévérence f.
disrespectful adj irrespectueux;

~**ly** adv irrespectueusement.
disrobe vt dévêtir.
disrupt vt interrompre.
disruption n interruption f.
dissatisfaction n mécontentement m.
dissatisfied adj mécontent.
dissect vt disséquer.
dissection n dissection f.
disseminate vt disséminer.
dissension n dissension f.
dissent vi être en dissension; * n dissension f.
dissenter n dissident m, -e f.
dissertation n thèse f.
dissident n dissident m, -e f.
dissimilar adj dissemblable.
dissimilarity n dissemblance f.
dissimulation n dissimulation f.
dissipate vt dissiper.
dissipation n dissipation f.
dissociate vt dissocier.
dissolute adj dissolu.
dissolution n dissolution f.
dissolve vt dissoudre; * vi se dissoudre.
dissonance n dissonance f.
dissuade vt dissuader.
distance n distance f; **at a ~** de loin; * vt distancer.
distant adj distant.
distaste n dégoût m.
distasteful adj désagréable.
distend vt distendre.
distil vt distiller.
distillation n distillation f.
distillery n distillerie f.
distinct adj distinct; ~**ly** adv distinctement.
distinction n distinction f.
distinctive adj distinctif.
distinctness n clarté f.
distinguish vt distinguer; discerner.
distort vt déformer.
distorted adj déformé.
distortion n distortion f.
distract vt distraire.
distracted adj distrait; ~**ly** adj distraitement.

distraction *n* distraction *f*; confusion *f*.

distraught *adj* fou.

distress *n* souffrance *f*; détresse *f*; * *vt* désoler; affliger.

distressing *adj* affligeant.

distribute *vt* distribuer, répartir.

distribution *n* distribution *f*.

distributor *n* distributeur *m*.

district *n* district *m*.

district attorney *n* procureur de la République *m*.

distrustful *adj* méfiant.

disturb *vt* déranger.

disturbance *n* dérangement *m*; trouble *m*.

disturbed *adj* troublé.

disturbing *adj* troublant.

disuse *n* désuétude *f*.

disused *adj* abandonné.

ditch *n* fossé *m*.

dither *vi* hésiter.

ditto *adv* idem.

ditty *n* chansonnette *f*.

diuretic *adj* (*med*) diurétique.

dive *vi* plonger.

diver *n* plongeur *m*, -euse *f*.

diverge *vi* diverger.

divergence *n* divergence *f*.

divergent *adj* divergent.

diverse *adj* divers, différent; ~ly *adv* différemment.

diversion *n* diversion *f*.

diversity *n* diversité *f*.

divert *vt* dévier; divertir.

divest *vt* dénuder; dépouiller.

divide *vt* diviser; * *vi* se diviser.

dividend *n* dividende *m*.

dividers *npl* (*math*) compas à pointes sèches *m*.

divine *adj* divin.

divinity *n* divinité *f*.

diving *n* plongeon *m*.

diving board *n* plongeoir *m*.

divisible *adj* divisible.

division *n* (*math*) division *f*.

divisor *n* (*math*) diviseur *m*.

divorce *n* divorce *m*; * *vi* divorcer.

divorced *adj* divorcé.

divulge *vt* divulguer.

dizziness *n* vertige *m*.

dizzy *adj* pris de vertige.

DJ *n* disc-jockey, DJ *m*.

do *vt* faire.

docile *adj* docile.

dock *n* dock *m*; * *vi* entrer aux docks.

docker *n* docker *m*.

dockyard *n* (*mar*) chantier naval *m*.

doctor *n* docteur *m*.

doctrinal *adj* doctrinal.

doctrine *n* doctrine *f*.

document *n* document *m*.

documentary *adj* documentaire.

dodge *vt* esquiver.

doe *n* biche *f*; ~ **rabbit** lapine *f*.

dog *n* chien *m*.

dogged *adj* tenace; ~ly *adv* tenacement.

dog kennel *n* refuge pour chiens *m*.

dogmatic *adj* dogmatique; ~ly *adv* dogmatiquement.

doings *npl* faits *mpl*.

do-it-yourself *n* bricolage *m*.

doleful *adj* lugubre, triste.

doll *n* poupée *f*.

dollar *n* dollar *m*.

dolphin *n* dauphin *m*.

domain *n* domaine *m*.

dome *n* dôme *m*.

domestic *adj* domestique.

domesticate *vt* domestiquer.

domestication *n* domestication *f*.

domesticity *n* domesticité *f*.

domicile *n* domicile *m*.

dominant *adj* dominant.

dominate *vi* dominer.

domination *n* domination *f*.

domineer *vi* dominer.

domineering *adj* dominant.

dominion *n* domination *f*.

dominoes *npl* domino *m*.

donate *vt* donner, faire don de.

donation *n* donation *f*.

done *p*, *adj* fait; cuit.

donkey *n* âne *m*.

donor *n* donneur *m*; donateur *m*.

doodle *vi* gribouiller.

doom n sort m.

door n porte f.

doorbell n sonnette f.

door handle n poignée de porte f.

doorman n portier m.

doormat n paillasson m.

doorplate n plaque f.

doorstep n pas de porte m.

doorway n entrée f.

dormant adj latent; dormant.

dormer window n lucarne f.

dormitory n dortoir m.

dormouse n loir m.

dosage n dose f; dosage m.

dose n dose f; * vt doser; donner une dose à.

dossier n dossier m.

dot n point m.

dote vi adorer.

dotingly adv avec adoration.

double adj double; * vt doubler; * n double m.

double bed n lit de deux personnes m.

double-breasted adj croisé.

double chin n double menton m.

double-dealing n duplicité f.

double-edged adj à double tranchant.

double entry n (com) comptabilité en partie double f.

double-lock vt fermer à double tour.

double room n chambre pour deux f.

doubly adv doublement.

doubt n doute m; * vt douter de.

doubtful adj douteux.

doubtless adv indubitablement.

dough n pâte f.

douse vt éteindre.

dove n colombe f.

dovecot n colombier m.

dowdy adj mal habillé.

down n duvet m; * prep en bas; **to sit ~** s'asseoir; **upside ~** à l'envers.

downcast adj démoralisé; baissé.

downfall n ruine f.

downhearted adj découragé.

downhill adv en descendant, dans la descente.

down payment n acompte m.

downpour n grosse averse f.

downright adj manifeste.

downstairs adv en bas.

down-to-earth adj pratique; terre à terre.

downtown adv dans le centre, en ville.

downward(s) adv vers le bas.

dowry n dot f.

doze vi somnoler.

dozen n douzaine f.

dozy adj somnolent.

drab adj gris; morne.

draft n brouillon m; traite f.

drag vt tirer; * n drague f; ennui m.

dragnet n seine f; filet m.

dragon n dragon m.

dragonfly n libellule f.

drain vt drainer; vider; * n tuyau d'écoulement m.

drainage n drainage m.

drainboard n égouttoir m.

drainpipe n tuyau d'écoulement m.

drake n canard mâle m.

dram n petit verre m.

drama n drame m.

dramatic adj dramatique; **~ally** adv dramatiquement.

dramatist n dramaturge mf.

dramatize vt dramatiser.

drape vt draper.

drapes npl tentures fpl.

drastic adj radical.

draught n courant d'air m.

draughts npl jeu de dames m.

draughty adj exposé aux courants d'air.

draw vt tirer; dessiner; **to ~ nigh** s'approcher.

drawback n désavantage, inconvénient m.

drawer n tiroir m.

drawing n dessin m.

drawing board n planche à dessin f.

drawing room n salon m.

drawl vi parler d'une voix traînante.

dread n terreur f; * vt redouter, craindre.

dreadful adj horrible; **~ly** adv horriblement.

dream n rêve m; * vi, vt rêver.

dreary adj triste, morne.

dredge vt draguer.

dregs npl lie f.

drench vt tremper.

dress vt habiller; panser; * vi s'habiller; * n robe f.

dresser n buffet m.

dressing n pansement m; sauce f.

dressing gown n peignoir m.

dressing room n loge f; garderobe f.

dressing table n coiffeuse f.

dressmaker n couturier m, -ière f.

dressy adj élégant.

dribble vi tomber goutte à goutte.

dried adj séché.

drift n amoncellement m; courant m; sens m; * vi aller à la dérive.

driftwood n bois flottant m.

drill n perceuse f; (mil) exercice m; * vt percer.

drink vt, vi boire; * n boisson f.

drinkable adj potable; buvable.

drinker n buveur m, -euse f.

drinking bout n beuverie f.

drinking water n eau potable f.

drip vi goutter; * n goutte f; goutte-à-goutte m.

dripping n graisse f.

drive vt conduire; pousser; * vi conduire; * n promenade en voiture f; allée, entrée f.

drivel n imbécilités fpl; * vi baver; dire des imbécilités.

driver n conducteur m, -trice f; chauffeur m.

driveway n allée, entrée f.

driving n conduite f.

driving instructor n moniteur (-trice) d'auto-école m(f).

driving licence n permis m de conduire.

driving school n auto-école f.

driving test n (examen du) permis de conduire m.

drizzle vi pleuvasser.

droll adj drôle.

drone n bourdon m.

droop vi tomber.

drop n goutte f; * vt laisser tomber; * vi tomber; **to ~ out** se retirer; abandonner.

drop-out n marginal m.

dropper n compte-gouttes m invar.

dross n scories fpl.

drought n sécheresse f.

drove n: **in ~s** en troupe.

drown vt noyer; * vi se noyer.

drowsiness n somnolence f.

drowsy adj somnolent.

drudgery n corvée f.

drug n drogue f; * vt droguer.

drug addict n drogué m, -e f.

druggist n pharmacien m, -ienne f.

drugstore n pharmacie f.

drum n tambour m; * vi jouer du tambour.

drum majorette n majorette f.

drummer n batteur m.

drumstick n baguette de tambour f.

drunk adj ivre.

drunkard n ivrogne mf.

drunken adj ivre.

drunkenness n ivresse f.

dry adj sec; * vt faire sécher; * vi sécher.

dry-cleaning n nettoyage à sec m.

dry-goods store n mercerie f.

dryness n sécheresse f.

dry rot n pourriture f.

dual adj double.

dual-purpose adj à double emploi.

dubbed adj doublé.

dubious adj douteux.

duck n canard m; * vt, vi plonger.

duckling n caneton m.

dud *adj* nul; faux.

due *adj* dû, *f* due; * *adv* exactement; * *n* droit *m*; chose due *f*.

duel *n* duel *m*.

duet *n* (*mus*) duo *m*.

dull *adj* terne; insipide; gris; * *vt* ternir; atténuer.

duly *adv* dûment; en temps voulu.

dumb *adj* muet; ~**ly** *adv* sans dire un mot.

dumbbell *n* haltère *m*; abruti *m*.

dumbfounded *adj* interloqué.

dummy *n* mannequin *m*; prête-nom *m*.

dump *n* tas *m*; * *vt* jeter; laisser tomber.

dumping *n* (*com*) dumping *m*.

dumpling *n* boulette de pâte *f*.

dumpy *adj* boulot.

dunce *n* cancre *m*.

dune *n* dune *f*.

dung *n* fumier *m*.

dungarees *npl* salopette *f*.

dungeon *n* donjon *m*; cachot *m*.

dupe *n* dupe *f*; * *vt* duper.

duplex *n* duplex *m*.

duplicate *n* duplicata *m*; copie *f*; * *vt* dupliquer.

duplicity *n* duplicité *f*.

durability *n* durabilité *f*.

durable *adj* durable.

duration *n* durée *f*.

during *prep* pendant.

dusk *n* crépuscule *m*.

dust *n* poussière *f*; * *vt* épousseter.

duster *n* plumier *m*.

dusty *adj* poussiéreux.

dutch courage *n* courage puisé dans la boisson *m*.

duteous *adj* fidèle, loyal.

dutiful *adj* obéissant, soumis; ~**ly** *adv* avec obéissance.

duty *n* devoir *m*; obligation *f*.

duty-free *adj* hors taxe.

dwarf *n* nain *m*, naine *f*; * *vt* rapetisser.

dwell *vi* habiter, vivre.

dwelling *n* habitation *f*; domicile *m*.

dwindle *vi* diminuer.

dye *vt* teindre; * *n* teinture *f*.

dyer *n* teinturier *m*.

dyeing *n* teinturerie *f*; teinture *f*.

dye-works *npl* teinturerie *f*.

dying *p*, *adj* mourant, agonisant; * *n* mort *f*.

dynamic *adj* dynamique.

dynamics *n* dynamique *f*.

dynamite *n* dynamite *f*.

dynamiter *n* dynamiteur *m*, -euse *f*.

dynamo *n* dynamo *f*.

dynasty *n* dynastie *f*.

dysentery *n* dysenterie *f*.

dyspepsia *n* (*med*) dyspepsie *f*.

dyspeptic *adj* dyspeptique.

E

each *pn* chacun; ~ **other** les uns les autres.

eager *adj* enthousiaste; ardent; ~**ly** *adv* avec enthousiasme; ardemment.

eagerness *n* enthousiasme *m*; ardeur *f*; désir *m*.

eagle *n* aigle *m*.

eagle-eyed *adj* aux yeux d'aigle.

eaglet *n* aiglon *m*.

ear *n* oreille *f*; ouïe *f*; **by** ~ en improvisant.

earache *n* mal d'oreille *m*.

eardrum *n* tympan *m*.

early *adj* premier; *adv* tôt, de bonne heure.

earmark *vt* destiner.

earn *vt* gagner.

earnest *adj* sérieux; ~**ly** *adv* sérieusement.

earnestness *n* sérieux *m*.

earnings *npl* revenus *mpl*.

earphones *npl* écouteurs *mpl*.

earring *n* boucle d'oreille *f*.

earth *n* terre *f*; * *vt* brancher à la terre.

earthen *adj* de terre.

earthenware *n* poterie *f*.

earthquake *n* tremblement de terre *m*.

earthworm *n* ver de terre *m*.

earthy *adj* pratique; truculent.

earwig *n* perce-oreille *m*.

ease *n* aise *f*; facilité *f*; **at ~** à l'aise; * *vt* apaiser; soulager.

easel *n* chevalet *m*.

easily *adv* facilement.

easiness *n* facilité *f*.

east *n* est *m*; orient *m*.

Easter *n* Pâques *fpl*.

Easter egg *n* oeuf de Pâques *m*.

easterly *adj* d'est.

eastern *adj* de l'est, oriental.

eastward(s) *adv* vers l'est.

easy *adj* facile; commode; **~ going** décontracté.

easy chair *n* fauteuil *m*.

eat *vt*, *vi* manger.

eatable *adj* comestible; mangeable; * **~s** *npl* vivres *mpl*.

eaves *npl* avant-toit *m*.

eau de Cologne *n* eau de Cologne *f*.

eavesdrop *vt* espionner; écouter discrètement.

ebb *n* reflux *m*; * *vi* refluer; décliner.

ebony *n* ébène *f*.

eccentric *adj* excentrique.

eccentricity *n* excentricité *f*.

ecclesiastic *adj* ecclésiastique.

echo *n* écho *m*; * *vi* résonner.

eclectic *adj* éclectique.

eclipse *n* éclipse *f*; * *vt* éclipser.

ecology *n* écologie *f*.

economic(al) *adj* économique; économe.

economics *npl* économie *f*.

economist *n* économiste *mf*.

economize *vt* économiser.

economy *n* économie *f*.

ecstasy *n* extase *f*.

ecstatic *adj* extatique; **~ally** *adv* avec extase.

eczema *n* eczéma *m*.

eddy *n* tourbillon *m*; * *vi* tourbillonner.

edge *n* fil *m*; pointe *f*; bord *m*; acrimonie *f*; * *vt* border; affiler.

edgeways, edgewise *adv* de côté.

edging *n* bordure *f*.

edgy *adj* nerveux.

edible *adj* mangeable; comestible.

edict *n* édit *m*; décret *m*.

edification *n* édification *f*.

edifice *n* édifice *m*.

edify *vt* édifier.

edit *vt* diriger; rédiger; couper.

edition *n* édition *f*.

editor *n* directeur *m*, -trice *f*; rédacteur *m*, -trice *f*.

editorial *adj* rédactionnel; * *n* éditorial *m*.

educate *vt* éduquer; instruire.

education *n* éducation *f*; instruction *f*.

eel *n* anguille *f*.

eerie *adj* inquiétant; surnaturel.

efface *vt* effacer.

effect *n* effet *m*; réalité *f*; **~s** *npl* biens *mpl*; * *vt* effectuer.

effective *adj* efficace; effectif; **~ly** *adv* effectivement, en effet.

effectiveness *n* efficacité *f*.

effectual *adj* efficace; **~ly** *adv* efficacement.

effeminacy *n* caractère efféminé *m*.

effeminate *adj* efféminé.

effervescence *n* effervescence *f*.

effete *adj* stérile; faible.

efficacy *n* efficacité *f*.

efficiency *n* efficacité *f*.

efficient *adj* efficace.

effigy *n* effigie *f*.

effort *n* effort *m*.

effortless *adj* sans effort.

effrontery *n* effronterie *f*.

effusive *adj* chaleureux; expansif.

egg n oeuf m; * **to ~ on** vt encourager.

eggcup n coquetier m.

eggplant n aubergine f.

eggshell n coquille d'oeuf f.

ego(t)ism n égoïsme m.

ego(t)ist n égoïste mf.

ego(t)istical adj égoïste.

eiderdown n édredon m.

eight adj, n huit m.

eighteen adj, n dix-huit m.

eighteenth adj, n dix-huitième mf.

eighth adj, n huitième mf.

eightieth adj, n quatre-vingtième mf.

eighty adj, n quatre-vingt.

either pn n'importe lequel, n'importe laquelle; * conj ou, soit.

ejaculate vi s'exclamer; éjaculer.

ejaculation n exclamation f; éjaculation f.

eject vt éjecter, expulser.

ejection n éjection, expulsion f.

ejector seat n siège éjectable m.

eke vt augmenter; prolonger.

elaborate vt élaborer; * adj élaboré; compliqué; ~**ly** adv avec soin.

elapse vi passer.

elastic adj élastique.

elasticity n élasticité f.

elated adj exultant.

elation n exultation f.

elbow n coude m; * vt pousser du coude.

elbow-room n espace m; (fig) liberté, latitude f.

elder n sureau m; * adj aîné.

elderly adj d'un âge avancé.

elders npl anciens mpl.

eldest adj aîné.

elect vt élire; choisir; * adj élu; choisi.

election n élection f; choix m.

electioneering n propagande électorale f.

elective adj facultatif.

elector n électeur m, -trice f.

electoral adj électoral.

electorate n électorat m.

electric(al) adj électrique.

electric blanket n couverture électrique f.

electric cooker n cuisinière électrique f.

electric fire n radiateur électrique m.

electrician n électricien m.

electricity n électricité f.

electrify vt électriser.

electron n électron m.

electronic adj électronique; ~**s** npl électronique f.

elegance n élégance f.

elegant adj élégant; ~**ly** adv élégamment.

elegy n élégie f.

element n élément m.

elemental, elementary adj élémentaire.

elephant n éléphant m.

elephantine adj immense; lourd.

elevate vt élever, hausser.

elevation n élévation f; hauteur f.

elevator n ascenseur m.

eleven adj, n onze m.

eleventh adj, n onzième mf.

elf n elfe m.

elicit vt tirer.

eligibility n éligibilité f.

eligible adj éligible.

eliminate vt éliminer, écarter.

elk n élan m.

elliptic(al) adj elliptique.

elm n orme m.

elocution n élocution f.

elocutionist n professeur d'élocution m.

elongate vt allonger.

elope vi s'échapper, s'enfuir.

elopement n fugue, évasion f.

eloquence n éloquence f.

eloquent adj éloquent; ~**ly** adv éloquemment.

else pn autre.

elsewhere adv ailleurs.

elucidate vt élucider, expliquer.

elucidation n élucidation, explication f.

elude vt éluder; éviter.

elusive, elusory adj insaisissable.

emaciated adj émacié.

emanate (from) vi émaner (de).

emancipate vt émanciper; affranchir.

emancipation n émancipation f; affranchissement m.

embalm vt embaumer.

embankment n talus m; quai m.

embargo n embargo m.

embark vt embarquer.

embarkation n embarcation f.

embarrass vt embarrasser.

embarrassed adj embarrassé.

embarrassing adj embarrassant.

embarrassment n embarras m.

embassy n ambassade f.

embed vt enchâsser; intégrer.

embellish vt embellir, orner.

embellishment n ornement m.

embers npl braise f.

embezzle vt détourner.

embezzlement n détournement de fonds m.

embitter vt rendre amer.

emblem n emblème m.

emblematic(al) adj emblématique, symbolique.

embodiment n incorporation f; incarnation f.

embody vt incorporer; incarner.

embrace vt étreindre; comprendre; * n étreinte f.

embroider vt broder.

embroidery n broderie f.

embroil vt impliquer.

embryo n embryon m.

emendation n correction f.

emerald n émeraude f.

emerge vi émerger; apparaître.

emergency n urgence f.

emergency cord n sonnette d'alarme f.

emergency exit n sortie de secours f.

emergency landing n atterrissage forcé m.

emergency meeting n réunion extraordinaire f.

emery n émeri m.

emigrant n émigré m, -e f.

emigrate vi émigrer.

emigration n émigration f.

eminence n hauteur f; éminence, excellence f.

eminent adj élevé; éminent, distingué; ~ly adv éminemment.

emission n émission f.

emit vt émettre.

emolument n émoluments mpl.

emotion n émotion f.

emotional adj émotionnel; ému.

emotive adj émotif.

emperor n empereur m.

emphasis n emphase f.

emphasize vt souligner, accentuer.

emphatic adj emphatique; ~ally adv avec emphase.

empire n empire m.

employ vt employer.

employee n employé m, -e f.

employer n employeur m.

employment n emploi, travail m.

emporium n grand magasin m.

empress n impératrice f.

emptiness n vide m; futilité f.

empty adj vide; vain; * vt vider.

empty-handed adj les mains vides.

emulate vt imiter.

emulsion n émulsion f.

enable vt permettre.

enact vt promulguer; représenter.

enamel n émail m; * vt émailler.

enamor vt s'éprendre de.

encamp vi camper.

encampment n campement m.

encase vt entourer.

enchant vt enchanter.

enchanting adj enchanteur.

enchantment n enchantement m.

encircle vt encercler.

enclose vt entourer; inclure, joindre.

enclosure n clôture f; enceinte f.

encompass *vt* comprendre.

encore *adv* encore.

encounter *n* rencontre *f*; combat *m*; * *vt* rencontrer.

encourage *vt* encourager.

encouragement *n* encouragement *m*.

encroach *vi* empiéter (sur).

encroachment *n* empiètement *m*.

encrusted *adj* incrusté.

encumber *vt* embarrasser.

encumbrance *n* embarras *m*.

encyclical *adj* encyclique.

encyclopedia *n* encyclopédie *f*.

end *n* fin *f*; extrémité *f*; bout *m*; dessein *m*; **to the ~ that** afin que; **to no ~** en vain; **on ~** debout; * *vt* terminer, conclure; * *vi* terminer.

endanger *vt* mettre en danger.

endear *vt* faire aimer.

endearing *adj* sympathique.

endearment *n* expression de tendresse *f*.

endeavour *vi* s'efforcer, tenter; * *n* effort *m*.

endemic *adj* endémique.

ending *n* fin, conclusion *f*; dénouement *m*; terminaison *f*.

endive *n* (*bot*) endive *f*.

endless *adj* infini, perpétuel; **~ly** *adv* sans fin, perpétuellement.

endorse *vt* endosser; approuver.

endorsement *n* endos *m*; approbation *f*.

endow *vt* doter.

endowment *n* dotation *f*.

endurable *adj* supportable.

endurance *n* endurance *f*; patience *f*.

endure *vt* supporter; * *vi* durer.

endways, endwise *adv* debout.

enemy *n* ennemi *mf*.

energetic *adj* énergique, vigoureux.

energy *n* énergie, force *f*.

enervate *vt* affaiblir, ramollir.

enfeeble *vt* affaiblir.

enfold *vt* envelopper.

enforce *vt* mettre en vigueur.

enforced *adj* forcé.

enfranchise *vt* émanciper.

engage *vt* aborder; engager.

engaged *adj* fiancé; occupé.

engagement *n* engagement *m*; combat *m*; fiançailles *fpl*. **engagement ring** *n* bague de fiançailles *f*.

engaging *adj* attrayant.

engender *vt* engendrer; produire.

engine *n* moteur *m*; locomotive *f*.

engine driver *n* conducteur *m*.

engineer *n* ingénieur *m*; mécanicien *m*.

engineering *n* ingénierie *f*.

engrave *vt* graver.

engraving *n* gravure *f*.

engrossed *adj* absorbé.

engulf *vt* submerger.

enhance *vt* améliorer; réhausser.

enigma *n* énigme *f*.

enjoy *vt* aimer; avoir; **to ~ oneself** s'amuser.

enjoyable *adj* agréable; amusant.

enjoyment *n* plaisir *m*; jouissance *f*.

enlarge *vt* agrandir; étendre; dilater.

enlargement *n* agrandissement *m*; extension *f*; dilatation *f*.

enlighten *vt* éclairer.

enlightened *adj* éclairé.

Enlightenment *n*: **the ~** le Siècle des lumières *m*.

enlist *vt* recruter.

enlistment *n* recrutement *m*.

enliven *vt* animer; égayer.

enmity *n* inimitié *f*; haine *f*.

enormity *n* énormité *f*; atrocité *f*.

enormous *adj* énorme; **~ly** *adv* énormément.

enough *adv* suffisamment; assez; * *n* assez *m*.

enounce *vt* déclarer.

enquire *vt* = inquire.

enrage *vt* rendre furieux.

enrapture *vt* enchanter, enthousiasmer.

enrich *vt* enrichir; orner.

enrichment n enrichissement m.

enrol vt enrôler; inscrire.

enrolment n inscription f.

en route adv en route.

ensign n (mil) drapeau m; porte-étendard m; (mar) pavillon m.

enslave vt asservir.

ensue vi s'ensuivre.

ensure vt assurer.

entail vt impliquer, entraîner.

entangle vt emmêler, embrouiller.

entanglement n emmêlement m.

enter vt entrer dans; inscrire; **to ~ for** se présenter à; **to ~ into** commencer; faire partie de.

enterprise n entreprise f.

enterprising adj entreprenant.

entertain vt divertir; recevoir; avoir.

entertainer n artiste mf.

entertaining adj divertissant, amusant.

entertainment n divertissement, passe-temps m.

enthralled adj captivé.

enthralling adj captivant.

enthrone vt introniser.

enthusiasm n enthousiasme m.

enthusiast n enthousiaste mf.

enthusiastic adj enthousiaste.

entice vt tenter; séduire.

entire adj entier, complet; parfait; **~ly** adv entièrement.

entirety n intégralité f.

entitle vt intituler; conférer un droit à.

entitled adj intitulé; **to be ~ to** avoir le droit de.

entity n entité f.

entourage n entourage m.

entrails npl entrailles fpl.

entrance n entrée f; admission f.

entrance examination n examen d'entrée m.

entrance fee n droit d'inscription m.

entrance hall n vestibule m.

entrance ramp n bretelle d'accès f.

entrant n participant m, -e f; candidat m, -e f.

entrap vt piéger.

entreat vt implorer, supplier.

entreaty n supplication, prière f.

entrepreneur n entrepreneur m.

entrust vt confier.

entry n entrée f.

entry phone n interphone m.

entwine vt entrelacer.

enumerate vt énumérer.

enunciate vt énoncer.

enunciation n énonciation f.

envelop vt envelopper.

envelope n enveloppe f.

enviable adj enviable.

envious adj envieux; **~ly** adv avec envie.

environment n environnement m.

environmental adj relatif à l'environnement.

environs npl environs mpl.

envisage vt envisager.

envoy n envoyé m, -e f.

envy n envie f; * vt envier.

ephemeral adj éphémère.

epic adj épique; * n récit épique m.

epidemic adj épidémique; * n épidémie f.

epilepsy n épilepsie f.

epileptic adj épileptique.

epilog(ue) n épilogue m.

Epiphany n Epiphanie f.

episcopacy n épiscopat m.

episcopal adj épiscopal.

episcopalian n épiscopal m.

episode n épisode m.

epistle n épître f.

epistolary adj épistolaire.

epithet n épithète f.

epitome n modèle m; résumé m.

epitomize vt incarner; résumer.

epoch n époque f.

equable adj uniforme; **~bly** adv uniformément.

equal adj égal; semblable; * n égal m, -e f; * vt égaler.

equality n égalité f.

equalize vt égaliser.

equalizer n point égalisateur m.
equally adv également.
equanimity n équanimité f.
equate vt égaliser.
equation n équation f.
equator n équateur m.
equatorial adj équatorial.
equestrian adj équestre.
equilateral adj équilatéral.
equilibrium n équilibre m.
equinox n équinoxe m.
equip vt équiper.
equipment n équipement m.
equitable adj équitable, impartial; **~bly** adv équitablement.
equity n équité, justice, impartialité f.
equivalent adj, n équivalent m.
equivocal adj équivoque, ambigu; **~ly** adv d'une manière équivoque.
equivocate vt équivoquer, user d'équivoques.
equivocation n équivoques fpl.
era n ère f.
eradicate vt supprimer; extirper.
eradication n suppression f; extirpation f.
erase vt effacer; gommer.
eraser n gomme f.
erect vt ériger; élever; * adj droit, debout.
erection n érection f; structure f.
ermine n hermine f.
erode vt éroder; ronger.
erotic adj érotique.
err vi se tromper.
errand n message m; commission f.
errand boy n garçon de courses, messager m.
errata npl errata m.
erratic adj changeant; irrégulier.
erroneous adj erroné, faux; **~ly** adv erronément, faussement.
error n erreur f.
erudite adj érudit.
erudition n érudition f.
erupt vi entrer en éruption; faire éruption.

eruption n éruption f.
escalate vi monter en flèche; s'intensifier.
escalation n montée en flèche f; intensification f.
escalator n escalier roulant m.
escapade n fredaine f.
escape vt éviter; échapper à; * vi s'évader, s'échapper; * n évasion, fuite f; **to make one's ~** prendre la fuite.
escapism n évasion de la réalité f.
eschew vt fuir; éviter.
escort n escorte f; * vt escorter.
esoteric adj ésotérique.
especial adj spécial; **~ly** adv spécialement.
espionage n espionnage m.
esplanade n (mil) esplanade f.
espouse vt épouser.
essay n essai m.
essence n essence f.
essential n essentiel m; * adj essentiel, principal; **~ly** adv essentiellement.
establish vt établir; fonder; démontrer.
establishment n établissement m; fondation f; institution f.
estate n état m; domaine m; biens mpl.
esteem vt estimer; apprécier; * n estime f; considération f.
esthetic adj esthétique; **~s** npl esthétique f.
estimate vt estimer; évaluer.
estimation n estimation, évaluation f; opinion f.
estrange vt éloigner, séparer.
estranged adj séparé.
estrangement n séparation f; distance f.
estuary n estuaire m.
etch vt graver à l'eau forte.
etching n gravure à l'eau forte f.
eternal adj éternel, perpétuel; **~ly** adv éternellement.
eternity n éternité f.
ether n éther m.

274

ethical *adj* éthique, moral; **~ly** *adv* éthiquement.

ethics *npl* éthique *f*.

ethnic *adj* ethnique.

ethos *n* génie *m*.

etiquette *n* étiquette *f*.

etymological *adj* étymologique.

etymologist *n* étymologiste *mf*.

etymology *n* étymologie *f*.

Eucharist *n* Eucharistie *f*.

eulogy *n* éloge *m*.

eunuch *n* eunuque *m*.

euphemism *n* euphémisme *m*.

evacuate *vt* évacuer.

evacuation *n* évacuation *f*.

evade *vt* éviter; échapper à.

evaluate *vt* évaluer.

evangelic(al) *adj* évangélique.

evangelist *n* évangéliste *m*.

evaporate *vt* faire évaporer; * *vi* s'évaporer; se volatiliser.

evaporated milk *n* lait condensé *m*.

evaporation *n* évaporation *f*.

evasion *n* dérobade *f*.

evasive *adj* évasif; **~ly** *adv* évasivement.

eve *n* veille *f*.

even *adj* égal; uni; pair; * *adv* même; encore; * *vt* égaliser; unir; * *vi*: **to ~ out** s'égaliser.

even-handed *adj* impartial, équitable.

evening *n* soir *m*, soirée *f*.

evening class *n* cours du soir *m*.

evening dress *n* robe du soir *f*; tenue de soirée *f*.

evenly *adv* également; uniment.

evenness *n* égalité *f*; uniformité *f*; régularité *f*; impartialité *f*.

event *n* événement *m*; épreuve *f*.

eventful *adj* mouvementé.

eventual *adj* final; **~ly** *adv* finalement, en fin de comptes.

eventuality *n* éventualité *f*.

ever *adv* toujours; jamais; déjà; **for ~ and ~** pour toujours; **~ since** depuis.

evergreen *adj* à feuilles persis-

tantes; * *n* arbre à feuilles persistantes *m*.

everlasting *adj* éternel.

evermore *adv* toujours.

every *adj* chacun, chacune; **~ where** partout; **~ thing** tout; **~ one**, **~ body** tout le monde.

evict *vt* expulser.

eviction *n* expulsion *f*.

evidence *n* évidence *f*; témoignage *m*; preuve *f*; * *vt* témoigner de.

evident *adj* évident; manifeste; **~ly** *adv* manifestement, de toute évidence.

evil *adj* mauvais; malveillant; * *n* mal *m*.

evil-minded *adj* malintentionné.

evocative *adj* évocateur.

evoke *vt* évoquer.

evolution *n* évolution *f*.

evolve *vt* développer; * *vi* se développer, évoluer.

ewe *n* brebis *f*.

exacerbate *vt* exacerber.

exact *adj* exact; * *vt* exiger.

exacting *adj* exigeant.

exaction *n* exaction *f*; extorsion *f*.

exactly *adj* exactement.

exactness, exactitude *n* exactitude *f*.

exaggerate *vt* exagérer.

exaggeration *n* exagération *f*.

exalt *vt* exalter; élever.

exaltation *n* exaltation *f*; élévation *f*.

exalted *adj* exalté; élevé.

examination *n* examen *m*.

examine *vt* examiner.

examiner *n* examinateur *m*, -trice *f*.

example *n* exemple *m*.

exasperate *vt* exaspérer, irriter.

exasperation *n* exaspération, irritation *f*.

excavate *vt* excaver, creuser.

excavation *n* excavation *f*.

exceed *vt* excéder, dépasser.

exceedingly *adv* trop; extrêmement.

excel *vt* surpasser; *vi* exceller.

excellence *n* excellence *f*; supériorité *f*.

Excellency *n* Excellence (titre) *f*.

excellent *adj* excellent; **~ly** *adv* excellemment, admirablement.

except *vt* excepter, exclure; **~(ing)** *prep* excepté, à l'exception de.

exception *n* exception *f*.

exceptional *adj* exceptionnel.

excerpt *n* extrait *m*.

excess *n* excès *m*.

excessive *adj* excessif; **~ly** *adv* excessivement.

exchange *vt* échanger; permuter; * *n* échange *m*; change *m*.

exchange rate *n* taux de change *m*.

excise *n* impôt *m*.

excitability *n* excitabilité *f*.

excitable *adj* excitable.

excite *vt* exciter; animer; enthousiasmer; stimuler.

excited *adj* animé, enthousiaste; excité.

excitement *n* animation *f*, enthousiasme *m*.

exciting *adj* passionnant; stimulant.

exclaim *vi* s'exclamer.

exclamation *n* exclamation *f*.

exclamation mark *n* point d'exclamation *m*.

exclamatory *adj* exclamatif.

exclude *vt* exclure.

exclusion *n* exclusion *f*; exception *f*.

exclusive *adj* exclusif; **~ly** *adv* exclusivement.

excommunicate *vt* excommunier.

excommunication *n* excommunion *f*.

excrement *n* excrément *m*.

excruciating *adj* atroce, horrible.

exculpate *vt* disculper; justifier.

excursion *n* excursion *f*; digression *f*.

excusable *adj* excusable.

excuse *vt* excuser; pardonner; * *n* excuse *f*.

execute *vt* exécuter.

execution *n* exécution *f*.

executioner *n* bourreau *m*.

executive *adj* exécutif.

executor *n* exécuteur testamentaire *m*.

exemplary *adj* exemplaire.

exemplify *vt* exemplifier.

exempt *adj* exempt.

exemption *n* exemption *f*.

exercise *n* exercice *m*; * *vi* prendre de l'exercice; * *vt* exercer; montrer.

excercise book *n* cahier *m*.

exert *vt* employer, exercer; **to ~ oneself** s'efforcer.

exertion *n* effort *m*.

exhale *vt* exhaler; expirer.

exhaust *n* échappement *m*; * *vt* épuiser.

exhausted *adj* épuisé.

exhaustion *n* épuisement *m*.

exhaustive *adj* exhaustif, complet.

exhibit *vt* exhiber; montrer; * *n* (*law*) pièce à conviction *f*.

exhibition *n* exposition, présentation *f*.

exhilarating *adj* stimulant.

exhilaration *n* joie *f*; stimulation *f*.

exhort *vt* exhorter.

exhortation *n* exhortation *f*.

exhume *vt* exhumer, déterrer.

exile *n* exil *m*; * *vt* exiler, déporter.

exist *vi* exister.

existence *n* existence *f*.

existent *adj* existant.

existing *adj* actuel, présent.

exit *n* sortie *f*; * *vi* sortir.

exit ramp *n* bretelle d'accès *f*.

exodus *n* exode *m*.

exonerate *vt* disculper; décharger.

exoneration *n* disculpation *f*; décharge *f*.

exorbitant *adj* exorbitant, excessif.

exorcise *vt* exorciser.

exorcism *n* exorcisme *m*.

exotic *adj* exotique.

expand *vt* étendre; dilater.

expanse *n* étendue *f*.

expansion *n* expansion *f*.

expansive *adj* expansif.

expatriate *vt* expatrier.

expect *vt* attendre; espérer; penser.

expectance, expectancy *n* attente *f*; espoir *m*.

expectant *adj* d'attente.

expectant mother *n* femme enceinte *f*.

expectation *n* expectative *f*; attente *f*.

expediency *n* convenance *f*; opportunité *f*.

expedient *adj* opportun; * *n* expédient *m*; **~ly** *adv* de manière opportune.

expedite *vt* accélérer; expédier.

expedition *n* expédition *f*.

expeditious *adj* expéditif; **~ly** *adv* de manière expéditive.

expel *vt* expulser.

expend *vt* dépenser; utiliser.

expendable *adj* jetable; remplaçable.

expenditure *n* dépense *f*.

expense *n* dépense *f*; coût *m*.

expense account *n* frais *mpl*.

expensive *adj* cher; coûteux; **~ly** *adv* de manière coûteuse; àgrands frais.

experience *n* expérience *f*; pratique *f*; * *vt* ressentir, éprouver; connaître.

experienced *adj* expérimenté.

experiment *n* expérience *f*; * *vi* expérimenter.

experimental *adj* expérimental; **~ly** *adv* expérimentalement.

expert *adj* expert.

expertise *n* habileté *f*.

expiration *n* expiration *f*; mort *f*.

expire *vi* expirer.

explain *vt* expliquer.

explanation *n* explication *f*.

explanatory *adj* explicatif.

expletive *adj* explétif.

explicable *adj* explicable.

explicit *adj* explicite; **~ly** *adv* explicitement.

explode *vt* faire exploser; *vi* exploser.

exploit *vt* exploiter; * *n* exploit *m*.

exploitation *n* exploitation *f*.

exploration *n* exploration *f*.

exploratory *adj* exploratoire.

explore *vt* explorer, examiner; sonder.

explorer *n* explorateur *m*, -trice *f*.

explosion *n* explosion *f*.

explosive *adj, n* explosif *m*.

exponent *n* (*math*) exposant *m*.

export *vt* exporter.

export, exportation *n* exportation *f*.

exporter *n* exportateur *m*, -trice *f*.

expose *vt* exposer; dévoiler.

exposed *adj* exposé.

exposition *n* exposition *f*; interprétation *f*.

expostulate *vi* débattre, discuter.

exposure *n* exposition *f*; temps de pose *m*; cliché *m*.

exposure meter *n* photomètre *m*.

expound *vt* exposer; interpréter.

express *vt* exprimer; * *adj* exprès; * *n* exprès *m*; (*rail*) rapide *m*.

expression *n* expression *f*; locution *f*.

expressionless *adj* inexpressif.

expressive *adj* expressif; **~ly** *adv* d'une manière expressive.

expressly *adv* expressément.

expressway *n* autoroute *f*.

expropriate *vt* exproprier.

expropriation *n* (*law*) expropriation *f*.

expulsion *n* expulsion *f*.

expurgate *vt* expurger.

exquisite *adj* exquis; **~ly** *adv* exquisément.

extant *adj* existant.

extempore *adv* à l'improviste.

extemporize *vi* improviser.
extend *vt* étendre; élargir; * *vi* s'étendre.
extension *n* extension *f*.
extensive *adj* étendu; important; **~ly** *adv* considérablement.
extent *n* extension *f*.
extenuate *vt* atténuer.
extenuating *adj* atténuant.
exterior *adj*, *n* extérieur *m*.
exterminate *vt* exterminer; supprimer.
extermination *n* extermination *f*; suppression *f*.
external *adj* externe; **~ly** *adv* extérieurement; **~s** *npl* extérieur *m*.
extinct *adj* disparu; éteint.
extinction *n* extinction *f*.
extinguish *vt* éteindre; supprimer.
extinguisher *n* extincteur *m*.
extirpate *vt* extirper.
extol *vt* louer, exalter.
extort *vt* extorquer; arracher.
extortion *n* extorsion *f*.
extortionate *adj* excessif.
extra *adv* particulièrement; *n* supplément *m*.
extract *vt* extraire; * *n* extrait *m*.
extraction *n* extraction *f*; origine *f*.
extracurricular *adj* périscolaire.
extradite *vt* extrader.
extradition *n* (*law*) extradition *f*.
extramarital *adj* extérieur au mariage.
extramural *adj* extra-muros.

extraneous *adj* superflu; sans rapport.
extraordinarily *adv* extraordinairement.
extraordinary *adj* extraordinaire.
extravagance *n* extravagance *f*; gaspillage *m*.
extravagant *adj* extravagant; exorbitant; gaspilleur; **~ly** *adv* de manière extravagante; en gaspillant.
extreme *adj* extrême; suprême; ultime; * *n* extrême *m*; **~ly** *adv* extrêmement.
extremist *adj*, *n* extrémiste *mf*.
extremity *n* extrémité *f*.
extricate *vt* extirper, démêler.
extrinsic(al) *adj* extrinsèque.
extrovert *adj*, *n* extraverti *m*, -e *f*.
exuberance *n* exubérance *f*.
exuberant *adj* exubérant; **~ly** *adv* avec exubérance.
exude *vi* exsuder.
exult *vi* exulter, triompher.
exultation *n* exultation *f*.
eye *n* oeil *m*; * *vt* regarder, observer; lorgner.
eyeball *n* globe oculaire *m*.
eyebrow *n* sourcil *m*.
eyelash *n* cil *m*.
eyelid *n* paupière *f*.
eyesight *n* vue *f*.
eyesore *n* monstruosité *f*.
eyetooth *n* canine *f*.
eyewitness *n* témoin oculaire *m*.
eyrie *n* aire *f*.

F

fable *n* fable *f*; légende *f*.
fabric *n* tissu *m*.
fabricate *vt* fabriquer; inventer.
fabrication *n* fabrication *f*; invention *f*.
fabulous *adj* fabuleux; **~ly** *adv* fabuleusement.

facade *n* façade *f*.
face *n* visage *m*, figure *f*; surface *f*; façade *f*; mine *f*; apparence *f*; * *vt* faire face à; affronter; **to ~ up to** faire face à.
face cream *n* crème pour le visage *f*.

face-lift *n* lifting *m*.
face powder *n* poudre de riz *f*.
facet *n* facette *f*.
facetious *adj* facétieux, plaisant, spirituel; **~ly** *adv* facétieusement.
face value *n* valeur nominale *f*.
facial *adj* facial.
facile *adj* facile; superficiel.
facilitate *vt* faciliter.
facility *n* facilité *f*; équipement *m*, infrastructure *f*.
facing *n* revers *m*; * *prep* en face de.
facsimile *n* fac-similé *m*.
fact *n* fait *m*; réalité *f*; **in ~** en fait.
faction *n* faction *f*; dissension *f*.
factor *n* facteur *m*.
factory *n* usine *f*.
factual *adj* factuel, basé sur les faits.
faculty *n* faculté *f*; le corps enseignant *m*.
fad *n* engouement *m*.
fade *vi* se faner; perdre son éclat.
fail *vt* échouer à; omettre; manquer à ses engagements envers; * *vi* échouer; faiblir; manquer.
failing *n* défaut *m*.
failure *n* échec *m*; panne *f*; raté *m*; faillite *f*; manquement *m*.
faint *vi* s'évanouir, défaillir; * *n* évanouissement *m*; * *adj* faible; **~ly** *adv* faiblement.
fainthearted *adj* timide, timoré, pusillanime.
faintness *n* faiblesse *f*; légèreté *f*.
fair *adj* beau; blond; clair; favorable; juste, équitable; considérable; passable; * *adv* loyalement; * *n* foire *f*.
fairly *adv* équitablement; absolument.
fairness *n* beauté *f*; justice *f*.
fair play *n* fair-play, franc-jeu *m*.
fairy *n* fée *f*.
fairy tale *n* conte de fées *m*.
faith *n* foi *f*; croyance *f*; fidélité *f*.
faithful *adj* fidèle, loyal; **~ly** *adv* fidèlement.

faithfulness *n* fidélité, loyauté *f*.
fake *n* falsification *f*; imposteur *m*; * *adj* faux; * *vt* feindre; falsifier.
falcon *n* faucon *m*.
falconry *n* fauconnerie *f*.
fall *vi* tomber; s'effondrer; diminuer, baisser; **to ~ asleep** s'endormir; **to ~ back** reculer; **to ~ back on** avoir recours à; **to ~ behind** être à la traîne; **to ~ down** tomber; **to ~ for** se faire avoir; tomber amoureux de; **to ~ in** s'effondrer; **to ~ short** échouer; **to ~ sick** tomber malade; **to ~ in love** tomber amoureux; **to ~ off** tomber; diminuer; **to ~ out** se produire; se quereller; * *n* chute *f*; automne *m*.
fallacious *adj* fallacieux, trompeur; **~ly** *adv* d'une manière fallacieuse.
fallacy *n* erreur *f*; sophisme *m*; tromperie *f*.
fallibility *n* faillibilité *f*.
fallible *adj* faillible.
fallout *n* retombées radioactives *fpl*.
fallout shelter *n* abri antiatomique *m*.
fallow *adj* en jachère; **~ deer** *n* daim *m*.
false *adj* faux; **~ly** *adv* faussement.
false alarm *n* fausse alerte *f*.
falsehood, falseness *n* mensonge *m*; fausseté *f*.
falsify *vt* falsifier.
falsity *n* fausseté *f*.
falter *vi* vaciller; faiblir.
faltering *adj* chancelant.
fame *n* réputation *f*; renommée, notoriété *f*.
famed *adj* célèbre.
familiar *adj* familier; domestique; **~ly** *adv* familièrement.
familiarity *n* familiarité *f*.
familiarize *vt* familiariser.
family *n* famille *f*.

family business n affaire de famille f.

family doctor n médecin de famille m.

famine n famine f; disette f.

famished adj affamé.

famous adj célèbre, fameux; ~ly adv fameusement.

fan n éventail m; ventilateur m; jeune admirateur m, -trice f; * vt éventer; attiser.

fanatic adj, n fanatique mf.

fanaticism n fanatisme m.

fan belt n courroie de ventilateur f.

fanciful adj fantasque, capricieux; ~ly adv capricieusement.

fancy n fantaisie, imagination f; caprice m; * vt avoir envie de; s'imaginer.

fancy-goods npl nouveautés fpl.

fancydress ball n bal masqué m.

fanfare n (mus) fanfare f.

fang n croc m.

fantastic adj fantastique; excentrique; ~ally adv fantastiquement.

fantasy n imagination f.

far adv loin; * adj lointain, éloigné; ~ and away de très loin; ~ off lointain.

faraway adj lointain.

farce n farce f.

farcical adj grotesque.

fare n prix (du voyage) m; tarif m; régime alimentaire m; voyageur m, -euse f; client m, -e f.

farewell n adieu m; ~! excl adieu!

farm n ferme f, exploitation agricole f; * vt cultiver.

farmer n fermier m; agriculteur m.

farmhand n ouvrier agricole m.

farmhouse n maison de ferme f.

farming n agriculture f.

farmland n terres arables fpl.

farmyard n cour de ferme f.

far-reaching adj d'une grande portée.

fart n (sl) pet; * vi péter.

farther adv plus loin; * adj plus éloigné.

farthest adv le plus lointain; le plus loin; au plus.

fascinate vt fasciner, captiver.

fascinating adj fascinant.

fascination n fascination f; charme m.

fascism n fascisme m.

fashion n manière, façon f; forme f; coutume f; mode f; style m; **people of ~** personnes élégantes fpl; * vt façonner, confectionner.

fashionable adj à la mode; chic; **the ~ world** le beau monde; ~bly adv à la mode.

fashion show n défilé de mode m.

fast vi jeûner; * n jeûne m; * adj rapide; ferme, stable; * adv rapidement; fermement; solidement.

fasten vt attacher; fixer; attribuer; * vi se fixer, s'attacher.

fastener, fastening n attache f; fermoir m.

fast food n restauration rapide f.

fastidious adj minutieux, méticuleux; ~ly adv minutieusement.

fat adj gros, gras; * n graisse f.

fatal adj mortel; néfaste; ~ly adv mortellement.

fatalism n fatalisme m.

fatalist n fataliste mf.

fatality n accident mortel m, fatalité f.

fate n destin, sort m.

fateful adj fatidique.

father n père m.

fatherhood n paternité f.

father-in-law n beau-père m.

fatherland n patrie f.

fatherly adj (adv) paternel(lement).

fathom n brasse (mesure) f; * vt sonder; pénétrer.

fatigue n fatigue f; * vt fatiguer, lasser.

fatten vt, vi engraisser.

fatty *adj* gras, graisseux.

fatuous *adj* imbécile, stupide, niais.

faucet *n* robinet *m*.

fault *n* défaut *m*, faute *f*; délit *m*; faille *f*.

faultfinder *n* chicaneur *m*, -euse *f*.

faultless *adj* irréprochable.

faulty *adj* défectueux.

fauna *n* faune *f*.

faux pas *n* impair *m*.

favor *n* faveur *f*; approbation *f*; avantage *m*; * *vt* favoriser, préférer.

favorable *adj* favorable, propice; **~bly** *adv* favorablement.

favored *adj* favorisé.

favorite *n* favori *m*; * *adj* favori.

favoritism *n* favoritisme *m*.

fawn *n* faon *m*; * *vi* flatter servilement.

fawningly *adv* d'une flatterie servile.

fax *n* télécopieur, fax *m*; télécopie *f*, fax *m*; * *vt* envoyer par fax, télécopier.

fear *vt* craindre; * *n* crainte *f*.

fearful *adj* effrayant; craintif, peureux; **~ly** *adv* terriblement; craintivement.

fearless *adj* intrépide, courageux; **~ly** *adv* courageusement.

fearlessness *n* intrépidité *f*.

feasibility *n* faisabilité *f*.

feasible *adj* faisable, réalisable.

feast *n* festin, banquet *m*; fête *f*; * *vi* banqueter.

feat *n* exploit *m*; prouesse *f*.

feather *n* plume *f*;.

feather bed *n* lit de plumes *m*.

feature *n* caractéristique *f*; trait *m*; * *vi* figurer.

feature film *n* long métrage *m*.

February *n* février *m*.

federal *adj* fédéral.

federalist *n* fédéraliste *mf*.

federate *vt* fédérer; * *vi* se fédérer.

federation *n* fédération *f*.

fed-up *adj*: **to be ~** en avoir marre.

fee *n* honoraires *mpl*; frais *mpl*.

feeble *adj* faible, frêle.

feebleness *n* faiblesse *f*.

feebly *adv* faiblement.

feed *vt* nourrir; alimenter; **to ~ on** se nourrir de; * *vi* manger; se nourrir; * *n* nourriture *f*; alimentation *f*.

feedback *n* réaction *f*.

feel *vt* sentir; toucher; croire; **to ~ around** tâtonner, fouiller; * *n* sensation *f*; toucher *m*.

feeler *n* antenne *f*; (*fig*) tentative *f*.

feeling *n* sensation *f*; sentiment *m*.

feelingly *adv* avec émotion.

feign *vt* inventer; feindre, simuler.

feline *adj* félin.

fellow *n* homme, type *m*; membre *m*.

fellow citizen *n* concitoyen *m* -enne *f*.

fellow countryman *n* compatriote *m*.

fellow feeling *n* sympathie *f*.

fellow men *npl* semblables *mpl*.

fellowship *n* camaraderie *f*; association *f*.

fellow student *n* copain (copine) de fac *m(f)*.

fellow traveller *n* compagnon (compagne) de voyage *m(f)*.

felon *n* criminel *m*, -elle *f*.

felony *n* crime *m*.

felt *n* feutre *m*.

felt-tip pen *n* feutre *m*.

female *n* femelle *f*; * *adj* de sexe féminin, femelle.

feminine *adj* féminin.

feminist *n* féministe *mf*.

fen *n* marais *m*.

fence *n* barrière *f*; clôture *f*; * *vt* clôturer; * *vi* faire de l'escrime.

fencing *n* escrime *f*.

fender *n* pare-chocs *m invar*.

fennel *n* (*bot*) fenouil *m*.

ferment n agitation f; * vi fermenter.

fern n (bot) fougère f.

ferocious adj féroce; ~ly adv férocement.

ferocity n férocité f.

ferret n furet m; * vt fureter; **to ~ out** découvrir, dénicher.

ferry n bac m; ferry m; * vt transporter.

fertile adj fertile, fécond.

fertility n fertilité, fécondité f.

fertilize vt fertiliser.

fertilizer n engrais m.

fervent adj fervent; ardent; ~ly adv avec ferveur.

fervid adj ardent, véhément.

fervor n ferveur, ardeur f.

fester vi suppurer; s'envenimer.

festival n fête f; festival m.

festive adj de fête.

festivity n fête f, réjouissances fpl.

fetch vt aller chercher.

fetching adj charmant, séduisant.

fête n fête f.

fetid adj fétide, nauséabond.

fetus n fœtus m.

feud n fief m; rivalité, dissension f.

feudal adj féodal.

feudalism n féodalité f.

fever n fièvre f.

feverish adj fiévreux.

few adj peu; **a ~** quelques; **~ and far between** rares.

fewer adj moins (de) ; * adv moins.

fewest adj le moins (de).

fiancé n fiancé m.

fiancée n fiancée f.

fib n bobard m; * vi raconter des bobards.

fibre n fibre f.

fibreglass n fibre de verre f.

fickle adj volage, inconstant.

fiction n fiction f; invention f.

fictional adj fictif.

fictitious adj fictif, imaginaire; feint; ~ly adv fictivement.

fiddle n violon m; combine f; * vi jouer du violon.

fiddler n violoniste mf.

fidelity n fidélité, loyauté f.

fidget vi s'agiter, s'impatienter.

fidgety adj agité, impatient.

field n champ m; étendue f; domaine m.

field day n (mil) jour de grandes manoeuvres m.

fieldmouse n mulot m.

fieldwork n recherches sur le terrain fpl.

fiend n démon m; mordu m.

fiendish adj diabolique.

fierce adj féroce, violent; acharné, furieux; ~ly adv férocement

fierceness n férocité, fureur f.

fiery adj ardent; fougueux.

fifteen adj, n quinze m.

fifteenth adj, n quinzième mf.

fifth adj, n cinquième mf; ~ly adv cinquièmement.

fiftieth adj, n cinquantième mf.

fifty adj, n cinquante m.

fig n figue f.

fight vt, vi se battre (contre); combattre; lutter ;* n bataille f; combat m; lutte f.

fighter n combattant m; lutteur m; chasseur m.

fighting n combat m.

fig-leaf n feuille de figuier f.

fig tree n figuier m.

figurative adj figuratif; ~ly adv figurativement.

figure n figure f; forme, silhouette f; image f; chiffre m; * vi figurer; avoir du sens; **to ~ out** comprendre.

figurehead n figure de proue f.

filament n filament m; fibre f.

filch vt chiper.

filcher n voleur m, -euse f.

file n file f; liste f; (mil) colonne, rangée f; ligne f; dossier m; fichier m; * vt enregistrer; limer; classer; déposer; * vi **to ~ in/out** entrer/sortir en file; **to ~ past** défiler devant.

filing cabinet *n* classeur (meuble) *m*.

fill *vt* remplir; **to ~ in** remplir; **to ~ up** remplir (jusqu'au bord).

fillet *n* filet *m*.

fillet steak *n* filet de boeuf *m*.

filling station *n* station-service *f*.

fillip *n* (*fig*) coup de fouet *m*.

filly *n* pouliche *f*.

film *n* pellicule *f*; film *f*; cellophane *m*; * *vt* filmer; * *vi* s'embuer.

film star *n* vedette de cinéma *f*.

filmstrip *n* film *m*.

filter *n* filtre *m*; * *vt* filtrer.

filter-tipped *adj* à bout filtre.

filth(iness) *n* immondice, ordure *f*; saleté, crasse *f*.

filthy *adj* crasseux, dégoûtant.

fin *n* nageoire *f*.

final *adj* dernier; définitif; **~ly** *adv* finalement.

finale *n* finale *m*.

finalist *n* finaliste *mf*.

finalize *vt* parachever, rendre définitif.

finance *n* finance *f*.

financial *adj* financier.

financier *n* financier *m*.

find *vt* trouver, découvrir; **to ~ out** découvrir; démasquer; **to ~ one's self** se retrouver; * *n* trouvaille *f*.

findings *npl* résultats *mpl*, conclusions *fpl*; verdict *m*.

fine *adj* fin; pur; aigu; raffiné; beau, *f* belle; délicat; subtil; élégant; * *n* amende *f*; * *vt* infliger une amende à.

fine arts *npl* beaux arts *mpl*.

finely *adv* magnifiquement.

finery *n* parure *f*.

finesse *n* finesse, subtilité *f*.

finger *n* doigt *m*; * *vt* toucher, manier.

fingernail *n* ongle *m*.

fingerprint *n* empreinte digitale *f*.

fingertip *n* bout du doigt *m*.

finicky *adj* pointilleux, difficile.

finish *vt* finir, terminer, achever; **to ~ off** finir; **to ~ up** terminer; * *vi*: **to ~ up** se retrouver.

finishing line *n* ligne d'arrivée *f*.

finishing school *n* école privée (pour jeunes filles) *f*.

finite *adj* fini.

fir (tree) *n* sapin *m*

fire *n* feu *m*; incendie *m*; * *vt* mettre le feu à; incendier; tirer; * *vi* s'enflammer, faire feu.

fire alarm *n* alarme d'incendie *f*.

firearm *n* arme à feu *f*.

fireball *n* boule de feu *f*.

fire department *n* pompiers *mpl*.

fire engine *n* voiture de pompiers *f*.

fire escape *n* escalier de secours *m*.

fire extinguisher *n* extincteur *m*.

firefly *n* luciole *f*.

fireman *n* pompier *m*.

fireplace *n* cheminée *f*, foyer *m*.

fireproof *adj* ignifugé.

fireside *n* coin du feu *m*.

fire station *n* caserne de pompiers *f*.

firewater *n* eau de vie *f*.

firewood *n* bois de chauffage *m*.

fireworks *npl* feu d'artifice *m*.

firing *n* fusillade *f*.

firing squad *n* peloton d'exécution *m*.

firm *adj* ferme, solide; constant; * *n* (*com*) compagnie *f*; **~ly** *adv* fermement.

firmament *n* firmament *m*.

firmness *n* fermeté *f*; résolution *f*.

first *adj* premier; * *adv* premièrement; **at ~** d'abord; **~ly** *adv* en premier lieu.

first aid *n* premiers secours *mpl*.

first-aid kit *n* trousse de premiers secours *f*.

first-class *adj* de première classe, de première catégorie.

first-hand *adj* de première main.

First Lady *n* première dame,

femme du président d'un pays
f.

first name n prénom m.

first-rate adj de première qualité.

fiscal adj fiscal.

fish n poisson m; * vi pêcher.

fishbone n arête f.

fisherman n pêcheur m.

fish farm n entreprise de pisciculture f.

fishing n pêche f.

fishing line n ligne de pêche f.

fishing rod n canne à pêche f.

fishing tackle n attirail de pêche m.

fish market n marché au poisson m.

fishseller n poissonnier m, -ière f.

fishstore n poissonnerie f.

fishy adj (fig) suspect.

fissure n fissure, crevasse f.

fist n poing m.

fit n accès m, attaque f; crise f; * adj en forme; capable; adapté à, qui convient; * vt aller à; ajuster, adapter; **to ~ out** équiper; * vi (bien) aller; **to ~ in** s'accorder avec; être en harmonie avec.

fitment n meuble encastré m.

fitness n forme physique f; aptitudes fpl.

fitted carpet n moquette f.

fitted kitchen n cuisine encastrée f.

fitter n monteur m.

fitting adj qui convient, approprié, juste; * n accessoire m; **~s** pl installations fpl.

five adj, n cinq m.

five spot n (sl) billet de cinq dollars m.

fix vt fixer, établir; **to ~ up** arranger.

fixation n obsession f.

fixed adj fixe.

fixings npl garniture f; accessoires mpl.

fixture n rencontre f.

fizz(le) vi pétiller.

fizzy adj gazeux.

flabbergasted adj abasourdi.

flabby adj mou, f molle, flasque.

flaccid adj flasque, mou, f molle.

flag n drapeau m; iris m; * vi s'affaiblir.

flagpole n mât aux drapeaux m.

flagrant adj flagrant.

flagship n vaisseau amiral m.

flagstop n arrêt facultatif m.

flair n flair m; talent m.

flak n tir antiaérien m; critiques fpl.

flake n flocon m; paillette f; * vi s'effriter, s'écailler.

flaky adj floconneux; friable.

flamboyant adj flamboyant; ostentatoire.

flame n flamme f; ardeur f.

flamingo n flamant m.

flammable adj inflammable.

flank n flanc m; (also mil); * vt flanquer.

flannel n flanelle f.

flap n battement m; rabat m; * vt, vi battre.

flare vi luire, briller; **to ~ up** s'embraser; se mettre en colère; éclater; * n flamme f.

flash n éclat m; éclair m; * vt faire briller; allumer.

flashbulb n ampoule de flash f.

flash cube n cube de flash m.

flashlight n fanal m.

flashy adj tape-à-l'oeil, voyant.

flask n flasque f; flacon m.

flat adj plat; uniforme; insipide; * n plaine f; plat m; (mus) si bémol m; **~ly** adv horizontalement; platement; également; catégoriquement.

flatness n égalité f; monotonie f.

flatten vt aplanir; aplatir.

flatter vt flatter.

flattering adj flatteur.

flattery n flatterie f.

flatulence n (med) flatulence f.

flaunt vt étaler, afficher.

flavour n saveur m; * vt parfumer; assaisonner.

flavoured adj savoureux; parfumé.

flavourless adj insipide.

flaw n défaut m; imperfection f.

flawless adj parfait.

flax n lin m.

flea n puce f.

flea bite n piqûre de puce f.

fleck n petite tache f; particule f.

flee vt fuir de; * vi s'enfuir; fuir.

fleece n toison f; * vt (sl) tondre.

fleet n flotte f; parc m.

fleeting adj fugace, fugitif.

flesh n chair f.

flesh wound n blessure superficielle f.

fleshy adj charnu.

flex n cordon m; * vt fléchir.

flexibility n flexibilité f.

flexible adj flexible, souple.

flick n petit coup m; * vt donner un petit coup à.

flicker vt vaciller; trembloter.

flier n aviateur m, -trice f.

flight n vol m; fuite f; volée f; (fig) envolée f.

flight attendant n steward m, hôtesse de l'air f.

flight deck n cabine de pilotage f.

flimsy adj léger; fragile.

flinch vi sourciller.

fling vt lancer, jeter.

flint n silex m.

flip vt lancer.

flippant adj désinvolte, cavalier.

flipper n nageoire f.

flirt vi flirter; * n charmeur m, -euse f.

flirtation n flirt f.

flit vi voler, voleter.

float vt faire flotter; lancer; * vi flotter; * n flotteur m; char (de carnaval) m; provision f.

flock n troupeau m; volée f; foule f, * vi affluer.

flog vt fustiger.

flogging n fustigation, flagellation f.

flood n inondation f; marée haute f; déluge m; * vt inonder.

flooding n inondation f.

floodlight n projecteur m.

floor n sol m; plancher m; étage m; * vt parqueter; déconcerter.

floorboard n planche f.

floor lamp n lampadaire m.

floor show n spectacle de cabaret m.

flop n four, fiasco m.

floppy adj lâche; * n disquette f.

flora n flore f.

floral adj floral.

florescence n floraison f.

florid adj fleuri.

florist n fleuriste mf.

florist's (shop) n boutique de fleuriste f.

flotilla n (mar) flotille f.

flounder n flet m; * vi patauger.

flour n farine f.

flourish vi fleurir; prospérer; * n fioriture f; (mus) fioriture f.

flourishing adj florissant.

flout vt mépriser, se moquer de.

flow vi couler; circuler; monter (marée); ondoyer; * n flux m; écoulement m; flot m.

flow chart n organigramme m.

flower n fleur f; * vi fleurir.

flowerbed n parterre de fleurs m.

flowerpot n pot de fleurs m.

flowery adj fleuri.

flower show n exposition de fleurs f.

fluctuate vi fluctuer.

fluctuation n fluctuation f.

fluency n aisance f.

fluent adj coulant; facile; **~ly** adv couramment.

fluff n peluche f; **~y** adj duveteux.

fluid adj, n fluide m.

fluidity n fluidité f.

fluke n (sl) veine f.

fluoride n fluorure m.

flurry n rafale f; agitation f.

flush vt: **to ~ out** nettoyer à grande eau; * vi rougir; * n rougeur f; éclat m.

flushed *adj* rouge.

fluster *vt* énerver.

flustered *adj* énervé.

flute *n* flûte *f*.

flutter *vi* voleter; s'agiter; * *n* agitation *f*; émoi *m*.

flux *n* flux *m*.

fly *vt* piloter; transporter par avion; * *vi* voler; fuir; **to ~ away/off** s'envoler; * *n* mouche *f*; braguette *f*.

flying *n* aviation *f*.

flying saucer *n* soucoupe volante *f*.

flypast *n* défilé aérien *m*.

flysheet *n* feuille volante *f*.

foal *n* poulain *m*.

foam *n* écume *f*; * *vi* écumer.

foam rubber *n* caoutchouc mousse *m*.

foamy *adj* écumeux.

focus *n* foyer *m*; centre *m*.

fodder *n* fourrage *m*.

foe *n* ennemi *m*, -e *f*, adversaire *mf*.

fog *n* brouillard *m*.

foggy *adj* brumeux.

fog light *n* feu de brouillard *m*.

foible *n* point faible *m*.

foil *vt* déjouer; * *n* papier d'aluminium *m*; fleuret *m*.

fold *n* pli *m*; parc à moutons *m*; * *vt* plier; **to ~ up** faire faillite; * *vi*: **to ~ up** plier, replier.

folder *n* chemise *f*; dépliant *m*.

folding *adj* pliant.

folding chair *n* chaise pliante *f*.

foliage *n* feuillage *m*.

folio *n* folio *m*.

folk *n* gens *mpl*.

folklore *n* folklore *m*.

folk song *n* chant folklorique *m*.

follow *vt* suivre; **to ~ up** suivre; exploiter; * *vi* suivre, s'ensuivre, résulter.

follower *n* serviteur *m*; disciple *mf*, partisan *m*, -e *f*; adhérent *m*, -e *f*; admirateur *m*, -trice *f*.

following *adj* suivant; * *n* partisans *mpl*.

folly *n* folie, extravagance *f*.

foment *vt* fomenter.

fond *adj* affectueux; **to be ~ of** aimer; **~ly** *adv* affectueusement.

fondle *vt* caresser.

fondness *n* prédilection *f*; affection *f*.

font *n* fonts baptismaux *mpl*.

food *n* nourriture *f*.

food mixer *n* mixer *m*.

food poisoning *n* intoxication alimentaire *f*.

food processor *n* robot *m*.

foodstuffs *npl* denrées alimentaires *fpl*.

fool *n* imbécile *mf*, idiot *m*, -e *f*; * *vt* duper.

foolhardy *adj* téméraire.

foolish *adj* idiot, insensé; **~ly** *adv* bêtement.

foolproof *adj* infaillible.

foolscap *n* papier ministre *m*.

foot *n* pied *m*; patte *f*; **on** *or* **by ~** à pied.

footage *n* métrage *m*.

football *n* football *m*; ballon de football *m*.

footballer *n* footballeur *m*, -euse *f*.

footbrake *n* frein à pied *m*.

footbridge *n* passerelle *f*.

foothills *npl* contreforts *mpl*.

foothold *n* prise (pour le pied) *f*.

footing *n* prise (pour le pied) *f*; statut *m*; situation *f*; plan *m*.

footlights *npl* feux de la rampe *mpl*.

footman *n* valet de pied *m*; soldat d'infanterie *m*.

footnote *n* note (de bas de page) *f*.

footpath *n* sentier *m*.

footprint *n* empreinte (de pas) *f*.

footsore *adj* aux pieds endoloris.

footstep *n* pas *m*.

footwear *n* chaussures *fpl*.

for *prep* pour; en raison de; pendant; * *conj* car; **as ~ me** quant à moi; **what ~?** pourquoi?; pourquoi faire?

forage *n* fourrage *m*; * *vt* fourrager; fouiller.

foray n incursion f.

forbid vt interdire, défendre; empêcher; **God ~!** pourvu que non!

forbidding adj menaçant; sévère.

force n force f; puissance, vigueur f; violence f; **~s** pl forces armées fpl; * vt forcer, obliger, contraindre; imposer.

forced adj forcé.

forced march n (mil) marche forcée f.

forceful adj énergique.

forceps n forceps m.

forcible adj énergique, vigoureux, puissant; **~bly** adv énergiquement, avec véhémence.

ford n gué m; * vt passer à gué.

fore n: **to the ~** en évidence.

forearm n avant-bras m.

foreboding n pressentiment m.

forecast vt prévoir; * n prévision f.

forecourt n avant-cour f.

forefather n aïeul, ancêtre m.

forefinger n index m.

forefront n: **in the ~ of** au premier plan de.

forego vt renoncer à, s'abstenir de.

foregone adj passé; anticipé.

foreground n premier plan m.

forehead n front m.

foreign adj étranger.

foreigner n étranger m, -ère f.

foreign exchange n devises fpl.

foreleg n patte de devant f.

foreman n contremaître m; (law) premier juré m.

foremost adj principal.

forenoon n matinée f.

forensic adj judiciaire.

forerunner n précurseur m; signe avant-coureur m.

foresee vt prévoir.

foreshadow vt présager.

foresight n prévoyance f; prescience f.

forest n forêt f.

forestall vt anticiper; prévenir.

forester n garde forestier m.

forestry n sylviculture f.

foretaste n avant-goût m.

foretell vt prédire.

forethought n prévoyance f; préméditation f.

forever adv toujours; un temps infini.

forewarn vt prévenir à l'avance.

foreword n préface f.

forfeit n amende f; confiscation f; * vt perdre.

forge n forge f; usine métallurgique f; * vt contrefaire * vi: **to ~ ahead** aller de l'avant.

forger n faussaire mf.

forgery n contrefaçon f.

forget vt, vi oublier.

forgetful adj étourdi; négligent.

forgetfulness n étourderie f; négligence f.

forget-me-not n (bot) myosotis m.

forgive vt pardonner.

forgiveness n pardon m; indulgence f.

fork n fourchette f; fourche f; * vi bifurquer; **to ~ out** (sl) casquer.

forked adj fourchu.

fork-lift truck n chariot élévateur m.

forlorn adj malheureux, abandonné.

form n forme f; formule f; formulaire m; formalité f; moule m; * vt former.

formal adj formel; méthodique; cérémonieux; **~ly** adv formellement.

formality n formalité f; cérémonie f.

format n format m; * vt formater.

formation n formation f.

formative adj formateur m, -trice f.

former adj précédent, ancien; **~ly** adv autrefois, jadis.

formidable adj effrayant, terrible.

formula n formule f.

formulate vt formuler.

forsake vt abandonner, renoncer à.

fort n fort m.

forte n fort m.

forthcoming adj prochain; sociable.

forthright adj franc.

forthwith adv immédiatement, tout de suite.

fortieth adj, n quarantième mf.

fortification n fortification f.

fortify vt fortifier, renforcer.

fortitude n stoïcisme m; courage m.

fortnight n quinze jours mpl; deux semaines fpl; * adj ~ly bimensuel; * adv ~ly tous les quinze jours.

fortress n (mil) forteresse f.

fortuitous adj fortuit; imprévu; ~ly adv fortuitement.

fortunate adj chanceux; ~ly adv heureusement.

fortune n chance f, sort m; fortune f.

fortune-teller n diseuse de bonne aventure f.

forty adj, n quarante m.

forum n forum m, tribune f.

forward adj avancé; précoce; présomptueux; ~(s) adv en avant, vers l'avant; * vt transmettre; promouvoir; expédier.

forwardness n précocité f; effronterie f.

fossil adj fossilisé; * n fossile m.

foster vt élever.

foster child n enfant adoptif m.

foster father n père adoptif m.

foster mother n mère adoptive f.

foul adj infect, ignoble; vil, déloyal ; ~ copy n copie illisible f; ~ly adv salement; ignoblement; * vt polluer.

foul play n jeu déloyal m; meurtre m.

found vt fonder, créer; établir, édifier; fondre.

foundation n foundation f; fondement m.

founder n fondateur m, -trice f;

fondeur m; * vi (mar) couler.

foundling n enfant trouvé(e) mf.

foundry n fonderie f.

fount, fountain n fontaine f.

fountainhead n source, origine f.

four adj, n quatre m.

fourfold adj quadruple.

four-poster (bed) n lit à baldaquin m.

foursome n groupe de quatre personnes m.

fourteen adj, n quatorze m.

fourteenth adj, n quatorzième mf.

fourth adj, n quatrième mf; * n quart m; ~ly adv quatrièmement.

fowl n volaille f.

fox n renard f; (fig) rusé m.

foyer n vestibule m.

fracas n rixe f.

fraction n fraction f.

fracture n fracture f; * vt fracturer.

fragile adj fragile; frêle.

fragility n fragilité f; faiblesse, délicatesse f.

fragment n fragment m.

fragmentary adj fragmentaire.

fragrance n parfum m.

fragrant adj parfumé, odorant; ~ly adv en eschalant un parfum.

frail adj frêle, fragile.

frailty n fragilité f; faiblesse f.

frame n charpente f; châssis m, armature f; cadre m; structure f; monture f; * vt encadrer; concevoir; construire; former.

frame of mind n état d'esprit m.

framework n charpente f; structure f, cadre m.

franchise n droit de vote m; franchise f.

frank adj franc, direct.

frankly adv franchement.

frankness n franchise f.

frantic adj frénétique, effréné.

fraternal adj, ~ly adv fraternel(lement).

fraternity n fraternité f.

fraternize *vi* fraterniser.

fratricide *n* fratricide *mf*.

fraud *n* fraude, tromperie *f*.

fraudulence *n* caractère frauduleux *m*.

fraudulent *adj* frauduleux; **~ly** *adv* frauduleusement.

fraught *adj* plein, chargé.

fray *n* rixe, bagarre, querelle *f*.

freak *n* caprice *m*; phénomène *m*.

freckle *n* tache de rousseur *f*.

freckled *adj* couvert de taches de rousseur.

free *adj* libre; autonome; gratuit; dégagé; * *vt* affranchir; libérer; débarrasser.

freedom *n* liberté *f*.

freehold *n* propriété libre *f*.

free-for-all *n* mêlée générale *f*.

free gift *n* prime *f*.

free kick *n* coup franc *m*.

freelance *adj* indépendant; * *adv* en indépendant.

freely *adv* librement; franchement; libéralement.

freemason *n* franc-maçon *m*.

freemasonry *n* franc-maçonnerie *f*.

freepost *n* port payé *m*.

free-range *adj* de ferme.

freethinker *n* libre-penseur *m*, -euse *f*.

freethinking *n* libre pensée *f*.

free trade *n* libre échange *m*.

freeway *n* autoroute *f*.

freewheel *vi* rouler au point mort.

free will *n* libre arbitre *m*.

freeze *vi* geler; * *vt* congeler; geler.

freeze-dried *adj* lyophilisé.

freezer *n* congélateur *m*.

freezing *adj* gelé.

freezing point *n* point de congélation *m*.

freight *n* cargaison *f*; fret *m*.

freighter *n* affréteur *m*.

freight train *n* train de marchandises *m*.

French bean *n* haricot vert *m*.

French fries *npl* frites *fpl*.

French window *n* porte-fenêtre *f*.

frenzied *adj* fou, frénétique.

frenzy *n* frénésie *f*; folie *f*.

frequency *n* fréquence *f*.

frequent *adj* fréquent; **~ly** *adv* fréquemment; * *vt* fréquenter.

fresco *n* fresque *f*.

fresh *adj* frais; nouveau, récent; **~ water** *n* eau douce *f*.

freshen *vt* rafraîchir; * *vi* se rafraîchir.

freshly *adv* nouvellement; récemment.

freshman *n* nouveau *m*, -elle *f*.

freshness *n* fraîcheur *f*.

freshwater *adj* d'eau douce.

fret *vi* s'agiter, se tracasser.

friar *n* moine *m*.

friction *n* friction *f*.

Friday *n* vendredi *m*; **Good ~** Vendredi Saint *m*.

friend *n* ami *m*, -e *f*.

friendless *adj* sans amis.

friendliness *n* amitié, bienveillance *f*.

friendly *adj* amical.

friendship *n* amitié *f*.

frieze *n* frise *f*.

frigate *n* (*mar*) frégate *f*.

fright *n* peur, frayeur *f*.

frighten *vt* effrayer.

frightened *adj* effrayé, apeuré.

frightening *adj* effrayant.

frightful *adj* épouvantable, effroyable; **~ly** *adv* affreusement, effroyablement.

frigid *adj* froid, glacé; frigide; **~ly** *adv* froidement.

fringe *n* frange *f*.

fringe benefits *npl* avantages en nature *mpl*.

frisk *vt* fouiller.

frisky *adj* vif, fringant.

fritter *vt*: **to ~ away** gaspiller.

frivolity *n* frivolité *f*.

frivolous *adj* frivole, léger.

frizz(le) *vt* faire trop griller; friser.

frizzy *adj* frisé.

fro *adv*: **to go to and ~** aller et venir.

frock *n* robe *f*.

frog *n* grenouille *f*.

frolic *vi* folâtrer, gambader.

frolicsome *adj* folâtre, gai.

from *prep* de; depuis; à partir de.

front *n* avant, devant *m*; façade *f*; front *m*; * *adj* de devant; premier.

frontal *adj* de front.

front door *n* porte d'entrée *f*.

frontier *n* frontière *f*.

front page *n* première page *f*.

front-wheel drive *n* (*auto*) traction avant *f*.

frost *n* gel *m*; gelée *f*; * *vt* geler.

frostbite *n* engelure *f*.

frostbitten *adj* gelé.

frosted *adj* gelé, givré.

frosty *adj* glacial; givré.

froth *n* écume *f*; * *vi* écumer.

frothy *adj* mousseux, écumeux.

frown *vt* froncer les sourcils; * *n* froncement de sourcils *m*.

frozen *adj* gelé.

frugal *adj* frugal; économique; simple; **~ly** *adv* frugalement.

fruit *n* fruit *m*.

fruiterer *n* fruitier *m*, -ière *f*.

fruiterer's (shop) *n* fruiterie *f*.

fruitful *adj* fécond, fertile; fructueux, utile; **~ly** *adv* fructueusement.

fruitfulness *n* fertilité *f*; caractère fructueux *m*.

fruition *n* réalisation *f*.

fruit juice *n* jus de fruit *m*.

fruitless *adj* stérile; infécond; **~ly** *adv* vainement, inutilement.

fruit salad *n* salade de fruits *f*.

fruit tree *n* arbre fruitier *m*.

frustrate *vt* contrecarrer; annuler.

frustrated *adj* frustré.

frustration *n* frustration *f*.

fry *vt* frire.

frying pan *n* poêle *f*.

fuchsia *n* (*bot*) fuchsia *m*.

fudge *n* caramel *m*.

fuel *n* combustible, carburant *m*.

fuel tank *n* réservoir à carburant *m*.

fugitive *adj*, *n* fugitif *m*, -ive *f*.

fugue *n* (*mus*) fugue *f*.

fulcrum *n* pivot *m*.

fulfill *vt* accomplir; réaliser.

fulfillment *n* accomplissement *m*.

full *adj* plein, rempli; complet; * *adv* pleinement, entièrement.

full-blown *adj* complet.

full-fledged *adj* diplômé, qualifié.

full-length *adj* en pied; de long métrage.

full moon *n* pleine lune *f*.

fullness *n* plénitude *f*; abondance *f*.

full-scale *adj* grandeur nature ; total, complet.

full-time *adj* à plein temps.

fully *adv* pleinement, entièrement.

fulsome *adj* exagéré.

fumble *vi* manier gauchement; farfouiller.

fume *vi* exhaler des vapeurs; rager, fumer; * **~s** *npl* exhalaisons *f pl*.

fumigate *vt* fumiger.

fun *n* amusement *m*; plaisir *m*; **to have ~** (bien) s'amuser.

function *n* fonction *f*.

functional *adj* fonctionnel.

fund *n* fonds *m*; * *vt* financer.

fundamental *adj* fondamental; **~ly** *adv* fondamentalement.

funeral service *n* office des morts *m*.

funeral *n* enterrement *m*.

funereal *adj* funèbre, lugubre.

fungus *n* champignon *m*; moisissure *f*.

funnel *n* entonnoir *m*; cheminée *f*.

funny *adj* amusant; curieux.

fur *n* fourrure *f*.

fur coat *n* manteau de fourrure *m*.

furious *adj* furieux; déchaîné; **~ly** *adv* furieusement.

furlong *n* mesure de longueur (220 yards = 201 mètres), furlong *m*.

furnace n fourneau m; chaudière f.

furnish vt meubler; fournir; pourvoir.

furnishings npl mobilier m.

furniture n meubles mpl.

furrow n sillon m; * vt sillonner; rider.

furry adj à poil.

further adj supplémentaire; plus lointain; * adv plus loin, plus avant; en outre; de plus; * vt faire avancer; favoriser; promouvoir.

further education n formation continue f.

furthermore adv de plus.

furthest adv le plus loin, le plus éloigné.

furtive adj furtif; secret; **~ly** adv furtivement.

fury n fureur f; furie f; colère f.

fuse vt fondre; faire sauter; * vi fondre, sauter; * n fusible m; amorce f.

fuse box n boîte à fusibles f.

fusion n fusion f.

fuss n tapage m; histoires fpl.

fussy adj tatillon, chipoteur.

futile adj futile, vain.

futility n futilité f.

future adj futur; * n futur m; avenir m.

fuzzy adj flou, confus; crépu.

G

gab n (fam) bavardage m.

gabble vi baragouiner; * n charabia m.

gable n pignon m.

gadget n gadget m.

gaffe n gaffe f.

gag n bâillon m; blague f; * vt bâillonner.

gaiety n gaieté f.

gaily adv gaiement.

gain n gain m; bénéfice m; * vt gagner; atteindre.

gait n démarche f; maintien m.

gala n gala m.

galaxy n galaxie f.

gale n grand vent m.

gall n bile f; fiel m.

gallant adj galant.

gall bladder n vésicule biliaire f.

gallery n galerie f.

galley n galère f; cuisine f.

gallon n gallon m (mesure).

gallop n galop m; * vi galoper.

gallows n potence f.

gallstone n calcul biliaire m.

galore adv en abondance.

galvanize vt galvaniser.

gambit n stratagème m.

gamble vi jouer; spéculer; * n risque m; pari m.

gambler n joueur m, -euse f.

gambling n jeu m.

game n jeu m; divertissement m; partie f; gibier m; * vi jouer.

gamekeeper n garde-chasse m.

gaming n jeu m.

gammon n jambon m.

gamut n (mus) gamme f.

gander n jars m.

gang n gang m, bande f.

gangrene n gangrène f.

gangster n gangster m.

gangway n passerelle f.

gap n trou m; vide m; intervalle, écart m.

gape vi être bouche bée; bâiller.

gaping adj béant.

garage n garage m.

garbage n ordures fpl.

garbage can n poubelle f.

garbage man n éboueur m.

garbled adj embrouillé; trompeur.

garden n jardin m.

garden hose n tuyau d'arrosage m.

gardener *n* jardinier *m*, -ière *f*.
gardening *n* jardinage *m*.
gargle *vi* se gargariser.
gargoyle *n* gargouille *f*.
garish *adj* tapageur.
garland *n* guirlande *f*.
garlic *n* ail *m*.
garment *n* vêtement *m*.
garnish *vt* garnir, décorer; * *n* garniture *f*.
garret *n* mansarde *f*.
garrison *n* (*mil*) garnison *f*; * *vt* (*mil*) mettre en garnison; protéger d'une garnison.
garrote *vt* étrangler.
garrulous *adj* locace, bavard.
garter *n* jarretelle *f*.
gas *n* gaz *m*; essence *f*.
gas burner *n* brûleur à gaz *m*.
gas cylinder *n* bouteille de gaz *f*.
gaseous *adj* gazeux.
gas fire *n* radiateur à gaz *m*.
gash *n* entaille *f*; fente *f*; * *vt* entailler.
gasket *n* joint d'étanchéité *m*.
gasp *vi* haleter; * *n* halètements *mpl*.
gas mask *n* masque à gaz *m*.
gas meter *n* compteur à gaz *m*.
gasoline *n* essence *f*.
gas pedal *n* accélérateur *m*.
gas ring *n* brûleur à gaz *m*.
gas station *n* poste d'essence *m*.
gassy *adj* gazeux.
gas tap *n* robinet de gaz *m*.
gastric *adj* gastrique.
gastronomic *adj* gastronomique.
gasworks *npl* usine de gaz *f*.
gate *n* porte *f*; portail *m*.
gateway *n* porte *f*.
gather *vt* rassembler; ramasser; comprendre; * *vi* se rassembler.
gathering *n* réunion *f*; récolte *f*.
gauche *adj* gauche.
gaudy *adj* criard.
gauge *n* calibre *m*; écartement *m*; * *vt* mesurer; calibrer.
gaunt *adj*, *n* maigre *mf*.
gauze *n* gaze *f*.
gay *adj* gai; vif; homosexuel.

gaze *vi* contempler, considérer; * *n* regard *m*.
gazelle *n* gazelle *f*.
gazette *n* gazette *f*.
gazetteer *n* répertoire géographique *m*.
gear *n* équipement *m*, matériel *m*; appareil *m*; affaires *fpl*; vitesse *f*.
gearbox *n* boîte de vitesses *f*.
gear shift *n* levier de vitesse *m*.
gear wheel *n* roue d'engrenage *f*.
gel *n* gel *m*.
gelatin(e) *n* gélatine *f*.
gelignite *n* gélignite *f*.
gem *n* pierre précieuse *f*; perle *f*.
Gemini *n* Gémeaux *mpl* (signe du zodiaque).
gender *n* genre *m*.
gene *n* gène *m*.
genealogical *adj* généalogique.
genealogy *n* généalogie *f*.
general *adj* général; commun, usuel; **in ~** en général; **~ly** *adv* généralement; * *n* général *m*; générale *f*.
general delivery *n* poste restante *f*.
general election *n* élections générales *fpl*.
generality *n* généralité; majeure partie *f*.
generalization *n* généralisation *f*.
generalize *vt* généraliser.
generate *vt* engendrer; produire; causer.
generation *n* génération *f*.
generator *n* générateur *m*.
generic *adj* générique.
generosity *n* générosité, libéralité *f*.
generous *adj* généreux.
genetics *npl* génétique *f*.
genial *adj* bienveillant; doux.
genitals *npl* organes génitaux *mpl*.
genitive *n* (*gr*) génitif *m*.
genius *n* génie *m*.
genteel *adj* élégant.
gentile *n* gentil *m*, -ille *f*.
gentle *adj* doux, *f* douce, modéré.

gentleman n gentleman m.

gentleness n douceur f.

gently adv doucement.

gentry n aristocratie f.

gents n toilettes pour hommes fpl.

genuflexion n génuflexion f.

genuine adj authentique; sincère; **~ly** adv authentiquement; sincèrement.

genus n genre m.

geographer n géographe mf.

geographical adj géographique.

geography n géographie f.

geological adj géologique.

geologist n géologue mf.

geology n géologie f.

geometric(al) adj géométrique.

geometry n géométrie f.

geranium n (bot) géranium m.

geriatric n malade gériatrique mf; * adj gériatrique.

germ n (bot) germe m.

germinate vi germer.

gesticulate vi gesticuler.

gesture n geste m.

get vt avoir; obtenir; atteindre; gagner; attraper; * vi devenir; aller; **to ~ the better** avoir l'avantage, surpasser.

geyser n geyser m; chauffe-eau m invar.

ghastly adj affreux; sinistre.

gherkin n cornichon m.

ghost n fantôme, spectre m.

ghostly adj spectral.

giant n géant m, -e f.

gibberish n charabia m; sornettes fpl.

gibe vi se moquer; * n moquerie f.

giblets npl abattis (de volaille) mpl.

giddiness n vertige m.

giddy adj vertigineux.

gift n cadeau m; don m; talent m.

gifted adj talentueux; doué.

gift voucher n bon-cadeau m.

gigantic adj gigantesque.

giggle vi rire bêtement.

gild vt dorer.

gilding, gilt n dorure f.

gill n quart de pinte m; **~s** pl branchies fpl.

gilt-edged adj de premier ordre.

gimmick n truc m.

gin n gin m.

ginger n gingembre m.

gingerbread n pain d'épice m.

ginger-haired adj roux, f rousse.

giraffe n girafe f.

girder n poutre f.

girdle n gaine f; ceinture f.

girl n fille f.

girlfriend n amie f; petite amie f.

girlish adj de fille.

giro n virement m.

girth n sangle f; circonférence f.

gist n essence f.

give vt donner; offrir; prononcer, faire; consacrer; **to ~ away** offrir; trahir; révéler; **to ~ back** rendre; **to ~ in** vi céder; vt remettre; **to ~ off** dégager; **to ~ out** distribuer; **to ~ up** vi abandonner; vt renoncer à.

gizzard n gésier m.

glacial adj glacial.

glacier n glacier m.

glad adj joyeux, content; **I am ~ to see that** je me réjouis de voir que; **~ly** adv avec joie, avec plaisir.

gladden vt réjouir.

gladiator n gladiateur m.

glamor n attrait m, séduction f.

glamorous adj attrayant, séduisant.

glance n regard m; * vi regarder; jeter un coup d'oeil.

glancing adj oblique.

gland n glande f.

glare n éclat m; regard féroce m; * vi éblouir, briller; lancer des regards indignés.

glaring adj éclatant; évident; furieux.

glass n verre m; longue-vue f; miroir m; **~es** pl lunettes fpl; * adj en verre.

glassware n verrerie f.

glassy adj vitreux, cristallin.

glaze *vt* vitrer; vernisser.

glazier *n* vitrier *m*.

gleam *n* rayon *m*; * *vi* rayonner, briller.

gleaming *adj* brillant.

glean *vt* glaner.

glee *n* joie *f*; exultation *f*.

glen *n* vallée *f*.

glib *adj* facile; volubile; **~ly** *adv* facilement; volubilement.

glide *vi* glisser; planer.

gliding *n* vol plané *m*.

glimmer *n* lueur *f*; * *vi* luire.

glimpse *n* aperçu *m*; vision *f*; * *vt* entrevoir.

glint *vi* briller, scintiller.

glisten, glitter *vi* luire, briller.

gloat *vi* exulter.

global *adj* global; mondial.

globe *n* globe *m*; sphère *f*.

gloom, gloominess *n* obscurité *f*; mélancolie, tristesse *f*; **~ily** *adv* sombrement; tristement.

gloomy *adj* sombre, obscur; triste, mélancolique.

glorification *n* glorification *f*.

glorify *vt* glorifier, célébrer.

glorious *adj* glorieux, illustre; **~ly** *adv* glorieusement.

glory *n* gloire, célébrité *f*.

gloss *n* glose *f*; lustre *m*; * *vt* gloser, interpréter; lustrer; **to ~ over** passer sur.

glossary *n* glossaire *m*.

glossy *adj* lustré, brillant.

glove *n* gant *m*.

glove compartment *n* boîte à gants *f*.

glow *vi* rougeoyer; rayonner; * *n* rougeoiment *m*; éclat *m*; feu *m*.

glower *vi* lancer des regards méchants.

glue *n* colle *f*; * *vt* coller.

gluey *adj* gluant, visqueux.

glum *adj* abattu, triste.

glut *n* surabondance *f*.

glutinous *adj* glutineux.

glutton *n* glouton *m*, -onne *f*.

gluttony *n* gloutonnerie *f*.

glycerine *n* glycérine *f*.

gnarled *adj* noueux.

gnash *vt*: **to ~ one's teeth** grincer des dents.

gnat *n* moucheron *m*.

gnaw *vt* ronger.

gnome *n* gnome *m*.

go *vi* aller; s'en aller, partir; disparaître; se perdre; **to ~ ahead** continuer; **to ~ away** s'en aller; **to ~ back** repartir; **to ~ by** passer; **to ~ for** *vt* se lancer sur; aimer; **to ~ in** entrer; **to ~ off** s'en aller, partir; se passer; se gâter; **to ~ on** continuer; se passer; **to ~ out** sortir; s'éteindre; **to ~ up** monter.

goad *n* aiguillon *m*; * *vt* aiguillonner; stimuler.

go-ahead *adj* entreprenant; * *n* feu vert *m*.

goal *n* but, objectif *m*.

goalkeeper *n* gardien de but *m*.

goalpost *n* poteau de but *m*.

goatherd *n* chevrier *m*, -ière *f*.

gobble *vt* engloutir, avaler.

go-between *n* intermédiaire *mf*.

goblet *n* coupe *f*.

goblin *n* lutin *m*.

God *n* Dieu *m*.

godchild *n* filleul *m*, -e *f*.

goddaughter *n* filleule *f*.

goddess *n* déesse *f*.

godfather *n* parrain *m*.

godforsaken *adj* perdu.

godhead *n* divinité *f*.

godless *adj* impie, athée.

godlike *adj* divin.

godliness *n* piété, dévotion, sainteté *f*.

godly *adj* pieux, dévot, religieux; droit.

godmother *n* marraine *f*.

godsend *n* don du ciel *m*.

godson *n* filleul *m*.

goggle-eyed *adj* aux yeux exorbités de surprise.

goggles *npl* lunettes *fpl*; lunettes de plongée *fpl*.

going *n* départ *m*; sortie *f*; progrès *m*.

gold *n* or *m*.

golden *adj* doré; d'or; excellent; **~ rule** *n* règle d'or *f*.

goldfish *n* poisson rouge *m*.

gold-plated *adj* plaqué or.

goldsmith *n* orfèvre *m*.

golf *n* golf *m*.

golf ball *n* balle de golf *f*.

golf club *n* club de golf *m*.

golf course *n* terrain de golf *m*.

golfer *n* golfeur *m*, -euse *f*.

gondolier *n* gondolier *m*.

gone *adj* parti; perdu; passé; fini; mort, disparu.

gong *n* gong *m*.

good *adj* bon; bienveillant; favorable; valable; * *adv* bien; * *n* bien *m*; avantage *m*; **~s** *pl* biens *mpl*; marchandises *fpl*.

goodbye ! *excl* au revoir!

Good Friday *n* Vendredi Saint *m*.

goodies *npl* gourmandises *fpl*.

good-looking *adj* beau.

good nature *n* bon caractère *m*.

good-natured *adj* qui a bon caractère.

goodness *n* bonté *f*; qualité *f*.

goodwill *n* bienveillance *f*.

goose *n* oie *f*.

gooseberry *n* groseille à maquereau *f*.

goosebumps *npl* chair de poule *f*.

goose-step *n* pas de l'oie *m*.

gore *n* sang *m*; * *vt* blesser d'un coup de corne.

gorge *n* gorge *f*; * *vt* engloutir, avaler.

gorgeous *adj* merveilleux.

gorilla *n* gorille *m*.

gorse *n* ajonc *m*.

gory *adj* sanglant.

goshawk *n* autour *m*.

gospel *n* évangile *m*.

gossamer *n* gaze *f*; toile d'araignée *f*.

gossip *n* commérages, cancans *mpl*; * *vi* cancaner, faire des commérages.

gothic *adj* gothique.

gout *n* goutte *f* (maladie).

govern *vt* gouverner, diriger.

governess *n* gouvernante *f*.

government *n* gouvernement *m*; administration publique *f*.

governor *n* gouverneur *m*.

gown *n* toge *f*; robe *f*; robe de chambre *f*.

grab *vt* saisir.

grace *n* grâce *f*; faveur *f*; pardon *m*; grâces *fpl*; **to say ~** dire le bénédicité; * *vt* orner; honorer.

graceful *adj* gracieux; **~ly** *adv* gracieusement.

gracious *adj* gracieux; favorable; **~ly** *adv* gracieusement.

gradation *n* gradation *f*.

grade *n* grade *m*; degré *m*; classe *f*.

grade crossing *n* passage à niveau *m*.

grade school *n* école primaire *f*.

gradient *n* (*rail*) rampe *f*.

gradual *adj* graduel; **~ly** *adv* graduellement.

graduate *vi* obtenir son diplôme.

graduation *n* remise des diplômes *f*.

graffiti *n* graffiti *mpl*.

graft *n* greffe *f*; * *vt* greffer.

grain *n* grain *m*; graine *f*; céréales *fpl*.

gram *n* gramme *m*.

grammar *n* grammaire *f*.

grammatical *adj*, **~ly** *adv* grammatical(lement).

granary *n* grenier *m*.

grand *adj* grandiose; magnifique.

grandchild *n* petit-fils *m*; petite-fille *f*; **grandchildren** *pl* petits-enfants *m pl*.

grandad *n* pépé *m*.

granddaughter *n* petite-fille *f*; **great- ~** arrière-petite-fille *f*.

grandeur *n* grandeur *f*; pompe *f*.

grandfather *n* grand-père *m*; **great- ~** arrière-grand-père *m*.

grandiose *adj* grandiose.

grandma *n* mémé *f*.

grandmother *n* grand-mère *f*; **great- ~** arrière-grand-mère *f*.

grandparents *npl* grands-parents *mpl*.

grand piano *n* piano à queue *m*.

grandson *n* petit-fils *m*; **great- ~** arrière-petit-fils *m*.

grandstand *n* tribune *f*.

granite *n* granit *m*.

granny *n* mémé *f*.

grant *vt* accorder; **to take for ~ed** considérer comme acquis; * *n* bourse *f*; allocation *f*.

granulate *vt* granuler.

granule *n* granule *m*.

grape *n* raisin *m*; **bunch of ~s** grappe de raisin *f*.

grapefruit *n* pamplemousse *m*.

graph *n* graphe, graphique *m*.

graphic(al) *adj* graphique; pittoresque; **~ally** *adv* graphiquement.

graphics *n* art graphique *m*; graphiques *mpl*.

grapnel *n* (*mar*) grappin *m*.

grasp *vt* saisir, empoigner; comprendre; * *n* poigne *f*; compréhension *f*; prise *f*.

grasping *adj* avide.

grass *n* herbe *f*.

grasshopper *n* sauterelle *f*.

grassland *n* prés *mpl*.

grass-roots *adj* populaire; de base.

grass snake *n* couleuvre *f*.

grassy *adj* herbeux.

grate *n* grille *f*; * *vt* râper; grincer (des dents); * *vi* grincer.

grateful *adj* reconnaissant; **~ly** *adv* avec reconnaissance.

gratefulness *n* gratitude, reconnaissance *f*.

gratification *n* satisfaction *f*.

gratify *vt* satisfaire; faire plaisir à.

gratifying *adj* réjouissant.

grating *n* grillage *m*; grincement *m*; * *adj* grinçant; énervant.

gratis *adv* gratis, gratuitement.

gratitude *n* gratitude, reconnaissance *f*.

gratuitous *adj* gratuit; volontaire; **~ly** *adv* gratuitement.

gratuity *n* gratification *f*.

grave *n* tombe *f*; * *adj* grave, sérieux; **~ly** *adv* gravement, sérieusement.

grave digger *n* fossoyeur *m*.

gravel *n* gravier *m*.

gravestone *n* pierre tombale *f*.

graveyard *n* cimetière *m*.

gravitate *vi* graviter.

gravitation *n* gravitation *f*.

gravity *n* gravité *f*.

gravy *n* jus de viande *m*; sauce *f*.

graze *vt* paître; effleurer; * *vi* paître.

grease *n* graisse *f*; * *vt* graisser.

greaseproof *adj* gras.

greasy *adj* gras.

great *adj* grand; important; fort; **~ly** *adv* énormément.

greatcoat *n* pardessus *m*.

greatness *n* grandeur *f*; importance *f*; pouvoir *m*; noblesse *f*.

greedily *adv* avidement.

greediness, greed *n* avidité *f*; gloutonnerie *f*.

greedy *adj* avide; glouton.

Greek *n* grec (langue) *m*.

green *adj* vert; inexpérimenté; * *n* vert *m*; verdure *f*; **~s** *npl* légumes verts *mpl*.

greenback *n* billet *m*.

green belt *n* zone verte *f*.

green card *n* carte verte *f*; permis de travail *m*.

greenery *n* verdure *f*.

greengrocer *n* marchand(e) de fruits et légumes *m(f)*.

greenhouse *n* serre *f*.

greenish *adj* verdâtre.

greenness *n* verdure *f*; manque d'expérience *m*.

green room *n* foyer des artistes *m*.

greet *vt* saluer; accueillir.

greeting *n* salutation *f*; accueil *m*.

greeting(s) card *n* carte de voeux *f*.

grenade *n* (*mil*) grenade *f*.

grenadier *n* grenadier *m*.

grey *adj* gris; * *n* gris *m*.

grey-haired adj aux cheveux gris.

greyhound n lévrier m.

greyish adj grisâtre; grisonnant.

greyness n couleur grise f; grisaille f.

grid n grille f; réseau m.

gridiron n gril m; terrain de football américain m.

grief n chagrin m, douleur, peine f.

grievance n grief m; doléance f; différend m; injustice f; tort m.

grieve vt peiner, affliger; * vi se chagriner, s'affliger.

grievous adj douloureux; grave, atroce; ~**ly** adv douloureusement; cruellement.

griffin n griffon m.

grill n gril m; grillade f; * vt faire griller; interroger, cuisiner.

grille n grille f.

grim adj peu engageant; sinistre.

grimace n grimace f; moue f.

grime n saleté f.

grimy adj crasseux.

grin n grimace f; sourire m; * vi grimacer; sourire.

grind vt moudre; piler, broyer; affûter, aiguiser; * vi grincer.

grinder n moulin m; rémouleur m; molaire f.

grip n prise f; poignée f; valise f; * vt saisir, agripper.

gripping adj passionnant.

grisly adj horrible; sinistre.

gristle n tendons, nerfs mpl.

gristly adj tendineux.

grit n gravillon m; cran m.

groan vi gémir; grogner; * n gémissement m; grognement m.

grocer n épicier m, -ière f.

groceries npl épicerie f, provisions fpl.

grocer's (shop) n épicerie f.

groggy adj sonné, étourdi.

groin n aine f.

groom n palefrenier m; valet m; marié m; * vt panser; préparer.

groove n rainure f.

grope vt chercher à tâtons; * vi tâtonner.

gross adj gros, corpulent; épais; grossier; brut; ~**ly** adv énormément.

grotesque adj grotesque.

grotto n grotte f.

ground n terre f, sol m; terrain, territoire m; fondement m; raison fondamentale f; fond m; * vt retenir au sol; fonder; mettre une prise de terre à.

ground floor n rez-de-chaussée m.

grounding n connaissances de base fpl.

groundless adj sans fondement; ~**ly** adv sans fondement.

ground staff n personnel au sol m.

groundwork n travaux de préparation mpl.

group n groupe m; * vt regrouper.

grouse n grouse f, coq de bruyère m; * vi grogner.

grove n bosquet m.

grovel vi se traîner; ramper.

grow vt cultiver; faire pousser; * vi pousser; grandir; augmenter; ~ **up** grandir.

grower n cultivateur m, -trice f; producteur m, -trice f.

growing adj croissant; grandissant.

growl vi grogner; * n grognement m.

grown-up n adulte mf.

growth n croissance f; augmentation f; poussée f.

grub n asticot m.

grubby adj sale.

grudge n rancune f; * vt accorder à contrecoeur; vi avoir de la rancune.

grudgingly adv à contrecoeur.

grueling adj difficile, pénible.

gruesome adj horrible.

gruff adj brusque; ~**ly** adv brusquement.

gruffness n brusquerie f.

grumble *vi* grogner; grommeler.

grumpy *adj* ronchon, grincheux.

grunt *vi* grogner; * *n* grognement *m*.

G-string *n* cache-sexe *m*.

guarantee *n* garantie *f*; * *vt* garantir.

guard *n* garde *f*; garde *m*; * *vt* garder; défendre.

guarded *adj* prudent; surveillé.

guardroom *n* (mil) corps de garde *m*.

guardian *n* tuteur *m*, -trice *f*; gardien *m*, -ienne *f*.

guardianship *n* tutelle *f*.

guerrilla *n* guérillero *m*.

guerrilla warfare *n* guérilla *f*.

guess *vt* deviner; supposer; * *vi* deviner; * *n* conjecture *f*.

guesswork *n* conjectures *fpl*.

guest *n* invité *m*, -ée *f*; client *m*, -e *f*.

guest room *n* chambre d'amis *f*.

guffaw *n* éclat de rire *m*.

guidance *n* guidage *m*; direction *f*.

guide *vt* guider, diriger; * *n* guide *m*.

guide dog *n* chien d'aveugle *m*.

guidelines *npl* directives *fpl*.

guidebook *n* guide *m*.

guild *n* association *f*; corporation *f*.

guile *n* astuce *f*.

guillotine *n* guillotine *f*; * *vt* guillotiner.

guilt *n* culpabilité *f*.

guiltless *adj* innocent.

guilty *adj* coupable.

guinea pig *n* cochon d'Inde, cobaye *m*.

guise *n* apparence *f*.

guitar *n* guitare *f*.

gulf *n* golfe *m*; abîme *m*.

gull *n* mouette *f*.

gullet *n* œsophage *m*.

gullibility *n* crédulité *f*.

gullible *adj* crédule.

gully *n* ravine *f*.

gulp *n* gorgée *f*; * *vi*, *vt* avaler.

gum *n* gomme *f*; gencive *f*; chewing-gum *m*; * *vt* coller.

gum tree *n* gommier *m*.

gun *n* pistolet *m*; fusil *m*.

gunboat *n* canonnière *f*.

gun carriage *n* affût de canon *m*.

gunfire *n* coups de feu *mpl*.

gunman *n* homme armé *m*.

gunmetal *n* bronze à canon *m*.

gunner *n* artilleur *m*.

gunnery *n* artillerie *f*.

gunpoint *n*: **at ~** sous la menace d'une arme à feu.

gunpowder *n* poudre à canon *f*.

gunshot *n* coup de feu *m*.

gunsmith *n* armurier *m*.

gurgle *vi* gargouiller.

guru *n* gourou *m*.

gush *vi* jaillir; bouillonner; * *n* jaillissement *m*.

gushing *adj* jaillissant; très exubérant.

gusset *n* soufflet *m*.

gust *n* rafale *f*; bouffée *f*.

gusto *n* plaisir *m*, délectation *f*.

gusty *adj* venteux.

gut *n* intestin *m*; **~s** *npl* coeur au ventre *m*; * *vt* vider.

gutter *n* gouttière *f*; caniveau *m*.

guttural *adj* guttural.

guy *n* mec, type *m*.

guzzle *vt* bouffer, engloutir; avaler.

gym(nasium) *n* gymnase *m*.

gymnast *n* gymnaste *mf*.

gymnastic *adj* gymnastique; **~s** *npl* gymnastique *f*.

gynecologist *n* gynécologue *mf*.

gypsy *n* gitan *m*, -e *f*.

gyrate *vi* tourner.

H

haberdasher *n* mercier *m*, -ière *f*.

haberdashery *n* mercerie *f*.

habit *n* habitude *f*.

habitable *adj* habitable.

habitat *n* habitat *m*.

habitual *adj* habituel; **~ly** *adv* d'habitude, habituellement.

hack *n* coupure, entaille *f*; * *vt* entailler, couper.

hackneyed *adj* rebattu.

haddock *n* aiglefin *m*.

haemorrhage *n* hémorragie *f*.

haemorrhoids *npl* hémorroïdes *fpl*.

hag *n* sorcière *f*.

haggard *adj* décharné; blême; hagard.

haggle *vi* marchander.

hail *n* grêle *f*; * *vt* saluer; * *vi* grêler.

hailstone *n* grêlon *m*.

hair *n* cheveu *m*; poil *m*.

hairbrush *n* brosse à cheveux *f*.

haircut *n* coupe de cheveux *f*.

hairdresser *n* coiffeur *m*, -euse *f*.

hairdryer *n* séchoir à cheveux *m*.

hairless *adj* chauve; sans poils.

hairnet *n* filet à cheveux *m*.

hairpin *n* épingle à cheveux *f*.

hairpin bend *n* virage en épingle à cheveux *m*.

hair remover *n* crème dépilatoire *f*.

hairspray *n* laque à cheveux *f*.

hairstyle *n* coiffure *f*.

hairy *adj* chevelu; poilu.

hale *adj* vigoureux.

half *n* moitié *f*; * *adj* demi; * *adv* à moitié.

half-caste *adj* métis.

half-hearted *adj* peu enthousiaste.

half-hour *n* demi-heure *f*.

half-moon *n* demi-lune *f*.

half-price *adj* à moitié prix.

half-time *n* mi-temps *f*.

halfway *adv* à mi-chemin.

hall *n* vestibule *m*.

hallmark *n* marque *f*.

hallow *vt* consacrer, sanctifier.

hallucination *n* hallucination *f*.

halo *n* halo *m*.

halt *vi* s'arrêter; * *n* arrêt *m*; halte *f*.

halve *vt* couper en deux.

ham *n* jambon *m*.

hamburger *n* hamburger *m*.

hamlet *n* hameau *m*.

hammer *n* marteau *m*; * *vt* marteler.

hammock *n* hamac *m*.

hamper *n* panier *m*; * *vt* embarrasser, entraver.

hamstring *vt* couper les jarrets à.

hand *n* main *f*; ouvrier *m*, -ière *f*; aiguille *f*; **at ~** à portée de main; * *vt* donner, passer.

handbag *n* sac à main *m*.

handbell *n* sonnette *f*.

handbook *n* manuel *m*.

handbrake *n* frein à main *m*.

handcuff *n* menotte *f*.

handful *n* poignée *f*.

handicap *n* handicap *m*.

handicapped *adj* handicapé.

handicraft *n* artisanat *m*.

handiwork *n* travail manuel *m*.

handkerchief *n* mouchoir *m*.

handle *n* manche *m*, queue *f*; anse *f*; poignée *f*; * *vt* manier; traiter, prendre.

handlebars *npl* guidon *m*.

handling *n* maniement *m*; traitement *m*.

handrail *n* garde-fou *m*.

handshake *n* poignée de mains *f*.

handsome *adj* beau; **~ly** *adv* élégamment.

handwriting *n* écriture *f*.

handy *adj* pratique; adroit.

hang *vt* accrocher; pendre; * *vi*

pendre, être accroché; être pendu.

hanger *n* cintre *m*.

hanger-on *n* parasite *m*.

hangings *npl* tapisserie *f*.

hangman *n* bourreau *m*.

hangover *n* gueule de bois *f*.

hang-up *n* complexe *m*.

hanker *vi* avoir envie.

haphazard *adj* fortuit.

hapless *adj* malheureux.

happen *vi* se passer; **I ~ to have one** il se trouve que j'en ai un.

happening *n* événement *m*.

happily *adv* heureusement; gaiement.

happiness *n* bonheur *m*.

happy *adj* heureux.

harangue *n* harangue *f*; * *vt* haranguer.

harass *vt* harceler; tourmenter.

harbinger *n* précurseur *m*.

harbour *n* port *m*; * *vt* héberger; entretenir, nourrir.

hard *adj* dur; pénible; sévère, rigide; **~ of hearing** dur d'oreille; **~ by** tout près.

harden *vt*, *vi* durcir.

hard-headed *adj* réaliste.

hard-hearted *adj* au coeur dur, insensible.

hardiness *n* robustesse *f*.

hardly *adv* à peine; **~ ever** presque jamais.

hardness *n* dureté *f*; difficulté *f*; sévérité *f*.

hardship *n* épreuve(s) *f(pl)*.

hard-up *adj* fauché, sans le sou.

hardware *n* matériel *m*; quincaillerie *f*.

hardwearing *adj* résistant.

hardy *adj* fort, robuste; résistant.

hare *n* lièvre *m*.

hare-brained *adj* écervelé.

hare-lipped *adj* qui a un bec de lièvre.

haricot *n* haricot blanc *m*.

harlequin *n* arlequin *m*.

harm *n* mal *m*; tort *m*; * *vt* faire du mal à; nuire à.

harmful *adj* nuisible.

harmless *adj* inoffensif.

harmonic *adj* harmonique.

harmonious *adj* harmonieux; **~ly** *adv* harmonieusement.

harmonize *vt* harmoniser.

harmony *n* harmonie *f*.

harness *n* harnais *m*; * *vt* harnacher.

harp *n* harpe *f*.

harpist *n* harpiste *mf*.

harpoon *n* harpon *m*.

harpsichord *n* clavecin *m*.

harrow *n* herse *f*.

harry *vt* harceler; dévaster.

harsh *adj* dur; austère; rude; **~ly** *adv* sévèrement; durement.

harshness *n* aspérité, dureté *f*; austérité *f*.

harvest *n* récolte *f*; moisson *f*; * *vt* récolter; moissonner.

harvester *n* moissonneur *m*, -euse *f*; moissonneuse *f* (machine).

hash *n* hachis *m*; gâchis *m*.

hassock *n* agenouilloir *m*.

haste *n* hâte *f*; **to be in ~** être pressé.

hasten *vt* accélérer, hâter; * *vi* se dépêcher.

hastily *adv* à la hâte, précipitamment.

hastiness *n* précipitation *f*.

hasty *adj* hâtif; irréfléchi.

hat *n* chapeau *m*.

hatbox *n* carton à chapeau *m*.

hatch *vt* couver; faire éclore; tramer; * *n* écoutille *f*.

hatchback *n* (*auto*) voiture à hayon arrière *f*.

hatchet *n* hachette *f*.

hatchway *n* (*mar*) écoutille *f*.

hate *n* haine *f*; * *vt* haïr, détester.

hateful *adj* odieux, détestable.

hatred *n* haine *f*.

hatter *n* chapelier *m*, -ière *f*.

haughtily *adv* hautainement.

haughtiness *n* orgueil *m*; hauteur *f*.

haughty *adj* hautain, orgueilleux.

haul *vt* tirer; * *n* prise *f*; butin *m*.

hauler *n* camionneur *m*.

haunch *n* hanche *f*.

haunt *vt* hanter; fréquenter; * *n* repaire *m*.

have *vt* avoir; posséder.

haven *n* refuge *m*.

haversack *n* sac à dos *m*.

havoc *n* ravages *mpl*.

hawk *n* faucon *m*; * *vi* chasser au faucon.

hawthorn *n* aubépine *f*.

hay *n* foin *m*.

hay fever *n* rhume des foins *m*.

hayloft *n* fenil *m*.

hayrick, haystack *n* meule de foin *f*.

hazard *n* risque, danger *m*; * *vt* risquer.

hazardous *adj* risqué, dangereux.

haze *n* brume *f*.

hazel *n* noisetier *m*; * *adj* noisette.

hazelnut *n* noisette *f*.

hazy *adj* brumeux.

he *pn* il.

head *n* tête *f*; chef *m*; esprit *m*; * *vt* conduire; **to ~ for** se diriger vers.

headache *n* mal de tête *m*.

headdress *n* coiffe *f*.

headland *n* promontoire *m*.

headlight *n* phare *m*.

headline *n* titre *m*.

headlong *adv* à toute allure.

headmaster *n* directeur *m*.

head office *n* siège social *m*.

headphones *npl* écouteurs *mpl*.

headquarters *npl* (*mil*) quartier général *m*; siège social *m*.

headroom *n* hauteur *f*.

headstrong *adj* têtu.

headwaiter *n* maître d'hôtel *m*.

headway *n* progrès *m(pl)*.

heady *adj* capiteux.

heal *vt*, *vi* guérir.

health *n* santé *f*.

healthiness *n* bonne santé *f*.

healthy *adj* en bonne santé; sain.

heap *n* tas *m*; * *vt* entasser.

hear *vt* entendre; écouter; * *vi* entendre; avoir des nouvelles.

hearing *n* ouïe *f*.

hearing aid *n* audiophone *m*.

hearsay *n* rumeur *f*.

hearse *n* corbillard *m*.

heart *n* coeur *m*; **by ~** par cœur; **with all my ~** de tout cœur.

heart attack *n* crise cardiaque *f*.

heartbreaking *adj* à fendre le cœur.

heartburn *n* acidité *f*.

heart failure *n* arrêt cardiaque *m*.

heartfelt *adj* sincère.

hearth *n* foyer *m*.

heartily *adv* sincèrement, cordialement.

heartiness *n* cordialité, sincérité *f*.

heartless *adj* cruel; **~ly** *adv* cruellement.

hearty *adj* cordial.

heat *n* chaleur *f*; * *vt* chauffer.

heater *n* radiateur *m*.

heather *n* (*bot*) bruyère *f*.

heathen *n* païen *m*, païenne *f*; **~ish** *adj* sauvage, barbare.

heating *n* chauffage *m*.

heatwave *n* onde de chaleur *f*.

heave *vt* lever; tirer; * *n* effort *m*.

heaven *n* ciel *m*.

heavenly *adj* divin.

heavily *adv* lourdement.

heaviness *n* lourdeur *f*.

heavy *adj* lourd, pesant; considérable.

Hebrew *n* hébreu *m* (langue).

heckle *vt* interrompre.

hectic *adj* agité.

hedge *n* haie *f*; * *vt* entourer d'une haie.

hedgehog *n* hérisson *m*.

heed *vt* tenir compte de; * *n* soin *m*; attention *f*.

heedless *adj* inattentif, étourdi; **~ly** *adv* étourdiment.

heel *n* talon *m*; **to take to one's ~s** prendre ses jambes à son cou.

hefty *adj* fort; gros.

heifer n génisse f.

height n hauteur f; altitude f.

heighten vt rehausser; augmenter; intensifier.

heinous adj atroce.

heir n héritier m; ~ **apparent** héritier présomptif m.

heiress n héritière f.

heirloom n héritage m.

helicopter n hélicoptère m.

hell n enfer m.

hellish adj infernal.

helm n (mar) barre f.

helmet n casque m.

help vt aider, secourir; **I cannot ~ it** je n'y peux rien; je ne peux pas m'en empêcher; * n aide f; secours m.

helper n aide mf.

helpful adj utile; qui rend service.

helping n portion f.

helpless adj impuissant; ~**ly** adv désespérément; sans pouvoir rien faire.

helter-skelter adv n'importe comment, en désordre.

hem n ourlet m; * vt ourler.

he-man n dur, mâle m.

hemisphere n hémisphère m.

hemp n chanvre m.

hen n poule f.

henchman n acolyte m.

henceforth, henceforward adv dorénavant.

hen-house n poulailler m.

hepatitis n hépatite f.

her pn son, sa, ses; elle; la; lui.

herald n héraut m.

heraldry n héraldique f.

herb n herbe f; ~**s** pl fines herbes fpl.

herbaceous adj herbacé.

herbalist n herboriste mf.

herbivorous adj herbivore.

herd n troupeau m.

here adv ici.

hereabout(s) adv dans les environs.

hereafter adv plus tard; ci-après.

hereby adv par la présente.

hereditary adj héréditaire.

heredity n hérédité f.

heresy n hérésie f.

heretic n, adj hérétique mf.

herewith adv avec ceci.

heritage n patrimoine, héritage m.

hermetic adj hermétique; ~**ly** adv hermétiquement.

hermit n ermite m.

hermitage n ermitage m.

hernia n hernie f.

hero n héros m.

heroic adj héroïque; ~**ally** adv héroïquement.

heroine n héroïne f.

heroism n héroïsme m.

heron n héron m.

herring n hareng m.

hers pn le sien, la sienne, le(s) sien(ne)s, à elle.

herself pn elle-même.

hesitant adj hésitant.

hesitate vi hésiter.

hesitation n hésitation f.

heterogeneous adj hétérogène.

heterosexual adj, n hétérosexuel m, -elle f.

hew vt tailler; couper.

heyday n apogée m.

hi excl salut!

hiatus n (gr) hiatus m.

hibernate vi hiberner.

hiccup n hoquet m; * vi avoir le hoquet.

hickory n noyer d'Amérique m.

hide vt cacher; * n cuir m; peau f.

hideaway n cachette f.

hideous adj hideux; horrible; ~**ly** adv horriblement.

hiding-place n cachette f.

hierarchy n hiérarchie f.

hieroglyphic adj hiéroglyphique; * n hiéroglyphe m.

hi-fi n hi-fi f invar.

higgledy-piggledy adv pêle-mêle.

high adj haut; élevé.

high altar n maître-autel m.

high chair n chaise haute f.

high-handed *adj* tyrannique.

highlands *npl* terres monta-gneuses *fpl*.

highlight *n* point fort *m*.

highly *adj* extrêmement, haute-ment.

highness *n* hauteur *f*; altesse *f*.

high school *n* lycée *m*.

high-strung *adj* nerveux, tendu.

high water *n* marée haute *f*.

highway *n* grande route *f*.

hike *vi* faire une randonnée.

hijack *vt* détourner.

hijacker *n* pirate de l'air *m*.

hilarious *adj* hilarant; hilare.

hill *n* colline *f*.

hillock *n* petite colline *f*.

hillside *n* coteau *m*.

hilly *adj* montagneux.

hilt *n* poignée *f*.

him *pn* lui; le.

himself *pn* lui-même; soi.

hind *adj* derrière; * *n* biche *f*.

hinder *vt* gêner, entraver.

hindrance *n* gêne *f*, obstacle *m*.

hindmost *adj* dernier.

hindquarter *n* arrière-train *m*.

hindsight *n*: **with ~** rétrospec-tivement.

hinge *n* charnière *f*; gond *m*.

hint *n* allusion *f*; insinuation *f*; * *vt* insinuer; suggérer.

hip *n* hanche *f*.

hippopotamus *n* hippopotame *m*.

hire *vt* louer; * *n* location *f*.

his *pn* son, sa, ses; le sien, la sienne, le(s) sien(ne)s; à lui.

Hispanic *adj* hispanique.

hiss *vt, vi* siffler.

historian *n* historien *m*, -ienne *f*.

historic(al) *adj* historique; **~ally** *adv* historiquement.

history *n* histoire *f*.

histrionic *adj* théâtral.

hit *vt* frapper; atteindre; heurter; * *n* coup *m*; succès *m*.

hitch *vt* accrocher; * *n* nœud *m*; anicroche *f*.

hitch-hike *vi* faire du stop.

hitherto *adv* jusqu'à présent, jusqu'ici.

hive *n* ruche *f*.

hoard *n* stock *m*; trésor caché *m*; * *vt* accumuler, amasser.

hoar-frost *n* givre *m*.

hoarse *adj* rauque; **~ly** *adv* d'une voix rauque.

hoarseness *n* voix rauque *f*.

hoax *n* canular *m*; * *vt* faire un canular à.

hobble *vi* boitiller.

hobby *n* passe-temps *m invar*.

hobbyhorse *n* cheval de bataille *m*.

hobo *n* vagabond *m*.

hockey *n* hockey *m*.

hodge-podge *n* confusion *f*.

hoe *n* binette *f*; * *vt* biner.

hog *n* porc *m*.

hoist *vt* hisser; * *n* grue *f*.

hold *vt* tenir; détenir; contenir; **to ~ on to** se tenir à; * *vi* valoir; * *n* prise *f*; pouvoir *m*.

holder *n* détenteur *m*, -trice *f*; titulaire *mf*.

holding *n* possession *f*.

holdup *n* hold-up *m*; retard *m*.

hole *n* trou *m*.

holiday *n* jour de congé *m*; jour férié *m*; **~s** *pl* vacances *fpl*.

holiness *n* sainteté *f*.

hollow *adj* creux; * *n* creux *m*; * *vt* creuser, vider.

holly *n* (*bot*) houx *m*.

hollyhock *n* rose trémière *f*.

holocaust *n* holocauste *m*.

holster *n* étui de révolver *m*.

holy *adj* saint; bénit; sacré.

holy water *n* eau bénite *f*.

holy week *n* semaine sainte *f*.

homage *n* hommage *m*.

home *n* maison *f*; patrie *f*; domi-cile *m*; **~ly** *adj* simple.

home address *n* domicile *m*.

homeless *adj* sans abri.

homeliness *n* simplicité *f*.

homely *adj* simple.

home-made *adj* fait maison.

homeopathist *n* homéopathe *mf*.

homeopathy n homéopathie f.
homesick adj nostalgique, qui a le mal du pays.
homesickness n nostalgie f, mal du pays m.
hometown n ville natale f.
homeward adj vers chez soi; vers son pays.
homework n devoirs mpl.
homicidal adj homicide.
homicide n homicide m; homicide mf.
homogeneous adj homogène.
homosexual adj, n homosexuel m, -elle f.
honest adj honnête; ~ly adv honnêtement.
honesty n honnêteté f.
honey n miel m.
honeycomb n rayon de miel m.
honeymoon n lune de miel f.
honeysuckle n (bot) chèvrefeuille m.
honor n honneur m; * vt honorer.
honorable adj honorable.
honorably adv honorablement.
honorary adj honoraire.
hood n capot m; capuche f.
hoodlum n truand m.
hoof n sabot m.
hook n crochet m; hameçon m; **by ~ or by crook** coûte que coûte; * vt accrocher.
hooked adj crochu.
hooligan n vandale m.
hoop n cerceau m.
hooter n sirène f.
hop n (bot) houblon m; saut m; * vi sauter.
hope n espoir m, espérance f; * vi espérer.
hopeful adj plein d'espoir; prometteur; ~ly adv avec espoir.
hopefulness n bon espoir m.
hopeless adj désespéré; ~ly adv désespérément.
horde n horde f.
horizon n horizon m.
horizontal adj horizontal; ~ly adv horizontalement.

hormone n hormone f.
horn n corne f.
horned adj à cornes.
hornet n frelon m.
horny adj calleux.
horoscope n horoscope m.
horrendous adj horrible.
horrible adj horrible.
horribly adv horriblement; énormément.
horrid adj horrible.
horrific adj horrible, affreux.
horrify vt horrifier.
horror n horreur f.
horror film n film d'horreur m.
hors d'oeuvre n hors-d'oeuvre m invar.
horse n cheval m.
horseback adv: **on ~** à cheval.
horse-breaker n dresseur (-euse) de chevaux m(f).
horse chesnut n marron d'Inde m.
horsefly n taon m.
horseman n cavalier m.
horsemanship n équitation f.
horsepower n cheval-vapeur m; puissance en chevaux f.
horse race n course de chevaux f.
horseradish n raifort m.
horseshoe n fer à cheval m.
horsewoman n cavalière f.
horticulture n horticulture f.
horticulturist n horticulteur m, -trice f.
hose-pipe n tuyau m.
hosiery n bonneterie f.
hospitable adj hospitalier.
hospitably adv avec hospitalité.
hospital n hôpital m.
hospitality n hospitalité f.
host n hôte m; hostie f.
hostage n otage m.
hostess n hôtesse f.
hostile adj hostile.
hostility n hostilité f.
hot adj chaud; épicé.
hotbed n foyer m.
hotdog n hot-dog m.

hotel *n* hôtel *m.*
hotelier *n* hôtelier *m*, -ière *f.*
hotheaded *adj* exalté.
hot-house *n* serre *f.*
hotline *n* téléphone rouge *m.*
hotplate *n* plaque chauffante *f.*
hotly *adv* violemment.
hound *n* chien de chasse *m.*
hour *n* heure *f.*
hour-glass *n* sablier *m.*
hourly *adv* toutes les heures.
house *n* maison *f*; maisonnée *f*;
  * *vt* loger.
houseboat *n* péniche *f.*
housebreaker *n* cambrioleur *m.*
housebreaking *n* cambriolage *m.*
household *n* famille *f*, ménage *m.*
householder *n* propriétaire *mf*;
  chef de famille *m.*
housekeeper *n* gouvernante *f.*
housekeeping *n* travaux ménagers *mpl.*
houseless *adv* sans abri.
house-warming party *n* pendai-
  son de crémaillère *f.*
housewife *n* ménagère *f.*
housework *n* travaux ménagers
  mpl.
housing *n* logement *m.*
housing development *n* urbanisation *f.*
hovel *n* taudis *m.*
hover *vi* planer.
how *adv* comme; comment; **~ do
  you do!** enchanté.
however *adv* de quelque manière
  que; cependant, néanmoins.
howl *vi* hurler; * *n* hurlement *m.*
hub *n* centre *m*; moyeu *m.*
hubbub *n* vacarme *m.*
hubcap *n* enjoliveur *m.*
hue *n* teinte *f*; nuance *f.*
huff *n*: **in a ~** fâché.
hug *vt* étreindre; * *n* étreinte *f.*
huge *adj* énorme; **~ly** *adv* énormément.
hulk *n* (*mar*) carcasse *f*; ponton *m.*
hull *n* (*mar*) coque *f.*
hum *vi* chantonner.
human *adj* humain.

humane *adj* humain; **~ly** *adv*
  humainement.
humanist *n* humaniste *mf.*
humanitarian *adj* humanitaire.
humanity *n* humanité *f.*
humanize *vt* humaniser.
humanly *adv* humainement.
humble *adj* humble, modeste; * *vt*
  humilier.
humbleness *n* humilité *f.*
humbly *adv* humblement.
humbug *n* blagues *fpl.*
humdrum *adj* monotone.
humid *adj* humide.
humidity *n* humidité *f.*
humiliate *vt* humilier.
humiliation *n* humiliation *f.*
humility *n* humilité *f.*
humming-bird *n* colibri *m.*
humorist *n* humoriste *mf.*
humorous *adj* humoristique; **~ly**
  adv avec humour.
humour *n* sens de l'humour *m*,
  humour *m*; * *vt* complaire à.
hump *n* bosse *f.*
hunch *n* bosse *f*; **~backed** *adj*
  bossu.
hundred *adj* cent; * *n* centaine *f.*
hundredth *adj* centième.
hundredweight *n* quintal *m.*
hunger *n* faim *f*; * *vi* avoir faim.
hunger strike *n* grève de la faim
  f.
hungrily *adv* avidement.
hungry *adj* qui a faim, affamé.
hunt *vt* chasser; poursuivre; chercher; * *vi* chasser; * *n* chasse *f.*
hunter *n* chasseur *m.*
hunting *n* chasse *f.*
huntsman *n* chasseur *m.*
hurdle *n* haie *f.*
hurl *vt* lancer avec violence, jeter.
hurricane *n* ouragan *m.*
hurried *adj* fait à la hâte; précipité; **~ly** *adv* hâtivement; précipitamment.
hurry *vt* presser; * *vi* se presser,
  se dépêcher; * *n* hâte *f.*
hurt *vt* faire mal à; blesser; * *n*
  mal *m.*

hurtful *adj* blessant; **~ly** *adv* de manière blessante.
husband *n* mari *m*.
husbandry *n* agriculture *f*.
hush! chut!, silence!; * *vt* faire taire; * *vi* se taire.
husk *n* coque *f*.
huskiness *n* voix rauque *f*.
husky *adj* rauque.
hustings *n* plate-forme électorale *f*.
hustle *vt* pousser avec force, bousculer.
hut *n* cabane, hutte *f*.
hutch *n* clapier *m*.
hyacinth *n* jacinthe *f*.
hydrant *n* bouche d'incendie *f*.
hydraulic *adj* hydraulique; **~s** *npl* hydraulique *f*.
hydroelectric *adj* hydroélectrique.
hydrofoil *n* hydrofoil *m*.

hydrogen *n* hydrogène *m*.
hydrophobia *n* hydrophobie *f*.
hyena *n* hyène *f*.
hygiene *n* hygiène *f*.
hygienic *adj* hygiénique.
hymn *n* hymne *m*.
hyperbole *n* hyperbole *f*.
hypermarket *n* hypermarché *m*.
hyphen *n* (*gr*) trait d'union *m*.
hypochondria *n* hypocondrie *f*.
hypochondriac *adj*, *n* hypocondriaque *mf*.
hypocrisy *n* hypocrisie *f*.
hypocrite *n* hypocrite *mf*.
hypocritical *adj* hypocrite.
hypothesis *n* hypothèse *f*.
hypothetical *adj*, **~ly** *adv* hypothétique(ment).
hysterical *adj* hystérique.
hysterics *npl* hystérie *f*; crise de nerfs *f*.

I

I *pn* je, j'; moi
ice *n* glace *f*; * *vt* glacer; geler.
ice-ax *n* piolet *m*.
iceberg *n* iceberg *m*.
ice-bound *adj* fermé par les glaces.
icebox *n* glacière *f*.
ice cream *n* glace *f*.
ice rink *n* patinoire *f*.
ice skating *n* patinage sur glace *m*.
icicle *n* stalactite *f*.
iconoclast *n* iconoclaste *mf*.
icy *adj* glacé.
idea *n* idée *f*.
ideal *adj* idéal; **~ly** *adv* idéalement.
idealist *n* idéaliste *mf*.
identical *adj* identique.
identification *n* identification *f*.
identify *vt* identifier.
identity *n* identité *f*.

ideology *n* idéologie *f*.
idiom *n* expression idiomatique *f*.
idiomatic *adj* idiomatique.
idiosyncrasy *n* idiosyncrasie *f*.
idiot *n* imbécile *mf*.
idiotic *adj* idiot, bête.
idle *adj* désœuvré; au repos; inutile.
idleness *n* paresse *f*; oisiveté *f*.
idler *n* paresseux *m*, -euse *f*.
idly *adv* oisivement; paresseusement; vainement.
idol *n* idole *f*.
idolatry *n* idôlatrie *f*.
idolize *vt* idôlatrer.
idyllic *adj* idyllique.
i.e. *adv* c.-à-d., c'est-à-dire.
if *conj* si; **~ not** sinon.
igloo *n* igloo *m*.
ignite *vt* allumer, enflammer.
ignition *n* (*chem*) ignition *f*; allumage *m*.

ignition key *n* clé de contact *f.*
ignoble *adj* ignoble; bas.
ignominious *adj* ignominieux;
  ~ly *adv* ignominieusement.
ignominy *n* ignominie, infamie *f.*
ignoramus *n* ignorant *m*, -e *f.*
ignorance *n* ignorance *f.*
ignorant *adj* ignorant; **~ly** *adv*
  par ignorance.
ignore *vt* ne pas tenir compte de.
ill *adj* malade; * *n* mal *m*; dommage *m*; * *adv* mal.
ill-advised *adj* malavisé.
illegal *adj* **~ly** *adv* illégal(ement).
illegality *n* illégalité *f.*
illegible *adj* illisible.
illegibly *adv* illisiblement.
illegitimacy *n* illégitimité *f.*
illegitimate *adj* illégitime; **~ly**
  adv illégitimement.
ill feeling *n* rancoeur *f.*
illicit *adj* illicite.
illiterate *adj* analphabète, illettré.
illness *n* maladie *f.*
illogical *adj* illogique.
ill-timed *adj* inopportun.
ill-treat *vt* maltraiter.
illuminate *vt* illuminer.
illumination *n* illumination *f.*
illusion *n* illusion *f.*
illusory *adj* illusoire.
illustrate *vt* illustrer.
illustration *n* illustration *f.*
illustrative *adj* qui illustre.
illustrious *adj* illustre.
ill-will *n* malveillance *f.*
image *n* image *f.*
imagery *n* images *fpl.*
imaginable *adj* imaginable.
imaginary *adj* imaginaire.
imagination *n* imagination *f.*
imaginative *adj* imaginatif.
imagine *vt* imaginer.
imbalance *n* déséquilibre *m.*
imbecile *adj* imbécile, idiot.
imbibe *vt* boire; imbiber; absorber.
imbue *vt* imprégner.
imitate *vt* imiter.
imitation *n* imitation *f.*

imitative *adj* imitatif.
immaculate *adj* immaculé.
immaterial *adj* insignifiant.
immature *adj* pas mûr.
immeasurable *adj* incommensu-
  rable.
immeasurably *adv* immensément.
immediate *adj* immédiat; **~ly**
  adv immédiatement.
immense *adj* immense; énorme;
  ~ly *adv* immensément.
immensity *n* immensité *f.*
immerse *vt* immerger.
immersion *n* immersion *f.*
immigrant *n* immigrant *m*, -e *f.*
immigration *n* immigration *f.*
imminent *adj* imminent.
immobile *adj* immobile.
immobility *n* immobilité *f.*
immoderate *adj* immodéré, excessif; **~ly** *adv* immodérément.
immodest *adj* immodeste.
immoral *adj* immoral.
immorality *n* immoralité *f.*
immortal *adj* immortel.
immortality *n* immortalité *f.*
immortalize *vt* immortaliser.
immune *adj* immunisé.
immunity *n* immunité *f.*
immunize *vt* immuniser.
immutable *adj* immuable.
imp *n* lutin *m.*
impact *n* impact *m.*
impair *vt* diminuer; affaiblir.
impale *vt* empaler.
impalpable *adj* impalpable.
impart *vt* communiquer.
impartial *adj* **~ly** *adv* impar-
  tial(ement).
impartiality *n* impartialité *f.*
impassable *adj* impraticable; infranchissable.
impasse *n* impasse *f.*
impassive *adj* impassible.
impatience *n* impatience *f.*
impatient *adj* impatient; **~ly** *adv*
  impatiemment.
impeach *vt* accuser.
impeccable *adj* impeccable.

impecunious *adj* impécunieux.
impede *vt* empêcher; entraver.
impediment *n* obstacle *m*.
impel *vt* pousser.
impending *adj* imminent.
impenetrable *adj* impénétrable.
imperative *adj* impératif.
imperceptible *adj* imperceptible.
imperceptibly *adv* imperceptiblement.
imperfect *adj*, **~ly** imparfait(ement); * *n* (*gr*) imparfait *m*.
imperfection *n* imperfection *f*; défaut *m*.
imperial *adj* impérial.
imperialism *n* impérialisme *m*.
imperious *adj* impérieux; **~ly** *adv* impérieusement.
impermeable *adj* imperméable.
impersonal *adj*, **~ly** *adv* impersonel(lement).
impersonate *vt* se faire passer pour.
impertinence *n* impertinence *f*.
impertinent *adj* impertinent; **~ly** *adv* impertinemment.
imperturbable *adj* imperturbable.
impervious *adj* imperméable; indifférent.
impetuosity *n* impétuosité *f*.
impetuous *adj* impétueux; **~ly** *adv* impétueusement.
impetus *n* élan *m*.
impiety *n* impiété *f*.
impinge (on) *vi* affecter; empiéter (sur).
impious *adj* impie.
implacable *adj* implacable.
implacably *adv* implacablement.
implant *vt* implanter.
implement *n* outil *m*; ustensile *m*.
implicate *vt* impliquer.
implication *n* implication *f*.
implicit *adj* implicite; **~ly** *adv* implicitement.
implore *vt* supplier.
imply *vt* supposer.
impolite *adj* impoli.
impoliteness *n* impolitesse *f*.

impolitic *adj* imprudent; impolitique.
import *vt* importer; * *n* importation *f*.
importance *n* importance *f*.
important *adj* important.
importation *n* importation *f*.
importer *n* importateur *m*, -trice *f*.
importunate *adj* importun.
importune *vt* importuner.
importunity *n* importunité *f*.
impose *vt* imposer.
imposing *adj* imposant.
imposition *n* imposition *f*.
impossibility *n* impossibilité *f*.
impossible *adj* impossible.
impostor *n* imposteur *m*.
impotence *n* impotence *f*.
impotent *adj* impotent; **~ly** *adv* faiblement.
impound *vt* confisquer.
impoverish *vt* appauvrir.
impoverished *adj* appauvri.
impoverishment *n* appauvrissement *m*.
impracticability *n* impraticabilité *f*.
impracticable *adj* impraticable.
impractical *adj* peu pratique.
imprecation *n* imprécation, malédiction *f*.
imprecise *adj* imprécis.
impregnable *adj* inexpugnable.
impregnate *vt* imprégner; féconder.
impregnation *n* fécondation *f*; imprégnation *f*.
impress *vt* impressionner.
impression *n* impression *f*; édition *f*.
impressionable *adj* impressionnable.
impressive *adj* impressionnant.
imprint *n* empreinte *f*; * *vt* imprimer; marquer.
imprison *vt* emprisonner.
imprisonment *n* emprisonnement *m*.
improbability *n* improbabilité *f*.

improbable *adj* improbable.

impromptu *adj* impromptu.

improper *adj* indécent; déplacé; impropre; **~ly** *adv* indécemment; de manière déplacée; improprement.

impropriety *n* impropriété *f*; inconvenance *f*.

improve *vt* améliorer; * *vi* s'améliorer.

improvement *n* amélioration *f*.

improvident *adj* imprévoyant.

improvise *vt* improviser.

imprudence *n* imprudence *f*.

imprudent *adj* imprudent.

impudence *n* impudence *f*.

impudent *adj* impudent; **~ly** *adv* impudemment.

impugn *vt* attaquer.

impulse *n* impulsion *f*.

impulsive *adj* impulsif.

impunity *n* impunité *f*.

impure *adj* impur; **~ly** *adv* impurement.

impurity *n* impureté *f*.

in *prep* dans; en.

inability *n* incapacité *f*.

inaccessible *adj* inaccessible.

inaccuracy *n* inexactitude *f*.

inaccurate *adj* inexact.

inaction *n* inaction *f*.

inactive *adj* inactif.

inactivity *n* inactivité *f*.

inadequate *adj* inadéquat.

inadmissible *adj* inadmissible.

inadvertently *adv* par inadvertance.

inalienable *adj* inaliénable.

inane *adj* inepte.

inanimate *adj* inanimé.

inapplicable *adj* inapplicable.

inappropriate *adj* impropre.

inasmuch *adv* attendu que.

inattentive *adj* inattentif.

inaudible *adj* inaudible.

inaugural *adj* inaugural.

inaugurate *vt* inaugurer.

inauguration *n* inauguration *f*.

inauspicious *adj* peu propice.

in-between *adj* intermédiaire.

inborn, inbred *adj* inné.

incalculable *adj* incalculable.

incandescent *adj* incandescent.

incantation *n* incantation *f*.

incapable *adj* incapable.

incapacitate *vt* mettre dans l'incapacité.

incapacity *n* incapacité *f*.

incarcerate *vt* incarcérer.

incarnate *adj* incarné.

incarnation *n* incarnation *f*.

incautious *adj* imprudent; **~ly** *adv* imprudemment.

incendiary *n* bombe incendiaire *f*; incendiaire *mf*.

incense *n* encens *m*; * *vt* exaspérer.

incentive *n* stimulant *m*; prime, aide *f*.

inception *n* commencement *m*.

incessant *adj* incessant, continuel; **~ly** *adv* continuellement.

incest *n* inceste *m*.

incestuous *adj* incestueux.

inch *n* pouce *m*; **~ by ~** petit à petit.

incidence *n* fréquence *f*.

incident *n* incident *m*.

incidental *adj* fortuit; **~ly** *adv* incidemment.

incinerator *n* incinérateur *m*.

incipient *adj* naissant.

incise *vt* inciser.

incision *n* incision *f*.

incisive *adj* incisif.

incisor *n* incisive *f*.

incite *vt* inciter, encourager.

inclement *adj* inclément.

inclination *n* inclination, propension *f*.

incline *vt* incliner; * *vi* s'incliner.

include *vt* inclure, comprendre.

including *prep* inclus, y compris.

inclusion *n* inclusion *f*.

inclusive *adj* inclus; tout compris.

incognito *adv* incognito.

incoherence *n* incohérence *f*.

incoherent *adj* incohérent; **~ly** *adv* d'une manière incohérente.

income *n* revenu *m*; recettes *fpl*.

income tax *n* impôt sur le revenu *m*.

incoming *adj* entrant; nouveau.

incomparable *adj* incomparable.

incomparably *adv* incomparablement.

incompatibility *n* incompatibilité *f*.

incompatible *adj* incompatible.

incompetence *n* incompétence *f*.

incompetent *adj* incompétent; ~ly *adv* de manière incompétente.

incomplete *adj* incomplet.

incomprehensibility *n* incompréhensibilité *f*.

incomprehensible *adj* incompréhensible.

inconceivable *adj* inconcevable.

inconclusive *adj* peu concluant; * *adv* d'une manière peu concluante.

incongruity *n* incongruité *f*.

incongruous *adj* incongru; ~ly *adv* incongrûment.

inconsequential *adj* inconséquent.

inconsiderate *adj* sans considération; inconsidéré; ~ly *adv* sans considération.

inconsistency *n* inconsistance *f*.

inconsistent *adj* inconsistant.

inconsolable *adj* inconsolable.

inconspicuous *adj* discret.

incontinence *n* incontinence *f*.

incontinent *adj* incontinent.

incontrovertible *adj* incontestable.

inconvenience *n* inconvénient, désagrément *m*; * *vt* incommoder.

inconvenient *adj* incommode; ~ly *adv* incommodément.

incorporate *vt* incorporer; * *vi* s'incorporer.

incorporated company *n* société constituée *f*.

incorporation *n* incorporation *f*.

incorrect *adj* incorrect, inexact; ~ly *adv* incorrectement.

incorrigible *adj* incorrigible.

incorruptibility *n* incorruptibilité *f*.

incorruptible *adj* incorruptible.

increase *vt, vi* augmenter; * *n* augmentation *f*.

increasing *adj* croissant; *adv* ~ly de plus en plus.

incredible *adj* incroyable.

incredulity *n* incrédulité *f*.

incredulous *adj* incrédule.

increment *n* augmentation *f*.

incriminate *vt* incriminer.

incrust *vt* incruster.

incubate *vi* couver.

incubator *n* couveuse *f*.

inculcate *vt* inculquer.

incumbent *adj* nécessaire; * *n* titulaire *mf*.

incur *vt* encourir.

incurability *n* incurabilité *f*.

incurable *adj* incurable.

incursion *n* incursion *f*.

indebted *adj* endetté; redevable.

indecency *n* indécence *f*.

indecent *adj* indécent; ~ly *adv* indécemment.

indecision *n* indécision, irrésolution *f*.

indecisive *adj* indécis, irrésolu.

indecorous *adj* inconvenant.

indeed *adv* vraiment.

indefatigable *adj* infatigable.

indefinite *adj*, ~ly *adv* indéfini(ment).

indelible *adj* indélébile.

indelicacy *n* indélicatesse *f*.

indelicate *adj* peu délicat.

indemnify *vt* indemniser.

indemnity *n* indemnité *f*.

indent *vt* bosseler; renfoncer.

independence *n* indépendance *f*.

independent *adj* indépendant; ~ly *adv* indépendamment.

indescribable *adj* indescriptible.

indestructible *adj* indestructible.

indeterminate *adj* indéterminé.

index *n* indice *m*.

index card *n* fiche *f*.

indexed *adj* indexé.

index finger *n* index *m*.

indicate *vt* indiquer.

indication *n* indication *f*; indice *m*.

indicative *adj, n* (*gr*) indicatif *m*.

indicator *n* indicateur *m*.

indict *vt* accuser.

indictment *n* accusation *f*.

indifference *n* indifférence *f*.

indifferent *adj* indifférent; **~ly** *adv* indifféremment.

indigenous *adj* indigène.

indigent *adj* indigent.

indigestible *adj* indigeste.

indigestion *n* indigestion *f*.

indignant *adj* indigné.

indignation *n* indignation *f*.

indignity *n* indignité *f*.

indigo *n* indigo *m*.

indirect *adj* indirect; **~ly** *adv* indirectement.

indiscreet *adj* indiscret; **~ly** *adv* indiscrètement.

indiscretion *n* indiscrétion *f*.

indiscriminate *adj*, **~ly** *adv* sans discernement.

indispensable *adj* indispensable.

indisposed *adj* indisposé.

indisposition *n* indisposition *f*.

indisputable *adj* indiscutable.

indisputably *adv* indiscutablement.

indistinct *adj* indistinct, confus; **~ly** *adv* indistinctement.

indistinguishable *adj* indistinctible.

individual *adj*, **~ly** *adv* individuel(lement); * *n* individu *m*.

individuality *n* individualité *f*.

indivisible *adv*, **~bly** *adv* indivisible(ment).

indoctrinate *vt* endoctriner.

indoctrination *n* endoctrinement *m*.

indolence *n* indolence *f*.

indolent *adj* indolent; **~ly** *adv* indolemment.

indomitable *adj* indomptable.

indoors *adv* à l'intérieur.

indubitably *adv* indubitablement.

induce *vt* persuader; causer, provoquer.

inducement *n* encouragement *m*; incitation *f*.

induction *n* induction *f*.

indulge *vt* céder à; *vi* se permettre, se laisser aller.

indulgence *n* indulgence *f*.

indulgent *adj* indulgent; **~ly** *adv* avec indulgence.

industrial *adj* industriel.

industrialist *n* industriel *m*.

industrialize *vt* industrialiser.

industrial park *n* zone industrielle *f*.

industrious *adj* travailleur.

industry *n* industrie *f*.

inebriated *vt* ivre.

inebriation *n* ivresse *f*.

inedible *adj* non comestible.

ineffable *adj* ineffable.

ineffective, ineffectual *adj* inefficace; **~ly** *adv* inefficacement.

inefficiency *n* inefficacité *f*.

inefficient *adj* inefficace.

ineligible *adj* inéligible.

inept *adj* inepte; déplacé.

ineptitude *n* ineptie *f*; manque d'à-propos *m*.

inequality *n* inégalité *f*.

inert *adj* inerte.

inertia *n* inertie *f*.

inescapable *adj* inévitable.

inestimable *adj* inestimable.

inevitable *adj* inévitable.

inevitably *adv* inévitablement.

inexcusable *adj* inexcusable.

inexhaustible *adj* inépuisable.

inexorable *adj* inexorable.

inexpedient *adj* imprudent, inopportun.

inexpensive *adj* bon marché.

inexperience *n* inexpérience *f*.

inexperienced *adj* inexpérimenté.

inexpert *adj* inexpert.

inexplicable *adj* inexplicable.

inexpressible *adj* indicible; inexprimable.

inextricably *adv* inextricablement.

infallibility *n* infaillibilité *f*.
infallible *adj* infaillible.
infamous *adj* vil, infâme; **~ly** *adv* vilement.
infamy *n* infamie *f*.
infancy *n* enfance *f*.
infant *n* bébé *m*; enfant *mf*.
infanticide *n* infanticide *mf*.
infantile *adj* infantile.
infantry *n* infanterie *f*.
infatuated *adj* fou.
infatuation *n* folie *f*; obsession *f*.
infect *vt* infecter.
infection *n* infection *f*.
infectious *adj* contagieux; infectieux.
infer *vt* inférer.
inference *n* inférence *f*.
inferior *adj* inférieur; * *n* subordonné *m*, -e *f*.
inferiority *n* infériorité *f*.
infernal *adj* infernal.
inferno *n* enfer *m*.
infest *vt* infester.
infidel *n* infidèle *mf*.
infidelity *n* infidélité *f*.
infiltrate *vi* s'infiltrer.
infinite *adj*, **~ly** *adv* infini(ment).
infinitive *n* (*gr*) infinitif *m*.
infinity *n* infini *m*; infinité *f*.
infirm *adj* infirme.
infirmary *n* infirmerie *f*.
infirmity *n* infirmité *f*.
inflame *vt* enflammer; * *vi* s'enflammer.
inflammation *n* inflammation *f*.
inflammatory *adj* inflammatoire.
inflatable *adj* gonflable.
inflate *vt* gonfler.
inflation *n* inflation *f*.
inflection *n* inflexion *f*.
inflexibility *n* inflexibilité *f*.
inflexible *adj* inflexible.
inflexibly *adv* inflexiblement.
inflict *vt* infliger.
influence *n* influence *f*; * *vt* influencer.
influential *adj* influent.
influenza *n* grippe *f*.
influx *n* affluence *f*.

inform *vt* informer.
informal *adj* informel; simple; familier.
informality *n* simplicité *f*.
informant *n* informateur *m*, -trice *f*
information *n* information *f*.
infraction *n* infraction *f*.
infra-red *adj* infrarouge.
infrastructure *n* infrastructure *f*.
infrequent *adj*, **~ly** *adv* rare(ment).
infringe *vt* enfreindre.
infringement *n* infraction *f*.
infuriate *vt* rendre furieux.
infuse *vt* infuser.
infusion *n* infusion *f*.
ingenious *adj* ingénieux; **~ly** *adv* ingénieusement.
ingenuity *n* ingéniosité *f*.
ingenuous *adj*, **~ly** *adv* ingénu(ment); sincère(ment).
inglorious *adj* honteux; **~ly** *adv* honteusement.
ingot *n* lingot *m*.
ingrained *adj* invétéré.
ingratiate *vi*: **~ with sb** chercher à entrer dans les bonnes grâces de qn.
ingratitude *n* ingratitude *f*.
ingredient *n* ingrédient *m*.
inhabit *vt*, *vi* habiter.
inhabitable *adj* habitable.
inhabitant *n* habitant *m*, -e *f*.
inhale *vt* inhaler.
inherent *adj* inhérent.
inherit *vt* hériter.
inheritance *n* héritage *m*.
inheritor *n* héritier *m*, -ière *f*.
inhibit *vt* inhiber.
inhibited *adj* inhibé.
inhibition *n* inhibition *f*.
inhospitable *adj* inhospitalier.
inhospitality *n* inhospitalité *f*.
inhuman *adj* inhumain; **~ly** *adv* inhumainement.
inhumanity *n* inhumanité, cruauté *f*.
inimical *adj* hostile, ennemi.
inimitable *adj* inimitable.

iniquitous *adj* inique, injuste.

iniquity *n* iniquité, injustice *f*.

initial *adj* initial; * *n* initiale *f*.

initially *adv* au début.

initiate *vt* commencer; initier.

initiation *n* début, commencement *m*; initiation *f*.

initiative *n* initiative *f*.

inject *vt* injecter.

injection *n* injection *f*.

injudicious *adj* peu judicieux.

injunction *n* injonction *f*; ordre
m.

injure *vt* blesser.

injury *n* blessure *f*; tort *m*.

injury time *n* arrêts de jeu *mpl*.

injustice *n* injustice *f*.

ink *n* encre *f*.

inkling *n* soupçon *m*.

inkstand *n* encrier *m*.

inlaid *adj* incrusté.

inland *adj* intérieur; * *adv* vers
l'intérieur, dans les terres.

in-laws *npl* belle-famille *f*.

inlay *vt* incruster.

inlet *n* entrée *f*; bras de mer *m*.

inmate *n* détenu *m*, -e *f*.

inmost *adj* le plus profond.

inn *n* auberge *f*; hôtel *m*.

innate *adj* inné.

inner *adj* intérieur.

innermost *adj* le plus profond.

inner tube *n* chambre à air *f*.

innkeeper *n* aubergiste *mf*, hôtelier *m*, -ière *f*.

innocence *n* innocence *f*.

innocent *adj* innocent; **~ly** *adv*
innocemment.

innocuous *adj* inoffensif; **~ly** *adv*
de manière inoffensive.

innovate *vt* innover.

innovation *n* innovation *f*.

innuendo *n* allusion *f*; insinuation *f*.

innumerable *adj* innombrable.

inoculate *vt* inoculer.

inoculation *n* inoculation *f*.

inoffensive *adj* inoffensif.

inopportune *adj* inopportun.

inordinately *adv* démesurément.

inorganic *adj* inorganique.

inpatient *n* patient(e) hospitali-
sé(e) *m(f)*.

input *n* entrée *f*; consommation *f*.

inquest *n* enquête *f*.

inquire *vt, vi* demander; **to ~
about** s'informer de; **to ~ after**
vt demander des nouvelles de;
to ~ into *vt* faire des recherches
sur; enquêter sur.

inquiry *n* demande de renseigne-
ments *f*; enquête *f*.

inquisition *n* investigation *f*.

inquisitive *adj* curieux.

inroad *n* incursion *f*.

insane *adj* fou, *f* folle.

insanity *n* folie *f*.

insatiable *adj* insatiable.

inscribe *vt* inscrire; dédier.

inscription *n* inscription *f*; dédicace *f*.

inscrutable *adj* impénétrable.

insect *n* insecte *m*.

insecticide *n* insecticide *m*.

insecure *adj* peu assuré.

insecurity *n* insécurité *f*.

insemination *n* insémination *f*.

insensible *adj* inconscient; insensible.

insensitive *adj* insensible.

inseparable *adj* inséparable.

insert *vt* introduire, insérer.

insertion *n* insertion *f*.

inshore *adj* côtier.

inside *n* intérieur *m*; * *adv* à
l'intérieur.

inside out *adv* à l'envers; à fond.

insidious *adj* insidieux; **~ly** insi-
dieusement.

insight *n* perspicacité *f*.

insignia *npl* insignes *mpl*.

insignificant *adj* insignifiant.

insincere *adj* peu sincère.

insincerity *n* manque de sincérité *m*.

insinuate *vt* insinuer.

insinuation *n* insinuation *f*.

insipid *adj* insipide.

insist *vi* insister.

insistence *n* insistance *f*.

insistent *adj* insistant.
insole *n* semelle intérieure *f.*
insolence *n* insolence *f.*
insolent *adj* insolent; ~ly *adv* insolemment.
insoluble *adj* insoluble.
insolvency *n* insolvabilité *f.*
insolvent *adj* insolvable.
insomnia *n* insomnie *f.*
insomuch *conj* à tel point.
inspect *vt* examiner, inspecter.
inspection *n* inspection *f.*
inspector *n* inspecteur *m*, -trice *f.*
inspiration *n* inspiration *f.*
inspire *vt* inspirer.
instability *n* instabilité *f.*
instal *vt* installer.
installation *n* installation *f.*
instalment *n* installation *f*; versement *m.*
instalment plan *n* plan de vente à tempérament *m.*
instance *n* exemple *m*; **for ~** par exemple.
instant *adj* instantané; ~ly *adv* immédiatement; * *n* instant, moment *m.*
instantaneous *adj*, ~ly *adv* instantané(ment).
instead (of) *pr* au lieu, à la place (de).
instep *n* cou-de-pied *m.*
instigate *vt* inciter; susciter.
instigation *n* incitation *f.*
instill *vt* instiller; inspirer.
instinct *n* instinct *m.*
instinctive *adj* instinctif; ~ly *adv* instinctivement, d'instinct.
institute *vt* instituer; * *n* institut *m.*
institution *n* institution *f.*
instruct *vt* instruire.
instruction *n* instruction *f.*
instructive *adj* instructif.
instructor *n* professeur *m*; moniteur *m*, -trice *f.*
instrument *n* instrument *m.*
instrumental *adj* instrumental.
insubordinate *adj* insubordonné.

insubordination *n* insubordination *f.*
insufferable *adj* insupportable.
insufferably *adv* insupportablement.
insufficiency *n* insuffisance *f.*
insufficient *adj* insuffisant; ~ly *adv* insuffisamment.
insular *adj* insulaire; borné.
insulate *vt* isoler; insonoriser.
insulating tape *n* ruban isolant *m.*
insulation *n* isolation *f*; insonorisation *f.*
insulin *n* insuline *f.*
insult *vt* insulter; * *n* insulte *f.*
insulting *adj* insultant.
insuperable *adj* insurmontable.
insurance *n* (*com*) assurance *f.*
insurance policy *n* police d'assurance *f.*
insure *vt* assurer.
insurgent *n* insurgé, rebelle *m.*
insurmountable *adj* insurmontable.
insurrection *n* insurrection *f.*
intact *adj* intact.
intake *n* admission *f*; consommation *f.*
integral *adj* intégrant; (*chem*) intégral; * *n* intégrale *f.*
integrate *vt* intégrer.
integration *n* intégration *f.*
integrity *n* intégrité *f.*
intellect *n* intellect *m.*
intellectual *adj* intellectuel.
intelligence *n* intelligence *f.*
intelligent *adj* intelligent.
intelligentsia *n* intelligentsia *f.*
intelligible *adj* intelligible.
intelligibly *adv* intelligiblement.
intemperate *adj*, ~ly *adv* immodéré(ment).
intend *vt* avoir l'intention de.
intendant *n* intendant *m*, -e *f.*
intended *adj* voulu.
intense *adj* intense; ~ly *adv* intensément.
intensify *vt* intensifier.
intensity *n* intensité *f.*

intensive *adj* intensif.

intensive care unit *n* service de soins intensifs *m*.

intent *adj* résolu; attentif; **~ly** *adv* attentivement; * *n* intention *f*, dessein *m*.

intention *n* intention *f*, dessein *m*.

intentional *adj* intentionnel; **~ly** *adv* à dessein, intentionnellement.

inter *vt* enterrer.

interaction *n* interaction *f*.

intercede *vi* intercéder.

intercept *vt* intercepter.

intercession *n* intercession *f*.

interchange *n* échange *m*.

intercom *n* interphone *m*.

intercourse *n* relations sexuelles *fpl*.

interest *vt* intéresser; * *n* intérêt *m*.

interesting *adj* intéressant.

interest rate *n* taux d'intérêt *m*.

interfere *vi* s'ingérer.

interference *n* ingérence *f*; interférence *f*.

interim *adj* intérimaire.

interior *adj* intérieur.

interior designer *n* décorateur (-trice) d'intérieur *m(f)*.

interjection *n* (*gr*) interjection *f*.

interlock *vi* s'entremêler.

interlocutor *n* interlocuteur *m*, -trice *f*.

interloper *n* intrus *m*, -e *f*.

interlude *n* intermède *m*.

intermarriage *n* intermariage *m*.

intermediary *n* intermédiaire *mf*.

intermediate *adj* intermédiaire.

interment *n* enterrement *m*.

interminable *adj* interminable.

intermingle *vt* entremêler; * *vi* s'entremêler.

intermission *n* entracte *m*; interruption *f*.

intermittent *adj* intermittent.

intern *n* interne *mf*.

internal *adj* intérieur; interne; **~ly** *adv* intérieurement.

international *adj* international.

interplay *n* interaction *f*.

interpose *vt* interposer.

interpret *vt* interpréter.

interpretation *n* interprétation *f*.

interpreter *n* interprète *mf*.

interregnum *n* interrègne *m*.

interrelated *adj* en corrélation.

interrogate *vt* interroger.

interrogation *n* interrogatoire *m*.

interrogative *adj* interrogatif.

interrupt *vt* interrompre.

interruption *n* interruption *f*.

intersect *vi* se croiser.

intersection *n* croisement *m*.

intersperse *vt* parsemer.

intertwine *vt* entrelacer.

interval *n* intervalle *m*; mi-temps *f*.

intervene *vi* intervenir.

intervention *n* intervention *f*.

interview *n* entrevue *f*; interview *f*; * *vt* faire passer une entrevue à; interviewer.

interviewer *n* interviewer *m*.

interweave *vt* entrelacer.

intestate *adj* intestat.

intestinal *adj* intestinal.

intestine *n* intestin *m*.

intimacy *n* intimité *f*.

intimate *n* intime *mf*; * *adj*, **~ly** *adv* intime(ment); * *vt* insinuer, laisser entendre.

intimidate *vt* intimider.

into *prep* dans, en.

intolerable *adj* intolérable.

intolerably *adv* intolérablement.

intolerance *n* intolérance *f*.

intolerant *adj* intolérant.

intonation *n* intonation *f*.

intoxicate *vt* enivrer.

intoxication *n* ivresse *f*.

intractable *adj* intraitable.

intransitive *adj* (*gr*) intransitif.

intravenous *adj* intraveineux.

in-tray *n* courrier à l'arrivée *m*.

intrepid *adj* intrépide; **~ly** *adv* intrépidement.

intrepidity *n* intrépidité *f*.

intricacy *n* complexité *f*.

intricate *adj* complexe, compliqué; **~ly** *adv* de manière compliquée.

intrigue *n* intrigue *f*; * *vi* intriguer.

intriguing *adj* intrigant.

intrinsic *adj*, **~ally** *adv* intrinsèque(ment).

introduce *vt* introduire.

introduction *n* introduction *f*.

introductory *adj* d'introduction.

introspection *n* introspection *f*.

introvert *n* introverti *m*, -ie *f*.

intrude *vi* s'ingérer, s'immiscer.

intruder *n* intrus *m*, -e *f*.

intrusion *n* intrusion *f*.

intuition *n* intuition *f*.

intuitive *adj* intuitif.

inundate *vt* inonder.

inundation *n* inondation *f*.

inure *vt* accoutumer, habituer.

invade *vt* envahir.

invader *n* envahisseur *m*, -euse *f*.

invalid *adj* invalide; * *n* invalide *mf*.

invalidate *vt* invalider, annuler.

invaluable *adj* inappréciable.

invariable *adj* invariable.

invariably *adv* invariablement.

invasion *n* invasion *f*.

invective *n* invective *f*.

inveigle *vt* persuader, entraîner.

invent *vt* inventer.

invention *n* invention *f*.

inventive *adj* inventif.

inventor *n* inventeur *m*, -trice *f*.

inventory *n* inventaire *m*.

inverse *adj* inverse.

inversion *n* inversion *f*.

invert *vt* inverser.

invest *vt* investir.

investigate *vt* faire des recherches sur; examiner.

investigation *n* investigation *f*; recherches *fpl*.

investigator *n* investigateur *m*, -trice *f*; chercheur *m*, -euse *f*.

investment *n* investissement *m*.

inveterate *adj* invétéré.

invidious *adj* odieux; désobligeant.

invigilate *vt* surveiller.

invigorating *adj* vivifiant.

invincible *adj* invincible.

invincibly *adv* invinciblement.

inviolable *adj* inviolable.

invisible *adj* invisible.

invisibly *adv* invisiblement.

invitation *n* invitation *f*.

invite *vt* inviter.

inviting *adj* attrayant, tentant.

invoice *n* (*com*) facture *f*.

invoke *vt* invoquer.

involuntarily *adv* involontairement.

involuntary *adj* involontaire.

involve *vt* impliquer, entraîner.

involved *adj* compliqué.

involvement *n* implication *f*; confusion *f*.

invulnerable *adj* invulnérable.

inward *adj* intérieur; intime; **~, ~s** *adv* vers l'intérieur.

iodine *n* (*chem*) iode *m*.

I.O.U. (I owe you) *n* reçu *m*.

irascible *adj* irascible.

irate, ireful *adj* irrité.

iris *n* iris *m*.

irksome *adj* fastidieux, ennuyeux.

iron *n* fer *m*; * *adj* de fer; * *vt* repasser.

ironic *adj*, **~ly** *adv* ironique(ment).

ironing *n* repassage *m*.

ironing board *n* table à repasser *f*.

iron ore *n* minerai de fer *m*.

ironwork *n* ferronnerie *f*; **~s** *pl* ferronneries *fpl*.

irony *n* ironie *f*.

irradiate *vt* irradier.

irrational *adj* irrationnel.

irreconcilable *adj* irréconciliable; inconciliable.

irregular *adj* irrégulier; **~ly** *adv* irrégulièrement.

irregularity *n* irrégularité *f*.
irrelevant *adj* hors de propos.
irreligious *adj* irréligieux.
irreparable *adj* irréparable.
irreplaceable *adj* irremplaçable.
irrepressible *adj* irrépressible.
irreproachable *adj* irréprochable.
irresistible *adj* irrésistible.
irresolute *adj*, **~ly** *adv* irrésolu(ment).
irresponsible *adj* irresponsable.
irretrievably *adv* irréparablement.
irreverence *n* irrévérence *f*.
irreverent *adj* irrévérencieux; **~ly** *adv* irrévérencieusement.
irrigate *vt* irriguer.
irrigation *n* irrigation *f*.
irritability *n* irritabilité *f*.
irritable *adj* irritable.
irritant *n* (*med*) irritant *m*.
irritate *vt* irriter.

irritating *adj* irritant.
irritation *n* irritation *f*.
Islam *n* Islam *m*.
island *n* île *f*.
islander *n* insulaire *mf*.
isle *n* île *f*.
isolate *vt* isoler.
isolation *n* isolement *m*.
issue *n* sujet *m*, question *f*; * *vt* publier; distribuer; fournir.
isthmus *n* isthme *m*.
it *pn* il, elle; le, la; cela, ça, ce, c'.
italic *n* italique *m*.
itch *n* démangeaison *f*; * *vi* avoir des démangeaisons.
item *n* article *m*.
itemize *vt* détailler.
itinerant *adj* ambulant, itinérant.
itinerary *n* itinéraire *m*.
its *pn* son, sa, ses.
itself *pn* lui-même, elle-même.
ivory *n* ivoire *m*.
ivy *n* lierre *m*.

J

jab *vt* planter, enfoncer.
jabber *vi* bafouiller.
jack *n* cric *m*; valet *m*.
jackal *n* chacal *m*.
jackboots *npl* bottes de militaire *fpl*.
jackdaw *n* choucas *m*.
jacket *n* veste *f*; couverture *f*.
jack-knife *vi* se mettre en travers.
jack plug *n* prise à fiche *f*.
jackpot *n* gros lot *m*.
jade *n* jade *m*.
jagged *adj* dentelé.
jaguar *n* jaguar *m*.
jail *n* prison *f*.
jailbird *n* prisonnier *m*, -ière *f*.
jailer *n* geôlier *m*, -ière *f*.
jam *n* confiture *f*; embouteillage *m*.
jangle *vi* cliqueter.

janitor *n* portier *m*.
January *n* janvier *m*.
jar *vi* se heurter; (*mus*) détonner; grincer; * *n* pot *m*.
jargon *n* jargon *m*.
jasmine *n* jasmin *m*.
jaundice *n* jaunisse *f*.
jaunt *n* promenade *f*.
jaunty *adj* enjoué.
javelin *n* javelot *m*.
jaw *n* mâchoire *f*.
jay *n* geai *m*.
jazz *n* jazz *m*.
jealous *adj* jaloux.
jealousy *n* jalousie *f*.
jeans *npl* jean *m*.
jeep *n* jeep *f*.
jeer *vi* se moquer, railler; * *n* raillerie, moquerie *f*.
jelly *n* gelée *f*.
jelly-fish *n* méduse *f*.

jeopardize *vt* risquer, mettre en péril.

jerk *n* secousse *f*; * *vt* donner une secousse à.

jerky *adj* saccadé.

jersey *n* jersey *m*.

jest *n* blague, plaisanterie *f*.

jester *n* bouffon *m*.

jestingly *adv* en plaisantant.

Jesuit *n* jésuite *m*.

Jesus *n* Jésus *m*.

jet *n* avion à réaction *m*; jet *m*; gicleur *m*.

jet engine *n* moteur à réaction *m*.

jettison *vt* se défaire de.

jetty *n* jetée *f*.

Jew *n* Juif *m*.

jewel *n* bijou *m*.

jeweller *n* bijoutier *m*, -ière *f*.

jewellery *n* bijoux *mpl*.

jewellery store *n* bijouterie *f*.

Jewess *n* Juive *f*.

jewish *adj* juif.

jib *n* (*mar*) foc *m*.

jibe *n* raillerie, moquerie *f*.

jig *n* gigue *f*.

jigsaw *n* puzzle *m*.

jilt *vt* laisser tomber.

jinx *n* porte-malheur *m invar*.

job *n* travail *m*.

jockey *n* jockey *m*.

jocular *adj* joyeux; facétieux.

jog *vi* faire du jogging.

jogging *n* jogging *m*.

join *vt* joindre, unir; **to ~ in** participer à; * *vi* se réunir; se joindre.

joiner *n* menuisier *m*.

joinery *n* menuiserie *f*.

joint *n* articulation *f*; * *adj* commun.

jointly *adv* conjointement.

joint-stock company *n* (*com*) société par actions *f*.

joke *n* blague, plaisanterie *f*; * *vi* blaguer, plaisanter.

joker *n* blagueur *m*, -euse *f*.

jollity *n* gaieté *f*.

jolly *adj* gai, joyeux.

jolt *vt* secouer; * *n* secousse *f*.

jostle *vt* bousculer.

journal *n* revue *f*.

journalism *n* journalisme *m*.

journalist *n* journaliste *mf*.

journey *n* voyage *m*; * *vi* voyager.

jovial *adj* jovial, gai; **~ly** *adv* jovialement.

joy *n* joie *f*.

joyful, joyous *adj* joyeux, gai; **~ly** *adv* joyeusement.

joystick *n* manche à balai *m*.

jubilant *adj* joyeux.

jubilation *n* jubilation *f*.

jubilee *n* jubilé *m*.

Judaism *n* judaïsme *m*.

judge *n* juge *m*; * *vt* juger.

judgment *n* jugement *m*.

judicial *adj*, **~ly** *adv* judiciaire(ment).

judiciary *n* pouvoir judiciaire *m*.

judicious *adj* judicieux.

judo *n* judo *m*.

jug *n* cruche *f*.

juggle *vi* jongler.

juggler *n* jongleur *m*, -euse *f*.

juice *n* jus *m*; suc *m*.

juicy *adj* juteux.

jukebox *n* juke-box *m*.

July *n* juillet *m*.

jumble *vt* mélanger; * *n* mélange *m*; fouillis *m*.

jump *vi* sauter; * *n* saut *m*.

jumper *n* pull *m*; sauteur *m*, -euse *f*.

jumpy *adj* nerveux.

juncture *n* conjoncture *f*.

June *n* juin *m*.

jungle *n* jungle *f*.

junior *adj* plus jeune.

juniper *n* (*bot*) genièvre *m*.

junk *n* cochonnerie *f*; bric-à-brac *m invar*.

junta *n* junte *f*.

jurisdiction *n* juridiction *f*.

jurisprudence *n* jurisprudence *f*.

jurist *n* juriste *mf*.

juror, juryman *n* juré *m*.

jury *n* jury *m*.

just *adj* juste; * *adv* justement,

exactement; ~ as juste quand; ~ now tout de suite.
justice n justice f.
justifiably adv légitimement.
justification n justification f.
justify vt justifier.
justly adv justement.

justness n justesse f.
jut vi; **to ~ out** faire saillie, dépasser.
jute n jute m.
juvenile adj juvénile; pour enfants.
juxtaposition n juxtaposition f.

K

kaleidoscope n kaléidoscope m.
kangaroo n kangourou m.
karate n karaté m.
kebab n brochette f.
keel n (mar) quille f.
keen adj aiguisé; vif; enthousiaste.
keenness n enthousiasme m.
keep vt garder, conserver; tenir.
keeper n gardien m, -ienne f.
keepsake n souvenir m.
keg n baril m.
kennel n niche f.
kernel n amande f; noyau m.
kerosene n kérosène m.
ketchup n ketchup m.
kettle n bouilloire f.
kettle-drum n timbale f.
key n clé, clef f; (mus) ton m; touche f.
keyboard n clavier m.
keyhole n trou de la serrure m.
keynote n (mus) tonique f.
key ring n porte-clefs m invar.
keystone n clef de voûte f.
khaki n kaki m.
kick vi (vt) donner un coup de pied (à); * n coup de pied m; plaisir m.
kid n gamin m, -e f.
kidnap vt kidnapper.
kidnapper n kidnappeur m, -euse f.
kidnapping n kidnapping m.
kidney n rein m; rognon m.
killer n assassin m.
killing n assassinat m.

kiln n four m.
kilo n kilo m.
kilobyte n kilo-octet m.
kilogram n kilogramme m.
kilometre n kilomètre m.
kilt n kilt m.
kin n parents mpl; **next of ~** parent proche m.
kind adj gentil; * n genre m, sorte f.
kindergarten n jardin d'enfants m.
kind-hearted adj bon.
kindle vt allumer; * vi s'allumer.
kindliness n gentillesse, bonté f.
kindly adj bon, bienveillant.
kindness n bonté f.
kindred adj apparenté.
kinetic adj cinétique.
king n roi m.
kingdom n royaume m.
kingfisher n martin-pêcheur m.
kiosk n kiosque m.
kiss n baiser m; * vt embrasser.
kissing n baisers mpl.
kit n équipement m.
kitchen n cuisine f.
kitchen garden n potager m.
kite n cerf-volant m.
kitten n chaton m.
knack n don, chic m.
knapsack n sac à dos m.
knave n fripouille f; (cards) valet m.
knead vt pétrir.
knee n genou m.
knee-deep adj jusqu'aux genoux.

kneel vi s'agenouiller.
knell n glas m.
knife n couteau m.
knight n chevalier m.
knit vt, vi tricoter; **to ~ the brows** froncer les sourcils.
knitter n tricoteur m, -euse f.
knitting pin n aiguille à tricoter f.
knitwear n tricots mpl.
knob n bouton m; nœud m (du bois).
knock vt, vi cogner, frapper; **to ~ down** abattre; * n coup m.
knocker n heurtoir m.

knock-kneed adj aux genoux cagneux.
knock-out n knock-out m.
knoll n butte f.
knot n nœud m; * vt nouer.
knotty adj emmêlé; épineux.
know vt, vi savoir; connaître.
know-all n je-sais-tout m.
know-how n savoir-faire m.
knowing adj entendu; **~ly** adv en connaissance de cause.
knowledge n connaissances fpl.
knowledgeable adj bien informé.
knuckle n articulation f.

L

label n étiquette f.
laboratory n laboratoire m.
labour n travail m; **to be in ~** être en train d'accoucher; * vi travailler.
labourer n ouvrier m.
labourious adj laborieux; pénible; **~ly** adv laborieusement.
labour union n syndicat m.
labyrinth n labyrinthe m.
lace n lacet m; dentelle f; * vt lacer.
lacerate vt lacérer.
lack vt manquer de; * vi manquer; * n manque m.
lackadaisical adj sans soin.
lackey n laquais m.
laconic adj laconique.
lacquer n laque f.
lad n garçon m.
ladder n échelle f.
ladle n louche f.
ladleful n louchée f.
lady n dame f.
ladybird n coccinelle f.
ladykiller n bourreau des coeurs m.
ladylike adj distingué.

ladyship n madame f.
lag vi se laisser distancer.
lager n bière blonde f.
lagoon n lagune f.
laidback adj décontracté.
lair n repaire m.
laity n laïcité f.
lake n lac m.
lamb n agneau m; * vi agneler.
lambswool n laine d'agneau f.
lame adj boiteux.
lament vt se lamenter sur; * vi lamenter; * n lamentation f.
lamentable adj lamentable, déplorable.
lamentation n lamentation f.
laminated adj laminé.
lamp n lampe f.
lampoon n satire f.
lampshade n abat-jour m invar.
lance n lance f; bistouri m; * vt inciser.
lancet n bistouri m.
land n pays m; terre f; * vt débarquer; * vi atterrir, débarquer.
land forces npl armée de terre f.
landholder n propriétaire terrien m.

landing n atterrissage m.

landing strip n piste d'atterrissage f.

landlady n propriétaire f.

landlord n propriétaire m.

landlubber n marin d'eau douce m.

landmark n point de repère m.

landowner n propriétaire terrien m.

landscape n paysage m.

landslide n glissement de terrain m.

lane n allée, ruelle f; file f.

language n langue f; langage m.

languid adj languissant; ~**ly** adv languissamment.

languish vi languir.

lank adj raide, plat.

lanky adj grand et maigre.

lantern n lanterne f.

lap n genoux mpl; * vt laper.

lapdog n chien d'appartement m.

lapel n revers m.

lapse n laps m; défaillance f; * vi expirer, se périmer; se relâcher.

larceny n vol m.

larch n mélèze m.

lard n saindoux m.

larder n garde-manger m invar.

large adj grand; **at ~** en liberté; ~**ly** adv en grande partie.

large-scale adj à grande échelle.

largesse n largesse f.

lark n alouette f.

larva n larve f.

laryngitis n laryngite f.

larynx n larynx m.

lascivious adj lascif; ~**ly** adv lascivement.

laser n laser m.

lash n coup de fouet m; * vt fouetter; attacher.

lasso n lasso m.

last adj dernier; **at ~** enfin; ~**ly** adv finalement; * n dernier m, dernière f; forme f (de cordonnier); * vi durer.

last-ditch adj ultime.

lasting adj, ~**ly** adv durable(ment).

last-minute adj de dernière minute.

latch n loquet m.

latch-key n clef de porte d'entrée f.

late adj en retard; défunt; (rail) **the train is ten minutes ~** le train a dix minutes de retard; * adv tard; ~**ly** adv récemment.

latecomer n retardataire mf.

latent adj latent.

lateral adj, ~**ly** adv latérale(ment).

lathe n tour m.

lather n mousse f.

latitude n latitude f.

latrine n latrine f.

latter adj dernier; ~**ly** adv récemment.

lattice n treillis m.

laudable adj louable.

laudably adv louablement.

laugh vi rire; **to ~ at** vt rire de, se moquer de; * n rire m.

laughable adj risible; dérisoire.

laughing stock n risée f.

laughter n rires mpl.

launch vt lancer; * vi se lancer; * n (mar) vedette f.

launching n lancement m.

launching pad n rampe de lancement f.

launder vt laver.

laundrette, laundromat n laverie automatique f.

laundry n lessive f.

laurel n laurier m.

lava n lave f.

lavatory n toilettes fpl.

lavender n (bot) lavande f.

lavish adj prodigue; ~**ly** adv avec prodigalité; * vt prodiguer.

law n loi f; droit m.

law-abiding adj respectueux de la loi.

law and order n ordre public m.

law court n tribunal m.

lawful adj légal; légitime; **~ly** adv légalement.

lawless adj anarchique.

lawlessness n anarchie f.

lawmaker n législateur m, -trice f.

lawn n pelouse f, gazon m.

lawnmower n tondeuse à gazon f.

law school n faculté de droit f.

law suit n procès m.

lawyer n avocat m; notaire m.

lax adj relâché.

laxative n laxatif m.

laxity n relâchement m; flou m.

lay vt coucher; mettre; pondre; **to ~ claim** réclamer; prétendre (à); * vi pondre.

layabout n paresseux m, -euse f.

layer n couche f.

layette n layette f.

layman n laïc m.

layout n disposition f; présentation f.

laze vi paresser.

lazily adv paresseusement.

laziness n paresse f.

lazy adj paresseux.

lead n plomb m; * vt, vi conduire, mener.

leader n chef m.

leadership n direction f.

leading adj principal; premier; **~ article** n article de fond m.

leaf n feuille f.

leaflet n feuillet m; prospectus m.

leafy adj feuillu.

league n ligue f; lieue f.

leak n fuite f; * vi (mar) faire eau.

leaky adj qui fuit.

lean vt appuyer; * vi s'appuyer; * adj maigre.

leap vi sauter; * n saut m.

leapfrog n saute-mouton m.

leap year n année bisextile f.

learn vt, vi apprendre.

learned adj instruit.

learner n élève mf; débutant m, -e f.

learning n érudition f.

lease n bail m; * vt louer.

leasehold n bail m.

leash n laisse f.

least adj moindre; **at ~** au moins; **not in the ~** pas du tout.

leather n cuir m.

leathery adj qui a l'aspect du cuir.

leave n permission f; congé m; **to take ~** prendre congé; * vt laisser.

leaven n levain m; * vt faire lever.

leavings npl restes mpl.

lecherous adj lascif.

lecture n conférence f; * vi faire une conférence.

lecturer n conférencier m, -ière f.

ledge n rebord m.

ledger n (com) grand livre m.

lee n (mar) côté sous le vent m.

leech n sangsue f.

leek n (bot) poireau m.

leer vt regarder d'un oeil lascif.

lees npl lie f.

leeward adj (mar) sous le vent.

leeway n liberté d'action f.

left adj gauche; **on the ~** à gauche.

left-handed adj gaucher.

left-luggage office n consigne f.

leftovers npl restes mpl.

leg n jambe f; patte f.

legacy n héritage, legs m.

legal adj légal, légitime; **~ly** adv légalement.

legal holiday n jour férié m.

legality n légalité, légitimité f.

legalize vt légaliser.

legal tender n monnaie légale f.

legate n légat m.

legatee n légataire mf.

legation n légation f.

legend n légende f.

legendary adj légendaire.

legible adj lisible.

legibly adv lisiblement.

legion n légion f.

legislate vi, vt légiférer.

legislation n législation f.

legislative *adj* législatif.

legislator *n* législateur *m*, -trice *f*.

legislature *n* corps législatif *m*.

legitimacy *n* légitimité *f*.

legitimate *adj* légitime; **~ly** *adv* légitimement; * *vt* légitimer.

leisure *n* loisir *m*; **~ly** *adj* tranquille; **at ~** au calme.

lemon *n* citron *m*.

lemonade *n* limonade *f*.

lemon tea *n* thé au citron *m*.

lemon tree *n* citronnier *m*.

lend *vt* prêter.

length *n* longueur *f*; durée *f*; **at ~** longuement; enfin.

lengthen *vt* allonger; * *vi* s'allonger.

lengthways, lengthwise *adv* dans le sens de la longueur.

lengthy *adj* long.

lenient *adj* indulgent.

lens *n* lentille *f*.

Lent *n* Carême *m*.

lentil *n* lentille *f*.

Leo *n* Lion *m* (signe du zodiaque).

leopard *n* léopard *m*.

leotard *n* justaucorps *m*.

leper *n* lépreux *m*, -euse *f*.

leprosy *n* lèpre *f*.

lesbian *n* lesbienne *f*.

less *adj* moins; * *adv* moins.

lessen *vt, vi* diminuer.

lesser *adj* moindre.

lesson *n* leçon *f*.

lest *conj* de crainte que.

let *vt* laisser, permettre; louer.

lethal *adj* mortel.

lethargic *adj* léthargique.

lethargy *n* léthargie *f*.

letter *n* lettre *f*.

letter bomb *n* lettre piégée *f*.

letter box boite aux lettres *f*.

lettering *n* inscription *f*.

letter of credit *n* lettre de crédit *f*.

lettuce *n* salade *f*.

leukaemia *n* leucémie *f*.

level *adj* plat, égal; à niveau; * *n* niveau *m*; * *vt* niveler.

level-headed *adj* sensé.

lever *n* levier *m*.

leverage *n* effet de levier *m*; prise *f*.

levity *n* légèreté *f*.

levy *n* levée *f*; prélèvement *m*; * *vt* prélever.

lewd *adj* obscène.

lexicon *n* lexique *m*.

liability *n* responsabilité *f*.

liable *adj* sujet (à); responsable.

liaise *vi* effectuer une liaison.

liaison *n* liaison *f*.

liar *n* menteur *m*, -euse *f*.

libel *n* diffamation *f*; * *vt* diffamer.

libellous *adj* diffamatoire.

liberal *adj* libéral; généreux; **~ly** *adv* libéralement.

liberality *n* libéralité, générosité *f*.

liberate *vt* libérer.

liberation *n* libération *f*.

libertine *n* libertin *m*, -ine *f*.

liberty *n* liberté *f*.

Libra *n* Balance *f* (signe du zodiaque).

librarian *n* bibliothécaire *mf*.

library *n* bibliothèque *f*.

libretto *n* livret *m*.

licence *n* licence *f*; permis *m*; permission *f*.

licentious *adj* licencieux.

lichen *n* (*bot*) lichen *m*.

lick *vt* lécher.

lid *n* couvercle *m*.

lie *n* mensonge *m*; * *vi* mentir; être allongé.

lieu *n*: **in ~ of** au lieu de.

lieutenant *n* lieutenant *m*.

life *n* vie *f*; **for ~** pour toute la vie.

life belt *n* gilet de sauvetage *m*.

lifeboat *n* canot de sauvetage *m*.

life-guard *n* maître nageur *m*; garde du corps *m*.

life jacket *n* gilet de sauvetage *m*.

lifeless *adj* mort; sans vie.

lifelike *adj* naturel.

lifeline *n* bouée de sauvetage *f*.

life sentence *n* condamnation à perpétuité *f*.

life-sized *adj* grandeur nature.

lifespan *n* durée de vie *f*.

lifestyle *n* style de vie *m*.

life-support system *n* système de respiration artificielle *m*.

lifetime *n* vie *f*.

lift *vt* lever.

ligament *n* ligament *m*.

light *n* lumière *f*; * *adj* léger; clair; * *vt* allumer; éclairer.

light bulb *n* ampoule *f*.

lighten *vi* s'éclaircir; * *vt* éclaircir; éclaircir; alléger.

lighter *n* briquet *m*.

light-headed *adj* étourdi.

lighthearted *adj* joyeux.

lighthouse *n* (*mar*) phare *m*.

lighting *n* éclairage *m*.

lightly *adv* légèrement.

lightning *n* éclair *m*.

lightning rod *n* paratonnerre *m*.

light pen *n* crayon optique *m*.

lightweight *adj* léger.

light year *n* année-lumière *f*.

ligneous *adj* ligneux.

like *adj* pareil; * *adv* comme; * *vt, vi* aimer.

likeable *adj* sympathique.

likelihood *n* probabilité *f*.

likely *adj* probable, vraisemblable.

liken *vt* comparer.

likeness *n* ressemblance *f*.

likewise *adv* pareillement.

liking *n* goût *m*.

lilac *n* lilas *m*.

lily *n* lis *m*; ~ **of the valley** muguet *m*.

limb *n* membre *m*.

limber *adj* flexible, souple.

lime *n* chaux *f*; lime *f*; ~ **tree** tilleul *m*.

limestone *n* pierre à chaux *f*.

limit *n* limite *f*; * *vt* limiter.

limitation *n* limitation *f*; restriction *f*.

limitless *adj* illimité.

limo(usine) *n* limousine *f*.

limp *vi* boiter; * *n* boitement *m*; * *adj* mou.

limpet *n* patelle *f*.

limpid *adj* limpide.

line *n* ligne *f*; ride *f*; * *vt* rayer; rider.

lineage *n* lignage *m*.

linear *adj* linéaire.

lined *adj* rayé; ridé.

linen *n* lin *m*.

liner *n* transatlantique *m*.

linesman *n* juge de ligne *m*.

linger *vi* traîner.

lingerie *n* lingerie *f*.

lingering *adj* long.

linguist *n* linguiste *mf*.

linguistic *adj* linguistique.

linguistics *n* linguistique *f*.

liniment *n* liniment *m*.

lining *n* doublure *f*.

link *n* chaînon *m*; * *vt* relier.

linnet *n* linotte *f*.

linoleum *n* linoléum *m*.

linseed *n* graine de lin *f*.

lint *n* peluche *f*.

lintel *n* linteau *m*.

lion *n* lion *m*.

lioness *n* lionne *f*.

lip *n* lèvre *f*; bord *m*.

lip-read *vi* lire sur les lèvres.

lip salve *n* pommade pour les lèvres *f*.

lipstick *n* rouge à lèvres *m*.

liqueur *n* liqueur *f*.

liquid *adj* liquide; * *n* liquide *m*.

liquidate *vt* liquider.

liquidation *n* liquidation *f*.

liquidize *vt* liquéfier.

liquor *n* spiritueux *m*.

liquorice *n* réglisse *m*/*f*.

liquor store *n* magasin de vins et spiritueux *m*.

lisp *vi* zézayer; * *n* zézaiement *m*.

list *n* liste *f*; * *vt* faire une liste de.

listen *vi* écouter.

listless *adj* indifférent.

litany *n* litanie *f*.

literal *adj* ~**ly** *adv* littéral(ement).

literary *adj* littéraire.

literate *adj* cultivé.

literature *n* littérature *f*.

lithe *adj* agile.

lithograph *n* lithographie *f*.

lithography *n* lithographie *f*.

litigation *n* litige *m*.

litigious *adj* litigieux.

litre *n* litre *m*.

litter *n* litière *f*; ordures *fpl*; * *vt* recouvrir.

little *adj* petit; ~ **by** ~ petit à petit; * *n* peu *m*.

liturgy *n* liturgie *f*.

live *vi* vivre; habiter; **to** ~ **on** *vt* se nourrir de; **to** ~ **up to** *vt* faire honneur à; * *adj* vivant.

livelihood *n* moyens de subsistance *mpl*.

liveliness *n* vivacité *f*.

lively *adj* vif.

liven up *vt* animer.

liver *n* foie *m*.

livery *n* livrée *f*.

livestock *n* bétail *m*.

livid *adj* livide; furieux.

living *n* vie *f*; * *adj* vivant.

living room *n* salle de séjour *f*.

lizard *n* lézard *m*.

load *vt* charger; * *n* charge *f*.

loaded *adj* chargé.

loaf *n* pain *m*.

loafer *n* paresseux *m*, -euse *f*.

loam *n* terreau *m*.

loan *n* prêt *m*.

loathe *vt* détester.

loathing *n* aversion *f*.

loathsome *adj* dégoûtant.

lobby *n* vestibule *m*.

lobe *n* lobe *m*.

lobster *n* langouste *f*.

local *adj* local.

local anaesthetic *n* anesthésique local *m*.

local government *n* administration municipale, administration locale *f*.

locality *n* localité *f*.

localize *vt* localiser.

locally *adv* localement.

locate *vt* localiser.

location *n* situation *f*.

loch *n* loch *m*.

lock *n* serrure *f*; * *vt* fermer à clé.

locker *n* casier *m*.

locket *n* médaillon *m*.

lockout *n* grève patronale *f*.

locksmith *n* serrurier *m*.

lock-up *n* cellule *f*.

locomotive *n* locomotive *f*.

locust *n* sauterelle *f*.

lodge *n* loge du gardien *f*; * *vi* se loger.

lodger *n* locataire *mf*.

loft *n* grenier *m*.

lofty *adj* haut.

log *n* bûche *f*.

logbook *n* (*mar*) journal de bord *m*.

logic *n* logique *f*.

logical *adj* logique.

logo *n* logo *m*.

loin *n* rein *m*.

loiter *vi* s'attarder.

loll *vi* se prélasser.

lollipop *n* sucette *f*.

lonely, lonesome *adj* seul, solitaire.

loneliness *n* solitude *f*.

long *adj* long, *f* longue; * *vi* désirer.

long-distance *n*: ~ **call** appel interurbain *m*.

longevity *n* longévité *f*.

long-haired *adj* aux cheveux longs.

longing *n* désir *m*.

longitude *n* longitude *f*.

longitudinal *adj* longitudinal.

long jump *n* saut en longueur *m*.

long-playing record *n* trente-trois tours *m*.

long-range *adj* à longue portée.

long-term *adj* à long terme.

long wave *n* grandes ondes *fpl*.

long-winded *adj* prolixe.

look *vi* regarder; sembler; **to** ~ **after** *vt* s'occuper de; garder; **to** ~ **for** *vt* chercher; **to** ~ **forward to** *vt* attendre avec impatience;

to ~ out for vt guetter; * n aspect m; regard m.

looking glass n miroir m.

look-out n (mil) sentinelle f; vigie f.

loom n métier à tisser m; * vi menacer.

loop n boucle f.

loophole n échappatoire f.

loose adj lâché; desserré; ~ly adv approximativement; ~, **loosen** vt lâcher; desserrer.

loot vt piller; * n butin m.

lop vt élaguer.

lop-sided adj de travers; déséquilibré.

loquacious adj loquace.

loquacity n loquacité f.

lord n seigneur m.

lore n savoir m.

lose vt, vi perdre.

loss n perte f; **to be at a ~** ne pas savoir que faire.

lost and found n objets trouvés mpl.

lot n sort f; lot m; **a ~** beaucoup.

lotion n lotion f.

lottery n loterie f.

loud adj fort, bruyant; ~ly adv bruyamment; haut.

loudspeaker n haut-parleur m.

lounge n salon m.

louse n (pl lice) pou m.

lousy adj minable.

lout n vaurien m.

lovable adj sympathique.

love n amour m; **to fall in ~** tomber amoureux; * vt aimer.

love letter n lettre d'amour f.

love life n vie sentimentale f.

loveliness n beauté f.

lovely adj beau.

lover n amant m.

love-sick adj fou amoureux.

loving adj affectueux.

low adj bas; * vi meugler.

low-cut adj décolleté.

lower adj plus bas; * vt baisser.

lowest adj le plus bas.

lowland n plaine f.

lowliness n humilité f.

lowly adj humble.

low-water n basse mer f.

loyal adj loyal, fidèle; ~ly adv loyalement.

loyalty n loyauté f; fidélité f.

lozenge n pastille f.

lubricant n lubrifiant m.

lubricate vt lubrifier.

lucid adj lucide.

luck n chance f.

luckily adv heureusement, par chance.

luckless adj malchanceux.

lucky adj chanceux, qui a de la chance.

lucrative adj lucratif.

ludricrous adj absurde.

lug vt traîner.

luggage n bagages mpl.

lugubrious adj lugubre, triste.

lukewarm adj tiède.

lull vt bercer; * n répit m.

lullaby n berceuce f.

lumbago n lumbago m.

lumberjack n bûcheron m.

lumber room n débarras m.

luminous adj lumineux.

lump n bosse f; grosseur f; morceau m; * vt réunir.

lump sum n somme globale f.

lunacy n folie f.

lunar adj lunaire.

lunatic adj fou, f folle.

lunch, luncheon n déjeuner m.

lungs npl poumons mpl.

lurch n embardée f.

lure n leurre m; attrait m; * vt séduire, attirer.

lurid adj blême; horrible.

lurk vi se cacher.

luscious adj délicieux.

lush adj luxuriant.

lust n luxure f; sensualité f; désir m; * vi désirer; **to ~ after** vt convoiter.

luster n lustre m.

lustful adj luxurieux, voluptueux; ~ly adv luxurieusement.

lustily adv vigoureusement.

lusty *adj* fort, vigoureux.
lute *n* luth *m*.
Lutheran *n* luthérien *m*, -ienne *f*.
luxuriance *n* exubérance, luxuriance *f*.
luxuriant *adj* exubérant, luxuriant.
luxuriate *vi* pousser de manière exubérante.

luxurious *adj* luxueux; **~ly** *adv* luxueusement.
luxury *n* luxe *m*.
lying *n* mensonges *mpl*.
lymph *n* lymphe *f*.
lynch *vt* lyncher.
lynx *n* linx *m*.
lyrical *adj* lyrique.
lyrics *npl* paroles *fpl*.

M

macaroni *n* macaronis *mpl*.
macaroon *n* macaron *m*.
mace *n* massue *f*; macis *m*.
macerate *vt* macérer.
machination *n* machination *f*.
machine *n* machine *f*.
machine gun *n* mitrailleuse *f*.
machinery *n* machinerie *f*; mécanisme *m*.
mackerel *n* maquereau *m*.
mad *adj* fou, *f* folle; furieux; insensé.
madam *n* madame *f*.
madden *vt* rendre fou; rendre furieux.
madder *n* (*bot*) garance *f*.
madhouse *n* asile de fous *m*.
madly *adv* à la folie; comme un fou.
madman *n* fou *m*.
madness *n* folie *f*.
magazine *n* magazine *m*, revue *f*; magasin *m*.
maggot *n* asticot *m*.
magic *n* magie *f*; * *adj*, **~ally** *adv* magique(ment).
magician *n* magicien *m*, -ienne *f*.
magisterial *adj*, **~ly** *adv* magistral(ement).
magistracy *n* magistrature *f*.
magistrate *n* magistrat *m*.
magnanimity *n* magnanimité *f*.
magnanimous *adj*, **~ly** *adv* magnanime(ment).
magnet *n* aimant *m*.

magnetic *adj* magnétique.
magnetism *n* magnétisme *m*.
magnificence *n* magnificence *f*.
magnificent *adj*, **~ly** *adv* magnifique(ment).
magnify *vt* grossir; exagérer.
magnifying glass *n* loupe *f*.
magnitude *n* magnitude *f*.
magpie *n* pie *f*.
mahogany *n* acajou *m*.
maid *n* bonne *f*.
maiden *n* jeune fille *f*.
maiden name *n* nom de jeune fille *m*.
mail *n* courrier *m*.
mailbox *n* boîte aux lettres *f*.
mail coach *n* malle-poste *f*.
mailing list *n* liste de publipostage *f*.
mail-order *n* vente par correspondance *f*.
mail train *n* (*rail*) train-poste *m*.
maim *vt* mutiler.
main *adj* principal; essentiel; **in the ~** en général.
mainland *n* continent *m*.
main line *n* (*rail*) grande ligne *f*.
mainly *adv* principalement, essentiellement.
main street *n* rue principale *f*.
maintain *vt* maintenir; soutenir.
maintenance *n* entretien *m*.
maize *n* maïs *m*.
majestic *adj* majestueux; **~ally** *adv* majestueusement.

majesty *n* majesté *f*.

major *adj* majeur; * *n* (*mil*) commandant *m*.

majority *n* majorité *f*.

make *vt* faire; to ~ for se diriger vers; to ~ up inventer; to ~ up for compenser; * *n* marque *f*.

make-believe *n* invention *f*.

makeshift *adj* improvisé, de fortune.

make-up *n* maquillage *m*.

make-up remover *n* démaquillant *m*.

malady *n* maladie *f*.

malaise *n* malaise *m*.

malaria *n* malaria *f*.

malcontent *adj, n* mécontent *m*, -e *f*.

male *adj* mâle; masculin; * *n* mâle *m*.

malevolence *n* malveillance *f*.

malevolent *adj* malveillant; ~ly *adv* avec malveillance.

malfunction *n* mauvais fonctionnement *m*.

malice *n* malice *f*.

malicious *adj* méchant; ~ly *adv* méchamment.

malign *adj* nocif; * *vt* calomnier.

malignant *adj* méchant; ~ly *adv* méchamment.

mall *n* centre commercial *m*.

malleable *adj* malléable.

mallet *n* maillet *m*.

mallows *n* (*bot*) mauve *f*.

malnutrition *n* malnutrition *f*.

malpractice *n* négligence *f*.

malt *n* malt *m*.

maltreat *vt* maltraiter.

mammal *n* mammifère *m*.

mammoth *adj* gigantesque.

man *n* homme *m*; * *vt* (*mar*) équiper en personnel.

manacle *n* entrave *f*; ~s *pl* menottes *fpl*.

manage *vt* diriger; réussir; * *vi* réussir.

manageable *adj* maniable.

management *n* direction *f*.

manager *n* directeur *m*.

manageress *n* directrice *f*.

managerial *adj* directorial.

managing director *n* directeur général *m*.

mandarin *n* mandarine *f*; mandarin *m*.

mandate *n* mandat *m*.

mandatory *adj* obligatoire.

mane *n* crinière *f*.

manfully *adv* vaillamment.

manger *n* mangeoire *f*.

mangle *n* essoreuse *f*; * *vt* mutiler.

mangy *adj* miteux.

manhandle *vt* maltraiter; manutentionner.

manhood *n* âge d'homme *m*; virilité *f*.

man-hour *n* heure-homme *f*.

mania *n* manie *f*.

maniac *n* maniaque *mf*.

manic *adj* maniaque.

manicure *n* manucure *f*.

manifest *adj* manifeste; * *vt* manifester.

manifestation *n* manifestation *f*.

manifesto *n* manifeste *m*.

manipulate *vt* manipuler.

manipulation *n* manipulation *f*.

mankind *n* humanité *f*.

manlike *adj* viril; d'homme.

manliness *n* virilité *f*; courage *m*.

manly *adj* viril.

man-made *n* artificiel.

manner *n* manière *f*; attitude *f*; ~s *pl* manières *fpl*.

manoeuvre *n* manœuvre *f*.

manpower *n* main-d'œuvre *f*.

mansion *n* château *m*.

manslaughter *n* homicide involontaire *m*.

mantelpiece *n* manteau de cheminée *m*.

manual *adj, n* manuel *m*.

manufacture *n* fabrication *f*; * *vt* fabriquer.

manufacturer *n* fabricant *m*.

manure *n* fumier *m*; engrais *m*; purin *m*; * *vt* bonifier.

manuscript *n* manuscrit *m*.

many *adj* beaucoup de; ~ a time

de nombreuses fois; **how ~?** combien?; **as ~ as** autant que.

map n carte f; plan m; * vt dessiner un plan de; **to ~ out** programmer.

maple n érable m.

mar vt gâter, gâcher.

marathon n marathon m.

marauder n maraudeur m, -euse f.

marble n marbre m; * adj marbré.

March n mars m.

march n marche f; * vi marcher.

marchpast n défilé m.

mare n jument f.

margarine n margarine f.

margin n marge f; bord m.

marginal adj marginal.

marigold n (bot) calendula f, souci m.

marijuana n marijuana f.

marinate vt mariner.

marine adj marin; * n soldat de marine m.

mariner n marin m.

marital adj matrimonial.

maritime adj maritime.

marjoram n marjolaine f.

mark n marque f; signe m; * vt marquer.

marker n marque f; marqueur m.

market n marché m.

marketable adj vendable.

marketing n marketing m.

marketplace n marché m.

market research n étude de marché f.

market value n valeur sur le marché f.

marksman n tireur d'élite m.

marmalade n confiture d'oranges f.

maroon adj marron.

marquee n tente f.

marriage n mariage m.

marriageable adj mariable.

marriage certificate n acte de mariage m.

married adj marié; conjugal.

marrow n moelle f.

marry vi se marier.

marsh n marécage m.

marshal n maréchal m.

marshy adj marécageux.

marten n martre f.

martial adj martial; **~ law** n loi martiale f.

martyr n martyr m, -e f.

martyrdom n martyre m.

marvel n merveille f; * vi s'émerveiller.

marvellous adj merveilleux; **~ly** adv merveilleusement.

marzipan n massepain m, pâte d'amandes f.

mascara n mascara m.

masculine adj masculin, viril.

mash n bouillie, purée f.

mask n masque m; * vt masquer.

masochist n masochiste mf.

mason n maçon m.

masonry n maçonnerie f.

masquerade n mascarade f.

mass n masse f; messe f; multitude f.

massacre n massacre m; * vt massacrer.

massage n massage m.

masseur n masseur m.

masseuse n masseuse f.

massive adj énorme.

mass media npl média mpl.

mast n mât m.

master n maître m; * vt maîtriser.

masterly adj magistral.

mastermind vt diriger.

masterpiece n chef-d'œuvre m.

mastery n maîtrise f.

masticate vt mastiquer.

mastiff n mastiff m.

mat n tapis m.

match n allumette f; match m; * vt égaler; * vi bien aller ensemble.

matchbox n boîte d'allumettes f.

matchless adj incomparable, sans pareil.

matchmaker n marieur m, -euse f.

mate *n* camarade *mf*; * *vt* accoupler.

material *adj*, **~ly** *adv* matériel(lement).

materialism *n* matérialisme *m*.

maternal *adj* maternel.

maternity dress *n* robe de grossesse *f*.

maternity hospital *n* maternité *f*.

math *n* maths *fpl*.

mathematical *adj*, **~ly** *adv* mathématique(ment).

mathematician *n* mathématicien *m*, -ienne *f*.

mathematics *npl* mathématiques *fpl*.

matinee *n* matinée *f*.

mating *n* accouplement *m*.

matins *npl* matines *fpl*.

matriculate *vt* immatriculer.

matriculation *n* immatriculation *f*.

matrimonial *adj* matrimonial.

mat(t) *adj* mat.

matted *adj* emmêlé.

matter *n* matière, substance *f*; sujet *m*; affaire *f*; **what is the ~?** que se passe-t-il? **a ~ of fact** un fait; * *vi* importer.

mattress *n* matelas *m*.

mature *adj* mûr; * *vi* mûrir.

maturity *n* maturité *f*.

maul *vt* meurtrir.

mausoleum *n* mausolée *m*.

mauve *adj* mauve.

maxim *n* maxime *f*.

maximum *n* maximum *m*.

may *v aux* pouvoir; **~ be** peut-être.

May *n* mai *m*.

Mayday *n* le Premier Mai *m*.

mayonnaise *n* mayonnaise *f*.

mayor *n* maire *m*.

mayoress *n* mairesse *f*.

maze *n* labyrinthe *m*.

me *pn* moi; me.

meadow *n* prairie *f*, pré *m*.

meagre *adj* pauvre.

meagreness *n* pauvreté *f*.

meal *n* repas *m*; farine *f*.

mealtime *n* heure du repas *f*.

mean *adj* avare, mesquin; moyen; **in the ~time, ~while** pendant ce temps-là; **~s** *npl* moyens *mpl*; * *vt*, *vi* signifier.

meander *vi* serpenter.

meaning *n* sens *m*, signification *f*.

meaningful *adj* significatif.

meaningless *adj* vide de sens.

meanness *n* avarice, mesquinerie *f*.

meantime, meanwhile *adv* pendant ce temps-là.

measles *npl* rougeole *f*.

measure *n* mesure *f*; * *vt* mesurer.

measurement *n* mesure *f*.

meat *n* viande *f*.

meatball *n* boulette de viande *f*.

meaty *adj* riche.

mechanic *n* mécanicien *m*.

mechanical *adj*, **~ly** *adv* mécanique(ment).

mechanics *npl* mécanique *f*.

mechanism *n* mécanisme *m*.

medal *n* médaille *f*.

medallion *n* médaillon *m*.

medallist *n* médaillé *m*, -e *f*.

meddle *vi* se mêler des affaires des autres.

meddler *n* fouineur *m*, -euse *f*, indiscret *m*, -ète *f*.

media *npl* média *mpl*.

median *n* médiane *f*.

mediate *vi* agir en tant que médiateur.

mediation *n* médiation *f*.

mediator *n* médiateur *m*, -trice *f*.

medical *adj* médical.

medicate *vt* traiter.

medicated *adj* médical.

medicinal *adj* médicinal.

medicine *n* médecine *f*; médicament *m*.

medieval *adj* médiéval.

mediocre *adj* médiocre.

mediocrity *n* médiocrité *f*.

meditate *vi* méditer.

meditation n méditation f.

meditative adj méditatif.

Mediterranean adj méditerranéen.

medium n milieu m; médium m; * adj moyen.

medium wave n ondes moyennes fpl.

medley n mélange m.

meek adj doux; ~ly adv doucement.

meekness n douceur f.

meet vt rencontrer; **to ~ with** retrouver; * vi se rencontrer; se retrouver.

meeting n réunion f; congrès m.

megaphone n mégaphone m.

melancholy n mélancolie f; * adj mélancolique.

mellow adj mûr; doux; * vi mûrir.

mellowness n maturité f.

melodious adj mélodieux; ~ly adv mélodieusement.

melody n mélodie f.

melon n melon m.

melt vt faire fondre; * vi fondre.

melting point n point de fusion m.

member n membre m.

membership n nombre de membres m.

membrane n membrane f.

memento n mémento m.

memo n note de service f.

memoir n mémoire m.

memorable adj mémorable.

memorandum n mémorandum m; note de service f.

memorial n monument commémoratif, mémorial m.

memorize vt mémoriser.

memory n mémoire f; souvenir m.

menace n menace f; * vt menacer.

menacing adj menaçant.

menagerie n ménagerie f.

mend vt réparer; raccommoder.

mending n réparation f; raccommodage m.

menial adj vil.

meningitis n méningite f.

menopause n ménopause f.

menstruation n menstruation f.

mental adj mental.

mentality n mentalité f.

mentally adv mentalement.

mention n mention f; * vt mentionner.

mentor n mentor m.

menu n menu m.

mercantile adj commercial.

mercenary adj, n mercenaire m.

merchandise n marchandise f.

merchant n négociant m, -e f.

merchantman n navire marchand m.

merchant marine n marine marchande f.

merciful adj miséricordieux.

merciless adj, ~ly adv impitoyable(ment).

mercury n mercure m.

mercy n pitié f.

mere adj, ~ly adv simple(ment).

merge vt, vi fusionner.

merger n fusion f.

meridian n méridien m.

meringue n meringue f.

merit n mérite m; * vt mériter.

meritorious adj méritoire.

mermaid n sirène f.

merrily adv joyeusement.

merriment n divertissement m; réjouissance f.

merry adj joyeux.

merry-go-round n manège m.

mesh n maille f.

mesmerize vt hypnotiser.

mess n désordre m; confusion f; (mil) mess m; **to ~ up** vt mettre en désordre.

message n message m.

messenger n messager m, -ère f.

metabolism n métabolisme m.

metal n métal m.

metallic adj métallique.

metallurgy n métallurgie f.

metamorphosis n métamorphose f.

metaphor n métaphore f.

metaphoric(al) *adj* métaphorique.

metaphysical *adj* métaphysique.

metaphysics *npl* métaphysique *f*.

mete (out) *vt* distribuer.

meteor *n* météore *m*.

meteorological *adj* météorologique.

meteorology *n* météorologie *f*.

meter *n* compteur *m*; mètre *m*.

method *n* méthode *f*.

methodical *adj*, **~ly** *adv* méthodique(ment).

Methodist *n* méthodiste *mf*.

metric *adj* métrique.

metropolis *n* métropole *f*.

metropolitan *adj* métropolitain.

mettle *n* courage *m*.

mettlesome *adj* courageux.

mew *vi* miauler.

mezzanine *n* mezzanine *f*.

microbe *n* microbe *m*.

microphone *n* microphone *m*.

microchip *n* microprocesseur *m*, puce *f*.

microscope *n* microscope *m*.

microscopic *adj* microscopique.

microwave *n* four à micro-ondes *m*.

mid *adj* demi; mi-.

midday *n* midi *m*.

middle *adj* moyen; du milieu; * *n* milieu *m*.

middle name *n* deuxième prénom *m*.

middleweight *n* poids moyen *m*.

middling *adj* moyen, passable.

midge *n* moucheron *m*.

midget *n* nain *m*, -e *f*.

midnight *n* minuit *m*.

midriff *n* diaphragme *m*; estomac *m*.

midst *n* milieu *m*.

midsummer *n* milieu de l'été *m*.

midway *adv* à mi-chemin.

midwife *n* sage-femme *f*.

midwifery *n* obstétrique *f*.

might *n* force *f*.

mighty *adj* fort, puissant.

migraine *n* migraine *f*.

migrate *vi* émigrer.

migration *n* émigration *f*.

migratory *adj* migratoire.

mike *n* micro *m*.

mild *adj* doux; modéré **~ly** *adv* doucement.

mildew *n* moisissure *f*; mildiou *m*.

mildness *n* douceur *f*.

mile *n* mille *m*.

mileage *n* kilométrage *m*.

milieu *n* milieu *m*.

militant *adj* militant.

military *adj* militaire.

militate *vi* militer.

militia *n* milice *f*.

milk *n* lait *m*; * *vt* traire; exploiter.

milkshake *n* milk-shake *m*.

milky *adj* laiteux; **M~ Way** *n* Voie lactée *f*.

mill *n* moulin *m*; * *vt* moudre.

millennium *n* millénaire *m*.

miller *n* meunier *m*.

millet *n* (*bot*) millet *m*.

milligram *n* milligramme *m*.

milliliter *n* millilitre *m*.

millimeter *n* millimètre *m*.

milliner *n* chapelier *m*, -ière *f*.

millinery *n* chapellerie *f*.

million *n* million *m*.

millionaire *n* millionaire *mf*.

millionth *adj*, *n* millionième *mf*.

millstone *n* meule *f*.

mime *n* mime *m*.

mimic *vt* mimer.

mimicry *n* mimique *f*.

mince *vt* hacher.

mind *n* esprit *m*; * *vt* prendre soin de; * *vi*: **do you ~?** est-ce que cela vous dérange?

minded *adj* disposé.

mindful *adj* conscient; attentif.

mindless *adj* insouciant.

mine *pn* le mien, la mienne, les miens, les miennes; à moi; * *n* mine *f*; * *vi* exploiter la mine.

minefield *n* champ de mines *m*.

miner *n* mineur *m*.

mineral *adj*, *n* minéral *m*.

mineralogy *n* minéralogie *f*.

mineral water *n* eau minérale *f*.

minesweeper *n* dragueur de mines *m*.

mingle *vt* mêler.

miniature *n* miniature *f*.

minimal *adj* minime.

minimize *vt* minimiser.

minimum *n* minimum *m*.

mining *n* exploitation minière *f*.

minion *n* larbin *m*; favorit(te) *m(f)*.

minister *n* ministre *m*; * *vt* servir.

ministerial *adj* ministériel.

ministry *n* ministère *m*.

mink *n* vison *m*.

minnow *n* vairon *m*.

minor *adj* mineur; * *n* mineur *m*, -e *f*.

minority *n* minorité *f*.

minstrel *n* ménestrel *m*.

mint *n* (*bot*) menthe *f*; hôtel de la Monnaie *m*; * *vt* frapper.

minus *adv* moins.

minute *adj* minuscule; ~**ly** *adv* minutieusement.

minute *n* minute *f*.

miracle *n* miracle *m*.

miraculous *adj* miraculeux.

mirage *n* mirage *m*.

mire *n* bourbe *f*.

mirky *adj* trouble; ténébreux.

mirror *n* miroir *m*.

mirth *n* allégresse *f*.

mirthful *adj* joyeux.

misadventure *n* mésaventure *f*.

misanthropist *n* misanthrope *mf*.

misapply *vt* mal appliquer.

misapprehension *n* méprise *f*.

misbehave *vi* se conduire mal.

misbehaviour *n* mauvaise conduite *f*.

miscalculate *vt* mal calculer.

miscarriage *n* fausse couche *f*.

miscarry *vi* faire une fausse couche; échouer.

miscellaneous *adj* divers, varié.

miscellany *n* mélange, assortiment *m*.

mischief *n* mal, tort *m*.

mischievous *adj* mauvais; espiègle.

misconception *n* méprise *f*.

misconduct *n* mauvaise conduite *f*.

misconstrue *vt* mal interpréter.

miscount *vt* mal compter.

miscreant *n* scélérat *m*.

misdeed *n* méfait *m*.

misdemeanour *n* délit *m*.

misdirect *vt* mal diriger.

miser *n* avare *mf*.

miserable *adj* malheureux.

miserly *adj* mesquin, avare.

misery *n* malheur *m*; misère *f*.

misfit *n* inadapté *m*, -e *f*.

misfortune *n* infortune *f*.

misgiving *n* doute *m*.

misgovern *vt* mal gouverner.

misguided *adj* malencontreux; malavisé.

mishandle *vt* mal traiter; mal s'y prendre avec.

mishap *n* mésaventure *f*.

misinform *vt* mal renseigner.

misinterpret *vt* mal interpréter.

misjudge *vt* méjuger.

mislay *vt* égarer.

mislead *vt* induire en erreur.

mismanage *vt* mal administrer.

mismanagement *n* mauvaise administration *f*.

misnomer *n* nom inapproprié *m*.

misogynist *n* misogyne *mf*.

misplace *vt* égarer.

misprint *vt* mal imprimer; * *n* coquille *f*.

misrepresent *vt* mal représenter.

Miss *n* Mlle, Mademoiselle *f*.

miss *vt* rater; s'ennuyer de.

missal *n* missel *m*.

misshape *n* déformation *f*.

missile *n* missile *m*.

missing *adj* perdu; absent.

mission *n* mission *f*.

missionary *n* missionnaire *mf*.

misspent *adj* gaspillé.

mist *n* brouillard *m*.

mistake *vt* confondre; * *vi* se

tromper; **to be mistaken** se
tromper; * n méprise f; erreur f.

Mister n Monsieur m.

mistletoe n (bot) gui m.

mistress n maîtresse f.

mistrust vt se méfier de; * n méfiance f.

mistrustful adj méfiant.

misty adj brumeux.

misunderstand vt mal comprendre.

misunderstanding n malentendu m.

misuse vt faire un mauvais usage
de; abuser de.

miter n mitre f.

mitigate vt atténuer.

mitigation n atténuation f.

mittens npl moufles fpl.

mix vt mélanger.

mixed adj mélangé; mixte.

mixed-up adj confus.

mixer n mixeur m.

mixture n mélange m.

mix-up n confusion f.

moan n gémissement m; * vi
gémir; se plaindre.

moat n fossé m.

mob n foule f; masse f.

mobile adj mobile.

mobile home n caravane f.

mobility n mobilité f.

mobilize vt (mil) mobiliser.

moccasin n mocassin m.

mock vt se moquer de.

mockery n moquerie f.

mode n mode m.

model n modèle m; * vt modeler.

moderate adj, **~ly** adv modé-
ré(ment); * vt modérer.

moderation n modération f.

modern adj moderne.

modernize vt moderniser.

modest adj, **~ly** adv modes-
te(ment).

modesty n modestie f.

modicum n minimum m.

modification n modification f.

modify vt modifier.

modulate vt moduler.

modulation n (mus) modulation
f.

module n module m.

mogul n magnat m.

mohair n mohair m.

moist adj humide.

moisten vt humidifier.

moisture n humidité f.

molar n molaire f.

molasses npl mélasse f.

mole n taupe f.

molecule n molécule f.

molehill n taupinière f.

molest vt importuner.

mollify vt apaiser.

mollusk n mollusque m.

mollycoddle vt dorloter.

molten adj fondu.

mom n maman f.

moment n moment m.

momentarily adv momentané-
ment.

momentary adj momentané.

momentous adj capital.

momentum n vitesse f; élan m.

mommy n maman f.

monarch n monarque m.

monarchy n monarchie f.

monastery n monastère m.

monastic adj monastique.

Monday n lundi m.

monetary adj monétaire.

money n argent m; pièce de monnaie f.

money order n mandat m.

mongol n (med) mongolien m,-ienne
f.

mongrel adj, n bâtard m, -e f.

monitor n moniteur m, -trice f.

monk n moine m.

monkey n singe m.

monochrome adj monochrome.

monocle n monocle m.

monologue n monologue m.

monopolize vt monopoliser.

monopoly n monopole m.

monosyllable n monosyllabe m.

monotonous adj monotone.

monotony n monotonie f.

monsoon n mousson f.

monster n monstre m.

monstrosity n monstruosité f.

monstrous adj monstrueux; **~ly** adv monstrueusement.

montage n montage m.

month n mois m.

monthly adj mensuel; adv mensuellement.

monument n monument m.

monumental adj monumental.

moo vi meugler.

mood n humeur f.

moodiness n mauvaise humeur f.

moody adj de mauvaise humeur; lunatique.

moon n lune f.

moonbeams npl rayons de lune mpl.

moonlight n clair de lune m.

moor n lande f; * vt (mar) amarrer.

moorland n lande f.

moose n élan m.

mop n lavette f; * vt frotter.

mope vi être triste.

moped n vélomoteur m.

moral adj, **~ly** adv moral(ement); **~s** npl moralité f.

morale n moral m.

moralist n moraliste mf.

morality n moralité f.

moralize vt, vi moraliser.

morass n marais m.

morbid adj morbide.

more adj, adv plus; **never ~** plus jamais; **once ~** encore une fois; **~ and ~** de plus en plus; **so much the ~** d'autant plus.

moreover adv de plus, en outre.

morgue n morgue f.

morning n matin m; **good ~** bonjour.

moron n imbécile mf.

morose adj morose.

morphine n morphine f.

morse n morse m.

morsel n bouchée f; morceau m.

mortal adj, **~ly** adv mortel(lement); * n mortel m, -elle f.

mortality n mortalité f.

mortar n mortier m.

mortgage n hypothèque f; * vt hypothéquer.

mortgage company n banque de prêts hypothécaires f.

mortgager n débiteur (-trice) hypothécaire m(f).

mortification n mortification f.

mortify vt mortifier.

mortuary n morgue f.

mosaic n mosaïque f.

mosque n mosquée f.

mosquito n moustique m.

moss n (bot) mousse f.

mossy adj moussu.

most adj, pn la plupart de; * adv extrêmement; **at ~** au maximum; **~ly** adv surtout, essentiellement.

motel n motel m.

moth n papillon de nuit m.

mothball n boule de naphtaline f.

mother n mère f.

motherhood n maternité f.

mother-in-law n belle-mère f.

motherless adj sans mère.

motherly adj maternel.

mother-of-pearl n nacre f.

mother-to-be n future maman f.

mother tongue n langue maternelle f.

motif n motif m.

motion n mouvement m.

motionless adj immobile.

motion picture n film m.

motivated adj motivé.

motive n motif m.

motley adj bigarré.

motor n moteur m.

motorbike n moto f.

motorboat n canot à moteur m.

motorcycle n motocyclette f.

motor vehicle n automobile f.

mottled adj bigarré.

motto n devise f.

mould n moule m; * vt mouler.

moulder vi s'effriter.

mouldy adj moisi.

moult vi muer.

mound n monticule m.

mount n mont m; * vt gravir.
mountain n montagne f.
mountaineer n alpiniste mf.
mountaineering n alpinisme m.
mountainous adj montagneux.
mourn vt pleurer.
mourner n personne en deuil f.
mournful adj, ~ly adv tris-
te(ment).
mourning n deuil m.
mouse n (pl mice) souris f.
mousse n mousse f.
moustache n moustache f.
mouth n bouche f; embouchure f.
mouthful n bouchée f.
mouth organ n harmonica m.
mouthpiece n bec m; microphone
m.
mouthwash n eau dentifrice f.
mouthwatering adj appétissant.
movable adj mobile.
move vt déplacer; toucher, émouvoir; * vi bouger; * n mouvement
m.
movement n mouvement m.
movie n film m.
movie camera n caméra f.
moving adj touchant, émouvant.
mow vt tondre.
mower n tondeuse f.
Mrs n Mme, Madame f.
much adj, pn beaucoup; adv beaucoup, très.
muck n saleté f.
mucous adj muqueux.
mucus n mucus m.
mud n boue f.
muddle vt confondre; embrouiller; * n confusion f; désordre m.
muddy adj boueux.
mudguard n garde-boue m invar.
muffle vt assourdir.
mug n tasse f.
muggy adj lourd.
mulberry n mûre f; ~ tree mû-
rier m.
mule n mulet m; mule f.
mull vt méditer.
multifarious adj divers.
multiple adj multiple.

multiplication n multiplication
f; ~ table table de multiplication
f.
multiply vt multiplier.
multitude n multitude f.
mumble vt, vi grommeler.
mummy n momie f.
mumps npl oreillons mpl.
munch vt mâcher.
mundane adj banal.
municipal adj municipal.
municipality n municipalité f.
munificence n munificence f.
munitions npl munitions fpl.
mural n mural m.
murder n assassinat, meurtre m;
homicide volontaire m; * vt assassiner.
murderer n assassin, meurtrier
m.
murderess n meurtrière f.
murderous adj meurtrier.
murky adj obscur.
murmur n murmure m; * vt, vi
murmurer.
muscle n muscle m.
muscular adj musculaire.
muse vi méditer, rêver.
museum n musée m.
mushroom n (bot) champignon
m.
music n musique f.
musical adj musical; mélodieux.
musician n musicien m, -ienne f.
musk n musc m.
muslin n mousseline f.
mussel n moule f.
must v aux devoir.
mustard n moutarde f.
muster vt rassembler.
musty adj moisi.
mute adj muet, silencieux.
muted adj sourd.
mutilate vt mutiler.
mutilation n mutilation f.
mutiny n mutinerie f; vi se mu-
tiner, se révolter.
mutter vt, vi grommeler, marmonner; * n grommellement m.
mutton n mouton m.

mutual *adj*, **~ly** *adv* mutuel(lement), réciproque(ment).
muzzle *n* muselière *f*; museau *m*;
* *vt* museler.
my *pn* mon, ma, mes.
myriad *n* myriade *f*.
myrrh *n* myrrhe *f*.
myrtle *n* myrte *m*.
myself *pn* moi-même.

mysterious *adj* mystérieux; **~ly**
adv mystérieusement.
mystery *n* mystère *m*.
mystic(al) *adj* mystique.
mystify *vt* mystifier; laisser perplexe.
mystique *n* mystique *f*.
myth *n* mythe *m*.
mythology *n* mythologie *f*.

N

nab *vt* attraper.
nag *n* bourrin *m*; * *vt* harceler.
nagging *adj* persistant; * *npl*
harcèlement *m*.
nail *n* ongle *m*; clou *m*; * *vt* clouer.
nailbrush *n* brosse à ongles *f*.
nailfile *n* lime à ongles *f*.
nail polish *n* vernis à ongles *m*.
nail scissors *npl* ciseaux à ongles
mpl.
naive *adj* naïf.
naked *adj* nu; dénudé; pur, simple.
name *n* nom *m*; réputation *f*, * *vt*
nommer; mentionner.
nameless *adj* anonyme.
namely *adv* à savoir.
namesake *n* homonyme *m*.
nanny *n* nourrice *f*.
nap *n* sieste *f*, somme *m*.
napalm *n* napalm *m*.
nape *n* nuque *f*.
napkin *n* serviette *f*.
narcissus *n* (*bot*) narcisse *m*.
narcotic *adj*, *n* narcotique *m*.
narrate *vt* narrer, raconter.
narrative *adj* narratif; * *n* narration *f*.
narrow *adj*, **~ly** *adv* étroit(e-
ment); * *vt* resserrer; limiter.
narrow-minded *adj* à l'esprit
étroit.
nasal *adj* nasal.
nasty *adj* méchant; mauvais; sale.
natal *adj* natal.

nation *n* nation *f*.
national *adj*, **~ly** *adv* national(e-
ment).
nationalism *n* nationalisme *m*.
nationalist *adj*, *n* nationaliste
mf.
nationality *n* nationalité *f*.
nationalize *vt* nationaliser.
nationwide *adj* au niveau national.
native *adj* natal; * *n* autochtone
mf.
native language *n* langue maternelle *f*.
Nativity *n* Nativité *f*.
natural *adj*, **~ly** *adv* naturel(lement).
natural gas *n* gaz naturel *m*.
naturalist *n* naturaliste *mf*.
naturalize *vt* naturaliser.
nature *n* nature *f*; sorte *f*.
naught *n* zéro *m*.
naughty *adj* méchant.
nausea *n* nausée, envie de vomir
f.
nauseate *vt* donner des nausées
à.
nauseous *adj* écœurant.
nautic(al), naval *adj* nautique.
nave *n* nef (d'église) *f*.
navel *n* nombril *m*.
navigate *vi* naviguer.
navigation *n* navigation *f*.
navy *n* marine *f*.
Nazi *n* nazi *m*, -e *f*.

near prep près de; * adv près; à côté; * adj proche.

nearby adj proche.

nearly adv presque.

near-sighted adj myope.

neat adj soigné; net, propre; **~ly** adv proprement; élégamment.

nebulous adj nébuleux.

necessarily adv nécessairement.

necessary adj nécessaire.

necessitate vt nécessiter.

necessity n nécessité f.

neck n cou m; * vi se bécoter.

necklace n collier m.

necktie n cravate f.

nectar n nectar m.

née adj: **~ Brown** née Brown.

need n besoin m; pauvreté f; * vt avoir besoin de, nécessiter.

needle n aiguille f.

needless adj superflu, inutile.

needlework n couture f.

needy adj nécessiteux, pauvre.

negation n négation f.

negative adj négatif; **~ly** adv négativement; * n négative f; négation f; négatif m.

neglect vt négliger; * n négligence f.

negligee n négligé, déshabillé m.

negligence n négligence f; manque de soin m.

negligent adj négligent; **~ly** adv négligemment.

negligible adj négligeable.

negotiate vt, vi négocier.

negotiation n négociation f.

Negress n Noire f.

Negro adj noir; * n Noire m.

neigh vi hennir; * n hennissement m.

neighbour n voisin m, -e f; * vt être voisin de.

neighbourhood n voisinage m.

neighbouring adj voisin.

neighbourly adj sociable.

neither conj ni; * pn aucun, ni l'un ni l'autre.

neon n néon m.

neon light n lumière au néon f.

nephew n neveu m.

nepotism n népotisme m.

nerve n nerf m; courage m; toupet m.

nerve-racking adj exaspérant.

nervous adj nerveux.

nervous breakdown n dépression nerveuse f.

nest n nid m; nichée f.

nest egg n (fig) économies fpl.

nestle vi, vt se blottir.

net n filet m.

netball n netball m.

net curtain n voile m.

netting n filet m.

nettle n ortie f.

network n réseau f.

neurosis n névrose f.

neurotic adj, n névrosé m, -e f.

neuter adj (gr) neutre.

neutral adj neutre.

neutrality n neutralité f.

neutralize vt neutraliser.

neutron n neutron m.

neutron bomb n bombe à neutrons f.

never adv jamais; **~ mind** ça ne fait rien.

never-ending adj interminable.

nevertheless adv cependant, néanmoins.

new adj neuf; nouveau; dernier; **~ly** adv nouvellement.

newborn adj nouveau-né, f nouveau-née.

newcomer n nouveau venu m, nouvelle venue f.

new-fangled adj moderne.

news npl nouvelles, informations fpl.

news agency n agence de presse f.

newscaster n présentateur m, -trice f.

newsdealer n marchand(e) de journaux m(f).

news flash n flash d'information m.

newsletter n bulletin m.

newspaper n journal m.

newsreel n actualités fpl.

New Year n Nouvel An m; **~'s Day** n Jour du Nouvel An m; **~'s Eve** Saint-Sylvestre f.

next adj prochain; **the ~ day** le jour suivant; * adv ensuite, après.

nib n pointe f; plume f.

nibble vt mordiller.

nice adj gentil, f gentille; agréable; joli; **~ly** adv gentiment; bien.

nice-looking adj beau, f belle.

niche n niche f.

nick n entaille f; * vt (sl) faucher.

nickel n nickel m; pièce de cinq cents (U.S.) f.

nickname n surnom m; * vt surnommer.

nicotine n nicotine f.

niece n nièce f.

niggling adj insignifiant.

night n nuit f; **by ~** de nuit; **good ~** bonne nuit.

nightclub n boîte de nuit f.

nightfall n tombée de la nuit f.

nightingale n rossignol m.

nightly adv tous les soirs; toutes les nuits; * adj nocturne.

nightmare n cauchemar m.

night school n cours du soir mpl.

night shift n équipe de nuit f.

nighttime n nuit f.

nihilist n nihiliste mf.

nimble adj léger; agile, souple.

nine adj, n neuf m.

nineteen adj, n dix-neuf m.

nineteenth adj, n dix-neuvième mf.

ninetieth adj, n quatre-vingt-dixième mf.

ninety adj, n quatre-vingt-dix m.

ninth adj, n neuvième mf.

nip vt pincer; mordre.

nipple n mamelon m; tétine f.

nit n lente f.

nitrogen n nitrogène m.

no adv non; * adj aucun; pas de.

nobility n noblesse f.

noble adj noble; * n noble mf.

nobleman n noble m.

nobody pn personne.

nocturnal adj nocturne.

nod n signe de tête m; * vi faire un signe de la tête; somnoler.

noise n bruit m.

noisily adv bruyamment.

noisiness n bruit, tapage m.

noisy adj bruyant.

nominal adj, **~ly** adv nominal(ement).

nominate vt nommer.

nomination n nomination f.

nominative n (gr) nominatif m.

nominee n candidat m, -e f.

non-alcoholic adj non alcoolisé.

non-aligned adj non-aligné.

nonchalant adj nonchalant.

non-committal adj réservé.

nonconformist n non-conformiste mf.

nondescript adj quelconque.

none pn aucun; personne.

nonentity n nullité f.

nonetheless adv cependant.

nonexistent adj inexistant.

nonfiction n ouvrages non romanesques mpl.

nonplussed adj perplexe.

nonsense n absurdité f.

nonsensical adj absurde.

nonsmoker n non-fumeur m.

nonstick adj anti-adhérent.

nonstop adj direct; * adv sans s'arrêter.

noodles npl nouilles fpl.

noon n midi m.

noose n nœud coulant m.

nor conj ni.

normal adj normal.

north n nord m; * adj du nord.

North America n Amérique du Nord f.

northeast n nord-est m.

northerly, northern adj du nord.

North Pole n pôle Nord m.

northward(s) adv vers le nord.

northwest n nord-ouest m.

nose n nez m.

nosebleed n saignement de nez m.

nosedive n piqué m.

nostalgia n nostalgie f.

nostril n narine f.

not adv pas; non.

notable adj notable.

notably adv notamment.

notary n notaire m.

notch n cran m, dent f; * vt denteler.

note n note f; billet m; mot m; marque f; * vt noter, marquer; remarquer.

notebook n carnet m.

noted adj célèbre, connu.

notepad n bloc-notes m.

notepaper n papier à lettres m.

nothing n rien m; **good for ~** bon à rien.

notice n notice f; avis m; * vt remarquer.

noticeable adj visible.

notification n notification f.

notify vt notifier.

notion n notion f; opinion f; idée f.

notoriety n notoriété f.

notorious adj notoire; **~ly** adv notoirement.

notwithstanding conj quoique.

nougat n nougat m.

nought n zéro m.

noun n (gr) nom, substantif m.

nourish vt nourrir, alimenter.

nourishing adj nourrissant.

nourishment n nourriture f, aliments mpl.

novel n roman m.

novelist n romancier m, -ière f.

novelty n nouveauté f.

November n novembre m.

novice n novice mf.

now adv maintenant; **~ and then** de temps en temps.

nowadays adv de nos jours, à l'heure actuelle.

nowhere adv nulle part.

noxious adj nocif.

nozzle n douille f.

nuance n nuance f.

nuclear adj nucléaire.

nucleus n noyau m.

nude adj nu.

nudge vt donner un coup de coude à.

nudist n nudiste mf.

nudity n nudité f.

nuisance n ennui m; gêne f.

nuke n (col) bombe atomique f; * vt atomiser.

null adj nul.

nullify vt annuler; invalider.

numb adj engourdi; * vt engourdir.

number n numéro, nombre m; quantité f; * vt numéroter; compter.

numberplate n plaque d'immatriculation f.

numbness n engourdissement m.

numeral n chiffre m.

numerical adj numérique.

numerous adj nombreux.

nun n religieuse f.

nunnery n couvent m.

nuptial adj nuptial; **~s** npl noces fpl.

nurse n infirmière f; * vt soigner; ménager.

nursery n crèche f; chambre d'enfant f.

nursery rhyme n comptine f.

nursery school n (école) maternelle f.

nursing home n maison de repos f.

nurture vt élever.

nut n noix f.

nutcrackers npl casse-noix m invar.

nutmeg n noix de muscade f.

nutritious adj nutritif.

nut shell n coquille de noix f.

nylon n nylon m; * adj en nylon.

O

oak *n* chêne *m*.

oar *n* rame *f*.

oasis *n* oasis *f*.

oat *n* avoine *f*.

oath *n* serment *m*.

oatmeal *n* flocons d'avoine *mpl*.

oats *npl* avoine *f*.

obedience *n* obéissance *f*.

obedient *adj* obéissant; ~**ly** *adv* avec obéissance.

obese *adj* obèse.

obesity *n* obésité *f*.

obey *vt* obéir à.

obituary *n* nécrologie *f*.

object *n* objet *m*; * *vt* objecter.

objection *n* objection *f*.

objectionable *adj* désagréable.

objective *adj*, *n* objectif *m*.

obligation *n* obligation *f*.

obligatory *adj* obligatoire.

oblige *vt* obliger; rendre service à.

obliging *adj* obligeant.

oblique *adj* oblique; indirect; ~**ly** *adv* obliquement.

obliterate *vt* effacer.

oblivion *n* oubli *m*.

oblivious *adj* oublieux.

oblong *adj* oblong.

obnoxious *adj* odieux.

oboe *n* hautbois *m*.

obscene *adj* obscène.

obscenity *n* obscénité *f*.

obscure *adj* obscur; ~**ly** *adv* obscurément; * *vt* obscurcir.

obscurity *n* obscurité *f*.

observance *n* observation *f*; observance *f*.

observant *adj* observateur; respectueux.

observation *n* observation *f*.

observatory *n* observatoire *m*.

observe *vt* observer.

observer *n* observateur *m*, -trice *f*.

observingly *adv* attentivement.

obsess *vt* obséder.

obsessive *adj* obsédant.

obsolete *adj* désuet.

obstacle *n* obstacle *m*.

obstinate *adj* obstiné; ~**ly** *adv* obstinément.

obstruct *vt* obstruer; entraver.

obstruction *n* obstruction *f*; encombrement *m*.

obtain *vt* obtenir.

obtainable *adj* disponible.

obtrusive *adj* importun.

obtuse *adj* obtus.

obvious *adj* évident; ~**ly** *adv* évidemment.

occasion *n* occasion *f*; * *vt* occasionner, causer.

occasional *adj* occasionnel; ~**ly** *adv* occasionnellement.

occupant, occupier *n* occupant *m*, -e *f*; locataire *mf*.

occupation *n* occupation *f*; emploi *m*.

occupy *vt* occuper.

occur *vi* se produire, arriver.

occurrence *n* incident *m*.

ocean *n* océan *m*.

ocean-going *adj* de haute mer.

oceanic *adj* océanique.

ocher *n* ocre *m*.

octave *n* octave *f*.

October *n* octobre *m*.

octopus *n* poulpe *m*.

odd *adj* impair; étrange; quelconque; ~**ly** *adv* étrangement.

oddity *n* singularité, particularité *f*.

odd jobs *npl* petits travaux *mpl*.

oddness *n* étrangeté *f*; singularité *f*.

odds *npl* chances *fpl*.

odious *adj* odieux.

odometer *n* compteur *m invar*.

odor *n* odeur *f*; parfum *m*.

odorous *adj* odorant.

of *prep* de; à.

off *adj* éteint; fermé; annulé; en congé; ~**!** *excl* du vent!

offend *vt* offenser, blesser; choquer; * *vi* pécher.

offender *n* délinquant *m*, -e *f*.

offense *n* offense *f*; injure *f*.

offensive *adj* offensant; injurieux; ~**ly** *adv* d'une manière offensante.

offer *vt* offrir; * *n* offre *f*.

offering *n* offrande *f*; offre *f*.

offhand *adj* désinvolte; * *adv* soudainement.

office *n* bureau *m*; poste *m*, fonctions *fpl*; service *m*.

office automation *n* bureautique *f*.

office building *n* immeuble de bureaux *m*.

office hours *npl* heures de bureau *fpl*.

officer *n* officier *m*; fonctionnaire *mf*.

office worker *n* employé(e) de bureau *m(f)*.

official *adj*, ~**ly** *adv* officiel(lement); * *n* employé *m*, -e *f*.

officiate *vi* officier.

officious *adj* officieux; ~**ly** *adv* officieusement.

off-line *adj*, *adv* hors ligne.

off-peak *adj* de basse saison.

off-season *adj*, *adv* hors-saison.

offset *vt* compenser; décaler.

offshoot *n* ramification *f*.

offshore *adj* côtier.

offside *adj* hors jeu.

offspring *n* progéniture *f*; descendance *f*.

offstage *adv* en coulisses.

off-the-rack *adj* prêt-à-porter.

ogle *vt* lorgner.

oil *n* huile *f*; * *vt* huiler.

oilcan *n* burette d'huile *f*; bidon d'huile *m*.

oilfield *n* gisement pétrolifère *m*.

oil filter *n* filtre à huile *m*.

oil painting *n* peinture à l'huile *f*.

oil rig *n* derrick *m*.

oil tanker *n* pétrolier *m*.

oil well *n* puits pétrolifère *m*.

oily *adj* huileux; gras.

ointment *n* onguent *m*.

O.K., okay *excl* O.K., d'accord; * *adj* bien; * *vt* approuver.

old *adj* vieux, *f* vieille.

old age *n* vieillesse *f*.

old-fashioned *adj* démodé.

olive *n* olivier *m*; olive *f*.

olive oil *n* huile d'olive *f*.

omelet(te) *n* omelette *f*.

omen *n* augure, présage *m*.

ominous *adj* menaçant.

omission *n* omission *f*; négligence *f*.

omit *vt* omettre.

omnipotence *n* omnipotence *f*.

omnipotent *adj* omnipotent, tout-puissant.

on *prep* sur, dessus; en; pour; * *adj* allumé, branché; ouvert; de service.

once *adv* une fois; **at** ~ tout de suite; **all at** ~ tout d'un coup; ~ **more** encore une fois.

oncoming *adj* qui arrive.

one *adj* un, une; ~ **by** ~ un par un.

one-day excursion *n* billet d'aller-retour valable une journée *m*.

one-man *adj* individuel.

onerous *adj* lourd; onéreux.

oneself *pn* soi-même.

one-sided *adj* partial.

one-to-one *adj* face à face.

ongoing *adj* continu; en cours.

onion *n* oignon *m*.

on-line *adj*, *adv* en ligne.

onlooker *n* spectateur *m*, -trice *f*.

only *adj* seul, unique; * *adv* seulement.

onset, onslaught *n* début *m*; attaque *f*.

onus *n* responsabilité *f*.

onward(s) *adv* en avant.

ooze *vi* suinter.

opaque *adj* opaque.

open *adj* ouvert; public; déclaré; sincère, franc; ~**ly** *adv* ouvertement; * *vt* ouvrir; * *vi* s'ouvrir;

commencer; **to ~ on to** donner lieu à; **to ~ up** *vt* ouvrir; *vi* s'ouvrir.

opening *n* ouverture *f*; *(com)* débouché *m*; inauguration *f*; commencement *m*.

open-minded *adj* aux idées larges.

openness *n* clareté *f*; franchise, sincérité *f*.

opera *n* opéra *m*.

opera house *n* théâtre de l'opéra *m*.

operate *vi* fonctionner; opérer.

operation *n* fonctionnement *m*; opération *f*.

operational *adj* opérationnel.

operative *adj* actif; en vigueur.

operator *n* opérateur *m*, -trice *f*; téléphoniste *mf*.

ophthalmic *adj* ophtalmique.

opine *vt* être d'avis (que).

opinion *n* opinion *f*; jugement *m*.

opinionated *adj* entêté.

opinion poll *n* sondage *m*.

opponent *n* opposant *m*, -e *f*; adversaire *mf*.

opportune *adj* opportun.

opportunist *n* opportuniste *mf*.

opportunity *n* occasion *f*.

oppose *vt* s'opposer à.

opposing *adj* opposé.

opposite *adj* opposé; contraire; * *adv* en face; *prep* en face de; * *n* contraire *m*.

opposition *n* opposition *f*; résistance *f*.

oppress *vt* opprimer.

oppression *n* oppression *f*.

oppressive *adj* oppressif.

oppressor *n* oppresseur *m*.

optic(al) *adj* optique; **~s** *npl* optique *f*.

optician *n* opticien *m*, -ienne *f*.

optimist *n* optimiste *mf*.

optimistic *adj* optimiste.

optimum *adj* optimum.

option *n* option *f*.

optional *adj* optionnel; facultatif.

opulent *adj* opulent.

or *conj* ou.

oracle *n* oracle *m*.

oral *adj* oral, verbal; **~ly** *adv* oralement.

orange *n* orange *f*.

orator *n* orateur *m*, -trice *f*.

orbit *n* orbite *f*.

orchard *n* verger *m*.

orchestra *n* orchestre *m*.

orchestral *adj* orchestral.

orchid *n* orchidée *f*.

ordain *vt* ordonner.

ordeal *n* épreuve *f*.

order *n* ordre *m*; commande *f*; mandat *m*; classe *f*; * *vt* ordonner; commander; mettre en ordre.

order form *n* bon de commande *m*.

orderly *adj* ordonné; réglé.

ordinarily *adv* ordinairement.

ordinary *adj* ordinaire.

ordination *n* ordination *f*.

ordnance *n* artillerie *f*.

ore *n* minerai *m*.

organ *n* organe *m*; orgue *m*.

organic(al) *adj* organique.

organism *n* organisme *m*.

organist *n* organiste *mf*.

organization *n* organisation *f*.

organize *vt* organiser.

orgasm *n* orgasme *m*.

orgy *n* orgie *f*.

oriental *adj* oriental.

orifice *n* orifice *m*.

origin *n* origine *f*.

original *adj* original; originel; **~ly** *adv* à l'origine; originalement.

originality *n* originalité *f*.

originate *vi* provenir (de); être originaire (de).

ornament *n* ornement *m*; * *vt* ornementer, décorer.

ornamental *adj* ornemental.

ornate *adj* ornementé.

orphan *adj, n* orphelin *m*, -e *f*.

orphanage *n* orphelinat *m*.

orthodox *adj* orthodoxe.

orthodoxy *n* orthodoxie *f*.

orthography n orthographe f.

orthopaedic adj orthopédique.

oscillate vi osciller.

osprey n balbuzard pêcheur m.

ostensibly adv selon les apparences.

ostentatious adj ostentatoire.

osteopath n ostéopathe mf.

ostracize vt frapper d'ostracisme.

ostrich n autruche f.

other pn autre.

otherwise adv autrement.

otter n loutre f.

ouch excl aïe!

ought v aux devoir; falloir.

ounce n once f.

our pn notre, pl nos.

ours pn le nôtre, la nôtre, les nôtres; à nous.

ourselves pn pl nous-mêmes.

oust vt évincer; déposséder.

out adv dehors; éteint.

outback n intérieur m.

outboard adj: ~ motor (moteur) hors-bord m.

outbreak n éruption f; explosion f.

outburst n explosion f.

outcast n paria m.

outcome n résultat m.

outcry n protestations fpl.

outdated adj démodé; périmé.

outdo vt surpasser.

outdoor adj de plein air, ~s adv à l'extérieur.

outer adj extérieur.

outermost adj extrême; le plus à l'extérieur.

outer space n espace m.

outfit n tenue f; équipement m.

outfitter n confectionneur m, -euse f.

outgoing adj extroverti; sortant.

outgrow vt devenir plus grand que.

outhouse n dépendances fpl.

outing n excursion f.

outlandish adj bizarre.

outlaw n hors-la-loi m; * vt proscrire.

outlay n dépenses fpl, frais mpl.

outlet n sortie f; débouché m.

outline n contour m; grandes lignes fpl.

outlive vt survivre à.

outlook n perspective f.

outlying adj distant, éloigné.

outmoded adj démodé.

outnumber vt être plus nombreux que.

out-of-date adj périmé; démodé.

outpatient n patient(e) en consultation externe m(f).

outpost n avant-poste m.

output n rendement m; sortie f.

outrage n outrage m; * vt outrager.

outrageous adj outrageant; atroce; ~ly adv outrageusement; atrocement.

outright adv absolument, complètement; * adj absolu, complet.

outrun vt gagner de vitesse, distancer.

outset n commencement m.

outshine vt éclipser.

outside n surface f; extérieur m; apparence f; * adv dehors; * prep en dehors de.

outsider n étranger m, -ère f.

outsize adj grande taille.

outskirts npl périphérie f, alentours mpl.

outspoken adj franc.

outstanding adj exceptionnel; en suspens.

outstretch vi s'étendre.

outstrip vt devancer; surpasser.

out-tray n courrier au départ m.

outward adj extérieur; vers l'extérieur; d'aller; ~ly adv à l'extérieur, extérieurement.

outweigh vt peser plus lourd que; l'emporter sur.

outwit vt être plus spirituel que.

oval n, adj ovale m.

ovary n ovaire m.

oven n four m.

ovenproof adj allant au four.

over *prep* sur, dessus; plus de; pendant; **all ~** de tous côtés; * *adj* fini; en trop, en plus; **~ again** à nouveau; **~ and ~** de nombreuses fois.

overall *adj* total; * *adv* dans l'ensemble; **~s** *npl* salopette *f*.

overawe *vt* impressionner.

overbalance *vi* perdre l'équilibre.

overbearing *adj* despotique.

overboard *adv* (*mar*) par-dessus bord.

overbook *vt* surréserver.

overcast *adj* couvert.

overcharge *vt* surcharger; faire payer un prix excessif à.

overcoat *n* pardessus *m*.

overcome *vt* vaincre; surmonter.

overconfident *adj* trop confiant.

overcrowded *adj* bondé; surpeuplé.

overdo *vi* exagérer.

overdose *n* overdose *f*.

overdraft *n* découvert *m*.

overdrawn *adj* à découvert.

overdress *vi* s'habiller trop élégamment.

overdue *adj* en retard; arriéré.

overeat *vi* trop manger.

overestimate *vt* surestimer.

overflow *vt* déborder de; * *vi* déborder; * *n* inondation *f*; surplus *m*.

overgrown *adj* envahi.

overgrowth *n* végétation envahissante *f*.

overhang *vt* surplomber.

overhaul *vt* réviser; * *n* révision *f*.

overhead *adv* en l'air, au-dessus.

overhear *vt* entendre par hasard.

overjoyed *adj* fou de joie.

overkill *n* exagération *f*.

overland *adj*, *adv* par voie de terre.

overlap *vi* se chevaucher.

overleaf *adv* au dos.

overload *vt* surcharger.

overlook *vt* dominer; donner sur;

oublier; laisser passer, tolérer; négliger.

overnight *adv* pendant la nuit; * *adj* de nuit.

overpass *n* pont surélevé *m*.

overpower *vt* dominer, écraser.

overpowering *adj* écrasant.

overrate *vt* surévaluer.

override *vt* outrepasser.

overriding *adj* prédominant.

overrule *vt* rejeter; annuler.

overrun *vt* envahir; infester; dépasser.

overseas *adv* à l'étranger; outremer; * *adj* étranger.

oversee *vt* inspecter, surveiller.

overseer *n* contremaître *m*.

overshadow *vt* éclipser.

overshoot *vt* dépasser.

oversight *n* oubli *m*; erreur *f*.

oversleep *vi* se réveiller en retard.

overspill *n* excédent de population *m*.

overstate *vi* exagérer.

overstep *vt* dépasser.

overt *adj* ouvert; public; **~ly** *adv* ouvertement.

overtake *vt* doubler.

overthrow *vt* renverser; détruire; * *n* renversement *m*; ruine, déroute *f*.

overtime *n* heures supplémentaires *fpl*.

overtone *n* harmonique *mf*; note *f*.

overture *n* ouverture *f*.

overturn *vt* renverser.

overweight *adj* trop lourd.

overwhelm *vt* écraser; submerger.

overwhelming *adj* écrasant; irrésistible.

overwork *vi* se surmener, trop travailler.

owe *vt* devoir; être redevable de.

owing *adj* dû; **~ to** en raison de.

owl *n* chouette *f*.

own *adj* propre; **my ~** mon, ma, mes propre(s); * *vt* posséder; **to**

~ **up** *vi* confesser.
owner *n* propriétaire *mf*.
ownership *n* possession *f*.
ox *n* boeuf *m*; ~**en** *pl* boeufs *mpl*.
oxidize *vt* oxyder.
oxygen *n* oxygène *m*.

oxygen mask *n* masque à oxygène *m*.
oxygen tent *n* tente à oxygène *f*.
oyster *n* huître *f*.
ozone *n* ozone *m*.

P

pa *n* papa *m*.
pace *n* pas *m*; allure *f*; * *vt* arpenter; * *vi* marcher.
pacemaker *n* meneur *m*, -euse *f* de train; (*med*) pacemaker *m*.
pacific(al) *adj* pacifique.
pacification *n* pacification *f*.
pacify *vt* pacifier.
pack *n* paquet *m*; jeu de cartes *m*; bande *f*; * *vt* empaqueter; remplier; * *vi* faire ses valises.
package *n* paquet *m*; accord *m*.
package tour *n* voyage organisé *m*.
packet *n* paquet *m*.
packing *n* emballage *m*.
pact *n* pacte *m*.
pad *n* bloc *m*; coussinet, tampon *m*; plateforme *f*; (*sl*) piaule *f*; * *vt* rembourrer.
padding *n* rembourrage *m*.
paddle *vi* ramer; * *n* pagaie *f*.
paddle steamer *n* vapeur à roues *m*.
paddock *n* paddock *m*.
paddy *n* rizière *f*.
pagan *adj*, *n* païen *m*, païenne *f*.
page *n* page *f*; page *m*.
pageant *n* grand spectacle *m*.
pageantry *n* pompe *f*.
pail *n* seau *m*.
pain *n* douleur *f*; mal *m*; peine *f*; * *vt* peiner.
pained *adj* peiné.
painful *adj* douloureux; pénible; ~**ly** *adv* douloureusement; péniblement; à grand-peine.
painkiller *n* analgésique *m*.

painless *adj* indolore; sans peine.
painstaking *adj* soigneux.
paint *vt* peindre.
paintbrush *n* pinceau *m*.
painter *n* peintre *m*.
painting *n* peinture *f*; tableau *m*.
paintwork *n* peinture *f*.
pair *n* pair *m*.
pajamas *npl* = **pyjamas**.
pal *n* copain *m*, copine *f*, pote *m*.
palatable *adj* savoureux.
palate *n* palais *m*.
palatial *adj* grandiose.
palaver *n* discussions *fpl*; situation embrouillée *f*.
pale *adj* pâle; clair.
palette *n* palette *f*.
paling *n* palissade *f*.
pall *n* nuage de fumée *m*; * *vi* perdre sa saveur.
pallet *n* palette *f*.
palliative *adj*, *n* palliatif *m*.
pallid *adj* pâle.
pallor *n* pâleur *f*.
palm *n* (*bot*) palme *f*, palmier *m*.
palmistry *n* chiromancie *f*.
Palm Sunday *n* Dimanche des Rameaux *m*.
palpable *adj* palpable; évident.
palpitation *n* palpitation *f*.
paltry *adj* dérisoire; mesquin.
pamper *vt* gâter, dorloter.
pamphlet *n* pamphlet *m*; brochure *f*.
pan *n* casserole *f*; poêle *f*.
panacea *n* panacée *f*.
panache *n* panache *m*.
pancake *n* crêpe *f*.

pandemonium n pandémonium m.

pane n vitre f.

panel n panneau m; comité m.

panelling n lambrissage m.

pang n angoisse f; tourment m.

panic adj, n (de) panique f.

panicky adj paniqué, affolé.

panic-stricken adj pris de panique.

pansy n (bot) pensée f.

pant vi haleter.

panther n panthère f.

panties npl (petite) culotte f.

pantihose n collant m.

pantry n placard m.

pants npl slip m; pantalon m.

papacy n papauté f.

papal adj papal.

paper n papier m; journal m; libellé d'examen m; exposé m, étude f; ~s pl documents mpl; (com) fonds mpl; * adj en papier; * vt garnir de papier; tapisser.

paperback n livre de poche m.

paper bag n sac en papier m.

paper clip n trombone m.

paperweight n presse-papiers m.

paperwork n paperasserie f.

paprika n paprica m.

par n équivalence f; égalité f; pair m; **at ~** (com) au pair.

parable n parabole f.

parachute n parachute m; * vi sauter en parachute.

parade n parade f; (mil) défilé m; * vt faire défiler, faire parader; * vi défiler, parader; se pavaner.

paradise n paradis m.

paradox n paradoxe m.

paradoxical adj paradoxal.

paragon n modèle absolu m.

paragraph n paragraphe m.

parallel adj parallèle; * n parallèle f; * vt mettre en parallèle; comparer.

paralyse vt paralyser.

paralysis n paralysie f.

paralytic(al) adj paralytique.

paramedic n auxiliaire médical(e) m(f).

paramount adj suprême, supérieur.

paranoid adj paranoïaque.

paraphernalia n affaires fpl; attirail m.

parasite n parasite m.

parasol n parasol m.

paratrooper n parachutiste m.

parcel n paquet m; parcelle f; * vt empaqueter, emballer.

parch vt dessécher.

parched adj mort de soif.

parchment n parchemin m.

pardon n pardon m; * vt pardonner.

parent n père m; mère f; ~s parents mpl.

parentage n parenté f; origine f.

parental adj paternel.

parenthesis n parenthèse f.

parish n paroisse f; * adj paroissial.

parishioner n paroissien m, -ienne f.

parity n parité f.

park n parc m; * vt garer; vi se garer.

parking n stationnement m.

parking lot n parking m.

parking meter n parcomètre m.

parking ticket n amende pour stationnement interdit f.

parlance n langage m.

parliament n parlement m.

parliamentary adj parlementaire.

parlour n parloir m; salon m.

parody n parodie f; * vt parodier.

parole n: **on ~** sur parole.

parricide n parricide m; parricide mf.

parrot n perroquet m.

parry vt parer.

parsley n (bot) persil m.

parsnip n (bot) navet m.

part n partie f; part f; rôle (d'acteur) m; raie f; ~s pl parties fpl; parages mpl; * vt séparer;

diviser; * *vi* se séparer; se diviser; **to ~ with** céder; se défaire de; donner; **~ly** *adv* en partie.

partial *adj* partial; **~ly** *adv* avec partialité; partiellement.

participant *n* participant *m*, -e *f*.

participate *vi* participer (à).

participation *n* participation *f*.

participle *n* (*gr*) participe *m*.

particle *n* particule *f*.

particular *adj* particulier, singulier; **~ly** *adv* particulièrement; * *n* particulier *m*; particularité *f*.

parting *n* séparation *f*; raie (dans les cheveux) *f*.

partisan *n* partisan *m*, -e *f*.

partition *n* partition, séparation *f*; * *vt* diviser en plusieurs parties, partager,

partner *n* associé *m*, -e *f*; cavalier *m*, -ière *f*.

partnership *n* association *f*; société *f*.

partridge *n* perdrix *f*.

party *n* parti *m*; fête *f*.

pass *vt* passer; dépasser; adopter; être admis à; * *vi* passer; * *n* permis *m*; passage *m*; **to ~ away** *vi* mourir; **to ~ by** *vi* passer; *vt* négliger, oublier; **to ~ on** *vt* transmettre; passer.

passable *adj* passable; praticable.

passage *n* passage *m*; traversée *f*; couloir *m*.

passbook *n* livret d'épargne *m*.

passenger *n* passager *m*, -ère *f*.

passer-by *n* passant *m*, -e *f*.

passing *adj* passager.

passion *n* passion *f*; amour *m*; emportement *m*.

passionate *adj* passionné; **~ly** *adv* passionnément; ardemment.

passive *adj* passif; **~ly** *adv* passivement.

passkey *n* passe-partout *m invar*.

Passover *n* Pâque *f*.

passport *n* passeport *m*.

passport control *n* contrôle des passeports *m*.

password *n* mot de passe *m*.

past *adj* passé; * *n* (*gr*) prétérit *m*; passé *m*; * *prep* au-delà de; après.

pasta *n* pâtes *fpl*.

paste *n* pâte *f*; colle *f*; * *vt* coller.

pasteurized *adj* pasteurisé.

pastime *n* passe-temps *m invar*; divertissement *m*.

pastor *n* pasteur *m*.

pastoral *adj* pastoral.

pastry *n* pâtisserie *f*.

pasture *n* pâture *f*.

pasty *adj* pâteux; pâle.

pat *vt* tapoter.

patch *n* pièce *f*; tache *f*; terrain *m*; * *vt* rapiécer; **to ~ up** réparer; faire la paix dans.

patchwork *n* patchwork *m*.

pâté *n* pâté *m*.

patent *adj* breveté; évident; * *n* brevet *m*; * *vt* faire breveter.

patentee *n* détenteur d'un brevet *m*.

patent leather *n* cuir verni *m*.

paternal *adj* paternel.

paternity *n* paternité *f*.

path *n* chemin, sentier *m*.

pathetic *adj*, **~ally** *adv* pathétique(ment); lamentable(ment).

pathological *adj* pathologique.

pathology *n* pathologie *f*.

pathos *n* pathétique *m*.

pathway *n* sentier *m*.

patience *n* patience *f*.

patient *adj* patient; **~ly** *adv* patiemment; * *n* patient *m*, -e *f*.

patio *n* patio *m*.

patriarch *m* patriarche *m*.

patriot *n* patriote *mf*.

patriotic *adj* patriotique.

patriotism *n* patriotisme *m*.

patrol *n* patrouille *f*; * *vi* patrouiller.

patrol car *n* voiture de patrouille *f*.

patrolman *n* agent de police *m*.

patron *n* protecteur *m*; client *m*, -e *f*.

patronage n patronage m; clientèle f.

patronize vt patronner, protéger.

patter n trottinement m; bavardage m; * vi trottiner.

pattern n motif m; modèle m.

paunch n panse f; ventre m.

pauper n pauvre mf.

pause n pause f; * vi faire une pause; hésiter.

pave vt paver; carreler.

pavement n trottoir m.

pavilion n pavillon m.

paving stone n pavé m.

paw n patte f; * vt tripoter.

pawn n pion m; gage m; * vt engager.

pawn broker n prêteur(-euse) sur gages m(f).

pawnshop n mont-de-piété m.

pay vt payer; **to ~ back** vt rembourser; **to ~ for** payer; **to ~ off** vt liquider; vi payer; rapporter; * n paie f; salaire m.

payable adj payable.

pay day n jour de paie m.

payee n porteur m.

pay envelope n enveloppe de paie f.

paymaster n caissier m.

payment n paiement m.

pay-phone n téléphone public m.

payroll n liste des employés f.

pea n pois m.

peace n paix f.

peaceful adj paisible; pacifique.

peach n pêche f.

peacock n paon m.

peak n pic m; maximum m.

peak hours, peak period n heures de pointe fpl.

peal n carillon m; grondement m.

peanut n cacahuète f.

pear n poire f.

pearl n perle f.

peasant n paysan m, -anne f.

peat n tourbe f.

pebble n caillou m; galet m.

peck n coup de bec m; * vt picoter.

pecking order n hiérarchie f.

peculiar adj étrange, singulier; **~ly** adv étrangement.

peculiarity n particularité, singularité f.

pedal n pédale f; * vi pédaler.

pedant n pédant m, -e f.

pedantic adj pédant.

peddler n vendeur ambulant m.

pedestal n piédestal m.

pedestrian n piéton m, -onne f; * adj pédestre.

pediatrics n pédiatrie f.

pedigree n généalogie f; pedigree m; * adj de race.

peek vi regarder à la dérobée.

peel vt peler; éplucher; * vi peler; * n peau f; pelure f.

peer n pair m.

peerless adj incomparable.

peeved adj fâché.

peevish adj maussade, ronchon (fam).

peg n cheville f; piquet m; * vt cheviller.

pelican n pélican m.

pellet n boulette f.

pelt n fourrure f; * vt arroser; * vi pleuvoir à verse.

pen n stylo m; plume f; enclos m.

penal adj pénal.

penalty n peine f; sanction f; amende f.

penance n pénitence f.

pence n = pl of penny.

pencil n crayon m.

pencil case n trousse f.

pendant n pendentif m.

pending adj pendant.

pendulum n pendule m.

penetrate vt pénétrer dans.

penguin n pingouin m.

penicillin n pénicilline f.

peninsula n péninsule f.

penis n pénis m.

penitence n pénitence f.

penitent adj, n pénitent m, -e f.

penitentiary n pénitencier m.

penknife n canif m.

pennant n fanion m.

penniless *adj* sans le sou.
penny *n* penny *m*.
penpal *n* correspondant *m*, -e *f*.
pension *n* pension *f*; * *vt* pensionner.
pensive *adj* pensif; ~**ly** *adv* pensivement.
pentagon *n*: **the P~** le Pentagone.
Pentecost *n* la Pentecôte *f*.
penthouse *n* appartement situé sur le toit d'un immeuble *m*.
pent-up *adj* reprimé, refoulé.
penultimate *adj* pénultième, avant-dernier.
penury *n* pénurie *f*.
people *n* peuple *m*; nation *f*; gens *mpl*; * *vt* peupler.
pep *n* énergie *f*; **to ~ up** *vt* animer.
pepper *n* poivre *m*; * *vt* poivrer.
peppermint *n* menthe poivrée *f*.
per *prep* par.
per annum *adv* par an.
per capita *adj*, *adv* par habitant.
perceive *vt* percevoir.
percentage *n* pourcentage *m*.
perception *n* perception *f*; notion *f*.
perch *n* perche *f*.
perchance *adv* par hasard.
percolate *vt* filtrer.
percolator *n* percolateur *m*.
percussion *n* percussion *f*.
perdition *n* perte, ruine *f*.
peremptory *adj* péremptoire; décisif.
perennial *adj* perpétuel.
perfect *adj* parfait; idéal; ~**ly** *adv* parfaitement; * *vt* parfaire, perfectionner.
perfection *n* perfection *f*.
perforate *vt* perforer.
perforation *n* perforation *f*.
perform *vt* exécuter; effectuer; * *vi* donner une représentation, tenir un rôle.
performance *n* exécution *f*; accomplissement *m*; rendement *m*; représentation *f*.
performer *n* exécutant *m*, -e *f*; acteur *m*, -trice *f*.

perfume *n* parfum *m*; * *vt* parfumer.
perhaps *adv* peut-être.
peril *n* péril, danger *m*.
perilous *adj* dangereux; ~**ly** *adv* dangereusement.
perimeter *n* périmètre *m*.
period *n* période *f*; époque *f*; règles *fpl*.
periodic(al) *adj* périodique; ~**ally** *adv* périodiquement.
periodical *n* journal *m*.
peripheral *adj* périphérique; * *n* unité périphérique *f*.
perish *vi* périr.
perishable *adj* périssable.
perjure *vt* parjurer.
perjury *n* parjure *m*.
perk *n* extra, à-côté *m*.
perky *adj* animé, plein d'entrain.
perm *n* permanente *f*.
permanent *adj* permanent; ~**ly** *adv* en permanence.
permeate *vt* pénétrer, traverser.
permissible *adj* permis.
permission *n* permission *f*.
permissive *adj* permissif.
permit *vt* permettre; * *n* permis *m*.
permutation *n* permutation *f*.
perpendicular *adj*, ~**ly** *adv* perpendiculaire(ment); * *n* perpendiculaire *f*.
perpetrate *vt* perpétrer, commettre.
perpetual *adj* perpétuel; ~**ly** *adv* perpétuellement.
perpetuate *vt* perpétuer, éterniser.
perplex *vt* confondre, laisser perplexe.
persecute *vt* persécuter; importuner.
persecution *n* persécution *f*.
perseverance *n* persévérance *f*.
persevere *vi* persévérer.
persist *vi* persister.
persistence *adj* persistance *f*.
persistent *adj* persistant.
person *n* personne *f*.
personable *adj* attrayant.

personage n personnage m.

personal adj, **~ly** adv personnel-(lement).

personal assistant n assistant m, -e f.

personal column n annonces personnelles fpl.

personal computer n ordinateur individuel m.

personality n personnalité f.

personification n personnification f.

personify vt personnifier.

personnel n personnel m.

perspective n perspective f.

perspiration n transpiration f.

perspire vi transpirer.

persuade vt persuader.

persuasion n persuasion f.

persuasive adj persuasif; **~ly** adv de manière persuasive.

pert adj plein d'entrain.

pertaining: ~ to prep relatif à.

pertinent adj pertinent; **~ly** adv de manière pertinente.

pertness n impertinence f; entrain m.

perturb vt perturber.

perusal n lecture f.

peruse vt lire; examiner attentivement.

pervade vt pénétrer, traverser.

perverse adj pervers, dépravé; **~ly** adv perversement.

pervert vt pervertir, corrompre.

pessimist n pessimiste mf.

pest n insecte nuisible m; casse-pieds (fam) mf invar.

pester vt importuner, fatiguer.

pestilence n peste f.

pet n animal domestique m; préféré m, -e f; * vt gâter; * vi se peloter (fam).

petal n (bot) pétale m.

petite adj menue.

petition n pétition f; * vt présenter une pétition à; supplier.

petrified adj pétrifié.

petroleum n pétrole m.

petticoat n jupon m.

pettiness n insignifiance f.

petty adj mesquin; insignifiant.

petty cash n argent destiné aux dépenses courantes m.

petty officer n second maître m.

petulant adj pétulant.

pew n banc m.

pewter n étain m.

phantom n fantôme m.

Pharisee n Pharisien m.

pharmaceutic(al) adj pharmaceutique.

pharmacist n pharmacien m, -ienne f.

pharmacy n pharmacie f.

phase n phase f.

pheasant n faisan m.

phenomenal adj phénoménal.

phenomenon n phénomène m.

phial n fiole f.

philanthropic adj philanthropique.

philanthropist n philanthrope mf.

philanthropy n philanthropie f.

philologist n philologue mf.

philology n philologie f.

philosopher n philosophe mf.

philosophic(al) adj, **~ally** adv philosophique(ment).

philosophize vi philosopher.

philosophy n philosophie f; **natural ~** sciences naturelles fpl.

phlegm n flegme m.

phlegmatic(al) adj flegmatique.

phobia n phobie f.

phone n téléphone m; * vt téléphoner à; **to ~ back** vt, vi rappeler; **to ~ up** vt appeler au téléphone.

phone book n annuaire m.

phone box, phone booth n cabine téléphonique f.

phone call n coup de téléphone m.

phosphorus n phosphore m.

photocopier n photocopieuse f.

photocopy n photocopie f.

photograph n photo(graphie) f; * vt photographier.

photographer *n* photographe *mf*.
photographic *adj* photographique.
photography *n* photo(graphie) *f*.
phrase *n* phrase *f*; locution *f*; * *vt* exprimer.
phrase book *n* guide de conversation *m*.
physical *adj*, **~ly** *adv* physique(ment).
physical education *n* éducation physique *f*.
physician *n* médecin *m*.
physicist *n* physicien *m*, -ienne *f*.
physiological *adj* physiologique.
physiologist *n* physiologiste, physiologue *mf*.
physiology *n* physiologie *f*.
physiotherapy *n* physiothérapie *f*.
physique *n* physique *m*.
pianist *n* pianiste *mf*.
piano *n* piano *m*.
piccolo *n* piccolo *m*.
pick *vt* choisir; cueillir; gratter; **to ~ on** *vt* s'en prendre à; **to ~ out** *vt* choisir; **to ~ up** *vi* s'améliorer; se remettre; * *vt* ramasser; décrocher; arrêter; acheter; * *n* pic *m*; choix *m*.
pickaxe *n* pic *m*.
picket *n* piquet *m*.
pickle *n* saumure *f*; * *vt* saumurer.
pickpocket *n* pickpocket *m*.
pickup *n* (*auto*) fourgonnette *f*.
picnic *n* pique-nique *m*.
pictorial *adj* pictural; illustré.
picture *n* image *f*; peinture *f*; photo *f*; * *vt* dépeindre; se figurer.
picture book *n* livre d'images *m*.
picturesque *adj* pittoresque.
pie *n* gâteau *m*; tarte *f*; pâté en croûte *m*.
piece *n* morceau *m*; pièce *f*; tranche *f*; * *vt* raccommoder.
piecemeal *adv* en morceaux; * *adj* partiel.
piecework *n* travail à la pièce *m*.
pier *n* jetée *f*.

pierce *vt* percer, transpercer.
piercing *adj* perçant.
piety *n* piété, dévotion *f*.
pig *n* cochon *m*.
pigeon *n* pigeon *m*.
pigeonhole *n* casier *m*.
piggy bank *n* tirelire *f*.
pigheaded *adj* têtu.
pigsty *n* porcherie *f*.
pigtail *n* natte *f*.
pike *n* brochet *m*; pique *f*.
pile *n* tas *m*; pile *f*; amas *m*; poil *m*; **~s** *pl* hémorroïdes *fpl*; * *vt* entasser, empiler.
pile-up *n* carambolage *m*.
pilfer *vt* chaparder.
pilgrim *n* pèlerin *m*.
pilgrimage *n* pèlerinage *m*.
pill *n* pilule *f*.
pillage *vt* piller, mettre à sac.
pillar *n* pilier *m*.
pillion *n* siège arrière *m*.
pillow *n* oreiller *m*.
pillow case *n* taie d'oreiller *f*.
pilot *n* pilote *m*; * *vt* piloter; (*fig*) mener.
pilot light *n* témoin *m*.
pimp *n* proxénète, maquereau (*fam*) *m*.
pimple *n* bouton *m*.
pin *n* épingle *f*; goupille *f*; **~s and needles** *npl* fourmis *fpl*; * *vt* épingler; goupiller.
pinafore *n* tablier *m*.
pinball *n* flipper *m*.
pincers *n* pinces, tenailles *fpl*.
pinch *vt* pincer; (*sl*) piquer, faucher; * *vi* serrer; * *n* pincement *m*; pincée *f*.
pincushion *n* pelote à épingles *f*.
pine *n* (*bot*) pin *m*; * *vi* languir.
pineapple *n* ananas *m*.
ping *n* tintement *m*.
pink *n*, *adj* rose *m*.
pinnacle *n* sommet *m*.
pinpoint *vt* préciser; souligner.
pint *n* pinte *f*.
pioneer *n* pionnier *m*.
pious *adj* pieux, dévot; **~ly** *adv* pieusement.

pip *n* pépin *m*.

pipe *n* tube, tuyau *m*; pipe *f*; **~s** tuyauterie *f*.

pipe cleaner *n* cure-pipe *m*.

pipe dream *n* rêve impossible *m*.

pipeline *n* canalisation *f*; oléoduc *m*; gazoduc *m*.

piper *n* joueur de cornemuse *m*.

piping *adj* bouillant; aigu, *f* aiguë.

pique *n* pique *f*; dépit *m*.

piracy *n* piraterie *f*.

pirate *n* pirate *m*.

pirouette *n* pirouette *f*; *vi* pirouetter.

Pisces *n* Poissons *mpl* (signe du zodiaque).

piss *n* (*sl*) pisse *f*; * *vi* pisser.

pistol *n* pistolet *m*.

piston *n* piston *m*.

pit *n* noyau *m*; mine *f*; fosse *f*.

pitch *n* lancement *m*; ton *m*; * *vt* lancer, jeter; * *vi* tomber; piquer du nez.

pitchblack *adj* noir comme dans un four.

pitcher *n* cruche *f*.

pitchfork *n* fourche *f*.

pitfall *n* piège *m*.

pithy *adj* moelleux.

pitiable *adj* pitoyable; déplorable.

pitiful *adj* pitoyable; lamentable; **~ly** *adv* pitoyablement.

pittance *n* salaire de misère *m*; pitance *f*.

pity *n* pitié *f*; * *vt* avoir pitié de.

pivot *n* pivot, axe *m*.

pizza *n* pizza *f*.

placard *n* affiche *f*.

placate *vt* apaiser.

place *n* endroit, lieu *m*; place *f*; * *vt* placer; mettre.

placid *adj* placide, calme; **~ly** *adv* placidement.

plagiarism *n* plagiat *m*.

plague *n* peste *f*; * *vt* tourmenter; infester.

plaice *n* carrelet *m*.

plaid *n* tartan *m*; plaid *m*.

plain *adj* uni; simple; clair, sincère; commun; évident; **~ly** *adv* simplement; clairement; * *n* plaine *f*.

plaintiff *n* (*law*) plaignant *m*, -e *f*.

plait *n* pli *m*; tresse *f*; * *vt* plier; tresser.

plan *n* plan *m*; projet *m*; * *vt* projeter.

plane *n* avion *m*; plan *m*; rabot *m*; * *vt* aplanir; raboter.

planet *n* planète *f*.

planetary *adj* planétaire.

plank *n* planche *f*.

planner *n* planificateur *m*, -trice *f*.

planning *n* planification *f*.

plant *n* plante *f*; usine *f*; machinerie *f*; * *vt* planter.

plantation *n* plantation *f*.

plaque *n* plaque *f*.

plaster *n* plâtre *m*; emplâtre *m*; * *vt* plâtrer; emplâtrer.

plastered *adj* (*sl*) bourré, soûl.

plasterer *n* plâtrier *m*.

plastic *adj* plastique.

plastic surgery *n* chirurgie esthétique *f*.

plate *n* assiette *f*; plaque *f*; lame *f*.

plateau *n* plateau *m*.

plate glass *n* vitre *f*.

platform *n* plateforme *f*.

platinum *n* platine *m*.

platitude *n* platitude *f*.

platoon *n* (*mil*) peloton *m*.

platter *n* écuelle *f*; plat *m*.

plaudit *n* applaudissement *m*.

plausible *adj* plausible.

play *n* jeu *m*; pièce de théâtre *f*; * *vt*, *vi* jouer; (*also mus*) **to ~ down** *vt* rabaisser; minimiser.

playboy *n* playboy *m*.

player *n* joueur *m*, -euse *f*; acteur *m*, -trice *f*.

playful *adj* enjoué, amusé; **~ly** *adv* d'une manière enjouée; pour s'amuser.

playmate *n* camarade de jeu *mf*.

playground *n* cour de récréation *f*; jardin d'enfants *m*.

playgroup *n* école maternelle *f*.
play-off *n* belle *f*.
playpen *n* parc pour enfant *m*.
plaything *n* jouet *m*.
playwright *n* dramaturge *mf*.
plea *n* appel *m*; excuse *f*, prétexte *m*.
plead *vt* plaider; prétexter.
pleasant *adj* agréable; plaisant; aimable; ~**ly** *adv* agréablement.
please *vt* faire plaisir à.
pleased *adj* content.
pleasing *adj* agréable, plaisant.
pleasure *n* plaisir *m*; gré *m*, volonté *f*.
pleat *n* pli *m*.
pledge *n* promesse *f*; gage *m*; * *vt* engager; promettre.
plentiful *adj* copieux; abondant.
plenty *n* abondance *f*; ~ **of** beaucoup de.
plethora *n* pléthore *f*.
pleurisy *n* pleurésie *f*.
pliable, pliant *adj* pliable, pliant; souple.
pliers *npl* tenailles *fpl*.
plight *n* épreuve *f*; situation difficile *f*.
plinth *n* plinthe *f*.
plod *vi* se traîner, avancer péniblement.
plot *n* petit morceau de terrain *m*; complot *m*; intrigue *f*; * *vt* tracer; comploter; conspirer.
plough *n* charrue *f*; * *vt* labourer; **to ~ back** *vt* réinvestir; **to ~ through** *vi* se faire un chemin; avancer péniblement.
ploy *n* truc *m*.
pluck *vt* tirer; arracher; déplumer; * *n* courage *m*.
plucky *adj* courageux.
plug *n* tampon *m*; bouchon *m*; bougie *f*; prise *f*; * *vt* boucher.
plum *n* prune *f*.
plumage *n* plumage *m*.
plumb *n* aplomb *m*; * *adv* d'aplomb; * *vt* plomber; sonder.
plumber *n* plombier *m*.
plume *n* plume *f*.

plump *adj* rondouillet, dodu.
plum tree *n* prunier *m*.
plunder *vt* mettre à sac, piller; * *n* pillage *m*; butin *m*.
plunge *vi* plonger; s'élancer.
plunger *n* piston *m*.
pluperfect *n* (*gr*) plus-que-parfait *m*.
plural *adj*, *n* pluriel *m*.
plurality *n* pluralité *f*.
plus *n* signe plus *m*; * *prep* plus.
plush *adj* en peluche.
plutonium *n* plutonium *m*.
ply *vt* manier avec vigueur; * *vi* s'appliquer; (*mar*) faire la navette.
plywood *n* contreplaqué *m*.
pneumatic *adj* pneumatique.
pneumatic drill *n* marteau pneumatique *m*.
pneumonia *n* pneumonie *f*.
poach *vt* pocher; braconner; *vi* braconner.
poached *adj* poché.
poacher *n* braconnier *m*.
poaching *n* braconnage *m*.
pocket *n* poche *f*; * *vt* empocher.
pocketbook *n* sac à main *m*.
pocket money *n* argent de poche *m*.
pod *n* cosse *f*.
podgy *adj* boudiné.
poem *n* poème *m*.
poet *n* poète *m*.
poetess *n* poétesse *f*.
poetic *adj* poétique.
poetry *n* poésie *f*.
poignant *adj* poignant.
point *n* pointe *f*; point *m*; promontoire *m*; ~ **of view** *n* point de vue *m*; * *vt* pointer; tailler en pointe; indiquer.
point-blank *adv* à bout portant; directement.
pointed *adj* pointu; acéré; ~**ly** *adv* subtilement.
pointer *n* auguille *f*; pointer *m*.
pointless *adj* inutile.
poise *n* attitude *f*; équilibre *m*.
poison *n* poison *m*; * *vt* empoisonner.

poisoning *n* empoisonnement *m*.

poisonous *adj* vénéneux.

poke *vt* attiser; donner un coup de coude à; pousser du doigt.

poker *n* tison *m*; poker *m*.

poker-faced *adj* au visage impassible.

poky *adj* exigu, *f* exiguë.

polar *adj* polaire.

pole *n* pôle *m*; mât *m*; perche *f*.

pole bean *n* haricot en rames *m*.

pole vault *n* saut à la perche *m*.

police *n* police *f*.

police car *n* voiture de police *f*.

policeman *n* agent de police *m*.

police state *n* état policier *m*.

police station *n* commissariat *m*.

policewoman *n* femme agent de police *f*.

policy *n* politique *f*; police d'assurance *f*.

polio *n* polio *f*.

polish *vt* polir; cirer; **to ~ off** *vt* parachever; expédier; * *n* poli *m*.

polished *adj* poli; ciré; élégant.

polite *adj*, **~ly** *adv* poli(ment), courtois(ement).

politeness *n* politesse, courtoisie *f*.

politic *adj* politique; rusé.

political *adj* politique.

politician *n* homme (femme) politique *m(f)*.

politics *npl* politique *f*.

polka *n* polka *f*; **~ dot** *n* pois *m*.

poll *n* liste électorale *f*; vote *m*; sondage *m*.

pollen *n* (*bot*) pollen *m*.

pollute *vt* polluer; corrompre.

pollution *n* pollution, contamination *f*.

polo *n* polo *m*.

polyester *n* polyester *m*.

polyethylene *n* polyéthylène *m*.

polygamy *n* polygamie *f*.

polystyrene *n* polystyrène *m*.

polytechnic *n* école d'enseignement technique *f*.

pomegranate *n* grenade *f*.

pomp *n* pompe *f*; splendeur *f*.

pompom *n* pompon *m*.

pompous *adj* pompeux.

pond *n* mare *f*; étang *m*.

ponder *vt* considérer; réfléchir à.

ponderous *adj* lourd, pesant.

pontiff *n* pontife *m*.

pontoon *n* ponton *m*.

pony *n* poney *m*.

ponytail *n* queue de cheval *f*.

pool *n* flaque d'eau *f*; piscine *f*; * *vt* grouper.

poor *adj* pauvre; mauvais; **~ly** *adv* pauvrement; **the ~** *n* les pauvres *mpl*.

pop *n* pop *m*; papa *m*; boisson gazeuse *f*; éclatement *m*; * **to ~ in/off** *vi* entrer/sortir un instant.

pop concert *n* concert de musique pop *m*.

popcorn *n* popcorn *m*.

Pope *n* pape *m*.

poplar *n* peuplier *m*.

poppy *n* (*bot*) pavot *m*.

popsicle *n* esquimau *m*.

populace *n* populace *f*.

popular *adj*, **~ly** *adv* populaire(ment).

popularity *n* popularité *f*.

popularize *vt* populariser.

populate *vi* peupler.

population *n* population *f*.

populous *adj* populeux.

porcelain *n* porcelaine *f*.

porch *n* porche *m*.

porcupine *n* porc-épic *m*.

pore *n* pore *m*.

pork *n* porc *m*.

pornography *n* pornographie *f*.

porous *adj* poreux.

porpoise *n* marsouin *m*.

porridge *n* porridge *m*, flocons d'avoine *mpl*.

port *n* port *m*; (*mar*) sabord *m*; porto (vin) *m*.

portable *adj* portable, portatif.

portal *n* portail *m*.

porter *n* portier *m*; garçon *m*.

portfolio *n* serviette *f*; carton *m*; portefeuille *m*.

porthole n hublot m.

portico n portique m.

portion n portion, part f.

portly adj corpulent.

portrait n portrait m.

portray vt faire le portrait de; dépeindre.

pose n posture f; pose f; * vi, vt poser.

posh adj chic; bourgeois.

position n position f; situation f; * vt mettre en position.

positive adj positif; réel; favorable; ~ly adv positivement; assurément.

posse n peloton m.

possess vt posséder.

possession n possession f.

possessive adj possessif.

possibility n possibilité f.

possible adj possible; ~ly adv peut-être.

post n courrier m; poste f; emploi m; poste m; pieu m; * vt poster; fixer.

postage n port m.

postage stamp n timbre m.

postcard n carte postale f.

postdate vt postdater.

poster n poster m.

posterior n postérieur m.

posterity n postérité f.

postgraduate n licencié m, -e f.

posthumous adj posthume.

postman n facteur m.

postmark n cachet de la poste m.

postmaster n receveur des postes m.

post office n poste f, bureau de poste m.

postpone vt remettre; différer.

postscript n post-scriptum m.

posture n posture f.

postwar adj d'après-guerre.

posy n petit bouquet de fleurs m.

pot n pot m; marmite f; (sl) marijuana f; * vt empoter; mettre en pot.

potato n pomme de terre, patate (fam) f.

potato peeler n couteau éplucheur m.

potbellied adj ventru.

potent adj puissant.

potential adj potentiel.

pothole n trou m.

potion n potion f.

potted adj en pot.

potter n potier m.

pottery n poterie f.

potty adj insignifiant; (sl) fou, maboul.

pouch n sac m.

poultice n cataplasme m.

poultry n volaille f.

pound n livre f; livre sterling f; fourrière f; * vt concasser; * vi taper fort.

pour vt verser; servir; * vi couler; pleuvoir à verse.

pout vi faire la moue.

poverty n pauvreté f.

powder n poudre f; * vt saupoudrer.

powder compact n poudrier m.

powdered milk n lait en poudre m.

powder puff n houppette f.

powder room n toilettes fpl.

powdery adj poudreux.

power n pouvoir m; puissance f; empire m; autorité f; force f; * vt propulser.

powerful adj puissant; ~ly adv puissamment; avec force.

powerless adj impotent.

power station n centrale électrique f.

practicable adj praticable; faisable.

practical adj, ~ly adv pratique(ment).

practicality n faisabilité f.

practical joke n farce f.

practice n pratique f; usage m; entraînement m; ~s pl agissements mpl.

practise vt pratiquer, exercer; * vi s'exercer, s'entraîner.

practitioner n médecin m.

pragmatic *adj* pragmatique.

prairie *n* prairie *f*.

praise *n* éloge *m*; louange *f*; * *vt* louer.

praiseworthy *adj* digne d'éloges.

prance *vi* cabrioler.

prank *n* folie, extravagance *f*.

prattle *vi* jacasser; * *n* jacasserie *f*.

prawn *n* crevette *f*.

pray *vi* prier.

prayer *n* prière *f*.

prayer book *n* livre de messe *m*.

preach *vt* prêcher.

preacher *n* prédicateur *m*.

preamble *n* préambule *m*.

precarious *adj* précaire, incertain; **~ly** *adv* précairement.

precaution *n* précaution *f*.

precautionary *adj* préventif.

precede *vt* précéder.

precedence *n* précédence *f*.

precedent *adj*, *n* précédent *m*.

precinct *n* limite *f*; enceinte *f*; circonscription *f*.

precious *adj* précieux.

precipice *n* précipice *m*.

precipitate *vt* précipiter; * *adj* précipité *m*.

precise *n* précis, exact; **~ly** *adv* précisément, exactement.

precision *n* précision, exactitude *f*.

preclude *vt* prévenir, empêcher.

precocious *adj* précoce, prématuré.

preconceive *vt* préconcevoir.

preconception *n* préjugé *m*; idée préconçue *f*.

precondition *n* condition préalable *f*.

precursor *n* précurseur *m*.

predator *n* prédateur *m*.

predecessor *n* prédécesseur *m*.

predestination *n* prédestination *f*.

predicament *n* situation difficile *f*.

predict *vt* prédire.

predictable *adj* prévisible.

prediction *n* prédiction *f*.

predilection *n* prédilection *f*.

predominant *adj* prédominant.

predominate *vt* prédominer.

preen *vt* nettoyer (ses plumes).

prefab *n* maison préfabriquée *f*.

preface *n* préface *f*.

prefer *vt* préférer.

preferable *adj* préférable.

preferably *adv* de préférence.

preference *n* préférence *f*.

preferential *adj* préférentiel.

preferment *n* promotion *f*; préférence *f*.

prefix *vt* préfixer; * *n* (*gr*) préfixe *m*.

pregnancy *n* grossesse *f*.

pregnant *adj* enceinte.

prehistoric *adj* préhistorique.

prejudice *n* préjudice, tort *m*; préjugé *m*; * *vt* préjudicier à, faire du tort à.

prejudiced *adj* qui a des préjugés; partial.

prejudicial *adj* préjudiciable.

preliminary *adj* préliminaire.

prelude *n* prélude *m*.

premarital *adj* préconjugal.

premature *adj*, **~ly** *adv* prématuré(ment).

premeditation *n* préméditation *f*.

premier *n* premier ministre *m*.

première *n* première *f*.

premise *n* prémisse *f*.

premises *npl* locaux *mpl*.

premium *n* prix *m*; indemnité *f*; prime *f*.

premonition *n* pressentiment *m*, prémonition *f*.

preoccupied *adj* préoccupé; absorbé.

prepaid *adj* port payé.

preparation *n* préparation *f*.

preparatory *adj* préparatoire.

prepare *vt* préparer; * *vi* se préparer.

preponderance *n* prépondérance *f*.

preposition *n* préposition *f*.

preposterous *adj* ridicule, absurde.

prerequisite n condition requise f.
prerogative n prérogative f.
prescribe vt prescrire.
prescription n prescription f; ordonnance f.
presence n présence f.
present n cadeau m; * adj présent; actuel; ~ly adv actuellement; * vt offrir, donner; présenter.
presentable adj présentable.
presentation n présentation f.
present-day adj actuel.
presenter n présentateur m, -trice f.
presentiment n pressentiment m, prémonition f.
preservation n préservation f.
preservative n préservatif m.
preserve vt préserver; conserver; faire des conserves de; * n conserve f; confiture f.
preside vi présider; diriger.
presidency n présidence f.
president n président m.
presidential adj présidentiel.
press vt appuyer sur; serrer; pressurer; * vi se presser; * n presse f; pressoir m; pression f.
press agency n agence de presse f.
press conference n conférence de presse f.
pressing adj pressant; urgent; ~ly adv de manière pressante; d'urgence.
pressure n pression f.
pressure cooker n autocuiseur m.
pressure group n groupe de pression m.
pressurized adj pressurisé.
prestige n prestige m.
presumable adj vraisemblable.
presumably adv vraisemblablement.
presume vt présumer, supposer.
presumption n présomption f.
presumptuous adj présomptueux.
presuppose vt présupposer.

pretence n prétexte m; simulation f; prétention f.
pretend vi prétendre; faire semblant.
pretender n prétendant m.
pretension n prétention f.
pretentious adj prétentieux.
preterite n prétérit m.
pretext n prétexte m.
pretty adj joli, mignon; * adv assez; plutôt.
prevail vi prévaloir; prédominer.
prevailing adj prédominant.
prevalent adj prédominant.
prevent vt prévenir; empêcher; éviter.
prevention n prévention f.
preventive adj préventif.
preview n avant-première f.
previous adj précédent; antérieur; ~ly adv auparavant.
prewar adj d'avant-guerre.
prey n proie f.
price n prix m.
priceless adj inappréciable.
price list n tarif m.
prick vt piquer; exciter; * n piqûre f; pointe f.
prickle n picotement m; épine f.
prickly adj épineux.
pride n orgueil m; vanité f; fierté f.
priest n prêtre m.
priestess n prêtresse f.
priesthood n sacerdoce m, prêtrise f.
priestly adj sacerdotal.
priggish adj affecté.
prim adj prude, affecté.
primacy n primauté f.
primarily adv principalement, surtout.
primary adj primaire; principal, premier.
primate n primate m.
prime n (fig) fleur f; commencement m; * adj premier; principal; excellent; * vt amorcer.
prime minister n premier ministre m.

primeval *adj* primitif.

priming *n* amorçage *m*.

primitive *adj* primitif; **~ly** *adv* primitivement.

primrose *n* (*bot*) primevère *f*.

prince *n* prince *m*.

princess *n* princesse *f*.

principal *adj*, **~ly** *adv* principal(ement); * *n* principal *m*.

principality *n* principauté *f*.

principle *n* principe *m*.

print *vt* imprimer; * *n* impression *f*; estampe *f*; caractères imprimés *mpl*; **out of ~** épuisé (livres).

printed matter *n* imprimés *mpl*.

printer *n* imprimeur *m*; imprimante *f*.

printing *n* impression *f*.

prior *adj* antérieur, précédent; * *n* prieur *m*.

priority *n* priorité *f*.

priory *n* prieuré *m*.

prism *n* prisme *m*.

prison *n* prison *f*.

prisoner *n* prisonnier *m*, -ière *f*.

pristine *adj* d'origine; intact.

privacy *n* intimité *f*.

private *adj* privé; secret; particulier; **~ soldier** *n* simple soldat *m*; **~ly** *adv* en privé.

private eye *n* détective privé *m*.

privet *n* troène *m*.

privilege *n* privilège *m*.

prize *n* prix *m*; * *vt* apprécier, évaluer; **to ~ open** ouvrir par la force, forcer.

prize-giving *n* distribution des prix *f*.

prizewinner *n* gagnant *m*, -e *f*.

pro *prep* pour.

probability *n* probabilité *f*; vraisemblance *f*.

probable *adj* probable, vraisemblable; **~bly** *adv* probablement.

probation *n* essai *m*; probation *f*.

probationary *adj* d'essai.

probe *n* sonde *f*; enquête *f*, * *vt* sonder; * *vi* faire des recherches.

problem *n* problème *m*.

problematical *adj*, **~ly** *adv* problématique(ment).

procedure *n* procédure *f*.

proceed *vi* procéder; provenir; poursuivre; **~s** *npl* produit *m*; montant *m*; **gross ~s** bénéfices bruts *mpl*; **net ~s** benéfices nets *mpl*.

proceedings *n* procédure *f*; procédé *m*; procès *m*.

process *n* processus *m*; procédé *m*.

procession *n* procession *f*.

proclaim *vt* proclamer; promulguer.

proclamation *n* proclamation *f*; décret *m*.

procrastinate *vt* différer, retarder.

proctor *n* censeur *m*.

procure *vt* procurer.

procurement *n* obtention *f*.

prod *vt* pousser.

prodigal *adj* prodigue.

prodigious *adj* prodigieux; **~ly** *adv* prodigieusement.

prodigy *n* prodige *m*.

produce *vt* produire; créer; fabriquer; * *n* produit *m*.

produce dealer *n* revendeur *m*, -euse *f*.

producer *n* producteur *m*, -trice *f*.

product *n* produit *m*; œuvre *f*; fruit *m*.

production *n* production *f*; produit *m*.

production line *n* ligne de production *f*.

productive *adj* productif.

productivity *n* productivité *f*.

profane *adj* profane.

profess *vt* professer; exercer; déclarer.

profession *n* profession *f*.

professional *adj* professionnel.

professor *n* professeur *m*.

proficiency *n* capacité *f*.

proficient *adj* compétent.

profile n profil m.

profit n bénéfice, profit m; avantage m; * vi profiter (de).

profitability n rentabilité f.

profitable adj profitable, avantageux.

profiteering n exploitation f, mercantilisme m.

profound adj, ~ly adv pro- fond(ément).

profuse adj profus; prodigue; ~ly adv à profusion.

program(me) n programme m.

programming n programmation f.

programmer n programmeur m, -euse f.

progress n progrès m; cours m; * vi progresser.

progression n progression f; avance f.

progressive adj progressif; ~ly adv progressivement.

prohibit vt prohiber; défendre.

prohibition n prohibition f.

project vt projeter; * n projet m.

projectile n projectile m.

projection n projection f.

projector n projecteur m.

proletarian adj prolétaire.

proletariat n prolétariat m.

prolific adj prolifique, fécond.

prolix adj prolixe, diffus.

prolog n prologue m.

prolong vt prolonger.

prom n bal m; concert-promenade m.

promenade n promenade f.

prominence n proéminence f; éminence f.

prominent adj proéminent.

promiscuous adj immoral, débauché.

promise n promesse f; * vt promettre.

promising adj prometteur.

promontory n promontoire m.

promote vt promouvoir.

promoter n promoteur m.

promotion n promotion f.

prompt adj, ~ly adv prompt(ement); * vt suggérer; inciter; souffler (au théâtre).

prompter n souffleur m, -euse f.

prone adj enclin (à).

prong n dent f.

pronoun n pronom m.

pronounce vt prononcer; déclarer.

pronounced adj marqué, prononcé.

pronouncement n déclaration f.

pronunciation n prononciation f.

proof n preuve f; * adj imperméable; résistant.

prop vt soutenir; * n appui, soutien m; tuteur m.

propaganda n propagande f.

propel vt propulser.

propeller n hélice f.

propensity n propension, tendance f.

proper adj propre; convenable; exact; approprié; ~ly adv convenablement; correctement.

property n propriété f.

prophecy n prophétie f.

prophesy vt prophétiser, prédire.

prophet n prophète m.

prophetic adj prophétique.

proportion n proportion f; symétrie f.

proportional adj proportionnel.

proportionate adj proportionné.

proposal n proposition f; offre f.

propose vt proposer.

proposition n proposition f.

proprietor n propriétaire mf.

propriety n propriété f.

pro rata adv au prorata.

prosaic adj prosaïque.

prose n prose f.

prosecute vt poursuivre en justice.

prosecution n poursuites fpl; accusation f.

prosecutor n plaignant m, -e f.

prospect n perspective f; espoir m; * vt, vi prospecter.

prospecting n prospection f.

prospective *adj* probable; futur.
prospector *n* prospecteur *m*,-trice *f*.
prospectus *n* prospectus *m*.
prosper *vi* prospérer.
prosperity *n* prospérité *f*.
prosperous *adj* prospère.
prostitute *n* prostituée *f*.
prostitution *n* prostitution *f*.
prostrate *adj* prostré.
protagonist *n* protagoniste *mf*.
protect *vt* protéger; abriter.
protection *n* protection *f*.
protective *adj* protecteur.
protector *n* protecteur *m*, -trice *f*.
protegé *n* protégé *m*, -e *f*.
protein *n* protéine *f*.
protest *vi* protester; * *n* protestation *f*.
Protestant *n* protestant *m*, -e *f*.
protester *n* manifestant *m*, -e *f*; protestataire *mf*.
protocol *n* protocole *m*.
prototype *n* prototype *m*.
protracted *adj* prolongé.
protrude *vi* déborder, ressortir.
proud *adj* fier, orgueilleux; **~ly** *adv* fièrement.
prove *vt* prouver; justifier; * *vi* s'avérer; se révéler.
proverb *n* proverbe *m*.
proverbial *adj*, **~ly** *adv* proverbial(ement).
provide *vt* fournir; **to ~ for** pourvoir aux besoins de; prévoir.
provided *conj*: **~ that** pourvu que.
providence *n* providence *f*.
province *n* province *f*; compétence *f*.
provincial *adj*, *n* provincial *m*, -e *f*.
provision *n* provision *f*; disposition *f*.
provisional *adj*, **~ly** *adv* provisoire(ment).
proviso *n* stipulation *f*.
provocation *n* provocation *f*.
provocative *adj* provocateur.

provoke *vt* provoquer.
prow *n* (*mar*) proue *f*.
prowess *n* prouesse *f*.
prowl *vi* rôder.
prowler *n* rôdeur *m*, -euse *f*.
proximity *n* proximité *f*.
proxy *n* procuration *f*; délégué *m*, -e *f*.
prudence *n* prudence *f*.
prudent *adj* prudent, circonspect; **~ly** *adv* prudemment.
prudish *adj* prude.
prune *vt* tailler; * *n* pruneau *m*.
prussic acid *n* acide prussique *m*.
pry *vi* espionner; **to ~ open** *vt* forcer.
psalm *n* psaume *m*.
pseudonym *n* pseudonyme *m*.
psyche *n* psyché *f*.
psychiatric *adj* psychiatrique.
psychiatrist *n* psychiatre *mf*.
psychiatry *n* psychiatrie *f*.
psychic *adj* psychique.
psychoanalysis *n* psychanalyse *f*.
psychoanalyst *n* psychanaliste *mf*.
psychological *adj* psychologique.
psychologist *n* psychologue *mf*.
psychology *n* psychologie *f*.
puberty *n* puberté *f*.
public *adj* public; commun; **~ly** *adv* publiquement; * *n* public *m*.
public address system *n* sonorisation *f*.
publican *n* patron(ne) de pub *m*(*f*).
publication *n* publication *f*; édition *f*.
publicity *n* publicité *f*.
publicize *vt* faire de la publicité pour.
public opinion *n* opinion publique *f*.
public school *n* école privée *f*.
publish *vt* publier.
publisher *n* éditeur *m*, -trice *f*.
publishing *n* édition *f*.
pucker *vt* plisser.
pudding *n* pudding *m*; dessert *m*.

puddle *n* flaque d'eau *f*.

puerile *adj* puéril.

puff *n* souple *m*; bouffée *f*; * *vt* souffler; dégager; * *vi* souffler; bouffer.

puff pastry *n* pâte feuilletée *f*.

puffy *adj* bouffi, gonflé.

pull *vt* tirer; arracher; **to ~ down** faire descendre; abattre; **to ~ in** *vi* s'arrêter; entrer en gare; **to ~ off** enlever; **to ~ out** *vi* partir; * *vt* arracher; **to ~ through** *vi* s'en sortir; se remettre; **to ~ up** *vi* s'arrêter; * *vt* arracher; arrêter; * *n* tirage *m*; secousse *f*.

pulley *n* poulie *f*.

pullover *n* pullover *m*.

pulp *n* pulpe *f*.

pulpit *n* chaire *f*.

pulsate *vi* battre.

pulse *n* pouls *m*; légumes *mpl*.

pulverize *vt* pulvériser.

pumice *n* pierre ponce *f*.

pummel *vt* battre.

pump *n* pompe *f*; * *vt* pomper; puiser.

pumpkin *n* citrouille *f*.

pun *n* jeu de mots *m*; * *vi* faire des jeux de mots.

punch *n* coup de poing *m*; poinçon *m*; punch *m*; * *vt* cogner; perforer; poinçonner.

punctual *adj* ponctuel, exact; **~ly** *adv* ponctuellement.

punctuate *vt* ponctuer.

punctuation *n* ponctuation *f*.

pundit *n* expert *m*.

pungent *adj* piquant, âcre; mordant.

punish *vt* punir.

punishment *n* châtiment *m*, punition *f*; peine *f*.

punk *n* punk *mf*; minable *mf*; **~ (music)** punk *m*.

punt *n* bateau plat *m*.

puny *adj* chétif, maigrelet.

pup *n* chiot *m*; * *vi* avoir des chiots, mettre bas.

pupil *n* élève *mf*; pupille *mf*.

puppet *n* marionnette *f*.

puppy *n* chiot *m*.

purchase *vt* acheter; * *n* achat *m*; acquisition *f*.

purchaser *n* acheteur *m*, -euse *f*.

pure *adj* pur; **~ly** *adv* purement.

purée *n* purée *f*.

purge *vt* purger.

purification *n* purification *f*.

purify *vt* purifier.

purist *n* puriste *mf*.

puritan *n* puritain *m*, -e *f*.

purity *n* pureté *f*.

purl *n* maille à l'envers *f*.

purple *adj*, *n* pourpre, violet *m*.

purport *vt*: **to ~ to** prétendre.

purpose *n* intention *f*; but, dessein *m*; **to the ~** à propos; **to no ~** en vain; **on ~** exprès, à dessein.

purposeful *adj* résolu.

purr *vi* ronronner.

purse *n* sac à main *m*; porte-monnaie *m invar*.

purser *n* commissaire *m*.

pursue *vi* poursuivre; suivre.

pursuit *n* poursuite *f*; occupation *f*.

purveyor *n* fournisseur *m*, -euse *f*.

push *vt* pousser; presser; **to ~ aside** écarter; **to ~ off** *vi* (*sl*) se casser; **to ~ on** *vi* continuer; * *n* poussée *f*; impulsion *f*; effort *m*; énergie *f*.

pusher *n* trafiquant de drogues *m*.

push-up *n* pompe *f*.

put *vt* mettre, poser; proposer; obliger; **to ~ away** ranger; **to ~ down** poser par terre; rabaisser; attribuer; **to ~ forward** avancer; **to ~ off** remettre; décourager; **to ~ on** mettre; allumer; prendre; affecter; **to ~ out** éteindre; faire sortir; déranger; **to ~ up** lever; augmenter; loger.

putrid *adj* putride.

putt *n* putt *m*; * *vt*, *vi* putter.

putty *n* mastic *m*.

puzzle *n* énigme *f*; casse-tête *m invar*.

puzzling *adj* étrange.
pyjamas *npl* pyjama *m*.
pylon *n* pylône *m*.

pyramid *n* pyramide *f*.
python *n* python *m*.

Q

quack *vi* cancaner; * *n* canard *m*; (*sl*) charlatan *m*.
quadrangle *n* quadrilatère *m*.
quadrant *n* quadrant *m*.
quadrilateral *adj* quadrilatéral.
quadruped *n* quadrupède *m*.
quadruple *adj* quadruple.
quadruplet *n* quadruplé *m*, -e *f*.
quagmire *n* marécage *m*.
quail *n* caille *f*.
quaint *adj* désuet; bizarre.
quake *vi* trembler.
Quaker *n* quaker *m*.
qualification *n* qualification *f*; diplôme *m*.
qualified *adj* qualifié; diplômé.
qualify *vt* qualifier; modérer; * *vi* se qualifier.
quality *n* qualité *f*.
qualm *n* scrupule *m*.
quandary *n* incertitude *f*, doute *m*.
quantitative *adj* quantitatif.
quantity *n* quantité *f*.
quarantine *n* quarantaine *f*.
quarrel *n* dispute, querelle *f*; * *vi* se disputer, se quereller.
quarrelsome *adj* querelleur.
quarry *n* carrière *f*.
quarter *n* quart *m*; **a ~ of an hour** un quart d'heure; * *vt* diviser en quatre.
quarterly *adj* trimestriel; * *adv* tous les trimestres.
quartermaster *n* (*mil*) intendant *m*.
quartet *n* (*mus*) quartette *m*; quatuor *m*.
quartz *n* (*min*) quartz *m*.
quash *vt* écraser; annuler.
quay *n* quai *m*.
queasy *adj* qui a des nausées; écœurant.

queen *n* reine *f*; femme *f*.
queer *adj* extrange; (*sl*) pédale *f*.
quell *vt* étouffer; apaiser.
quench *vt* assouvir; éteindre.
query *n* question *f*; * *vt* demander.
quest *n* recherche *f*.
question *n* question *f*; sujet *m*; doute *m*; * *vt* douter de; mettre en question; questionner.
questionable *adj* discutable; douteux.
questioner *n* interrogateur *m*.
question mark *n* point d'interrogation *m*.
questionnaire *n* questionnaire *m*.
quibble *vi* chicaner.
quick *adj* rapide; vif; prompt; **~ly** *adv* rapidement, vite.
quicken *vt* presser; accélérer; * *vi* s'accélérer.
quicksand *n* sables mouvants *mpl*.
quicksilver *n* mercure *m*.
quick-witted *adj* à l'esprit vif.
quiet *adj* calme; silencieux; **~ly** *adv* calmement.
quietness *n* calme *m*, tranquillité *f*; silence *m*.
quinine *n* quinine *f*.
quintet *n* (*mus*) quintette *m*.
quintuple *adj* quintuple.
quintuplet *n* quintuplé *m*, -e *f*.
quip *n* sarcasme *m*; * *vt* railler.
quirk *n* particularité *f*.
quit *vt* arrêter de; quitter; * *vi* abandonner; démissionner; * *adj* quitte.
quite *adv* assez; complètement, absolument.
quits *adj* quitte.

quiver vi trembler.
quixotic adj donquichottesque.
quiz n concours m; examen m; * vt interroger.
quizzical adj railleur.
quota n quota m.

quotation n citation f.
quotation marks npl guillemets mpl.
quote vt citer.
quotient n quotient m.

R

rabbi n rabbi, rabbin m.
rabbit n lapin m.
rabbit hutch n clapier m.
rabble n cohue f.
rabid adj forcené, enragé.
rabies n rage f.
race n course f; race f; * vt faire une course avec; * vi courir; faire une course; aller très vite; foncer.
racer n cheval de course m.
racial adj racial; ~ist adj, n raciste mf.
raciness n vivacité f.
racing n courses fpl.
rack n casier m; étagère f; * vt soumettre au supplice du chevalet; tourmenter.
racket n vacarme m; raquette f.
rack-rent n loyer démesuré m.
racy adj piquant, plein de verve.
radiance n rayonnement m, éclat m.
radiant adj rayonnant, radieux.
radiate vt, vi rayonner, irradier.
radiation n irradiation f.
radiator n radiateur m.
radical adj, ~ly adv radical(ement).
radicalism n radicalisme m.
radio n radio f.
radioactive adj radioactif.
radish n radis m.
radius n radius m.
raffle n tombola f; * vt mettre en tombola.
raft n radeau, train de flottage m.
rafter n chevron m.
rag n lambeau m, loque f.

ragamuffin n va-nu-pieds m invar; galopin m.
rage n rage f; fureur f; * vi être furieux; faire rage.
ragged adj déguenillé.
raging adj furieux, déchaîné, enragé.
ragman, ~ picker n chiffonnier m.
raid n raid m; * vt faire un raid sur.
raider n raider m.
rail n rambarde f, garde-fou m; (rail) rail, chemin de fer m; * vt entourer d'une barrière.
raillery n taquinerie f.
railroad, railway n chemin de fer m.
raiment n vêtements mpl.
rain n pluie f; * vi pleuvoir.
rainbow n arc-en-ciel m.
rainwater n eau de pluie f.
rainy adj pluvieux.
raise vt lever, soulever; ériger; édifier; élever.
raisin n raisin sec m.
rake n râteau m; libertin m; * vt ratisser.
rakish adj libertin, débauché.
rally vt (mil) rallier; * vi se rallier.
ram n bélier m; navire bélier m; * vt enfoncer.
ramble vi errer; faire une randonnée; * n excursion à pied, randonnée f.
rambler n excursionniste mf.
ramification n ramification f.
ramify vi se ramifier.
ramp n rampe f.

rampant adj exubérant.

rampart n terre-plein m; (mil) rempart m.

ramrod n baguette f; refouloir m.

ramshackle adj délabré.

ranch n ranch m.

rancid adj rance.

rancour n rancœur f.

random adj fortuit, fait au hasard; **at ~** au hasard.

range vt ranger, classer; * vi s'étendre; * n rangée f; ordre m; portée f; chaîne f; champ de tir m; fourneau de cuisine m.

ranger n garde forestier m.

rank adj exubérant; fétide; flagrant; * n rang m, classe f, grade m.

rankle vi rester sur le coeur.

rankness n exubérance f; odeur rance f.

ransack vt saccager, piller.

ransom n rançon f.

rant vi déclamer.

rap vi donner un coup sec; * n petit coup sec m.

rapacious adj rapace; ~ly adv avec rapacité.

rapacity n rapacité f.

rape n viol m; rapt m; (bot) colza m; * vt violer.

rapid adj, ~ly adv rapide(ment).

rapidity n rapidité f.

rapier n rapière f.

rapist n violeur m.

rapt adj extasié; absorbé.

rapture n ravissement m; extase f.

rapturous adj de ravissement.

rare adj, ~ly adv rare(ment).

rarity n rareté f.

rascal n vaurien m.

rash adj imprudent, téméraire; ~ly adv sans réfléchir; * n vague f; éruption (cutanée) f.

rashness n imprudence f.

rasp n râpe f; * vt râper.

raspberry n framboise f; ~ **bush** framboisier m.

rat n rat m.

rate n taux, prix, cours m; classe f; vitesse f; * vt estimer, évaluer.

rather adv plutôt; quelque peu.

ratification n ratification f.

ratify vt ratifier.

rating n estimation f; classement m; indice m.

ratio n rapport m.

ration n ration f; (mil) vivres mpl.

rational adj rationnel; raisonnable; ~ly adv rationnellement.

rationality n rationalité f.

rattan n (bot) rotin m.

rattle vi s'entrechoquer; cliqueter * vt faire s'entrechoquer; * n fracas m; cliquetis m.

rattlesnake n serpent à sonnettes m.

ravage vt ravager, piller; dévaster; * n ravage m.

rave vi délirer.

raven n corbeau m.

ravenous adj ~ly adv vorace(ment).

ravine n ravin m.

ravish vt enchanter; ravir.

ravishing adj enchanteur.

raw adj cru; brut; novice.

rawboned adj décharné; maigre.

rawness n crudité f; inexpérience f.

ray n rayon m; (fish) raie f.

raze vt raser.

razor n rasoir m.

reach vt atteindre; arriver à; * vi s'étendre, porter; * n portée f.

react vi réagir.

reaction n réaction f.

read vt, vi lire.

readable adj lisible.

reader n lecteur m, -trice f.

readily adv volontiers; facilement.

readiness n bonne volonté f; empressement m.

reading n lecture f.

reading room n salle de lecture f.

readjust vt réajuster, réadapter.

ready adj prêt; enclin; disposé.

real adj réel, vrai; **~ly** adv vraiment.

reality n réalité f.

realization n réalisation f.

realize vt se rendre compte de; réaliser.

realm n royaume m.

ream n rame f.

reap vt moissonner.

reaper n moissonneuse f (machine).

reappear vi réapparaître.

rear n arrière m; derrière m; * vt élever, dresser.

rearmament n réarmement m.

reason n raison f; cause f; * vt, vi raisonner.

reasonable adj raisonnable.

reasonableness n bon sens m, sagesse f.

reasonably adv raisonnablement.

reasoning n raisonnement m.

reassure vt rassurer; (com) réassurer.

rebel n rebelle mf; * vi se rebeller.

rebellion n rébellion f.

rebellious adj rebelle.

rebound vi rebondir.

rebuff n rebuffade f; * vt repousser.

rebuild vt reconstruire.

rebuke vt réprimander; * n réprimande f.

rebut vt réfuter

recalcitrant adj récalcitrant.

recall vt (se) rappeler; retirer; * n retrait m.

recant vt rétracter, désavouer.

recantation n rétractation f.

recapitulate vt, vi récapituler.

recapitulation n récapitulation f.

recapture n reprise f.

recede vi reculer.

receipt n reçu m; réception f; **~s** npl recettes fpl.

receivable adj recevable.

receive vt recevoir; accueillir.

recent adj récent, neuf; **~ly** adv récemment.

receptacle n récipient m.

reception n réception f.

recess n vacance f; renfoncement m; recoin m.

recession n recul m; (com) récession f.

recipe n recette f.

recipient n destinataire mf.

reciprocal adj, **~ly** adv réciproque(ment).

reciprocate vi rendre la pareille.

reciprocity n réciprocité f.

recital n récit m.

recite vt réciter; exposer, énumérer.

reckless adj téméraire; **~ly** adv imprudemment.

reckon vt compter, calculer; * vi calculer.

reckoning n compte m; calcul m.

reclaim vt assainir; récupérer.

reclaimable adj asséchable; récupérable.

recline vt reposer; * vi être allongé.

recluse n reclus m, -e f.

recognition n reconnaissance f.

recognize vt reconnaître.

recoil vi reculer.

recollect vt se rappeler, se souvenir de.

recollection n souvenir m.

recommence vt recommencer.

recommend vt recommander.

recommendation n recommandation f.

recompense n récompense f; * vt récompenser.

reconcilable adj conciliable.

reconcile vt réconcilier.

reconciliation n réconciliation f.

recondite adj abstrus, obscur.

reconnoiter vt (mil) reconnaître.

reconsider vt reconsidérer.

reconstruct vt reconstruire.

record vt enregistrer; consigner par écrit; * n rapport m, registre *m*; disque *m*; record *m*; **~s** *pl* archives *fpl*.

recorder *n* magnétophone *m*, archiviste *mf*; (*mus*) flûte à bec *f*.

recount *vt* raconter.

recourse *n* recours *m*.

recover *vt* retrouver; reprendre; récupérer; * *vi* se remettre, se rétablir.

recoverable *adj* récupérable.

recovery *n* guérison *f*; reprise *f*.

recreation *n* détente *f*; récréation *f*.

recriminate *vi* récriminer.

recrimination *n* récrimination *f*.

recruit *vt* recruter; * *n* (*mil*) recrue *f*.

recruiting *n* recrutement *m*.

rectangle *n* rectangle *m*.

rectangular *adj* rectangulaire.

rectification *n* rectification *f*.

rectify *vt* rectifier.

rectilinear *adj* rectiligne.

rectitude *n* rectitude *f*.

rector *n* pasteur *m*.

recumbent *adj* couché, étendu.

recur *vi* se reproduire.

recurrence *n* répétition *f*.

recurrent *adj* répétitif.

red *adj* rouge; * *n* rouge *m*.

redden *vt*, *vi* rougir.

reddish *adj* rougeâtre.

redeem *vt* racheter, rembourser.

redeemable *adj* rachetable.

Redeemer *n* Rédempteur *m*.

redemption *n* rachat *m*.

redeploy *vt* reconvertir.

redhanded *adj*: **to catch sb ~** prendre quelqu'un la main dans le sac.

redhot *adj* brûlant, ardent.

red-letter day *n* jour à marquer d'une pierre blanche *m*.

redness *n* rougeur, rousseur *f*.

redolent *adj* parfumé, odorant.

redouble *vt*, *vi* redoubler.

redress *vt* réparer ; corriger; redresser; * *n* réparation *f*, redressement *m*.

redskin *n* Peau-Rouge *mf*.

red tape *n* (*fig*) paperasserie *f*.

reduce *vt* réduire; diminuer; abaisser.

reducible *adj* réductible.

reduction *n* réduction *f*; baisse *f*.

redundancy *n* licenciement *m*.

redundant *adj* superflu.

reed *n* roseau *m*.

reedy *adj* couvert de roseaux.

reef *n* (*mar*) ris *m*; récif *m*.

reek *n* puanteur *f*; * *vi* empester; puer.

reel *n* bobine *f*; bande *f*; dévidoir *m*; * *vi* chanceler.

re-election *n* réélection *f*.

re-engage *vt* rengager.

re-enter *vt* rentrer.

re-establish *vt* rétablir; réhabiliter.

re-establishment *n* rétablissement *m*; restauration *f*.

refectory *n* réfectoire *m*.

refer *vt* soumettre, renvoyer; se référer à; * *vi* se référer.

referee *n* arbitre *m*.

reference *n* référence, allusion *f*.

refine *vt* raffiner, affiner.

refinement *n* raffinement *m*; raffinerie *f*; culture *f*.

refinery *n* raffinerie *f*.

refit *vt* réparer; (*also mar*).

reflect *vt* réfléchir, refléter; * *vi* réfléchir.

reflection *n* réflexion, pensée *f*.

reflector *n* réflecteur *m*; cataphote *m*.

reflex *adj* réflexe.

reform *vt* réformer; * *vi* se réformer.

reform, reformation *n* réforme *f*.

reformer *n* réformateur *m*, -trice *f*.

reformist *n* réformiste *mf*.

refract *vt* réfracter.

refraction *n* réfraction *f*.

refrain *vi*: **to ~ from something** s'abstenir de quelque chose.

refresh *vt* rafraîchir.

refreshment *n* rafraîchissement *m*.

refrigerator *n* glacière *f*; réfrigérateur *m*.

refuel *vi* se ravitailler (en carburant).

refuge *n* refuge, asile *m*.

refugee *n* réfugié *m*, -e *f*.

refund *vt* rembourser; * *n* remboursement *m*.

refurbish *vt* rénover.

refusal *n* refus *m*.

refuse *vt* refuser; * *n* déchets *mpl*.

refute *vt* réfuter.

regain *vt* recouvrer, reprendre.

regal *adj* royal.

regale *vt* régaler.

regalia *n* insignes *mpl*.

regard *vt* regarder; considérer; * *n* considération *f*; respect *m*.

regarding *pr* en ce qui concerne.

regardless *adv* quand même, malgré tout.

regatta *n* régate *f*.

regency *n* régence *f*.

regenerate *vt* régénérer; * *adj* régénéré.

regeneration *n* régénération *f*.

regent *n* régent *m*.

regime *n* régime *m*.

regiment *n* régiment *m*.

region *n* région *f*.

register *n* registre *m*; * *vt* enregistrer; ~ed letter *n* lettre recommandée *f*.

registrar *n* officier d'état civil *m*.

registration *n* enregistrement *m*.

registry *n* enregistrement *m*.

regressive *adj* régressif.

regret *n* regret *m* * *vt* regretter.

regretful *adj* plein de regrets.

regular *adj* régulier; ordinaire; ~ly *adv* régulièrement; * *n* habitué *m*, -e *f*.

regularity *n* régularité *f*.

regulate *vt* régler, réglementer.

regulation *n* règlement *m*; réglementation *f*.

regulator *n* régulateur *m*.

rehabilitate *vt* réhabiliter.

rehabilitation *n* réhabilitation *f*.

rehearsal *n* répétition *f*.

rehearse *vt* répéter; raconter.

reign *n* règne *m*; * *vi* régner.

reimburse *vt* rembourser.

reimbursement *n* remboursement *m*.

rein *n* rêne *f*; * *vt* contenir.

reindeer *n* renne *m*.

reinforce *vt* renforcer.

reinstate *vt* réintégrer.

reinsure *vt* (*com*) réassurer.

reissue *n* réédition *f*.

reiterate *vt* réitérer.

reiteration *n* réitération, répétition *f*.

reject *vt* rejeter.

rejection *n* refus, rejet *m*.

rejoice *vt* réjouir; * *vi* se réjouir.

rejoicing *n* réjouissance *f*.

relapse *vi* retomber; * *n* rechute *f*.

relate *vt* relater; rapprocher; * *vi* se rapporter.

related *adj* apparenté.

relation *n* rapport *m*; parent *m*.

relationship *n* lien de parenté *m*; relation *f*; rapport *m* .

relative *adj* relatif; ~ly *adv* relativement; * *n* parent *m*, -e *f*.

relax *vt* relâcher ; détendre; * *vi* se relâcher; se détendre.

relaxation *n* relâchement *m*; détente *f*.

relay *n* relais *m*; * *vt* retransmettre.

release *vt* libérer, relâcher; * *n* libération *f*; décharge *f*.

relegate *vt* reléguer.

relegation *n* relégation *f*.

relent *vi* s'adoucir.

relentless *adj* implacable.

relevant *adj* pertinent.

reliable *adj* fiable, digne de confiance.

reliance *n* confiance *f*.

relic *n* relique *f*.

relief *n* soulagement *m*; secours *m*.

relieve *vt* soulager, alléger; secourir.

religion *n* religion *f*.

religious *adj* religieux; ~ly *adv* religieusement.

relinquish vt abandonner, renoncer à.

relish n saveur f; goût m; attrait m; * vt savourer, se délecter de.

reluctance n répugnance f.

reluctant adj peu disposé.

rely vi compter sur, avoir confiance en.

remain vi rester, demeurer.

remainder n reste, restant m.

remains npl restes, vestiges mpl; dépouille f.

remand vt: **to ~ in custody** mettre en détention préventive.

remark n remarque, observation f; * vt (faire) remarquer, (faire) observer.

remarkable adj remarquable, notable.

remarkably adv remarquablement.

remarry vi se remarier.

remedial adv de rattrapage.

remedy n remède, recours m; * vt remédier à.

remember vt se souvenir de; se rappeler.

remembrance n mémoire f; souvenir m.

remind vt rappeler.

reminiscence n réminiscence f.

remiss adj négligent.

remission n rémission f.

remit vt remettre, pardonner; * vi diminuer.

remittance n remise f.

remnant n reste, restant m.

remodel vt remodeler.

remonstrate vi protester.

remorse n remords m.

remorseless adj implacable.

remote adj lointain, éloigné; **~ly** adv au loin, de loin.

remoteness n éloignement m; isolement m.

removable adj amovible.

removal n suppression f; déménagement m.

remove vt enlever; * vi déménager.

remunerate vt rémunérer.

remuneration n rémunération f.

render vt rendre, remettre; traduire; rendre.

rendezvous n rendez-vous m; point de ralliement m.

renegade n renégat m, -e f.

renew vt renouveler.

renewal n renouvellement m.

rennet n présure f.

renounce vt renoncer à.

renovate vt rénover.

renovation n rénovation f.

renown n renommée f; célébrité f.

renowned adj célèbre, renommé.

rent n loyer m; location f; * vt louer.

rental n loyer m.

renunciation n renonciation f.

reopen vt rouvrir.

reorganization n réorganisation f.

reorganize vt réorganiser.

repair vt réparer; * n réparation f.

reparable adj réparable.

reparation n réparation f.

repartee n répartie, réplique f.

repatriate vt rapatrier.

repay vt rembourser; rendre, récompenser.

repayment n remboursement m.

repeal vt abroger, annuler; * n abrogation, annulation f.

repeat vt répéter.

repeatedly adv à plusieurs reprises.

repeater n montre à répétition f.

repel vt repousser, rebuter.

repent vi se repentir.

repentance n repentir m.

repentant adj repentant.

repertory n répertoire m.

repetition n répétition, réitération f.

replace vt replacer; remplacer.

replant vt replanter.

replenish vt remplir de nouveau.

replete adj rempli, plein de.

reply n réponse f; * vi répondre.

report vt rapporter, relater; rendre compte de; * n rapport m; compte rendu m; rumeur f.

reporter n journaliste mf.

repose vi (se) reposer; * n repos m.

repository n dépôt m.

repossess vt reprendre possession de.

reprehend vt condamner.

reprehensible adj répréhensible.

represent vt représenter.

representation n représentation f.

representative adj représentatif; * n représentant(e) m(f).

repress vt réprimer, contenir.

repression n répression f.

repressive adj répressif.

reprieve vt accorder un sursis ou un répit à; * n sursis m.

reprimand vt réprimander, blâmer; * n blâme m; réprimande f.

reprint vt réimprimer.

reprisal n représailles fpl.

reproach n reproche, opprobre m; * vt reprocher.

reproachful adj réprobateur; ~ly adv d'un air de reproche.

reproduce vt reproduire.

reproduction n reproduction f.

reptile n reptile m.

republic n république f.

republican adj, n républicain m, -e f.

republicanism n républicanisme m.

repudiate vt renier.

repugnance n répugnance f, dégoût m.

repugnant adj répugnant; ~ly adv avec répugnance.

repulse vt repousser, rejeter; * n rebuffade f; refus m.

repulsion n répulsion f.

repulsive adj répulsif.

reputable adj honorable.

reputation n réputation f.

repute vt passer pour.

request n demande, requête f; * vt demander.

require vt demander, nécessiter.

requirement n besoin m; exigence f.

requisite adj nécessaire, indispensable; * n objet(s) nécessaire(s) m(pl).

requisition n demande; (mil) réquisition f.

requite vt rembourser.

rescind vt annuler, abroger.

rescue vt sauver, secourir; * n secours m, délivrance f.

research vt faire des/de la recherche(s); * n recherche(s) f(pl).

resemblance n ressemblance f.

resemble vt ressembler à.

resent vt être contrarié/irrité par.

resentful adj plein de ressentiment; amer; ~ly adv avec ressentiment.

resentment n ressentiment m.

reservation n réserve f; réservation f.

reserve vt réserver; * n réserve f.

reservedly adv avec réserve.

reservoir n réservoir m.

reside vi résider.

residence n résidence f; séjour m.

resident adj résidant; * n résident m, -e f.

residuary adj restant; ~ **legatee** n (law) légataire universel m.

residue n reste, résidu m.

residuum n (chem) résidu m.

resign vt démissionner de, renoncer à, céder; se résigner à; * vi démissionner.

resignation n démission f.

resin n résine f.

resinous adj résineux.

resist vt résister, s'opposer.

resistance n résistance f.

resolute adj, ~ly adv résolu(ment).

resolution n résolution f.

resolve vt resoudre; * vi (se) résoudre, (se) décider.

resonance n résonance f.

resonant adj résonant.

resort vi recourir; * n lieu de vacances m; recours m.

resound vi résonner.

resource n ressource(s) f(pl); expédient m.

respect n respect m; égard m; rapport m; ~s pl respects mpl; * vt respecter.

respectability n respectabilité f.

respectable adj respectable; considérable; ~bly adv convenablement.

respectful adj respectueux; ~ly adv respectueusement.

respecting prep en ce qui concerne.

respective adj respectif; ~ly adv respectivement.

respirator n respirateur m.

respiratory adj respiratoire.

respite n répit m; (law) sursis m; * vt repousser, différer.

resplendence n resplendissement m, splendeur f.

resplendent adj resplendissant.

respond vi répondre; réagir.

respondent n (law) défendeur m, -deresse f.

response n réponse, réaction f.

responsibility n responsabilité f.

responsible adj responsable.

responsive adj sensible à, réceptif.

rest n repos m; (mus) pause f; reste, restant m; * vt faire/or laisser reposer; appuyer; * vi se reposer, reposer.

resting place n lieu de repos m.

restitution n restitution f.

restive adj rétif, récalcitrant; agité.

restless adj agité; instable.

restoration n restauration f.

restorative adj fortifiant.

restore vt restituer, restaurer.

restrain vt retenir, contenir.

restraint n contrainte, entrave f.

restrict vt restreindre, limiter.

restriction n restriction f.

restrictive adj restrictif.

rest room n toilettes fpl.

result vi résulter; * n résultat m.

resume vt reprendre; résumer.

resurrection n résurrection f.

resuscitate vt réanimer.

retail vt vendre au détail, détailler; * n vente au détail f.

retain vt retenir, conserver.

retainer n serviteur m; ~s pl arrhes fpl; suite f.

retake vt reprendre.

retaliate vi se venger.

retaliation n représailles fpl.

retardation n retard m.

retarded adj retardé.

retch vi se forcer à vomir.

retention n conservation f.

retentive adj qui retient bien.

reticence n réticence f.

reticule n réticule m.

retina n rétine f.

retire vt retirer; mettre à la retraite; * vi se retirer; prendre sa retraite.

retired adj retraité, à la retraite.

retirement n isolement m; retraite f.

retort vt rétorquer; * n réplique f.

retouch vt retoucher.

retrace vt retracer.

retract vt rétracter; retirer.

retrain vt recycler.

retraining n reformation du personnel m.

retreat n repli m; * vi se retirer.

retribution n châtiment m; récompense f.

retrievable adj récupérable; réparable.

retrieve vt récupérer, recouvrer.

retriever n chien d'arrêt m.

retrograde adj rétrograde.

retrospect, retrospection n regard rétrospectif m.

retrospective adj rétrospectif.

return vt rendre; restituer; renvoyer; * n retour m; renvoi m;

récompense *f*; revenu *m*; remboursement *m*.

reunion *n* réunion *f*.

reunite *vt* réunir; * *vi* se réunir.

reveal *vt* révéler.

revel *vi* faire la fête.

revelation *n* révélation *f*.

reveller *n* fêtard *m*.

revelry *n* fête *f*.

revenge *vt* venger; * *n* vengeance *f*.

revengeful *adj* vindicatif.

revenue *n* revenu *m*; rente *f*.

reverberate *vt* réverbérer; * *vi* résonner, retentir; se réverbérer.

reverberation *n* répercussion *f*; réverbération *f*.

revere *vt* révérer, vénérer.

reverence *n* vénération *f*; * *vt* révérer.

reverend *adj* révérend; vénérable; * *n* curé *m*.

reverent, reverential *adj* révérenciel, respectueux.

reversal *n* renversement *m*; annulation *f*.

reverse *vt* renverser; annuler; * *vi* faire marche arrière; * *n* inverse *m*; contraire *m*; revers *m*.

reversible *adj* révocable; réversible.

reversion *n* retour *m*; réversion *f*.

revert *vi* revenir; retourner.

review *vt* revoir; (*mil*) passer en revue; * *n* revue *f*; examen *m*.

reviewer *n* critique *m*.

revile *vt* injurier; insulter.

revise *vt* réviser; mettre à jour.

reviser *n* réviseur *m*.

revision *n* révision *f*.

revisit *vt* retourner voir.

revival *n* reprise *f*; renouveau *m*.

revive *vt* ranimer; raviver; * *vi* reprendre connaissance; reprendre.

revocation *n* révocation *f*.

revoke *vt* révoquer, annuler.

revolt *vi* se révolter; * *n* révolte *f*.

revolting *adj* exécrable.

revolution *n* révolution *f*.

revolutionary *adj*, *n* révolutionnaire *mf*.

revolve *vt* (re)tourner; * *vi* tourner.

revolver *n* revolver *m*.

revolving *adj* tournant.

revue *n* revue *f*.

revulsion *n* écœurement *m*.

reward *n* récompense *f*; * *vt* récompenser.

rhapsody *n* r(h)apsodie *f*.

rhetoric *n* rhétorique *f*.

rhetorical *adj* rhétorique.

rheumatic *adj* rhumatisant.

rheumatism *n* rhumatisme *m*.

rhinoceros *n* rhinocéros *m*.

rhombus *n* rhombe *m*.

rhomboid *n* rhomboïd *m*.

rhubarb *n* rhubarbe *f*.

rhyme *n* rime *f*; vers *mpl*; * *vi* rimer.

rhythm *n* rythme *m*.

rhythmical *adj* rythmique.

rib *n* côte *f*.

ribald *adj* paillard.

ribbon *n* ruban *m*; guides *fpl*.

rice *n* riz *m*.

rich *adj* riche; somptueux; abondant; ~ly *adv* richement.

riches *npl* richesse *f*.

richness *n* richesse *f*; abondance *f*.

rickets *n* rachitisme *m*.

rickety *adj* rachitique.

rid *vt* débarrasser; se débarrasser de.

riddance *n*: good ~! bon débarras!

riddle *n* énigme *f*; crible *m*; * *vt* cribler.

ride *vi* monter à cheval; aller en voiture; * *n* promenade à cheval *ou* en voiture *f*.

rider *n* cavalier *m*, -ière *f*.

ridge *n* arête, crête *f*; chaîne *f*; * *vt* rider.

ridicule *n* ridicule *m*; raillerie *f*; * *vt* ridiculiser.

ridiculous *adj*, ~ly *adv* ridicule(ment).

riding n équitation f; monte f.
riding habit n tenue d'amazone f.
riding school n manège m.
rife adj répandu, abondant.
riffraff n racaille f.
rifle vt dévaliser, piller; strier, rayer; * n fusil m.
rifleman n fusilier m.
rig vt équiper; truquer; (mar) gréer; * n gréement m; plateforme de forage f.
rigging n (mar) gréement m.
right adj droit, bien; juste; équitable; ~! bien!, bon! ~ly adv bien; correctement; à juste titre; * n justice f; raison f; droit m; droite f; * vt redresser.
righteous adj droit, vertueux; ~ly adv vertueusement.
righteousness n droiture f; vertu f.
rigid adj rigide; sévère, strict; ~ly adv rigidement.
rigidity n rigidité f; sévérité f.
rigmarole n galimatias m.
rigorous adj rigoureux; ~ly adv rigoureusement.
rigour n rigueur f; sévérité f.
rim n bord m, monture f.
rind n peau, écorce f.
ring n anneau, cercle, rond m; bague f; cloche f; * vt sonner; * vi sonner, retentir; **to ~ the bell** sonner.
ringer n carillonneur m.
ringleader n meneur m.
ringlet n anglaise f.
ringworm n (med) teigne f.
rink n (also **ice ~**) patinoire f.
rinse vt rincer.
riot n émeute f; * vi se livrer à une émeute.
rioter n manifestant m, -e f.
riotous adj séditieux; dissolu; ~ly adv de façon tapageuse.
rip vt déchirer, fendre.
ripe adj mûr.
ripen vt, vi mûrir.
ripeness n maturité f.
rip-off n (sl): **it's a ~!** c'est du vol!

ripple vt rider; * vi se rider; * n ondulation f, ride f.
rise vi se lever; naître; se soulever; monter; provenir de; s'élever; croître; ressusciter; * n hausse f; augmentation f; montée f; lever m; source f.
rising n insurrection f; levée, clôture f.
risk n risque, danger m; * vt risquer.
risky adj risqué.
rissole n rissole f.
rite n rite m.
ritual adj, n rituel m.
rival adj rival; * n rival m, -e f; * vt rivaliser avec, concurrencer.
rivalry n rivalité f.
river n rivière f.
rivet n rivet m; * vt riveter, river.
rivulet n petit ruisseau m.
roach n blatte f.
road n route f.
roadsign n panneau de signalisation m.
roadstead n (mar) rade f.
roadworks npl travaux routiers mpl.
roam vt parcourir; errer dans; * vi errer.
roan adj rouan.
roar vi hurler, rugir; mugir; * n hurlement m; rugissement, mugissement m; grondement m.
roast vt rôtir; griller.
roast beef n rôti de boeuf m.
rob vt voler.
robber n voleur m, -euse f.
robbery n vol m.
robe n robe (de cérémonie) f; peignoir de bain m; * vt revêtir d'une robe de cérémonie.
robin (redbreast) n rouge-gorge m.
robust adj robuste.
robustness n robustesse f.
rock n roche f; rocher m; roc m; * vt bercer; balancer; ébranler; * vi (se) balancer.
rock and roll n rock (and roll) m.

rock crystal n cristal de roche m.

rocket n fusée f.

rocking chair n fauteuil à bascule m.

rock salt n sel gemme m.

rocky adj rocheux.

rod n baguette, tringle, canne f.

rodent n rongeur m.

roe n chevreuil m; oeufs mpl.

roebuck n chevreuil (mâle) m.

rogation n rogations fpl.

rogue n coquin, polisson m; gredin m.

roguish adj coquin.

roll vt rouler; étendre; enrouler; * vi (se) rouler; * n roulement m; rouleau m; liste f; catalogue m; liasse f; petit pain m.

roller n rouleau, cylindre m.

roller skates npl patins à roulettes mpl.

rolling pin n rouleau à pâtisserie m.

Roman Catholic adj, n catholique mf.

romance n romance f; roman m; conte m; fable f.

romantic adj romantique.

romp vi jouer bruyamment.

roof n toit m; voûte f; * vt couvrir.

roofing n toiture f.

rook n freux m; tour f (aux échecs).

room n pièce, salle f; place f, espace m; chambre f.

roominess n grande envergure f.

rooming house n pension f.

roomy adj spacieux.

roost n perchoir m; * vi se percher.

root n racine f; origine f; * vt, vi; **to ~ out** vt extirper; dénicher.

rooted adj enraciné; ancré.

rope n corde f; cordage m; * vi filer.

ropemaker n cordier m.

rosary n rosaire m.

rose n rose f.

rosebed n massif de roses m.

rosebud n bouton de rose m.

rosemary n (bot) romarin m.

rose tree n rosier m.

rosette n rosette f.

rosé wine n (2vin) rosé m.

rosewood n bois de rose m.

rosiness n couleur rosée f.

rosy adj rosé.

rot vi pourrir; * n pourriture f.

rotate vt faire tourner; * vi tourner.

rotation n rotation f.

rote n cœur m; routine f.

rotten adj pourri; corrompu.

rottenness n pourriture f.

rotund adj rond, replet, arrondi.

rouble n rouble m.

rouge n rouge (à joues) m.

rough adj accidenté, inégal, rugueux; rude, brutal, brusque; houleux; **~ly** adv rudement.

roughcast n crépi m.

roughen vt rendre rugueux.

roughness n rugosité f; rudesse, brusquerie f; agitation f.

roulette n roulette f.

round adj rond, circulaire; rondelet; franc; * n cercle m; rond m; tour m; tournée f; partie f; ronde f; canon m; série f; * adv autour de; environ; **~ly** adv rondement; franchement; * vt contourner; arrondir.

roundabout adj détourné, indirect; * n rond-point m.

roundness n rondeur f.

rouse vt réveiller; exciter.

rout n déroute, débâcle f; * vt mettre en déroute.

route n itinéraire m; route f.

routine adj habituel; * n routine f; numéro m.

rove vi vagabonder, errer.

rover n vagabond m, -e f; pirate m.

row n querelle f; vacarme m.

row n rangée, file f; * vt (mar) faire aller à la rame.

rowdy n hooligan, voyou m.

rower n rameur m, -euse f.

royal adj royal; princier; **~ly** adv royalement.

royalist n royaliste mf.

royalty *n* royauté *f*; droits d'auteur *mpl*; royalties *fpl*; redevance *f*; membres de la famille royale *mpl*.

rub *vt* frotter; irriter; * *n* frottement *m*; (*fig*) ennui *m*; difficulté *f*.

rubber *n* caoutchouc *m*, gomme *f*; préservatif *m*.

rubber band *n* élastique *m*.

rubbish *n* détritus *mpl*; ordures *fpl*; bêtises *fpl*; décombres *mpl*.

rubric *n* rubrique *f*.

ruby *n* rubis *m*.

rucksack *n* sac à dos *m*.

rudder *n* gouvernail *m*.

ruddiness *n* teint vif *m*, rougeur *f*.

ruddy *adj* coloré, rouge.

rude *adj* impoli, rude, brusque; grossier, primitif; **~ly** *adv* impoliment, grossièrement.

rudeness *n* impolitesse *f*; rudesse, insolence *f*.

rudiment *n* rudiments *mpl*.

rue *vt* regretter amèrement; * *n* (*bot*) rue *f*.

rueful *adj* triste.

ruffian *n* voyou *m*, brute *f*; * *adj* brutal.

ruffle *vt* ébouriffer, déranger; rider.

rug *n* tapis *m*, carpette *f*.

rugby *n* rugby *m*.

rugged *adj* accidenté, déchiqueté; rude; robuste.

ruin *n* ruine *f*; perte *f*; ruines *fpl*; * *vt* ruiner; détruire.

ruinous *adj* ruineux.

rule *n* règle *f*; règlement *m*; pouvoir *m*; domination *f*; * *vt* gouverner, dominer; décider, régler; diriger.

ruler *n* dirigeant *m*, -e *f*; règle *f*.

rum *n* rhum *m*.

rumble *vi* gronder, tonner.

ruminate *vt* ruminer.

rummage *vi* fouiller.

rumour *n* rumeur *f*; * *vt* faire courir le bruit.

rump *n* croupe *f*.

run *vt* diriger; organiser; faire couler; passer; **to ~ the risk** courir le risque; * *vi* courir; fuir, se sauver; filer; fonctionner; aller; couler; concourir; * *n* course, compétition *f*; parcours *m*; cours *m*; série *f*; mode *f*; ruée *f*.

runaway *n* fugitif *m*, -ive *f*, fuyard *m*.

rung *n* barreau, échelon *m*.

runner *n* coureur *m*; concurrent *m*, -e *f*; messager *m*.

running *n* course *f*; direction *f*.

runway *n* piste de décollage *f*.

rupture *n* rupture *f*; hernie *f*; * *vt* rompre; * *vi* se rompre.

rural *adj* rural, champêtre.

ruse *n* ruse *f*, stratagème *m*.

rush *n* jonc *m*; ruée *f*; hâte *f*; * *vt* pousser vivement; * *vi* se précipiter, s'élancer.

rusk *n* biscotte *f*.

russet *adj* roux.

rust *n* rouille *f*; * *vi* se rouiller.

rustic *adj* rustique; * *n* paysan, rustaud *m*.

rustiness *n* rouille *f*.

rustle *vi* bruire; * *vt* faire bruire; froisser.

rustling *n* vol de bétail *m*; bruissement *m*.

rusty *adj* rouillé; roux.

rut *n* rut *m*; ornière *f*.

ruthless *adj* cruel, impitoyable; **~ly** *adv* sans pitié.

rye *n* (*bot*) seigle *m*.

S

Sabbath *n* sabbat *m*; dimanche *m*.

saber *n* sabre *m*.

sable *n* zibeline *f*.

sabotage *n* sabotage *m*.

saccharin *n* saccharine *f*.

sachet *n* sachet *m*.

sack *n* sac *m*; * *vt* mettre à sac; renvoyer.

sacrement *n* sacrement *m*; Eucharistie *f*.

sacramental *adj* sacramentel.

sacred *adj* saint, sacré; inviolable.

sacredness *n* (caractère) sacré *m*.

sacrifice *n* sacrifice *m*; * *vt* sacrifier.

sacrificial *adj* sacrificiel.

sacrilege *n* sacrilège *m*.

sacrilegious *adj* sacrilège.

sad *adj* triste, déprimé; attristant; regrettable; **~ly** *adv* tristement.

sadden *vt* attrister.

saddle *n* selle *f*; col *m*; * *vt* seller.

saddlebag *n* sacoche de selle *f*.

saddler *n* sellier *m*.

sadness *n* tristesse *f*.

safari *n* safari *m*.

safe *adj* sûr; en sécurité; hors de danger; sans danger; **~ly** *adv* sans accident; **~ and sound** sain et sauf; * *n* coffre-fort *m*.

safe-conduct *n* sauf-conduit *m*.

safeguard *n* sauvegarde *f*; * *vt* sauvegarder, protéger.

safety *n* sécurité *f*; sûreté *f*.

safety belt *n* ceinture de sécurité *f*.

safety pin *n* épingle de nourrice *f*.

saffron *n* safran *m*.

sage *n* (*bot*) sauge *f*; sage *m*; * *adj* sage; **~ly** *adv* avec sagesse.

Sagittarius *n* Sagittaire *m* (signe du zodiaque).

sago *n* (*bot*) sagou *m*.

sail *n* voile *f*; * *vt* piloter; * *vi* aller à la voile, naviguer.

sailing *n* navigation *f*.

sailor *n* marin *m*.

saint *n* saint *m*, -e *f*.

sainted, saintly *adj* saint.

sake *n* bien *m*, égard *m*; **for God's ~** pour l'amour de Dieu.

salad *n* salade *f*.

salad bowl *n* saladier *m*.

salad dressing *n* vinaigrette *f*.

salad oil *n* huile de table *f*.

salamander *n* salamandre *f*.

salary *n* salaire *m*.

sale *n* vente *f*; solde *m*.

saleable *adj* vendable.

salesman *n* vendeur *m*.

saleswoman *n* vendeuse *f*.

salient *adj* saillant.

saline *adj* salin.

saliva *n* salive *f*.

sallow *adj* jaunâtre, cireux.

sally *n* (*mil*) sortie, saillie *f*; * *vi* saillir.

salmon *n* saumon *m*.

salmon trout *n* truite saumonée *f*.

saloon *n* bar *m*.

salt *n* sel *m*; * *vt* saler.

salt cellar *n* salière *f*.

saltness *n* salinité *f*.

saltpetre *n* salpêtre *m*.

saltworks *npl* salin *m*.

salubrious *adj* salubre, sain.

salubrity *n* salubrité *f*.

salutary *adj* salutaire.

salutation *n* salutation(s) *f(pl)*.

salute *vt* saluer; * *n* salut *m*.

salvage *n* (*mar*) droit de sauvetage *m*.

salvation *n* salut *m*.

salve *n* baume, onguent *m*.

salver *n* plateau *m*.

salvo *n* salve *f*; réserve *f*.

same *adj* même, identique.

sameness *n* identité *f*.

sample *n* échantillon *m*; prélèvement *m*; * *vt* goûter.

sampler n échantillonneur m, -euse f; modèle m.

sanatorium n sanatorium m.

sanctify vt sanctifier.

sanctimonious adj cagot.

sanction n sanction f; * vt sanctionner.

sanctity n sainteté f.

sanctuary n sanctuaire m; asile m.

sand n sable m; * vt sabler.

sandal n sandale f.

sandbag n (mil) sac de terre m.

sandpit n carrière de sable f.

sandstone n grès m.

sandwich n sandwich m.

sandy adj sablonneux, sableux.

sane adj sain.

sanguinary adj sanguinaire, sanglant.

sanguine adj sanguin.

sanitary towel n serviette hygiénique f.

sanity n santé mentale, raison f.

sap n sève f; * vt miner.

sapient adj sage, prudent.

sapling n jeune arbre m.

sapphire n saphir m.

sarcasm n sarcasme m.

sarcastic adj sarcastique, caustique; ~ally adv d'une manière sarcastique.

sarcophagus n sarcophage m.

sardine n sardine f.

sash n écharpe f; ceinture f.

sash window n fenêtre à guillotine f.

sassy adj insolent.

Satan n Satan m.

satanic(al) adj satanique.

satchel n cartable m.

satellite n satellite m.

satiate, sate vt rassasier, assouvir.

satin n satin m; * adj en ou de satin.

satire n satire f.

satiric(al) adj satirique; ~ly adv d'une manière satirique.

satirist n écrivain satirique m.

satirize vt faire la satire de.

satisfaction n satisfaction f.

satisfactorily adv d'une manière satisfaisante.

satisfactory adj satisfaisant.

satisfy vt satisfaire; convaincre.

saturate vt saturer.

Saturday n samedi m.

saturnine adj saturnien, sombre.

satyr n satyre m.

sauce n sauce f; assaisonnement m; * vt assaisonner.

saucepan n casserole f.

saucer n soucoupe f.

saucily adv avec impertinence.

sauciness n impertinence, insolence f.

saucy adj impertinent.

saunter vi flâner, se balader.

sausage n saucisse f.

savage adj sauvage, barbare; ~ly adv sauvagement; * n sauvage mf.

savageness n sauvagerie f; barbarie f.

savagery n sauvagerie, barbarie f.

savannah n savane f.

save vt sauver; économiser; épargner; éviter; conserver; * adv sauf, à l'exception de; * n (sport) arrêt m.

saveloy n cervelas m.

saver n libérateur m, -trice f ; épargnant m, -e f.

saving adj économique, économe; * prep sauf, à l'exception de; * n sauvetage m; ~s pl économies fpl, épargne f.

savings account n compte d'épargne m.

savings and loan association n organisme de crédit immobilier m.

savings bank n caisse d'épargne f.

Saviour n Sauveur m.

savour n saveur f; goût m; * vt déguster, savourer.

savouriness n goût m; saveur f.

savoury adj savoureux.

saw *n* scie *f*; * *vt* scier.

sawdust *n* sciure *f*.

sawfish *n* poisson scie *m*.

sawmill *n* scierie *f*.

sawyer *n* scieur *m*.

saxophone *n* saxophone *m*.

say *vt* dire.

saying *n* dicton, proverbe *m*.

scab *n* gale *f*; croûte *f*.

scabbard *n* gaine *f*; fourreau *m*.

scabby *adj* galeux.

scaffold *n* échafaud *m*; échafaudage *m*.

scaffolding *n* échafaudage *m*.

scald *vt* échauder; * *n* brûlure *f*.

scale *n* balance *f*; échelle *f*; gamme *f*; écaille *f*; * *vt* escalader; écailler.

scallion *n* échalote *f*.

scallop *n* feston *m*; * *vt* festonner.

scalp *n* cuir chevelu *m*; * *vt* scalper.

scamp *n* coquin *m*.

scamper *vi* galoper.

scampi *npl* langoustines *fpl*.

scan *vt* scruter; explorer; scander.

scandal *n* scandale *m*; infamie *f*.

scandalize *vt* scandaliser.

scandalous *adj* scandaleux; ~**ly** *adv* scandaleusement.

scant, scanty *adj* rare, insuffisant.

scantily *adv* pauvrement, insuffisamment.

scantiness *n* insuffisance, pauvreté *f*.

scapegoat *n* bouc émissaire *m*.

scar *n* cicatrice *f*; * *vt* marquer d'une cicatrice.

scarce *adj* rare; ~**ly** *adv* à peine.

scarcity *n* rareté *f*; pénurie *f*.

scare *vt* effrayer; * *n* peur; panique *f*.

scarecrow *n* épouvantail *m*.

scarf *n* écharpe *f*.

scarlatina *n* scarlatine *f*.

scarlet *n* écarlate *f*; * *adj* écarlate.

scarp *n* escarpement *m*.

scat *interj* (*sl*) ouste!

scatter *vt* éparpiller; disperser.

scavenger *n* charognard *m*; éboueur *m*.

scenario *n* scénario *m*; (*also fig*).

scene *n* scène *f*; lieu *m*; spectacle *m*, vue *f*.

scenery *n* vue *f*; décor (de théâtre) *m*.

scenic *adj* scénique.

scent *n* parfum *m*, odeur *f*; odorat *m*; piste *f*; * *vt* parfumer.

scent bottle *n* flacon à parfum *m*.

scentless *adj* sans odeur; inodore.

sceptic *n* sceptique *mf*.

sceptic(al) *adj* sceptique.

scepticism *n* scepticisme *m*.

sceptre *n* sceptre *m*.

schedule *n* horaire *m*; programme *m*; liste *f*.

scheme *n* projet, plan *m*; schéma *m*; système *m*; machination *f*; * *vt* machiner; * *vi* intriguer.

schemer *n* conspirateur *m*, -trice *f*, intrigant *m*, -e *f*.

schism *n* schisme *m*.

schismatic *n* schismatique *mf*.

scholar *n* élève *mf*; érudit *m*, -e *f*.

scholarship *n* savoir *m*, science *f*; bourse (d'études) *f*.

scholastic *adj* scolaire.

school *n* école *f*; * *vt* instruire.

schoolboy *n* écolier, élève *m*.

schoolgirl *n* écolière, élève *f*.

schooling *n* instruction, éducation *f*.

schoolmaster *n* instituteur, maître (d'école) *m*.

schoolmistress *n* institutrice, maîtresse (d'école) *f*.

schoolteacher *n* instituteur/trice *mf*; professeur *mf*.

schooner *n* (*mart*) goélette *f*.

sciatic *n* sciatique *f*.

science *n* science *f*.

scientific *adj*, ~**ally** *adv* scientifique(ment).

scientist *n* scientifique *mf*.

scimitar *n* cimeterre *m*.

scintillate *vi* scintiller, étinceler.

scintillating *adj* brillant, scintillant.

scission *n* scission, division *f*.

scissors *npl* ciseaux *mpl*.

scoff *vi* se moquer.

scold *vt* réprimander; * *vi* grogner.

scoop *n* louche *f*; pelle *f*; exclusivité *f*; * *vt* évider; écoper.

scooter *n* scooter *m*; trottinette *f*.

scope *n* portée, envergure, étendue *f*; zone de compétence *f*; liberté d'action *f*.

scorch *vt* brûler; roussir, griller; * *vi* se brûler, roussir.

score *n* score *m*; marque *f*; entaille, rayure *f*; titre, égard *m*; compte *m*; (*mus*) partition *f*; vingtaine *f*; * *vt* marquer; souligner; * *vi* marquer un/des point(s).

scoreboard *n* tableau (d'affichage) *m*.

scorn *vt* mépriser; dédaigner; * *n* dédain, mépris *m*.

scornful *adj* dédaigneux; **~ly** *adv* avec mépris.

Scorpio *n* Scorpion *m* (signe du zodiaque).

scorpion *n* scorpion *m*.

scotch *vt* mettre fin à.

Scotch *n* whisky *m*.

Scotch tape *n* scotch *m*.

scoundrel *n* vaurien *m*.

scour *vt* récurer, frotter; nettoyer; * *vi* battre la campagne.

scourge *n* fouet *m*; châtiment *m*; * *vt* fouetter; châtier.

scout *n* (*mil*) éclaireur *m*, -euse *f*; guetteur *m*; reconnaissance *f*; * *vi* aller en reconnaissance.

scowl *vi* se renfrogner; * *n* mine renfrognée *f*.

scragginess *n* décharnement *m*, maigreur extrême *f*; rugosité *f*.

scraggy *adj* rugueux; famélique.

scramble *vi* avancer à quatre pattes; grimper; se battre, se disputer; * *n* bousculade, ruée *f*; ascension *f*.

scrap *n* bout *m*; restes *mpl*; petit morceau *m*; bagarre *f*; ferraille *f*.

scrape *vt*, *vi* racler, gratter; * *vt* érafler; * *n* embarras *m*, ennui *m*.

scraper *n* racloir *m*.

scratch *vt* griffer, égratigner; gratter, griffonner; * *n* égratignure *f*.

scrawl *vt*, *vi* gribouiller; * *n* griffonnage *m*.

scream, screech *vi* hurler, pousser des cris; * *n* cri perçant, hurlement *m*.

screen *n* écran *m*; paravent *m*; rideau *m*; écran de cheminée *m*; * *vt* abriter, cacher; projeter; passer au crible, sélectionner.

screenplay *n* scénario *m*.

screw *n* vis *f*; * *vt* visser; extorquer, soutirer.

screwdriver *n* tournevis *m*.

scribble *vt* gribouiller; * *n* gribouillage *m*.

scribe *n* scribe *m*.

scrimmage *n* mêlée *f*.

script *n* scénario *m*; script *m*.

scriptural *adj* biblique.

Scripture *n* Ecriture sainte *f*.

scroll *n* rouleau (de papier *ou* parchemin) *m*.

scrub *vt* nettoyer à la brosse, récurer; annuler; * *n* broussailles *fpl*.

scruffy *adj* mal soigné.

scruple *n* scrupule *m*.

scrupulous *adj* scrupuleux; **~ly** *adv* scrupuleusement.

scrutinize *vt* étudier minutieusement, examiner.

scrutiny *n* examen minutieux *m*.

scuffle *n* échauffourée, rixe *f*; * *vi* se bagarrer.

scull *n* aviron *m*.

scullery *n* arrière-cuisine *f*.

sculptor *n* sculpteur *m*, -trice *f*.

sculpture *n* sculpture *f*; * *vt* sculpter.

scum *n* écume *f*; crasse *f*; rebut *m*.

scurrilous *adj* injurieux; vil,

ignoble; **~ly** *adv* injurieusement.

scurvy *n* scorbut *m*; * *adj* vil,
mesquin.

scuttle *n* corbeille *f*; * *vi* courir
précipitamment.

scythe *n* faux *f*.

sea *n* mer *f*; * *adj* marin; **heavy ~**
mer houleuse *f*.

sea breeze *n* brise de mer *f*.

seacoast *n* côte *f*.

sea fight *n* combat naval *m*.

seafood *n* fruits de mer *mpl*.

sea front *n* bord de mer *m*.

seagreen *adj* vert glauque.

seagull *n* mouette *f*.

sea horse *n* hippocampe *m*.

seal *n* sceau *m*; phoque *m*; * *vt*
sceller.

sealing wax *n* cire à cacheter *f*.

seam *n* couture *f*; * *vt* faire une
couture.

seaman *n* marin *m*.

seamanship *n* habileté à naviguer *f*.

seamstress *n* couturière *f*.

seamy *adj* sordide.

sea plane *n* hydravion *m*.

seaport *n* port de mer *m*.

sear *vt* cautériser.

search *vt* fouiller; inspecter; examiner; scruter, sonder; * *n*
fouille *f*; recherche *f*; perquisition *f*.

searchlight *n* projecteur *m*.

seashore *n* rivage *m*, bord de mer
m.

seasick *adj* sujet au mal de mer.

seasickness *n* mal de mer *m*.

seaside *n* bord de mer *m*.

season *n* saison *f*; moment opportun *m*; assaisonnement *m*; * *vt*
assaisonner; dessécher.

seasonable *adj* opportun, à propos.

seasonably *adv* de façon opportune, à propos.

seasoning *n* assaisonnement *m*.

season ticket *n* carte d'abonnement *f*.

seat *n* siège *m*; place *f*; derrière
m; fond *m*; * *vt* (faire) asseoir;
placer.

seat belt *n* ceinture de sécurité *f*.

seaward *adj* du large; **~s** *adv* vers
le large.

seaweed *n* algue *f*.

seaworthy *adj* en état de naviguer.

secede *vi* faire sécession, se séparer.

secession *n* sécession *f*; séparation *f*.

seclude *vt* éloigner, isoler.

seclusion *n* solitude *f*; isolement
m.

second *adj*, **~(ly)** *adv* deuxiè-
me(ment); * *n* second *m*; seconde
f; (*mus*) seconde *f*; * *vt* aider;
seconder.

secondary *adj* secondaire.

secondary school *n* collège d'enseignement secondaire *m*.

secondhand *n* article d'occasion
m.

secrecy *n* secret *m*; discrétion *f*.

secret *adj*, *n* secret *m*; **~ly** *adv*
secrètement.

secretary *n* secrétaire *mf*.

secrete *vt* cacher; (*med*) sécréter.

secretion *n* sécrétion *f*.

secretive *adj* secret, dissimulé.

sect *n* secte *f*.

sectarian *n* sectaire *mf*.

section *n* section *f*.

sector *n* secteur *m*.

secular *adj* séculaire.

secularize *vt* séculariser.

secure *adj* sûr; en sûreté **~ly** *adv*
en sécurité; * *vt* mettre en
sûreté; assurer.

security *n* sécurité *f*; sûreté *f*;
protection *f*; caution *f*.

sedan *n* chaise à porteurs *f*.

sedate *adj*, **~ly** *adv* calme(ment),
posé(ment).

sedateness *n* calme *m*.

sedative *n* sédatif *m*.

sedentary *adj* sédentaire.

sedge *n* (*bot*) carex *m*.

sediment n sédiment m; lie f; dépôt m.

sedition n sédition f.

seditious adj séditieux.

seduce vt séduire; corrompre.

seducer n séducteur m, -trice f.

seduction n séduction f.

seductive adj séduisant.

sedulous adj assidu; ~ly adv assidûment.

see vt voir, remarquer, découvrir; connaître; juger; comprendre; * vi voir; comprendre; ~! regarde!; tu vois!

seed n graine, semence f; * vi monter en graine.

seedling n semis m.

seedsman n grainetier m.

seed time n (époque des) semailles f(pl).

seedy adj minable.

seeing conj: ~ vu que.

seek vt chercher; demander.

seem vi paraître, sembler.

seeming n apparence f; ~ly adv apparemment.

seemliness n bienséance f.

seemly adj convenable, bienséant.

seer n prophète m.

seesaw n bascule f; * vi osciller.

seethe vi bouillir, bouillonner.

segment n segment m.

seize vt saisir, attraper; opérer la saisie de.

seizure n capture f; saisie f.

seldom adv rarement, peu souvent.

select vt sélectionner, choisir; * adj choisi, sélectionné.

selection n sélection f.

self n soi-même; **the** ~ le moi; * pref auto-.

self-command n maîtrise de soi f.

self-conceit n vanité f.

self-confident adj sûr de soi.

self-defence n autodéfense f.

self-denial n abnégation de soi f.

self-employed adj indépendant.

self-evident adj évident, qui va de soi.

self-governing adj autonome.

self-interest n intérêt personnel m.

selfish adj, ~ly adv égoïste(ment).

selfishness n égoïsme m.

self-pity n apitoiement sur soi-même m.

self-portrait n autoportrait m.

self-possession n sang-froid m, assurance f.

self-reliant adj indépendant.

self-respect n respect de soi m.

selfsame adj exactement le même, identique.

self-satisfied adj suffisant.

self-seeking adj égoïste.

self-service adj libre-service.

self-styled adj soi-disant.

self-sufficient adj autosuffisant.

self-taught adj autodidacte.

self-willed adj obstiné, volontaire.

sell vt vendre; attraper; * vi se vendre.

seller n vendeur m, -euse f.

selling-off n liquidation f.

semblance n semblant m, apparence f.

semen n sperme m.

semester n semestre m.

semicircle n demi-cercle m.

semicircular adj semi-circulaire.

semicolon n point-virgule m.

semiconductor n semi-conducteur m.

seminary n séminaire m.

semitone n (mus) demi-ton m.

senate n sénat m.

senator n sénateur m, -trice f.

senatorial adj sénatorial.

send vt envoyer, expédier, adresser; émettre; pousser.

sender n expéditeur m, -trice f.

senile adj sénile.

senility n sénilité f.

senior n aîné m, -e f; * adj aîné; supérieur.

seniority n ancienneté f.

senna n (bot) séné m.

sensation n sensation f.

sense n sens m; sensation f; raison f; bon sens m; sentiment m.

senseless adj insensé; sans connaissance; **~ly** adv stupidement.

senselessness n manque de bon sens m; absurdité f.

sensibility n sensibilité f.

sensible adj sensé, raisonnable; sensible.

sensibly adj raisonnablement.

sensitive adj sensible.

sensual, sensuous adj, **~ly** adv sensuel(lement).

sensuality n sensualité f.

sentence n phrase f; condamnation f; * vt condamner, prononcer une sentence contre.

sententious adj sentencieux; **~ly** adv sentencieusement.

sentient adj sensible.

sentiment n sentiment m; opinion f.

sentimental adj sentimental.

sentinel, sentry n sentinelle f.

sentry box n guérite f.

separable adj séparable.

separate vt séparer; * vi se séparer; * adj séparé; distinct; **~ly** adv séparément.

separation n séparation f.

September n septembre m.

septennial adj septennal.

septuagenarian n septuagénaire m.

sepulchre n sépulcre m.

sequel n conséquence f; suite f.

sequence n ordre m, série f.

sequester, sequestrate vt séquestrer.

sequestration n séquestration f.

seraglio n sérail m.

seraph n séraphin m.

serenade n sérénade f; * vt jouer une sérénade pour.

serene adj serein; **~ly** adv sereinement.

serenity n sérénité f.

serf n serf m, serve f.

serge n serge f.

sergeant n sergent m; caporal-chef m; brigadier m.

serial adj de/en série; * n feuilleton m; téléroman m.

series n série f.

serious adj sérieux, grave; **~ly** adv sérieusement.

sermon n sermon m.

serous adj séreux.

serpent n serpent m.

serpentine adj sinueux; * n (chem) serpentine f.

serrated adj en dents de scie.

serum n sérum m.

servant n domestique mf.

servant-girl n servante, bonne f.

serve vt servir; desservir; faire; accomplir; * vi servir; être utile; **to ~ a warrant** remettre un mandat.

service n service m; office m; entretien m; * vt entretenir; réviser.

service station n station-service f.

serviceable adj utilisable; pratique.

servile adj servile.

servitude n servitude f, esclavage m.

session n séance, session f; réunion f.

set vt mettre, poser, placer; fixer, déterminer; * vi se coucher (soleil); se figer; se mettre; * n jeu m; service m; ensemble m; (cine) plateau m; set m; groupe m, bande f; * adj fixe, figé; prêt; déterminé.

settee n canapé m.

setter n setter m.

setting n disposition f; cadre m; monture f; **~ of the sun** coucher du soleil m.

settle vt poser, installer, arranger; régler; calmer; * vi se poser; s'installer; se calmer.

settlement n règlement m; établissement m; accord m; résolution f; colonie f; colonisation f.

settler *n* colon *m*, colonisateur *m*, -trice *f.*

set-to *n* lutte *f*; combat *m.*

seven *adj*, *n* sept *m.*

seventeen *adj*, *n* dix-sept *m.*

seventeenth *adj*, *n* dix-septième *mf.*

seventh *adj*, *n* septième *mf.*

seventieth *adj*, *n* soixante-dixième *mf.*

seventy *adj*, *n* soixante-dix *m.*

sever *vt* séparer.

several *adj*, *pn* plusieurs.

severance *n* séparation *f.*

severe *adj* sévère, rigoureux, austère, dur; **~ly** *adv* sévèrement.

severity *n* sévérité *f.*

sew *vt*, *vi* coudre.

sewer *n* égout *m.*

sewerage *n* (système d') égouts *mpl*; eaux d'égout *fpl.*

sex *n* sexe *m.*

sewing machine *n* machine à coudre *f.*

sexist *adj*, *n* sexiste *mf.*

sextant *n* sextant *m.*

sexton *n* sacristain *m.*

sexual *adj* sexuel.

sexy *adj* sexy.

shabbily *adv* petitement, mesquinement.

shabbiness *n* aspect décrépit *ou* miteux *m.*

shabby *adj* miteux.

shackle *vt* enchaîner; **~s** *npl* chaînes *fpl.*

shade *n* ombre, obscurité *f*; nuance *f*; abat-jour *m*; * *vt* ombrager; abriter; atténuer.

shadiness *n* ombre *f*; ombrage *m.*

shadow *n* ombre *f.*

shadowy *adj* ombragé; sombre; indistinct.

shady *adj* ombreux, ombragé; sombre.

shaft *n* flèche *f*; fût *m*; puits *m*; (*tech*) arbre *m*; rayon *m.*

shag *n* tabac *m*; cormoran huppé *m.*

shaggy *adj* hirsute.

shake *vt* secouer; agiter; * *vi* trembler; chanceler; **to ~ hands** se serrer la main; * *n* secousse *f*; tremblement *m.*

shaking *adj* tremblant.

shaky *adj* tremblant.

shallow *adj* peu profond, superficiel; futile.

shallowness *n* manque de profondeur *m*; futilité *f.*

sham *vt* feindre; * *n* imitation *f*; imposture *f*; * *adj* feint, simulé.

shambles *npl* désordre *m.*

shame *n* honte *f*; * *vt* faire honte à, déshonorer.

shamefaced *adj* honteux, confus.

shameful *adj* honteux; scandaleux; **~ly** *adv* honteusement.

shameless *adj*, **~ly** *adv* effronté(ment).

shamelessness *n* effronterie, impudeur *f.*

shammy *n* chamois *m.*

shampoo *vt* faire un shampooing à; * *n* shampooing *m.*

shamrock *n* trèfle *m.*

shank *n* jambe *f*; hampe *f*; tuyau (de pipe) *m*; canon *m.*

shanty *n* baraque *f.*

shanty town *n* bidonville *m.*

shape *vt* former; façonner; modeler; * *vi* prendre forme; * *n* forme, figure *f*; modèle *m.*

shapeless *adj* informe.

shapely *adj* bien proportionné.

share *n* part, portion *f*; (*com*) action *f*; soc (de charrue) *m*; * *vt* partager; répartir; * *vi* partager.

sharer *n* participant *m.*

shark *n* requin *m.*

sharp *adj* aigu, acéré; malin; fin; pénétrant; âpre, mordant, cinglant; perçant; vif, violent; * *n* (*mus*) dièse *m*; * *adv* pile .

sharpen *vt* aiguiser, affûter.

sharply *adv* brusquement; sévèrement; vivement; nettement.

sharpness *n* tranchant *m*; finesse, acuité *f*; aigreur *f.*

shatter vt fracasser, détruire; * vi se fracasser.

shave vt raser, raboter; * vi se raser; n rasoir électrique m.

shaver n rasoir électrique m.

shaving n rasage m.

shaving brush n blaireau m.

shaving cream n crème à raser f.

shawl n châle m.

she pn elle.

sheaf n gerbe f; liasse f.

shear vt tondre; ~s npl cisailles fpl.

sheath n fourreau m.

shed vt verser, répandre; perdre; * n hangar m; cabane f.

sheen n lustre m.

sheep n mouton m.

sheepfold n parc à moutons m.

sheepish adj penaud; timide.

sheepishness n timidité f, air penaud m.

sheep-run n patûrage pour moutons m.

sheepskin n peau de mouton f.

sheer adj pur, absolu, véritable; abrupt; * adv abruptement.

sheet n drap m; plaque f; feuille (de papier) f; (mar) écoute f.

sheet anchor n ancre de veille f.

sheeting n toile pour draps f.

sheet iron n tôle f.

sheet lightning n éclairs en nappes mpl.

shelf n étagère f; (mar) écueil m; saillie f; **on the ~** au rancart.

shell n coquille f; carcasse f; écorce f; obus m; * vt écosser, décortiquer; bombarder; * vi se décortiquer.

shellfish npl invar crustacé m; fruits de mer mpl.

shelter n abri m; asile, refuge m; * vt abriter; protéger; * vi s'abriter.

shelve vt mettre au rancart.

shelving n rayonnage m.

shepherd n berger m.

shepherdess n bergère f.

sherbet n sorbet m.

sheriff n shérif m.

sherry n xérès m.

shield n bouclier m; écran protecteur m; * vt protéger.

shift vi changer; se déplacer; * vt changer, bouger; transférer; * n changement m; roulement m.

shinbone n tibia m.

shine vi briller, reluire, illuminer; * vt cirer; * n éclat m.

shingle n galets mpl; ~s pl (med) zona m.

shining adj resplendissant; * n éclat m.

shiny adj brillant, reluisant.

ship n bateau m; navire m; bâtiment m; * vt embarquer; transporter.

shipbuilding n construction navale f.

shipmate n (mar) camarade de bord m.

shipment n cargaison f.

shipowner n armateur m.

shipwreck n naufrage m.

shirt n chemise f.

shit excl (sl) merde!

shiver vi frissonner.

shoal n banc m.

shock n choc m; décharge f; coup m; * vt bouleverser; choquer.

shock absorber n amortisseur m.

shoddy adj de mauvaise qualité.

shoe n chaussure f; fer (à cheval) m; * vt chausser; ferrer (un cheval.

shoeblack n cireur de chaussures m.

shoehorn n chausse-pied m.

shoelace n lacet de chaussure m.

shoemaker n cordonnier m.

shoestring n lacet de chaussure m.

shoot vt tirer, lancer, décocher; * vi pousser, bourgeonner; passer en flèche; s'élancer; * n pousse f.

shooter n tireur m, -euse f.

shooting n fusillade f; tir m.

shop n magasin m; atelier m.

shopfront n devanture f.

shoplifter n voleur(-euse) à l'étalage m(f).

shopper n acheteur m, -euse f.

shopping n courses fpl.

shopping centre n centre commercial m.

shore n rivage, bord m, côte f.

short adj court, bref, succinct, concis; ~ly adv brièvement; rapidement.

shortcoming n insuffisance f; défaut m.

shorten vt raccourcir; abréger.

shortness n petitesse f; brièveté f.

short-sighted adj myope.

short-sightedness n myopie f.

shortwave n ondes courtes fpl.

shot n coup m; décharge f; plomb m; tentative f; prise f.

shotgun n fusil de chasse m.

shoulder n épaule f; accotement m; * vt charger sur son épaule.

shout vi crier; * vt crier; * n cri m, acclamation f.

shouting n cris mpl.

shove vt, vi pousser; * n poussée f.

shovel n pelle f; * vt pelleter.

show vt montrer; faire voir, présenter; prouver; expliquer; * vi se voir; * n exposition f; spectacle m; manifestation f; salon m.

show business n monde du spectacle m.

shower n averse f; douche f; (fig) torrent m; * vi pleuvoir.

showery adj pluvieux.

showroom n salle d'exposition f.

showy adj voyant, ostentatoire.

shred n lambeau m, parcelle f; * vt mettre en lambeaux.

shrew n mégère f; musaraigne f.

shrewd adj astucieux; perspicace; ~ly adv astucieusement.

shrewdness n astuce f.

shriek vt, vi hurler; * n hurlement m.

shrill adj aigu, strident.

shrillness n ton aigu m.

shrimp n crevette f; nabot m, -e f, avorton m.

shrine n lieu saint m.

shrink vi rétrécir; se réduire, rapetisser.

shrivel vi se ratatiner, se flétrir; * vt ratatiner.

shroud n voile m; linceul m; * vt envelopper, voiler; ensevelir.

Shrove Tuesday n Mardi gras m.

shrub n arbuste m.

shrubbery n massif d'arbustes m.

shrug vt hausser les épaules; * n haussement d'épaules m.

shudder vi frissonner; * n frisson m.

shuffle vt mélanger; battre.

shun vt fuir, éviter.

shunt vt (rail) aiguiller.

shut vt fermer; vi (se) fermer.

shutter n volet m.

shuttle n navette f.

shuttlecock n volant m.

shy adj timide; réservé; embarrassé, gauche; ~ly adv timidement.

shyness n timidité f.

sibling n enfants de mêmes parents mpl.

sibyl n sibylle f.

sick adj malade; écœuré.

sicken vt rendre malade; * vi tomber malade.

sickle n faucille f.

sick leave n congé de maladie m.

sickliness n état maladif m.

sickly adj maladif.

sickness n maladie f.

sick pay n indemnité de maladie f.

side n côté m; flanc m; camp m; parti m; * adj latéral; secondaire; * vi se ranger du côté de.

sideboard n buffet m.

sidelight n veilleuse f.

sidelong adj oblique.

sideways adv de côté, obliquement.

siding n (rail) voie de garage f.

sidle vi avancer de côté; avancer furtivement.

siege n (mil) siège m.

sieve n tamis m; crible m; passoire f; * vt tamiser.

sift vt tamiser; passer au crible; dégager.

sigh vi soupirer, gémir; * n soupir m.

sight n vue f; mire f; spectacle m.

sightless adj aveugle.

sightly adj agréable à regarder; séduisant.

sightseeing n tourisme m.

sign n signe m, indication f; panneau m; geste m; trace f; * vt signer.

signal n signal m; * adj insigne, remarquable.

signalize vt signaler.

signal lamp n (rail) lampe de signalisation f.

signalman n (rail) aiguilleur m.

signature n signature f.

signet n sceau m.

significance n importance f.

significant adj considérable.

signify vt signifier.

signpost n poteau indicateur m.

silence n silence m; * vt imposer le silence à.

silent adj silencieux; ~ly adv silencieusement.

silex n silex m.

silicon chip n puce de silicium f.

silk n soie f.

silken adj soyeux; satiné.

silkiness n soyeux m.

silkworm n ver à soie m.

silky adj soyeux; satiné.

sill n rebord m; seuil m.

silliness n stupidité, bêtise, niaiserie f.

silly adj bête, stupide.

silver n argent m; * adj en argent.

silversmith n orfèvre m.

silvery adj argenté.

similar adj semblable; similaire; ~ly adv de la même façon.

similarity n ressemblance f.

simile n comparaison f.

simmer vi cuire à feux doux, mijoter.

simony n simonie f.

simper vi minauder; * n sourire affecté m.

simple adj simple; naïf.

simpleton n nigaud m, -e f.

simplicity n simplicité f; naïveté f.

simplification n simplification f.

simplify vt simplifier.

simply adv simplement; seulement.

simulate vt simuler, feindre.

simulation n simulation f.

simultaneous adj simultané.

sin n péché m; * vi pécher.

since adv depuis; * prep depuis; * conj depuis que; puisque.

sincere adj, ~ly adv sincère(ment); **yours ~ly** veuillez agréer, Monsieur/Madame, l'expression de mes salutations distinguées.

sincerity n sincérité f.

sinecure n sinécure f.

sinew n tendon m; nerf m.

sinewy adj nerveux; tendineux.

sinful adj coupable, honteux; ~ly adv honteusement.

sinfulness n corruption f, péché m.

sing vi, vt chanter; (poet) vt célébrer.

singe vt roussir.

singer n chanteur m, -euse f.

singing n chant m.

single adj seul, unique, simple; célibataire; * n aller simple m; 45 tours m; * vt distinguer; séparer.

singly adv séparément.

singular adj singulier, rare; * n singulier m; ~ly adv singulièrement.

singularity n singularité f.

sinister adj sinistre; de mauvais augure, funeste.

sink *vi* couler; sombrer; s'affaisser; tomber très bas, baisser; * *vt* couler, faire sombrer; ruiner; * *n* évier *m*.

sinking fund *n* fonds d'amortissement *m*.

sinner *n* pécheur *m*; pécheresse *f*.

sinuosity *n* sinuosité *f*.

sinuous *adj* sinueux.

sinus *n* sinus *m*.

sip *vt* boire à petites gorgées; * *n* petite gorgée *f*.

siphon *n* siphon *m*.

sir *n* monsieur *m*.

sire *n* étalon *m*.

siren *n* sirène *f*.

sirloin *n* aloyau (de boeuf) *m*.

sister *n* soeur *f*.

sister-in-law *n* belle-soeur *f*.

sisterhood *n* solidarité féminine *f*.

sisterly *adj* de soeur.

sit *vi* s'asseoir; se trouver; * *vt* se présenter à.

site *n* emplacement *m*; site *m*.

sit-in *n* sit-in *m*, manifestation avec occupation de lieux publics *f*.

sitting *n* séance, réunion *f*; position assise *f*.

sitting room *n* salle de séjour *f*.

situated *adj* situé.

situation *n* situation *f*.

six *adj*, *n* six *m*.

sixteen *adj*, *n* seize *m*.

sixteenth *adj*, *n* seizième *mf*.

sixth *adj*, *n* sixième *mf*.

sixtieth *adj*, *n* soixantième *mf*.

sixty *adj*, *n* soixante *m*.

size *n* taille, grandeur *f*; volume *m*; dimension *f*; ampleur *f*; étendue *f*.

sizeable *adj* assez grand.

skate *n* patin *m*; * *vi* patiner.

skateboard *n* planche à roulettes *f*, skateboard *m*.

skating *n* patinage *m*.

skating rink *n* patinoire *f*.

skein *n* écheveau *m*.

skeleton *n* squelette *m*.

skeleton key *n* passe(-partout) *m*.

sketch *n* croquis *m*; esquisse *f*; * *vt* equisser, faire un croquis de.

skewer *n* broche *f*; brochette *f*; * *vt* embrocher.

ski *n* ski *m*; * *vi* skier.

ski boot *n* chaussure de ski *f*.

skid *n* dérapage *m*; * *vi* déraper.

skier *n* skieur *m*, -euse *f*.

skiing *n* ski *m*.

skill *n* habileté, adresse, dextérité *f*.

skilled *adj* adroit; qualifié.

skilful *adj*, **~ly** *adv* adroit(ement), habile(ment).

skilfulness *n* habileté *f*.

skim *vt* écrémer; effleurer.

skimmed milk *n* lait écrémé *m*.

skimmer *n* écumoire *f*.

skin *n* peau *f*; * *vt* écorcher.

skin diving *n* plongée sous-marine *f*.

skinned *adj* dépouillé.

skinny *adj* maigre, efflanqué.

skip *vi* sautiller, gambader; * *vt* sauter, passer; * *n* saut, bond *m*; benne *f*.

ski pants *npl* fuseau (de ski) *m*.

skipper *n* capitaine *m*.

skirmish *n* escarmouche *f*; * *vi* s'engager dans une escarmouche.

skirt *n* jupe *f*; bordure *f*; * *vt* contourner.

skit *n* parodie, satire *f*.

skittish *adj* espiègle, fantasque; coquet; inconstant; **~ly** *adv* d'une manière espiègle.

skittle *n* quille *f*.

skulk *vi* se cacher, rôder furtivement.

skull *n* crâne *m*.

skullcap *n* calotte *f*.

sky *n* ciel *m*.

skylight *n* lucarne *f*.

skyrocket *n* fusée *f*.

skyscraper *n* gratte-ciel *m invar*.

slab *n* dalle *f*.

slack *adj* lâche, mou, indolent, négligent.

slack(en) *vt* relâcher; ralentir; diminuer; * *vi* se relâcher; ralentir.

slackness *n* manque d'énergie, ralentissement *m*; laisser-aller *m*.

slag *n* scories *fpl*.

slam *vt* claquer violemment; * *vi* se refermer en claquant.

slander *vt* calomnier, dire du mal de; * *n* calomnie *f*.

slanderer *n* calomniateur *m*, -trice *f*.

slanderous *adj* calomnieux; ~ly *adv* calomnieusement.

slang *n* argot *m*.

slant *vi* pencher; être incliné; * *n* inclinaison *f*; point de vue *m*.

slanting *adj* en pente, incliné.

slap *n* claque *f*; (*on the face*) gifle *f*; * *adv* en plein; * *vt* donner une claque à, gifler.

slash *vt* entailler; * *n* entaille *f*.

slate *n* ardoise *f*.

slater *n* ardoisier *m*.

slating *n* recouvrement en ardoises *m*.

slaughter *n* carnage, massacre *m*; * *vt* abattre; massacrer.

slaughterer *n* tueur, meurtrier *m*.

slaughterhouse *n* abattoir *m*.

slave *n* esclave *mf*; * *vi* travailler comme un nègre.

slaver *n* bave *f*; * *vi* baver.

slavery *n* esclavage *m*.

slavish *adj* servile, d'esclave; ~ly *adv* servilement.

slavishness *n* servilité *f*.

slay *vt* tuer.

slayer *n* tueur *m*, -euse *f*.

sleazy *adj* louche, sordide.

sledge, sleigh *n* traîneau *m*.

sledgehammer *n* marteau de forgeron *m*.

sleek *adj* lisse et brillant, luisant.

sleep *vi* dormir; * *n* sommeil *m*.

sleeper *n* dormeur *m*, -euse *f*.

sleepily *adv* d'un air endormi.

sleepiness *n* envie de dormir *f*.

sleeping bag *n* sac de couchage *m*.

sleeping pill *n* somnifère *m*.

sleepless *adj* sans sommeil.

sleepwalking *n* somnambulisme *m*.

sleepy *adj* qui a envie de dormir; endormi.

sleet *n* neige fondue *f*.

sleeve *n* manche *f*.

sleight *n*: ~ of hand tour de passe-passe *m*.

slender *adj* svelte, mince, élancé; faible; ~ly *adv* faiblement.

slenderness *n* sveltesse *f*, minceur *f*; faiblesse *f*.

slice *n* tranche *f*; spatule *f*; * *vt* couper (en tranches).

slide *vi* glisser; faire des glissades; * *n* glissade *f*; coulisse *f*; diapositive *f*; toboggan *m*.

sliding *adj* glissant; coulissant.

slight *adj* léger, mince, petit; * *n* affront *m*; * *vt* manquer d'égards pour.

slightly *adv* légèrement.

slightness *n* fragilité *f*; insignifiance *f*.

slim *adj* mince; * *vi* maigrir.

slime *n* vase *f*; dépôt visqueux *m*.

sliminess *n* viscosité *f*.

slimming *n* amaigrissement *m*.

slimy *adj* visqueux, gluant.

sling *n* fronde *f*; écharpe *f*; * *vt* lancer.

slink *vi* s'en aller furtivement; s'éclipser.

slip *vi* (se) glisser, se faufiler; * *vt* glisser; * *n* glissade *f*; faux pas *m*; oubli *m*; fiche *f*.

slipper *n* pantoufle *f*.

slippery *adj* glissant.

slipshod *adj* négligé.

slipway *n* cale *f*.

slit *vt* fendre, inciser; * *n* fente, incision *f*.

slobber *n* bave *f*.

sloe *n* prunelle *f*.

slogan *n* slogan *m*.

sloop n (mar) sloop m.

slop n fange f; bouillon m; ~s pl eaux sales fpl.

slope n inclinaison f; pente f; déclivité f; versant m; * vt incliner.

sloping adj en pente; incliné.

sloppy adj négligé; peu soigné.

sloth n paresse f.

slouch vi manquer de tenue; se tenir d'une façon négligée.

slovenliness n négligence f; manque de soin m.

slovenly adj négligé, sale, débraillé.

slow adj lent; lourd; ennuyeux; ~ly adv lentement.

slowness n lenteur, lourdeur f, manque d'intérêt m.

slow worm n orvet m.

slug n lingot m; limace f; jeton m; coup m.

sluggish adj paresseux; léthargique; ~ly adv paresseusement.

sluggishness n paresse, mollesse f.

sluice n écluse f; * vt lâcher les vannes.

slum n taudis m; quartier pauvre m.

slumber vi dormir paisiblement; * n sommeil paisible m.

slump n récession f.

slur vt dénigrer; calomnier; mal articuler; * n calomnie f.

slush n neige fondante f.

slut n traînée f.

sly adj rusé; ~ly adv de façon rusée.

slyness n ruse, finesse f.

smack n léger goût m; claque f; gros baiser retentissant m; * vi sentir; embrasser bruyamment; * vt donner une claque à.

small adj petit, menu.

smallish adj assez petit.

smallness n petitesse f.

smallpox n variole f.

smalltalk n conversation f.

smart adj élégant; rapide; astucieux; vif; * vi brûler.

smartly adv astucieusement, vivement; avec élégance; habilement.

smartness n astuce, vivacité, finesse f.

smash vt casser, briser; détruire; * vi se briser (en mille morceaux), se fracasser; * n fracas m; coup violent m.

smattering n connaissances superficielles fpl.

smear n (med) frottis m; * vt enduire; salir.

smell vt, vi sentir; * n odorat m; odeur f; mauvaise odeur f.

smelly adj malodorant.

smelt n éperlan m; * vt fondre.

smelter n fondeur m.

smile vi sourire; * n sourire m.

smirk vi sourire d'un air affecté.

smite vt frapper.

smith n forgeron m.

smithy n forge f.

smock n blouse f.

smoke n fumée f; vapeur f; * vt, vi fumer.

smokeless adj sans fumée.

smoker n fumeur m, -euse f.

smoke shop n bureau de tabac m.

smoking : 'no ~' "interdiction de fumer".

smoky adj enfumé; qui fume.

smooth adj lisse, uni, égal; doucereux, mielleux; * vt lisser; aplanir; adoucir.

smoothly adv facilement; doucement.

smoothness n douceur f; aspect lisse m; air doucereux m.

smother vt étouffer; réprimer.

smoulder vi couver.

smudge vt salir; * n tache f.

smug adj suffisant.

smuggle vt passer en contrebande.

smuggler n contrebandier m, -ière f.

smuggling n contrebande f.

smut n saleté f; trace de suie f.

smuttiness n suie f; obscénité f.

smutty adj noirci; obscène.

snack n collation f.

snack bar n snack-bar m.

snag n obstacle m.

snail n escargot m.

snake n serpent m.

snaky adj sinueux.

snap vt casser net; * vi se casser net; claquer; mordre; parler sèchement; **to ~ one's fingers** faire claquer ses doigts; * n claquement m; photographie f.

snapdragon n (bot) gueule-de-loup f.

snap fastener n bouton-pression m.

snare n piège m; collet m.

snarl vi gronder férocement.

snatch vt saisir; s'emparer de; * n geste vif m; vol m; fragment m.

sneak vi se glisser furtivement; * n faux-jeton m.

sneakers npl chaussures de basket fpl.

sneer vi parler d'un ton méprisant; ricaner.

sneeringly adv d'un ton méprisant.

sneeze vi éternuer.

sniff vt renifler; * vi renifler.

snigger vi rire sous cape.

snip vt donner de petits coups de ciseaux dans; * n petit coup de ciseaux m; petit bout m.

snipe n bécassine f.

sniper n franc-tireur m.

snivel n pleurnicherie f; * vi pleurnicher.

sniveller n pleurnicheur m, -euse f.

snob n snob mf.

snobbish adj snob.

snooze n petit somme m; * vi faire un somme.

snore vi ronfler.

snorkel n tube respiratoire m.

snort vi renifler fortement.

snout n museau m; groin m.

snow n neige f; * vi neiger.

snowball n boule de neige f.

snowdrop n (bot) perce-neige m invar.

snowman n bonhomme de neige m.

snowplough n chasse-neige m invar.

snowy adj neigeux; enneigé.

snub vt repousser, rejeter.

snub-nosed adj au nez retroussé.

snuff n tabac à priser m.

snuffbox n tabatière f.

snuffle vi parler d'une voix nasillarde, nasiller.

snug adj confortable, douillet; bien abrité.

so adv si, tellement, aussi; ainsi.

soak vi tremper; * vt faire tremper.

soap n savon m; * vt savonner.

soap bubble n bulle de savon f.

soap opera n feuilleton à l'eau de rose m.

soap powder n lessive f.

soapsuds n mousse de savon f.

soapy adj savonneux.

soar vi monter en flèche.

sob n sanglot m; * vi sangloter.

sober adj sobre; sérieux; **~ly** adv sobrement; sérieusement.

sobriety n sobriété f; sérieux, calme m.

soccer n football m.

sociability n sociabilité f.

sociable adj sociable, liant.

sociably adv sociablement.

social adj social, sociable; **~ly** adv socialement.

socialism n socialisme m.

socialist n socialiste mf.

social work n assistance sociale f.

social worker n assistant(e) social(e) m(f).

society n société f; compagnie f.

sociologist n sociologue mf.

sociology n sociologie f.

sock n chaussette f.

socket n prise de courant f.

sod n gazon m.

soda n soude f; eau de Seltz f, soda m.

sofa n sofa m.

soft adj doux, moelleux; aimable, gentil; **~ly** adv doucement; tendrement .

soften vt (r)amollir, adoucir; atténuer.

soft-hearted adj compatissant.

softness n douceur, mollesse f.

soft-spoken adj à la voix douce.

software n logiciel m.

soil vt salir, souiller; * n salissure, souillure f; sol m; terre f.

sojourn vi séjourner; * n séjour m.

solace vt consoler, soulager; * n consolation f.

solar adj solaire.

solder vt souder; * n soudure f.

soldier n soldat m.

soldierly adj militaire.

sole n plante du pied f; semelle (de chaussure) f; sole f; * adj seul, unique.

solecism n (gr) solécisme m.

solemn adj, **~ly** adv solennel(lement).

solemnity n solennité f.

solemnize vt solenniser.

solicit vt solliciter; quémander.

solicitation n sollicitation f.

solicitor n notaire m.

solicitous adj plein de sollicitude; **~ly** adv avec sollicitude.

solicitude n sollicitude f.

solid adj solide, compact; * n solide m; **~ly** adv solidement.

solidify vt solidifier.

solidity n solidité f.

soliloquy n soliloque m.

solitaire n solitaire m.

solitary adj solitaire, retiré; * n anachorète m.

solitude n solitude f.

solo n (mus) solo m.

solstice n solstice m.

soluble adj soluble.

solution n solution f.

solve vt résoudre.

solvency n solvabilité f.

solvent adj solvable; n (chem) solvant m.

some adj du, de la, de l', des; quelques; quelconque; certain(e)s; quelque.

somebody pn quelqu'un.

somehow adv d'une façon ou d'une autre.

someplace adv quelque part.

something pn quelque chose.

sometime adv au cours de, un jour ou l'autre.

sometimes adv quelquefois, parfois.

somewhat adv quelque peu.

somewhere adv quelque part.

somnambulism n somnambulisme m.

somnambulist n somnambule mf.

somnolence n somnolence f.

somnolent adj somnolent.

son n fils m.

sonata n (mus) sonate f.

song n chanson f.

son-in-law n gendre m.

sonnet n sonnet m.

sonorous adj sonore.

soon adv bientôt; **as ~ as** dès que.

sooner adv plus tôt; plutôt.

soot n suie f.

soothe vt calmer, apaiser; flatter.

soothsayer n devin m.

sop n pain trempé m.

sophism n sophisme m.

sophist n sophiste mf.

sophistical adj sophistiqué.

sophisticate vt falsifier; sophistiquer.

sophisticated adj sophistiqué.

sophistry n sophistique f.

sophomore n étudiant(e) de seconde année m(f).

soporific adj soporifique.

sorcerer n sorcier m.

sorceress n sorcière f.

sorcery n sorcellerie f.

sordid adj sordide, sale; avide.

sordidness n aspect sordide m, saleté f.

sore n plaie, blessure f; * adj douloureux, sensible; contrarié; **~ly** adv gravement.

sorrel n (bot) oseille f; * adj alezanroux.

sorrow n peine f; chagrin m; * vi se lamenter.

sorrowful adj triste, affligé; **~ly** adv tristement.

sorry adj désolé, navré; déplorable; **I am ~** je suis désolé.

sort n sorte f; genre m; espèce f; race f; manière f; * vt classer; trier.

soul n âme f; essence f; personne f.

sound adj sain; solide; valide; **~ly** adv sainement, solidement; * n son m; bruit m; * vt sonner (de); * vi sonner, retentir; ressembler; sembler.

sounding board n table d'harmonie f; abat-voix m.

sound effects npl bruitage m.

soundings npl (mar) sondages mpl; (mar) fonds mpl.

soundness n santé f; solidité f.

soundtrack n bande sonore f.

soup n soupe f.

sour adj aigre, acide; acerbe; revêche; **~ly** adv aigrement; * vt aigrir, faire tourner; * vi s'aigrir; tourner.

source n source f; origine f.

sourness n acidité, aigreur f; acrimonie f.

souse n (sl) soûlard m, -e f; * vt mariner; faire tremper.

souvenir n souvenir m.

south n sud m; * adj sud, du sud, au sud; * adv au sud; vers le sud.

southerly, southern adj du sud, sud, méridional.

southward(s) adv vers le sud.

southwester n (mar) vent du sud-ouest m; suroît m.

sovereign adj, n souverain m, -e f.

sovereignty n souveraineté f.

sow n truie f.

sow vt semer; disperser.

sowing time n époque des semailles f.

soy n soja m.

space n espace m; intervalle m; * vt espacer.

spacecraft n vaisseau spatial m.

spaceman/woman n astronaute mf.

spacious adj spacieux, ample; **~ly** adv spacieusement.

spaciousness n dimensions spacieuses fpl, espace m.

spade n bêche f; pique m.

spaghetti n spaghetti mpl.

span n envergure f; * vt enjamber; embrasser.

spangle n paillette f; * vt orner de paillettes.

spaniel n épagneul m.

Spanish adj espagnol; * n espagnol m; Espagnol m, -e f.

spar n (mar) espar m; * vi s'entraîner.

spare vt, vi épargner; ménager; éviter; se passer de; * adj de trop; de réserve.

sparing adj limité, modéré, économe; **~ly** adv frugalement, avec modération.

spark n étincelle f.

sparkle n scintillement m, étincelle f; * vi étinceler; briller.

spark plug n bougie f.

sparrow n moineau m.

sparrowhawk n épervier m.

sparse adj clairsemé; épars; **~ly** adv faiblement.

spasm n spasme m.

spasmodic adj spasmodique.

spatter vt éclabousser; * vi gicler.

spatula n spatule f.

spawn n frai m; * vt pondre; engendrer.

spawning n frai m.

speak vt parler; dire; * vi parler, s'entretenir; prendre la parole.

speaker n haut-parleur m; interlocuteur m, -trice f; orateur m.

spear n lance f; harpon m; * vt transpercer d'un coup de lance.

special *adj* spécial, particulier; **~ly** *adv* spécialement.

speciality *n* spécialité *f.*

species *n* espèce *f.*

specific *adj* spécifique; * *n* remède spécifique *m.*

specifically *adv* spécifiquement; explicitement.

specification *n* spécification *f.*

specify *vt* spécifier.

specimen *n* spécimen *m*; exemple *m.*

specious *adj* spécieux.

speck(le) *n* grain, tache *f*; * *vt* tacheter, moucheter.

spectacle *n* spectacle *m.*

spectator *n* spectateur *m*, -trice *f.*

spectral *adj* spectral; **~ analysis** *n* analyse spectrale *f.*

spectre *n* spectre *m.*

speculate *vi* spéculer; méditer.

speculation *n* spéculation *f*; conjecture *f*; méditation *f.*

speculative *adj* spéculatif, méditatif.

speculum *n* spéculum *m.*

speech *n* parole *f*; discours *m*; langage *m*; élocution *f.*

speechify *vi* discourir.

speechless *adj* muet.

speed *n* vitesse *f*; rapidité *f*; * *vt* presser; accélérer; * *vi* se presser.

speedboat *n* vedette *f.*

speedily *adv* rapidement, vite.

speediness *n* rapidité, promptitude, célérité *f.*

speed limit *n* limitation de vitesse *f.*

speedometer *n* compteur de vitesse *m.*

speedway *n* piste de course *f.*

speedy *adj* rapide, prompt.

spell *n* charme, sortilège *m*; période *f*; * *vt* écrire; épeler; ensorceler, envoûter; * s'écrire; s'épeler.

spelling *n* orthographe *f.*

spend *vt* dépenser; passer; épuiser; gaspiller.

spendthrift *n* dépensier *m*, -ière *f.*

spent *adj* épuisé.

sperm *n* sperme *m.*

spermaceti *n* spermaceti *m.*

spew *vi* (*sl*) vomir.

sphere *n* sphère *f.*

spherical *adj* sphérique; **~ly** *adv* de forme sphérique.

spice *n* épice *f*; * *vt* épicer.

spick-and-span *adj* impeccable; tiré à quatre épingles.

spicy *adj* épicé.

spider *n* araignée *f.*

spigot *n* clef de robinet *f.*

spike *n* pointe *f*; clou *m*; * *vt* clouter.

spill *vt* renverser, répandre; * *vi* se répandre.

spin *vt* filer; inventer, fabriquer; faire tourner; * *vi* tourner; * *n* tournoiement *m*; tour (en voiture) *m.*

spinach *n* épinard *m.*

spinal *adj* spinal.

spindle *n* fuseau *m*; broche *f.*

spine *n* colonne vertébrale, épine dorsale *f.*

spinet *n* (*mus*) épinette *f.*

spinner *n* fileur *m*; fileuse *f.*

spinning wheel *n* rouet *m.*

spin-off *n* sous-produit *m.*

spinster *n* célibataire *f.*

spiral *adj*, **~ly** *adv* en spirale.

spire *n* flèche *f*; aiguille *f*; tige *f.*

spirit *n* esprit *m*; âme *f*; caractère *m*, disposition *f*; courage *m*; humeur *f*; * *vt* encourager; animer; **to ~ away** faire disparaître comme par enchantement.

spirited *adj* vif, fougueux; **~ly** *adv* fougueusement.

spirit lamp *n* lampe à alcool *f.*

spiritless *adj* sans entrain, abattu.

spiritual *adj*, **~ly** *adv* spirituel(lement).

spiritualist *n* spiritualiste *mf.*

spirituality *n* spiritualité *f.*

spit *n* crachat *m*; salive *f*; * *vt*, *vi* cracher; crépiter.

spite *n* dépit *m*, rancune *f*; **in ~ of** en dépit de, malgré; * *vt* vexer.

spiteful *adj* rancunier, malveillant; **~ly** *adv* par méchanceté, par rancune.

spitefulness *n* méchanceté *f*; rancune *f*.

spittle *n* salive *f*; crachat *m*.

splash *vt* éclabousser, faire gicler; * *vi* barboter; * *n* éclaboussure *f*; tache *f*.

spleen *n* rate *f*; spleen *m*.

splendid *adj* splendide, magnifique; **~ly** *adv* splendidement.

splendour *n* splendeur *f*; magnificence *f*.

splice *vt* (*mar*) épisser, abouter.

splint *n* éclisse *f*.

splinter *n* éclat *m*; esquille *f*; écharde *f*; * *vt* (*vi*) (se) fendre en éclats.

split *n* fente *f*; rupture *f*, * *vt* fendre, diviser; * *vi* se fendre.

spoil *vt* abîmer; gâter; gâcher.

spoiled *adj* abîmé; gâté.

spoke *n* rayon (de roue) *m*.

spokesman *n* porte-parole *m invar*.

spokeswoman *n* porte-parole *f invar*.

sponge *n* éponge *f*; * *vt* éponger; * *vi* être un parasite.

sponger *n* parasite *m*.

sponginess *n* spongiosité *f*.

spongy *adj* spongieux.

sponsor *n* caution *m*; parrain *m*; marraine *f*.

sponsorship *n* parrainage *m*.

spontaneity *n* spontanéité *f*.

spontaneous *adj*, **~ly** *adv* spontané(ment).

spool *n* bobine *f*; rouleau *m*.

spoon *n* cuiller *f*.

spoonful *n* cuillerée *f*.

sporadic(al) *adj* sporadique.

sport *n* sport *m*; jeu *m*; divertissement, amusement *m*.

sport jacket *n* veste sport *f*.

sports car *n* voiture de sport *f*.

sportsman *n* sportif *m*.

sportswear *n* vêtements de sport *mpl*.

sportswoman *n* sportive *f*.

spot *n* tache *f*; point *m*; endroit *m*; pois *m*; * *vt* apercevoir; tacher.

spotless *adj* impeccable, immaculé.

spotlight *n* feu de projecteur *m*.

spotted, spotty *adj* tacheté; à pois.

spouse *n* époux *m*; épouse *f*.

spout *vi* jaillir; gicler; déblatérer; * *vt* faire jaillir; * *n* bec *m*; gargouille *f*; jet *m*.

sprain *adj* foulé; * *n* entorse *f*.

sprat *n* sprat *m*.

sprawl *vi* s'étaler.

spray *n* spray *m*; pulvérisation *f*; embruns *mpl*.

spread *vt* étendre, étaler; répandre, propager; * *vi* s'étendre, se répandre; * *n* propagation, diffusion *f*.

spree *n* fête *f*.

sprig *n* brin *m*.

sprightliness *n* vivacité *f*, entrain *m*.

sprightly *adj* alerte, vif, fringant.

spring *vi* bondir, sauter; provenir, découler; émaner, naître; * *n* printemps *m*; élasticité *f*; ressort *m*; saut *m*; source *f*.

springiness *n* élasticité *f*.

springtime *n* printemps *m*.

springwater *n* eau de source *f*.

springy *adj* élastique.

sprinkle *vt* arroser.

sprinkling *n* arrosage *m*.

sprout *n* pousse *f*, germe *m*; **~s** *npl* choux de Bruxelles *mpl*; * *vi* germer.

spruce *adj* net, impeccable; **~ly** *adv* tiré à quatre épingles; * *vt* se mettre sur son trente-et-un.

spruceness *n* élégance *f*.

spur *n* éperon *m*; ergot (coq) *m*; stimulant *m*; * *vt* éperonner; stimuler.

spurious *adj* faux, feint; falsifié, de contrefaçon; bâtard.

spurn *vt* repousser avec mépris.

sputter *vi* postillonner; bredouiller; bafouiller.

spy *n* espion *m*, -onne *f*; * *vt* apercevoir; espionner; *vi* espionner.

squabble *vi* se disputer, se quereller; * *n* querelle, dispute *f*.

squad *n* escouade *f*; brigade *f*; équipe *f*.

squadron *n* (*mil*) escadron *m*.

squalid *adj* misérable, sordide.

squall *n* rafale *f*; bourrasque *f*; * *vi* piailler.

squally *adj* qui souffle en rafales.

squalor *n* saleté *f*; misère *f*.

squander *vt* gaspiller, dilapider.

square *adj* carré; catégorique; honnête; * *n* carré *m*; place *f*; équerre *f*; * *vt* cadrer; mettre en ordre, régler; * *vi* cadrer.

squareness *n* forme carrée *f*.

squash *vt* écraser; * *n* squash *m*.

squat *vi* s'accroupir; * *adj* accroupi; trapu, courtaud.

squatter *n* squatter *m*.

squaw *n* squaw, femme peaurouge *f*.

squeak *vi* grincer, crier; * *n* cri, couinement *m*.

squeal *vi* pousser un cri aigu, couiner.

squeamish *adj* exigeant; délicat.

squeeze *vt* presser, tordre; comprimer; * *n* pression *f*; serrement de main *m*; cohue *f*.

squid *n* calmar *m*.

squint *adj* atteint de strabisme; * *vi* loucher; * *n* strabisme.

squirrel *n* écureuil *m*.

squirt *vt* faire gicler; * *n* giclée *f*; jet *m*; seringue *f*.

stab *vt* poignarder; * *n* coup de couteau *m*.

stability *n* stabilité, solidité *f*.

stable *n* écurie *f*; * *vt* mettre à l'écurie; * *adj* stable.

stack *n* pile *f*; * *vt* empiler.

staff *n* personnel *m*; bâton *m*; soutien *m*.

stag *n* cerf *m*.

stage *n* étape *f*; scène *f*; échafaudage *m*; théâtre *m*; stade *m*; estrade *f*.

stagger *vi* vaciller, tituber; hésiter; * *vt* stupéfier; échelonner.

stagnation *n* stagnation *f*.

stagnant *adj* stagnant.

stagnate *vi* stagner.

staid *adj* posé, sérieux.

stain *vt* tacher; ternir; * *n* tache *f*.

stainless *adj* sans tache; immaculé.

stair *n* marche *f*; ~s *pl* escalier *m*.

staircase *n* escalier *m*.

stake *n* pieu *m*; enjeu *m*; * *vt* marquer; délimiter.

stale *adj* rassis, rance.

staleness *n* manque de fraîcheur *m*; rance *m*.

stalk *vi* avancer d'un air majestueux; * *n* tige, queue *f*, trognon *m*.

stall *n* stalle *f*; stand, étalage *m*; (fauteuil d') orchestre *m*; emplacement *m*; * *vt* caler; * *vi* caler; atermoyer.

stallion *n* étalon *m*.

stalwart *n* partisan fidèle *m*.

stamen *n* étamine *f*.

stamina *n* résistance *f*.

stammer *vi* bégayer; * *n* bégaiement *m*.

stamp *vt* trépigner; timbrer; affranchir; tamponner; * *vi* trépigner; * *n* timbre *m*; cachet *m*; tampon *m*; empreinte *f*; estampille *f*.

stampede *n* débandade *f*.

stand *vi* être debout, se tenir; se maintenir; résister ; être situé, se trouver; rester, durer; s'arrêter, faire halte; * *vt* poser; résister; soutenir, supporter; * *n* position, prise de position *f*; pied, support *m*; étalage *m*; état *m*; tribune *f*; stand *m*.

standard *n* étendard *m*; modèle *m*; étalon *m*; norme *f*; * *adj* normal.

standing *adj* permanent, fixe, établi; en pied; * *n* durée *f*; importance *f*; rang *m*.

standstill *n* arrêt *m*; immmobilisation *f*.

staple *n* agrafe *f*; * *adj* principal, de base; * *vt* agrafer.

star *n* étoile *f*; astérisque *m*.

starboard *n* tribord *m*.

starch *n* amidon *m*; * *vt* amidonner.

stare *vi*: **to ~ at** regarder fixement; * *n* regard fixe *m*.

stark *adj* raide, rigide; pur; * *adv* complètement.

starling *n* étourneau *m*.

starry *adj* étoilé.

start *vi* commencer, débuter; sursauter, tressaillir; démarrer, se mettre en route; * *vt* commencer; amorcer; lancer; mettre en marche; * *n* début *m*; ouverture *f*; sursaut *m*; départ *m*; avance *f*.

starter *n* starter, démarreur *m*.

starting point *n* point de départ *m*.

startle *vt* faire sursauter.

startling *adj* surprenant, alarmant.

starvation *n* inanition, faim *f*.

starve *vi* mourir de faim.

state *n* état *m*; condition *f*; pompe *f*, apparat *m*; **the S~s** les Etats-Unis *mpl*; * *vt* déclarer; exposer.

stateliness *n* majesté, grandeur *f*.

stately *adj* majestueux, imposant.

statement *n* déclaration, affirmation *f*.

statesman *n* homme d'Etat *m*.

statesmanship *n* qualité d'homme politique *f*.

static *adj* statique; * *n* parasites *mpl*.

station *n* station *f*; place, position *f*; condition *f*, rang *m*; situation *f*; condition *f*; (*rail*) gare *f*; * *vt* placer.

stationary *adj* stationnaire, immobile.

stationer *n* papetier *m*, -ière *f*.

stationery *n* papeterie *f*.

station wagon *n* break *m*.

statistical *adj* statistique.

statistics *npl* statistiques *fpl*.

statuary *n* statuaire *f*.

statue *n* statue *f*.

stature *n* stature, taille *f*.

statute *n* statut *m*; loi *f*.

stay *n* séjour *m*; **~s** *npl* corset *m*; * *vi* rester, demeurer; tenir; loger; **to ~ in** rester à la maison; **to ~ on** rester encore quelque temps; **to ~ up** ne pas se coucher.

stead *n* place *f*, lieu *m*.

steadfast *adj* ferme, résolu, inébranlable; **~ly** *adv* fermement, résolument .

steadily *adv* fermement; régulièrement.

steadiness *n* fermeté, stabilité *f*.

steady *adj* stable, solide; * *vt* affermir.

steak *n* biftek *m*; steak *m*.

steal *vt*, *vi* voler.

stealth *n* vol *m*; **by ~** à la dérobée.

stealthily *adv* furtivement.

stealthy *adj* furtif.

steam *n* vapeur *f*; buée *f*; * *vt* cuire à la vapeur; * *vi* fumer.

steam engine *n* locomotive à vapeur *f*.

steamer, steamboat *n* (bateau à) vapeur, paquebot *m*.

steel *n* acier *m*; * *adj* d'acier.

steelyard *n* balance romaine *f*.

steep *adj* abrupt; excessif; * *vt* tremper.

steeple *n* clocher *m*; flèche *f*.

steeplechase *n* steeple (course) *m*.

steepness *n* raideur *f*; escarpement *m*.

steer *n* bouvillon *m*; * *vt* conduire; diriger; gouverner; * *vi* tenir le gouvernail.

steering *n* direction *f*.

steering wheel *n* volant *m*.

stellar *adj* stellaire.

stem *n* tige *f*, tronc *m*; souche *f*; pied *m*; tuyau *m*; * *vt* endiguer.

stench *n* odeur fétide *f*.

stencil *n* stencil *m*.

stenographer *n* sténographe *mf*.

stenography *n* sténographie *f*.

step *n* pas *m*, marche *f*; trace *f*; * *vi* faire un pas; marcher.

stepbrother *n* demi-frère *m*.

stepdaughter *n* belle-fille *f*.

stepfather *n* beau-père *m*.

stepmother *n* belle-mère *f*.

stepping stone *n* pierre de gué *f*.

stepsister *n* demi-soeur *f*.

stepson *n* beau-fils *m*.

stereo *n* stéréo *f*.

stereotype *n* stéréotype *m*; * *vt* stéréotyper.

sterile *adj* stérile.

sterility *n* stérilité *f*.

sterling *adj* de bon aloi, vrai, véritable; * *n* livres sterling *fpl*.

stern *adj* sévère, rigide, strict; * *n* (*mar*) poupe *f*; ~**ly** *adv* sévèrement.

stethoscope *n* (*med*) stéthoscope *m*.

stevedore *n* (*mar*) docker *m*.

stew *vt* faire cuire à l'étouffée; * *n* ragoût *m*.

steward *n* intendant *m*; (*mar*) steward *m*.

stewardess *n* hôtesse de l'air *f*.

stewardship *n* intendance *f*.

stick *n* bâton *m*; canne *f*; baguette *f*; * *vt* coller; piquer, planter; supporter; * *vi* tenir; se planter; rester fidèle.

stickiness *n* viscosité *f*.

stick-up *n* braquage, hold-up *m*.

sticky *adj* collant, poisseux.

stiff *adj* raide, rigide; inflexible; dur; entêté; ~**ly** *adv* raidement; obstinément.

stiffen *vt* raidir, renforcer; * *vi* se raidir.

stiff neck *n* torticolis *m*.

stiffness *n* raideur, rigidité *f*; opiniâtreté *f*.

stifle *vt* étouffer.

stifling *adj* suffocant.

stigma *n* stigmate *m*.

stigmatize *vt* stigmatiser.

stile *n* tourniquet *m*.

stiletto *n* stylet *m*; talon aiguille *m*.

still *vt* calmer, apaiser; faire taire; * *adj* silencieux, calme; * *n* alambic *m*; * *adv* encore; toujours; quand même, tout de même.

stillborn *adj* mort-né.

stillness *n* calme *m*, tranquillité *f*.

stilts *npl* échasses *fpl*.

stimulant *n* stimulant *m*.

stimulate *vt* stimuler.

stimulation *n* stimulant *m*; stimulation *f*.

stimulus *n* stimulant *m*.

sting *vt* piquer; * *vi* brûler; * *n* dard *m*; piqûre *f*; aiguillon *m*.

stingily *adv* avec avarice.

stinginess *n* mesquinerie, avarice *f*.

stingy *adj* mesquin, avare, pingre.

stink *vi* puer; * *n* puanteur *f*.

stint *n* tâche assignée *f*.

stipulate *vt* stipuler.

stipulation *n* stipulation *f*.

stir *vt* remuer; agiter; exciter; * *vi* remuer, bouger; * *n* agitation *f*; émoi *m*.

stirrup *n* étrier *m*.

stitch *vt* coudre; * *n* point *m*; point de suture *m*.

stoat *n* hermine *f*.

stock *n* réserve *f*; provision *f*; bouillon *m*; souche *f*; lignée *f*; capital *m*; fonds *mpl*; ~**s** *pl* valeurs mobilières *fpl*; * *vt* approvisionner, stocker.

stockade *n* prison militaire *f*.

stockbroker *n* agent de change *m*.

stock exchange *n* Bourse *f*.

stockholder *n* actionnaire *mf*.

stocking *n* bas *m*.

stock market *n* Bourse *f*.

stoic n stoïque mf.

stoical adj, **~ly** adv stoï-que(ment).

stoicism n stoïcisme m.

stole n étole f.

stomach n estomac m; ventre m; * vt digérer; endurer.

stone n pierre f; caillou m; noyau m; * adj de pierre; * vt lancer des pierres sur; dénoyauter; empierrer.

stone deaf adj sourd comme un pot.

stoning n empierrement m.

stony adj pierreux, rocailleux; dur.

stool n tabouret m; rebord, appui m.

stoop vi se baisser, se pencher; * n inclination en avant f.

stop vt arrêter, interrompre; boucher; * vi s'arrêter, cesser; * n arrêt m; halte f; pause f; point m.

stopover n escale; étape f.

stoppage, stopping n obstruction f; engorgement m; (rail) suppression f.

stopwatch n chronomètre m.

storage n emmagasinage m; entreposage m.

store n provision f; réserve f; entrepôt m, magasin m; * vt mettre en réserve, accumuler, emmagasiner.

storekeeper n marchand m, -e f.

stork n cigogne f.

storm n tempête f, orage m; assaut m; * vt prendre d'assaut; * vi faire rage.

stormily adv violemment.

stormy adj orageux; houleux.

story n histoire f; récit m; étage m.

stout adj corpulent, robuste, vigoureux; solide; **~ly** adv solidement; vaillamment; résolument.

stoutness n vigueur f; puissance f; corpulence f.

stove n poêle m; cuisinière f.

stow vt ranger, mettre en place; (mar) arrimer.

straggle vi être disséminé.

straggler n traînard m, -e f.

straight adj droit; direct; franc; * adv droit; directement.

straightaway adv immédiatement, tout de suite.

straighten vt redresser.

straightforward adj honnête; franc; direct.

straightforwardness n honnêteté f.

strain vt tendre; fouler; forcer; mettre à l'épreuve; * vi peiner; * n tension f; effort m; entorse f; contrainte f; lignée f; accent m; ton m.

strainer n passoire f.

strait n détroit m; embarras m; situation critique f.

strait-jacket n camisole de force f.

strand n brin m; rivage m, rive f.

strange adj inconnu; étrange; **~ly** adv étrangement, curieusement.

strangeness n étrangeté f; nouveauté f.

stranger n inconnu(e) m(f), étranger m, -ère f.

strangle vt étrangler.

strangulation n strangulation f.

strap n lanière, sangle f; courroie f; * vt attacher avec une courroie.

strapping adj robuste, charpenté.

stratagem n stratagème m.

strategic adj stratégique m.

strategy n stratégie f.

stratum n strate f.

straw n paille f.

strawberry n fraise f.

stray vi s'égarer; vagabonder; * adj perdu; errant.

streak n raie, bande f; filet m; * vt strier.

stream n ruisseau m, rivière f; torrent m; * vi ruisseler.

streamer n serpentin m.

street n rue f.

streetcar n tramway m.

strength n force, puissance f; vigueur f; robustesse f.

strengthen vt fortifier; confirmer, renforcer.

strenuous adj ardu; vigoureux.

stress n pression f; stress m; tension f; contrainte f; importance f; accent m; * vt souligner; accentuer.

stretch vt étendre, étirer; élargir; forcer; * vi s'étendre, s'étirer; * n extension f; étendue f; période f.

stretcher n brancard m.

strew vt éparpiller; semer.

strict adj strict, sévère; exact, rigoureux, précis; ~**ly** adv strictement, sévèrement.

strictness n sévérité f; rigueur f.

stride n grand pas m; * vi marcher à grandes enjambées.

strife n conflit m, lutte f.

strike vt frapper; heurter; attaquer; rayer; * vi frapper; se mettre en grève; sonner; * n coup m; grève f; découverte f.

striker n gréviste mf.

striking adj frappant; saisissant; ~**ly** adv remarquablement.

string n ficelle f; corde f; cordon m; rang m; fibre f; * vt munir d'une corde; enfiler; suspendre.

stringent adj rigoureux.

stringy adj filandreux.

strip vt déshabiller, dévêtir; * vi se déshabiller; * n bande f; langue f; bandelette f.

stripe n raie, rayure f; coup de fouet m; * vt rayer.

strive vi s'efforcer; s'évertuer; lutter, se battre.

stroke n coup m; trait m; course f; caresse f; apoplexie f; * vt caresser.

stroll n petit tour; * vi flâner.

strong adj fort, vigoureux, robuste; puissant; intense; ~**ly** adv fortement, énergiquement.

strongbox n coffre-fort m.

stronghold n forteresse f.

strophe n strophe f.

structure n structure f; construction f.

struggle vi lutter; se battre; se démener; * n lutte f.

strum vt (mus) tapoter de.

strut vi se pavaner; * n démarche affectée f.

stub n souche f; bout m; talon m.

stubble n chaume m; barbe de plusieurs jours f.

stubborn adj entêté, obstiné; ~**ly** adv obstinément.

stubbornness n entêtement m, obstination f.

stucco n stuc m.

stud n clou m; crampon m; écurie f.

student n, adj étudiant m, -e f.

stud horse n étalon m.

studio n studio, atelier m.

studio apartment n studio m.

studious adj studieux; sérieux; ~**ly** adv studieusement, sérieusement.

study n étude f; études fpl; méditation f; * vt étudier; observer; * vi étudier; faire des études.

stuff n matière f; matériaux mpl; étoffe f; * vt (rem)bourrer, remplir; empailler.

stuffing n rembourrage m.

stuffy adj mal aéré; collet monté.

stumble vi trébucher; * n faux pas, trébuchement m.

stumbling block n hésitation f; pierre d'achoppement f.

stump n souche f; moignon m; bout m.

stun vt étourdir; stupéfier.

stunner n personne ou chose extraordinaire f.

stunt n cascade f; coup de publicité m; * vt empêcher de croître.

stuntman n cascadeur m.

stupefy vt hébéter; stupéfier.

stupendous adj prodigieux, remarquable.

stupid *adj*, **~ly** *adv* stupide(ment).

stupidity *n* stupidité *f*.

stupor *n* stupeur *f*.

sturdily *adv* fortement.

sturdiness *n* force, robustesse *f*; résolution *f*.

sturdy *adj* vigoureux, robuste, fort; hardi, résolu.

sturgeon *n* esturgeon *m*.

stutter *vi* bégayer.

sty *n* porcherie *f*; taudis *m*.

stye *n* orgelet *m*.

style *n* style *m*; mode *f*; * *vt* appeler, dénommer; créer, dessiner.

stylish *adj* élégant, qui a du chic.

suave *adj* suave.

subdivide *vt* subdiviser.

subdivision *n* subdivision *f*.

subdue *vt* subjuguer, assujettir; contenir, réfréner; adoucir.

subject *adj* soumis; sujet à; * *n* sujet *m*; thème *m*; * *vt* soumettre; exposer.

subjection *n* sujétion *f*.

subjugate *vt* subjuguer, assujettir.

subjugation *n* subjugation *f*.

subjunctive *n* subjonctif *m*.

sublet *vt* sous-louer.

sublimate *vt* sublimer.

sublime *adj* sublime, suprême; **~ly** *adv* sublimement; * *n* sublime *m*.

sublimity *n* sublimité *f*.

submachine gun *n* mitraillette *f*.

submarine *adj*, *n* sous-marin *m*.

submerge *vt* submerger.

submersion *n* submersion *f*.

submission *n* soumission *f*.

submissive *adj* soumis, docile; **~ly** *adv* avec soumission.

submissiveness *n* docilité *f*; soumission *f*.

submit *vt* soumettre; * *vi* se soumettre.

subordinate *adj* subalterne, inférieur; * *vt* subordonner.

subordination *n* subordination *f*.

subpoena *n* citation *f*; * *vt* citer.

subscribe *vi* souscrire; * *vt* apposer; signer.

subscriber *n* souscripteur *m*, -trice *f*.

subscription *n* souscription *f*.

subsequent *adj*, **~ly** *adv* ultérieur(ement).

subservient *adj* subordonné; utile.

subside *vi* s'affaisser, baisser.

subsidence *n* affaissement *m*.

subsidiary *adj* subsidiaire.

subsidize *vt* subventionner, fournir des subsides à.

subsidy *n* subvention *f*; subside *m*.

subsist *vi* subsister; exister.

subsistence *n* existence *f*; subsistance *f*.

substance *n* substance *f*; fond *m*; essentiel *m*.

substantial *adj* considérable; réel, substantiel; solide; **~ly** *adv* considérablement.

substantiate *vt* justifier.

substantive *n* substantif *m*.

substitute *vt* substituer; * *n* remplaçant *m*, -e *f*.

substitution *n* substitution *f*.

substratum *n* substrat *m*.

subterfuge *n* subterfuge *m*; faux-fuyant *m*.

subterranean *adj* souterrain.

subtitle *n* sous-titre *m*.

subtle *adj* subtile.

subtlety *n* subtilité *f*.

subtly *adv* subtilement.

subtract *vt* (*math*) soustraire.

suburb *n* banlieue *f*.

suburban *adj* de banlieue.

subversion *n* subversion *f*.

subversive *adj* subversif.

subvert *vt* subvertir, renverser.

subway *n* métro *m*.

succeed *vi* réussir; succéder; avoir du succès; * *vt* succéder à, suivre.

success *n* succès *m*.

successful *adj* couronné de succès, qui réussit; **~ly** *adv* avec succès.

succession *n* succession *f*.

successive *adj* successif; **~ly** *adv* successivement.

successor *n* successeur *m*.

succinct *adj* succinct, concis; **~ly** *adv* succinctement.

succulent *adj* succulent.

succumb *vi* succomber.

such *adj* tel, pareil; **~ as** tel que.

suck *vt, vi* sucer; *vi* téter.

suckle *vt* allaiter.

suckling *n* nourrisson *m*.

suction *n* (*med*) succion *f*.

sudden *adj*, **~ly** *adv* soudain(ement), subit(ement).

suddenness *n* soudaineté *f*.

suds *npl* mousse de savon *f*.

sue *vt* poursuivre en justice; supplier.

suede *n* daim *m*.

suet *n* graisse de rognon *f*.

suffer *vt* souffrir, subir; tolérer, endurer; * *vi* souffrir.

suffering *n* souffrance *f*; douleur *f*.

suffice *vi* suffire, être suffisant.

sufficiency *n* quantité suffisante *f*; aisance *f*.

sufficient *adj* suffisant; **~ly** *adv* suffisamment.

suffocate *vt, vi* étouffer.

suffocation *n* suffocation *f*.

suffrage *n* suffrage, vote *m*.

suffuse *vt* baigner, se répandre sur.

sugar *n* sucre *m*; * *vt* sucrer.

sugar beet *n* betterave à sucre *f*.

sugar cane *n* canne à sucre *f*.

sugar loaf *n* pain de sucre *m*.

sugar plum *n* bonbon *m*.

sugary *adj* sucré.

suggest *vt* suggérer.

suggestion *n* suggestion *f*.

suicidal *adj* suicidaire.

suicide *n* suicide *m*; suicidé *m*, -e *f*.

suit *n* procès *m*; pétition *f*; costume *m*; tailleur *m*; requête *f*;

* *vt* convenir à; aller à; arranger, adapter.

suitable *adj* qui convient, approprié.

suitably *adv* convenablement.

suitcase *n* valise *f*.

suite *n* suite *f*; escorte *f*; mobilier *m*; cortège *m*.

suitor *n* plaideur *m*; prétendant *m*.

sulkiness *n* bouderie *f*.

sulky *adj* boudeur, maussade; **~ly** *adv* d'un air maussade; de mauvaise grâce.

sullen *adj* maussade; sombre; **~ly** *adv* d'un air maussade; de mauvaise grâce.

sullenness *n* maussaderie *f*; silence *m*.

sulphur *n* soufre *m*.

sulphurous *adj* sulphureux.

sultan *n* sultan *m*.

sultana *n* sultane *f*; raisin sec *m*.

sultry *adj* étouffant; chaud.

sum *n* somme *f*; total *m*; **to ~ up** *vt* résumer; récapituler; * *vi* résumer.

summarily *adv* sommairement.

summary *adj*, *n* résumé *m*.

summer *n* été *m*.

summerhouse *n* gloriette *f*, pavillon de jardin *m*.

summit *n* sommet *m*; cime *f*.

summon *vt* convoquer, citer à comparaître; sommer; (*mil*) sommer de se rendre.

summons *n* convocation *f*; sommation *f*.

sumptuous *adj* somptueux; **~ly** *adv* somptueusement.

sun *n* soleil *m*.

sunbathe *vi* prendre un bain de soleil, se faire bronzer.

sunburnt *adj* bronzé, hâlé.

Sunday *n* dimanche *m*.

sundial *n* cadran solaire *m*.

sundry *adj* divers, différent.

sunflower *n* tournesol *m*.

sunglasses *npl* lunettes de soleil *fpl*.

sunless *adj* sans soleil.

sunlight *n* lumière du soleil *f*.

sunny *adj* ensoleillé; radieux.
sunrise *n* lever du soleil *m*.
sun roof *n* toit ouvrant *m*.
sunset *n* coucher du soleil *m*.
sunshade *n* parasol *m*.
sunshine *n* (lumière du) soleil *m*; ensoleillement *m*.
sunstroke *n* insolation *f*.
suntan *n* bronzage *m*.
suntan oil *n* huile solaire *f*.
super *adj* (*fam*) sensationnel.
superannuated *adj* en retraite.
superannuation *n* retraite, pension de retraite *f*.
superb *adj*, **~ly** *adv* superbe(ment).
supercargo *n* (*mar*) subrécargue *m*.
supercilious *adj* hautain, dédaigneux; **~ly** *adv* avec dédain.
superficial *adj*, **~ly** *adv* superficiel(lement).
superfluity *n* surabondance, superfluité *f*.
superfluous *adj* superflu.
superhuman *adj* surhumain.
superintendent *n* directeur *m*, -trice *f*.
superior *adj*, *n* supérieur *m*, -e *f*.
superiority *n* supériorité *f*.
superlative *adj*, *n* superlatif *m*; **~ly** *adv* extrêmement, au suprême degré.
supermarket *n* supermarché *m*.
supernatural *n* surnaturel.
supernumerary *adj* surnuméraire.
superpower *n* superpuissance *f*.
supersede *vt* remplacer; supplanter.
supersonic *adj* supersonique.
superstition *n* superstition *f*.
superstitious *adj* superstitieux; **~ly** *adv* superstitieusement.
superstructure *n* superstructure *f*.
supertanker *n* gros pétrolier, supertanker *m*.
supervene *vi* survenir.

supervise *vt* surveiller, superviser.
supervision *n* surveillance *f*.
supervisor *n* surveillant *m*, -e *f*.
supine *adj* couché, étendu sur le dos; indolent.
supper *n* dîner *m*.
supplant *vt* supplanter.
supple *adj* souple, flexible; obséquieux.
supplement *n* supplément *m*.
supplementary *adj* supplémentaire.
suppleness *n* souplesse *f*.
suppli(c)ant *n* suppliant *m*, -e *f*.
supplicate *vt* supplier.
supplication *n* supplique, supplication *f*.
supplier *n* fournisseur *m*.
supply *vt* fournir, approvisionner; suppléer à, remédier à; * *n* approvisionnement *m*; provision *f*.
support *vt* soutenir; supporter, appuyer; * *n* appui *m*.
supportable *adj* supportable.
supporter *n* partisan *m*; supporter *m*, adepte *mf*.
suppose *vt*, *vi* supposer.
supposition *n* supposition *f*.
suppress *vt* supprimer.
suppression *n* suppression *f*.
supremacy *n* suprématie *f*.
supreme *adj*, **~ly** *adv* suprême(ment).
surcharge *vt* surcharger; * *n* surtaxe *f*.
sure *adj* sûr, certain; infaillible; **to be ~** certainement; **~ly** *adv* sûrement, certainement, sans doute.
sureness *n* certitude, sûreté *f*.
surety *n* certitude *f*; caution *f*.
surf *n* (*mar*) ressac *m*.
surface *n* surface *f*; * *vt* revêtir; * *vi* remonter à la surface.
surfboard *n* planche (de surf) *f*.
surfeit *n* excès *m*.
surge *n* vague, montée *f*; * *vi* déferler.
surgeon *n* chirurgien *m*.

surgery n chirurgie m.
surgical adj chirurgical.
surliness n air revêche, bourru m.
surly adj revêche, bourru.
surmise vt conjecturer; * n conjecture f.
surmount vt surmonter.
surmountable adj surmontable.
surname n nom de famille m.
surpass vt surpasser, dépasser.
surpassing adj sans pareil, incomparable.
surplice n surplis m.
surplus n excédent m; surplus m; * adj en surplus.
surprise vt surprendre; * n surprise f.
surprising adj surprenant.
surrender vt rendre; céder; * vi se rendre; * n reddition f.
surreptitious adj, ~ly adv subreptice(ment).
surrogate vt remplacer; * n substitut m.
surrogate mother n mère-porteuse f.
surround vt entourer, cerner, encercler.
survey vt examiner, inspecter; faire le relevé de; * n enquête f; relevé (des plans) m.
survive vi survivre; * vt survivre à.
survivor n survivant m, -e f.
susceptibility n sensibilité f.
susceptible adj sensible.
suspect vt soupçonner; * n suspect m, -e f.
suspend vt suspendre.
suspense n incertitude f; suspense m.
suspension n suspension f.
suspension bridge n pont suspendu m.
suspicion n soupçon m.
suspicious adj soupçonneux; ~ly adv soupçonneusement.
suspiciousness n caractère soupçonneux m.

sustain vt soutenir, supporter, maintenir; subir.
sustenance n (moyens de) subsistance f.
suture n suture f.
swab n tampon m; prélèvement m.
swaddle vt emmailloter.
swaddling-clothes npl langes mpl.
swagger vi plastronner.
swallow n hirondelle f; * vt avaler.
swamp n marais m.
swampy adj marécageux.
swan n cygne m.
swap vt échanger; * n échange m.
swarm n essaim m; grouillement m; nuée f; * vi fourmiller; grouiller de monde; pulluler.
swarthy adj basané.
swarthiness n teint basané m.
swashbuckling adj fanfaron.
swath n andain m.
swathe vt emmailloter; * n bande f.
sway vt balancer; * vi se balancer, osciller; * n balancement m; emprise, domination, puissance f.
swear vt jurer; faire prêter serment; * vi jurer.
sweat n sueur f; * vi suer, transpirer.
sweater, sweatshirt n pullover m.
sweep vt balayer; ramoner; * vi s'étendre; avancer rapidement, majestueusement; * n coup de balai m; grand geste m; champ m.
sweeping adj rapide; ~s pl balayures fpl.
sweepstake n sweepstake m.
sweet adj sucré, doux, agréable; suave; gentil; mélodieux; adorable; * adv doux; sucré; * n bonbon m.
sweetbread n ris de veau m.
sweeten vt sucrer; adoucir; assainir; purifier.

sweetener n édulcorant m.

sweetheart n petit(e) ami(e) m(f); chéri m, -e f.

sweetmeats npl sucreries fpl.

sweetness n goût sucré m, douceur f.

swell vi gonfler; enfler; augmenter; * vt gonfler, enfler, grossir; * n houle f; * adj (fam) génial, épatant.

swelling n gonflement m; boursouflure, tuméfaction f.

swelter vi étouffer de chaleur.

swerve vi faire un écart; * vt dévier.

swift adj rapide, prompt, vif; * n martinet m.

swiftly adv rapidement.

swiftness n rapidité, promptitude f.

swill vt boire avidemment; * n pâtée f.

swim vi nager; * vt traverser à la nage; * n baignade f.

swimming n natation f; vertige m.

swimming pool n piscine f.

swimsuit n maillot de bain m.

swindle vt escroquer.

swindler n escroc m.

swine n pourceau, porc m.

swing vi se balancer, osciller; virer; * vt balancer; faire tourner; influencer; * n balancement m; rythme m.

swinging adj (fam) rythmé.

swinging door n porte battante f.

swirl n tourbillon.

switch n baguette f; interrupteur m; (rail) aiguille f; * vt changer de; **to ~ off** éteindre; **to ~ on** allumer.

switchboard n standard (téléphonique) m.

swivel vt faire pivoter.

swoon vi s'évanouir; * n éva-

nouissement m, défaillance f.

swoop vi fondre sur; * n descente en piqué f; descente, rafle f; **in one ~** d'un seul coup.

sword n épée f.

swordfish n espadon m.

swordsman n tireur d'épée m.

sycamore n sycomore m.

sycophant n sycophante mf.

syllabic adj syllabique.

syllable n syllabe f.

syllabus n programme d'un cours m.

syllogism n syllogisme m.

sylph n sylphe m; sylphide f.

symbol n symbole m.

symbolic(al) adj symbolique.

symbolize vt symboliser.

symmetrical adj, **~ly** adv symétrique(ment).

symmetry n symétrie f.

sympathetic adj compatissant; **~ally** adv avec compassion.

sympathize vi compatir.

sympathy n compassion f.

symphony n symphonie f.

symposium n symposium m.

symptom n symptôme m.

synagogue n synagogue f.

synchronism n synchronisme m.

syndicate n syndicat m.

syndrome n syndrome m.

synod n synode m.

synonym n synonyme m.

synonymous adj synonyme; **~ly** adv de façon synonyme.

synopsis n synopsis f; résumé m.

synoptical adj synoptique.

syntax n syntaxe f.

synthesis n synthèse f.

syringe n seringue f; * vt seringuer.

system n système m.

systematic adj, **~ally** adv systématique(ment).

systems analyst n analyste de systèmes mf.

T

tab *n* patte *f*; étiquette *f*.

tabernacle *n* tabernacle *m*.

table *n* table *f*; * *vt* mettre en forme de tableau; ajourner; ~ **d'hôte** repas à prix fixe *m*.

tablecloth *n* nappe *f*.

tablespoon *n* grande cuiller *f*.

tablet *n* tablette *f*; comprimé *m*.

table tennis *n* ping-pong *m*.

taboo *adj, n* tabou *m*; * *vt* proscrire.

tabular *adj* tabulaire.

tacit *adj*, **~ly** *adv* tacite(ment).

taciturn *adj* taciturne.

tack *n* broquette *f*; bord *m*; * *vt* clouer; * *vi* tirer des bordées.

tackle *n* attirail, équipement, matériel *m*; plaquage *m*; (*mar*) appareil de levage *m*, apparaux *mpl*.

tact *n* tact *m*.

tactician *n* tacticien *m*.

tactics *npl* tactique *f*.

tadpole *n* têtard *m*.

taffeta *n* taffetas *m*.

tag *n* ferret *m*; * *vt* ferrer.

tail *n* queue *f*; basque *f*; * *vt* suivre, filer.

tailgate *n* hayon arrière *m*.

tailor *n* tailleur *m*.

tailoring *n* métier de tailleur *m*.

tailor-made *adj* fait sur mesure.

tailwind *n* vent arrière *m*.

taint *vt* infecter, polluer; vicier; * *n* tache, souillure *f*.

tainted *adj* infecté; souillé.

take *vt* prendre, saisir; apporter; emporter; conduire; enlever, retirer; passer; * *vi* prendre; **to ~ away** *vt* enlever; emporter; **to ~ back** *vt* reprendre; raccompagner; **to ~ down** *vt* descendre; prendre (notes); **to ~ in** *vt* saisir, comprendre; recevoir; **to ~ off** *vi* décoller; *vt* enlever; imiter; **to ~ on** *vt* accepter; engager; s'attaquer à; **to ~ out** *vt* sortir; enlever; **to ~ to** *vt* se prendre d'amitié pour; **to ~ up** *vt* monter; occuper; se mettre à; * *n* prise *f*.

takeoff *n* décollage *m*.

takeover *n* prise de possession *f*.

takings *npl* recette *f*.

talc *n* talc *m*.

talent *n* talent *m*; don *m*.

talented *adj* talentueux.

talisman *n* talisman *m*.

talk *vi* parler, bavarder; causer; * *n* conversation *f*; discussion *f*; entretien *m*.

talkative *adj* loquace.

talk show *n* débat télévisé *m*.

tall *adj* grand, élevé; incroyable.

tally *vi* correspondre.

talon *n* serre *f*.

tambourine *n* tambourin *m*.

tame *adj* apprivoisé, domestiqué; **~ly** *adv* docilement; fadement; * *vt* apprivoiser, domestiquer.

tameness *n* nature apprivoisée *f*; soumission *f*.

tamper *vi* toucher à.

tampon *n* tampon *m*.

tan *vt, vi* bronzer; * *n* bronzage *m*.

tang *n* saveur forte *f*.

tangent *n* tangente *f*.

tangerine *n* mandarine *f*.

tangible *adj* tangible.

tangle *vt* enchevêtrer, embrouiller.

tank *n* réservoir *m*; citerne *f*.

tanker *n* pétrolier *m*; camion-citerne *m*.

tanned *adj* bronzé.

tantalizing *adj* tentant.

tantamount *adj* équivalent (à).

tantrum *n* accès de colère *m*.

tap *vt* taper doucement; exploiter; inciser; * *n* petite tape *f*; robinet *m*.

tape *n* ruban *m*; * *vt* enregistrer.

tape measure *n* mètre à ruban *m*.

taper n cierge m.

tape recorder n magnétophone m.

tapestry n tapisserie f.

tar n goudron m.

target n cible f.

tariff n tarif m.

tarmac n piste f.

tarnish vt ternir.

tarpaulin n bâche (goudronnée) f.

tarragon n (bot) estragon m.

tart adj acidulé, âpre; * n tarte, tartelette f.

tartan n tartan m.

tartar n tartre m.

task n tâche f.

tassel n gland m.

taste n goût m; saveur f; pincée f; penchant m; * vt sentir le goût de; goûter à; déguster; savourer; * vi avoir du goût.

tasteful adj de bon goût; ~ly adv avec goût.

tasteless adj insipide, sans goût.

tasty adj savoureux.

tattoo n tatouage m; * vt tatouer.

taunt vt railler; accabler de sarcasmes; * n raillerie f, sarcasme m.

Taurus n Taureau m (signe du zodiaque).

taut adj tendu.

tautological adj tautologique.

tautology n tautologie f.

tawdry adj tapageur, voyant, clinquant.

tax n impôt m; contribution f; * vt imposer; mettre à l'épreuve.

taxable adj imposable.

taxation n imposition f.

tax collector n percepteur m.

tax-free adj exonéré d'impôts.

taxi n taxi m; * vi rouler sur la piste.

taxi driver n chauffeur de taxi m.

taxi stand n station de taxis f.

tax payer n contribuable mf.

tax relief n dégrèvement fiscal m.

tax return n déclaration d'impôts f.

tea n thé m.

teach vt enseigner, apprendre; * vi enseigner.

teacher n professeur m; instituteur m, -trice f.

teaching n enseignement m.

teacup n tasse à thé f.

teak n teck m.

team n équipe f.

teamster n routier m.

teamwork n travail d'équipe m.

teapot n théière f.

tear vt déchirer; **to ~ up** mettre en morceaux.

tear n larme f.

tearful adj larmoyant; ~ly adv en pleurant.

tear gas n gaz lacrymogène m.

tease vt taquiner.

tea-service, tea-set n service à thé m.

teaspoon n petite cuiller f.

teat n tétine f, mamelon m.

technical adj technique.

technicality n technicité f.

technician n technicien m, -ienne f.

technique n technique f.

technological adj technologique.

technology n technologie f.

teddy (bear) n ours en peluche m.

tedious adj ennuyeux, fastidieux; ~ly adv fastidieusement.

tedium n ennui, manque d'intérêt m.

tee n tee m.

teem vi grouiller (de).

teenage adj adolescent; ~r n adolescent(e) m(f).

teens npl adolescence (de 13 à 20 ans) f.

tee-shirt n T-shirt m.

teeth npl de tooth.

teethe vi faire ses premières dents.

teetotal adj antialcoolique, qui ne boit jamais d'alcool.

teetotaller n personne qui ne boit jamais d'alcool f.

telegram n télégramme m.

telegraph n télégraphe m.

telegraphic adj télégraphique.

telegraphy n télégraphie f.

telepathy n télépathie f.

telephone n téléphone m.

telephone booth n cabine téléphonique f.

telephone call n appel téléphonique m.

telephone directory n annuaire m.

telephone number n numéro de téléphone m.

telescope n télescope m.

telescopic adj télescopique.

televise vt téléviser.

television n télévision f.

television set n téléviseur, poste de télévision m.

telex n télex m; vt envoyer par télex.

tell vt dire; raconter.

teller n caissier m, -ière f.

telling adj révélateur.

telltale adj dénonciateur.

temper vt tempérer, modérer; * n colère f.

temperament n tempérament m.

temperance n tempérance, modération f.

temperate adj tempéré, modéré, mesuré.

temperature n température f.

tempest n tempête f.

tempestuous adj de tempête.

template n gabarit m.

temple n temple m; tempe f.

temporarily adv temporairement.

temporary adj temporaire.

tempt vt tenter.

temptation n tentation f.

tempting adj tentant.

ten adj, n dix m.

tenable adj défendable.

tenacious adj tenace, ~ly adv avec ténacité.

tenacity n ténacité f.

tenancy n location f.

tenant n locataire mf.

tend vt garder, surveiller; * vi avoir tendance (à).

tendency n tendance f.

tender adj tendre, délicat; sensible; ~ly adv tendrement; * n offre f; * vt offrir.

tenderness n tendresse f.

tendon n tendon m.

tenement n appartement m.

tenet n doctrine f; principe m.

tennis n tennis m.

tennis court n court ou terrain de tennis m.

tennis player n joueur(-euse) de tennis m(f).

tennis racket n raquette de tennis f.

tennis shoes npl chaussures de tennis fpl.

tenor n (mus) ténor m; sens m; substance f.

tense adj tendu; * n (gr) temps m.

tension n tension f.

tent n tente f.

tentacle n tentacule m.

tentative adj timide, hésitant; ~ly adv à titre d'essai.

tenth adj, n dixième mf.

tenuous adj ténu.

tenure n titularisation f.

tepid adj tiède.

term n terme m; trimestre m; mot m; condition, clause f; * vt appeler, nommer.

terminal adj terminal; * n aérogare f; terminal m.

terminate vt terminer.

termination n fin, conclusion f.

terminus n terminus m.

terrace n terrace f.

terrain n terrain m.

terrestrial adj terrestre.

terrible adj terrible.

terribly adv terriblement.

terrier n terrier m.

terrific adj terrifiant; fantastique.

terrify vt terrifier, épouvanter.

territorial adj territorial.

territory n territoire m.

terror n terreur f.

terrorism *n* terrorisme *m.*

terrorist *n* terroriste *mf.*

terrorize *vt* terroriser.

terse *adj* concis, net.

test *n* essai *m;* épreuve *f;* * *vt* essayer; examiner.

testament *n* testament *m.*

tester *n* contrôleur *m,* -euse *f.*

testicles *npl* testicules *mpl.*

testify *vt* témoigner, déclarer sous serment.

testimonial *n* certificat *m.*

testimony *n* témoignage *m.*

test pilot *n* pilote d'essai *m.*

test tube *n* éprouvette *f.*

testy *adj* irritable.

tetanus *n* tétanos *m.*

tether *vt* attacher.

text *n* texte *m.*

textbook *n* manuel *m.*

textiles *npl* textiles *mpl.*

textual *adj* textuel.

texture *n* texture *f;* tissu *m.*

than *adv* que; de.

thank *vt* remercier, dire merci à.

thankful *adj* reconnaissant; **~ly** *adv* avec reconnaissance.

thankfulness *n* reconnaissance *f.*

thankless *adj* ingrat.

thanks *npl* remerciement(s) *m(pl).*

thanksgiving *n* action de grâce *f.*

that *pn* cela, ça, ce; qui, que; celui-là; * *conj* que; afin que; **so ~** pour que.

thatch *n* chaume *m;* * *vt* couvrir de chaume.

thaw *n* dégel *m;* * *vi* fondre, dégeler.

the *art* le, la, l', les.

theatre *n* théâtre *m.*

theatre-goer *n* habitué(e) du théâtre *m(f).*

theatrical *adj* théâtral.

theft *n* vol *m.*

their *pn* leur(s); **~s** le leur; la leur; les leurs; à elles; à eux.

them *pn* les; leur.

theme *n* thème *m.*

themselves *pn pl* eux-mêmes *mpl,* elles-mêmes *fpl;* se.

then *adv* alors, à cette époque-là; ensuite; en ce cas; * *conj* donc; en ce cas; * *adj* d'alors; **now and ~** de temps en temps.

theologic(al) *adj* théologique.

theologian *n* théologien *m,* -ne *f.*

theology *n* théologie *f.*

theorem *n* théorème *m.*

theoretic(al) *adj,* **~ly** *adv* théorique(ment).

theorist *n* théoricien *m,* -ne *f.*

theorize *vt* théoriser.

theory *n* théorie *f.*

therapeutics *n* thérapeutique *f.*

therapist *n* thérapeute *mf.*

therapy *n* thérapie *f.*

there *adv* y, là.

thereabout(s) *adv* par là, près de là.

thereafter *adv* par la suite; après.

thereby *adv* de cette façon.

therefore *adv* donc, par conséquent.

thermal *adj* thermal.

thermal printer *n* imprimante thermique *f.*

thermometer *n* thermomètre *m.*

thermostat *n* thermostat *m.*

thesaurus *n* trésor *m;* dictionnaire de synonymes *m.*

these *pn pl* ceux-ci, celles-ci.

thesis *n* thèse *f.*

they *pn pl* ils, elles.

thick *adj* épais, gros; dense; obtus.

thicken *vi* (s')épaissir, grossir.

thicket *n* fourré *m.*

thickness *n* épaisseur *f.*

thickset *adj* trapu; râblé.

thick-skinned *adj* à la peau épaisse.

thief *n* voleur *m,* -euse *f.*

thigh *n* cuisse *f.*

thimble *n* dé (à coudre) *m.*

thin *adj* mince, fin, maigre; clair; * *vt* amincir; délayer; éclaircir.

thing *n* chose *f;* objet *m;* truc *m.*

think vi penser, réfléchir, imaginer; * vt penser, croire, juger; **to ~ over** vt réfléchir à; **to ~ up** vt imaginer.

thinker n penseur m, -euse f.

thinking n pensée f; réflexion f; opinion f.

third adj troisième; * n troisième mf; tiers m; **~ly** adv troisièmement.

third rate adj médiocre, de mauvaise qualité.

thirst n soif f.

thirsty adj assoiffé.

thirteen adj, n treize m.

thirteenth adj, n treizième mf.

thirtieth adj, n trentième mf.

thirty adj, n trente m.

this adj ce, cet, cette, ces; * pn ceci, ce.

thistle n chardon m.

thorn n épine f; aubépine f.

thorny adj épineux.

thorough prep à travers, par; * adj consciencieux, approfondi; **~ly** adv minutieusement, à fond.

thoroughbred adj pur-sang, de race.

thoroughfare n rue, artère f.

those pn pl ceux-là, celles-la; * adj ces, ces...là.

though conj bien que, malgré le fait que; * adv pourtant.

thought n pensée, réflexion f; opinion f; intention f.

thoughtful adj pensif.

thoughtless adj étourdi; irréfléchi; **~ly** adv étourdiment, à la légère.

thousand adj, n mille m.

thousandth adj, n millième mf.

thrash vt battre; rouer de coups.

thread n fil m; filetage m; * vt enfiler.

threadbare adj râpé, élimé.

threat n menace f.

threaten vt menacer.

three adj, n trois m.

three-dimensional adj à trois dimensions, tridimensionnel.

three-ply adj à trois fils ou épaisseurs.

threshold n seuil m.

thrifty adj économe.

thrill vt faire frissonner; * n frisson m.

thriller n film ou roman à suspense m.

thrive vi prospérer; bien se développer.

throat n gorge f.

throb vi palpiter; vibrer; lanciner.

throne n trône m.

throng n foule f; * vi affluer.

throttle n accélérateur m; * vt étrangler.

through prep à travers; pendant; par, grâce à; * adj direct; * adv complètement.

throughout prep partout dans; * adv partout.

throw vt jeter, lancer, projeter; * n jet m; lancement m; **to ~ away** vt jeter; **to ~ off** vt rejeter; **to ~ out** vt jeter dehors; **to ~ up** vt, vi vomir.

throwaway adj à jeter.

thru = through.

thrush n grive f.

thrust vt pousser violemment; enfoncer; * n poussée f.

thud n bruit sourd m.

thug n voyou m.

thumb n pouce m.

thumbtack n punaise f.

thump n coup de poing m; * vi frapper, cogner; * vt cogner à.

thunder n tonnerre m; * vi tonner.

thunderbolt n coup de foudre m.

thunderclap n coup de tonnerre m.

thunderstorm n orage m.

thundery adj orageux.

Thursday n jeudi m.

thus adv ainsi, de cette manière.

thwart vt contrecarrer.

thyme n (bot) thym m.

thyroid n thyroïde f.

tiara n tiare f.

tic n tic m.

tick *n* tic-tac *m*; instant *m*; * *vt* cocher; **to ~ over** *vi* tourner au ralenti; aller doucement.

ticket *n* billet, ticket *m*; étiquette *f*; carte *f*.

ticket collector *n* (*rail*) contrôleur *m*, -euse *f*.

ticket office *n* guichet *m*.

tickle *vt* chatouiller.

ticklish *adj* chatouilleux.

tidal *adj* (*mar*) de la marée.

tidal wave *n* raz-de-marée *m*.

tide *n* époque *f*; marée *f*.

tidy *adj* rangé, en ordre; ordonné; soigné.

tie *vt* attacher, nouer; * *vi* se nouer; **to ~ up** *vt* ficeler; attacher; amarrer; conclure; * *n* attache *f*; lacet *m*; égalité *f*.

tier *n* gradin *m*; étage *m*.

tiger *n* tigre *m*.

tight *adj* raide, tendu; serré; hermétique; * *adv* très fort.

tighten *vt* (re)serrer, tendre.

tightfisted *adj* avare.

tightly *adv* très fort.

tightrope *n* corde raide *f*.

tigress *n* tigresse *f*.

tile *n* tuile *f*; carreau *m*; * *vt* couvrir de tuiles.

tiled *adj* en tuiles, carrelé.

till *n* caisse *f*; * *vt* labourer, cultiver.

tiller *n* barre du gouvernail *f*.

tilt *vt* pencher; * *vi* s'incliner.

timber *n* bois de construction *m*; arbres *mpl*.

time *n* temps *m*; période *f*; heure *f*; moment *m*; (*mus*) mesure *f*; **in ~** à temps; **from ~ to ~** de temps en temps; * *vt* fixer; chronométrer.

time bomb *n* bombe à retardement *f*.

time lag *n* décalage *m*.

timeless *adj* éternel.

timely *adj* opportun.

time off *n* temps libre *m*.

timer *n* sablier *m*; minuteur *m*.

time scale *n* durée *f*.

time zone *n* fuseau horaire *m*.

timid *adj* timide, timoré; **-ly** *adv* timidement.

timidity *n* timidité *f*.

timing *n* chronométrage *m*.

tin *n* étain *m*; boîte (de conserve) *f*.

tinfoil *n* papier d'aluminium *m*.

tinge *n* teinte *f*.

tingle *vi* picoter; vibrer, frissonner.

tingling *n* picotement *m*; frisson *m*.

tinker *n* rétameur *m*; romanichel *m*, -elle *f*.

tinkle *vi* tinter.

tinplate *n* fer-blanc *m*.

tinsel *n* guirlande *f*.

tint *n* teinte *f*; * *vt* teinter.

tinted *adj* teinté; fumé.

tiny *adj* minuscule, tout petit.

tip *n* pointe *f*, bout *m*; pourboire *m*; conseil, tuyau *m*; * *vt* donner un pourboire à; pencher; effleurer.

tip-off *n* avertissement *m*.

tipsy *adj* gai, éméché.

tiptop *adj* excellent, de premier ordre.

tirade *n* diatribe *f*.

tire *n* pneu *m*; * *vt* fatiguer; * *vi* se fatiguer; se lasser.

tireless *adj* infatigable.

tire pressure *n* pression des pneus *f*.

tiresome *adj* ennuyeux, fatigant.

tiring *adj* fatigant.

tissue *n* tissu *m*; mouchoir en papier *m*.

tissue paper *n* papier de soie *m*.

titbit *n* friandise *f*; bon morceau *m*.

titillate *vt* titiller.

title *n* titre *m*.

title deed *n* titre de propriété *m*.

title page *n* page de titre *f*.

titter *vi* rire sottement; * *n* petit rire sot *m*.

titular *adj* titulaire.

to *prep* à; vers; en; chez; moins; de.

toad n crapaud m.

toadstool n (bot) champignon vénéneux m.

toast vt (faire) griller; porter un toast à la santé de; * n toast m.

toaster n grille-pain m invar.

tobacco n tabac m.

tobacconist n marchand(e) de tabac m(f).

tobacco pouch n blague à tabac f.

tobacco shop n bureau de tabac m.

toboggan n toboggan m.

today adv aujourd'hui.

toddler n enfant qui commence à marcher m.

toddy n grog m.

toe n orteil m; pointe f.

together adv ensemble; en même temps.

toil vi travailler dur, peiner; se donner du mal; * n dur travail m; labeur m; peine f.

toilet n toilette f; toilettes fpl; * adj de toilette.

toilet bag n trousse de toilette f.

toilet bowl n cuvette des toilettes f.

toilet paper n papier hygiénique m.

toiletries npl articles de toilette mpl.

token n signe m; marque f; souvenir m; bon m; jeton m.

tolerable adj tolérable; passable.

tolerance n tolérance f.

tolerant adj tolérant.

tolerate vt tolérer.

toll n péage m; nombre de victimes m; * vi sonner.

tomato n tomate f.

tomb n tombeau m; tombe f.

tomboy n garçon manqué m.

tombstone n pierre tombale f.

tomcat n matou m.

tomorrow adv, n demain m.

ton n tonne f.

tone n ton m; tonalité f; * vi s'harmoniser; **to ~ down** vt adoucir.

tone-deaf adj qui n'a pas d'oreille.

tongs npl pinces fpl.

tongue n langue f.

tongue-tied adj muet.

tongue-twister n phrase difficile à prononcer f.

tonic n (med) tonique m.

tonight adv, n ce soir (m).

tonnage n tonnage m.

tonsil n amygdale f.

tonsure n tonsure f.

too adv aussi; trop.

tool n outil m; ustensile m.

tool box n caisse à outils f.

toot vi klaxonner.

tooth n dent f.

toothache n rage de dents f.

toothbrush n brosse à dents f.

toothless adj édenté.

toothpaste n dentifrice m.

toothpick n cure-dent m.

top n sommet m, cime f; haut m; tête f; dessus m; couvercle m; étage supérieur m; * adj du haut; premier; * vt dépasser; être au sommet de; **to ~ off** couronner.

topaz n topaze f.

top floor n dernier étage m.

top-heavy adj instable, déséquilibré.

topic n sujet m; **~al** adj d'actualité.

topless adj torse nu, aux seins nus.

top-level adj au plus haut niveau.

topmost adj le plus haut.

topographic(al) adj topographique.

topography n topographie f.

topple vt renverser; * vi basculer.

top-secret adj ultra-secret.

topsy-turvy adv sens dessus dessous.

torch n torche f.

torment vt tourmenter; * n tourment m.

tornado n tornade f.

torrent *n* torrent *m*.

torrid *adj* torride.

tortoise *n* tortue *f*.

tortoiseshell *adj* en écaille de tortue.

tortuous *adj* tortueux, sinueux.

torture *n* torture *f*; * *vt* torturer.

toss *vt* lancer, jeter; agiter, secouer.

total *adj* total, global; ~**ly** *adv* totalement.

totalitarian *adj* totalitaire.

totality *n* totalité *f*.

totter *vi* chanceler.

touch *vt* toucher; **to ~ on** ; **to ~ up** retoucher; * *n* toucher *m*; contact *m*; touche *f*.

touch-and-go *adj* incertain, précaire.

touchdown *n* atterrissage *m*; but *m*.

touched *adj* touché; timbré.

touching *adj* touchant, attendrissant.

touchstone *n* pierre de touche *f*.

touchwood *n* amadou *m*.

touchy *adj* susceptible.

tough *adj* dur; pénible; résistant; fort; * *n* dur *m*.

toughen *vt* durcir.

toupee *n* postiche *m*.

tour *n* voyage *m*; visite *f*; * *vt* visiter.

touring *n* voyages touristiques *mpl*.

tourism *n* tourisme *m*.

tourist *n* touriste *mf*.

tourist office *n* office de tourisme *m*.

tournament *n* tournoi *m*.

tow *n* remorquage *m*; * *vt* remorquer.

toward(s) *prep* vers, dans la direction de; envers, à l'égard de.

towel *n* serviette *f*.

towelling *n* tissu éponge *m*.

towel rack *n* porte-serviette *m invar*.

tower *n* tour *f*.

towering *adj* imposant.

town *n* ville *f*.

town clerk *n* secrétaire de mairie *mf*.

town hall *n* mairie *f*.

towrope *n* câble de remorquage *m*.

toy *n* jouet *m*.

toyshop *n* magasin de jouets *m*.

trace *n* trace, piste *f*; * *vt* tracer, esquisser; retrouver.

track *n* trace *f*; empreinte *f*; chemin *m*; voie *f*; piste *f*; * *vt* suivre à la trace.

tracksuit *n* survêtement *m*.

tract *n* étendue, région *f*; période *f*; brochure *f*.

traction *n* traction *f*.

trade *n* commerce *m*, affaires *fpl*; échange *m*; métier *m*; * *vi* faire le commerce (de), commercer.

trade fair *n* foire commerciale *f*.

trademark *n* marque de fabrique *f*.

trade name *n* raison commerciale *f*.

trader *n* négociant *m*, -e *f*.

tradesman *n* fournisseur, commerçant *m*.

trade(s) union *n* syndicat *m*.

trade unionist *n* syndicaliste *mf*.

trading *n* commerce *m*; * *adj* commercial.

tradition *n* tradition *f*

traditional *adj* traditionnel.

traffic *n* circulation *f*; négoce *m*; * *vi* faire le commerce (de).

traffic circle *n* rond-point *m*.

traffic jam *n* embouteillage *m*.

trafficker *n* trafiquant *m*, -e *f*.

traffic lights *npl* feux de signalisation *mpl*.

tragedy *n* tragédie *f*.

tragic *adj*, ~**ally** *adv* tragique(ment).

tragicomedy *n* tragi-comédie *f*.

trail *vt* suivre la piste de; traîner; *vi* traîner; * *n* traînée *f*; trace *f*; queue *f*.

trailer *n* remorque *f*; caravane *f*; bande-annonce *f*.

train *vt* entraîner; former; * *n* train *m*; traîne *f*; file *f*.

trained *adj* qualifié; diplômé.

trainee *n* stagiaire *mf*.

trainer *n* entraîneur *m*.

training *n* formation *f*; entraînement *m*.

trait *n* trait *m*.

traitor *n* traître *m*.

tramp *n* clochard *m*, -e *f*; (*sl*) putain *f*; * *vi* marcher d'un pas lourd; * *vt* piétiner.

trample *vt* piétiner.

trampoline *n* trampoline *m*.

trance *n* transe *f*; extase *f*.

tranquil *adj* tranquille.

tranquillize *vt* tranquilliser.

tranquillizer *n* tranquillisant *m*.

transact *vt* traiter.

transaction *n* transaction *f*; opération *f*.

transatlantic *adj* transatlantique.

transcend *vt* transcender, dépasser; surpasser.

transcription *n* transcription *f*; copie *f*.

transfer *vt* transférer, déplacer; * *n* transfert *m*; mutation *f*; décalcomanie *f*.

transform *vt* transformer.

transformation *n* transformation *f*.

transfusion *n* transfusion *f*.

transient *adj* transitoire, passager.

transit *n* transit *m*.

transition *n* transition *f*; passage *m*.

transitional *adj* de transition.

transitive *adj* transitif.

translate *vt* traduire.

translation *n* traduction *f*.

translator *n* traducteur *m*, -trice *f*.

transmission *n* transmision *f*.

transmit *vt* transmettre.

transmitter *n* transmetteur *m*; émetteur *m*.

transparency *n* transparence *f*.

transparent *adj* transparent.

transpire *vi* transpirer; arriver.

transplant *vt* transplanter; * *n* transplantation *f*.

transport *vt* transporter; * *n* transport *m*.

transportation *n* moyen de transport *m*.

trap *n* piège *m*; * *vt* prendre au piège; bloquer.

trap door *n* trappe *f*.

trapeze *n* trapèze *m*.

trappings *npl* ornements *mpl*.

trash *n* camelote *f*; inepties *fpl*.

trash can *n* poubelle *f*.

trashy *adj* sans valeur, de mauvaise qualité.

travel *vi* voyager; * *vt* parcourir; * *n* voyage *m*.

travel agency *n* agence de voyages *f*.

travel agent *n* agent de voyages *m*.

traveller *n* voyageur *m*, -euse *f*.

traveller's cheque *n* chèque de voyage *m*.

travelling *n* voyages *mpl*.

travel sickness *n* mal de mer/de l'air *m*.

travesty *n* parodie *f*.

trawler *n* chalutier *m*.

tray *n* plateau *m*; tiroir *m*.

treacherous *adj* traître, perfide.

treachery *n* traîtrise *f*.

tread *vi* marcher; écraser; * *n* pas *m*; bruit de pas *m*; bande de roulement *f*.

treason *n* trahison *f*; **high ~** haute trahison *f*.

treasure *n* trésor *m*; * *vt* conserver précieusement.

treasurer *n* trésorier *m*, -ière *f*.

treat *vt* traiter; offrir; * *n* cadeau *m*; plaisir *m*.

treatise *n* traité *m*.

treatment *n* traitement *m*.

treaty *n* traité *m*.

treble *adj* triple; * *vt*, *vi* tripler; * *n* (*mus*) soprano *m*.

treble clef *n* clef de sol *f*.

tree n arbre m.

trek n randonnée f; étape f.

trellis n treillis m.

tremble vi trembler.

trembling n tremblement m; frisson m.

tremendous adj terrible; énorme; formidable.

tremor n tremblement m.

trench n fossé m; (mil) tranchée f.

trend n tendance f; direction f; mode f.

trendy adj dernier cri.

trepidation n vive inquiétude f.

trespass vt transgresser, violer.

tress n boucle de cheveu f; tresse f.

trestle n tréteau, chevalet m.

trial n procès m; épreuve f; essai m; peine f.

triangle n triangle m.

triangular adj triangulaire.

tribal adj tribal.

tribe n tribu f.

tribulation n tribulation f.

tribunal n tribunal m.

tributary adj, n tributaire m.

tribute n tribut m.

trice n instant m.

trick n ruse, astuce f, tour m; blague f; pli m; * vt attraper.

trickery n supercherie f.

trickle vi couler goutte à goutte; * n filet m.

tricky adj délicat; difficile.

tricycle n tricycle m.

trifle n bagatelle, vétille f; * vi jouer; badiner.

trifling adj futile, insignifiant.

trigger n détente f; **to ~ off** vt déclencher.

trigonometry n trigonométrie f.

trill n trille f; * vi triller.

trim adj net, soigné; bien tenu; en parfait état; * vt arranger; tailler; orner.

trimmings npl ornements mpl.

Trinity n Trinité f.

trinket n bibelot m, babiole f; colifichet m.

trio n (mus) trio m.

trip vt faire trébucher; * vi trébucher; faire un faux pas; **to ~ up** vi trébucher; vt faire trébucher; * n faux pas m; voyage m.

tripe n tripes fpl; bêtises fpl.

triple adj triple; * vt, vi tripler.

triplets npl triplés mpl.

triplicate n copie en trois exemplaires f.

tripod n trépied m.

trite adj banal; usé.

triumph n triomphe m; * vi triompher.

triumphal adj triomphal.

triumphant adj triomphant; victorieux; ~ly adv triomphalement.

trivia npl futilités fpl.

trivial adj insignifiant, sans importance; ~ly adv banalement.

triviality n banalité f.

trolley n chariot m.

trombone n trombone m.

troop n bande f; ~s npl troupes fpl.

trooper n soldat de cavalerie m.

trophy n trophée m.

tropical adj tropical.

trot n trot m; * vi trotter.

trouble vt affliger; tourmenter; * n problème m; ennui m; difficulté f; affliction, peine f.

troubled adj inquiet; agité.

troublemaker n agitateur m, -trice f.

troubleshooter n médiateur m.

troublesome adj pénible.

trough n abreuvoir m; auge f.

troupe n troupe f.

trousers npl pantalon m.

trout n truite f.

trowel n truelle f.

truce n trêve f.

truck n camion m; wagon m.

truck driver n routier m.

truck farm n jardin maraîcher m.

truculent adj brutal, agressif.

trudge vi marcher lourdement.

true *adj* vrai, véritable; sincère; exact.

truelove *n* bien-aimé *m*, -e *f*.

truffle *n* truffe *f*.

truly *adv* vraiment; sincèrement.

trump *n* atout *m*.

trumpet *n* trompette *f*.

trunk *n* malle *f*, coffre *m*; trompe *f*.

truss *n* botte *f*; * *vt* botteler; trousser.

trust *n* confiance *f*; trust *m*; fidéicommis *m*; * *vt* avoir confiance en; confier à.

trusted *adj* de confiance.

trustee *n* fidéicommissaire *m*, curateur *m*, -trice *f*.

trustful *adj* confiant.

trustily *adj* fidèlement.

trusting *adj* confiant.

trustworthy *adj* digne de confiance.

trusty *adj* fidèle, loyal; sûr.

truth *n* vérité *f*; **in ~** en vérité.

truthful *adj* véridique; qui dit la vérité.

truthfulness *n* véracité *f*.

try *vt* essayer, tâcher, chercher à; expérimenter; mettre à l'épreuve; tenter; juger; * *vi* essayer; **to ~ on** *vt* essayer; **to ~ out** *vt* essayer; * *n* tentative *f*; essai *m*.

trying *adj* pénible; fatigant.

tub *n* cuve *f*, bac *m*; baignoire *f*.

tuba *n* tuba *m*.

tube *n* tube *m*; métro *m*.

tuberculosis *n* tuberculose *f*.

tubing *n* tuyaux *mpl*.

tuck *n* pli *m*; * *vt* mettre.

tucker *vt* fatiguer.

Tuesday *n* mardi *m*.

tuft *n* touffe *f*; houppe *f*.

tug *vt* remorquer; * *n* remorqueur *m*.

tuition *n* cours, enseignement *m*.

tulip *n* tulipe *f*.

tumble *vi* tomber, faire une chute; se jeter; * *vt* renverser; culbuter; * *n* chute *f*; culbute *f*.

tumbledown *adj* délabré.

tumbler *n* verre *m*.

tummy *n* ventre *m*.

tumour *n* tumeur *f*.

tumultuous *adj* tumultueux.

tuna *n* thon *m*.

tune *n* air *m*; accord *m*; harmonie *f*; * *vt* accorder; syntoniser.

tuneful *adj* mélodieux, harmonieux.

tuner *n* syntonisateur *m*.

tunic *n* tunique *f*.

tuning fork *n* (*mus*) diapason *m*.

tunnel *n* tunnel *m*; * *vt* creuser un tunnel dans.

turban *n* turban *m*.

turbine *n* turbine *f*.

turbulence *n* turbulence, agitation *f*.

turbulent *adj* turbulent, agité.

tureen *n* soupière *f*.

turf *n* gazon *m*; * *vt* gazonner.

turgid *adj* turgide.

turkey *n* dinde *f*.

turmoil *n* agitation *f*; trouble *m*.

turn *vi* (se) tourner; devenir; changer; se retourner; se changer, se transformer; **to ~ around** se retourner; tourner; **to ~ back** revenir; **to ~ down** *vt* rejeter; rabattre; **to ~ in** aller se coucher; **to ~ off** *vi* tourner; *vt* éteindre; fermer; **to ~ on** *vt* allumer; ouvrir; **to ~ out** s'avérer; **to ~ over** *vi* se retourner; *vt* tourner; **to ~ up** *vi* arriver; se présenter; *vt* monter; * *n* tour *m*; tournure *f*; virage *m*; tendance *f*.

turncoat *n* renégat *m*.

turning *n* embranchement *m*.

turnip *n* navet *m*.

turn-off *n* sortie (d'autoroute) *f*; embranchement *m*.

turnout *n* production *f*.

turnover *n* chiffre d'affaires *m*.

turnpike *n* autoroute à péage *f*.

turnstile *n* tourniquet *m*.

turntable *n* platine *f*.

turpentine *n* (essence de) térébenthine *f*.

turquoise *n* turquoise *f*.

turret n tourelle f.
turtle n tortue marine f.
turtledove n tourterelle f.
tusk n défense f.
tussle n lutte f.
tutor n professeur particulier m; directeur d'études m; * vt enseigner, donner des cours particuliers à.
tuxedo n smoking m.
twang n bruit sec m; ton nasillard m.
tweezers npl pince à épiler f.
twelfth adj, n douzième mf.
twelve adj, n douze m.
twentieth adj, n vingtième mf.
twenty adj, n vingt m.
twice adv deux fois.
twig n brindille f; * vi comprendre.
twilight n crépuscule m.
twin n jumeau m, -elle f.
twine vi s'enrouler; serpenter; * n ficelle f.
twinge vt élancer; * n élancement m; remords m.
twinkle vi scintiller; clignoter.
twirl vt faire tournoyer; * vi tournoyer; * n tournoiement m.
twist vt tordre, tortiller; entortiller; * vi serpenter; * n torsion f; tournant m; rouleau m.
twit n (sl) crétin m, -e f.
twitch vi avoir un mouvement nerveux; * n tic m.
twitter vi gazouiller; * n gazouillis m.
two adj, n deux m.
two-door adj à deux portes.
two-faced adj hypocrite.
twofold adj double; * adv au double.
two-seater n voiture/avion à deux places f/m.
twosome n paire f; couple m.
tycoon n magnat m.
type n type m; caractère m; exemple m; * vi taper à la machine.
typecast adj enfermé dans un rôle.
typeface n œil de caractère m.
typescript n texte dactylographié m.
typewriter n machine à écrire f.
typewritten adj dactylographié.
typical adj typique.
tyrannical adj tyrannique.
tyranny n tyrannie f.
tyrant n tyran m.

U

ubiquitous adj doué d'ubiquité.
udder n pis m.
ugh excl pouah!, berk!
ugliness n laideur f.
ugly adj laid; inquiétant.
ulcer n ulcère m.
ulterior adj ultérieur.
ultimate adj final; ~ly adv finalement; à la fin.
ultimatum n ultimatum m.
ultramarine n, adj outremer m.
ultrasound n ultrason m.
umbilical cord n cordon ombilical m.
umbrella n parapluie m.
umpire n arbitre m.
umpteen adj un très grand nombre de, beaucoup de.
unable adj incapable.
unaccompanied adj non accompagné, seul.
unaccomplished adj inaccompli, inachevé.
unaccountable adj inexplicable.
unaccountably adv inexplicablement.
unaccustomed adj inaccoutumé, inhabituel.
unacknowledged adj non reconnu; (resté) sans réponse.

unacquainted *adj* qui ignore, qui n'a pas connaissance de.

unadorned *adj* sans ornement.

unadulterated *adj* pur; sans mélange.

unaffected *adj* sincère; non affecté.

unaided *adj* sans aide.

unaltered *adj* inchangé.

unambitious *adj* sans ambition.

unanimity *n* unanimité *f*.

unanimous *adj*, **~ly** *adv* unanime(ment).

unanswerable *adj* incontestable.

unanswered *adj* sans réponse.

unapproachable *adj* inaccessible.

unarmed *adj* non armé, désarmé.

unassuming *adj* sans prétention, modeste.

unattached *adj* indépendant; libre.

unattainable *adj* inaccessible.

unattended *adj* sans surveillance.

unauthorized *adj* sans autorisation.

unavoidable *adj* inévitable.

unavoidably *adv* inévitablement.

unaware *adj* ignorant; inconscient.

unawares *adv* à l'improviste; par mégarde.

unbalanced *adj* déséquilibré; non soldé.

unbearable *adj* insupportable.

unbecoming *adj* malséant, déplacé.

unbelievable *adj* incroyable.

unbend *vi* se détendre; * *vt* redresser.

unbiased *adj* impartial.

unblemished *adj* sans tache, sans défaut.

unborn *adj* à naître, pas encore né.

unbreakable *adj* incassable.

unbroken *adj* non brisé; intact; ininterrompu; indompté .

unbutton *vt* déboutonner.

uncalled-for *adj* injustifié.

uncanny *adj* mystérieux.

unceasing *adj* incessant, continu.

unceremonious *adj* brusque.

uncertain *adj* incertain, douteux.

uncertainty *n* incertitude *f*.

unchangeable *adj* immuable.

unchanged *adj* inchangé.

unchanging *adj* invariable, immuable.

uncharitable *adj* peu charitable.

unchecked *adj* non maîtrisé.

unchristian *adj* peu chrétien.

uncivil *adj* impoli, grossier.

uncivilized *adj* barbare, non civilisé.

uncle *n* oncle *m*.

uncomfortable *adj* inconfortable; incommode; désagréable.

uncomfortably *adv* inconfortablement; mal; désagréablement.

uncommon *adj* rare, extraordinaire.

uncompromising *adj* intransigeant.

unconcerned *adj* indifférent.

unconditional *adj* inconditionnel, absolu.

unconfined *adj* illimité, sans bornes.

unconfirmed *adj* non confirmé.

unconnected *adj* sans rapport.

unconquerable *adj* invincible, insurmontable.

unconscious *adj* inconscient; **~ly** *adv* inconsciemment, sans s'en rendre compte.

unconstrained *adj* non contraint, libre.

uncontrollable *adj* irrésistible; qui ne peut être maîtrisé.

unconventional *adj* peu conventionnel.

unconvincing *adj* peu convaincant.

uncork *vt* déboucher.

uncorrected *adj* non corrigé.

uncouth *adj* grossier.

uncover *vt* découvrir.

uncultivated *adj* inculte.

uncut *adj* non taillé, intégral.

undamaged *adj* non endommagé, indemne.

undaunted *adj* intrépide.

undecided *adj* indécis.

undefiled *adj* pur, immaculé.

undeniable *adj* indéniable, incontestable; **~bly** *adv* incontestablement.

under *prep* sous; dessous; moins de; selon; * *adv* au-dessous, en-dessous.

under-age *adj* mineur.

undercharge *vt* ne pas faire payer assez.

underclothing *n* sous-vêtements *mpl*.

undercoat *n* première couche *f*.

undercover *adj* secret, clandestin.

undercurrent *n* courant sous-marin *m*.

undercut *vt* vendre moins cher que.

underdeveloped *adj* sous-développé, insuffisamment développé.

underdog *n* opprimé *m*, -e *f*.

underdone *adj* pas assez cuit.

underestimate *vt* sous-estimer.

undergo *vt* subir; supporter.

undergraduate *n* étudiant(e) en licence *m(f)*.

underground *n* mouvement clandestin *m*.

undergrowth *n* brouissailles *fpl*, sous-bois *m*.

underhand *adv* en cachette; * *adj* secret, clandestin.

underlie *vi* être à la base de.

underline *vt* souligner.

undermine *vt* saper.

underneath *adv* (en) dessous; * *prep* sous, au-dessous de.

underpaid *adj* sous-payé.

underprivileged *adj* défavorisé.

underrate *vt* sous-estimer.

undersecretary *n* sous-secrétaire *mf*.

undershirt *n* maillot de corps *m*.

undershorts *npl* caleçon *m*.

underside *n* dessous *m*.

understand *vt* comprendre.

understandable *adj* compréhensible.

understanding *n* compréhension *f*; intelligence *f*; entendement *m*; accord *m*; * *adj* compréhensif.

understatement *n* affirmation en dessous de la vérité *f*.

undertake *vt* entreprendre.

undertaking *n* entreprise *f*; engagement *m*.

undervalue *vt* sous-estimer.

underwater *adj* sous-marin; * *adv* sous l'eau.

underwear *n* sous-vêtements *mpl*, dessous *mpl*.

underworld *n* pègre *f*.

underwrite *vt* souscrire à; assurer contre.

underwriter *n* assureur *m*.

undeserved *adj* immérité; **~ly** *adv* à tort, indûment.

undeserving *adj* peu méritant.

undesirable *adj* peu souhaitable.

undetermined *adj* indéterminé; indécis.

undigested *adj* non digéré.

undiminished *adj* non diminué.

undisciplined *adj* indiscipliné.

undisguised *adj* non déguisé.

undismayed *adj* non découragé.

undisputed *adj* incontesté.

undisturbed *adj* non dérangé, paisible.

undivided *adj* indivisé, entier.

undo *vt* défaire; détruire.

undoing *n* ruine *f*.

undoubted *adj*, **~ly** *adv* indubitable(ment).

undress *vi* se déshabiller.

undue *adj* excessif; injuste.

undulating *adj* ondulant.

unduly *adv* trop, excessivement.

undying *adj* éternel.

unearth *vt* déterrer.

unearthly *adj* surnaturel.

uneasy *adj* inquiet; troublé, gêné.

uneducated *adj* sans instruction.

unemployed *adj* au chômage.
unemployment *n* chômage *m*.
unending *adj* interminable.
unenlightened *adj* peu éclairé.
unenviable *adj* peu enviable.
unequal *adj* , **~ly** *adv* inégal(ement).
unequaled *adj* inégalé.
unerring *adj* , **~ly** *adv* infaillible(ment).
uneven *adj* inégal; impair; **~ly** *adv* inégalement.
unexpected *adj* inattendu; inopiné; **~ly** *adv* de manière inattendue; inopinément.
unexplored *adj* inexploré.
unfailing *adj* infaillible, certain.
unfair *adj* injuste; inéquitable; **~ly** *adv* injustement.
unfaithful *adj* infidèle.
unfaithfulness *n* infidélité *f*.
unfaltering *adj* ferme, assuré.
unfamiliar *adj* peu familier, peu connu.
unfashionable *adj* démodé; **~bly** *adv* sans se préoccuper de la mode.
unfasten *vt* détacher, défaire.
unfathomable *adj* insondable, impénétrable.
unfavourable *adj* défavorable.
unfeeling *adj* insensible, impitoyable.
unfinished *adj* inachevé, incomplet.
unfit *adj* inapte; impropre.
unfold *vt* déplier; révéler; * *vi* s'ouvrir.
unforeseen *adj* imprévu.
unforgettable *adj* inoubliable.
unforgivable *adj* impardonnable.
unforgiving *adj* implacable.
unfortunate *adj* malheureux, malchanceux; **~ly** *adv* malheureusement, par malheur.
unfounded *adj* sans fondement.
unfriendly *adj* inamical.
unfruitful *adj* stérile; infructueux.
unfurnished *adj* non meublé.

ungainly *adj* gauche.
ungentlemanly *adj* peu galant.
ungovernable *adj* ingouvernable, irrépressible.
ungrateful *adj* ingrat; peu reconnaissant; **~ly** *adv* avec ingratitude.
ungrounded *adj* infondé.
unhappily *adv* malheureusemnt.
unhappiness *n* tristesse *f*.
unhappy *adj* malheureux.
unharmed *adj* indemne, sain et sauf.
unhealthy *adj* malsain; maladif.
unheard-of *adj* inédit, sans précédent.
unheeding *adj* insouciant; distrait.
unhook *vt* décrocher; dégrafer.
unhoped(-for) *adj* inespéré.
unhurt *adj* indemne.
unicorn *n* licorne *f*.
uniform *adj* uniforme; **~ly** *adv* uniformément; * *n* uniforme *m*.
uniformity *adj* uniformité *f*.
unify *vt* unifier.
unimaginable *adj* inimaginable.
unimpaired *adj* non diminué, intact.
unimportant *adj* sans importance.
uninformed *adj* mal informé.
uninhabitable *adj* inhabitable.
uninhabited *adj* inhabité, désert.
uninjured *adj* indemne, sain et sauf.
unintelligible *adj* inintelligible.
unintelligibly *adj* inintelligiblement.
unintentional *adj* involontaire.
uninterested *adj* indifférent.
uninteresting *adj* inintéressant.
uninterrupted *adj* ininterrompu, continu.
uninvited *adj* sans être invité.
union *n* union *f*; syndicat *m*.
unionist *n* syndicaliste *mf*.
unique *adj* unique, exceptionnel.
unison *n* unisson *m*.

unit *n* unité *f*.

unitarian *n* unitarien *m*, -ienne *f*.

unite *vt* unir; * *vi* s'unir.

unitedly *adv* conjointement, ensemble.

United States (of America) *npl* Etats-Unis *mpl*.

unity *n* unité, harmonie *f*, accord *m*.

universal *adj* , **~ly** *adv* universel(lement).

universe *n* univers *m*.

university *n* université *f*.

unjust *adj*, **~ly** *adv* injuste(ment).

unkempt *adj* négligé; débraillé.

unkind *adj* peu aimable; méchant.

unknowingly *adv* inconsciemment.

unknown *adj* inconnu.

unlawful *adj* illégal, illicite; **~ly** *adv* illégalement.

unlawfulness *n* illégalité *f*.

unleash *vt* lâcher, déchaîner.

unless *conj* à moins que/de, sauf.

unlicensed *adj* illicite.

unlike, unlikely *adj* différent, dissemblable; improbable; invraisemblable; **~ly** *adv* improbablement.

unlikelihood *n* improbabilité *f*.

unlimited *adj* illimité.

unlisted *adj* ne figurant pas sur une liste/sur l'annuaire.

unload *vt* décharger.

unlock *vt* ouvrir, dévérouiller.

unluckily *adv* malheureusement.

unlucky *adj* malchanceux.

unmanageable *adj* difficile, peu maniable, impossible.

unmannered *adj* mal élevé, impoli.

unmannerly *adj* mal élevé, impoli.

unmarried *adj* célibataire, qui n'est pas marié.

unmask *vt* démasquer.

unmentionable *adj* qu'il ne faut pas mentionner.

unmerited *adj* immérité.

unmindful *adj* oublieux, indifférent.

unmistakable *adj* indubitable; **~ly** *adv* sans aucun doute.

unmitigated *adj* absolu.

unmoved *adj* insensible, impassible.

unnatural *adj* non naturel; pervers; affecté.

unnecessary *adj* inutile, superflu.

unneighbourly *adj* peu aimable avec ses voisins, peu sociable.

unnoticed *adj* inaperçu.

unnumbered *adj* innombrable.

unobserved *adj* inaperçu.

unobtainable *adj* impossible à obtenir; introuvable.

unobtrusive *adj* discret.

unoccupied *adj* inoccupé.

unoffending *adj* inoffensif, innocent.

unofficial *adj* non officiel.

unorthodox *adj* hétérodoxe; peu orthodoxe.

unpack *vt* défaire; déballer.

unpaid *adj* non payé.

unpalatable *adj* désagréable au goût.

unparalleled *adj* incomparable; sans pareil.

unpleasant *adj* , **~ly** *adv* désagréable(ment).

unpleasantness *n* caractère désagréable *m*.

unplug *vt* débrancher.

unpolished *adj* non ciré; fruste, rude.

unpopular *adj* impopulaire.

unpractised *adj* inexpérimenté, inexercé.

unprecedented *adj* sans précédent.

unpredictable *adj* imprévisible.

unprejudiced *adj* impartial.

unprepared *adj* qui n'est pas préparé.

unprofitable *adj* inutile; peu rentable.

unprotected *adj* sans protection; exposé.

unpublished *adj* inédit.

unpunished *adj* impuni.

unqualified *adj* non qualifié; sans réserve.

unquestionable *adj* incontestable, indiscutable; **~ly** *adv* indiscutablement, sans conteste.

unquestioned *adj* incontesté, indiscuté.

unravel *vt* débrouiller.

unread *adj* qui n'a pas été lu; inculte.

unreal *adj* irréel.

unrealistic *adj* irréaliste.

unreasonable *adv* déraisonnable.

unreasonably *adj* déraisonnablement.

unregarded *adj* négligé; dont on fait peu de cas.

unrelated *adj* sans rapport; sans lien de parenté.

unrelenting *adj* implacable.

unreliable *adj* peu fiable.

unremitting *adj* inlassable, constant.

unrepentant *adj* impénitent.

unreserved *adj* sans réserve; franc; **~ly** *adv* sans réserve.

unrest *n* agitation *f*; troubles *mpl*.

unrestrained *adj* non contenu; non réprimé.

unripe *adj* vert, pas mûr.

unrivalled *adj* sans égal, sans pareil.

unroll *vt* dérouler.

unruliness *n* indiscipline *f*; turbulence *f*.

unruly *adj* indiscipliné.

unsafe *adj* dangereux, peu sûr.

unsatisfactory *adj* peu satisfaisant.

unsavoury *adj* désagréable, insipide.

unscathed *adj* indemne.

unscrew *vt* dévisser.

unscrupulous *adj* sans scrupules.

unseasonable *adj* hors de saison, inopportun.

unseemly *adj* inconvenant.

unseen *adj* invisible; inaperçu.

unselfish *adj* généreux.

unsettle *vt* perturber.

unsettled *adj* perturbé; instable; variable.

unshaken *adj* inébranlable, ferme.

unshaven *adj* non rasé.

unsightly *adj* disgracieux, laid.

unskilled *adj* inexpérimenté.

unskilful *adj* maladroit, malhabile.

unsociable *adj* insociable, sauvage.

unspeakable *adj* ineffable, indicible.

unstable *adj* instable.

unsteadily *adv* d'un pas chancelant; d'une manière mal assurée.

unsteady *adj* instable.

unstudied *adj* naturel; spontané.

unsuccessful *adj* infructueux, vain; **~ly** *adv* sans succès.

unsuitable *adj* peu approprié; inopportun.

unsure *adj* peu sûr.

unsympathetic *adj* peu compatissant.

untamed *adj* sauvage.

untapped *adj* non exploité.

untenable *adj* insoutenable.

unthinkable *adj* inconcevable.

unthinking *adj* irréfléchi, étourdi.

untidiness *n* désordre *m*.

untidy *adj* en désordre; peu soigné.

untie *vt* dénouer, défaire.

until *prep* jusqu'à; * *conj* jusqu'à ce que.

untimely *adj* intempestif.

untiring *adj* infatigable.

untold *adj* jamais révélé; indicible; incalculable.

untouched *adj* intact.

untoward *adj* fâcheux; indiscipliné.

untried *adj* qui n'a pas été essayé *ou* mis à l'épreuve.

untroubled *adj* tranquille, paisible.

untrue *adj* faux.

untrustworthy *adj* indigne de confiance.

untruth *n* mensonge *m*, fausseté *f*.

unused *adj* neuf, inutilisé.

unusual *adj* inhabituel, exceptionnel; **~ly** *adv* exceptionnellement, rarement.

unveil *vt* dévoiler.

unwavering *adj* inébranlable.

unwelcome *adj* importun.

unwell *adj* indisposé, souffrant.

unwieldy *adj* peu maniable.

unwilling *adj* peu disposé; **~ly** *adv* de mauvaise grâce.

unwillingness *n* mauvaise grâce, mauvaise volonté *f*.

unwind *vt* dérouler; * *vi* se détendre.

unwise *adj* imprudent.

unwitting *adj* involontaire.

unworkable *adj* impraticable.

unworthy *adj* indigne.

unwrap *vt* défaire.

unwritten *adj* non écrit.

up *adv* en haut, en l'air; levé; * *prep* au haut de; vers.

upbringing *n* éducation *f*.

update *vt* mettre à jour.

upheaval *n* bouleversement *m*.

uphill *adj* difficile, pénible; * *adv* en montant.

uphold *vt* soutenir.

upholstery *n* tapisserie *f*.

upkeep *n* entretien *m*.

uplift *vt* élever.

upon *prep* sur.

upper *adj* supérieur; (plus) élevé.

upper-class *adj* aristocratique.

upper-hand *n* (*fig*) dessus *m*.

uppermost *adj* le plus haut, le plus élevé; **to be ~** prédominer.

upright *adj* droit, vertical; droit, honnête.

uprising *n* soulèvement *m*.

uproar *n* tumulte, vacarme *m*.

uproot *vt* déraciner.

upset *vt* renverser; déranger, bouleverser; * *n* désordre *m*; bouleversement *m*; * *adj* vexé; bouleversé.

upshot *n* résultat *m*; aboutissement *m*; conclusion *f*.

upside-down *adv* sens dessus dessous.

upstairs *adv* en haut (d'un escalier).

upstart *n* parvenu *m*, -e *f*.

uptight *adj* très tendu.

up-to-date *adj* à jour.

upturn *n* amélioration *f*.

upward *adj* ascendant; **~s** *adv* vers le haut; en montant.

urban *adj* urbain.

urbane *adj* courtois.

urchin *n* oursin *m*.

urge *vt* pousser; * *n* impulsion *f*; désir ardent *m*.

urgency *n* urgence *f*.

urgent *adj* urgent.

urinal *n* urinoir *m*.

urinate *vi* uriner.

urine *n* urine *f*.

urn *n* urne *f*.

us *pn* nous.

usage *n* traitement *m*; usage *m*.

use *n* usage *m*; utilisation *f*, emploi *m*; * *vt* se servir de, utiliser.

used *adj* usagé.

useful *adj* , **~ly** *adv* utile(ment).

usefulness *n* utilité *f*.

useless *adj*, **~ly** *adv* inutile(ment).

uselessness *n* inutilité *f*.

user-friendly *adj* facile à utiliser.

usher *n* huissier *m*; placeur *m*.

usherette *n* ouvreuse *f*.

usual *adj* habituel, courant; **~ly** *adv* habituellement.

usurer *n* usurier *m*, -ière *f*.

usurp *vt* usurper.

usury *n* usure *f*.

utensil *n* ustensile *m*.

uterus *n* utérus *m*.

utility *n* utilité *f*.

utilize *vt* utiliser.

utmost *adj* extrême, le plus grand; dernier.

utter *adj* complet; absolu; total; * *vt* prononcer; proférer; émettre.

utterance *n* expression *f.*

utterly *adv* complètement, tout à fait.

V

vacancy *n* chambre libre *f.*

vacant *adj* vacant; inoccupé; libre.

vacant lot *n* terrain vague *m.*

vacate *vt* quitter; démissionner.

vacation *n* vacances *fpl.*

vacationer *n* vacancier *m,* -ière *f.*

vaccinate *vt* vacciner.

vaccination *n* vaccination *f.*

vaccine *n* vaccin *f.*

vacuous *adj* vide.

vacuum *n* vide *m.*

vacuum bottle *n* thermos *m.*

vagina *n* vagin *m.*

vagrant *n* vagabond *m,* -e *f.*

vague *adj,* ~**ly** *adv* vague(ment).

vain *adj* vain, inutile; vaniteux.

valet *n* valet de chambre *m.*

valiant *adj* courageux, brave.

valid *adj* valide, valable.

valley *n* vallée *f.*

valour *n* courage *m,* bravoure *f.*

valuable *adj* précieux, de valeur; ~**s** *npl* objets de valeur *mpl.*

valuation *n* évaluation, estimation *f.*

value *n* valeur *f;* * *vt* évaluer; tenir à, apprécier.

valued *adj* précieux, estimé.

valve *n* soupape *f.*

vampire *n* vampire *m.*

van *n* camionnette *f.*

vandal *n* vandale *mf.*

vandalism *n* vandalisme *m.*

vandalize *vt* saccager.

vanguard *n* avant-garde *f.*

vanilla *n* vanille *f.*

vanish *vi* disparaître, se dissiper.

vanity *n* vanité *f.*

vanity case *n* vanity-case *m.*

vanquish *vt* vaincre.

vantage point *n* position avantageuse *f.*

vapour *n* vapeur *f.*

variable *adj* variable; changeant.

variance *n* désaccord, différend *m.*

variation *n* variation *f.*

varicose vein *n* varice *f.*

varied *adj* varié.

variety *n* variété *f.*

variety show *n* spectacle de variétés *m.*

various *adj* divers, différent.

varnish *n* vernis *m;* * *vt* vernir.

vary *vt, vi* varier; *vi* changer.

vase *n* vase *m.*

vast *adj* vaste; immense.

vat *n* cuve *f.*

vault *n* voûte *f;* cave *f,* caveau *m;* saut *m;* * *vi* sauter.

veal *n* veau *m.*

veer *vi* (*mar*) virer.

vegetable *adj* végétal; * *n* végétal *m;* ~**s** *pl* légumes *mpl.*

vegetable garden *n* (jardin) potager *m.*

vegetarian *n* végétarien *m,* -ienne *f.*

vegetate *vi* végéter.

vegetation *n* végétation *f.*

vehemence *n* véhémence, fougue *f.*

vehement *adj* véhément, violent; ~**ly** *adv* avec véhémence.

vehicle *n* véhicule *m.*

veil *n* voile *m;* * *vt* voiler, dissimuler.

vein *n* veine *f;* nervure *f;* disposition *f.*

velocity *n* vitesse *f.*

velvet n velours m.

vending machine n distributeur automatique m.

vendor n vendeur m.

veneer n placage m; vernis m.

venerable adj vénérable.

venerate vt vénérer.

veneration n vénération f.

venereal adj vénérien.

vengeance n vengeance f.

venial adj véniel.

venison n venaison f.

venom n venin m.

venomous adj vénéneux; ~ly adv avec animosité.

vent n orifice m; conduit m; * vt décharger.

ventilate vt aérer.

ventilation n ventilation, aération f.

ventilator n ventilateur m.

ventriloquist n ventriloque mf.

venture n entreprise f; * vi s'aventurer; * vt risquer, hasarder.

venue n lieu de réunion m.

veranda(h) n véranda f.

verb n (gr) verbe m.

verbal adj verbal, oral; ~ly adv verbalement.

verbatim adv textuellement, mot pour mot.

verbose adj verbeux.

verdant adj verdoyant.

verdict n (law) verdict m; jugement m.

verification n vérification f.

verify vt vérifier.

veritable adj véritable.

vermin n vermine f.

vermouth n vermout(h) m.

versatile adj doué de talents multiples; versatile.

verse n vers m; verset m.

versed adj versé.

version n version f.

versus prep contre.

vertebra n vertèbre f.

vertebral, vertebrate adj vertébral.

vertex n sommet m.

vertical adj , ~ly adv vertical(ement).

vertigo n vertige m.

verve n verve f.

very adj vrai, véritable; exactement, même; * adv très, fort, bien.

vessel n récipient m; vase m; navire m.

vest n gilet m.

vestibule n vestibule m.

vestige n vestige m.

vestment n vêtement de cérémonie m; chasuble f.

vestry n sacristie f.

veteran adj, n vétéran m.

veterinarian n vétérinaire mf.

veterinary adj vétérinaire.

veto n véto m; * vt opposer son véto à.

vex vt contrarier.

vexed adj contrarié.

via prep via, par.

viaduct n viaduc m.

vial n fiole, ampoule f.

vibrate vi vibrer.

vibration n vibration f.

vicarious adj par personne interposée.

vice n vice m; défaut m; étau m.

vice-chairman n vice-président m.

vice versa adv vice versa.

vicinity n voisinage m, proximité f.

vicious adj méchant; ~ly adv méchamment.

victim n victime f.

victimize vt prendre pour victime.

victor n vainqueur m.

victorious adj victorieux.

victory n victoire f.

video n vidéo f; vidéocassette f; magnétoscope m.

video tape n bande vidéo f.

viewer n téléspectateur m, -trice f.

vie vi rivaliser.

view n vue f; perspective f; opinion f; panorama m; * vt voir; examiner.

viewfinder n viseur m.

viewpoint n point de vue m.

vigil n veille f; vigile f.

vigilance n vigilance f.

vigilant adj vigilant, attentif.

vigor n vigueur f; énergie f.

vigorous adj vigoureux; ~ly adv vigoureusement.

vile adj vil, infâme; exécrable.

vilify vt diffamer.

villa n pavillon m; maison de campagne f.

village n village m.

villager n villageois m, -e f.

villain n scélérat m.

vindicate vt venger, défendre.

vindication n défense f; justification f.

vindictive adj vindicatif.

vine n vigne f.

vinegar n vinaigre m.

vineyard n vignoble m.

vintage n vendange(s) f(pl).

vinyl n vinyle m.

viola n (mus) viole f.

violate vt violer.

violation n violation f.

violence n violence f.

violent adj violent; ~ly adv violemment.

violet n (bot) violette f.

violin n (mus) violon m.

violinist n violiniste mf.

violoncello n (mus) violoncelle m.

viper n vipère f.

virgin n, adj vierge f.

virginity n virginité f.

Virgo n Vierge f (signe du zodiaque).

virile adj viril.

virility n virilité f.

virtual adj , ~ly adv de fait, pratiquement.

virtue n vertu f.

virtuous adj virtueux.

virulent adj virulent.

virus n virus m.

visa n visa m.

vis-a-vis prep vis-à-vis.

viscous adj visqueux, gluant.

visibility n visibilité f.

visible adj visible.

visibly adv visiblement.

vision n vision f; vue f.

visit vt visiter; * n visite f.

visitation n visite f.

visiting hours npl heures de visite fpl.

visitor n visiteur m, -euse f; touriste mf.

visor n visière f.

vista n vue, perspective f.

visual adj visuel.

visual aid n support visuel m.

visualize vt s'imaginer.

vital adj vital; essentiel; indispensable; ~ly adv vitalement; ~s npl organes vitaux mpl.

vitality n vitalité f.

vital statistics npl statistiques démographiques fpl.

vitamin n vitamine f.

vitiate vt vicier.

vivacious adj vif.

vivid adj vif; vivant; frappant; ~ly adv de façon éclatante; de façon frappante.

vivisection n vivisection f.

vocabulary n vocabulaire m.

vocal adj oral.

vocation n vocation f; profession f, métier m; ~al adj professionnel.

vocative n vocatif m.

vociferous adj bruyant.

vodka n vodka f.

vogue n vogue f; mode f.

voice n voix f; * vt exprimer.

void adj vide; * n vide m.

volatile adj volatile; versatile.

volcanic adj volcanique.

volcano n volcan m.

volition n volonté f.

volley n volée f; salve f; grêle f.

volleyball n volley-ball m.

volt n volt m.

voltage n voltage m.

voluble adj volubile, loquace.

volume *n* volume *m*.
voluntarily *adv* volontairement.
voluntary *adj* volontaire.
volunteer *n* volontaire *mf*; * *vi* se porter volontaire .
voluptuous *adj* voluptueux.
vomit *vt*, *vi* vomir; * *n* vomissement *m*.
voracious *adj* ~**ly** *adv* vorace(ment).
vortex *n* tourbillon *m*.
vote *n* vote, suffrage *m*; voix *f*; * *vt* voter.

voter *n* électeur *m*, -trice *f*.
voting *n* vote *m*.
voucher *n* bon *m*.
vow *n* vœu *m*; * *vt* jurer.
vowel *n* voyelle *f*.
voyage *n* voyage par mer *m*; traversée *f*.
vulgar *adj* vulgaire; grossier.
vulgarity *n* grossièreté *f*; vulgarité *m*.
vulnerable *adj* vulnérable.
vulture *n* vautour *m*.

W

wad *n* tampon *m*; bouchon *m*.
waddle *vi* se dandiner.
wade *vi* patauger.
wading pool *n* petit bassin (pour enfants) *m*.
wafer *n* gaufrette *f*; plaque *f*.
waffle *n* gaufre *f*.
waft *vt* porter, apporter; * *vi* flotter.
wag *vt*, *vi* remuer.
wage *n* salaire *m*.
wage earner *n* salarié *m*, -e *f*.
wager *n* pari *m*; * *vt* parier.
wages *npl* salaire *m*.
waggle *vt* remuer.
waggon *n* chariot *m*; (*rail*) wagon *m*.
wail *n* gémissement *m*, plainte *f*; * *vi* gémir.
waist *n* taille *f*.
waistline *n* taille *f*.
wait *vi* attendre; * *n* attente *f*; arrêt *m*.
waiter *n* serveur *m*.
waiting list *n* liste d'attente *f*.
waiting room *n* salle d'attente *f*.
waive *vt* renoncer à.
wake *vi* se réveiller; * *vt* réveiller; * *n* veillée *f*; (*mar*) sillage *m*.
waken *vt* réveiller; * *vi* se réveiller.

walk *vi* marcher, aller à pied; * *vt* parcourir; * *n* promenade *f*; marche *f*.
walker *n* marcheur *m*, -euse *f*.
walkie-talkie *n* talkie-walkie *m*.
walking *n* marche à pied *f*.
walking stick *n* canne *f*.
walkout *n* grève *f*.
walkover *n* (*sl*) victoire facile *f*, gâteau *m*.
walkway *n* passage pour piétons *m*.
wall *n* mur *m*; muraille *f*; paroi *f*.
walled *adj* muré.
wallet *n* portefeuille *m*.
wallflower *n* (*bot*) giroflée *f*.
wallow *vi* se vautrer.
wallpaper *n* papier peint *m*.
walnut *n* noix *f*; noyer *m*.
walrus *n* morse *m*.
waltz *n* valse *f*.
wan *adj* pâle.
wand *n* baguette (magique) *f*.
wander *vi* errer; aller sans but.
wane *vi* décroître.
want *vt* vouloir; demander; * *vi* manquer; * *n* besoin *m*; manque *m*.
wanting *adj* manquant, qui manque, qui fait défaut.
wanton *adj* lascif; capricieux.

war n guerre f.

ward n salle f; pupille mf.

wardrobe n garde-robe f, penderie f.

warehouse n entrepôt m.

warfare n guerre f.

warhead n ogive f.

warily adv avec circonspection.

wariness n circonspection, prudence f.

warm adj chaud; chaleureux; * vt réchauffer; **to ~ up** vi se réchauffer; s'échauffer; s'animer; vt réchauffer.

warm-hearted adj affectueux.

warmly adv chaudement, chaleureusement.

warmth n chaleur f.

warn vt prévenir; avertir.

warning n avertissement m.

warning light n voyant lumineux m.

warp vi se voiler; * vt voiler; fausser.

warrant n garantie f; mandat m.

warranty n garantie f.

warren n terrier m.

warrior n guerrier m, -ière f.

warship n navire de guerre m.

wart n verrue f.

wary adj prudent, circonspect.

wash vt laver; * vi se laver; * n lavage m; lessive f.

washable adj lavable.

washbowl n lavabo m.

washcloth n gant de toilette m.

washer n rondelle f.

washing n linge à laver m; lessive f.

washing machine n machine à laver f.

washing-up n vaisselle f.

wash-out n (sl) fiasco m.

washroom n toilettes fpl.

wasp n abeille f.

wastage n gaspillage m; perte f.

waste vt gaspiller; dévaster, saccager; perdre; * vi se perdre; * n gaspillage m; détérioration f; terre inculte f; déchets mpl.

wasteful adj gaspilleur; prodigue; **~ly** adv avec prodigalité.

waste paper n vieux papiers mpl.

waste pipe n tuyau d'échappement m.

watch n montre f; surveillance f; garde f; * vt regarder; observer; surveiller; faire attention à; * vi regarder; monter la garde.

watchdog n chien de garde m.

watchful adj vigilant; **~ly** adv avec vigilance.

watchmaker n horloger m.

watchman n veilleur de nuit m; gardien m.

watchtower n tour de guet f.

watchword n mot de passe m; mot d'ordre m.

water n eau f; * vt arroser, mouiller; * vi pleurer, larmoyer.

water closet n W.C. mpl.

watercolour n aquarelle f.

waterfall n cascade f.

water heater n chauffe-eau m invar.

watering-can n arrosoir m.

water level n niveau de l'eau m.

waterlily n nénuphar m.

water line n ligne de flottaison f.

waterlogged adj imprégné d'eau.

water main n conduite principale d'eau f.

watermark n filigrane m.

water melon n pastèque f.

watershed n moment critique m.

watertight adj étanche.

waterworks npl usine hydraulique f.

watery adj aqueux; détrempé; délavé.

watt n watt m.

wave n vague f; lame f; onde f; * vi faire signe de la main; onduler; * vt agiter.

wavelength n longueur d'ondes f.

waver vi vaciller, osciller.

wavering adj hésitant.

wavy adj ondulé.

wax n cire f; * vt cirer; * vi croître.

wax paper n papier paraffiné m.

waxworks n musée de cire m.

way n chemin m; voie f; route f; manière f; direction f; **to give ~** céder.

waylay vt attirer dans une embuscade.

wayward adj capricieux.

we pn nous.

weak adj , **~ly** adv faible(ment).

weaken vt affaiblir.

weakling n personne faible f.

weakness n faiblesse f; point faible m.

wealth n richesse f; abondance f.

wealthy adj riche.

wean vt sevrer.

weapon n arme f.

wear vt porter; user; * vi s'user; **to ~ away** vt user; vi s'user; **to ~ down** vt user; épuiser; **to ~ off** vi s'effacer; **to ~ out** vi s'user; s'épuiser; vt user; * n usage m; usure f.

weariness n lassitude f; fatigue f; ennui m.

wearisome adj fatigant.

weary adj las, fatigué; ennuyeux.

weasel n belette f.

weather n temps m; * vt surmonter.

weather-beaten adj ayant souffert des intempéries.

weather cock n girouette f.

weather forecast n prévisions météorologiques fpl.

weave vt tisser; entrelacer.

weaving n tissage m.

web n tissu m; toile f; palmure f.

wed vt épouser; * vi se marier.

wedding n mariage m; noces fpl.

wedding day n jour du mariage m.

wedding dress n robe de mariée f.

wedding present n cadeau de mariage m.

wedding ring n alliance f.

wedge n cale f; * vt caler; enfoncer.

wedlock n mariage m.

Wednesday n mercredi m.

wee adj petit.

weed n mauvaise herbe f; * vt désherber.

weedkiller n désherbant m.

weedy adj envahi par les mauvaises herbes.

week n semaine f; **tomorrow ~** demain en huit; **yesterday ~** il y a eu une semaine hier.

weekday n jour de semaine, jour ouvrable m.

weekend n week-end m, fin de semaine f.

weekly adj de la semaine, hebdomadaire; * adv chaque semaine, par semaine.

weep vt, vi pleurer.

weeping willow n saule pleureur m.

weigh vt, vi peser.

weight n poids m.

weightily adv pesamment.

weightlifter n haltérophile m.

weighty adj lourd; important.

welcome adj opportun; **~!** bienvenue !; * n accueil m; * vt accueillir.

weld vt souder; * n soudure f.

welfare n bien-être m; assistance sociale f.

welfare state n Etat-providence m.

well n source f; fontaine f; puits m; * adj bien, bon; * adv bien; **as ~ as** aussi bien que, en plus de, comme.

well-behaved adj bien élevé.

well-being n bien-être m.

well-bred adj bien élevé.

well-built adj bien bâti, solide.

well-deserved adj bien mérité.

well-dressed adj bien habillé.

well-known adj connu, célèbre.

well-mannered adj poli, bien élevé.

well-meaning adj bien intentionné.

well-off adj aisé, dans l'aisance.

well-to-do *adj* aisé, riche.

well-wisher *n* admirateur *m*, -trice *f*.

wench *n* jeune fille, jeune femme *f*.

west *n* ouest, Occident *m*; * *adj* ouest, de/à l'ouest; * *adv* vers/à l'ouest.

westerly, western *adj* (d')ouest.

westward *adv* vers l'ouest.

wet *adj* mouillé, humide; * *n* humidité *f*; * *vt* mouiller.

wet-nurse *n* nourrice *f*.

wet suit *n* combinaison de plongée *f*.

whack *vt* donner un grand coup à; * *n* grand coup *m*.

whale *n* baleine *f*.

wharf *n* quai *m*.

what *pn* qu'est-ce qui,(qu'est-ce) que, quoi; que, qui; ce qui, ce que; quel(le), que; * *adj* quel(s), quelle(s); * *excl* quoi! comment!.

whatever *pn* quoi que; tout; n'importe quoi.

wheat *n* blé *m*.

wheedle *vt* cajoler, câliner.

wheel *n* roue *f*; volant *m*; gouvernail *m*; * *vt* tourner; pousser, rouler; * *vi* tourner en rond, tournoyer.

wheelbarrow *n* brouette *f*.

wheelchair *n* fauteuil roulant *m*.

wheel clamp *n* sabot *m*.

wheeze *vi* respirer bruyamment.

when *adv*, *conj* quand.

whenever *adv* quand; chaque fois que.

where *adv* où; * *conj* où; **any~** n'importe où; **every~** partout.

whereabout(s) *adv* où.

whereas *conj* tandis que; attendu que.

whereby *pn* par lequel (laquelle), au moyen duquel (de laquelle).

wherever *adv* où que.

whereupon *conj* sur quoi; après quoi.

wherewithal *npl* ressources *fpl*.

whet *vt* aiguiser.

whether *conj* si.

which *pn* lequel, laquelle; celui/ celle(s)/ceux que, celui/celle(s)/ ceux qui; ce qui, ce que; quoi, ce dont * *adj* quel(s), quelle(s).

whiff *n* bouffée, odeur *f*.

while *n* moment *m*; **a ~** quelque temps; * *conj* pendant que; alors que; quoique.

whim *n* caprice *m*.

whimper *vi* gémir, pleurnicher.

whimsical *adj* capricieux, fantasque.

whine *vi* gémir, se plaindre; * *n* gémissement *m*, plainte *f*.

whinny *vi* hennir.

whip *n* fouet *m*; cravache *f*; * *vt* fouetter; battre.

whipped cream *n* crème fouettée *f*.

whirl *vi* tourbillonner, tournoyer; aller à toute allure; * *vt* faire tourbillonner, faire tournoyer.

whirlpool *n* tourbillon *m*.

whirlwind *n* tornade *f*.

whisky *n* whisky *m*.

whisper *vi* chuchoter; murmurer.

whispering *n* chuchotement *m*; murmure *m*.

whistle *vi* siffler; * *n* sifflement *m*.

white *adj* blanc; pâle; * *n* blanc *m*; blanc d'oeuf *m*.

white elephant *n* objet superflu *m*.

white-hot *adj* chauffé à blanc.

white lie *n* petit mensonge, mensonge innocent *m*.

whiten *vt*, *vi* blanchir.

whiteness *n* blancheur *f*; pâleur *f*.

whitewash *n* blanc de chaux *m*; * *vt* blanchir à la chaux; disculper.

whiting *n* merlan *m*.

whitish *adj* blanchâtre.

who *pn* qui.

whoever *pn* quiconque, qui que ce soit, quel(le) que soit.

whole *adj* tout, entier; intact,

complet; sain; * *n* tout *m*; ensemble *m*.

wholehearted *adj* sincère.

wholemeal *adj* complet.

wholesale *n* vente en gros *f*.

wholesome *adj* sain, salubre.

wholewheat *adj* complet.

wholly *adv* complètement.

whom *pn* qui; que.

whooping cough *n* coqueluche *f*.

whore *n* putain *f*.

why *n* pourquoi *m*; * *conj* pourquoi; * *excl* eh bien!, tiens!

wick *n* mèche *f*.

wicked *adj* méchant, mauvais; ~**ly** *adv* méchamment.

wickedness *n* méchanceté, perversité *f*.

wicker *n* osier *m*; * *adj* en osier.

wide *adj* large, ample; grand; ~**ly** *adv* partout; **far and** ~ de tous côtés.

wide-awake *adj* bien réveillé.

widen *vt* élargir, agrandir.

wide open *adj* en grand.

widespread *adj* très répandu.

widow *n* veuve *f*.

widower *n* veuf *m*.

width *n* largeur *f*.

wield *vt* manier, brandir.

wife *n* femme *f*; épouse *f*.

wig *n* perruque *f*.

wiggle *vt* agiter; * *vi* s'agiter.

wild *adj* sauvage, féroce; désert; fou; furieux.

wilderness *n* étendue déserte *f*.

wild life *n* faune *f*.

wildly *adv* violemment; furieusement; follement.

wilful *adj* délibéré; entêté.

wilfulness *n* obstination *f*.

wiliness *n* ruse, astuce *f*.

will *n* volonté *f*; testament *m*; * *vt* vouloir.

willing *adj* prêt, disposé; ~**ly** *adv* volontiers, de bon coeur.

willingness *n* bonne volonté *f*, empressement *m*.

willow *n* saule *m*.

willpower *n* volonté *f*.

wilt *vi* se fâner.

wily *adj* astucieux.

win *vt* gagner, conquérir; remporter.

wince *vi* tressaillir.

winch *n* treuil *m*.

wind *n* vent *m*; souffle *m*; gaz *mpl*.

wind *vt* enrouler; envelopper; donner un tour de; * *vi* serpenter.

windfall *n* fruit abattu par le vent *m*.

winding *adj* tortueux.

windmill *n* moulin à vent *m*.

window *n* fenêtre *f*.

window box *n* jardinière *f*.

window cleaner *n* laveur(-euse) de carreaux *m(f)*.

window ledge *n* rebord de fenêtre *m*.

window pane *n* carreau *m*.

window sill *n* rebord de fenêtre *m*.

windpipe *n* tranchée *f*.

windscreen *n* pare-brise *m invar*.

windscreen washer *n* lave-glace *m invar*.

windscreen wiper *n* essuie-glace *m invar*.

windy *adj* venteux.

wine *n* vin *m*.

wine cellar *n* cave (à vin) *f*.

wine glass *n* verre à vin *m*.

wine list *n* carte des vins *f*.

wine merchant *n* négociant en vins *m*.

wine-tasting *n* dégustation de vins *f*.

wing *n* aile *f*.

winged *adj* ailé.

winger *n* ailier *m*.

wink *vi* faire un clin d'oeil; * *n* clin d'oeil *m*; clignement *m*.

winner *n* gagnant *m*, -e *f*; vainqueur *m*.

winning post *n* poteau d'arrivée *m*.

winter *n* hiver *m*; * *vi* hiverner.

winter sports *npl* sports d'hiver *mpl*.

wintry *adj* d'hiver, hivernal.

wipe *vt* essuyer; effacer.

wire *n* fil *m*; télégramme *m*; * *vt* installer des fils électriques à; télégraphier.

wiring *n* installation électrique *f*.

wiry *adj* effilé et nerveux.

wisdom *n* sagesse, prudence *f*.

wisdom teeth *npl* dents de sagesse *fpl*.

wise *adj* sage, avisé, judicieux, prudent.

wisecrack *n* bon mot *m*, plaisanterie *f*.

wish *vt* souhaiter, désirer; * *n* souhait, désir *m*.

wishful *adj* désireux.

wisp *n* brin *m*; mince volute *f*.

wistful *adj* nostalgique, rêveur.

wit *n* esprit *m*, intelligence *f*.

witch *n* sorcière *f*.

witchcraft *n* sorcellerie *f*.

with *prep* avec; à; de; contre.

withdraw *vt* retirer; rappeler; annuler; * *vi* se retirer.

withdrawal *n* retrait *m*.

withdrawn *adj* réservé.

wither *vi* se flétrir, se faner.

withhold *vt* détenir, retenir, empêcher.

within *prep* à l'intérieur de; * *adv* dedans; à l'intérieur.

without *prep* sans.

withstand *vt* résister à.

witless *adj* sot, stupide.

witness *n* témoin *m*; témoignage *m*; * *vt* être témoin de; attester.

witness stand *n* barre des témoins *f*.

witticism *n* mot d'esprit *m*.

wittily *adv* spirituellement.

wittingly *adv* sciemment, à dessein.

witty *adj* spirituel, plein d'esprit.

wizard *n* sorcier, magicien *m*.

wobble *vi* trembler.

woe *n* malheur *m*; affliction *f*.

woeful *adj* triste, malheureux; **~ly** *adv* tristement.

wolf *n* loup *m*; **she ~** louve *f*.

woman *n* femme *f*.

womanish *adj* de femme.

womanly *adj* féminin, de femme.

womb *n* utérus *m*.

women's lib *n* mouvement de libération de la femme *m*.

wonder *n* merveille *f*; miracle *m*; émerveillement *m*; * *vi* s'émerveiller.

wonderful *adj* merveilleux; **~ly** *adv* merveilleusement.

wondrous *adj* merveilleux.

won't *abrev* de will not.

wont *n* coutume *f*.

woo *vt* faire la cour à.

wood *n* bois *m*.

wood alcohol *n* alcool méthylique *m*.

wood carving *n* sculpture sur bois *f*.

woodcut *n* gravure sur bois *f*.

woodcutter *n* graveur sur bois *m*; bûcheron *m*.

wooded *adj* boisé.

wooden *adj* de bois, en bois.

woodland *n* région boisée *f*.

woodlouse *n* cloporte *m*.

woodman *n* forestier *m*; garde-forestier *m*.

woodpecker *n* pic *m*.

woodwind *n* bois *mpl*.

woodwork *n* menuiserie *f*.

woodworm *n* ver du bois *m*.

wool *n* laine *f*.

woollen *adj* de laine.

woollens *npl* lainages *mpl*.

woolly *adj* laineux, de laine.

word *n* mot *m*; parole *f*; * *vt* exprimer; rédiger.

wordiness *n* verbosité *f*.

wording *n* rédaction *f*.

word processing *n* traitement de texte *m*.

word processor *n* machine à traitement de texte *f*.

wordy *adj* verbeux.

work *vi* travailler; opérer; fonctionner; fermenter; * *vt* (faire) travailler, faire fonctionner; façonner; * **to ~ out** *vi* marcher;

* *vt* résoudre; * *n* travail *m*; œuvre *f*; ouvrage *m*; emploi *m*.

workable *adj* exploitable.

workaholic *n* drogué du travail *m*.

worker *n* travailleur *m*, -euse *f*; ouvrier *m*, -ère *f*.

workforce *n* main-d'œuvre *f*.

working-class *adj* ouvrier.

workman *n* ouvrier, artisan *m*.

workmanship *n* exécution *f*; qualité du travail *f*.

workmate *n* camarade de travail *mf*.

workshop *n* atelier *m*.

world *n* monde *m*; * *adj* du monde; mondial.

worldliness *n* mondanité *f*; attachement aux choses matérielles *m*.

worldly *adj* mondain; terrestre.

worldwide *adj* mondial.

worm *n* ver *m*; filet *m*.

worn-out *adj* épuisé; usé.

worried *adj* inquiet.

worry *vt* inquiéter; *n* souci *m*.

worrying *adj* inquiétant.

worse *adj*, *adv* pire; * *n* le pire.

worship *n* culte *m*; adoration *f*; **your** ~ Monsieur le Maire, Monsieur le Juge; * *vt* adorer, vénérer.

worst *adj* le pire; * *adv* le plus mal; * *n* le pire *m*.

worth *n* valeur *f*, prix *m*; mérite *m*.

worthily *adv* dignement, à juste titre.

worthless *adj* sans valeur; inutile.

worthwhile *adj* qui vaut la peine; louable.

worthy *adj* digne; louable.

would-be *adj* soi-disant.

wound *n* blessure *f*; * *vt* blesser.

wrangle *vi* se disputer; *n* dispute *f*.

wrap *vt* envelopper.

wrath *n* colère *f*.

wreath *n* couronne, guirlande *f*.

wreck *n* naufrage *m*; ruines *fpl*; destruction *f*; épave *f*; * *vt* causer le naufrage de; démolir.

wreckage *n* naufrage *m*; épave *f*, débris *mpl*.

wren *n* roitelet *m*.

wrench *vt* tordre; forcer; tourner violemment; * *n* clé *f*; torsion violente *f*.

wrest *vt* arracher.

wrestle *vi* lutter.

wrestling *n* lutte *f*.

wretched *adj* malheureux, misérable.

wriggle *vi* remuer, se tortiller.

wring *vt* tordre; essorer; arracher.

wrinkle *n* ride *f*; * *vt* rider; * *vi* se rider.

wrist *n* poignet *m*.

wristband *n* manchette de chemise *f*.

wristwatch *n* montre-bracelet *f*.

writ *n* écriture *f*; assignation *f*; acte judiciaire *m*.

write *vt* écrire; composer; **to ~ down** consigner par écrit; **to ~ off** annuler; réduire; **to ~ up** rédiger.

write-off *n* perte *f*.

writer *n* écrivain *m*; auteur *m*.

writhe *vi* se tordre.

writing *n* écriture *f*; oeuvres *fpl*; écrit *m*.

writing desk *n* bureau *m*.

writing paper *n* papier à lettres *m*.

wrong *n* mal *m*; injustice *f*; tort *m*; injure *f*; * *adj* mauvais, mal; injuste; inopportun; faux, erroné; * *adv* mal, inexactement; * *vt* faire du tort à, léser.

wrongful *adj* injuste.

wrongly *adv* injustement.

wry *adj* ironique.

X

xenon *n* xénon *m*.
xenophobe *n* xénophobe *mf*.
xenophobia *n* xénophobie *f*.
xenophobic *adj* xénophobique.

Xmas *abbr* Noël *m*.
X-ray *n* rayon X *m*.
xylophone *n* xylophone *m*.

Y

yacht *n* yacht *m*.
yachting *n* navigation de plaisance *f*.
Yankee *n* yankee *m*.
yard *n* yard (0,914 m) *m*; cour *f*.
yardstick *n* critère d'évaluation *m*.
yarn *n* longue histoire *f*; fil *m*.
yawn *vi* bâiller; * *n* bâillement *m*.
yawning *adj* béant.
yeah *adv* oui, ouais (*fam*).
year *n* année *f*.
yearbook *n* annuaire *m*.
yearling *n* animal âgé d'un an *m*.
yearly *adj*, *adv* annuel(lement).
yearn *vi* languir.
yearning *n* désir ardent *m*.
yeast *n* levure *f*.
yell *vi* hurler; * *n* hurlement *m*.
yellow *adj*, *n* jaune *m*.
yellowish *adj* jaunâtre.
yelp *vi* japper, glapir; * *n* jappement *m*.
yes *adv*, *n* oui *m*.
yesterday *adv*, *n* hier (*m*).
yet *conj* pourtant; cependant; * *adv* encore.
yew *n* if *m*.

yield *vt* donner, produire; rapporter; * *vi* se rendre; céder; * *n* production f; récolte *f*; rendement *m*.
yoga *n* yoga *m*.
yog(h)urt *n* yaourt *m*.
yoke *n* joug *m*.
yolk *n* jaune d'oeuf *m*.
yonder *adv* là-bas.
you *pn* vous; tu; te; toi.
young *adj* jeune; ~**er** *adj* plus jeune.
youngster *n* jeune *mf*.
your(s) *pn* ton, ta, tes; votre, vos; le tien, la tienne, les tiens, les tiennes; le/la vôtre, les vôtres; **sincerely** ~**s** je vous prie d'agréer, Monsieur/Madame, l'expression de mes sentiments les meilleurs.
yourself *pn* toi-même; vous-même(s).
youth *n* jeunesse, adolescence *f*; jeune homme *m*.
youthful *adj* jeune.
youthfulness *n* jeunesse *f*.
yuppie (*adj*) *n* (de) jeune cadre dynamique *m*.

Z

zany *adj* farfelu.
zap *vt* flinguer.

zeal *n* zèle *m*; ardeur *f*.
zealous *adj* zélé.

zebra *n* zèbre *m*.
zenith *n* zénith *m*.
zero *n* zéro *m*.
zest *n* enthousiasme *m*.
zigzag *n* zigzag *m*.
zinc *n* zinc *m*.
zip, zipper *n* fermeture éclair *f*.
zip code *n* code postal *m*.

zodiac *n* zodiaque *m*.
zone *n* zone *f*; secteur *m*.
zoo *n* zoo *m*.
zoological *adj* zoologique.
zoologist *n* zoologiste *mf*.
zoology *n* zoologie *f*.
zoom *vi* vrombir.
zoom lens *n* zoom *m*.

Verbes Irréguliers en Anglais

	Prétérit	Participe du passé		Prétérit	Participe du passé
arise	arose	arisen	draw	drew	drawn
awake	awoke	awaked,	dream	dreamed,	dreamed
awoken				dreamt	dreamt
be [I am, you/we/they are, he/she/it			drink	drank	drunk
is, *gérondif* being]			drive	drove	driven
	was, were	been	dwell	dwelt,	dwelt,
bear	bore	borne		dwelled	dwelled
beat	beat	beaten	eat	ate	eaten
become	became	become	fall	fell	fallen
begin	began	begun	feed	fed	fed
behold	beheld	beheld	feel	felt	felt
bend	bent	bent	mistake	mistook	mistaken
beseech	besought,	besought,	fight	fought	fought
beseeched	beseeched		find	found	found
beset	beset	beset	flee	fled	fled
bet	bet, betted	bet, betted	fling	flung	flung
bid	bade, bid	bade, bid,	fly [he/she/it flies]		
		bidden		flew	flown
bite	bit	bitten	forbid	forbade	forbidden
bleed	bled	bled	forecast	forecast	forecast
bless	blessed	blessed,	forget	forgot	forgotten
		blest	forgive	forgave	forgiven
blow	blew	blown	forsake	forsook	forsaken
break	broke	broken	forsee	foresaw	foreseen
breed	bred	bred	freeze	froze	frozen
bring	brought	brought	get	got	got, gotten
build	built	built	give	gave	given
burn	burnt,	burnt,	go [he/she/it goes]		
	burned	burned		went	gone
burst	burst	burst	grind	ground	ground
buy	bought	bought	grow	grew	grown
can	could	(been able)	hang	hung,	hung,
cast	cast	cast		hanged	hanged
catch	caught	caught	have [I/you/we/they have,		
choose	chose	chosen	he/she/it has, *gérondif* having]		
cling	clung	clung		had	had
come	came	come	hear	heard	heard
cost	cost	cost	hide	hid	hidden
creep	crept	crept	hit	hit	hit
cut	cut	cut	hold	held	held
deal	dealt	dealt	hurt	hurt	hurt
dig	dug	dug	keep	kept	kept
do [he/she/it does]			kneel	knelt,	knelt
	did	done		kneeled	kneeled

	Prétérit	Participe du passé		Prétérit	Participe du passé
know	knew	known	shoot	shot	shot
lay	laid	laid	show	showed	shown,
lead	led	led			showed
lean	leant,	leant,	shrink	shrank	shrunk
	leaned	leaned	shut	shut	shut
leap	leapt,	leapt,	sing	sang	sung
leaped	leaped		sink	sank	sunk
learn	learnt,	learnt	sit	sat	sat
learned	learned		slay	slew	slain
leave	left	left	sleep	slept	slept
lend	lent	lent	slide	slid	slid
let	let	let	sling	slung	slung
lie [gérondif lying]	lay		smell	smelt,	smelt,
lain			smelled	smelled	
light	lighted,	lighted,	sow	sowed	sown,
lit	lit				sowed
lose	lost	lost	speak	spoke	spoken
make	made	made	speed	sped,	sped,
may	might	-		speeded	speeded
mean	meant	meant	spell	spelt,	spelt,
meet	met	met	spelled	spelled	
mow	mowed	mowed,	spend	spent	spent
		mown	spill	spilt,	spilt
must	(had to)	(had to)	spilled	spilled	
overcome	overcame	overcome	spin	spun	spun
pay	paid	paid	spit	spat	spat
put	put	put	split	split	split
quit	quitted	quitted	spoil	spoilt,	spoilt,
read	read	read	spread	spread	spread
rid	rid	rid	spring	sprang	sprung
ride	rode	ridden	stand	stood	stood
ring	rang	rung	steal	stole	stolen
rise	rose	risen	stick	stuck	stuck
run	ran	run	sting	stung	stung
saw	sawed	sawn	stink	stank	stunk
say	said	said	stride	strode	stridden
see	saw	seen	strike	struck	struck
seek	sought	sought	strive	strove	striven
sell	sold	sold	swear	swore	sworn
send	sent	sent	sweep	swept	swept
set	set	set	swell	swelled	swelled,
sew	sewed	sewn			swollen
shake	shook	shaken	swim	swam	swum
shall	should	-	swing	swung	swung
shear	sheared	sheared,	take	took	taken
		shorn	teach	taught	taught
shed	shed	shed	tear	tore	torn
shine	shone	shone	tell	told	told

	Prétérit	Participe du passé		Prétérit	Participe du passé
think	thought	thought	wed	wed, wedded	wed, wedded
throw	threw	thrown	weep	wept	wept
thrust	thrust	thrust	win	won	won
tread	trod	trodden	wind	wound	wound
understand	understood	understood	withdraw	withdrew	withdrawn
upset	upset	upset	withhold	withheld	withheld
wake	woke	woken	withstand	withstood	withstood
wear	wore	worn	wring	wrung	wrung
weave	wove, weaved	wove, weaved	write	wrote	written

French Verbs

Regular

infinitive	donn**er**	fin**ir**	vend**re**
	to give	*to finish*	*to sell*
gerund	donn**ant**	fin**issant**	vend**ant**
past participle	donn**é**	fin**i**	vend**u**
present	je donn**e**	je fin**is**	je vend**s**
	tu donn**es**	tu fin**is**	tu vend**s**
	il donn**e**	il fin**it**	il vend
	nous donn**ons**	nous fin**issons**	nous vend**ons**
	vous donn**ez**	vous fin**issez**	vous vend**ez**
	ils donn**ent**	ils fin**issent**	ils vend**ent**
imperfect	donn**ais**	fin**issais**	vend**ais**
	donn**ais**	fin**issais**	vend**ais**
	donn**ait**	fin**issait**	vend**ait**
	donn**ions**	fin**issions**	vend**ions**
	donn**iez**	fin**issiez**	vend**iez**
	donn**aient**	fin**issaient**	vend**aient**
future	donn**erai**	fin**irai**	vend**rai**
	donn**eras**	fin**iras**	vend**ras**
	donn**era**	fin**ira**	vend**ra**
	donn**erons**	fin**irons**	vend**rons**
	donn**erez**	fin**irez**	vend**rez**
	donn**eront**	fin**iront**	vend**ront**
conditional	donn**erais**	fin**irais**	vend**rais**
	donn**erais**	fin**irais**	vend**rais**
	donn**erait**	fin**irait**	vend**rait**
	donn**erions**	fin**irions**	vend**rions**
	donn**eriez**	fin**iriez**	vend**riez**
	donn**eraint**	fin**iraient**	vend**raient**
past historic	donn**ai**	fin**is**	vend**is**
	donn**as**	fin**is**	vend**is**
	donn**a**	fin**it**	vend**it**
	donn**âmes**	fin**îmes**	vend**îmes**
	donn**âtes**	fin**îtes**	vend**îtes**
	donn**èrent**	fin**irent**	vend**irent**
present	donn**e**	fin**isse**	vend**e**
subjunctive	donn**es**	fin**isses**	vend**es**
	donn**e**	fin**isse**	vend**e**

	donnions	finissions	vendions
	donniez	finissiez	vendiez
	donnent	finissent	vendent
imperfect	donnasse	finisse	vendisse
subjunctive	donnasses	finisses	vendisses
	donnât	finît	venît
	donnassions	finissions	vendissions
	donnassiez	finissiez	vendissiez
	donnassent	finissent	vendissent

Auxiliary verbs

infinitive		*conditional*	
être	**avoir**	serais	aurais
to be	*to have*	serais	aurais
present participle		serait	aurait
étant	ayant	serions	aurions
past participle		seriez	auriez
été	eu	seraient	auraient
present		*past historic*	
je suis	j'ai	fus	eus
tu es	tu as	fus	eus
il est	il a	fut	eut
nous sommes	nous avons	fûmes	eûmes
vous êtes	vous avez	fûtes	eûtes
ils sont	ils ont	furent	eurent
imperfect		*present subjunctive*	
étais	avais	sois	aie
étais	avais	sois	aies
était	avait	soit	ait
étions	avions	soyons	ayons
étiez	aviez	soyez	ayez
étaient	avaient	soient	aient
future		*imperfect subjunctive*	
serai	aurai	fusse	eusse
seras	auras	fusses	eusses
sera	aura	fût	eût
serons	aurons	fussions	eussions
serez	aurez	fussiez	eussiez
seront	auront	fussent	eussent

Irregular Verbs

acheter	**acquérir**	**aller**	**appeler**
to buy	*to acquire*	*to go*	*to call*
present			
achète	acquiers	vais	appelle
achètes	acquiers	vas	appelles
achète	acquiert	va	appelle
achetons	acquérons	allons	appelons
achetez	acquérez	allez	appelez
achètent	acquièrent	vont	appellent
imperfect			
achetais	acquérais	allais	apellais
achetais	acquérais	allais	apellais
achetait	acquérait	allait	apellait
achetions	acquérions	allions	apelions

achetiez	acquériez	alliez	apelliez
achetaient	acquérient	allaient	apellaient

future

achèterai	acquerrai	irai	apellerai
achèteras	acquerras	iras	apelleras
achètera	acquerra	ira	appellera
achèterons	acquerrons	irons	appellerons
achèterez	acquerrez	irez	appellerez
achèteront	acquerront	iront	appelleront

conditional

achèterais	acquerrais	irais	apellerais
achèterais	acquerrais	irais	apellerais
achèterait	acquerrait	iriat	appellerait
achèterions	acquerrions	irions	appellerions
achèteriez	acquerriez	iriez	appelleriez
achèterient	acquerrient	iraient	appelleriont

past historic

achetai	acquis	allai	appelai
achetas	acquis	allas	appelas
acheta	acquit	alla	appela
achetâmes	acquîmes	allâmes	appelâmes
achetâtes	acquîtes	allâtes	appelâtes
achetèrent	acquirent	allèrent	appelèrent

present subjunctive

achète	acquière	aille	appelle
achètes	acquières	ailles	appelles
achète	acquière	aille	appelle
achetions	acquiérions	aillions	appelions
achetiez	acquiériez	ailliez	appeliez
achètent	acquièrent	aillent	appellent

imperfect subjunctive

achetasse	acquisse	allasse	appelasse
achetasses	acquisses	allasses	appelasses
achetât	acquî	allât	appelât
achetassions	acquissions	allassions	appelassions
achetassiez	acquissiez	allassiez	appelassiez
achetassent	acquissent	allassent	appelassent

appuyer	**s'asseoir**	**battre**	**boire**
to lean	*to sit down*	*to hit*	*to drink*

present

appuie	m'assieds	bats	bois
appuies	t'assieds	bats	bois
appuie	s'assied	bat	boit
appuyons	nous asseyons	battons	buvons
appuyez	vous asseyez	battez	buvez
appuient	s'asseyent	battent	boivent

imperfect

appuyais	m'asseyais	battais	buvais
appuyais	t'asseyais	battais	buvais
appuyait	s'asseyait	battait	buvait
appuyions	nous asseyion	battions	buvions
appuyiez	vous asseyiez	battiez	buviez
appuyaient	s'asseyaient	battaient	buvaient

future

appuierai	m'assiérai	battrai	boirai
appuieras	t'assiéras	battras	boiras

appuiera	s'assiéra	battra	boira
appuierons	nous assiérons	battrons	boirons
appuierez	vous assiérez	battrez	boirez
appuieront	s'assiéront	battront	boiront

conditional

appuierais	m'assiérais	battrais	boirais
appuierais	t'assiérais	battrais	boirais
appuierait	s'assiérait	battrait	boirait
appuierions	nous assiérions	battrions	boirions
appuieriez	vous assiériez	battriez	boiriez
appuieraient	s'assiéraient	battraient	boiraient

past historic

appuyai	m'assis	battis	bus
appuyas	t'assis	battis	bus
appuya	s'assit	battit	but
appuyâmes	nous assîmes	battîmes	bûmes
appuyâtes	vous assîtes	battîtes	bûtes
appuyèrent	s'assirent	battirent	burent

present subjunctive

appuie	m'asseye	batte	boive
appuies	t'asseyes	battes	boives
appuie	s'asseye	batte	boive
appuyions	nous asseyions	battions	buvions
appuyiez	vous asseyiez	battiez	buviez
appuient	s'asseyent	battent	boivent

imperfect subjunctive

appuyasse	m'assisse	battisse	busse
appuyasses	t'assisses	battisses	busses
appuyât	s'assît	battît	bût
appuyassions	nous assissions	battissions	bussions
appuyassiez	vous assissiez	battissiez	bussiez
appuyassent	s'assissent	battissent	bussent

| **commencer** | **conduire** | **connaître** | **courir** |
| *to begin* | *to drive* | *to know* | *to run* |

present

commence	conduis	connais	cours
commences	conduis	connais	cours
commence	conduit	connaît	court
commençons	conduisons	connaissons	courons
commencez	conduisez	connaissez	courez
commencent	conduisent	connaissent	courent

imperfect

commençais	conduisais	connaissais	courais
commençais	conduisais	connaissais	courais
commençait	conduisait	connaissait	courait
commencions	conduisions	connaissions	courions
commenciez	conduisiez	connaissiez	couriez
commençaient	conduisaient	connaissaient	couraient

future

commencerai	conduirai	connaîtra	courrai
commenceras	conduiras	connaîtras	courras
commencera	conduira	connaîtra	courra
commencerons	conduirons	connaîtrons	courrons
commencerez	conduirez	connaîtrez	courrez
commenceront	conduiront	connaîtront	courront

conditional

commencerais	conduirais	connaîtrais	courrais
commencerais	conduirais	connaîtrais	courrais
commencerait	conduirait	connaîtrait	courrait
commencerions	conduirions	connaîtrions	courrions
commenceriez	conduiriez	connaîtriez	courriez
commenceraient	conduiraient	connaîtraient	couraient

past historic

commençai	conduisis	connus	courus
commenças	conduisis	connus	courus
commença	conduisit	connut	couru
commençâmes	conduisîmes	connûmes	courûmes
commençâtes	conduisîtes	connûtes	courûtes
commencèrent	conduisirent	connurent	coururent

present subjunctive

commence	conduise	connaisse	coure
commences	conduises	connaisses	coures
commence	conduise	connaisse	coure
commencions	conduisions	connaissions	courions
commenciez	conduisiez	connaissiez	couriez
commencent	conduisent	connaissent	courent

imperfect subjunctive

commençasse	conduisisse	connusse	courusse
commençasses	conduisisses	connusses	courusses
commençât	conduisît	connût	courût
commençassions	conduisissions	connussions	courussions
commençassiez	conduisissiez	connussiez	courussiez
commençassent	conduisissent	connussent	courussent

couvrir	**craindre**	**croire**	**devoir**
to cover	*to fear*	*to believe*	*to owe, have to*

present

couvre	crains	crois	dois
couvres	crains	crois	dois
couvre	craint	croit	doit
couvrons	craignons	croyons	devons
couvrez	craignez	croyez	devez
couvrent	craignent	croient	doivent

imperfect

couvrais	craignais	croyais	devais
couvrais	craignais	croyais	devais
couvrait	craignait	croyait	devait
couvrions	craignions	croyions	devions
couvriez	craigniez	croyiez	deviez
couvraient	craignient	croyaient	devaient

future

couvrirai	craindrai	croirai	devrai
couvriras	craindras	croiras	devras
couvrira	craindra	croira	devra
couvrirons	craindrons	croirons	devrons
couvrirez	craindrez	croirez	devrez
couvriront	craindront	croiront	devront

conditional

couvrirais	craindrais	croirais	devrais
couvrirais	craindrais	croirais	devrais
couvrirait	craindrait	croirait	devrait
couvririons	craindrions	croirions	devrions

441

couvririez	craindriez	croiriez	devriez
couvriront	craindraient	croiraient	devraient
past historic			
couvris	craignis	crus	dus
couvris	craignis	crus	dus
couvrit	craignit	crut	dut
couvrîmes	craignîmes	crûmes	dûmes
couvrîtes	craignîtes	crûtes	dûtes
couvrirent	craignirent	crurent	durent
present subjunctive			
couvre	craigne	croie	doive
couvres	craignes	croies	doives
couvre	craigne	croie	doive
couvrions	craignions	croyions	devions
couvriez	craigniez	croyiez	deviez
couvrent	craignent	croient	doivent
imperfect subjunctive			
couvrisse	craignisse	crusse	dusse
couvrisses	craignisses	crusses	dusses
couvrît	craignît	crût	dût
couvrissions	craignissions	crussions	dussions
couvrissiez	craignissiez	crussiez	dussiez
couvrissent	craignissent	crussent	dussent

dire	**écrire**	**envoyer**	**faire**
to say	*to write*	*to send*	*to do; to make*
present			
dis	écris	envoie	fais
dis	écris	envoies	fais
dit	écrit	envoie	fait
disons	écrivons	envoyons	faisons
dites	écrivez	envoyez	faites
disent	écrivent	envoient	font
imperfect			
disais	écrivais	envoyais	faisais
disais	écrivais	envoyais	faisais
disait	écrivait	envoyait	faisait
disions	écrivions	envoyions	faisions
disiez	écriviez	envoyiez	faisiez
disaient	écrivaient	envoyaient	faisaient
future			
dirai	écrirai	enverrai	ferai
diras	écriras	enverras	feras
dira	écrira	enverra	fera
dirons	écrirons	enverrons	ferons
direz	écrirez	enverrez	ferez
diront	écrivaient	enverront	feront
conditional			
dirais	écrirais	enverrais	ferais
dirais	écrirais	enverrais	ferais
dirait	écrirait	enverrait	ferait
dirions	écririons	enverrions	ferions
diriez	écririez	enverriez	feriez
diraient	écriraient	enverraient	feraient
past historic			
dis	écrivis	envoyai	fis
dis	écrivis	envoyas	fis

442

dit	écrivit	envoya	fit
dîmes	écrivîmes	envoyâmes	fîmes
dîtes	écrivîtes	envoyâtes	fîtes
dirent	écrivirent	envoyèrent	firent

present subjunctive

dise	écrive	envoie	fasse
dises	écrives	envoies	fasses
dise	écrive	envoie	fasse
disions	écrivions	envoyions	fassions
disiez	écriviez	envoyiez	fassiez
disent	écrivent	envoient	fassent

imperfect subjunctive

disse	écrivisse	envoyasse	fisse
disses	écrivisses	envoyasses	fisses
dit	écrivît	envoyât	fit
dissions	écrivissions	envoyassions	fissions
dissiez	écrivissiez	envoyassiez	fissiez
dissent	écrivissent	envoyassent	fissent

| **fuir** | **haïr** | **jeter** | **lire** |
| *to flee* | *to hate* | *to throw* | *to read* |

present

fuis	hais	jette	lis
fuis	hais	jettes	lis
fuit	hait	jette	lit
fuyons	haïssons	jetons	lisons
fuyez	haïssez	jetez	lisez
fuient	haïssent	jettent	lisent

imperfect

fuyais	haïssais	jetais	lisais
fuyais	haïssais	jetais	lisais
fuyait	haïssait	jetait	lisait
fuyions	haïssions	jetions	lisions
fuyiez	haïssiez	jetiez	lisiez
fuyaient	haïssaient	jetaient	lisaient

future

fuirai	haïrai	jetterai	lirai
fuiras	haïras	jetteras	liras
fuira	haïra	jettera	lira
fuirons	haïrons	jetterons	lirons
fuirez	haïrez	jetterez	lirez
fuiront	haïront	jetteront	liront

conditional

fuirais	haïrais	jetterais	lirais
fuirais	haïrais	jetterais	lirais
fuirait	haïrait	jetterait	lirait
fuirions	haïrions	jetterions	lirions
fuiriez	haïriez	jetteriez	liriez
fuiraient	haïraient	jetteraient	liraient

past historic

fuis	haïs	jetai	lus
fuis	haïs	jetas	lus
fuit	haït	jeta	lut
fuîmes	haïmes	jetâmes	lûmes
fuîtes	haïtes	jetâtes	lûte
fuirent	haïrent	jetèrent	lurent

present subjunctive

fuie	haïsse	jette	lise
fuies	haïsses	jettes	lises
fuie	haïsse	jette	lise
fuyions	haïssions	jetions	lisions
fuyiez	haïssiez	jetiez	lisiez
fuient	haïssent	jettent	lisent

imperfect subjunctive

fuisse	haïsse	jetasse	lusse
fuisses	haïsses	jetasses	lusses
fuît	haït	jetât	lût
fuissions	haïssions	jetassions	lussions
fuissiez	haïssiez	jetassiez	lussiez
fuissent	haïssent	jetassent	lussent

manger	**mettre**	**mourir**	**mouvoir**
to eat	*to put*	*to die*	*to drive, to move*

present

mange	mets	meurs	meus
manges	mets	meurs	meus
mange	met	meurt	meut
mangeons	mettons	mourons	mouvons
mangez	mettez	mourez	mouvez
mangent	mettent	meurent	meuvent

imperfect

mangeais	mettais	mourais	mouvrais
mangeais	mettais	mourais	mouvrais
mangeait	mettait	mourait	mouvrait
mangions	mettions	mourions	mouvrions
mangiez	mettiez	mouriez	mouvriez
mangeaient	mettaient	mouraient	mouvraient

future

mangerai	mettrai	mourrai	mouvrai
mangeras	mettras	mourras	mouvras
mangera	mettra	mourra	mouvra
mangerons	mettrons	mourrons	mouvrons
mangerez	mettrez	mourrez	mouvrez
mangeront	mettront	mourront	mouvront

conditional

mangerais	mettrais	mourrais	mouvrais
mangerais	mettrais	mourrais	mouvrais
mangerait	mettrait	mourrait	mouvrait
mangerions	mettrions	mourrions	mouvrions
mangeriez	mettriez	mourriez	mouvriez
mangeraient	mettraient	mourraient	mouvraient

past historic

mangeai	mis	mourus	mus
mangeas	mis	mourus	mus
mangea	mit	mourut	mut
mangeâmes	mîmes	mourûmes	mûmes
mangeâtes	mîtes	mourûtes	mûtes
mangèrent	mirent	moururent	murent

present subjunctive

mange	mette	meure	meuve
manges	mettes	meures	meuves
mange	mette	meure	meuve
mangions	mettions	mourions	mouvions

| mangiez | mettiez | mouriez | mouviez |
| mangent | mettent | meurent | meuvent |

imperfect subjunctive

mangeasse	misse	mourusse	musse
mangeasses	misses	mourusses	musses
mangeât	mît	mourût	mût
mangeassions	missions	mourussions	mussions
mangeassiez	missiez	mourussiez	mussiez
mangeassent	missent	mourussent	mussent

| **naître** | **partir** | **plaire** | **pouvoir** |
| *to be born* | *to leave* | *to please* | *to be able; can* |

present

nais	pars	plais	peux
nais	pars	plais	peux
naît	part	plaît	peut
naissons	partons	plaison	pouvons
naissez	partez	plaisez	pouvez
naissent	partent	plaisent	peuvent

imperfect

naissais	partais	plaisais	pouvais
naissais	partais	plaisais	pouvais
naissait	partait	plaisait	pouvait
naissions	partions	plaisions	pouvions
naissiez	partiez	plaisiez	pouviez
naissaient	partaient	plaisaient	pouvaient

future

naîtrai	partirai	plairai	pourrai
naîtras	partiras	plairas	pourras
naîtra	partira	plaira	pourra
naîtrons	partirons	plairons	pourrons
naîtrez	partirez	plairez	pourrez
naîtront	partiront	plairont	pourront

conditional

naîtrais	partirais	plairais	pourrais
naîtrais	partirais	plairais	pourrais
naîtrait	partirait	plairait	pourrait
naîtrions	partirions	plairions	pourrions
naîtriez	partiriez	plairiez	pourriez
naîtraient	partiraient	plairaient	pourraient

past historic

naquis	partis	plus	pus
naquis	partis	plus	pus
naquit	partit	plut	put
naquîmes	partîmes	plûmes	pûmes
naquîtes	partîtes	plûtes	pûtes
naquirent	partirent	plurent	purent

present subjunctive

naisse	parte	plaise	puisse
naisses	partes	plaises	puisses
naisse	parte	plaise	puisse
naissions	partions	plaisions	puissions
naissiez	partiez	plaisiez	puissiez
naissent	partent	plaisent	puissent

imperfect subjunctive

| naquisse | partisse | plusse | pusse |
| naquisses | partisses | plusses | pusses |

naquît	partît	plût	pût
naquissions	partissions	plussions	pussions
naquissiez	partissiez	plussiez	pussiez
naquissent	partissent	plussent	pussent

| **préférer** | **prendre** | **recevoir** | **rire** |
| *to prefer* | *to take* | *to receive* | *to laugh* |

present

préfère	prends	reçois	ris
préfères	prends	reçois	ris
préfère	prend	reçoit	rit
préférons	prenons	recevons	rions
préférez	prenez	recevez	riez
préfèrent	prennent	reçoivent	rient

imperfect

préférais	prenais	recevais	riais
préférais	prenais	recevais	riais
préférait	prenait	recevait	riait
préférions	prenions	recevions	riions
préfériez	preniez	receviez	riiez
préféraient	prenaient	recevaient	riaient

future

préférerai	prendrai	recevrai	rirai
préféreras	prendras	recevras	riras
préférera	prendra	recevra	rira
préférerons	prendrons	recevrons	rirons
préférerez	prendrez	recevrez	rirez
préféreront	prendront	recevront	riront

conditional

préférerais	prendrais	recevrais	rirais
préférerais	prendrais	recevrais	rirais
préférerait	prendrait	recevrait	rirait
préférerions	prendrions	recevrions	ririons
préféreriez	prendriez	recevriez	ririez
préféreraient	prendraient	recevraient	riraient

past historic

préférai	pris	reçus	ris
préféras	pris	reçus	ris
préféra	prit	reçut	rit
préférâmes	prîmes	reçûmes	rîmes
préférâtes	prîtes	reçûtes	rîtes
préférèrent	prirent	reçurent	rirent

present subjunctive

préfère	prenne	reçoive	rie
préfères	prennes	reçoives	ries
préfère	prenne	reçoive	rie
préférions	prenions	recevions	riions
préfériez	preniez	receviez	riiez
préfèrent	prennent	reçoivent	rient

imperfect subjunctive

préférasse	prisse	reçusse	risse
préférasses	prisses	reçusses	risses
préférât	prît	reçût	rît
préférassions	prissions	reçussions	rissions
préférassiez	prissiez	reçussiez	rissiez
préférassent	prissent	reçussent	rissent

savoir	**suffire**	**suivre**	**tenir**
to know	*to be enough*	*to follow*	*to hold*
present			
sais	suffis	suis	tiens
sais	suffis	suis	tiens
sait	suffit	suit	tient
savons	suffisons	suivons	tenons
savez	suffisez	suivez	tenez
savent	suffisent	suivent	tiennent
imperfect			
savais	suffisais	suivais	tenais
savais	suffisais	suivais	tenais
savait	suffisait	suivait	tenait
savions	suffisions	suivions	tenions
saviez	suffisiez	suiviez	teniez
savaient	suffisiaent	suivaient	tenaient
future			
saurai	suffirai	suivrai	tiendrai
sauras	suffiras	suivras	tiendras
saura	suffira	suivra	tiendra
saurons	suffirons	suivrons	tiendrons
saurez	suffirez	suivrez	tiendrez
sauront	suffiront	suivront	tiendront
conditional			
saurais	suffirias	suivrais	tiendrais
saurais	suffirias	suivrais	tiendrais
saurait	suffirait	suivrait	tiendrait
saurions	suffirions	suivrions	tiendrions
sauriez	suffiriez	suiviez	tiendriez
sauraient	suffiraient	suivraient	tiendraient
past historic			
sus	suffis	suivis	tins
sus	suffis	suivis	tins
sut	suffit	suivit	tint
sûmes	suffîmes	suivîmes	tînmes
sûtes	suffîtes	suivîtes	tîntes
surent	suffirent	suivirent	tinrent
present subjunctive			
sache	suffise	suivre	tienne
saches	suffises	suivres	tiennes
sache	suffise	suive	tienne
sachions	suffisions	suivions	tenions
sachiez	suffisiez	suiviez	teniez
sachent	suffisent	suivent	tiennent
imperfect subjunctive			
susse	suffisse	suivisse	tinsse
susses	suffisses	suivisses	tinsses
sût	suffît	suivît	tînt
sussions	suffissions	suivissions	tinssions
sussiez	suffissiez	suivissiez	tinssiez
sussent	suffissent	suivissent	tinssent

valoir	**venir**	**vivre**	**voir**
to be worth	*to come*	*to live*	*to see*
present			
vaux	viens	vis	vois
vaux	viens	vis	vois

vaut	vient	vit	voit
valons	venons	vivons	voyons
valez	venez	vivez	voyez
valent	viennent	vivent	voient

imperfect

valais	venais	vivais	voyais
valais	venais	vivais	voyais
valait	venait	vivait	voyait
valions	venions	vivions	voyions
valiez	veniez	viviez	voyiez
valaient	venaient	vivaient	voyaient

future

vaudrai	viendrai	vivrai	verrai
vaudras	viendras	vivras	verras
vaudra	viendra	vivra	verra
vaudrons	viendrons	vivrons	verrons
vaudrez	viendrez	vivrez	verrez
vaudront	viendront	vivront	verront

conditional

vaudrais	viendrais	vivrais	verrais
vaudrais	viendrais	vivrais	verrais
vaudrait	viendrait	vivrait	verrait
vaudrions	viendrions	vivrions	verrions
vaudriez	viendriez	vivriez	verriez
vaudraient	viendraient	vivraient	verraient

past historic

valus	vins	vécus	vis
valus	vins	vécus	vis
valut	vint	vécut	vit
valûmes	vînmes	vécûmes	vîmes
valûtes	vîntes	vécûtes	vîtes
valurent	vinrent	vécurent	virent

present subjunctive

vaille	vienne	vive	voie
vailles	viennes	vives	voies
vaille	vienne	vive	voie
valions	venions	vivions	voyions
vailiez	veniez	viviez	voyiez
vaillent	viennent	vivent	voient

imperfect subjunctive

valusse	vinsse	vécusse	visse
valusses	vinsses	vécusses	visses
valût	vînt	vécût	vît
valussions	vinssions	vécussions	vissions
valussiez	vinssiez	vécussiez	vissiez
valussent	vinssent	vécussent	vissent